Theology of Discontent

Theology of Discontent

The Ideological Foundations of the
Islamic Revolution in Iran

Hamid Dabashi

NEW YORK UNIVERSITY PRESS
NEW YORK AND LONDON

NEW YORK UNIVERSITY PRESS
New York and London

Library of Congress Cataloging-in-Publication Data
Dabashi, Hamid, 1951–
Theology of discontent: the ideological foundations of the Islamic
Revolution in Iran / Hamid Dabashi.
p.   cm.
Includes bibliographical references (p. 595–622) and index.
ISBN 0-8147-1839-6 (alk. paper) ISBN 0-8147-1840-X
(pbk. : alk. paper)
1. Shiʿah—Iran—History—20th century.   2. Islam and state—Iran.
3. Iran—Politics and government—1979–   I. Title.
BP63.I68D33   1992   92-25276
320.5′5—dc20   CIP

New York University Press books are printed on acid-free paper,
and their binding materials are chosen for strength and durability.

Manufactured in the United States of America

c 10 9 8 7 6 5 4 3 2 1
p 10 9 8 7 6 5 4 3 2 1

In Memoriam
Ali Alemohammad (1922–1991)
more than a father

Contents

Preface

A revolution has happened in our time. The Islamic Revolution in Iran has exploded right at the doorsteps of modern history, posing a dual task for serious students of the event. The Islamic Revolution is predicated on "the Islamic Ideology," now the militant voice of Muslim discontent. The wider wings of this soaring ideology are yet to be stretched out, much further than in Iran, deep into the Islamic heartland, as far as North Africa, Central Asia, the Near, Middle, and Far East. Its central occurrence in Iran thus needs careful understanding. While the vast body of literature in Persian and Arabic ought to be collected and analyzed gradually, it will have to be exposited in analytical studies of detailed accuracy to compensate for the lack of good and reliable translations. I have written this book with this dual objective, among others, in mind. While working with the vast body of diffused literature produced by the revolutionary ideologues, I have tried to convey what they have actually said. Only then would I take a few steps further and convey the significance of what they have said, and, perhaps even more important, what is at stake in their saying what they have said.

In my discussions of "what they have said" I have done my best to think myself in their minds. This is not to say that I have found a golden key to the "value-neutrality" box or to its illusive apparition called "objectivity." But insofar as I have conscious access to my own political motivations, let me confess, at the very outset, that, for a sociologist, I am incurably apolitical. Approaching the Deuteronomical number of punishment, forty, I lay no claim to this Revolution or any other orchestration of political (un)truth. I am neither for nor against the late Shah, for or against the Ayatollah, to take the two personal codes of larger claims to political (dis)loyalty. One has to be, I daresay, an individual to write about society, apolitical about politics, composed about Revolution. Too much entrapment in inherited social categories ("we Iranians, you Americans") dulls the wit. The result of this finding myself, as I say, in these ideologues' minds, it should be emphasized, is that this book has a special kind of voice, a multiple kind of voice. Without paying primary attention to how this voice speaks, and how it shifts its narrative, it would not be possible to follow what it actually says.

Somewhere among those multiple narratives, I author this book. In that authorial voice, I do not write as an Iranian, which I am, or as a sociologist, which I am also. I write as an individual who happens to be an Iranian who happens to be a sociologist—in that particular order. And even in that particular order, I still refuse all the stereotypes that chase me around. I escape them all. I have been guided through these texts and their authors and audiences, wherever they lead me, by the inner composition of their logic or sentiments, anger or illusion. Thus, one should not be quick to detect and define the omniscient authorial voice. Every chapter in this book is narrated from a multiple, yet its subject's voice most dominant, perspective. The authorial voice may fade into the subject's and then fade out for some necessary fresh air. There is a design, a point of contention, in this multiple, interlaced, kind of voice, adopted and abandoned. Insofar as Herr Dr. Freud has divided my mind into conscious and unconscious components, in paradoxical denial/confirmation of each other, obviously I, speaking for the conscious, cannot speak for the unconscious—nor it for me. Yet it has become something of a customary ritual for Iranian observers of the Iranian Revolution to announce in their prefaces—in a voice audible only in the preface, never to be heard again in the text itself—their tacit or explicit prejudices of method or anxieties of objectivity. In his introductory note to his masterful reconstruction of a narrative of religion and politics in Iran, *The Mantle of the Prophet*, Roy Mottahedeh felt obliged to draw a line between those who find his portrayal of Ali Hashemi too sympathetic and those who would see it as not reverential enough. Mottahedeh located himself between these two groups, announcing his preference for Iranian individuals, rather than archetypes. Said Amir Arjomand excused his "measured intrusion of . . . value judgments in Chapters 6 and 7" of his indispensable contribution to our understanding of the Revolution, *Turban for the Crown*. Ervand Abrahamian, too, thought it necessary, at the very outset of his *Radical Islam,* to share with his readers "the author's own biases." In writing his definitive statement about the Mojahedin-e Khalq, Abrahamian explained that he is "an Armenian-Iranian by birth; a skeptic by intellectual training; a democratic Socialist by political preference." As for his "religious conviction," Abrahamian confessed to be "an agnostic on most days—on other days, an atheist."

Here, then, is my confessional statement. In the solitude of my study, where I am an individual, not an archetype, I have no stand vis-à-vis the Revolution. In that solitude I do not really know whether the Revolution was a good or a bad thing that happened to my country. Yet I have no categorical claim to value-neutrality. Quite the contrary. I have no reason to have remained aloof from a cataclysmic event that has shaken my homeland to its bones. I am more an insider than an observer, more a self than an other. I am very much present in my text, in the pages you are about to read. I take this Kierkegaardian dictum (recorded in his diary in 1854) quite seriously that: "It is with most systematicians in relation to their system as with a man who has built a vast palace and himself occupies a barn close by: they do not themselves live in their vast systematic structures. But in matters of the mind and spirit this is and remains a definite objection. Spiritually speaking, a man's thoughts must inhabit the house in which he lives—or else there is something wrong."

For more than a decade, I have dwelt in this text. I have abandoned all anxieties of "value-neutrality." But if there is any sign of salvation in what Weber code-named "value-neutrality," it is precisely in its promise to engage us in a language, a level of discourse, the operation of a theoretical voice, that denies the comfort of good and evil, the certainty of choosing sides between believers and atheists, or the bliss of having "truth on our side." That sense of wonder spells out the particulars of our "Wissenschaft als Beruf." Whether or not we are saved in this post-Protestant assumption is an uncertainty that Weber, among other religiously amusicals, taught us to celebrate.

Acknowledgments

Different parts of this book have been researched and written in various libraries in a number of universities and countries. The conception and initial research occurred at my alma mater, the University of Pennsylvania. I am grateful to Brian Spooner and William Hanaway for their support, particularly for having facilitated my access to the Van Pelt Library. My occasional lunches with Renata Holod have always proved to be intellectually stimulating. What I have learned from her wisdom and erudition far exceeds her immediate recognition; for this and for her enduring friendship I am most grateful. A large portion of this book was documented while I was visiting the University of Texas at Austin. My sincere gratitude to Hafez Farmayan, Michael Hillmann, Ian Manners, and Abazar Sepehri for their ceaseless support, precious guidance, and, most of all, indispensable friendship. My Wednesday luncheon meetings with Mohammad Valady and Mohammad Reza Ghanoonparvar, the year I was in Austin, were engaging moments of conversation and reflection. I am privileged by their friendship.

Over a few Christmas and summer holidays I went to Oxford and consulted related material. I am grateful to Homa Katouzian and John Gurney for their wealth of advice, support, and hospitality. During these visits I benefited from my long conversations with Homa Katouzian who generously hosted me from one cafe to another, guided me from Bodleian to St. Anthony to anywhere else, and all the while even more generously shared with me his vast and penetrating knowledge of modern Iranian history. Our long strolls through the streets and back alleys of Oxford have given me much otherwise unteachable insight that only a wise friend can impart. He also carefully read my chapter on Al-e Ahmad and the Chronology. His corrections have saved me from some factual errors. His suggestions have enriched the chapter. He, of course, remains a tabula rasa saved from all my interpretations of Al-e Ahmad's character and texts, with which he may or may not agree. A segment of my introductory chapter, the section on Zoroastrian cosmology, was also read by my distinguished colleague at Columbia, Professor James Russel. I am grateful for his constructive comments.

Mr. Jamal Hashemi, at the al-Huda Bookshop in London, gave me sound advice for locating materials and, even better, discounts for purchasing them. I am grateful to him. But my gratitude and debt to Mr. and Mrs. Shirzad, the owners and operators of Iran Books, Inc., in Washington, DC, cannot be expressed properly in a few words. They have given me reliable advice in locating books; they have lent books to me indefinitely; and they have been most generous in giving me discounts for the books I purchased. They are noble souls, credits to the Iranian community abroad. On the subject of locating books, purchasing and shipping them from Iran, there is no more valiant soul than my mother-in-law, Mrs. Felor Alemohammad. To her and to Karim and Goli Emami, the owners and operators of Zamineh Bookstore, I am eternally grateful.

As a postdoctoral fellow at Harvard, I benefited from the good advice and friendship of Roy Motahhedeh. I am most grateful for his continuous support for and interest in my work. The year I spent at Harvard gave me peace of mind, indispensable during the crucial period of writing this book. Habib Ladjevardi and Houchang Chehabi were instrumental in making the short period of my fellowship precious and enduring. I am most grateful for their good company and friendship. I am also grateful to John Emerson and Mahdokht Homa'i, of Widener Library at Harvard, for locating obscure pamphlets for me, some of them published in preeternity in Qom or God-knows-where.

I am most grateful to Peter Chelkowski, Frank Peters, Caroline Persell, and Denis Wrong for having made possible and pleasant my research and teaching at New York University. The publication of this book is made possible, in effect, by the relentless support of Peter Chelkowski, for whom I am reluctant to unpack the depth of my gratitude and affection. He knows too much about the Persian proclivity for hyperbole. I am afraid he might misread me. I wish I knew Polish. I also thank Farhad Kazemi and Michael Carter for facilitating my access to the Middle East Collection at the Bobst Library. Ervand Abrahamian made available to me some crucial materials otherwise inaccessible. I have also had a number of constructive conversations with him about the mechanics of this book. For this and for the model of scholarship he establishes for all of us I am grateful. Said Amir Arjomand has also given me important advice at various stages of this endeavor. Ahmad Ashraf and Ali Banuazizi have been constant sources of inspiration and exemplary models for collecting and analyzing archival materials.

My understanding of modern Iranian history is due, in large part, to long conversations with my late father-in-law, Mr. Ali Alemohammad. His knowledge of and active participation in the crucial events of the 1940s and 1950s never ceased to teach me the minutiae of Iranian politics. Dedicating this book to him is a mere token of my gratitude for his having taught me otherwise unteachable truths about Iranian politics. For this and for so much more, I am eternally grateful to him. It deeply saddens me that he saw me all the way through my writing this book and now he is not to see it out.

For the past several years I have had the rare privilege of having instructive conversations—I mostly listening, he generously teaching—with Ebrahim Golestan—that last truly Renaissance Iranian, whose vast erudition, intimate knowledge, and deep insights of the most essential events, political and literary, in Iran, and of much more, have taught me many unwritten truths about the country he and I call home. Confident acceptance into the gracious presence of Ebrahim Golestan is an experience in the precision of insight, the playful working of irony, the perplexing joy of paradox, and yet the happy sobriety of intellectucal rectitude that only a fortunate few have had. I am most grateful and honored to have been one of these happy few.

Without his knowing so, yet another rare Iranian intellectual, my dear friend Farhad Mechkat, for years the music director and the principal conductor of the Tehran Symphony Orchestra, has opened my ears and my eyes to realities of contemporary Iranian cultural history otherwise so brutally concealed to naked, and perhaps even prejudiced, organs of perception. I am honored by his friendship.

Two of my brilliant graduate students, Laura Miller and Jacque Berlinerblau, have been delightful sources of insight into a work they are yet to read but which they have influenced in ways beyond their immediate recognition. I thank them both.

How can I ever properly thank Selma Pastor: my decipherist, word-processor magician, primary editor, demanding alter ego. She has choreographed my endless revisions of these pages, the words you are about to read. She has recorded faithfully every move I have made with these words, forcing, as I do, my escaping ideals to have a firm foot in the ground. From a maddening pile of scattered manuscripts, jotted down on a variety of odd objects—including credit card receipts, airline ticket envelopes, and McDonald's napkins—she has always managed to produce readable and clear passages. For her masterful deciphering of my scribbles, for her superb word-processing and editing skills, and, most of all, for her gracious humor and good nature, I salute Selma Pastor and offer her my most sincere gratitude.

In my chapters on Shari'ati, Taleqani, and Khomeini, I have used the revised and expanded versions of my articles on them, already published elsewhere. I am grateful to the Islamic Cultural Centre, St. Martin's Press, and Sage Publications for their kind permission to use these articles. I am equally grateful to Penguin, U.S.A., and Mage Publishers for permission to quote passages from James Joyce's *A Portrait of the Artist as a Young Man* and Simin Daneshvar's *Savushun,* respectively.

All these fine institutions and wise individuals have given freely and readily of their resources in order to make this book possible. On behalf of "this book," I wish to thank them for the generosity of their spirit. But in no way, shape, or form is anyone other than myself responsible for any deficiency or malediction that may, for whatever reason, persist. I wrote it.

A wise friend once said that it takes two to make one academic life. The implications of this wisdom go far beyond the limitations of that ephemeral vanity we suffer or celebrate as our academic career. It reaches deep into the making of our intellectual disposition. Without the loving care of my wife, Afsaneh, I would have been unable to attain that serenity of mind and spirit without which no mere word can survive the vicinity of its printing house. If I have uttered a word in this book worth reading beyond the immediate significance of the Iranian Revolution of 1979, it is because of the indispensable serenity of mind, that composure of character, only she knows how to give and sustain. For all that, for gracefully managing a household, two children, and an absent-minded husband, while pursuing her own graduate degree, for giving a sense of perfect sanity to an otherwise perfectly insane world, and for so much more I am eternally grateful to her.

Long after I had written parts of this acknowledgment, I read John Maxwell Hamilton's brutal satire on the perfunctory nature that such sincere expressions of gratitude can assume ("The Mistakes in This Essay Are My Own," *New York Times Book Review,* April 15, 1990). "Acknowledgments," he decreed, "are a curious achievement of pretension, hyperbole and banality." Here is the dilemma. Should I, as the author of this acknowledgment, accept the charges and thus add to his curiosity, or should I rewrite it in a different tone or, better yet, not write it at all? Closing with a paradox or two is, "Dear Mr. Hamilton," the best way to open a quintessentially Iranian text to an American audience, or is it a quintessentially American text to an Iranian audience?

A Note on Transliteration

Except for Anglicized names such as "Ayatollah Khomeini," "Tehran," or "Qom," I have tried to follow the transliteration rules of the *International Journal of the Middle Eastern Studies*. For the sake of simplicity, however, I have dispensed with all diacritical notes. I have also dropped all initial *hamzah*s and ʿ*ayn*s, thus *Ershad* and not *'Irshad*, and Ali, and not ʿAli. But because I deal with both Persian and Arabic words, and because occasionally I have to give Arabic words in their Persian pronunciations, inconsistencies, alas, persist. For a combination of bizarre, yet serious, reasons, the roots of which are to be traced back to a battle in the seventh century (C.E.) in which a certain Iranian general (who among all things was called "Rostam") was miserably defeated by his Arab counterpart, it has now become a matter of political choice whether one writes "Al-e Ahmad" or "Al-i Ahmad," "Abolhasan" or "Abu al-Hasan." The latent anxiety in all this is so unreal, I do not know how to make a choice without appearing to favor one side over the other. The result of my final choices would, I hope, half-please the Iranists and half-please the Arabists; and yet I fear it might half-anger both, doubly damn the result. There it is. The second paradox. A double paradox: to herald the rest.

Chronology of the Revolution: 1921–1979

1921	The Qajar dynasty is abolished by means of a coup d'etat led by Reza Khan (1878–1944).
1925	Reza Khan becomes Reza Shah and the Pahlavi dynasty is officially established (1925–1979).
1925–1941	The reign of Reza Shah the Great, with a ruthless determination to give a "modern" look to the ancient land.
1928	Reza Shah's Dress Law restricts the use of the clerical robe to a limited number of clerics.
1929	Reza Shah bans the Muharram celebration.
1934	Reza Shah constructs the trans-Iranian Railway; Tehran University is established.
1936	Reza Shah orders women unveiled. Ayatollah Haj Shaykh Abdolkarim Ha'eri, the founder of the Qom seminary, dies.
1941	The Allied occupation of Iran; Reza Shah is forced to abdicate; Mohammad Reza Shah (1919–1980) ascends the peacock throne; the Tudeh (Communist) Party is established.
1942	Khomeini's *Kashf al-Asrar (Unveiling of the Secrets)* is published. It is harshly critical of the growing secularism of the state and society.
1944	Reza Shah dies in exile; the Tudeh Party has its first congress.
1946	Navvab Safavi creates the Fada'ian-e Islam, a radical organization devoted to the militant propagation of Islamic ideals.
1948	There is a major split in the Tudeh Party following Sayyid

	Ja'far Pishehvari's failure to establish an "Autonomous Republic" in Azarbaijan—backed by the Red Army.
1949–1953	Ayatollah Kashani actively supports the nationalization of the oil industry; for a time he also supports the government of Mohammad Mosaddeq (1882–1967).
1949	The National Front is established by Mosaddeq; failed assassination attempt against the Shah by Nasir Fakhr-ara'i; Abdolhossein Hajir, the court minister, is assassinated by Fada'ian-e Islam.
1951	Premier Ali Razmara is assassinated by Fada'ian-e Islam; Premier Mosaddeq nationalizes the Iranian oil industry.
1953	Ayatollah Kashani splits with Mosaddeq; Mosaddeq's government is toppled by a CIA-sponsored coup; Fazl Allah Zahedi becomes Premier of the newly installed government.
1954	Mossadeq's Foreign Minister, Sayyid Hossein Fatemi, is executed.
1955	Fada'ian-e Islam attempts to assassinate Premier Husayn Ala'.
1957	The Shah's notorious secret police, SAVAK, is formed.
1958	The Iranian monarch creates a nominal two-party system.
1960	Ayatollah Khomeini publishes his *Tawzih al-Masa'il (Explication of Questions)* and is thus recognized as a "Source of Exemplary Conduct" by Shi'i believers.
1960–1961	Premiership of Ja'far Sharif-Imami.
1961	Ayatollah Borujerdi, the highest-ranking Shi'i authority, dies in Qom; Ayatollah Hakim in Najaf succeeds him.
1961–1962	Premiership of Ali Amini.
1962	Jalal Al-e Ahmad publishes *Westoxication*.
1962–1963	Premiership of Asadollah Alam.
1963	
January	The Shah goes to Qom to demonstrate his force before he lauches his "White Revolution."
March	The Shah's army quells a demonstration at Feyziyyah Seminary.
April	Ayatollah Khomeini denounces the Shah for the Feyziyyah incident; the Shah orders the punitive act of drafting the clerics for military service.
May	The Shah admits that his "White Revolution" had been bloodied; he denounces Khomeini without mentioning his name; later he denounces Khomeini publicly.
June	Ayatollah Khomeini lashes out against the Shah. He is arrested; massive demonstrations ensue throughout Iran;

	other people already arrested include Mehdi Bazargan and Sayyid Mahmud Taleqani.
July	Ayatollah Khomeini is released but put under house arrest.
November	Haj Reza'i brothers (Tayyeb and Isma'il), supporters of Khomeini's uprising, are executed.
1964–1965	Premiership of Hasan Ali Mansur.
1964	
April	Premier Hasan Ali Mansur releases Ayatollah Khomeini.
October	The Shah gives diplomatic immunity to Americans working in Iran; Khomeini delivers his famous "anticapitulation" speech.
November	Khomeini is exiled to Turkey; he stays there for eleven months before leaving for Iraq in October 1965.
1965–1977	Premiership of Amir Abbas Hoveyda.
1965	
January	Fada'ian-e Islam assassinates Premier Mansur; Amir Abbas Hoveyda becomes Premier.
April	Reza Shamsabadi attempts but fails to assassinate the Shah.
October	Khomeini leaves Turkey and goes to Iraq.
1967	Mohammad Mosaddeq dies; the Family Protection Laws are passed, granting women greater rights in marriage.
April	Khomeini's letter to Premier Hoveyda protesting the coronation expenses is widely circulated in the Tehran Bazaar and Qom.
October	Coronation of the Shah Mohammad Reza Pahlavi.
November	Khomeini's second letter to Premier Hoveyda protesting the coronation is published.
1968	Al-e Ahmad is instrumental in founding the Iranian Writers Association; compulsory military service for women is drafted.
1970	Massive increase in the Iranian military budget and build-up.
1971	A considerable increase in the price of crude oil; Iran's military power in the Persian Gulf is increased; a significant guerrilla movement in the Siahkal region of Northern Iran challenges the Iranian monarchy; the Fada'ian-e Khalq organization (leftist) is established; the Mojahedin-e Khalq organization (Islamic leftist) is established; the Iranian monarch expands his relations with Communist China; the Religious Corps is created; the 2,500th anniversary of the Persian monarchy is celebrated at Persepolis; Ayatollah Khomeini condemns both the Religious Corps and the 2,500th anniversary celebrations.

1972   The Iranian army battles the Communists in Oman; massive purchases of U.S.-built arms by the Iranian monarch; Mojahedin-e Khalq bombs the U.S. Information Center to protest President Nixon's visit to Iran.

1973   The Arab oil embargo; Iran does not participate; massive increase in Iranian oil revenues; the Mojahedin-e Khalq organization assassinates an American military advisor; following the discovery of a kidnapping plot against members of the royal family, two prominent Marxists, Khosrow Golsorkhi and Keramatollah Daneshian, are executed.

1975   The Resurrection Party *(Hezb-e Rastakhiz)* is established in Iran; membership is mandatory for all Iranians; Iran and Iraq draw up a peace treaty in Algeria; two U.S. Air Force officers are assassinated in Iran.

1976   Execution of Iranian guerrillas for having assassinated American advisors; three American employees of Rockwell International are assassinated in Tehran; the Shah changes the origin of the Iranian calendar from the migration of the Prophet Mohammad from Mecca to Medina to the coronation of Cyrus the Great; Jimmy Carter—the "human rights" president—is elected in the United States.

1977   President Carter assumes office; prompted by President Carter's "human rights" campaign, the Shah begins a rapid process of liberalization; the National Front sends an open letter to the Shah, criticizing abuses of power; President Carter refuses to deliver AWACS to Iran; Premier Jamshid Amuzegar succeeds Hoveyda; Ayatollah Khomeini's son, Haj Aqa Mostafa', dies; demonstrations follow in Tehran and Qom; Iranian intellectuals and literati gather in the Goethe Institute to read political poetry.

1978
January   President Carter visits Iran and praises the Shah's "Island of Stability"; the publication of a newspaper article against Ayatollah Khomeini causes anger and demonstrations in Qom; the police fire into a crowd; casualties are reported.

February   Riots break out in Tabriz; banks and movie houses are burned down.

March   Demonstrations continue in many Iranian cities; casualties are reported in Yazd.

April   The residences of Bazargan and Sanjabi and a number of other opposition leaders are bombed; the government organizes pro-Shah demonstrations; antigovernment riots expand to Tehran University.

May	Antigovernment riots are reported in Tehran, Shiraz, Isfahan, Tabriz, and many other cities; two seminarians are killed in Qom; the Shah leaves Iran for a visit to Eastern Europe.
June	Commemorating the anniversary of the June 1963 uprising, a general strike is called by supporters of Ayatollah Khomeini; General Ni'matollah Nasiri, the hated and feared chief of SAVAK, is dismissed.
July	The Shah tries to control corruption in the royal family by issuing a "Code of Conduct"; Ayatollah Shari'atmadari, for much of this period the effective leader of the Islamic opposition inside the country, calls for free parliamentary elections; high numbers of casualties are reported in clashes between police and demonstrators in Mashhad.
August	Riots break out in Isfahan and the city is put under martial law; a cinema is set ablaze in Abadan, hundreds are burned to death; Premier Sharif-Imami succeeds Amuzegar; the Shah promises free elections and much more.
September	Tehran is under martial law; hundreds of demonstrators are killed in Zhaleh Square ("Black Friday"); telecommunications employees go on strike; demonstrators in Tehran call for the return of Ayatollah Khomeini and the establishment of an "Islamic Republic"; some 11,000 are reported dead in an earthquake in Tabas, in eastern Iran; oil workers go on strike against the Shah's government.
October	Ayatollah Khomeini leaves Iraq and comes to France; President Carter endorses the Shah; demonstrations and strikes continue.
November	General Azhari forms a government to succeed Sharif-Imami; the National Television employees go on strike; employees of the Iranian Central Bank go on strike; Ayatollah Taleqani is released from prison; Sanjabi meets with Khomeini in Neauphle-le-Chateau and concedes to an "Islamic Republic"; the Shah admits past mistakes and promises freedom in the future; some prominent government officials, including former Premier Hoveyda, are arrested on charges of corruption and abuses of power.
December	Massive anti-Shah demonstrations continue; Premier Shahpour Bakhtiar succeeds General Azhari; strikes continue; oil production is reduced drastically; U.S. Marines use tear gas to disperse angry crowds around the American Embassy.

1979

January	The Shah leaves Iran; Ayatollah Khomeini returns to Tehran; General Huyser is reported to be in Tehran.
February	Bakhtiar's government falls; Ayatollah Khomeini nominates Mehdi Bazargan to head the Provisional Government.
March	Women protest against new veiling codes suggested by members of the clergy; Khomeini leaves for Qom; oil exports are resumed; a referendum is proposed for people to choose between monarchy and the "Islamic Republic."
April	Through a referendum, the Islamic Republic is established; Hoveyda is executed.
May	Morteza Motahhari is assassinated.
June	U.S. Ambassador-designate to Iran is rejected; secular intellectuals are threatened by Khomeini; the draft of the new constitution is publicized; massive nationalization of Iranian banks and industries is reported.
July	Fighting between the Revolutionary Guards and the Kurds is reported.
August	The Assembly of Experts convenes to ratify the Islamic Constitution; a new press law goes into effect, curtailing the freedom of mass communication.
September	Sayyid Mahmud Taleqani dies; the Kurds continue to fight the Islamic government.
October	The Shah is admitted to a New York hospital; fighting between the Revolutionary Guards and the Kurds intensifies.
November	American diplomats are taken hostage in Tehran; Bazargan resigns; the Revolutionary Council takes charge.
December	The Islamic Constitution is ratified.

Introduction: Formative Forces of "the Islamic Ideology"

I have written this book primarily, but not exclusively, to facilitate the access of a larger community of readers to the revolutionary ideas of the most important ideologues of the Islamic Revolution. There is nothing available to the community of interpreters trying to understand the Islamic Revolution of 1979 that examines the ideas of these revolutionary figures comprehensively. The few scattered pieces that do exist on a few of these ideologues are nowhere near a comprehensive coverage of their essential ideas. The fewer translations of their works that are available in English, or any other European language, are even less accurate, trustworthy, or representative. A great deal of liberty is taken when the primary sources of the Revolution are translated into a European language.

This book has emerged out of my conviction that a larger community of readers and interpreters—whether those who, because of language barriers, have no direct access to these original ideas or those who find the mass of scattered and repetitive writings too troublesome to tackle—needs to have a thorough and authoritative command over these sources. Beyond the necessity of producing authoritative monographs on every one of these ideologues, ideally we would need to have critical editions, translations, annotations of, and introductions to their collected writings. Pending that ideal, I hope the present volume will suffice in providing a comprehensive view of eight prominent figures who were instrumental in giving the Iranian Revolution of 1979 its ultimate ideological shape.

In preparing this expository aspect of the present volume, I have reduced my own voice to an indispensable minimum. This does not mean that I have not provided my particular reading of these texts or that I have not suggested a particular order in the logic of their production. But all these have been executed with the most detailed attention to the minutiae of these ideologues and their writings.

How does such attention to the minutiae of the Revolution stand vis-à-vis the more grandiloquent theories of the Revolution? A comprehensive theory of the Iranian Revolution of 1979, taking into account all the relevant material and ideological factors, may take decades to address, analyze, synthesize, and formulate. Zhou En-lai, the revolutionary Chinese Premier, is reported to have considered a mere lapse of two centuries still "too soon to tell" the story of the French Revolution.[1] Even if a hyperbole, there is still a strong element of truth in waiting for a thorough collection of primary studies before addressing the theoretical issues of the Iranian Revolution of 1979. But between the two extreme levels of delegating all our theoretical joys to future generations—and being suffocated in the basements and attics of our archival tortures—there is a happy medium where we can tame our theoretical urges by channeling them into constructive attention to the historical immediacy and empirical exegencies of the event. I realize that there is no collecting, analyzing, or discussing data without a theoretical lense, or even a number of them. But that is quite different from designing theoretical sand castles on the seashore of our imagination, neglecting the very historicity of the event. With a built-in and invincible theoretical bent in the very cast of my mind, I would be the last person to recommend getting lost in the midst and maze of speechless facticities. But what a feast a theoretical sight can provide when casting a long and sustained look upon the factual particularities of the Iranian Revolution!

My aim in writing this book has been to reconstruct, as best I know how, that generic spirit of "the Islamic Ideology," the single most important construction of the revolutionary movement that preceded the Revolution and, I suggest, was instrumental in the course and consequences of the event. I have deliberately ended the chronology of my analysis in the vicinity of the 1977–79 period which generated a new momentum in the revolutionary discourse of the living ideologues, that is, those of Motahhari, Taleqani, Bazargan, Bani-Sadr, and Khomeini.

The Word Behind the Sword

The public currency of these ideological voices was, of course, crucial to their contributions to making possible the Islamic Revolution. Yet, there is no way of knowing or retrospectively ascertaining how many people actually read and responded positively to these writings. We can establish only certain organizational and institutional forums, such as the Muslim Students Association or the Association of (Muslim) Engineers, through which these voices were publicized. That these texts were produced by the primary architects of the revolutionary movement and that they were widely disseminated in religious and professional organizations during the prerevolutionary period are evidence enough to give them the status of having, if not caused then at least, occasioned the Revolution.

Beyond the political significance of the ideologues I examine in this book and beyond the range of their prerevolutionary public reception, the underlying assumption of my discussion of "the Islamic Ideology"—and its central significance in the making of the Iranian Revolution of 1979—is the mobilizing power of ideas. In giving voice to the common miseries of a people—actual or perceived, absolute or relative—revolutionary ideas have an instrumental presence in the course and consequences of the revolutionary movement. The focal point of convergence for all revolutionary ideas is a particular reading of the status quo and, more specifically, its highest symbolic expression: the state. The mobilizing power of ideas can generate and accumulate unmanageable difficulties for the state, both internal and external. Before structural and multidirectional pressures are brought to bear on the state, someone has to call for a strike, and someone has to call for a press conference to draw international attention to the common miseries of a nation—factual or imaginary. That someone perforce uses a language of conviction—congenial to the material conditions of the revolution and conducive to revolutionary mobilization. That language, code-named "the Islamic Ideology" in the Iranian case, draws from the deepest and most enduring convictions of its constituency, and, at the same time, addresses the highest and most distant ideals of those who are, literally, willing and able to put their lives on the line.

At this point, revolutionary movements are much indebted to the rising appeal of radical ideas. "Let us have the kingdom of heaven right here on earth," says the revolutionary sage. Translating the theological into the political, the revolutionary ideologues draw from the most sacred in order to advance the most tangible. From the sacred to the tangible there is an indispensable line of communication that "the ideology" virtually draws and energizes.

There should be no ambiguity in the central significance of this ideological line. Without seeking in any way "to explain" the Revolution, I do unabashedly confess my conviction in the primacy of an ideological build-up in "occasioning" a revolutionary situation that may or may not necessarily lead to an actual revolution. What ultimately accounts for that "may or may not" is a set of other material and structural forces that can shift the balance of power between the state and the organizing opposition to topple it.

Revolutions are acts of communal denial. Every revolution begins with a "no." Conviction of a denial is the mother of all revolutions. Men act out of convictions, revolutionary men out of radical convictions. Convictions are made of opinions, radical convictions of revolutionary ideologies. Religious ideologies, set on a revolutionary course, have the added incentive of calling God on their side, of bordering their radical convictions with Truth. Thus circumscribed, social actions are political extensions of otherwise mute ideological convictions. For these convictions to be translated effectively to politically significant social actions, more concrete and material forces are necessary too. Only the revolutionary elite, the absolutely convinced, may be presumed not in need of material incentives. For them ideological convictions, a deep sense of moral jeopardy, will do. But for the masses of revolutionary zeal to be mobilized, convictions are extended into politically significant social actions with and through the active agency of more concrete material forces of absolute or relative deprivation. Khomeini may not have led a revolution for the price of melon, but many of his followers thought they did.

Thus confronting the challenge of reexamining the constellation of ideas that "occasioned" the Revolution, I wish to reconstruct in this study perhaps the most important ideological build-up that preceded the Islamic Revolution in Iran. "The Islamic Ideology" was the crucial, perhaps even indispensable, mobilizing force behind the massive demonstration of public discontent with the Pahlavi regime. Although other, patently secular, ideologues were equally instrumental, if less persuasive in their mass appeal, in the penultimate making of the 1979 Revolution, it was "the Islamic Ideology" that, for the most part, established the universe and particulars of discourse in terms of which the revolutionary episode narrated itself.

What precisely were the specific features of this "Islamic Ideology"? Who were its primary architects? How did it construct the ideological frames of its contemporary reference? How did it project the specifics of a future utopian design? These are among the questions for which I wish to provide accurate and thoroughly documented answers.

The Stated Agenda

Tracing the Islamic Revolution back to "the Islamic Ideology," I shall first and foremost present the crucial ideas of eight figures who were instrumental in the making of this ideology.

Second, beyond my primary objective of systematizing and analyzing these ideological statements that preceded the Revolution, I have also tried to put them in their proper social and historical contexts. This contextualization of ideas in their respective settings has inevitably led me to introduce cultural, social, political, and historical materials.[2] Some of these contextualizations would be known, but most are unknown, at least in my particular reading of them, to the range of readers I hope this book will reach.

Locating these ideas in their proper social context inevitably gives an occasional language of cultural history and/or political culture to the text.

Third, beyond these revolutionary ideas and their respective contexts, I shall also be charting the course of how a significant revolutionary discourse was developed. The language of this discourse was not a given; it was not just there. It was concocted gradually and consistently. The construction of this revolutionary discourse, its vicissitudes, internal logic, premises, and inherent possibilities and limitations are all crucial aspects of the Revolution itself. A revolution cannot but speak and act its ideology, cannot talk but with its own language, cannot persuade but on the level of its own discourse. These features and aspects of the revolutionary momentum, its simultaneous construction of ideology and utopia, concern me as well.

Fourth, the construction of this revolutionary discourse leads, inevitably, to the collective construction of a commonly held mythology of revolt. This mythology, its method and manner of persuasion, and the modes and modalities of public participation in it are central to the build-up of the revolutionary momentum. Ideologized into revolutionary claims to truth, realities of Iranian social life were transformed into compelling components of a commonly held set of myths that held its participants in the grip of a forceful alternative to the existing status quo. The nature and organization of this metamorphosis was the most powerful mobilizing force in the course of the Revolution.

But, ultimately, beyond the expositions of these revolutionary ideas, beyond contextualizing them in their respective social settings, beyond the specifics of a revolutionary discourse in the making, and beyond the constructions of a common mythology to mobilize the masses, beyond all these aspects of a language of revolt, we ought to know the specifics of what this language speaks, the message it conveys. The message of this revolutionary language is discontent, which necessitates an injured Self and a hostile Other. The injured Self, as it was collectively created, is the most compelling force in the contemporary Iranian psyche; the hostile Other is the visceral denial of "The West." More than anything else, it is this collective discontent against an imaginative construction called "The West" that deeply animated the revolutionary movement. This discontent was expressed essentially in ethical, moral, normative, and spiritual terms. But ultimately the language of the revolt, the magical terms of this discontent, was theological. The theological language of discontent was inevitable, perhaps, because theology is the ultimate language of truth. It is in theological terms, whatever the god-terms of a culture may be, that every disenchantment furnishes the parameters of the coming reenchantment, the very disillusion that serves the coming reillusion. Alternatives to this theological language have only economic, social, cultural, or, at best, ideological claims to truth. All these fade in light of a theological claim to having God at the top of your political agenda.

Four Clerics and Four Laymen

To meet this agenda, I have selected eight seminal revolutionary thinkers whose ideas have shaped the nature and constitution of the Islamic Revolution. It was only after I had selected these eight ideologues that I realized that four of them are clerics and the other four "lay" intellectuals, if, indeed, such a term may be applied to religiously minded ideologues. Motahhari, Taleqani, Tabataba'i, and Khomeini were clericals of medium to high order. Motahhari and Taleqani had pursued their scholastic studies and then distinguished themselves not by writing in classical discourses of their received learning, *fiqh* and *usul,* but by propagating a revolutionary and politically demanding reading of their faith, whether in the form of Qur'anic exegesis or otherwise. Tabataba'i was a philospher-mystic in the tradition of his medieval predecessors. His writings contributed only inadvertently to the making of "the Islamic Ideology" and with it the Islamic Revolution. Khomeini was a cleric of the highest order. His interests in philosophical and mystical discourses notwithstanding, he gradually established himself as a high-ranking "source of exemplary conduct" *(marja'-e taqlid).*

   The other four ideologues received no systematic or serious scholastic training. Although Al-e Ahmad, Shari'ati, Bazargan, and Bani-Sadr were all born to highly religious families and although they were exposed to some preliminary scholastic training, it was essentially in a nonclerical discourse that they found their revolutionary voice. Al-e Ahmad found the primary medium of his political and ideological concerns in literary and social criticism as well as fiction. Shari'ati benefited greatly from his religiously conscious and erudite father. Although he, too, never received any systematic scholastic education, he was widely exposed to a range of religious discourses. Bazargan also received his religious education primarily from his father and then continued on his own. Bani-Sadr was born to a family of religious dignitaries in Hamadan; but his education took place in secular schools and universities in Tehran and Paris. The diversities of these religious and secular backgrounds were translated effectively into the respective revolutionary discourses of these ideologues and, in turn, won them a variety of diverse political constituencies. It was the cumulative effect of these multiple discourses, centered around the core construction of "the Islamic Ideology," that ultimately contributed to the making of the Islamic Revolution.

"The Islamic Ideology"

"The Islamic Ideology" was the quintessential prerequisite of "the Islamic Revolution" in Iran. Although I am not suggesting that this ideology caused the Revolution, I do submit that "the Islamic Revolution" could not have occurred without "the Islamic Ideology."

"The Islamic Ideology," as the penultimate construction of the contemporary Muslim revolutionary urges, went through what have been identified as the three simultaneous processes of externalization, objectification, and internalization[3] in the four decades that preceded the Iranian Revolution of 1979. The construction of "the Islamic Ideology" renders questionable any simplistic notion of secularization.[4] In this particular case, as probably in many others, there does not seem to be a simple release of social and cultural forces from the supremacy of religious doctrines and symbols. An outward appearance of religious signs and doctrines may, in fact, conceal a deeply rooted process of internal secularization. And, conversely, patently secular rhetorics of left and liberal persuasions may, in fact, conceal the deepest forms of religiosity. That no Islamic ideologue noted the thunderous contradiction in terms of "the Islamic Ideology" is a clear indication of how deeply and convincingly secular ideas, with the almost magical touch of "The West," had penetrated and shaped the very constitution of "the Islamic Ideology."

The constitutional build-up of "the Islamic Ideology" was a politically necessitated hybrid between innate Islamic (Shiʿi) revolutionary dispositions and imported secular (left and liberal) ideologies. At the same time that "the Islamic Ideology" harshly condemned these secular ideologies, it borrowed heavily from their language and logic, their rhetoric and romance, to construct its own claim on political truth. Some preliminary observations about some salient factors in Iranian political culture are necessary for this aspect of "the Islamic Ideology" to become more evident.

Legitimacy in Iranian Political Culture

Two prominent motifs of legitimate authority, one Iranian and the other Islamic, have historically constituted the dual basis of justified rulership in the Iranian political culture. The Iranian element that bestows divine grace, *Xᵛaranah*, upon the king predates Islam. According to this notion, the earthly king, endowed with the divine grace, shall lead all the forces of good, in alliance with the supreme Good of the Lord Wisdom (Ahura Mazda), against all the forces of evil, mobilized by the Destructive Spirit (Angra Mainyu).[5] The Islamic element extends from the supreme figure of political authority: first Muhammad and then the archetypal caliph or any

number of his historical substitutes. Having gradually appropriated the
political dimension of Muhammad's charismatic legacy, the caliph held and
subsequently bestowed political power over various segments of the Islamic
empire.[6]

Although increasingly demoralized and delegitimized in modern history,
monarchy has been the institutional expression of the Iranian political
culture. Its pre-Islamic roots extend far beyond the Iranian plateau. As the
shadow of God on earth, the Shah exercised universal authority.[7] As the
terrestrial expression of the Zoroastrian cosmological order, the kingdom,
headed by one king, was providentially preordained. The Zoroastrian cosmo-
historical theory of creation had stipulated the first stage of creation as a
total absence of evil, that is, a spiritual and immaterial—or *menog*—state.
This first stage leads to the materialization of the creation—or *getig*—
existence. These two stages, together called *Bundahishn* in Pahlavi, set the
stage for the introduction of evil in creation, because it is in the second,
getig stage that the materialization of the universe occasions the advance of
evil, spearheaded by Angra Mainyu, into the world. This period of mixture
—or *gumezishn* in Pahlavi—is the historical setting of human experience.[8]
The social order, as regulated by the priestly caste and dominated by the
kingly, is located within this sacred cosmological order. At this stage the
direction of the earthly battle waged by all the elements of good against the
forces of evil is spearheaded by the historical king. The battle is waged in
the common spirit of mankind and the divinities to recreate the original
order. *Frashokereti,* or renovation, is that ultimate moment when the final
victory of Good over Evil is achieved. Upon this victory the third phase in
Zoroastrian cosmo-history will begin, that of *Wizarishn,* or the absolute
separation of Good from Evil.

As the surviving inscriptions of the Achaemanid kings indicate, all royal
pronouncements of earthly victory are proclaimed in the name of Ahura
Mazda,[9] that is, the supreme figure of authority in the celestial realm. The
suggestion that the Iranian King was, in fact, primus inter pares and that
Mesopotamian, mainly Babylonian, influences put him at the center of the
universe,[10] even if tenable, does not alter in any significant way the centrality of monarchy in the received Iranian political culture.

Thus interwoven with the sacred Zoroastrian cosmo-history, the sanctified and supreme status of the king survived for millennia until the fall of
the Sasanids in the mid-seventh century.

Throughout its viscissitudes in the Islamic period, the status of the king
received an added dimension of legitimacy. As early as the ninth century,
semi-independent Iranian dynasties began to emerge—from within the
Islamic empire—that would include, inevitably, Islamic elements of legitimacy. This added factor was a mode of authority derived from the caliphate, which was itself based on that of the prophet Muhammad. After its

initial changes during the reign of the Rightly Guided Caliphs (632–661) and the early Umayyads, the caliph, as understood and recognized by the majority of Muslims, became the supreme political figure, gradually delegating other spheres of authority to different figures and institutions.[11]

With the advent of the semi- or totally independent Iranian states, the supreme position of political authority, whether identified as Shah or with some other title, claimed two bases of legitimacy: Iranian and Islamic. The Iranian factor was the surviving, however latent, notion of the king as the earthly expression of Ahura Mazda, or the supreme figure of Good waging universal war against Evil. The Islamic factor was the derivative authority extended from the caliph to those who received their legitimacy from him. After the Islamic invasion of Iran in the mid-seventh century, the paradigmatic expression of political authority was so thoroughly established in such terms that no claimant to political authority could escape it.[12]

With the emergence of independent Iranian states, this dual basis of legitimacy became increasingly evident and operative. Occasionally there were dynasties such as the Bawandids (665–1349) in the Caspian coastland, or political uprisings such as the Khorramdinan (c. 816), or cultural movements such as the Shuʿubiyyah (from the end of the seventh century onward) that defied the central caliphate and claimed independent authority on a primarily pre-Islamic basis. But on the whole, from the Taherids (821–873) to the Samanids (819–1005) and the Saffarids (867–1495), the dual basis of legitimacy, consciously or otherwise, persisted. The Persianized Turkish dynasties of the Ghaznavids (977–1186) and the Seljuqs (1038–1194) did not alter or supersede the kingly and caliphal dichotomy of legitimacy. The Il-Khanids (1256–1353) added certain Mongolian elements to the kingly notion but continued with the dual Iranic/Islamic sources of their legitimacy. The same is true about the Timurids (1370–1506), the Qara Quyunlu (1380–1468), and the Aq Quyunlu (1378–1508). The Safavids (1501–1732) began by underlining the Islamic (Shiʿite) element of dual legitimacy but continued by upholding the Iranic as well. From the Afsharids (1736–1795) through the Zands (1750–1794) to the Qajars (1779–1924), no significant change could alter the by then established, consolidated, and historically validated pattern of legitimacy based on a fundamental duality: Iranic and Islamic.

The Pahlavi dynasty (1925–1979), begun by Reza Shah (1878–1944) and continued by his son Mohammad Reza Shah (1919–1980), again founded the basis of its legitimacy on both Iranic and Islamic sources. However, towards the end of his reign, Mohammad Reza Shah began to advance further certain tendencies begun by his father and to propagate more and more an exclusively Iranian frame of reference for the legitimation of his kingship. Certain symbolic gestures, with important and far-reaching ideological implications, began to surface. The honorific title attached to the Shah's name, *Aryamehr* ("the sun of the Aryan race"), immediately symbolized this change of direction. The 1971 celebration of the 2,500 years of the establishment of the Persian Empire was equally directed at the same objective of upgrading the Iranic aspect of political legitimacy, at the expense of the Islamic. Another step taken by the Shah was to change the Iranian solar calendar from its historical origin in the migration of Prophet Muhammad from Mecca to Medina to the putative date of the coronation of Cyrus the Great. Finally the introduction of the Zoroastrian symbol of fire into the national celebration of the Shah's birthday clearly demonstrated that less and less significance was being attributed to (Shiʿite) Islam as the legitimating force of kingship.

In part, the Islamic Revolution in Iran can be seen as a direct (Shiʿite) Islamic reaction against the artificial over-Persianization of Iranian political culture at the expense of its Islamic component. In the face of diverse ideological alternatives that were actively challenging the monarchy, this lopsided emphasis on the Iranic heritage, supporting the political apparatus, began to lose its legitimacy. Having gradually lost its reliance on the forces of "inner justification,"[13] the Shah's regime increasingly relied on the necessity of the "external means," that is, the use of physical force. The nature and organization of the ideological alternatives shaped the course of events and the outcome of the revolution that would follow.

Four Sources of Strain in the System of Pahlavi Legitimacy

The revolutionary ideologies that challenged the established order of the *ancien régime* could not but be derived from the operative modalities of command and obedience that have historically characterized the Iranian political culture. However, the century-old exposure to secular ideas, liberal and radical, had left its mark on the Iranian political culture. These secular forces also offered and organized ideological alternatives to the established order. This much is perhaps inevitable and obvious. But there was also the equally inevitable, however less obvious, outcome of ideological constructions of a hybrid nature. Here, certain religious ideologies began to develop that had latent secular twists; and, conversely, certain secular ideologies were propagated that concealed deep religious sentiments. As a result, ideological forces began to challenge the established order from four complementary fronts: (1) the obviously and essentially religious, (2) the blatantly and patently secular, (3) the cryptosecular religious, and, finally, (4) the cryptoreligious secular. Each of these ideological dispositions, which are constructed here as ideal-types, had its legitimating apparatus; and each was driven by the profound immediacy of certain charismatic elements inherent to its ideological origins.

The Religious

In retrospect, perhaps the most significant ideological antecedent of the Islamic Revolution in Iran in an ideal-typically "religious" context was the doctrinal propagation of *velayat-e faqih,* or "the authority of the jurist," as formulated by Ayatollah Khomeini. Although Khomeini occasionally referred to such non-Islamic political ideas as the division of power into the executive, legislative, and judicial branches, the doctrinal formulation of *velayat-e faqih* is based on innate Islamic (Shi'i) references.[14] Consequently, the formulation of this revolutionary doctrine, as perhaps the most significant example of Khomeini's political ideas, represents the typically and quintessentially "religious" alternative to the status quo.

As a specifically Shi'ite doctrine, *velayat-e faqih* derives its dogmatic force from its close association with a number of other crucial tenets in Shi'ism, equally congenial to Mahdistic outbursts and utopian movements.[15] Although the historical and symbolic sources of this doctrine go back to the very origin of Shi'ite Islam, its recent developments are of particular significance. The most important characteristic of this doctrine is its appropriation of certain political authority for the figure of the Shi'i jurist *(faqih).* The specifics of this authority, as articulated by Khomeini, transcend the institutionalized organization of command and obedience in the context of the Shi'ite hierocracy. Although of immediate significance for the Islamic Revolution, the political boundaries of this doctrine extend outside Iran.[16]

The transcendental notion of *Imamah,* the collective belief in a charismatic figure of continuity central in human history, has postulated the legitimate de jure authority of the line of historical Imams that begins with Ali and continues through the Great Occultation *(Ghaybah al-kubra')* of the Twelfth (Hidden) Imam. In the physical absence of the Hidden Imam there is an innate proclivity in Shi'ism towards the periodic outbursts of charismatic movements. With the doctrine of *velayat-e faqih,* Khomeini sought to provide an institutional basis for the figure of the jurist to assume the latent charismatic forces in Shi'ism. However, the success of a given *faqih* in establishing a large enough political constituency to claim a share of power depends, to a considerable degree, on the range and depth of the actual authority he commands. If that optimum of popular obedience is attained, through the credal agency of the doctrine of *velayat-e faqih,* then the explicit or tacit argument of vox populi, vox dei becomes politically active and consequential.

The most prominent proponent of a political reading of *velayat-e faqih* in nineteenth-century Iran was Mollah Ahmad Naraqi (1771–1829) whose *Awa'id al-ayyam* offers the most elaborate treatment of the subject, mobilizing many prophetic traditions *(hadith)* in support of his interpretation.[17]

Among the traditions that Mollah Ahmad quotes is the following: "The kings have authority over the people and the religious scholars have authority over kings *(Al-muluk hukkam ala' al-nas wa al-ulama' hukkam ala' al-muluk)*."[18]

Ayatollah Khomeini's further elaboration of this doctrine[19] mobilized perhaps the most important ideological challenge to the established political order. The predominance of a political overtone is the chief characteristic of his emendation of the *faqih*'s juridical authority to the point of attributing a political connotation to every ritualistic aspect of Shi'ism. On the basis of the *velayat-e faqih* doctrine, Khomeini mobilized the most crucial and consequential segment of the anti-Shah movement. In his reading, *velayat-e faqih* constituted that legitimating apparatus that would grant the jurisconsult every right to challenge the validity of a Muslim ruler. After Ayatollah Khomeini, his student and once heir-apparent Ayatollah Montazeri became a radical proponent and expositor of the idea of *velayat-e faqih*.[20] Later, postrevolutionary developments added more drastic elements to this idea, giving rise to the notion of the "absolute *velayat-e faqih*."[21]

Next to Khomeini's orchestrated appeals for the authority of the jurist, launched primarily in a "religious" language, were competing, however less powerful, ideological alternatives that commanded no less consequential obedience of other constituencies.

The Secular

A trinity of commonly held political claims to truth—nationalism, democracy, and socialism—imposed itself on the Iranian (among other Muslim) intelligentsia towards the middle of the nineteenth century.[22] These alternative ideological forces divided among themselves, with obvious overlapping constituencies, the adherence of selected segments of the Iranian society. The intelligentsia became physically and mentally separated from the core of the Iranian society by being ideologically engaged in political and ethical questions not traditionally sanctioned by the Islamic political culture.[23] Responsive to these imported ideologies, the Iranian intelligentsia began to incorporate their ideals into an active political frame of reference.

Nationalism in Iran was not just an alien utopian scheme "forced upon the Muslim mind from outside—from the Western challenge to the credibility and integrity of Islam."[24] This ought to be augmented with the nationalistically (in the sense of ethnically and culturally distinct) charged participation of Iranians as Muslims in the long course of Islamic history. Always conscious of their ethnic and cultural identity, Iranians, before and after the Shu'ubiyyah movement (seventh century), have participated in the collective Muslim history with a distinct voice and identity. The thriving persistence of the Persian language, the monumental epic of Ferdowsi (the *Shahnamah*), the towering achievements of Persian literature, the Iranian solar calendar, and seasonal holidays and festivities are among the innumerable motifs of Iranian cultural identity that have secured a distinct position for Iranians among other Muslims.

As a primarily modern secular political motif, however, nationalism has played a considerable role in contemporary Iranian history.[25] In the course of the Revolution, nationalist sentiments were expressed in more ways than just their primary institutionalization in the National Front. To be sure, the National Front claimed descendance from the revered legacy of Mohammad Mosaddeq (1882–1967)[26] and thus mobilized enough political force to make Ayatollah Khomeini receive Karim Sanjabi, former Minister of Education to Mosaddeq and, in the wake of the Revolution, the de facto leader of the National Front, in Neauphle-le-Château, France.[27]

Democracy was a utopian banner raised higher rhetorically than achieved in political practice. In the political lexicon of the Iranian intelligentsia, democracy postulated certain freedoms predicated on the principles of free will and individualism. Devoid of any meaningful institutional bases of support, ideals of democracy have always remained at a merely rhetorical level, at quintessential contradiction with the formal and informal forces of the Iranian traditional political culture. The contradictions that such encounters created for a Muslim audience[28] were chiefly responsible for restricting the democratic ideals to secluded pockets of devotion among the detached intelligentsia. The persistent propagation of democratic rhetorics to modern Iranian political culture was forceful enough, however, to infiltrate revolutionary semantics. This was manifested particularly in the ideological and political revolt against the repressive measures that the gradually delegitimated monarchy was forced to undertake.

Socialism, too, was pervasive in modern Iranian political culture beyond its institutionalization in the Tudeh and other socialist parties. In fact, socialist motifs have been more powerful in their noninstitutionalized settings. The doctrinal and metaphysical contradictions of Islam and socialism notwithstanding,[29] the political ideals of many Iranian intellectuals were directed away from traditional forms sanctioned in their received political culture and towards the powerful revolutionary motifs imported from the secular minds. From the Russian Revolution onward, socialism has been a powerful source of Iranian social movements.[30] In the course of the Islamic Revolution, it manifested itself not only clearly in the Tudeh and the Fada'ian-e Khalq sectors but also more tacitly in such diverse socialist figures and institutions as Ali Shari'ati, Mehdi Bazargan, Abolhasan Bani-Sadr, and the Mojahedin-e Khalq Organization.[31]

The dominance of the secular triumvirate of nationalism, democracy, and socialism appealed to a significant minority in the Iranian political community that, in turn, became a significant Other in terms of which religious ideologies began to redefine and relocate themselves. The principle problem with these secular ideological alternatives to the existing monarchical order was their exogenous origin, which was too heavy a burden for their targeted constituencies. The symbolic sources that nourished these ideologies were essentially alien to the constituencies that the secular intellectuals wished to lead. This created an ideological impasse that led a few prominent intellectuals to seek to disguise their ideals, consciously or otherwise, in Islamic rhetoric.

The (Cryptosecular) Religious: "The Islamic Ideology"

The failure of secular ideologies to attain a measure of legitimacy in Muslim societies is due in part to their attempt to activate a rhetoric that is Islamically mute. "The Islamic Ideology," the subject of the present study, however, was a set of religiously charged, Islamically informed, and ideologically alert political notions articulating the specific ways through which the status quo had to be altered. As articulated by its chief ideologues, "the Islamic Ideology" was an attempt to assimilate contemporary (secular) political objectives into "Islamic" ideas.[32]

The most eminent proponents of "the Islamic Ideology" in Iran were Jalal Al-e Ahmad (1923–1969), Ali Shariʿati (1933–1977), and Morteza Motahhari (1920–1979). Other prominent figures, as we shall see in the course of the present study, contributed to the making of this ideology. Having witnessed the failure of the Tudeh Party to communicate its ideological designs to its purported audience, Al-e Ahmad envisioned the possibility of an alternative language that could be delivered in a more Islamic cast. In his *Gharbzadegi (Westoxication),* and as the most compelling hidden agenda of the text, Al-e Ahmad tried to convince himself and others that the Shiʿite political ideas were the best possible forms through which an alternative system of political persuasions could be formulated.[33]

But the most serious exponent of "the Islamic Ideology" was Ali Shariʿati who undertook the task of rewriting the entire Islamic history in a utopian language that would convince his young constituency of the political viability of his version of Shiʿite Islam.[34] He embarked on an extensive approximation of the Marxist utopian motifs based on specifically Shiʿite terms.[35] The success of his reideologization of Islam still reverberates in diverse political groupings such as the organs of the Islamic Republic and the Mojahedin-e Khalq Organization. Beyond the initial endeavors of Al-e Ahmad and Shariʿati, and even beyond the massive erudition that Morteza Motahhari brought to bear on the validity of the neologistic construct, a whole generation of Islamic ideologues substantiated the specifics of "the Islamic Ideology."

While the patently secular ideologies could not mobilize enough revolutionary momentum to become politically viable, and thus gave rise to cryptosecular religious ideologies, patently religious motifs and sensibilities found their way into the pronouncedly secular movements and thus gave certain metaphysical impetus to otherwise this-worldly claims to political salvation.

The (Cryptoreligious) Secular: the Tudeh Party as a Prototype

The myths through which social orders sustain themselves are not realities sui generis. They are always indications of a political culture more enduring than its specific manifestations. Certain religious motifs of Islamic and Iranian origin found their way into patently secular ideologies which, if successful, would have subverted the metaphysical authority of that very political culture. That secular schemata of revolutionary energy are susceptible to such infiltration of religious motifs has to do with, first, the deep penetration of religious symbolics into the character of individuals despite their actively professing otherwise and, second, the inescapable urge of all utopian ideals, sacred or secular, to sustain themselves mythologically. Modernity and its secular ideologies have not in any way surpassed this urge.

In Iran the strongest cryptoreligious movement, perhaps the latest anti-credal creed of modernity, in this century was Marxism à la Tudeh Party. As the most successful and pervasive expression of Marxism, the Tudeh Party was the embodiment of the great socialist hope. The history of the actual organizational development of the Tudeh Party into the most widespread radical movement in modern Iranian history is also the chronicle of a unique fabrication of a particular mode of political myths.

In the Kabalistic tradition, the Tudeh Party had its share of sacred numbers, the first and most essential of which was "Fifty-Three," the number of original Marxists who planted the seeds that would later grow into the Tudeh Party. One of the Fifty-Three, Bozorg Alavi, permanently registered this figure in a literary rendition of their lives and thoughts.[36] Registration of this semisacred number in modern Iranian literary culture has rooted the Kabalistic number in the fertile soil of creative imagination.

After Alavi, Anvar Khame'i, another apostolic figure in the hagiographical history, added his twist to the sacred figure by dividing the number into "Fifty" and "Three," thus making three of the original Marxists, that is, Taqi Erani, Abdolsamad Kambakhsh, and Muhammad Shureshian, prominent and distinguished from the others.[37] In his hagiographical homage to this triumvirate, Anvar Khame'i canonizes them as three archetypal figures of almost metaphysical authority: Erani is the Immortal of wisdom, courage, and sacrifice;[38] Kambakhsh the angelic figure of organization, the chief mobilizer, the man of action and of few words;[39] Shureshian the archetypal commoner, the vile, as real and down-to-earth as all human fallacies require.[40] An archetype, Shureshian is the antithesis of both Erani, the supremely courageous and wise, and Kambakhsh, the supremely tactical and practical.

In both personal and collective consciousness, the Tudeh Party mobilized the most pervasive sentiments of hero worshipping and cults of "saintly" individuals. Such sentiments were directed towards figures with superhuman attributes. Taqi Erani and Khosrow Ruzbeh have constantly remained revered names whose invocation stirs the deepest respect and awe and the noblest of aspirations among the true believers.

There is also the pantheon of the Patristic generation whose names and thoughts are invoked as the supreme spells of truth. Marx, Engels, Lenin, and Stalin are Immortals whose words should be invoked to begin any discourse or settle any argument. The Gospels have been authoritative, bearing canonical weight: *Das Kapital* has always been in the background, rarely to be read and understood critically, always to be recited authoritatively; the *Communist Manifesto* is more readily accessible—the Prayer Book for every occasion. But Lenin and Stalin's exegeses should remain matters of essential party liturgy. Other than the canonical texts of the Patristic generation, there is also the native expositions of the principle dogmas. Here, the journal that Erani founded and edited, *Donya (The World)*, is of ecclesiastical authority. The demeanor and dogma of Marxism have fitted easily and perfectly with those of Shi'ism or any other creed of revealed truth.

The religious bent of the Tudeh Party was later followed closely by the Fada'ian-e Khalq Organization, some of whose founding fathers, such as Mas'ud Ahmadzadeh and Amir Parviz Pouyan, in fact, came from religious backgrounds.[41] The tradition of martyrdom, hero worship, and the cult of the individual persisted around such real/mythical figures as Bizhan Jazani, Abbas Sourki, Ali Akbar Safa'i Farahani, Muhammad Ashtiyani, and Hamid Ashraf. Even today the names and hagiographies of their heroic deeds carry the hallowed ring of sanctity. The details of the Siyahkal incident, in which the Shah's army annihilated the "rural team" of the Fada'ian, have assumed epic and romantic proportions, giving rise to volumes of poetry.[42] Bahman 19, 1350 (February 8, 1971), the day of the Siyahkal incident, entered the Kabalistic numerology of this Iranian revolutionary sect.

Ideologies and the Revolution

The relationship between these multiple ideological forces and the historical unfolding of the Revolution of 1979 is perhaps the most crucial impulse of modern Iranian history. Narrated on this impulse, the Islamic Revolution in Iran was a unique historical case in which these diverse ideological visions challenged the status quo ante. All contenders derived their ideological energies from two interpenetrating sources: (1) the traditional Iranic-Islamic culture and (2) modern secular motifs. The authority of the former was rooted in the metaphysical apparatus that had sustained its legitimacy for millennia. The power of the latter was derived from the hegemonic continuities of imperialism and colonialism, "The West" as the new supreme god-term. Both were present at diverse societal levels from the mid-nineteenth century onward. Perhaps without the Islamic Revolution providing a historical test of these two sources, it would have been impossible to ascertain which one carried more political and moral weight. But the Islamic Revolution testifies, among other things, to the preponderance of Islamic and Iranian ideas in securing the active obedience of a proportionately larger number of people. This suggestion is not merely founded on the historical fact of a *faqih* having led the Revolution or the Islamic Republican Party having appropriated all its political organs or the clergy having monopolized all the figures and institutions of the postrevolutionary authority. Even in their most professedly secular movements—the Tudeh Party and the Fada'ian-e Khalq Organization—the Iranian revolutionary intelligentsia could not escape the legacy of their Shi'ite heritage.

This is not to suggest that the fate of secular motifs is terminal in the Iranian political culture. Quite the contrary, the deep penetration of secular motifs—the persistence of the very word "ideology" in the revolutionary lexicon of the Islamic Republic—is too pervasive to be denied or easily eradicated. As a significant sign of their success, secular motifs persist totally undetected in the organs of the Islamic Republic. But such contradictions are inevitable in the transitional course of a victorious utopia becoming an established ideology.

Forces of Revolutionary Conviction: Between Ideology and Utopia

Upon such forces of revolutionary conviction and between the ideological and utopian constructions of "reality" are set forth the specific terms of the victory of "the Islamic Ideology." These specific terms, and with them those of the Revolution, are defined and circumscribed in ways more enduring than a given historical realization. Whether in ideological or in utopian reconstructions, constituent symbolic forces become operative at every social and cultural setup. Revolutionary circumstances are exaggerated conditions of ideological and utopian confrontations. States have a stake in picturing realities as being better than they actually are. Social revolutionary movements have an equally compelling motive to show the same realities as being worse than they are so that the terms and forces of the coming Kingdom of Heaven on Earth are made legitimate. Between states and social revolutions challenging their respective counterlegitimacy there exists a vast arena of conflict wherein every cultural symbol is reactivated for larger claims on the untapped energies of a mass constituency.

In such terms we cross the limits of a particular ideological revolution into more universal rules governing all symbolic breaks with the immediate past. Between a state ideology and a revolutionary utopia (itself expressed in ideological terms) there exists a volatile tension upon which the specific terms of discontent, longing for yet another reenchantment with the world, are articulated. "If every ideology," Paul Ricoeur has stipulated, "tends finally to legitimate a system of authority, does not every utopia, the moment of the other, attempt to come to grips with the program of power itself?"[43] This "power itself" is the mobilizing force behind every utopian denial of the status quo. The answer to Ricoeur's rhetorical question—"Is it not because a credibility gap exists in all systems of legitimation, all authority, that a place for utopia exist too?"—is self-evident. In every mechanism of legitimation, constructed on the Weberian bifocal bases of "external means" and "inner justification,"[44] dwells its undoing, rendering it, while still legitimate, illegitimate. It is precisely this possibility that makes legitimacy more a process than an absolute actuality. This process, always narrated in terms of a given political culture, must respond to changing historical circumstances or else fail. As Khomeini said upon his arrival in Tehran in February 1979, suppose our forefathers accepted constitutional monarchy as their preferred mode of government. They were in no position to decide for us what form of government we should follow.[45] Thus "the function of utopia," as Ricouer suggests, is "to expose the credibility gap wherein all systems of authority exceed . . . both our confidence in them and our belief in their legitimacy."[46] Ideologically formulated for mass political mobilization, such possibilities of utopian promises are realized in the course of the revolutionary movement.

The transformation of the discernible discrepancy between the state ideology and the revolutionary utopia into the ideology of revolt shall always remain contingent upon the immediacies of the historical exegencies —absolute or relative, actual or imaginary. Marx's insistence may be extended here beyond a mere economic determinism. "The production of ideas, of conceptions, of consciousness," Marx insisted, "is at first directly interwoven with the material activity and the material intercourse of men, the language of real life."[47] The reality of that life, particularly in its conceptual transformation into a language, however, goes beyond the specifically material conditions of the economic production of life. If "conceiving, thinking, the mental intercourse of men, appear . . . as the direct efflux of their material behavior,"[48] the compelling discrepancies between ideological claims of state to legitimacy and the revolutionary utopias denying it can be as material to generations of mobilizing forces as the most economic of all reasons. Particularly since those ideological claims, locating man, as they do, on a concrete correspondence to his being-in-the-world, are deeply rooted in their historical matter-of-factness—much beyond the economic means of production.

Absolute or relative, perceived deprivation from imagined standards of life become moving reasons for rebellion. Actual or imaginary, conventions of injustice, tyranny, corruption, and immorality can be the most compelling forces of ideological formation for revolutionary mobilization. "The phantoms formed in the human brain are," as Marx insisted, "necessarily, sublimates of their material life-process, which is empirically verifiable and bound to material premises."[49] Sublimates of material life as they may be, phantoms of liberty, equality, and moral certitude become realities sui generis capable of drastically altering the same material life. Conceptions of truth and reality emerge from man's being materially in the world. From these conceptions, in turn, revolutionary claims can emerge to redefine the world and all realities in it.

The Function of Social Fantasy

Althusser's structural integration of ideology and utopia into the formative forces of social consciousness gives credence to the assumption of their historical importance in social movements. "[A]n organic part of every social reality,"[50] ideology in Althusser's reading, informs, as it is formed by, every particular of the movement (as the most exaggerated form of social reality) it inspires and gives rise to. Althusser's apparent hyperbole that "it is as if human societies could not survive without these specific [ideological] formations, these systems of representations . . ., their ideologies,"[51] underlies the integral, and perhaps even inevitable, function of social fantasies in any mode of communal identity. Fantasy makes meaning possible; and meaning, interpreted in revolutionary terms, prompts political action. Whether representations of otherwise mute and meaningless facts into ingredients of a social cosmology of conviction or else their collective sublimation into active commands of revolt and resurrection, ideologies render the world meaningful and trustworthy even as they put systemic demands upon their memberships. "[T]he very element and atmosphere indispensable to . . . historical inspiration and life,"[52] as Althusser called them, ideologies, in fact, facilitate the cultural continuity of otherwise utterly unrelated facticities. At moments of revolutionary rejuvenations, ideologies, as momentarily supreme symbolic constructions of common mythologies, elevate communal Self-consciousness in sharp and radical contradistinction to Other-consciousness. With the prolonged agency of this dual imperative, these Self- and Other-consciousnesses, societies, as their individual memberships, leave and read their marks on history. "Only an ideological world outlook," Althusser suggested, "could have imagined societies without ideology and accepted the utopian ideas of a world in which ideology . . . would disappear without a trace, to be replaced by science."[53] To be replaced by science, as one radical expectation, or by religion, as another, utopian dreams of an end to ideology inevitably assume an ironically and paradoxically ideological language. An end of ideology is an ideology. So, too, is the beginning of every revolutionary movement which, defying the mortality of men and their societies, seeks to rejuvenate the communal identity by a set of new enchantments.

The irresistible propensity to be enchanted by successive ideological imperatives raises the all-too-essential question of "obedience." "When and why do men obey?"[54] Weber's formulation of the question—and the devotion of a lifetime to answer it—still remains the quintessential statement of modernity. "Upon what inner justifications and upon what external means does this domination rest?"[55] The bifocal direction of the answer also lies in the formulation of the Weberian question. No ideological construction of legitimacy, in stable or revolutionary directions, can rely solely on a monopoly of the physical force at its disposal. Such external means, whether appropriated by the state or claimed by the revolutionary opposition, will always have to be augmented by the equally compelling necessity of the "inner justification." The moving, convincing, and mobilizing call of this inner voice can echo from the "eternal yesterday" of all shared memories, can be receptive to "the extraordinary and personal *gift of grace*," or else can invoke the letter of some law as the basis of its legitimacy.[56] Perhaps the traditional is more convincing than the legal; perhaps the charismatic is stronger than both; but the ideological voice of legitimacy is always the most compelling force of Self- and Other-perception. Where forces of the cultural symbolic come to bear on the borderline of social psychology, modes of legitimate authority, whether in stable or revolutionary phases, not only move and mobilize, they also define and locate. Ideology, not the mere mechanics of the factual language, is the house of being. Right at the kernel of the "inner justification," where the dominant ideology yields to the rising utopia, lies the quintessential recipe of all revolutionary semantics—from the social psychology of obedience to the political culture of legitimacy.

The nature of this legitimacy, in physical or metaphysical terms, is at the foundation of the state apparatus, as it is at the very heart of the revolutionary challenge against it. Habermas's stipulation about the nature and orientation of this legitimacy unpacks a central problem of contention in the battle between every state and its revolutionary opposition. "If belief in legitimacy," Habermas noted, "is conceived as an empirical phenomenon without an immanent relation to truth, the grounds upon which it is explicitly based have only psychological significance."[57] It is very difficult to imagine a "belief" in legitimacy that is operative at a merely "empirical" level. All claims and beliefs in legitimacy must, by definition, operate at some measurable proximity to truth—self-proclaimed, self-sustained, however in reference to some higher reality. Otherwise, the continued validity of that legitimacy is always subject to counterinterpreted facts.

Yet it is possible to see, in comparative terms, two modes of legitimacy, with one having a more "immanent relation to truth" than the other. If such two modes of legitimacy face each other as two opposing claims over one territorial constituency, such as a social revolution, the one with the closer affinity to truth will always be at a moral, if not material, advantage. The psychological significance of an empirically based legitimacy is no match for a claim of political truth with God on its side. An ideology of legitimacy is no match for a theology of discontent. The theological choice between the Shah and the Ayatollah is self-evident.

Habermas is quite emphatic on the precarious nature of a merely empirically based legitimacy.

Whether such [empirically based psychological] grounds can sufficiently stabilize a given belief in legitimacy depends on the institutionalized prejudices and observable behavioral dispositions of the group in question.[58]

But neither "institutionalized prejudices" nor "observable behavioral dispositions" can be a match for symbolic suggestions that higher authorities are involved.

If ... every effective belief in legitimacy is assumed to have an immanent relation to truth, the grounds on which it is explicitly based contain a rational validity claim that can be tested and criticized independently of the psychological effect of these grounds.[59]

The assumed proximity of the legitimacy to truth invariably grounds the rationality of the choice in profound metarational figments of shared imagination. The more collectively held a belief, the larger its rational claims of metaphysical legitimacy.

Insufficiency of the Bare Necessities

It is this presumed proximity to truth—sustained by cultural, sociological, and psychological terms of legitimacy—that gives the ideological proposition its inner strength vis-à-vis the existing social concerns. Whether in stable or revolutionary phases, "the ideological guidance," as Clifford Geertz has suggested for Indonesia, has to face "this forest of problems."[60] The observation is equally valid for any other national culture. It is impossible for a political culture to confront the realities of its problems with its bare necessities.

The motivation to seek ... technical skill and knowledge, the emotional resilience
to support the necessary patience and resolution, and the moral strength to sustain
self-sacrifice and incorruptibility must come from somewhere, from some vision of
public purpose anchored in a compelling image of social reality.[61]

Whether the technical skill is to build a dam or to print a revolutionary
poster, the emotional resilience necessary for its achievement cannot be
derived from a mechanical accumulation of expertise. "The moral strength
to sustain self-sacrifice," or *sabr-e enqelabi* ("revolutionary patience") as
the Iranian activists called it in the course of the Revolution, not only puts
the movement at a moral advantage over the status quo, it also translates
the morality of this self-sacrifice into calculable matters of mass mobilization. As for the self-deceptive illusions that all this enterprise entails, Geertz's
insight about Indonesia is frighteningly applicable to the Iranian case too:

That all these qualities may not be present; that the present drift to revivalistic
irrationalism and unbridled fantasy may continue; that the next ideological phase
may be even farther from the ideals for which the revolution was ostensibly fought
than is the present one; that Indonesia may continue to be ... the scene of political
experiments from which others profit much but she herself very little; or that the
ultimate outcome may be viciously totalitarian and wildly zealotic is all very true.[62]

The cultural forces, beyond the sociological and the psychological, that
become operative in postrevolutionary disenchantments are the very causes
that were instrumental in the originating enchantments. In fact, no mobilizing enchantment, no engaged preoccupation with a convincing illusion, is
possible without their terms of legitimacy deeply rooted in cultural mores,
in the sanctifying memory of that eternal yesterday that simply refuses to
let go of any present or future.

The Hegelian proposition, so favored by Mannheim's conception of
"Ideology and Utopia," provides further clues as to the dialectical roots of
this primacy of enchantment in any received imperative of the political
culture: "All movements in the historical world go on in this way: Thought,
which is the ideal counterpart of things as they really exist, develops itself
as things ought to be."[63] No political culture is conceivable in a static or
stagnant stage. That would be a contradiction in terms. A political apparatus can claim a cultural underpinning only to the degree that it attends its
historicity with such symbolic imperatives that transcend, as they define, its
immediate exegencies. The historical world would thus be rendered into a
heap of memoryless facticities if denied the cultural parameters of its realization, the power of its remembrance, the symbolic terms of its own
transcendence. The primacy of thought over action can only be conceivable
for the cultural man, for the symbolic artifact who acts with concepts and
conceives with actions. Things as they really exist—a contingency always
there by virtue of a figment of imagination—are, in fact, the battlefield

between the ideological and utopian alternatives, fighting over larger portions of mass loyalties. By virtue of collective subscription to an ideological or utopian reality of "things as they really exist," states and social revolutions measure their chances of combat and victory. Whether in the pre- or postrevolutionary imagination, "as things ought to be" divides the royalties of potential followers to competing utopias, to rival claims to political truth. Throughout this relentless enterprise of culture-building political activitism, no battle is launched, no revolution made, no state toppled without such compelling terms of ideological construction, of utopian design, of semiotic transfiguration of what is into what will have to be.

Is there any direction or sense of purpose in this relentless transfigurative force that closes every ideological certainty by a utopian doubt and then, in turn, metamorphoses the utopian doubt into the illusion of the coming ideological crisis? Having reviewed the utopian designs of Saint-Simon and Fowler, Paul Ricoeur suggests that "We cannot get out of the circle of ideology and utopia, but the judgment of appropriateness may help us to understand how the circle can become spiral." [64] There is a rational mind immune to the forces of history.

For the circle to become a spiral, with the necessary stipulation of an upward mobility, a metaphysical Hegelian inevitability must be assigned to the presumed rhymes and reasons of history. The challenges to the continuous construction of such spirals out of the circularity of ideology and utopia come not only from the historical inevitability of rational and traditional forces, in the Weberian understanding, constantly advancing and regressing the movement in diametrically opposed directions, permanently undoing the spiral. The more compelling challenge comes from charismatic movements that, by totally reconstituting the legitimate and operative moral demand systems, suggest—and occasionally succeed in implementing—a whole new geometrical proposition.

Upon the selfsame circularity of ideology and utopia a host of alternatives to a spiral movement may be suggested, may be implemented, may succeed, and may fail. Or even more fundamentally, the construction of any geometrical purpose in life may be altogether challenged. The circularity of the ideological-utopian alternates neither sees nor recognizes itself as such. Any ideological or utopian episode locates itself, to use Habermas's language, in the closest possible vicinity of truth. The sense of purpose and direction beyond its contemporary political verification, or beyond its distant metaphysical claims, cannot be stipulated as a constituent force of any ideological or utopian design for mass mobilization.

Authority of the Text

Between institutions and texts, ideologies and utopias divide their respective realms of authority. If institutions are the active loci for the ideological legitimacy of the status quo, texts are where utopias begin to rest their case for the coming paradise on earth. Whether ideological or utopian, massive orchestrations of the shared symbolics need to have either institutional or textual frames of self-reference. As states construct ministries and parliaments, festivals and monuments, in their legitimizing terms, social revolutions are predicated on textual testimonies to their ideological veracity. For the utopian language to choreograph its claim to legitimacy on pages of its advancement to ideological maturity (because ideology is the dramatization of language into political corners of legitimacy), generations of mobilizing vocabulary ought to be reetymologized.

Whether reinterpreted or neologized, the terms of the coming revolution derive their energy from the distant and immediate roots of their claim to legitimacy. "The Islamic Ideology," as the supreme ideological construct of the Islamic modernity, draws on both "Islam" reinterpreted and "ideology" reinvented.[65] Quintin Skinner's textual-contextual dialectics of historical hermeneutics allows the contemporaneity of such constructs to come forward.

For it is evident that the nature and limits of the normative vocabulary available at any given time will also help to determine the ways in which particular questions come to be singled out and discussed.[66]

Such a "normative vocabulary" is formed through the dialectics of "ideology" and "utopia," each denying the other legitimacy. Thus the same vocabulary that normalizes patterns of social behavior sows the seeds of the coming revolution, the terms of the coming reenchantment. "The nature and limits of the normative vocabulary" cannot be assumed as the essentialist terms of a permanent enchantment with the possibilities of being. The questions a generation of ideologues come to pose postulate the terms of the coming revolution, even as they seek to render the status quo (il)legitimate.

The haunting questions that animate a generation emerge from the deepest layers of its moral convictions. The existential imperative of the ideologues is to help such collective sentiments come to surface. To Merton's question, "Where is the existential basis of mental productions located?" there are more than social structural and cultural answers.[67] The institutional bases of ideological production, whether in contemporary or historical diameters, can respond only belatedly to more compelling activities of deeper cultural origins. This is not to suggest that the economic production or political sustenance of history succeeds their aesthetic or normative celebration. Both institutions and figures of authority, whether in economic or political spheres of social construction of reality, are but more tangible manifestations of the deeper symbolics of authority that assume a reality almost sui generis. Changes in the symbolics of authority —who is to rule and why and through what particular set of legitimate ceremonials—occur long before a king is chased out of his sovereignty or an ayatollah out of his jurisdiction. A cleric would succeed a monarch in assuming supreme political authority long after the royal regalia have yielded their symbolic legitimacy to the juridical robe. A minister of finance is chosen on the basis of the number of years he has spent in prison— rather than the extent of his education and experience—long after ties and three-piece suits have yielded their authorities to a tieless shirt, a compelling black beard, and all the semiotic regalia of a "downtrodden" appearance.

Mental productions of some essentialist views of past, present, and future in ideological or utopian terms always rest on an all-out battle for symbolic realms of legitimacy. For the legitimacy-nervous Shah there was the 2,500th anniversary of Persian monarchy, constructed from a fragmented historical memory to make him feel more secure in his power. But for Khomeini the selfsame 2,500 years are records of shame and tyranny. Between the Shah's construction of fabricated glory and Khomeini's imagination of collective shame, each for his particular political purpose, there is only one set of a common repertoire of shared symbolics. Use it as they do to their stated and hidden agenda, it is at this symbolic level of manipulation that battles are fought and revolutions launched. Changes in figures and institutions of authority—from Mohammad Reza Shah, "the Sun of the Aryan Race," to Imam Khomeini, "the Leader of the poor people of the world," from Constitutional Monarchy to the Islamic Republic—occur only after the battles over the symbolic sources of their legitimacy are launched, fought, and won. The rhetoric of the symbolics, fought at ideological and utopian battlelines, is much more compelling and immediate than the brick and mortars of domestic and foreign affairs.

Where do these symbols find their home, their Self- and Other-references, their power of enchantment? This question is at the heart of revolutionary mobilization. Mannheim's attempt to search behind the structural foundations of ideological formations led him to stipulate a "total ideological superstructure"[68] as the ultimate aim of the sociology of ideology. Sociological determinants are incapable of reducing ideological formations "to the last detail."[69] Two additional angles are necessary to narrow in on the forceful presence of ideological constructs: social-psychological and what Mannheim calls "the specialized contents" of ideologies.

For the social-psychological forces conducive to ideological constructions, Mead is more persuasive than Mannheim in his analytical stipulation of "Self" and "Other" in the social production of identity and whatever else goes with it. In the social construction of identity—as the quintessential locus of ideology-making enterprise—not only a "Self," consisting of the premise of a "me" and the active agency of an "I," but also a "generalized Other" are of central significance.[70] Between the "Self" and the "generalized Other" there develops an active enterprise of dialectical cross-confirmation in terms of which realities are perceived. Otherwise mute and irrelevant, facts assume meaning and significance only to the degree that they make sense in that tacit but binding contract negotiated between the "Self" and the "generalized Other." Although Mead did not follow his own theoretical lead in this particular direction, there is a significant contribution to the sociology of ideology in his social psychology of personal and communal identity. As dramatized occasions of social-psychological identity, ideologies and utopias invariably operate on the ebb and flow of the borderlines between the "Self" and the "generalized Other." Moreover, whereas Mead saw this "generalized Other" as an essentially communal enterprise in which the individual bearer of a "Self" participates, there is also the historically recognizable possibility of a "hostile Other" in terms of its hegemonic perceptions the "Self" may remake itself. As the supreme deification of the Muslim self-consciousness, "The West" has come to constitute the ultimate "hostile Other" against whose domineering terms modern Islam has a deep *ressentiment*. It is precisely in terms of this *ressentiment* that Islam attends its modern history.

In the Mannheimian recognition of "the specialized contents" of ideological formations, nothing can be more revealing than symbolic referents of the specificities of mental constructs—whether political or aesthetic. Here Geertz has given us the necessary clue in his conception of art as a cultural system:

The chief problem presented by the sheer phenomenon of aesthetic force . . . is how to place it within the other mode of social activity, how to incorporate it into the texture of a particular pattern of life. And such placing, the giving to art objects a cultural significance, is always a local matter; what art is in classical China or classical Islam . . . is just not the same thing, no matter how universal the intrinsic qualities that actualize its emotional power may be.[71]

Nothing is more central to, more constitutional in the making of, an aesthetic construction of reality that has an ideological force of its own than its formative (local) symbolic forces. Geertz's insistence on the locality of the artistic force is merely an indication of the superior force of symbolic constructs—always compelling only to the degree of their local and native registrability—that form and signify the artifact. The whole process and spectrum of signification in the aesthetic artifact, whether visual or literary, cannot begin to become simultaneously illuminative and operative before the local repertoire of collective symbolics is registered at both the ontological and epistemological levels. These two angles, in fact, focus on precisely "the specialized contents," as Mannheim calls them, or the locality of the artifact, as does Geertz. Through either of the two theoretical lenses—or preferably both—the primacy of symbolic registration in ideological constructions, political or aesthetic in medium, becomes evident. Historicized symbolics is where politics and culture meet.

The Function of Intellectuals

If, as we see now, symbolic forces and constructs, rehistoricized, are the quintessential terms of the ideological fabrication of reality, we already have a significant clue as to the specific social grouping that always acts as the agency of change. The intellectuals, in the broadest sense of the term, are the master manipulators of the received symbolics, the agents of rehistoricizing their received culture. "Make it new!" Ezra Pound's public revelation speaks precisely to this relentless intellectual preoccupation with the sacrosanct of all received symbolics.[72] "There is in every society," as begins a convincing definition of the intellectuals by Edward Shils,

a minority of persons who, more than the ordinary run of their fellow men, are enquiring, and desirous of being in frequent communion with symbols which are more general than the immediate concrete situation of everyday life, and remote in their reference in both time and space.[73]

The intellectuals are always in the minority. There are only a few, perhaps a happy yet anxious few, who dare to look the most sacrosanct forces of their collective destiny in the eye and reach for their Achilles' heel. Shils's emphatic parameters of "more general" or "remote in their reference" may create the impression of an ivory tower detachment that is simply not there. In the most "immediate concrete situation of everyday life" intellectuals perceive their quintessential symbolic origins of historical legitimacy. It is precisely the relentless preoccupation with the originating force of these symbolics that energizes the intellectuals' "need to externalize this quest in oral and written discourse, in poetic or plastic expressions, in historical reminiscence or writing, in ritual performance and acts of worship."[74] The intellectuals' "historical reminiscence" is the very stuff of which contending realities are remade. What Shils calls "this interior need to penetrate beyond the screen of immediate concrete experience"[75] is the intellectual's very reason for being, his condito sine qua non. The existential presence of the intellectuals in every society is the social-structural realization of formative cultural forces that seek measures of manifestation and continuity through the selfsame agencies they engender and animate, doubt and destroy, rethink and reconstruct.

The End of Ideology?

With the Mannheimian understanding of the term—and with such social-structural, cultural, and rehistoricized symbolic forces operative in its perpetuation—"the end of ideology," "the end of history," "the end of Hegel," or any other such illusions is a figment of an anxious imagination, a negligence of man's coexistential need to redefine his human existence in ever more updated terms. If anything, this is the most significant lesson of the Islamic Revolution in Iran. Contrary to Daniel Bell's otherwise brilliant articulation of its demise, there is no "dead end"[76] for ideology. As a "secular religion,"[77] ideological constructs have no less claim on the modernity of human symbolic repertoires and obedience than "real religions" did on the archaic repertoire and faith.

What difference does it make which ultimate source of authority legitimates an exclusive claim on symbolic authority—God, "eternal yesterday," or "the inevitable force of history." Conviction is conviction is conviction. With Mannheim's sociology of knowledge now a mere set of truisms, Bell's differentiation between a "scholar," as someone "less involved with his 'self,' " and an "intellectual," as someone who "begins with *his* experience, *his* individual perceptions of the world, *his* privileges and deprivations, and [who] judges the world by these sensibilities,"[78] has a more dubious claim on our credulity.

Particular ideologies, from new Hegelians to post-Marxists, may indeed have exhausted themselves. But man's need to define and redefine his existential location in opposing universes of meaning and significance continues. The language of that quintessential need, always speaking with suggestions and symbols, is irreversibly ideological. Bell is closer to this truth when he admits that "the end of ideology is not—should not be—the end of utopia as well."[79] What is "utopia" but "ideology" turned upside down in the very same cast?

Of course ideologues are "terrible simplifiers." The subjects of this book testify to that fact. But it is precisely in the terrible simplicity of their argument that they manage to have access to the most public convictions of men out of their most sincere solitudes. Translating private virtues into public convictions, ideologies are the primary movers of human history through the active agency of the most enduring human need for Self-and Other-definition. As history moves with time, so does the innate human need to relocate man in the newly coined terms of security and legitimacy—remaking the world, as they do, meaningful and trustworthy.

"The end of history" is as meaningless as "the end of ideology." A mere redundancy, "the end of history" is a disingenious sensationalizing of "the end of ideology." Issued from the surface of a bureaucratic vulgarization of a much deeper insight provided by Weber earlier in the century, Fukuyama's assumption of "the trimph of the West, of the Western *idea*," which is supposed to be "evident first of all in the total exhaustion of viable systematic alternatives to Western liberalism,"[80] is a mere self-congratulatory pat on the back at a moment of deep anxiety for the same "West." The same "West" that through selective amnesia forgets that for more than a decade now "liberalism" is an almost four-letter word in American politics. That Allan Bloom—the same Bloom who, a volume earlier, had imagined "the Western Culture" closed to the American mind[81]—and many other "defenders" of "the Western civilization" have jumped on the bandwagon of self-congratulation[82] is perhaps the strongest indication that this is more a symptom of deep anxiety than any genuine insight into the state of our presumed ideological exhaustion. Except for its bureaucratic version, there is nothing new in Fukuyama's assumption of "the end of history." Almost seventy years earlier, Weber's brilliant insight into the conditions of disenchantment of the world articulated the terms of what he thought was the coming spiritual crisis.[83] Even before Weber, the brutal pronouncements of Nietzche in the nineteenth century or, even earlier, Pascal's reflections on the changing cosmology of man's self-reference in the seventeenth century anticipated or lamented, in vain, a "perpetual" loss of compelling illusions giving meaning and significance to an otherwise meaningless and insignificant location of man in the universe.

What is particular to our age is perhaps, and only perhaps, the historical exhaustion of only one particular ideology, Marxism, vis-à-vis another, "Western liberalism." But even after all inner contradictions of "Western liberalism" have been exhausted, after all the quintessential cross-negations of the Jesse Jacksons and Jesse Helmses of "The West," the David Dukes and Mario Cuomos of American Politics, have levelled each other out, there will emerge yet another set of enchantments, another cast of ideological anchor on which men will hang their human destiny. As in the Manichaen preeternal cosmogony, world history commences when particles of good and evil begin to recognize themselves—and with themselves their opposites—in some universal frame of reference. Insofar as that recognition in terms of two opposing dialectics continues to be the quintessential mechanism of human self-knowledge, history continues. If not this ideology, then another; if not this utopia, then another. Every disenchantment paves the way for the coming reenchantment. Every disillusion marks the coming reillusion. History cannot have an end if the historical men and women are to people it.

The Aesthetics of Discontent

Nowhere is this inevitability of the ideological discourse, within which history, in one form or another, keeps narrating itself, more evident than in its coeternality with the aesthetics. The revolutionary posters, stamps, and murals in Tehran testify to that. Based on the specifics of the Kantian imaginary, Terry Eagleton has narrowed in on the precise nature of this affinity:

The ideologico-aesthetic is that indeterminate region, stranded somewhere between the empirical and theoretical, in which abstractions seem flushed with irreducible specificity and accidental particulars raised to pseudocognitive status. The loose contingencies of subjective experience are imbued with the binding force of law, but a law which can never be known in abstraction from them. Ideology constantly offers to go beyond the concrete to some debatable proposition, but that proposition constantly eludes formulation and disappears back into the things themselves. In this particular condition of being, the individual subject becomes the bearer of a universal, ineluctable structure which impresses itself upon it as the very essence of its identity.[84]

In their indeterminancy, in their quasi-aesthetic allusions to realities that are there and are not there, ideologies provoke the awe of obedient uncertainty that is most congenial to revolutionary mobilization. Before being transferred to the theoretical comfort of academic speculations, the empirical world, from the streets of Tehran to the Shah's palaces, is always the subject of ideological reconstructions into a meaningful and moving picture of reality—always socially constituted. Thus constructed, it is more a matter of theoretical choice if we call ideological claims to our obedience "pseudocognitive" or otherwise. False consciousness is as compelling as any other. Although the abstracted laws that emanate from the particulars of an ideology cannot be known except in terms of those particulars, there still exists a reciprocal relationship between facts, ideologically reconstructed, and ideologies, factually redocumented. What is permanent in ideological reconstructions of reality—and what is permanent in man's ideological disposition—is precisely this illusion that not their imaginative apparition but "the things themselves" have a solitary claim on truth. Beginning with a benign factual indeterminancy, mundane realities—or the accidental particulars of a totally shapeless world—are sublimated and obediently raised to the level of ideological particles. Then that universal call to truth that animates this particular ideology, or another, gives meaning and significance, function and thrust, to those speechless and voiceless realities and only then throws them back to us as elements of our historical narrative.

Whether theological, hagiographical, or simply ideological, the historical narrative feeds on such sublimated particles of accidental reality, obediently raised to meet the terms of their ideological signification. True to the ideological—and as Terry Eagleton says for the aesthetic—state of man's being-in-the-world, this compelling force of myth- and history-making enterprise, always a joint venture, puts a negating question mark at the dead end of any proposition of "the end of history?"

Between Interdicts and Transgressions

The continuity and, as we can see, the historical inevitability of the ideological ordering of reality cannot be separated from the permanent hierarchical order of authority. For every departing Shah there is a returning Ayatollah. From this permanence ideology derives its force. Perhaps it is a condition of radical contemporaneity, as Philip Rieff has taught us, perhaps an indication of "shifting conditions, [when] all justifications [are] exposed as ideologies."[85] But mythological constructs, sacred or secular figments of the imagination, have a habit of universalizing themselves into some reading of an abiding "eternal yesterday," condemning "the terrible conditions of today," promising "the kingdom of heaven to come." The expanse of "remissive occasions," in Rieff's stipulation, is precisely the territory where the "interdicts" and the "transgressives" fight their historical battle, settle their accounts. All the "Thou Shalt Nots" first yield to "Thou Mayest" before they succumb to total reversals. Ideologies are the heightened languages of the remissives—transferring one political culture to another. Revolutionary movements, in Rieff's reading, operate at three interrelated levels of engagement—the cultural, the social-structural, and the psychological. The cultural order of interdictions and transgressions, the social order of privileges and deprivations, and the psychological order of impulse and inhibitions must all undergo fundamental transmutations before a revolutionary movement may be assumed to be in full gear. The active agencies of such revolutionary changes always work "through the symbolic and beyond it."[86] That beyond is the collective set of god-terms specific to every ideology, and with it to the political culture that creates and sustains it.

Anxiety-provoking transgressions render the legitimate interdictory motifs the commanding truths of every living and thriving culture—political or aesthetic. Ideological constructions, themes and battle cries of the coming revolution, redefine the existing moral demand system by investing in its interdictory and transgressive motifs. Although social revolutions—and their originating ideological testaments—aim at the institutional redefinition of politics and culture, they register their most enduring effects at the symbolic level. Symbolic subversion of the existing order always precedes and invariably succeeds the more visible institutional transmutations. It is through poetry, painting, and ideological pamphleteering that the terms of the coming revolution are first articulated. And it is through the same modes of the symbolic manipulation of the culture that the utopian illusion of the next revolt comes to discredit the preceding disenchantment. Between them, ideology and utopia divide the human history into relentless successive phases of "yes" and "no," of denial and approval.

Within the framework of the inevitable authority—constant in its hierarchical form, varied in its constitutional content—the elusive nature of the relationship between ideas (in ideological orchestrations) and social actions (in specific political direction) is quite crucial. Here, Parsons' division of ideas—in their relation to social action—into "existential" and "normative" categories, discounting, for our purposes, the further subdivision of the "existential" into "empirical" and "nonempirical,"[87] could carry us some distance. "Existential" ideas, empirical or otherwise, may or may not be conducive to radical social actions. If ideas, regardless of their origin, are indicative of grave material reasons for revolutions, they will, in fact, be so used. But they may also be grasped in some existential recognition as supportive of the status quo. The same is true about the "normative" ideas: They, too, may hinder or advance the legitimacy of the status quo.

Lacking in the Parsonian stipulations here is the crucial role of the orchestration of ideas, existential or normative, into particular political melodies—ideological or utopian, conservative or revolutionary. Ideas as facts, pure and simple, will always be lacking in registering a responsive cord in a politically significant constituency. Unless harmonized into some existential or normative pattern of meaning and mobilization, ideas as such, whether existential or normative in origin, are mute and set in an irreversible course of counterinterpretations. In their isolated individualities, ideas as facts are invitations to conflicting readings. Only when organized into a convincing system of command and obedience do historical facts assume their relevant role in directing social actions.

Max Scheler's attempt to designate, even beyond Husserl, a "phenomenological fact" that is not (1) naturally or (2) cognitively mediated[88] shall always remain a cognitive philosophical proposition, plausible theoretically but uncontrollable sociologically. The notion of a "phenomenological fact . . . independent of all factors which are not grounded in the things themselves,"[89] however philosophically plausible, is sociologically problematic. Unless ideologically constructed, whether through natural or cognitive processes, facts, in their phenomenological abstractions, are meaningless or at least subject to relentless and paralyzing counterinterpretations. Every ideological reading of facts, backed by the politics of power and the metaphysics of certainty, blocks, ipso facto, all other counterinterpretations. Then they become socially significant.

Obviously such ideological readings of reality and facticity are somehow "grounded in the things themselves," and here phenomenology can open a window from the facticity of being-in-the-world unto its historicity. But in which specific directions the branches of this tree move, the root has very little to say. There is quite a distance between Muhammad and Khomeini, between history "objectively" ascertained, if ever, and ideology imaginatively reconstructed. "Natural facts," as Scheler understood them, are phenomenological facticities intermediated by sense perceptions. Cognitive or "scientific facts" are those constructed through what Scheler called "scientific reduction."[90] "The carriers of scientific facts," Alfred Schultz paraphrases Scheler, "are symbols, which receive a particular content merely by way of a science definition."[91] Because what Scheler calls "scientific fact" stands at a higher level of abstracted construction, it yields more fruit for a sociological reading of reality. But we may expand this "scientific fact" to include any form of "cognitive" construction of reality. In this more general sense, any cognitive construction of reality involves the symbolic assignment of meaning to an otherwise mute abundance of facticities. Symbolic, historically charged, interventions between the phenomenological reality of an overabundance of facticities and their cognitive reconstruction into meaningful social forces is at the very heart of the sociology of ideology. It is precisely in this process of rendering facts into meaningful realities that multiple and simultaneous ideological invitations to political truths and pious obedience measure their degree of success or failure. The social revolutions, anticipated or achieved, projected by such ideological reconstructions of reality, are dramatized moments in a never-ending quest for meaning and justification in an otherwise meaningless and unjustifiable world.

The Age of Disenchantment?

How are we to reconcile between such relentless and timeless human urges for ideologically remaking sense of the world through successive revolutions and Weber's prophetic vision that ours is the age of "disenchantment"? The key word here, perhaps, is "disenchantment" which must embody the seeds of future "reenchantment" in it. "The fate of our time," Weber proclaimed as early as 1918, "is characterized by rationalization and intellectualization and, above all, by the 'disenchantment of the world.' "[92] Paving the way for this compelling disenchantment, rationalization and intellectualization have had the best of intentions. In the process, however, all heavenly forces have been redomesticated and repoliticized, even the Almighty Himself.

But in what precise term, other than the particulars of our existential choice, can we assume that "the ultimate and most sublime values have retreated from public life"?[93] Neither "the transcendental realm of mystic life" nor "the brotherliness of direct and personal human relations," in the precise sense of the terms, have—or could have—exhausted the possibilities of the "ultimate and most sublime values." The fountainhead of such

"ultimate and most sublime values" is not in any specific historical materialization of their ideals, but in the collective imagination of man as an
exclusively symbolizing, myth-making animal. Insofar as that fountainhead
is there, a coeternal of all human collectivities, so, too, is the relentless
reenchantment with "the ultimate and most sublime values." As the example of the Iranian Revolution testifies, both "the transcendental realm of
mystic life" (Khomeini objectified) and "the brotherliness of direct and
personal human relations" ("the Islamic Ideology" subjectified) could very
well be the agencies of reenchantment with a newly improved reconstruction of "ultimate and most sublime values." Discounting their aesthetic
qualities, or the lack thereof, the Iranian revolutionary art defies all intima-
cies and aspires to monumental presence. Khomeini's mausoleum exemplifies everything about the Islamic Revolution. Resembling the Dome of the
Rock, where Prophet Muhammad is believed to have ascended to the
Seventh Heaven to be with God Almighty Himself, Khomeini's mausoleum
is the monumental artistic expression of a reenacted enchantment with
some rather old "ultimate and most sublime values."

For his time, which he called "our time," Weber observed that it is not
accidental "that today only within the smallest and intimate circles . . .
something is pulsating" that corresponds to the prophetic *pneuma,* which
in former times swept through the great communities like a firebrand,
welding them together." [94] But look at the Iranian Revolution. The reverberating pulse of a "smallest and intimate" circle, the ideologues of the
Islamic Revolution, did precisely that: sweeping through a great community, welding them together. Insofar as "the transcendental realm of mystic
life," "the brotherliness of direct and personal human relations," or "the
smallest and intimate circles" continue to safeguard the seeds of that "prophetic *pneuma,*" what is there to prevent a charismatic translation of all
such private pieties into a firebrand of the most compelling communal
concerns?

Yes, indeed, artificial attempts at artistic revival of the monumental style
may lead to "miserable monstrosities" [95] of Weber's contemporary examples—or ours. Yes, indeed, the same would ensue if there is an "intellectual" effort "to construe new religions without a new and genuine prophecy." [96] But did Weber underestimate the power of reinterpretation,
Verstehendemethode radicalized from sociology to ideology? From "Zionism" to "Liberation Theology" to "the Islamic Ideology" there is, in a
modern history to which Weber was not a witness, a relentless reinterpretation of what was into what should be. Weber was right in characterizing
any "intellectual" attempts towards a "religious" movement, a contradiction in terms, as "miserable monstrosities." But did he underestimate the
power of his own brilliant construction of "charismatic authority" in manipulating the still stirring common symbolics into new and ecstatic heights?

Old symbols die hard, and new symbols are born even harder. A mere masterful manipulating hand can reorganize older convictions for newer ambitions. "Academic prophecy," again a contradiction in terms (because intellectuals are terrible prophets), may indeed lead to "fanatical sects but never a genuine community."[97] The only two Islamic ideologues who came near universities, Shari'ati and Motahhari, despised everything about formal training. Compare the dismal number of dissertations they supervised to the avalanche of their ideological outpourings. No comparison there. But "the demon who holds the fibers of his very life," to use Weber's profoundest assessment of academic intellectuality for ideologues, is of an entirely different origin and orientation. Not academic but ideological prophecy—the tireless urge to reinterpret the old convictions for the newly formed political agenda—is at the heart of every renewed social movement to create not just "fanatical sects" but "a genuine community"—formed only to be reenchanted.

With Weber's ultimatum, "To the person who cannot bear the fate of the times like a man," we already cross the realm of inquiry into the nature and organization of ideology and enter the existential vicinity of the scholar himself, the author, the student of the (Iranian) revolution. "[M]ay he rather return silently, without the usual publicity build-up of renegades, but simply and plainly"[98] is the advice we may give many contemporary students of the Iranian Revolution who cannot keep their religious convictions to themselves and to their private pieties. "The arms of the old churches are opened widely and compassionately for him."[99] The "old churches," or mosques, no difference here, might have been renovated or even completely reconstructed, but the open arms are there. Weber put "the intellectual sacrifice" for such transfers of royalty into quotation marks then and, nonexistent as it is now too, it should stay there perhaps permanently. The rest of Weber's indictment against the misplaced piety of academic prophets is so eloquently clear in his own words, uttered at the beginning of the twentieth century, that they need no updating for the 1990s or modifying for the Iranists.

". . . One Way or Another

He has to bring his 'intellectual sacrifice'—that is inevitable. If he can really do it, we shall not rebuke him. For such an intellectual sacrifice in favor of an unconditional religious devotion is ethically quite a different matter than the evasion of the plain duty of intellectual integrity, which sets in if one lacks the courage to clarify one's own ultimate standpoint and rather facilitates this duty by feeble relative judgments. In my eyes, such religious return stands higher than the academic prophecy, which does not clearly realize that in the lecture rooms of the university no other virtue holds but plain intellectual integrity. Integrity, however, compels us to state that for the many who today tarry for new prophets and saviors, the situation is the same as resounds in the beautiful Edomite watchman's song of the period of exile that has been included among Isaiah's oracles:

He calleth to me out of Seir, Watchman, what of the night? The watchman said, The morning cometh, and also the night: if he will enquire, enquire ye: return, come." [100]

Now is the Winter of our Discontent
Made glorious Summer. . . .

Richard III
Act I, Scene I

CHAPTER I

Jalal Al-e Ahmad: The Dawn of "the Islamic Ideology"

"You seem to think that I want to convert you to a doctrine," George Sand conjectured once in a letter to Gustave Flaubert.[1] "Not at all, I don't think of such a thing. Everyone sets off from a point of view, the free choice of which I respect. In a few words, I can give a resume of mine, not to place oneself behind an opaque glass through which one can see only the reflection of one's own nose. To see as far as possible the good, the bad, about, around, yonder, everywhere; to perceive the continual gravitation of all tangible and intangible things towards the necessity of the decent, the good, the true, the beautiful."[2] Beyond the realm of individual conversions, doctrines of social and revolutionary concerns seek to operate at a mass politicized level. Individual agencies can merely mediate otherwise saturated revolutionary messages. "A point of view," under such circumstances of enticed collective treaty, sheds all pretensions of humility and relativism aside and calls all the gods of truth and certitude to its side. But even under these circumstances, it takes a certain bottomless pit of energy to reach for a spectacular visionary height from which to gaze at "the good, the bad, about, around, yonder, everywhere." There the individual stands, a testimony to his time perhaps, not necessarily the voice and visage of what is best or what is most enduring in the society that chooses to celebrate him for the moment. But there is something fundamentally typical about the man, his voice, and his vision that corresponds perfectly to what makes his moral and political community tick. "The necessity of the decent, the good, the true, the beautiful" is the underlying conviction that drives the man. The conviction may be false, its assumption pretentious. It may merely reflect the glorified image of a dehumanized society projected onto an individual, upon an ideal, towards a utopian ideology, invested in a denial. Yet it defines the ideologue thus conceived; and, in

39

doing so, it reflects back on the society that celebrates him and its collective self-consciousness. Such individuals, in dialogue with their history, stand at the threshold of their national destiny. There is no cause and effect here, no individual vs. material (economic) forces. Here the active imagination of a living collectivity, the excited shared memory of a nation, reaches for ideals it can hardly define, objectives it can barely articulate. Denial is the cost of all discontent.

To Live by the Pen

"No!" objects Mirza Asadollah, a conscious self-projection of Jalal Al-e Ahmad in his most successful fiction, By the Pen,

If for all the blessings that I have wasted I am able to give something in return, I will have given meaning to my life. My children are the natural continuation of my life. . . . They are not the human meaning of my life. . . . Anyone else could have been . . . the father of these or any other children. But no one else can . . . be Mirza Asadollah the Scribe, who writes letters at the door of the mosque. I am the only one who has carried this load. I cannot leave it halfway down the road and run away. I must carry it to the end.[3]

Although Al-e Ahmad himself could not share the dismissive vanity of his created Mirza Asadollah in having natural children, or perhaps because he was denied the ability to father his own natural continuity, he always felt obligated to do something in return for the abundance of blessings that mere living entails. Al-e Ahmad was biologically incapable of having a child. In his vociferous writings and activities, he sublimated a biological inability into a tireless social force. Driving that force towards specific political objectives was an equally sublimated sense of "obligation."

This sense of obligation animated every aspect of Al-e Ahmad's relentless, tireless, and restless life. Like Mirza Asadollah the Scribe, Al-e Ahmad attended life with a commanding conviction that as he had theoretically, if not biologically, conceived himself, he had to register himself ideologically in the most active self-consciousness of his contemporaries. The load Al-e Ahmad felt compelled to carry—the burden of responsibility, the certitude of a seer—moved him from politics to literature to existentialism to the vast emptiness of Iranian deserts, and then around the world, to Europe, the United States, the Soviet Union, Israel, and, most important perhaps, to Mecca. Then he returned, even more convinced of the heavy load of his responsibility, the feelings and agonies of a man who only halfheartedly thought he had seen the light but fullheartedly tried to convince masses of his fellow countrymen of the utopia at their disposal.

His success or failure, fame or notoriety, cannot and should not be measured in the veracity or falsehood of his political message. Men of conviction like Al-e Ahmad speak with their sentiments not their minds, act with their courage not their prudence, write with their anxieties not their deliberations, and lead with their hopes not their strategies. The place their historical exegencies afford them can be assayed only in terms of the aspirations they invoke, the convictions they personify, the maledictions they ideologize, and ultimately the public and private miseries they so deeply resent. The "No" they ever so loudly deliver screams of the insidious tyranny that has robbed them of their public and private dignity. Speaking for generations of betrayed hopes and against the overwhelming indignities of his own time, Al-e Ahmad simply said "No."

Ten Years Before the Revolution

Jalal Al-e Ahmad (1923–1969) died exactly ten years before the Islamic Revolution of 1979. If someone would have told him in 1969 that precisely a decade later a vast revolutionary movement would mobilize the Iranians and lead to the downfall of the Pahlavi monarchy and the establishment of a Republic, either he would have refused to believe this sequence of events or else, if he were somehow convinced of its actual future occurrence, he would have guessed its precise ideological composition with almost 100 percent accuracy. There is a claim worth examining further.

There is enough evidence in Al-e Ahmad's writings to show that he would have anticipated the ideological disposition of any serious revolutionary movement in Iran to be religious in nature. It is precisely an examination of this "evidence" that is the subject of this chapter. This examination will demonstrate that Al-e Ahmad's cumulative writings during the three decades that led to the Revolution were more instrumental than those of any other single individual in pointing elements of a mobilizing ideological language towards a revolutionary discourse, indispensable in the making of the Islamic Revolution.

Al-e Ahmad's writings thus constitute the first crucial link in a chain of cumulative ideological statements that collectively constitute what was later to be called "the Islamic Ideology." The writings of Ali Shari'ati, Morteza Motahhari, and others, as we shall examine them later, were, of course, central in the constitution of "the Islamic Ideology." But the collective writings of Al-e Ahmad, as well as the course of his political activities, were equally indispensable in making "the Islamic Ideology" the single most important mobilizing force prior to the Revolution. Although Al-e Ahmad never used this term in so many words, more than anyone else he prepared the necessary groundwork for its neologistic coinage and subsequent currency.

The origin and composition of Al-e Ahmad's contribution to the making of "the Islamic Ideology" and, in turn, to that of the Islamic Revolution can be traced back to his experience with the Tudeh Party, the most pervasive political event of Al-e Ahmad's generation. But his attraction to the Tudeh Party must be prefaced with a brief overview of his early life.

Early Life

Al-e Ahmad was born in 1923 to a respectable religious family. The effects of his religious upbringing, at a time when the society at large was experiencing a vast and pervasive period of secularization, would remain with Al-e Ahmad for the rest of his life.[4]

The 1920s was a decade of some fundamental changes in Iran, as Reza Shah established his autocratic rule at the expense of both the remnants of the defunct Qajar aristocracy and the relatively deactivated and subdued clerics. While the old Qajar aristocrats, stripped of their claims to nobility, competed for the lucrative bureaucratic posts in the new regime, a conservative and apolitical generation of clerics, headed by the distinguished resuscitator of the Qom scholastic seminary, Ayatollah Ha'eri, was putting to rest the tumultuous memories of the Constitutional period.[5]

Although the rule of Reza Shah in the 1920s increasingly curtailed the public and political domains of the Shi'i clerics, the latter continued to receive communal respect in the immediate context of their lives. Al-e Ahmad's grandfather, Sayyid Taqi Taleqani, was a locally prominent and respected cleric who led the public prayer at his local mosque in Tehran. Deeply revered and honored, Sayyid Taqi Taleqani would attract crowds of well-wishers who would seek to kiss his hands and pay their respects when they spotted him on his way to the mosque.[6] Al-e Ahmad's father, Ahmad, the first son of Sayyid Taqi Taleqani, was an equally respected cleric who followed in his father's footsteps in religious piety and practice.

Much of Al-e Ahmad's childhood in the 1920s and his adolescence in the 1930s was spent in the shadow of his religious family. His father obviously wore the religious habit. So did Jalal Al-e Ahmad himself, up to and including his final high school years in the early 1940s. Wearing the religious habit in those days was more than merely an identification with Islam and the clerical order. It had been turned into a political statement. When, in 1928, Reza Shah restricted the use of the clerical habit, in the hope of substituting the tie and chapeau for the turban and aba, the measure caused much resentment in many religious circles. The young turbaned and robed Al-e Ahmad must have felt particularly antagonized by Reza Shah's determination to give his Iranian subjects a European look. The effects of these antagonisms would later surface in Al-e Ahmad's *Gharbzadegi (Westoxication)*, his most powerful indictment of blind "Westernization." At the time, however, wearing of the religious habit was a particularly isolating factor, going against, as it were, the tide of the time.[7]

Two Mutually Exclusive Father Figures

Al-e Ahmad grew up with an exacting and demanding father whose religiosity had been aggravated by a society assuming an increasingly secular bend and by an absolutist tyrant determined to hasten the implementation of that secularism. In 1929 Reza Shah banned Muharram ceremonies, the annual commemoration of the death of al-Husayn, the third Shi'i Imam, in 628 c.e. Such policies greatly dismayed Al-e Ahmad's father. The six-year-old Al-e Ahmad's experience of the annual ceremony was thus partially curtailed by the abrupt cessation. In 1936 Reza Shah ordered the unveiling of Iranian women. This would greatly aggravate Al-e Ahmad's father. The lives of the young Al-e Ahmad's female relatives became much more restricted. Al-e Ahmad, in particular, felt the moral pressure of a father whose frustrations with society at large spelled ethical absolutism for his own household. Under the imposing shadow of two mutually exclusive father figures—one his own, the other Reza Shah—Al-e Ahmad was raised with paradoxical demands upon his character. These dual demands, aggravated in their intensity by being mutually exclusive and yet juxtaposed, pulled the young Al-e Ahmad in two diametrically opposed directions: one, the faith and practices of his biological father and ancestry, representing the old Persia; the other, the ideology and policies of an autocratic patriarch, forging the new Iran. Although later in life Al-e Ahmad would adopt a series of ideological stands fundamentally opposed to those of Reza Shah and his successor, Mohammad Reza Shah, the innate opposition between the authority of his own father, representing the old Shi'i Persia, and the father figure of a changing world, promising a new secular Iran, would remain with him permanently. Westoxication, his most celebrated contribution to modern Iranian political culture, is a crucial battlefield for this lifelong paradox.[8]

The 1940s was a decade of formidable turmoil and challenge for Iran in general and for the young Jalal Al-e Ahmad in particular. In 1941, two years into World War II, Iran was occupied by the Allied Forces. Reza Shah's flirtations with Hitler had made the Allied Forces particularly uneasy about the southern borders of the Soviet Union. Following the occupation, the Allied Forces forced Reza Shah to abdicate in favor of his son, Mohammad Reza Shah, and to retire to South Africa. In the confusion and turmoil of these drastic events, Iranian political life received a highly charged impetus. In 1941, the Tudeh Party, the chief institutional form of a socialist party in Iran and the most significant political movement of the period, was founded, ostensibly to promote the cause of socialism through blatant advocacy of the Soviet interest.

Those were years of great changes, grand ideals, and minute atrocities. A dictatorial monarch had left, a young and inexperienced king had been nominally put on the peacock throne, and a massive political party was organized with the grandiloquent claim of leading the deprived Iranian masses into the paradise of the socialist camp. Hopes were high, fears abundant, tantalizing expectations prevalent. Hopes for an unarticulated democratic future, perceived as the mother of all progress, and fears from an equally unarticulated past, conceived as the cause of all malice, drove the young and restless generation of the 1940s. Among the young and restless, determined in will and yet confused in ideals, was Jalal Al-e Ahmad.

In the early years of the 1940s, Al-e Ahmad entered Dar al-Fonun, a prestigious high school that was the distant memory—yet still a true heir —of the Polytechnique College that Amir Kabir, the celebrated Qajar Prime Minister, had established in 1851 on the model of the École Polytechnique of Paris.

At that time, students concentrated on a particular subject in their senior high school years: natural sciences, mathematics or literature. Literature was Al-e Ahmad's choice. Although his high school friends do not remember him as a particularly good writer,[9] his choice of major foretold his later literary interests and achievements. Both natural sciences and mathematics were areas of concentration with the longest positivistic distance from Al-e Ahmad's notions of doctrinal religiosity. Concentrations in such areas would have committed the sophomore Al-e Ahmad to a frame of modern and positivistic conceptual references beyond his accustomed piety. Literature, on the other hand, was an area with a curriculum that included a healthy dose of Iranian history, prose and poetry, philosophy and logic—all the necessary ingredients for keeping Al-e Ahmad, albeit with a modern twist, tuned to his father's inherited discourse.

Al-e Ahmad's classmates remember him strolling through the school yard with his long aba, distributing religious pamphlets, attending various meetings of the Muslim Students Association, and actively propagating up-to-date Islamic causes.[10] Thus, well into his last years in high school, he could have expected to pursue a life—though not entirely of a traditional and scholastic nature—of piety, subservient to received notions of religious propriety, and congenial to his father's self-perception. That self-perception was increasingly antagonized by drastic secular changes in the larger society of Al-e Ahmad's youth.

Between Tehran and Najaf

The indications of Al-e Ahmad's break with his father and, through him, with his own received Islamic identity, became more evident when he left Iran for Najaf, Iraq, in 1943. He did not stay in Najaf for more than a few months and soon returned to Iran. Had he decided to follow his father's wishes and remain in Najaf, he would have been trained at the juridical capital of the Shi'i world and could have returned to Iran a full-fledged cleric. But Al-e Ahmad returned to Iran to finish high school and receive his diploma from Dar al-Fonun. If we remember that Dar al-Fonun was established in 1851, to the great dismay of some clerics, Al-e Ahmad's decision in 1943 to receive his high school diploma from a secular school in Tehran rather than continue his studies as a seminarian in Najaf becomes quite symbolic and gives a crucial hint as to his future ideological disposition: a disposition more in tune with Al-e Ahmad's self-created notion of cultural identity than with his active perceptions of his father's expectations.

A Side Step to Kasravi

The year 1943 turned out to be crucial in the life of the now twenty-year-old Al-e Ahmad. He was in his senior year at Dar al-Fonun when he was attracted to the ideas of Sayyid Ahmad Kasravi (d. 1946), who was to have an immediate and transitory impact on Al-e Ahmad, but perhaps with some crucial, lasting effects.

Sayyid Ahmad Kasravi, a social reformist with strong anticlerical views, was a self-styled historian and linguist. His book on the Iranian Constitutional Revolution of 1906–1911 was the first major step towards collecting crucial primary data and providing a social reformist reading of them. Kasravi became increasingly attracted to social issues and felt compelled to propagate his literalist opinions about everything—from linguistics to poetry to theology. Because of his radical positivism, which included book-burning rituals, he attracted a group of followers who wished to reform the Iranian society on a perceived rational model. Within his extremely utilitarian frame of reference, Kasravi severely criticized all forms of popular piety. This put him in direct opposition to petit-clericals, religious functionaries, and radical Muslim activists. His tangles with the petit-clerics inevitably led to his assuming a flat literalism in his political discourse. The result was bizarre ideological statements, denouncing Hafez's poetry as much as Shi'i doctrinal principles, of both of which he had a crude and rather artificial understanding. Kasravi finally paid for his radical anticlericalism with his life. He was assassinated in 1946, at the doorstep of the Ministry of Justice in Tehran. His assassin, who escaped punishment, was Sayyid Hossein

Imami Kashani, a member of the radical "Devotees of Islam" organization
(Fada'ian-e Islam).[11]

Kasravi's ideas represent a crucial phase in the history of modern Iranian
political discourse. His writings constitute a necessary and perhaps inevitable internal phase in the aborted metamorphosis of Iranian political culture
from an innately religious to a patently secular frame of reference. His
audience in the 1930s and 1940s consisted of semiliberated Muslim youths
who were disillusioned with what they perceived to be the political ineptitude of their faith, but not radically enough to go to the other extreme and
join the Tudeh Party. Many former members of the Tudeh Party report
that Kasravi's group was always considered a stepping stone towards full
membership in their Party.[12] The process seems quite natural. Kasravi
stripped his followers of their last vestiges of common religiosity but failed
to give them a strong enough ideological conviction in a promised utopia.
That was offered by the Tudeh Party, to which many former Kasravites
turned.

The son of a turbaned cleric, Al-e Ahmad's attraction to Ahmad Kasravi
must have been quite turbulent to him and disquieting to his father. It
indicates signs of a break, not only with his father, who must have considered Kasravi an infidel, but, perhaps more important, with his own
religious identity. This was a significant but relatively minor step for Al-e
Ahmad compared to his next move—becoming a full-fledged member of
the Tudeh Party. But the anxieties and the courage required for the son of
a cleric to join the Kasravi camp should never be underestimated. This
particular characteristic of going against his peer pressure and making a
decision that would antagonize his immediate cohorts would remain a
permanent trait of Al-e Ahmad's character. His attraction to Kasravi also
indicates an enlargement of Al-e Ahmad's political concerns from merely
local and communal to national, regional, and, given Kasravi's quasi-
European discourse, even global. Kasravi represented a new breed of Iranian intelligentsia who, although their roots were in a traditional scholastic
system, sought to appropriate the European positivistic legacy without
necessarily subscribing to a radical political ideology. Al-e Ahmad's participation in this experience would engross his political perception of the
world and, along with it, his horizons and definitions of political activity.

Joining the Tudeh Party

Jalal Al-e Ahmad joined the Tudeh Party in 1943, only one year after he
had been to Najaf, which could have led him to become a Shi'i cleric. The
road from Najaf to Moscow, however, was paved by Ahmad Kasravi in
Tehran.

The Tudeh Party was established in 1941 in the wake of the Allied occupation of Iran and the subsequent abdication of Reza Shah. The origin of the Iranian Communist movements dates back to the early twentieth century when, following the ideological acquaintance of Iranian intellectuals with socialism, the stage was set for active political involvement.[13] Iranian intellectuals became acquainted with Marxist ideas in Baku and Constantinople, among other major urban centers in the area, in the late nineteenth century.[14] Communist activities in the 1910s led to the establishment of the Adalat (Justice) Committee in 1916 as the first institutional form of Communism. In June 1920, the seed of the Adalat Committee flowered into the Persian Communist Party, with active engagement in and support from the young Soviet Union. As the Persian Communist Party continued its activities well into the Reza Shah's period, the circle of Taqi Erani commenced its activities in Europe in 1933, moved to Iran in 1935, and was brought to closure in April 1937 when Erani and fifty-two other members of his circle were arrested by the Reza Shah's police. Erani died in the prison hospital on 4 February 1940. More than a year later, following the Allied occupation of Iran and with the Red Army in the north, the Tudeh Party was founded in October 1941 by some members of "the 53" group of the Erani circle in conjunction with some "older Communists" they had met in Reza Shah's prison.[15]

Al-e Ahmad advanced very quickly within the Tudeh leadership. Only two years after joining the Party, he was sent to Abadan in 1945 to promote the cause of socialism and organize the workers in that crucial industrial city. The year 1945 was one of great hopes for and radical expectations from the Tudeh Party. The young and energetic party promised to deliver Iranian masses, as they said, from their avid miseries and, at the same time, gave the Iranian urban intellectuals a share of the glory for participating in the universal struggle on the side of the oppressed. This "universal struggle," however, carried within its glory some troubling seeds of discontent. Where would universal concerns end and national interests begin? How is one to see one's immediate and unique national identity as opposed to a remote and vague universal brotherhood of humankind under the banner of socialism? "The Pishehvari incident" would induce such issues to come to the surface.

Assuming a more radical foreign policy towards the Iranian government, the Soviet Union actively supported Sayyid Jaʿfar Pishehvari, a true Communist believer from the province of Azarbaijan, and his aspiration to establish a Soviet satellite state in his home province.[16] In September 1945, Pishehvari, supported by the Tudeh provincial committee in Azarbaijan, effectively called for insurrection and the establishment of an "autonomous state." By November, the movement, under the protection of the Red Army, had begun to capture the army garrisons. In early December the Pishehvari Democratic Party held elections for the autonomous Republic and was overwhelmingly elected to the newly formed Azarbaijan parliament. The Tudeh Party in Tehran officially and unconditionally supported the insurrection. "With the successful seizure of power in Azarbaijan," it has been documented, "this group [the members of the Tudeh Party] in parliament became the official voice of the insurrection in the capital, and it used every occasion to advance its cause."[17] Despite these official statements, however, seeds of disapproval were being sown within the leading ranks of the Tudeh Party.

Leaving the Tudeh Party

Al-e Ahmad's famous break, the enshe'ab, with the Tudeh Party occurred in 1948. This break was led by Khalil Maleki, ostensibly because of the ill-fated attempt, led by Pishehvari's Democratic Party, to establish a Soviet satellite state in the Iranian Azarbaijan province. This break, however, could have been caused by other forces internal to the composition of the Tudeh leadership.[18] Prior to their break, Al-e Ahmad and Eshaq Eprim jointly wrote Hezb-e Tudeh bar Sar-e Do Rah (The Tudeh Party at a Crossroads), in which they reflected on the inner tensions within the Party.

Al-e Ahmad's relationship with Khalil Maleki was always ambivalent. Although he followed Maleki in his break with the Tudeh Party, Al-e Ahmad did not like the idea of playing second fiddle to Maleki. He made an ex post facto reference to this fact in a comment about Ebrahim Golestan who, according to Al-e Ahmad, agreed with the secessionists but refused to join them, resigning from the Tudeh Party separately and on his own terms:

Our first serious experience . . . with Golestan was in the course of [our] secession episode. He was with us. But he did not come along with us. When we seceded, he did too, but alone, and wrote a letter of resignation to the party, having maintained in it that "since my closest friends have left, I do not belong here anymore." He did confess that it was on the basis of our support that he had resigned from the party. But he was too selfish to come out among a group and remain anonymous. Because Khalil Maleki was our leader, and inevitably he would, like me, remain second or third rate.[19]

In another related comment to a fellow party member,[20] Al-e Ahmad had emphasized that he did not leave the Tudeh Party because of Maleki and that he did not consider himself any less significant than the maverick socialist. There are indications, however, that Al-e Ahmad may have reached an independent decision to leave the Tudeh Party after the episode of the oil crisis between Iran and the Soviet Union.

While the Soviet army was still in Iran, as part of the Allied Forces during World War II, Stalin tried to extract an oil concession from the

Iranian government. The demonstrations of the Tudeh Party on behalf of this concession were conducted literally under the military protection of the Red Army. Al-e Ahmad felt an accute feeling of shame for having organized demonstrations against his own government to give an oil concession to a foreign state, under the military protection of that state.[21]

Following the Pishehvari incident and the oil crisis, Khalil Maleki actively participated in the movement to break with the Tudeh Party, ostensibly because of these and other such extremes of pro-Soviet policies of the Central Committee of the Tudeh Party. However, his dissatisfaction with the party may also have had something to do with his initial ambition within the Tudeh Party hierarchy. When the Azarbaijan incident occurred in 1946, many members of the Party who, for a variety of reasons, were having second thoughts about their membership may have used the occasion as an excuse to leave. But even more essentially, it is important to distinguish between the Central Committee and the rank and file of the Tudeh organization, particularly in matters related to blind obedience to Soviet policies. From very early on, there were younger members of the Party who felt ill at ease in conforming to the pro-Soviet attitudes slavishly adopted by the Central Committee.

The possible ad hominem considerations of Maleki's personal ambitions, however, should not detract from genuine political and tactical objections to, as well as a general feeling of disillusion with, the whole Tudeh enterprise. Quite apart from questions of personal ambitions, Khalil Maleki demonstrated some genuine misapprehensions about the Party and its acting as a fifth column for the Soviet interests in Iran. As Al-e Ahmad once observed, Maleki objected to Sovietism—or, even worse, Stalinism—much sooner than Tito did.[22]

Politics After the Tudeh Party

Immediately after breaking with the Tudeh Party in 1948, the Maleki group, Al-e Ahmad among them, sought to organize the Socialist Tudeh League of Iran and tried to receive recognition from the Soviets. Three years later, in 1951, Al-e Ahmad joined Khalil Maleki and Mozaffar Baqa'i in organizing the Toilers Party of the Iranian Nation. Then, in 1952, he once again joined Khalil Maleki in founding the Third Force. During the Mosaddeq era, which led to the CIA coup d'état of 1953, Al-e Ahmad advocated the liberal-democratic programs of the Iranian prime minister.

Following his break with the Tudeh Party, Al-e Ahmad did not remain loyal to or steadfast with any particular political organization. Once the Tudeh Party, with all its might and promises, had failed his ideals—and perhaps ambitions—Al-e Ahmad could not remain confined within any less grandiose political apparatus. He joined Khalil Maleki and others in establishing these various political organizations chiefly to express his independence from the Tudeh Party. But very soon the whole idea of organized political action and, perhaps more important, the very secular and imported ideological foundations of these movements seem to have lost their interest or relevance for Al-e Ahmad. He was all prepared now for a new phase in his active and diversified career.

Turning to Literature

Before we focus our attention on some of Al-e Ahmad's crucial texts, instrumental in making "the Islamic Ideology" possible, we need a general grasp of the range of his extrapolitical activities, from literature to ethnographics, etc.

Al-e Ahmad's unique position among the major ideologues of the Islamic Revolution in Iran was writing not only critical social essays but also works of fiction. In a general assessment of his ideas, his works of fiction are at least as important as his essays. In formulating his contribution to the making of "the Islamic Ideology" and Revolution, both his literary and nonliterary output must be considered.

In 1945 Al-e Ahmad inaugurated a long and sustained contribution to the making of the modern Persian literature by publishing a short story, "Ziarat" (Pilgrimage), in *Sokhan* magazine, one of the leading literary journals of the time, which paid some attention to aspects of the modernist movements in Persian literature.[23] Al-e Ahmad had already made the acquaintance of Sadeq Hedayat, the founder of the modern Persian fiction, in 1945, and, although his creative imagination must have been active much earlier, the occasion further encouraged his literary aspirations. Al-e Ahmad's first collection of short stories, *Did va Bazdid* (Visit), appeared that same year.

Throughout his active intellectual life, Al-e Ahmad was at the very center of the most innovative movements in modernist Persian literature. Because of the political and engagé nature of this literature, Al-e Ahmad's acquaintance with and active participation in it made him particularly aware of the political pulse and posture of his time—a privilege other contributors to "the Islamic Ideology," perhaps with the exception of Ali Shariʿati, lacked.

In 1946 Al-e Ahmad made the acquaintance of Nima Yushij, the founding father of modernist Persian poetry. His dual acquaintance with Sadeq Hedayat and Nima Yushij put Al-e Ahmad in immediate contact with the two towering figures of modernist Persian literature. His friendship with Nima Yushij lasted a lifetime. In 1953, Al-e Ahmad and his wife moved to a new house next door to Nima Yushij and his wife Aliyah. This made their earlier friendship even stronger. Nima's closeness and confidence in Al-e Ahmad, as much as the old man's invincible suspicion of others permitted him to trust anyone, became particularly evident when, upon his death, he entrusted the publication of his unpublished poems to three individuals, one of them Jalal Al-e Ahmad, who would later pay great homage to Nima by writing one of the earliest and most influential essays on Nima's life and poetry.

Whatever the critical merits of this essay, "The Old Man Was Our Eyes," it reflects Al-e Ahmad's unswerving courage in defending Nima's revolutionary changes in the received notions of Persian poetics, which Iranian classicists guarded with their lives. Al-e Ahmad saw and sought to utilize the great revolutionary potentials that Nima's poetry entailed. Modernist Persian literature was attracting an increasingly significant young intellectual milieu with considerable political possibilities as it forged a new politically charged symbolic frame of reference, energetic and active in its emerging semiotic organs, that for a time seemed as if it would supercede the received notions and norms of aesthetic authority. By participating in this frame of reference, quite apart from his other political activities, Al-e Ahmad sought and successfully gained a prominent place in the emerging political agenda of this literature.

Al-e Ahmad also secured in that literature an important niche for his own fiction. His fictional characters, however, are thinly disguised personae deeply rooted in his own biographical experiences. Simin Daneshvar, his distinguished wife who is a prominent writer in her own right, once observed that her major literary criticism of Al-e Ahmad's fiction was his constant presence in his own stories.[24] Others have verified this observation.[25] Whatever its literary merits, or lack thereof, Al-e Ahmad's recognizable personal voice in his fiction gave an immediacy and sincerity to his creative imagination that rendered them akin to actual experiences of his social milieu. This had a dual effect: It forced Al-e Ahmad into a realistic appreciation of his social and cultural context, and, at the same time, it brought his fiction to a wider reading constituency.

Both aspects distinguish Al-e Ahmad from most of his contemporary secular intellectual peers. Centered primarily in Tehran, and even in their secluded cafés, à la Quartier Latin, the Iranian secular intellectuals had but a romantic and thus condescending understanding of what they would call "common life" or "ordinary people." Deeply concerned with new experiments in artistic achievements, their creative imaginations set them worlds apart from their presumed constituency, let alone purported followers. But Al-e Ahmad's fictions demonstrate less concern with aesthetic experimentations and articulated techniques than with simply getting "the point" across. To keep this major thrust of his literary work operative, he had to remain always a realistic observer of Iranian cultural realities. Social realism thus remained the quintessential feature of his fiction.

As an indication of his primary concern with ordinary life as it is socially experienced, the question of religion is very much present in Al-e Ahmad's short stories. This aspect of his fictions has been summarized as follows:

On the whole, his characters are divided into two religious orientations: one is spiritually affected by all religious factors and reflections. His words, expressions, terminologies, similarities, invocations, and curses all have superstitious tone and form. It is obvious that [this type of character] has spent much of his life amongst staunch old believers, as well as the intimidated young believers. The other [type] is a character who wants to rebel against all religious and superstitious fetters and turn to science and to the real meaning of life. But since we simultaneously see both of these personae in him [that is, in Al-e Ahmad], we inevitably see him as a doubtful and spurious kind of individual who does not want to be recognized [as one type or another].[26]

The duality of Al-e Ahmad's character, negationally reflected in his fiction in terms of the degree and mode of religiosity, looms prominently in his intellectual disposition. What is crucial here is the functional expressions of this dual, on the surface mutually exclusive, disposition, this ambivalence towards religion in general, Islam in particular. Although this ambivalence could not have been resolved one way or another in Al-e Ahmad's fiction, it is quite evident, judging from his later nonfiction works, that in his actual political disposition, he moved increasingly towards a greater recognition of the symbolic hold religions command over people's receptive minds and active imaginations. If the aim were to change those minds and alter the course of those imaginations with politically mandated revolutionary zeal, then the whole plethora of religious symbolic commitments could not be ignored.

Phases and Forces in Al-e Ahmad's Fiction

Five distinct phases in Al-e Ahmad's short stories have been identified, in the course of which he moves from an enthusiastic youth constantly present in his plots to a mature artist who develops his characters more carefully and who then occasionally lets them do their own things.[27] "Their own things," however, are always socially and culturally circumscribed. From political commitments to social isolation to economic destitution—all the major concerns of Al-e Ahmad's generation appear in his fiction.

In *Nefrin-e Zamin (The Curse of the Land)* (1967), Al-e Ahmad had one of his characters severely criticize an economy that, with its total dependency on oil revenues, aborts the possibility of internal growth and infra-structural build-up.[28] But such economic mismanagements are merely symptoms of more serious problems. In this story, Al-e Ahmad would find the opportunity to examine the extent of "Westoxication" in his contemporary society, for him the central source of all problems:

They have kept pounding into our heads for a lifetime that Europe is the Paradise on Earth. The book says so. The teacher, the radio, the government, the newspapers. You are a student at the Teacher's College, and they tell you if you are the head of your class, you'll be sent to Europe.[29]

Having been to Europe then would become a measure of success: "The tourist comes back [from Europe] with his eyes fully opened; the student with the robe of ministership, the merchant with the agency of [a European] company."[30] The proportions of "Westoxication" are extended deep into the Iranian economic structure, thereby threatening a self-sustained communal infrastructure:

Now we have reached a point that people who until recently were selling cotton shoes from Sedeh are today importing plastic shoes from Indonesia; and those who were making samovar or silverware in Borujerd are selling electrical samovar and iron made by General Electric, along with high fidelity radiogram and 33 LP records.[31]

In the same book, Al-e Ahmad would seriously take issue with Marxism, an ideology that, despite its appeal to secular intellectuals, was still a product of "The West" and attraction to it a sign of "Westoxication":

Would that mean that the means of production identifies the individual, that is, it is his Identification Card? ... And these are all what that old bearded German has said, when more than a hundred years ago he emulated Moses and then we used to gargle his ideas in the Teachers College. But what about language? History? Religion? Customs?[32]

From religion to economics, Al-e Ahmad's fiction was always concerned with the most vital social issues. Preoccupation with the political and social implications of Iranian oil, for example, was a permanent feature of Al-e Ahmad's fiction. In *Sargozasht-e Kandu-ha (The Story of the Beehives)* (1958), he used the analogy of a "beehive" to suggest how the Iranian oil industry was being robbed by England and other colonial powers. Great Britain was depicted here as an ant that steals other people's property.[33] In this story, Al-e Ahmad also returned to an old theme, his anger against the leading elite of the Tudeh Party who fled the country following the 1953 coup d'état. Here he demonstrated a greater affinity with the younger generation who would continue their struggle against tyranny rather than go abroad and issue ill-suited manifestos:

The young believe that exile is a grand euphemism the old have put on their flight. It's better calling it flight. Flight is what the scared do, those who cannot go through life's battle. If the old prefer flight, that is their prerogative. But the young have the stamina and can face the difficulties.[34]

By the Pen

In perhaps his most successful work of fiction, *Nun wa al-Qalam (By the Pen)* (1961), which dealt with the nature and multiplicity of these difficulties, Al-e Ahmad achieved in folkloric symbolism what he could not, because of a peculiar combination of his literary temperament and official censorship, do in his political essays. While it would have been impossible for him to describe publicly his feelings about the Shah's departure from Iran during the premiership of Mosaddeq in 1953, he could very easily have one of his characters in *Nun wa al-Qalam* proclaim:

Our forefathers have not seen such things [that is, kings escaping]. . . . Every five or six generations or so, at best, such things would happen. . . . To tell you the truth, these days I give much importance to myself, especially to my eyes which have witnessed the evacuation of a court with all its pomp and ceremonies. . . . Which one of our fathers had witnessed such a thing?[35]

The primary success of *Nun wa al-Qalam* lies in its astonishing ability to operate at two levels: the internal logic of the fable itself, which is universal in tone and delivery, and the external political context that was time-specific to modern Iranian history. The following example clarifies this point:

Don't keep asking me "what is to be done?" How do I know. Why don't you go and ask the leaders of the land, who as soon as something happens escape, or else go into forty-day seclusion?[36]

At the internal level of the fable the forty-day seclusion was a ritualistic and symbolic gesture that the Calendars, the revolutionaries who momentarily take power, did in the face of grave difficulties. But at the same time and referring to the actual historical context of the book, many would-be national leaders either escaped the turmoils of the 1951–53 Mosaddeq experience or else remained silent and secluded. The secondary meaning, perhaps more immediate for Al-e Ahmad, works at such a delicate, tangential, and referral level that it is precisely in its subtlety and nuanced intonation that it is successful and effective. The primary textual level of the fable gives Al-e Ahmad's insight symbolic and universal validity; its secondary contextual level gives it specific historical articulation. The result is a deep penetration into the workings of the Iranian political culture. It is precisely such abilities, however less frequently utilized, that set Al-e Ahmad worlds apart from the rest of his cohorts on the secular intellectual side. His acute sensitivity to the making of public mythologies and fables, best demonstrated in *Nun wa al-Qalam,* enabled him to see the simple, yet much neglected, workings of a political culture still in touch with its originating popular signals.

Al-e Ahmad's Prose

Related to Al-e Ahmad's literary achievements is his unique prose, which was particularly instrumental in widely propagating his political ideas. Much has been said about Al-e Ahmad's prose—for and against.[37] Some consider him a revolutionary stylist who advanced Persian literary prose to new frontiers. Others have severely criticized his defiance of the classical rules of grammar and diction, particularly his habitual verbless sentences. Many have pointed out in detail the technical flaws in Al-e Ahmad's use of grammatical Persian in both his essays and his works of fiction.[38] The fact remains, however, that Al-e Ahmad did introduce and develop a unique prose of his own, compelling and powerful in its furious and relentless diction. An entire generation of prose writers imitated Al-e Ahmad's diction —occasionally successfully, sometimes with ridiculous results. The result, at any rate, was a major impact on contemporary literary and political prose.

Al-e Ahmad's prose is characterized by a quick and telegraphic urgency that twists and turns and occasionally even bypasses traditional conventions of literary diction. The result is an immediacy of purpose, an intimacy of context, and, perhaps more important, a compelling urgency that grips the attention and does not easily let go. His prose flies in the face of time and patience. He wants to say something important; but the urgency of the message breaks apart the rhythm and reasons of the prose. He wants to say something fast in the shortest time and with the fewest possible words, leaving much to bear on the Persian equivalent of "etc."

The significance of Al-e Ahmad's prose should be understood in the context of an essential, almost ideological, bifurcation between the official academic prose, deeply entrenched in the rules and requirements of classical Persian diction, and the more spontaneously developed modern literary prose, in conceptual and terminological contact with colloquial speech. During the early twentieth century, about the time of the Constitutional Revolution, a modern literary prose gradually developed that consciously sought to draw from the vast pool of folkloric imagery. The resulting language had demonstrated great possibilities in reaching deep into the collective contemporaneity of historical identity with which an increasing number of secularly educated Iranians identified themselves. The official academic prose, however, was advocated by the leading professoriate of Persian literature who considered themselves the besieged custodians of the greatest prize and pride of the Iranian literary and cultural heritage.

With a deeply felt animosity, almost a *ressentiment,* towards the official academic prose, Al-e Ahmad identified with, and considerably contributed to, the efflorescence of a thriving engagé prose that, while changing in itself, sought to change its social context. In developing his unique prose, Al-e

Ahmad was perhaps the most influential essayist whose particular and unique diction became the model for many aspiring and even accomplished young writers. The appeal of his prose was due to a successful balance that he was able to create between a free adaptation of such classic prose writers as Saʿdi and Naser Khosrow and a vigorous attention to contemporary Persian colloquialism. The stylish classicism of his intonations and the abrupt immediacy of his discourse gave Al-e Ahmad a biting and satirical language that was particularly suited to social criticism. The result of this generally successful prose was a traditional flavor that intimidated and yet attracted the seculars, while it harbored a modern twist that the orthodox classicists rejected. The immediate consequence of this paradoxical prose was an angry flow of critical consciousness that facilitated effective communication precisely because of the sincerity it expressed so effortlessly.

As a social essayist, master of this prose of his own making, Al-e Ahmad wrote, consciously, for a wide range of audience. Consequently, it would be a case of misplaced significance to try to detect the presence or lack of a systematic and careful exposition of an issue in his collected essays. He would rarely footnote an observation, document a claim, or sustain an elaborate argument. When he occasionally did footnote a proposition, it would appear mostly as an artificial faking of a discourse for which Al-e Ahmad was not prepared. Yet in doing so, he did occasionally try, as in his last important work, "On the Services and Treasons of the Intellectuals," to appeal to the academic and particularly social scientific discourse. But if he was not successful at convincing the specialist in a given field, Al-e Ahmad did manage to communicate his ideas to a relatively vast audience with a certain air of authority. This authority was extended to a range of contemporary political and cultural issues that Al-e Ahmad addressed. The contemporaneity and secular significance of such issues as the Iranian oil reserves and its economic management would render Al-e Ahmad's prose sensitive to the very pulses of his *Zeitgeist*. None of the other Islamic ideologues examined in this book shared Al-e Ahmad's penchant for matters of contemporary secular significance. From Shariʿati to Khomeini, every major religious ideologue saw the world from a specifically and pronouncedly "Islamic" point of view. This ipso facto alienated a wide range of putatively secular political activists. The significance of Al-e Ahmad's unique prose and discourse was that while it increasingly signalled the political necessity, or perhaps even inevitability, of the religious symbols, it did so with an acute reflection of the most compelling political realities of the time, speaking, in their own language, to secular intellectuals.

Al-e Ahmad's Translations

In conjunction with developing his unique political prose, translating contemporary European sources on a variety of political and literary subjects was an occasion for Al-e Ahmad to convey specific ideological messages. When he found a prominent European author, someone like Albert Camus or André Gide, having said, as he thought they did, precisely what he had in mind, he would choose to translate him. This would give an added air of authority to the message. In translating André Gide's *Retour de L'U.R.S.S.* *(Return from the Soviet Union)*, for example, he meant to cast a soul-searching glance at his years with the Tudeh Party:

In our own country how many enthusiastic souls have gotten in this path of deceit, and how many innocent lives have been wasted. How many young people have withered away their enthusiasm, ecstacy and youthful energy, and thus what a tremendous human asset we have lost! A regret for that lost asset and a deep sorrow for this prolonged deceit are among the causes of translating this book.[39]

These translations were also among the first initial steps that Al-e Ahmad was taking towards a full recognition of the primacy of local religious sentiments in the Iranian political culture. Before he would come to grips with the futility of the patently secular political language in Iran (by definition the displacement of a "Western" artifact for Al-e Ahmad), he could not have grasped the revolutionary potentials of the religiously charged messages. In his introduction to Andre Gide's *Return from the Soviet Union,* Al-e Ahmad would speak of the Soviet experience as a "deceitful mirage"[40] that had captivated the minds and souls of many European and, by extension, Muslim intellectuals.

The significance of Al-e Ahmad's translations of his contemporary literary sources from "The West" may be seen as providing him with an individualistic haven from the collective commitments of his years with the Tudeh Party. While the socialist ideals of the Tudeh Party had emphasized public virtues and collective salvations, almost all the "Western" literary sources he chose to translate reflected an existentialist emphasis on the primacy of the individual and private virtues. From his translations of Dostoyevski's *The Gambler* in 1948 to Camus' *The Stranger* in 1949 to Sartre's *Dirty Hands* in 1952 to Eugène Ionesco's *Rhinoceros* in 1966, Al-e Ahmad demonstrated a particular preoccupation with the major themes of the Existentialist movement. These translations, all dated after his break with the Tudeh Party, seem to have provided Al-e Ahmad with a necessary existentialist break from collective concerns with the potential revolutionary achievements of public virtues. Before he would reach for the specifics of his immediate political culture towards yet another (religious) version of collective salvation, his passage from this existentialist and individualistic phase was all but inevitable.

Translating European sources into Persian, a crucial cultural phenomenon that has so far remained completely unexamined, was perhaps the single most important mechanism for creating "The West" as the most significant Other in the Muslim (Iranian) collective imagination. In this context, Al-e Ahmad's translations served two interrelated purposes. At a more immediate level, they provided him with an existentialist path out of the ideological impasse he had faced after his break with the Tudeh Party. Sartre and Camus, Dostoyevski and Gide became his sources of salvation. In them he found, whether he consciously recognized it or not, a meaningful refuge from collective commitments to organizational causes. But at the same time, these, and similar, translations contributed to the collective construction of the compelling image of "The West" as the most important generalized Other in the Iranian collective imagination. Importer of the most sensitive symbolic artifacts from "The West," Al-e Ahmad's generation continued to measure elements of its own identity in terms of a constructed dominant myth: "The West."

Turning to Ethnography

But at the same time, any contribution to translating "Western" intellectual sources smacked of "Westoxication": for Al-e Ahmad a debilitating disease. To balance the sentiments and impressions of such a self-inflicted "disease," Al-e Ahmad vigorously attended to the most rugged realities of his homeland: an attendance that would put him in touch with the most compelling facts of rural Iranians leading meager lives in the remotest part of the country. In 1955, Al-e Ahmad began a series of monographs on various Iranian villages, a kind of ad hoc ethnography that he undertook and encouraged others to do with no disciplinary preparation and yet with surprisingly impressive results. The primary purpose of these studies, as Al-e Ahmad himself testified, was to measure and analyze the exposure of typically Iranian villages to the "onslaught of machine and machine civilization."[41] While in the first two of these three studies, *Tat-neshin-ha-ye Boluk-e Zahra'* and *Urazan*, Al-e Ahmad managed to muster a neutral and almost social scientific language, in the last one, *Karg: Dorr-e Yatim-e Khalij*, he openly criticized "the devastation of an economic and cultural unit of this country"[42] in the face of "machine and machine civilization," his alternative terms for "The West."

The first of this series of ethnographies, the result of his trips to the villages of Qazvin in northwestern Iran, was a monograph called *Tat-neshin-ha-ye Boluk-e Zahra' (The Tatis of the Zahra Block)*. Al-e Ahmad knew very well he was no trained ethnographer. He knew he was trespass-

ing into territories unknown to him. He conducted his ethnographic studies, as he did most other things, knowing full well the limitations that
affected him and his output: "You have run for a lifetime," Al-e Ahmad
once addressed himself:

searched every corner, and before you reach some understanding of yourself, you
have committed stupidities, have gone ways astray, banged your head on walls, and
from all these you have none but fragmented records. This too [*Tat-neshin-ha-ye
Boluk-e Zahra'*] is one such fragmentary note. . . . And what can one do? . . . [Y]ou
cannot throw away and burn even fragmentary notes. Because they are part of you,
part of your juvenile enthusiasms, of a water that went into marshes, and no branch
grew out of it.[43]

In June 1958, Al-e Ahmad was invited by the Oil Consortium, an
invitation which was arranged by Ebrahim Golestan, to visit Kharg Island.
The result of this trip was *Karg: Dorr-e Yatim-e Khalij (Kharg: The Or-
phaned Pearl of the Gulf)*, in which he gathered some historical records
and a collection of fieldwork he conducted while on the island. Here, too,
Al-e Ahmad's primary concern was to attend to matters of popular beliefs
and myths in the area. His interest in Kharg Island had much to do with
the fact that here was an almost abandoned part of the country, where
political activists and criminals were exiled, recently rejuvenated because of
its oil installations to facilitate the flow of "black gold" to "The West." As
Al-e Ahmad saw it, while oil installations on Kharg Island would create a
relative economic and cultural expansion in the area, the development was
isolated and irrelevant to the rest of the country, where "half of its fifty
thousand villages still do not know what a match is,"[44] and that it was
bound to isolate the economy and culture of the area from the rest of the
nation.

He attended to his task of documenting the local culture of Kharg on the
verge of destruction by the invading "Westernization" with the spirit of an
observer who knows the object of his inquiry will soon be obliterated. He
compared Iran to the weak and exhausted body of a sick man with an
unnaturally big and strong head that was the oil industry, artificially drag-
ging the country just to feed "The West." Beyond matters of economy, it
was more this deep cultural alienation that Al-e Ahmad resented. Gradually, he anticipated, "the entire local and cultural identity and existence will
be swept away. And why? So that a factory can operate in 'The West,' or
that workers in Iceland or Newfoundland are not jobless."[45]

In *Urazan*, which Al-e Ahmad published in 1954, the most elementary
unit of social organization, namely a small village, came under close scrutiny. There was nothing particular about this village except that Al-e Ahmad's ancestors had come from there.[46] His essay on this village is something of an ethnography with the prose and diction of a travelogue. Al-e

Ahmad had his introduction to this ethnography translated into English by his wife, Simin Daneshvar, presumably having a larger audience in mind. The book consists of religious beliefs, problems of irrigation, ceremonies around death, local diets, clothing, wedding festivities, social organization, and aspects of the local dialect. In identifying this village, Al-e Ahmad pointed out that

it is one of several thousand Persian villages where ploughing is done in a primitive way, and the villagers often fight over the water supply and are deprived of public bath and a sufficient supply of sugar for their tea.[47]

In *Urazan* there is neither a school nor a hospital; there is no police department; the villagers had not yet seen a match.[48] Between 1947, when Al-e Ahmad last visited Urazan and took his notes, and 1977, when the book went through its seventh printing, not much improvement could have changed this particular unit of "the Japan of the Middle East." Such direct experiences of the most rugged realities of Iran gave Al-e Ahmad the moral authority, if nothing else, to speak of the most rudimentary lores of his native political culture.

Al-e Ahmad the Journalist

Such ethnographic studies, however, remained isolated writings with a limited readership. Journalism, of a particular sort, was Al-e Ahmad's key to the widest range of audience available to a writer of grave social and political concerns. In 1946, he became the manager of Sholehvar Printing House and launched a long and crucial career not only as a leading journalist but as an acute observer of Iranian periodicals from the 1940s through the 1960s. His tenure with the Tudeh Party from 1943 to 1948 gave him ample experience in journalism. For a while, in 1946, he contributed to *Rahbar,* the organ of the Tudeh Party. At the age of twenty-three, he was on the editorial staff of *Mardom,* the chief ideological journal of the Party. This put him on a par with the leading organizational and ideological patriarchs of the Party—in particular Fereydun Keshavarz and Ehsan Tabari.

Early in 1950, Al-e Ahmad joined the editorial board of *Shahed,* a journal published by Mozaffar Baqa'i. Later in his life he would attribute a redeeming quality to having edited this journal, suggesting that his disappointing affiliation with the Tudeh Party had caused in him a mental disease that was very difficult to get rid of:

If I escaped the evil of this disease (which I am not quite sure I did), it was first because I sought a haven in writing, and second because the section of "searching in the papers" which lasted in *Shahed* for a year (1950–51) extracted all the poisons of this disease from my body and put it on paper, with my signature on it.[49]

Al-e Ahmad also collaborated in 1952 with Khalil Maleki in publishing the *Nabard-e Zendegi (The Battle of Life,* also published as *Elm va Zendegi [Science and Life]*) journal. Perhaps the most important effect of his career as a journalist was a sort of acrobatic prose Al-e Ahmad could perform in his writings about contemporary political issues. To be diligently aware of the pitfalls of treacherous politics, to be conscious of the rising expectations of a new generation of revolutionary youth, and to watch for the curves and slopes of Iranian intellectual and cultural exposure to "The West" were among the principal challenges that Al-e Ahmad successfully met in his extended writing career. Tightly controlled by state-sponsored and self-inflicted censorship, Iranian journalism from the 1950s to the 1960s gave Al-e Ahmad ample opportunity to develop a political prose—concealing in its revelations, revealing in its concealments—closely reflective of the most crucial problems of his generation.

Al-e Ahmad the Essayist

Journalism, with the tight hand of censorship holding its throat, had its inherent limitations for Al-e Ahmad. The overflow of social concerns inevitably sought a different channel of expression. Al-e Ahmad's long and impressive career in virtually making the engagé genre of modern Iranian social essays began in 1946 when he wrote a series of "reports" on the condition of high schools in Iran. By 1946, he had gained sufficient experience to justify his formidable acumen for sharp social criticism and had already been through a gamut of ideological commitments, leading him to the highest echelons of the Tudeh Party. In active and engaging command of a vibrant Persian prose, he had already published his first collection of short stories in 1945. His acquaintance with Hedayat and Nima had put him in touch with the avant garde literary movements of his day. By the time he launched his essay-writing career, Al-e Ahmad had also been among the editorial staffs of both *Mardom* and *Rahbar,* the chief ideological organ of the Tudeh Party.

Perhaps the lasting effect of the Tudeh Party on Al-e Ahmad was his critical eye for social maladies. Although he commenced his writing career in 1945 by publishing a short story, *Did va Bazdid* ("Visit"), it was in the collection of his essays, launched in 1946, that Al-e Ahmad ultimately left his mark on the modern Iranian political culture. In 1954 he published his *Seven Essays (Haft Maqaleh).* Some eight years later he published *Three More Essays (Seh Maqaleh-ye Digar).* The Three-Year Balance Sheet (Karnameh-ye Seh Saleh) also appeared in 1962. His *Hurried Appraisal (Arzyabi-ye Shetab Zadeh),* which was published in 1965, was the last collection of short, critical, and provocative essays he wrote. Although such long essays as *Gharbzadegi* (1962), *Yik Chah Va Do Chaleh* (1977), and *Dar*

Khedmat Va Khiyanat-e Roshanfekran (1977) are technically considered in this genre, their content requires separate examination.

Throughout these essays, Al-e Ahmad attends to the particular problems of his rapidly changing environment. But he occasionally ventures into what exactly is to be done. In addressing questions of crucial importance for his contemporary concerns, "The West" is always the dominant force:

> We need to take certain things from the West. But not everything. From the West, or in the West, we are looking for technology. Technology we have to import. We will also learn the science that goes with it. That [in itself] is not Western; it is universal. But not the social sciences and humanities. These, that is, from literature to history, economics, and jurisprudence, I [as an Iranian] have and know well. One can learn the scientific method from someone who knows. But as it pertains to the subject of social sciences and humanities, those I have. I have written on many occasions that Naser Khosrow almost a thousand years ago has told us how to do it. He has taught me how to write, not Newton or Sartre. Newton has written on mechanics, that is, on the foundation of hard sciences. Thus I inevitably need him. Electrical shaver and this tape recorder [I talk to], we need. That's all good and well. But what about our thoughts which are made up through social sciences and humanities? At the moment do we have anything other than these as tokens of our Iranian identity? [50]

That Iranians had lost their sense of historical identity was, for Al-e Ahmad, a premeditated scheme of European colonialism and its commercial interests: "The West and the [oil] companies not only do not care for local orders, forms and traditions, they even try to destroy . . . [them] as soon as possible." [51]

In his social essays, Al-e Ahmad paid particular attention to matters of common mythologies. Among the architects of Persian mythologies, Ferdowsi was particularly dear to Al-e Ahmad. "You and I," Al-e Ahmad once said, "if we are very healthy and powerful, will have exploded after seventy years, with no trace." [52] He realized the persistence with which collective mythologies endure the test of time in a society. Iranians, in fact, have expressed their deepest appreciation for Ferdowsi's preservation of their ancient myths by incorporating the poet himself into the corpus of their mythologies.

But such mythologies, Al-e Ahmad believed, were no idle entertainment. He was convinced that myths are "the most real of all realities." [53] Such realities constitute the most essential and immediate frames of reference within which members of a common culture assume their measures of social action. Such attention to the inner workings of common mythologies was instrumental in the final disposition of Al-e Ahmad's political agenda. He complained bitterly of the substitution of an artificial knowledge of Greek mythology for a genuine understanding of Iranian myths. "Still no average literate Iranian knows our national mythology," he regretted. "Who is Zarir or Garshasp? Or what is the myth of creation in this part of the world? But every newspaper is full of Greek mythology. . . . Why?"[54]

Al-e Ahmad's concern with the spread of "Westoxication" was a simultaneous fear for the future of Iranian identity. Here, as elsewhere, his ideological disposition, which was always sensitive to common myths, coincided with his political agenda of constructing an "anti-Western" Iranian identity. This identity was rooted, more than anything else, in the Persian language; and yet today " 'start,' 'consortium,' 'festival,' and 'exposition' are the passwords, even for the doroshky driver of yesterday who has just sold the horses, bought a cab on credit, and turned up as 'Mr. Driver.' "[55]

Al-e Ahmad's ultimate concern, perhaps even more crucial than pushing Iranian politics towards the mainstream of common symbolic (Islamic) consciousness, was for Iran to have an independent cultural identity on a par with "The Western" nation-states:

Infrastructure, superstructure, struggle, peace, etc., are all good and well; but for me the problem is that so far as my infrastructure is oil and superstructure is gargling the chewed-out literary and industrial leftovers of the West, they will not take me that seriously. After living for forty years in this country, I at least have to have understood so much that in this international circus first you have to be a rival in order to be taken seriously. Then you can talk of war or peace.[56]

Al-e Ahmad persistently tried to instill a sense of self-respect and dignity in being an "Easterner." "Beware that the epoch of grand ideals should not be past for us."[57] But contrary to such grand ideals, the urban and bureaucratic corruption, a product of "Westernization" for Al-e Ahmad, was now spreading to Iranian villages.[58] The key industrial malaise was total dependency, ruining, as it had, the Iranian economy.[59]

Confronted with such grave difficulties, faced with the responsibility of assuming the ideological, if not the political, leadership of his nation, Al-e Ahmad saw himself as something between a teacher and a preacher:

I am a teacher. . . . But here the situation is such that I cease to be a teacher. Yet I do not wish to change my definition as a teacher. Because there is a difference between a teacher and a preacher. A preacher usually invests in the emotions of a large crowd. While [a] teacher emphasizes the intelligence of a small group. The other difference is that a preacher begins and preaches with certitude. But a teacher begins and speaks with doubt. . . . Professionally, I am a teacher. Yet, I am not completely devoid of preaching either. I don't know what I am.[60]

Al-e Ahmad's Travels

Whenever such debilitating questions began to bother Al-e Ahmad, he left home and went on a long journey. He traveled extensively throughout his life. His travels were always occasions for reflection and thorough reconsideration of his ideas. These journeys expanded and enriched his political disposition—whatever that might have been at any given time. It would not be an exaggeration to suggest that Al-e Ahmad's travels, in and out of Iran, were as instrumental in shaping his political ideas as his readings or the company he kept. Although he usually went abroad with more or less set and determined ideas about the places he was about to visit, his trips to the United States, the Soviet Union, Israel, and Mecca led him to reconsider his ideas, radical at times, about "Westoxication," Stalinism, Zionism, and Islam, respectively. The Meccan trip, in fact, led to a thorough reconsideration of the political impact Islam could, might, and should have.

To Najaf with Faith?

Al-e Ahmad's first major trip abroad was to Najaf in 1943 to study at this historical site of Shi'i learning. In Iraq he visited Basrah, Khaniqayn, Samara, Karbala, Najaf, and Kazimayn. He had made this trip at his father's insistence in order to complete his scholastic learning, which he had pursued, simultaneously with his formal (secular) school, at a preliminary level at the Marvi School in Tehran. In Najaf he was meant to join his older brother, Mohammad Taqi Taleqani, and, under the guidance of an eminent Shi'i scholar, Shaykh Aqa Bozorg Tehrani, who was also a distant relative, study with Ayatollah Sayyid Abolhasan Isfahani, the leading Shi'i authority of the time. Al-e Ahmad would later reflect some of his impressions from this trip in his stories.[61]

Although he did not stay in Najaf for more than a few months, and although the wishes of his father to have another turbaned cleric as his son (Al-e Ahmad's older brother had become a rather prominent cleric) were not to be fulfilled, still this first trip to the scholastic capital of Shi'i jurisprudence must have left an indelible impression on the young Al-e Ahmad. For the rest of his political and intellectual life, he would possess a close intimacy with the received imperatives of his faith, one that most of his cohorts on the secular humanist side would not and could not share. This affinity had far-reaching impressions on Al-e Ahmad's political disposition, not the least of which was immediate support for Ayatollah Khomeini's June 1963 uprising. But these were affinities Al-e Ahmad would feel most defensive about. Years after he had abandoned his father's wishes of becoming a cleric, he would still become agitated at the mere suggestion that he was an "Akhond" after all.[62]

To Abadan with a Mission

Al-e Ahmad's first major trip inside Iran was in 1945 when, on a mission for the Tudeh Party, he went to organize the cause of socialism in Abadan.

Those were years of high hopes: years when Al-e Ahmad used his fresh but inexperienced political drive for a cause he thought was the most noble endeavor a man could undertake. His experiences in Abadan gave him an acute understanding of the inner workings of politics and, of course, harbored an appropriate dose of cynicism and disillusion that would not leave him unaffected.

To Qazvin to Know

Al-e Ahmad's trip to Qazvin in 1955 was the beginning of a long and sustained program of getting to know Iran at its most rustic, rugged, and realistic depths. He would gradually write ethnographic records of these trips. Whatever the ethnographic validity of these reports, a validity to which Al-e Ahmad had no printed claim, they demonstrate a deep and concentrated concern for the lowest and most common denominator of the Iranian society. These trips also gave Al-e Ahmad a realistic understanding of the diversified masses of people and their valid and legitimate cultural frames of reference. As opposed to the typical Iranian secular intellectual, who was an essentially urban creature with a minimum to nonexistent understanding of rural life, Al-e Ahmad, through these systematically planned excursions into the Iranian heartland, felt the very pulse of the people he wished to lead to a promised land, even though, as he grew older, he increasingly lost all presumptions of knowing precisely what constitution this promised land would have.

To Europe, to "The West"

In the summer of 1957, Al-e Ahmad made his first trip to Europe. His wife, Simin Daneshvar, accompanied him in this trip, which lasted for two months. They spent their vacations in France and England. He did not write a travelogue on this trip; but he reportedly kept a journal.[63]

His trips to Europe, and later to the United States, were perhaps logical and inevitable continuations of his primary concern, cultural and political, with "The West." Although in his *Westoxication* he severely criticized the awkward imitation of matters and manners "Western," he was, given the limitations of an intellectual of his generation, relatively well informed and, one might even say, erudite about his contemporary European intellectual scene. This erudition was particularly instrumental in a crucial phase of Al-e Ahmad's intellectual curve when, removed from his communal identity with the Tudeh Party, he became increasingly attracted to Existentialism and the freedom of experience it afforded the individual. It is later, upon this individuality, that Al-e Ahmad would construct his own unique definition of political commitment.

To Walk Through the Land

In 1958, Al-e Ahmad went to Khuzestan, a southern Iranian province, and traveled on foot from Behbahan to Kazerun, a distance of some 300 miles. In olden days, his ancestors would have performed their Hajj pilgrimage— or sometimes even their ordinary trips—on foot. From the distant provinces of Khorasan, Fars, or Azarbaijan, Iranians walked to Arabia, Syria, or Iraq. It was believed that a pilgrimage to a sacred precinct performed on foot would enhance the nobility and honor of one's religious duty in this world and would increase one's other-worldly rewards proportionately. Al-e Ahmad's walking through and around the Iranian deserts provides a glimpse of his replaced piety, his reconstituted enchantment.

Again to "The West"

Al-e Ahmad returned to Europe for four months in 1962, this time without his wife. On this trip he went to France, Switzerland, West Germany, Holland, and England. He had reportedly prepared his notes from this trip for publication in a book; but his sudden death aborted this plan.[64] Years later, when the autobiographical sketch *Sangi bar Guri* ("A Tombstone") was published, we would learn that during this trip he had a brief extramarital affair. "A Tombstone" deserves particular attention.

"A Tombstone" is a remarkable autobiographical document of unsurpassed sincerity in the modern history of the Iranian literary tradition. With a rare courage very few Iranians could have mustered and sustained, Al-e Ahmad articulated the darkest emotions of a man tradition-bound in his quintessential disposition and yet artificially exposed to the imported ideals of a liberal mind. His primary dilemma in "A Tombstone" is a translation in sexual terms of what he actually faced in the political arena. "A Tombstone" is the private confessions of Al-e Ahmad who had been told by physicians that he could not father his own children because of the low number of sperm in his semen. The technicalities of the problem aside, Al-e Ahmad gives a sincere and detailed account of a tormented traditionalist at once attracted to and repelled by the allure of a liberal mind, of a technological age, and, ultimately, of "The West." For the first time in his received history it had become conceivable for an Iranian man to accompany his wife to a male gynecologist. Only one generation earlier, Al-e Ahmad's father would have rather seen his wife dead than examined by a male gynecologist. With Al-e Ahmad's generation, however, the idea had begun to assume a certain degree of uneasy acceptability among the presumably liberal intellectuals. Those intellectuals would not have dared to speak publicly about the darker corners of their tormented privacies, which still saw something quintessentially troublesome in having a man (call him a physician, what difference does it make?) see, touch, and examine the most private parts of their wives. Al-e Ahmad had the courage to record his outrage when he took his wife to a male gynecologist:

Do you really know what it means to be a pimp? I experienced it that very day. Yes. He laid my wife on the operation bed . . . just as I would on our bed. And then he rolled up his sleeves, his instruments in hand, and then the look in his eyes was such that I, all of a sudden, remembered my sister who finally did not consent to having an operation, to having the hands of a male stranger touch her. And that was [only] her breast. Cancer had eaten her up, and yet she ultimately did not consent to having an operation. The hair on the man's hand had been left out of the [surgical] gloves, and my wife had laid down in a position which I really could not. . . . But I did not even scream. I just saw I could not take it anymore. Just like pimps.[65]

Here was the trouble with "The West." Al-e Ahmad's experience in having to take his wife to a male gynecologist was a symbol of his central problems with "The West." On one hand, the realities of the circumstances, that Al-e Ahmad and his wife needed to have a child but could not, necessitated their seeking the most technologically advanced help possible. And yet in the process of doing so, they, now representing the entire modern Iranian society, had to sacrifice what was most dear and significant to them: their dignity as they defined it. No one in Al-e Ahmad's generation had the moral courage to admit this ethical paradox. And no ideologue could, or would, articulate the moral dilemma in a more compelling and personal narrative.

And to Israel

In the winter of 1962, following his European trip, Al-e Ahmad traveled to Israel for two weeks, where he was joined by his wife. His travel notes from this trip initially appeared in two journals in 1964 and 1967 and were later reedited and published by his brother Shams Al-e Ahmad in 1984.[66] On this trip, which lasted from 4 to 17 February 1963, Al-e Ahmad and his wife were guests of the Israeli government.[67] By 1963, the non-Stalinist socialist experiences of the Israeli kibbutzim held much interest and appeal for a non-Tudeh generation of Iranian socialists. Articles and essays by post-Tudeh socialists such as Khalil Maleki created and sustained a very positive image of the Israeli kibbutzim among many Iranian intellectuals.[68] Much to the dismay of the clericals at Qom, the non-Tudeh socialists, led by Khalil Maleki, projected a positive image of Israel and its socialist experiences with kibbutzim.

Publication of a portion of Al-e Ahmad's travelogue to Israel in September 1964 caused quite a stir among his clerical readers and followers in Qom. The future leader of the Islamic Republic, Sayyid Ali Khamenei, was one of the disenchanted followers who, in fact, came to Tehran, contacted Al-e Ahmad and registered, kindly though, his dismay on behalf of the young clericals in Qom.[69] When, some three years later, Al-e Ahmad's travelogue to Israel appeared in a journal, the Shah's government immediately banned the journal and confiscated its last issue. This chapter, however, was very much welcomed in Qom because it was critical of the State of Israel. It is important to note that while the secular intellectuals in Tehran did not quite get to read this piece, the young clericals in Qom reprinted it first in five thousand and then in fifty thousand copies, wrote an introduction to it, and published it under the title of "Israel: The Agent of Imperialism" (its actual title, as it later appeared in the book, was "The Beginning of a Hatred").[70]

Al-e Ahmad occasionally appears not to share Maleki's and the other non-Tudeh socialists' optimism and enthusiasm for Israel. In fact, the publication of the second portion of his travelogue in 1967, which was critical of the Israeli government, angered Khalil Maleki considerably.[71] It has also been suggested, perhaps with some justification, that the publication of Al-e Ahmad's fragmented critical pieces on Israel in the late 1960s caused, or at least was partially responsible for, the appearance of a generation of publications critical of the state of Israel.[72]

In the first chapter of the book, however, which was partially published in 1964 and caused much anger among the young clericals in Qom, Al-e Ahmad saw the state of Israel not merely as a threat to Arab dreams of a united caliphate, for which he obviously had no sympathy, but also as the promising possibility of a new emergence for "The East" to balance the power of "The West":

In the eyes of this Easterner, Israel, despite all its defects and despite all contradictions it harbors, is the basis of a power: The first step in the promise of a future which is not that late.[73]

As Al-e Ahmad saw it, from Tel Aviv to Tokyo there were the beginning signs of a new emergence for "The East" to stand, once again, vis-à-vis "The West." He saw essentially two negative attributes in the very presence of the state of Israel: First, it was a "Western" stronghold at the very gate of "The East"; and second, it was the price that the poor "East" had to pay for the atrocities "The West" had committed in Dachau and Buchenwald. But more than anything else, he saw Israel as an inspiring, almost symbolic, statement and position vis-à-vis "The West":

For me as an Easterner, Israel is a model, [better] than any other model, of how to deal with the West. How to extract from its industries by the spiritual power of a [mass] martyrdom, how to take remunition from it and spend the capital thus obtained to advance the country, and how with the price of a short time of political dependency give permanence to our newly established enterprise.[74]

To top it all, Al-e Ahmad also appealed to the vast arena of Irano-Judaic relationships, and claimed Esther and Mordecai, Daniel and the reconstruction of the Temple by Cyrus. Yet the more immediate attraction of Al-e Ahmad, which dated back to his secession from the Tudeh Party in 1948, had to do with a non-Stalinist experience with socialist cooperatives — kibbutzim — that he and a number of other like-minded anti-Stalinist socialists began to know about and propagate in the late 1940s.

Al-e Ahmad confessed that this propagation of something positive about Israel was much to the dismay of the Qom clericals.[75] But he pursued his interest in Israel by reading the proceedings of the Nuremburg Trials, rereading the Old Testament, and writing two fictions about these experiences, one of which has apparently disappeared.[76] Al-e Ahmad goes a step further and genuinely expresses his approval of the state of Israel, simply because he has never seen, nor does he pretend to harbor, any sympathy from, or for, the Arabs. As a Shiʿi Iranian, he lists a host of grievances — from being called an *Ajam* ("a non-Arab") and a *rafidi* ("a Shiʿi" — both terms are derogatory) by the Arabs to the Egyptian dream of leading all the Muslim world — that prevents him from having any genuine historical (either religious or ethnic) identification with the Arab cause. Thus, Al-e Ahmad daringly concludes:

Having so much suffered at the hands of these rootless Arabs, I am happy to see the presence of Israel in the East. The presence of Israel that can cut off the oil pipe of the Arab sheikhs, and that can implant the seed of seeking justice and equanimity in the heart of every Beduin Arab and that can cause much headache for the illegitimate and archaic regimes. These rotten scales on the stem of the old but strong tree of Islam . . . ought to be blown away by the whirlwind awe of the Israeli presence so that I as an Easterner can rid myself of the tyranny of the puppet regimes installed by the oil [companies].[77]

The duality of the immigrant character, the division between the Sephardim and the Ashkenazim, also interested Al-e Ahmad. As he saw it, the Israeli attempt to establish Hebrew as the national language was a conscious, and apparently successful, attempt to meld the cultural differences of the Sephardim and the Ashkenazim into a new monolithic self-image — neither Eastern nor Western, almost like the Israeli territory that has only a North-South axis and lacks an East-West bar.

In Al-e Ahmad's version of the establishment of the state of Israel, not surprisingly, it is the British who emerge as the essential villains, systematically aborting all historical possibilities between 1918 and 1948 for a Jewish-Palestinian state.[78] Al-e Ahmad's sympathy for the Palestinians, however, in no way detracts from his admiration for the Israelis.

In the last chapter of this book Al-e Ahmad's tone of language changes completely. This chapter, which, according to Al-e Ahmad's brother was first published in July 1967, after the June 1967 Arab-Israeli war, demonstrates a visceral contempt for the European left and liberal intellectuals who were rallying their support for the Israeli cause. This radical change of voice in the last chapter can create some doubts about its authenticity. Although it is hard to prove that this chapter was actually concocted by someone else and injected in this volume, which has been edited by Al-e Ahmad's brother Shams, still its visceral anti-Israeli content makes it drastically different from the preceding four chapters of the book. What further substantiates this doubt is the abrupt ending of the preceding chapter that ends not with a complete sentence but with a subordinate clause. Further challenging a complete re-Islamization of Al-e Ahmad's memory are the tone and diction of this last chapter which are in radical opposition, in manner and matter, to what he has argued for in previous parts. While the other chapters carry the unmistakable charm and character of Al-e Ahmad's essay diction, this last chapter is actually in the form of a letter written by someone who was in Europe at the time and addressed to a like-minded individual in Iran. It is also quite evident from the content of this letter-cum-chapter that its author was actually in France some time around June and July of 1967. It is, however, quite possible that Al-e Ahmad did, in fact, write this chapter with a different tone and diction some four years after his initial reactions to Israel. Indeed, the June 1967 Arab-Israeli war and "The Western" support for Israel might very well have angered Al-e Ahmad enough to cause him to revise thoroughly his previous ideas about the state of Israel. In the absence of further reliable documents, we must leave this question unresolved.

This last chapter, at any rate, is a visceral condemnation of Israel, "The West," and "The Western" intellectuals:

Because Nazism, this flowering achievement of Western bourgeoisie, dragged six million wretched Jews into man-baking furnaces, today two to three million Arabs of Palestine, Gaza, and Western Jordan ought to be massacred and scattered around under the auspices of Wall Street capitalists and Rothschild Bank. And because the European intellectuals, so called, were partially responsible for Hitler's atrocities, and yet did not utter a word at the time, now they are giving the same Jews the green light in the Middle East so that the people of Egypt, Syria, Algeria, and Iraq are whipped enough to forget about fighting against the Western colonialism, and would never again close the Suez Canal to the civilized nations![79]

In this last section, Al-e Ahmad—or whoever wrote the piece—contradicts everything he had written about Arabs or about the socialist experiences in Israel in the earlier sections of the book. In this part, Israel is no longer the hope of the East for emancipation from tyrant sheikhs. It is "the puppet supreme of capitalism and Western colonialism in the Middle East."[80] Arabs here are not the historical enemies of the Persians, but "Muslim brothers."[81] While in the earlier sections Al-e Ahmad projects himself as a pro-Jewish and benevolent observer, here he shows no hesitation in using such racist comments as "the proverbial Jewish stinginess" that prevents Israelis from capturing the Egyptian soldiers in Sinai and thus having to feed them.[82]

Lost in the Crowd

In the spring of 1964 Al-e Ahmad made perhaps the most crucial trip of his life: a pilgrimage to Mecca. In 1965 he edited his notes, and in 1966 he published them in a book called *Khasi dar Miqat (Lost in the Crowd)*.[83] The depth and intensity of the impact of this pilgrimage on Al-e Ahmad are hard to exaggerate. In retrospect, it seems that since his short trip to Najaf in 1943 and his father's aborted wishes for him to follow a career as a religious scholar, Al-e Ahmad had postponed his return to the birthplace of his faith, the most compelling source of his identity. But whereas Najaf is the intellectual and juridical capital of Shiʿism, Mecca is the very physical and spiritual heart of Islam, its proclamation to the world. This is not to read anachronistic existential values into Al-e Ahmad's pilgrimage. In view of his later political ideas, Islam in general and Shiʿism in particular assumed an increasingly pronounced significance for his ideological disposition. It is true that by 1964 Al-e Ahmad was too much in the sun. He had simply seen and experienced too much to turn through this pilgrimage into a full-fledged Muslim. A reconstitution of his religious disposition, an immediate personal reenchantment, is beyond the immediate impact of his spiritual experiences during this pilgrimage. This certainly was not a trip through which Al-e Ahmad would rediscover an undiluted Muslim, whatever that creature might be, within himself. Yet the very act of pilgrimage at the very heart of a decade that Al-e Ahmad's generation of intellectuals was exposed and thus transformed to the most varied forms of secularization testifies to the validity of something deeply religious in him.

Thus the crucial publication of 1966 was *Lost in the Crowd*, Al-e Ahmad's version of a profound confession of faith, however convoluted. This is where Al-e Ahmad's belated religiosity came to meet his updated political agenda. His pilgrimage to Mecca gave him ample opportunity to develop a rhetorical discourse that combines political engagement with a religiously sensitive prose:

Under the cover of that sky and in that infinity, I recited every poem I'd ever memorized, mumbling to myself, looking into myself as carefully as I could until dawn. . . . It appears that even Kaʿbah will have been built with steel-reinforced concrete by next year, just like the Prophet's mosque.[84]

Al-e Ahmad's reconstituted religiosity would find new, unconventional, and disguised forms of expressing itself. Here three dates are crucially interrelated: Al-e Ahmad published *Westoxication* in 1962, performed his pilgrimage to Mecca in 1964, and published his travel notes from Mecca, *Lost in the Crowd,* in 1966. Within the expanse of these four years, 1962–66, he outwardly expressed his deepest sense of recognized religiosity by performing his Hajj pilgrimage, once he had first intellectualized it into the most successfully disguised form of Islamicity in his conceptualization of *Westoxication.*

Here is how the relation between *Westoxication* and *Lost in the Crowd* works: Although chronologically *Westoxication* was published before *Lost in the Crowd,* in terms of its intellectual conception, it comes after. In effect, the reason behind this reversal can work out very well. Years before 1964, the germane idea of a pilgrimage to Mecca incubates in Al-e Ahmad's subconscious mind. But he cannot actually perform it before he has intellectually rationalized this most symbolic expression of a Muslim's belief. He finally provides this intellectual rationalization of his deepest desire to go to Mecca in *Westoxication:* his Islamicity expressed in terms of animosity to "the abode of war" or, more precisely, to "The West." Once, through the writing of *Westoxication,* Al-e Ahmad has rationalized an otherwise inexplicable religiosity in his secular modernity and thus extracted it from his subconscious, he comfortably and without the slightest sense of self-contradiction performs his pilgrimage in 1964. The interval between 1964, when Al-e Ahmad performed his pilgrimage, and 1966, when he published his travel notes, is accounted for, in part, by the time it naturally took to write and publish it, but also by the time necessary to reconcile the a priori intellectualization of the pilgrimage in *Westoxication* and its actual day-to-day record in *Lost in the Crowd.*

Off to the Socialist Paradise

In the same year that Al-e Ahmad performed his pilgrimage to Mecca, he made a trip, over the summer, to the Soviet Union. What a coincidence—if a coincidence! He was invited to go to the Soviet Union to participate in an International Anthropological Conference. By then his ethnographic monographs, *Urazan* (1954) and *Tat-neshin-ha-ye Boluk-e Zahra'* (1955) had been published. This trip took more than a month. Al-e Ahmad completed his notes from this trip in 1966 and published them in a journal, *Baru.* That journal was immediately banned and its issues confiscated by SAVAK. Shams Al-e Ahmad, his brother, is reportedly preparing a new edition of this book.[85]

With Kissinger at Harvard

In the summer of 1965 Al-e Ahmad traveled to the United States and participated in a conference at Harvard hosted by Henry M. Kissinger. This trip, which lasted close to three months, included a short visit to Canada. He wrote close to 180 pages of notes on this trip, parts of which were rewritten and published in *Karnameh-ye Seh Saleh (The Three-Year Balance Sheet)*. But the complete notes have not yet been published.[86]

Four Ka'bahs

Al-e Ahmad's wife, Simin Daneshvar, and his brother, Shams Al-e Ahmad, have a reference to a manuscript Al-e Ahmad was working on during his last days in 1969 which is worth considering here. They both report that he meant to publish four of his travelogues—to Mecca, Jerusalem, Europe and the United States, and the Soviet Union—under the general title of "Four Ka'bahs."[87] "Four directions of prayers" was the telling title that best characterized Al-e Ahmad's wandering soul in search of a communal identity for himself and his generation. Europe and the United States constituted one qiblah, the direction of obedience and prostration, tightly connected under the general rubric of "The West." This was the most compelling, the most appealing, and thus the most negationally charged direction to face and follow. Jerusalem, the new Israeli Jerusalem, was the intermediary direction, once faced in prayer by early Muslims, to which "Easterners" were to look in reconstructing a hopeful and appealing alternative to "The West." The Soviet Union was once the qiblah of Al-e Ahmad's choice, the direction to an earthly and immediate paradise. But ultimately, the qiblah closest to Al-e Ahmad's home and, perhaps, heart was Mecca, where he once saw that the unity of purpose of the Muslim collective self-consciousness could be reengendered. It would be presumptuous on our part to assume any particular preference of qiblah, direction of identity, towards the end of Al-e Ahmad's life. We best leave his wandering soul undetermined among these "four ka'bahs."

Westoxication

In 1967, Al-e Ahmad made two trips, one to Ardabil and Dasht-e Moghan, the other to Tabriz. His trip to Mashhad in 1968 brought him face to face with a man who would later carry forward the major ideological thrust that was his lasting legacy. In Mashhad, Al-e Ahmad met with Ali Shari'ati. His final trip was to Asalem, a village in Gilan, where he died of a heart attack in 1969.

But men of Al-e Ahmad's character live beyond their death, as crucial components of their contemporary spirit. Contributing to the remaking of that spirit was the most significant publication of 1962 for Al-e Ahmad and for the entire formative political culture of the 1960s—the appearance of *Westoxication*. In terms of its appeal to a generation of social activists, this was perhaps the single most important essay published in modern Iranian history. In creating a wide range of positive and negative reactions, in constituting the very vocabulary of Iranian social criticism in the two decades preceding the Revolution, and in formulating the most essential "anti-Western" disposition of the Islamic revolutionary discourse, no other single text comes even close to *Westoxication*. The term "Westoxication" *(Gharbzadegi)* became so deeply entrenched in the Iranian political vocabulary of the 1960s and beyond that even Ayatollah Khomeini used it when he delivered his lectures and wrote his letters and proclamations in Iraq. No other term has captured the quintessential *Zeitgeist* of a generation like *Gharbzadegi*. Its ideological construction was a matter of political inevitability.

The fact that while Al-e Ahmad severely criticized "Westoxication" as a form of disease he himself, in his own highly alert discourse, was markedly "West-stricken" is an acute, however ironic, testimony to his own insight. He, for example, criticized—and occasionally even ridiculed—the secular-minded intellectuals' almost exclusive attention to "The Western" cultural heritage, at the expense of their own; and yet he himself was chiefly responsible for translating into Persian books by Sartre, Gide, Dostoyevski, Camus, and others. Al-e Ahmad's own "Westoxication," however, was the result of a more complicated process. He obviously believed in the theoretical validity of his own observation about the predominance of "The West" in modern Iranian political culture. He repeatedly referred to the fact that he was surprised at how well the book had been received. But he verified the validity of his own observation, a biting criticism of a social malaise, not on its own merits, but on its proximity to a German writer, Ernst Jünger, of whom he had already translated an essay into Persian. But the theoretical validity of his observation notwithstanding, the mere criticism of "Westoxication" would immediately put Al-e Ahmad on the defensive as a propagator of reactionary obscurantism. The accusation of being an "akhond" was always there. To counter this, he would always be alert to *prove* his "not being an akhond" by demonstrating his affinity for "high Western" culture: art, literature, and, yes, of course, good wine and palatable French cheese.[88]

The patent intention of *Westoxication* was to identify and criticize "Westoxication" as a pervasive social phenomenon that deeply disturbed Al-e Ahmad. By this term he meant the excessive and rather awkward preoccupation of certain influential segments of Iranian society with manners and matters "Western" in origin. He considered this preoccupation a major malady that had gradually but incessantly weakened the Iranian national character, the major component of which he considered to be the Shi'i ethos. "Westoxication," as Al-e Ahmad articulated it, was gradually eroding the essence of the Iranian national spirit more than anything else.

Although he was too close to see it, the extreme modes of Iranian nationalism or Shi'i religiosity were also being expressed in "Westoxicated" terms.
And perhaps the greatest irony of Al-e Ahmad's lifelong achievements was
that the ideological frame of reference he helped to shape, "the Islamic
Ideology," was the deepest, most effective form of "Westoxication" ever.
The mere juxtaposition of "Islam," which could not be an "ideology" in its
own sacred self-understanding, and "Ideology," which, by definition, is a
postreligious proposition, "false" in its Marxist stipulation, belies the contradiction that is resolved only in admitting the troublesome fact that in the
very terms and terminologies of their opposing "Westoxication," Muslims
have become even more "Westoxicated."

Much accidental affinity has gone into the construction of this text.
Although *Westoxication* turned out to be the manifesto of "anti-Westerni-
zation," it begins with a verbatim translation of the lyrics of a popular
American record. Here, on the very first page of the book, is a token of Al-
e Ahmad's self-contradiction, which, in fact, goes a long way towards
proving him right in his observations. The message of the American lyric
appealed to Al-e Ahmad because it is narrated by a miner who keeps telling
St. Peter to forget about his soul since he had sold it to the "company." [89]
The narration, in Al-e Ahmad's reconstruction, became a symbolic statement for those who believed that individuals and societies were forfeiting
their spiritual and intellectual authorities and legitimacies to abstract and
technological entities institutionalized in industrial bureaucracies and deified into "The Machine," both of which abstractions had for Al-e Ahmad
a "Western" ring to them.

The story of the publication of *Westoxication* is perhaps the most telling
example of how ideas and forces of ideological consequence were generated
in the 1960s. The ever-present force of censorship gave, inadvertently, a
certain degree of legitimacy to these texts when they appeared in the Iranian
underground political culture. The specifics of how Al-e Ahmad's essays
were published, confiscated, censored, and secretly republished became the
forceful elements of the urban legends that surrounded him. The case of
Westoxication is the epitome of this crucial part of the political tone of the
period. The content of *Westoxication,* or at least an earlier version of it,
was first delivered to "the Committee for the Guidance of the Iranian
Culture" *(Shora-ye Hedayat-e Farhang-e Iran)* in November-December 1961.
When the committee published the proceedings of its meetings in February
1962, Al-e Ahmad's contribution was omitted. He spoke very bitterly
about this:

Ministry of Culture was neither worthy nor capable of publishing this report. . . .
The time had not yet come for one of the offices at the Ministry of Culture to
publish a report like this officially. The time had come, however, for the honorable
members of that committee to tolerate listening to it. [90]

Al-e Ahmad first published *Westoxication* in 1962 privately and circulated it among his friends and cohorts, among whom was Mahmud Human, who taught philosophy at the Teacher's College in Tehran. Prompted by Al-e Ahmad's ideas, Human introduced him to the German nihilist Ernst Jünger. Eventually Human, assisted by Al-e Ahmad, translated a short book of Jünger's, titled, in its Persian translation, *Ubur az Khat (Crossing the Line; Über die Linie* is the German title). Human told Al-e Ahmad that he and Jünger "had seen one issue but with two eyes; had said one thing but with two languages."[91]

Westoxication was intended to be published in the first issue of *Ketab-e Mah*, a journal of the Keyhan Publishing Company. Although the first chapter of Ernst Jünger's *Crossing the Line*, translated by Human and Al-e Ahmad, was published in this issue, *Westoxication* was censored out.[92] Al-e Ahmad subsequently published the first version of the book in October 1962 in one thousand copies. Late in 1963 he revised *Westoxication* for a second, pocket-sized, printing. But this printing was confiscated by the government, and the publisher went bankrupt.[93] Early in 1964 he completely rewrote the book and sent this version to Europe so that Iranian students there could get it published; but they did not. It is this penultimate version that Al-e Ahmad wished to revise but did not and published it rather apologetically.[94]

Al-e Ahmad admits that he borrowed the term "Westoxication" from Ahmad Fardid, a professor of philosophy at the Teachers Training College. Fardid had used the term in the same committee at which Al-e Ahmad had delivered his report.[95]

The Success of a Text

There is no underestimating the influence this single text had on the political culture of the 1960s. From its very inception, and while Al-e Ahmad was still alive, *Westoxication* immediately became a success. Numerous photocopies were prepared and distributed clandestinely in Iran and beyond. Al-e Ahmad himself spoke sarcastically about this state of publication which led to his book being "more trumpeted than discussed."[96] But *Westoxication* was read and discussed in high schools and universities as the first bibliographical item on a hidden syllabus with which the Iranian youth of the 1960s came to political self-consciousness. You were accepted into cliques of political activists by virtue of your ability to quote passages from the text verbatim. This popularity was achieved more on symbolic rites of initiation than on any meaningful critical ground. Al-e Ahmad was acutely aware of the ideologically charged language of his treatise. His apology to the readers belies his aspirations for a more conceptually balanced and theoretically nuanced language: "You must forgive [me]," he said, "that after so many distillations, still my pen is rebellious."[97]

Al-e Ahmad was particularly conscious of the fact that he wrote in a hurried and inaccurate discourse. This self-conscious recognition of the methodic inaccuracies of the language was a feature that both Shariʿati and Motahhari would share with Al-e Ahmad. The common leitmotif of Al-e Ahmad, Shariʿati, Motahhari, and, in fact, most other ideologues of the Islamic Revolution in Iran is that they would have been more accurate and careful in their writings had they only had more time to develop their thoughts. Al-e Ahmad's self-consciousness was best evidenced when he felt he was trespassing into territories of sociological and economic disciplines:

This report does not operate at a level to provide a definition of these two poles (the East and the West) of economic, political, sociological, psychological planes, or that of two civilizations. [That would] be an accurate task. . . . But as you shall see, not knowing better, I have had to seek help, every once in a while, from certain generalities in these fields.[98]

Again in a reference to his not being qualified to address the problem properly, he gave the example of detecting a coming earthquake:

At any rate, it is time that the exact features of an earthquake will have to be inquired from the seismograph at a university. Yet, before the seismograph registers anything, the peasant's horse, ignoble as it might be, has escaped to the safe desert. This author wants, at least, to see something with a sense of smell sharper than that of a shepherd's dog, and a sight reaching further than a crow—that others have missed, or have not seen anything . . . [worth] exposing it.[99]

The success of *Westoxication* ought to be attributed to its having captured the imagination of a generation in search of a revolutionary identity, a language of revolt. During the 1940s, the Tudeh Party gave massive institutional and ideological expression to secular tendencies dormant in Iran at least since the turn of the century. During this decade, Islam, as a bona fide and relevant revolutionary language, was in its quietest and most defensive posture. After the 1953 coup and the debacle of the Tudeh Party with the Mosaddeq experience, the predominance of secular ideologies, particularly institutionalized Marxism, began to dwindle. From the post-Mosaddeq era onward, the Iranians became increasingly receptive to other modes of ideological persuasions, whether localized nationalism and liberalism or the non-Tudeh Marxism of various urban guerrilla groups. Al-e Ahmad's *Westoxication,* coming from a former member of the Tudeh Party, suddenly exposed a whole new set of possibilities, in terms of ideological build-ups, for potential revolutionary activities.

To be sure, Al-e Ahmad himself did not grasp the full range of ideological potentials he had made possible:

I myself believe that it was just a discussion of a contemporary problem, and at best one or two years later it would disappear. But as you see the pain is still in the organs, and the sickness increases its circles of contamination wider and wider.[100]

For Al-e Ahmad, "Westoxication" was a kind of disease[101] that had infected the Iranian (Eastern) body. The disease obviously had come from "The West," but the Iranian (or even Islamic) body was weak enough to give it momentum and space to spread. "Westoxication" was thus an abnormality, a distortion, a sickness, an aberration from the normal, the natural, and the healthy. Al-e Ahmad took "The West" and "Westoxication" not merely in their reference to the material dimensions of an advanced level of economic production, but also, and more important, in the ideological sense of a complex organization of intellectual and artistic achievements.[102] This dual power of "The West" made annihilation of "The East" into its ever-larger circles ever more comprehensive and exhaustive.

A Hidden Agenda

In addition to its manifest and stated objectives, Westoxication had a hidden, more serious, agenda than simply identifying a social disease. The nonstated, or perhaps even unintended, agenda was, in fact, so hidden that even Al-e Ahmad himself did not fully see it. The hidden, yet actual, agenda of the book was to disclose, to a degree Al-e Ahmad could not have foreseen, the range of possibilities inherent in concocting a vital and ideologically potent Islamic political discourse. Although his secular cohorts failed to see it, Al-e Ahmad's recognition was very simple and derived from mere observations from experienced history. The experiences of the Tobacco Revolt of 1890–91 and the Constitutional Revolution of 1906 had clearly demonstrated that the clerics' call for political action was followed more immediately than the similar intentions of the lay politicians. The Mosaddeq episode had proven to Al-e Ahmad that even lay politicians with closer affinities to the clericals had a better and more nuanced response to their call than those with latent or blatant anticlerical commitments. The Tudeh Party and its catastrophic failures to mobilize a mass movement had proven to him beyond any doubt that alien symbolics, translated and executed by crude, deceptive, and theoretically illiterate locals, had no chance of striking a responsive chord in their presumed constituency. A year after the publication of Westoxication (1962), Khomeini's June 1963 revolt would further verify Al-e Ahmad's accurate but limited observation that clerical figures of authority carry more clout with the masses than any other (secular) claimant.

But this observation, accurate and historically verifiable as it was, was not carried out to its logical theoretical conclusions in *Westoxication*. That was a different matter, realized in other texts by other ideologues. As for Al-e Ahmad, he was too much in the sun. He saw something in the shadow of Shi'ism, but was unable to articulate it precisely. In two successive books, *Westoxication* and "On the Services and Treasons of the Intellectuals," Al-e Ahmad narrowed in on the necessity and viability of the clerical order, politicized into mass revolutionary mobilization. Between that objective and what was finally achieved through the collective effort of all the ideologues of "the Islamic Ideology," there is a considerable distance Al-e Ahmad could not see or measure. It was left primarily to Shari'ati and Motahhari to see through the vast ideological gamut the Shi'i tradition had in store. Other ideologues discussed in this book, knowingly or inadvertently, added further material and momentum, dimensions and angles, to the ideological structure constructed by the Al-e Ahmad-Shari'ati-Motahhari triumverate. The penultimate result, the inevitable revolutionary precondition, was a coming together, in the course of the three to four prerevolutionary decades, of a monolithic claim on the viability of "the Islamic Ideology" as a supreme revolutionary doctrine.

Although Al-e Ahmad merely tangentially saw and addressed, as if in serendipity, this possibility of a Shi'i-born political consciousness and discourse, and although its actual fulfillment was the work of others, still without Al-e Ahmad having actually bridged, in the Iranians' collective political consciousness of the post-World War II era, a necessary epistemological gap between the historical exegencies of the day and the politically mute Islamic discourse of the time, the almost simultaneous development of an engagé language of Shari'ati and Motahhari would not have been as socially relevant as it later proved to be.

Perhaps the crucial factor in this link is Al-e Ahmad's sympathetic treatment of the clerical establishment in an otherwise patently secular discourse. His sympathy for the clerics and his condemnation of the government's crackdown on their demonstrations was quite evident in *Westoxication:*

In a world where the fates of governments and international borders are determined at conference tables not at battlefields ... preparing parachuters and commando regiments only becomes handy to suppress the demonstration of the university students or to quell the demonstrations of the students at Feyziyyah.[103]

Taking sides with the clerics was concomitant with a deep-rooted, almost obsessive, suspicion of all foreign elements. Thus, sharing a particular proclivity of his generation of political observers, Al-e Ahmad articulated the deep-rooted Iranian propensity for the conspiratorial theories of history, always concomitant with bestowing omnipotent power on the mighty "West" and, by doing so, refusing to assume the slightest responsibility for national calamities and yet, at the same time, claiming every false presumption of honor for a presumed past glory. Here is how he saw the whole episode of the Mosaddeq experience and the coup that followed it:

There is a minimum of freedom until 1951 when the oil is nationalized, and then the United States checkmates and the pawns are changed, one after the other. One has to be put into the box of nonexistence,[104] the other checkmated, so that the American capitalism can take away 40% of the consortium shares, precisely the share that belonged to the British Admiralty. And that is the story of 28 Mordad 1332 (19 August 1953) national uprising![105]

Islam and the Necessity of a Modern Political Discourse

Catering to such conspiratorial conceptions of history further endeared the text of Al-e Ahmad's political discourse to its immediate circle of interpreters. Substantiating this feeling of trust and comfort was Al-e Ahmad's attendance to what was most dear to an Iranian sense of self-perceived identity: the Persian language. Thus, in *Westoxication* Al-e Ahmad developed a successful polemical discourse that sought to connect modern political issues to the traditional conceptual setting of the Persian language, perhaps the single most important ingredient in the Iranian identity. The origin of this modern political discourse goes back to the constitutional period and the emergence of a simplified Persian prose, exorcised of its breathtaking formalism. Al-e Ahmad's persistent move towards a historically updated sensitivity in his prose, diction, and discourse does not in any way imply a simultaneous refutation of traditional modes and modalities of writing. In fact, he persistently criticized the Iranian educational system for the artificiality of its approach to classical studies:

In the programs of all these schools, there is no indication of reliance on tradition, no trace of the culture of the past, no relationship whatsoever between home and school, between society as a whole and the individual.[106]

Such possibilities that energize a religiously charged revolutionary discourse may, however, be turned against it. Attending the specific revolutionary potentials of his received religious language, Al-e Ahmad had to confront its particular political pitfalls. His ultimate attention to the necessity of religious consciousness in uniting and mobilizing the Iranian masses inevitably caused the anger and animosity of many secularists, especially the radical revolutionaries who insisted on instilling a Marxist class consciousness in their purported constituency. These critics have periodically accused Al-e Ahmad of backwardness and fanaticism.[107] And at the same time, many religiously oriented critics have refused to believe in what they consider to be the politically motivated intrusions into the totality of religious dogmas. They, too, refuse to acknowledge Al-e Ahmad except for precisely the opposite charge of opportunism with Islamic doctrines.[108]

Yet there can be little doubt that Al-e Ahmad was quite serious in his conception of an Islamically charged political ideology. In fact, his attention to the essentiality of religious symbolism in the Iranian political culture is gradually surfacing. It has now become evident that he had approached a number of people for a translation of the Qur'an into Persian, but this time with "a more easily understandable language."[109] The existing translations of the Qur'an into Persian were merely verbatim renditions, because of a doctrinal belief in the immutability of the word of God and, as such, rather difficult to comprehend. A politically charged and relevant translation of the Qur'an, despite its doctrinal inhibition, would have put the Holy Text more readily at the disposal of the ideologues of "the Islamic Ideology."

Al-e Ahmad's reawakened alertness to religious symbolics in general and his attention to the Qur'an in particular are also evident in Ayatollah Taleqani's recollections of him. "The first thing you ought to know," Taleqani once wrote about Al-e Ahmad, "is that Jalal was my cousin."[110] Of Al-e Ahmad's father, Taleqani said that he was "dogmatic" in his faith and that Jalal's turn to the Tudeh Party was a reaction to this dogmatism. Taleqani regretted that Al-e Ahmad had been diverted to the Tudeh Party. But he was happy that, in his estimation, "later, after the demise of the Tudeh gang, [and] once his erudition deepened, he *almost* [emphasis is Taleqani's] returned to our own people, to our own habits and customs, and became attracted to religion."[111] It is also interesting to note that Taleqani identified *Westoxication* and *Lost in the Crowd* as Al-e Ahmad's best books. These two books, as noted earlier, have an intimate relationship in revealing the inner tensions of Al-e Ahmad in reconstructing his religious identity. Taleqani also testifies that when he had his classes in Qur'anic exegesis, Al-e Ahmad attended them regularly. "Lately," Taleqani concluded,

Jalal had become very good [in his faith] and grown interested in the Islamic tradition. Two weeks before his death, we were coming down from Shemiran. He insisted that I should visit him in his cottage in Asalem. . . . He said, "Let's go and chat." I was looking forward to going there when I heard of his death.[112]

When Al-e Ahmad advanced his rather mute ideas of using Islam for revolutionary purposes, he was not intellectually prepared to fortify his proposals with ideological legitimacy. In fact, he was not himself totally aware of the revolutionary potentials of his acutely political "return to self." But as a necessary first step in *Westoxication,* he reached a full recognition of the ineptitude of Iranian political activism (particularly that of the Tudeh Party) in mobilizing Iranians for a meaningful program of revolt:

They [the critics] have taken issue with me as to why in this book [*Westoxication*] I have ignored people's struggle in political matters: from the constitutional period to the present time. I have not ignored this struggle. I have passed by it in silence. Because if the leadership of so much struggle (despite all its afflictions, imprisonment, murder, and exile) was proper, our conditions nowadays would have been much better. Of course, the people are not to be blamed for so much defeat. It is the impervious (*ghalat*) leadership of these movements that has caused such an outcome.[113]

"The impervious leadership" was Al-e Ahmad's judgment against the secular (if not outright antireligious) ideologies of the Tudeh and other similar political parties. With *Westoxication,* Al-e Ahmad mobilized whatever was at his limited disposal to point towards an Islamically sensitive discourse. He had much too little to mobilize in terms of his actual working knowledge of the Islamics, but, for the last decade of his life, he was increasingly distanced, insofar as his ideological disposition may be assayed, from the Iranian secular intellectuals. While the disappointment of Al-e Ahmad's secular contemporaries with his apparent religiosity was expressed in mild and benign sarcasm during his lifetime, it turned into rather bitter denouncements after the success of the Islamic Revolution.[114]

Constructing a Revolutionary Identity

Al-e Ahmad's increasing attention to the political validity of the Islamic ideological discourse was not only charged against rival oppositional forces in the secular realm; it also condemned the state-sponsored emphasis on the pre-Islamic Iranian identity. He considered the early Pahlavi insistence on the pre-Islamic history as an essentially "Western" plot to distort the contemporary Iranian notion of historical identity. He accused "The Western" colonial powers and their local cohorts of having

stirred only one passion, that of the ancient Iran. Passion for Cyrus, Darius, and Zoroaster. Belief in pre-Islamic Iranian history. . . . As if from the Sassanid period until the government of [Reza Shah's] coup d'état only two and a half days had passed, and that even in sleep.[115]

On the whole, Al-e Ahmad considered the early Pahlavi period, the 1920s, an era of massive "Westernization," predicated on a calculated denial of the Iranian Islamic heritage. During this period, even Bayer Aspirin, he complained, advertised its product through an appeal to Achaemanid symbols.[116] There was also a systematic resuscitation of Zoroastrian symbols, congenial to the spirit of denying the relevance of Islam. These were also designed, Al-e Ahmad proposed, to sever the Iranian link to its Islamic heritage and identity.

That Islamic identity, reinterpreted with contemporary historical exegencies, was instrumental in Al-e Ahmad's reconstruction of a religiously charged political ideology. In opposing a positivistic definition of politics, he clearly demonstrated an acute understanding of how religion and what he called "superstitions" are relevant in the making of a collective political consciousness. In this, he was a pioneer in his generation:

Even if politics is a science, it is one of those very loosely defined [branches of the] humanities, with its foundations on the latent collective consciousness—from religion to superstitious behaviors, from language to codes of etiquette.[117]

But while attentive to such symbolic features of his political culture, he had no false assumptions about the realities of his historical immediacies. One of his characters in *Nun wa al-Qalam (By the Pen)* proclaims: "I am principally opposed to every kind of government. Because every government is necessarily founded on violence."[118] This almost identical phrasing of Al-e Ahmad's and Weber's definitions of state,[119] stripped his understanding of politics of all false presumptions of justice and fairness about the nature of political activity and led him to search for what was realistically feasible in his society and usable for revolutionary purposes.

Unless properly located in specific historical circumstances, revolutionary purposes shall always remain at a tangential theoretical level, incapable of mobilizing the masses. In *Westoxication,* Al-e Ahmad clearly saw the significance of what he aptly called "the historical consciousness of a nation"[120] that he thought was being jeopardized by the onslaught of "Western" cultural hegemony. The clearest expression of this cultural hegemony was where the myth of the Pahlavi dynasty was being constructed by the colonial power, at which time Al-e Ahmad suggested,

in order to create confusion in a nation's historical consciousness, they wanted to ignore its immediate historical period and connect the might of the [1920] coup d'état straight to the tails of Cyrus the Great and Ardashir, as if there is no distance of some thirteen hundred years in between. Note this very crucial issue, and that only through this and by loosening the "religio-cultural" background of the contemporary man, would it be possible to pave the way for the onslaught of Westoxication . . . unveiling [of women], the European hat, prevention of religious ceremonies, the demolition of *Tekyeh-ye Dowlat,* prevention of *ta'ziyeh,* restricting the ulama'. . . .[121]

The gradual but persistent loss of this crucial dimension of the Iranian collective identity was, in Al-e Ahmad's perception, concurrent with a massive but artificial exposure to manners and matters "Western." His concern with "Westoxication" led him to believe in the immediate, yet artificial, subjugation of the Iranian national character to convoluted per-

ceptions about and from "The West." That subjugation went deep into the
primacy of technology in "The West":

We have not been able to preserve our "cultural-historical" identity in the face of
the machine and its inevitable onslaught. Instead, we have been dissolved. The point
is that we have not been able to assume a calculated and evaluated position vis-à-
vis this monster of our time.[122]

The primacy of the "machine" in "The Western" technological age spelled
confusion in the national character of the Iranians. Far from formulating
"a calculated and evaluated position vis-à-vis this monster of our time"
(that is, the machine), the Iranians of Al-e Ahmad's generation either were
massively petrified out of their wits by its awe, were significantly assimilated into its orbit, or rejected it altogether along with its presumed moral
corruption. Al-e Ahmad was, of course, far from having formulated a
sustained program of exactly how "a calculated and evaluated response"
should be attempted. But the operational impact of *Westoxication* was to
signal the presence of a process that, if unchecked, would have thoroughly
metamorphosized the Iranian collective consciousness in a pseudo-"Western" direction. Put simply, Al-e Ahmad captured the heart of his disillusioned age: a rising political and intellectual elite who increasingly saw
themselves as a people wronged, their hopes betrayed, their dreams misinterpreted, all at the hands of a massive abstraction they called "The West."
The alienation went deep into the (un)making of the Iranian character:

We have now altogether forgotten the sense of competition. It has been substituted
by the sense of helplessness, the sense of servitude. We no longer see ourselves as
deserving any right. . . . Nay, even if we seek to justify an aspect of our this- or
other-worldly affairs we evaluate them on their ["The Westerners' "] principles,
following the injunctions of their advisers and counselors. We study like them; take
census like them; do research like them. But even that is all right, because science
has assumed a kind of universal methodology. Scientific methods have no sign of
any specific country. But the interesting thing is that we get married like the
Westerners do; imitate liberalism like they do; evaluate the world, dress, and write
like they do. As if our own principles have all been superseded. . . . Yes, now from
those two old rivals finally one has ended up cleaning after the circus; the other one
runs the show. And what a show! A pornograhic scandal, stupefying, stultifying
assininity. So that they can plunder the oil.[123]

To the degree that the terms corresponded to a collectively presumed
reality, the decades of sustained "Westoxication" had not penetrated deep
enough to create a sense of self-hatred. Al-e Ahmad's *Westoxication* may,
in fact, be considered the alert response of a living organism rejecting what
it considered to be a "foreign" element. The "foreign" element, that is, the
collectively presumed forceful imposition of "Western" cultural hegemony,

had never been faced in equal terms but as an extension of an uneven relation of power: "The West" vs. (the Islamic) Iran.

A face-to-face interaction with "The West," as presumed in pre-Islamic Iranian history or early Islamic history, would have resulted in much fruitful interpenetration of cultural mores. But on unequal terms with "The West," the Iranian collective consciousness was translating "The Western" military might into the equally mighty moral hegemony. On the surface, Al-e Ahmad's *Westoxication* was a harsh and lasting blow against "The Western" morality and its presumed universal validity. But in effect it could not but further substantiate the mythical construction of "The West" as the most compelling generalized "Other" in the Iranian "Self"-understanding. In a celebrated and also much disputed passage in *Westoxication*, Al-e Ahmad stated:

that the religious leader siding with *mashru'eh* [= literally "based on religious law," a term coined to rhyme but negate *mashruteh*, "Constitutionalism"] was hanged in the course of the Constitutional Revolution was itself a sign of retreat [in the face of overflowing "Westernization"]. I agree . . . that the martyred master [Shaykh Fazlollah] Nuri had to be hanged not because he opposed "Constitutionalism"— which he initially had supported—but because he had favored a form of government based on sacred Islamic law. But I also add that because he defended the totality of Islam. . . . At any rate, it is from that day that the seal of Westoxication like a stigma was cauterized on our brow. And thus I consider the body of that most revered [man] upon the gallows a flag mounted on the roof of this land as a sign of the predomination of Westoxication after a two-hundred-year struggle.[124]

Besieged by the overwhelming force of the Constitutionalists to "Westernize" the Iranian government, Shaykh Fazlollah Nuri had been killed by secular Westoxicated liberals so that Islam would be eliminated as a viable political force. Recognizing the significance of Islam as a legitimate source of a revolutionary ideology, Al-e Ahmad sought to resuscitate the opposition to the influx of "Western" ideological forces during the constitutional period.

Shaykh Fadlollah Nuri was defeated and hanged and his pleas silenced. "Westernization" triumphed over the local forces of the Islamic culture and religion. In order to carry out the resurrection and the political requirements of an Islamically charged ideology, a new breed of intellectuals was needed. In *Westoxication*, Al-e Ahmad's notion of an intellectual par excellence returned to the nineteenth-century models.

If in those days [the nineteenth century] only Atabak and Amir Kabir were subjects of indoctrination, each a wise old man with a bundle of experience gained in a lifetime and through their traditions and oriental criteria, and with their feet fettered with beliefs, customs, and habits of this part of the world, nowadays the subject of conversion or indoctrination of European admirers is the group of intellectuals who are deeply Westoxicated, lacking both the stamina of Atabak and Amir Kabir, and the shrewdness of Hajj Mirza Aqasi.[125]

What is remarkable here is that as late as the mid-1960s—or as early as the 1960s in retrospect—Al-e Ahmad perceived "age," "experience," "tradition," "Oriental criteria," "beliefs," "customs," and "habits" as valid and bona fide principles in terms of which an Iranian intellectual should be characterized and with which matters of collective behavior, constructive or revolutionary, organized. Such perceptions of political propriety would put Al-e Ahmad immediately at odds with his secular intellectual cohorts. But at the same time it would make him more conscious of the hidden possibilities of the Shi'i political culture.

Hidden Possibilities

Al-e Ahmad's intuitive sensitivities to the Shi'i political culture began to discern a range of possibilities within the received specifics of people's shared memory. Without, for example, having any serious grasp of the juridical complexities of the question of "the Hidden Imam," he had an acute understanding of the political ramifications of this canonical belief:

90 percent of the dearly beloved people of this country think of the government as the instrument of tyranny, and the usurper of the legitimate right of "His Majesty the Prince of the Age, May God Almighty Hasten His Appearance." So they have every right not to pay their taxes, cheat the government authorities, escape conscription through all kinds of excuses, and don't give a straight answer to any census official.[126]

Because of the prevalence of such sentiments, people were more conducive to calls for revolutionary mobilizations when issued by religious authorities. The example in modern Iranian history that Al-e Ahmad thought best demonstrated how the common Islamic bounds can be used politically was the episode of the nationalization of oil by Mosaddeq in the early 1950s. Al-e Ahmad ardently believed that if the nationalization of oil movement was successful, it was due to a symbiotic cooperation, a coincidence of interest, between political and religious forces, that is, between Mosaddeq and some of the clerical elements:

The leaders in those days were shrewd enough to lead the struggle in such a way that through collaboration with the religious leaders every uneducated common person would identify the government as the instrument of tyranny which gave the oil to the [British] company and then treated its own subjects harshly. This is the greatest lesson that intellectuals and [political] leaders ought to have learned from that incident.[127]

Whereas here, and elsewhere, Al-e Ahmad thought of using the existing and operative religious sentiments politically, Shari'ati would go one step further and seek to instill new and powerful political commitments by selectively reactivating aspects of Islamic historical and mythological tradition. Motahhari, in turn, would lend intellectual credence to Al-e Ahmad's timid but groundbreaking suggestions and Shariᶜati's revolutionary achievements. In a footnote to the above passage, Al-e Ahmad would also suggest, again tacitly and through a reference to a French observer,[128] that not only in Iran but throughout the Muslim world the infusion of religious sentiments into politics is bound to produce effective results. This is attainable, Al-e Ahmad argued through Grousset, despite the Sunni-Shiᶜi schism that divides Iranians from most of the Arabs. At the end of this footnote,[129] Al-e Ahmad repeats that "what I have said in concealment, this [French] gentleman has said a bit more clearly," which is again a reference to how openly Al-e Ahmad was willing, or able, to discuss his notion of the political uses of Islam. This is a kind of dual censorship on Al-e Ahmad's part: one obviously by the government officials, the other from the religious establishment in Qom, of whose reactions to suggestions of the political uses of Islam, with the exception of Khomeini, he was unsure.

It is worth remembering that until 1961—that is, a year before the publication of *Westoxication*—Ayatollah Borujerdi was the supreme juridical figure in Iran. His political quietism would make Al-e Ahmad doubtful of how actively the religious establishment would react to his ideas. But a year after the publication of *Westoxication*, Khomeini's June 1963 uprising against the Shah would inevitably leave Al-e Ahmad more convinced of the serious implications of his ideas.

Al-e Ahmad's conviction was well founded. The key concept of "Westoxication" had reached deep into the collective political commitments of his contemporaries, and he thought of taking full advantage of that:

let's stick to something, perhaps we can hold on to our identity. Not the way Turkey ended up. You see what I mean? That's why I keep thinking about this issue, and am rather hoping that after five years these dime-a-dozen things I have said in *Westoxication* will have subsided, like water, under the foundation. . . . [Thus the book] is still alive. While I thought it would not last for two months, and it shall die out, that is to say, it would be forgotten. But apparently it has not. Because they still talk about it.[130]

Al-e Ahmad's political concern for the revolutionary uses of Islam, however, cannot in any way be interpreted as concern for the future relevance of religion, understood in an abstract sense. In fact, he clearly saw how religion and other traditional thrusts of collective symbolics could be used effectively for counterrevolutionary and colonialist objectives:

In the kind of world we live in, the more national boundaries are tightened, the more powerful the ethnic traditions, the more serious the raw ambitions of ye old king, the more widespread the religious dogmas, so much deeper would be the jail dungeons of nations and peoples.[131]

"On the Services and Treasons of the Intellectuals"

The final formulation of Al-e Ahmad's political uses of Islam was to be realized in his long essay, *Dar Khedmat va Khiyanat-e Roshanfekran*, "On the Services and Treasons of the Intellectuals" (hereafter "On the Intellectuals"). This essay was difficult to publish.[132] Al-e Ahmad began working on the text of "On the Intellectuals" right after Khomeini's 1963 uprising and its bloody suppression.[133] He thought the Iranian secular intellectuals were to blame for the failure of the movement.[134] At one of his regular weekly luncheons with some of his Dar al-Fonun and Tudeh Party friends, Al-e Ahmad harshly criticized his former Tudeh comrades and accused them of sharing responsibility for the failure of the movement.[135] In fact, after Al-e Ahmad's violent criticism, these weekly luncheons were effectively cancelled.

"On the Intellectuals" is the strongest and most eloquently argued condemnation of the secular intellectuals. With a combined experience of more than three decades in Iranian political culture, Al-e Ahmad concluded that the secular intellectuals were a spineless bunch of self-centered hypocrites who could only look to "The West" for hopes, aspirations, and guidance:

The Iranian intellectual has gradually turned into a root which is not [planted] in the soil of this land. He always has his eyes on Europe, and always dreams of escaping there. . . . When the BBC [the British Broadcasting Corporation] insults the deposed First Person [Reza Shah] of the ruling class personally, the intellectual cannot but jump on the bandwagon! Thus all of a sudden everyone joins the Tudeh Party, . . . condemning religion as reactionary, and the government as despotic.[136]

Here Al-e Ahmad took the Tudeh Party as the supreme example of a group of "rootless" secular intellectuals. His accusations went much further than that. He clearly accused the Tudeh Party, and all its historical experience, of not merely mistakes but of graver misdeeds:

During all this time [the 1940s], it was only the Tudeh Party that had a voice and moved a group of people and had some impact, upon which there were also many mistakes, wrongdoings, and even treason, and for these very reasons we seceded from it in 1948.[137]

Upon such conclusions, Al-e Ahmad moved towards a more realistic understanding of the Iranian political culture. He clearly saw what set of specific operations of collective symbols could eventually move the people. Specific historical episodes have demonstrated that revolutionary movements can be successful only when directed by figures and symbolics of authority

closest to the masses of Iranian sentiments. A good example occurred
during the Mosaddeq era when

in the nationalization of oil episode, because the clerics and liberal intellectuals of
the day were united in their anticolonial move, people of the street were mobilized,
and the movement was ultimately so powerful that for breaking it the [oil] companies had to intervene directly.[138]

Al-e Ahmad's principal criticism of the Tudeh Party, and the main
experience he took away from his term with it, particularly in the course of
the Mosaddeq episode, was its inability to translate grandiloquent Marxist
ideals into practical local issues, attuned to the specifics of the Iranian
political culture. "Because the Tudeh Party could not give itself local and
national form, and thus solve people's problems," Al-e Ahmad thought, "it
could not but found its roots on waves, not in the social depth."[139] Because
the Tudeh Party failed to respond to the most basic concerns of its constituency, it could not but add to the existing problems, "nay it was the source
of many problems in the country."[140]

As Al-e Ahmad saw it, particularly towards the end of his life, the
clerical organization, as a viable political apparatus, was potentially capable of moving and mobilizing the nation. Among his chief criticisms of the
Tudeh Party was its refusal to work in coalition with such socialist movements as the Third Force, which he and Khalil Maleki had founded upon
their break with the Party in 1948, or with the National Front, which Al-e
Ahmad thought robbed the Tudeh Party of all its potential grassroots
constituency and thus public legitimacy, and most of all directly with the
clerics:

Thus while the Tudeh Party was present, no other ideological order could find the
necessary persistence and stamina so that when that Party was removed from the
scene, there could be a kind of substitute.[141]

To be sure, Al-e Ahmad slightly exaggerates here the lack of an alternative
political ideology to mobilize discontent. It is true that the Tudeh Party had
monopolized the Iranian political scene for some time. But this monopoly
was the result of two things. First, the Tudeh Party offered a new, provocative, and unprecedented mode of political consciousness that appealed to
the young and the restless. Second, the Tudeh Party was the most effectively
organized political group in modern Iranian history. Through effective
strategies—which did not shy away from Machiavellian uses of terror,
intimidation, campaigns of lies and libel, fabrication of ethical misconduct,
pacification of opponents by gangs of thugs, and even assassination of
ideological adversaries—the Tudeh Party had maintained its ideological
and organizational supremacy over the Iranian political scene. But all these
efforts could not but remain at a superficial level, incapable of substituting

the larger, deeper, and more pervasive common myths of the Shiʿi political culture—the clericals its primary custodians.

It is precisely as "a kind of substitute" that Al-e Ahmad perceived the Shiʿi clerical organization and its potential political machinery. Whatever the degree of his sincere religiosity and piety, resumed in the latter part of his life, a disposition that cannot be ascertained in any meaningful way, Al-e Ahmad did realize the great political force potentially present in the Shiʿi clerical order. His recognition of this revolutionary urge in the political dimension of Shiʿism was a direct response to, or recognition of, the deficiencies in the experience of the Tudeh Party. In one sentence, Al-e Ahmad summarized the success and failure of the Party:

On one hand it criticized the government as the representative of the ruling class (and that was its strength and the cause of its expansion); and on the other hand it criticized every [other] ideological and religious movement (and that was its weakness and the cause of its failure).[142]

The effective alienation of the Tudeh Party from the society it was supposed to lead became particularly evident during the nationalization of oil episode, when Mosaddeq championed this cause and yet the Tudeh Party opposed it and sought to safeguard the Iranian oil fields in the North for their Russian comrades. In a memorable passage in "On the Intellectuals" there is a genuine and heartfelt sense of guilt and shame in Al-e Ahmad when he captures the precise moment of his disenchantment with the Tudeh Party:

There was a time when there was the Tudeh Party. It had something to say for itself. It had launched a revolution. It tackled colonialism. It defended the workers and the peasants. And what great ideals it had! What enthusiasm it generated! We were young and members of the Tudeh Party, not having the slightest idea who was pulling the strings. We were evading our youth and collecting experience. But [the disillusion] started for me the day I was in charge of security and order in one of the Party's demonstrations, on behalf of Kaftardze's mission to secure the North oil. . . . From the entrance of the Tudeh Party headquarters (on Ferdowsi Avenue) to Mokhberoldoleh crossroads: what a fuss I made with the security brassard around my arm. But at the beginning of Shah-abad [Street] I had a glimpse of the Russian personnel carriers in the street, all in a row, full of soldiers, watching over and protecting our demonstration. All of a sudden I was startled and became so ashamed that I [left the demonstration,] headed into Sayyid Hashim alley, and tossed my brassard [into the air].[143]

Al-e Ahmad saw the defeat of not only the Tudeh Party, with its socialist disposition, but also that of the National Front, with its nationalist posture, as specific symptoms in the "Westoxication" syndrome. In yet another memorable passage in "On the Intellectuals," he gave a full and accurate assessment of why he thought imported ideologies were incapable of moving the Iranian masses for specific revolutionary purposes:

If the Tudeh Party was defeated, and so was the National Front, . . . it is because of this principal reason that all these gentlemen have ventured into the battlefield of politics with imported ideas: Bragging about Communism and Socialism (and even that in secret and not openly), and not even trying to conform those "isms" to the local conditions. [This resulted in] confronting the foundations of people's traditional beliefs. In the general scheme of politics, [they] completely disregarded the clerics. (If the National Front had a larger impact on people in a shorter time [than the Tudeh Party], it was because it relied on the clerics.) In the absence of a massive proletariate, pretending to defend the benefits of a working class, and in the presence of the great majority of the peasants, completely ignoring the problems of peasantry and lands, and other problems that I cannot elaborate [here, contributed to the defeat of the Tudeh Party].[144]

Al-e Ahmad praised the National Front precisely for its having accommodated both religious sentiments and the clerical order:

The National Front . . . was the meeting place of anticolonial parties, and it was the first post-[Constitutional] Revolutionary political organization to have given credit to the clerics, and precisely for this reason it had more grassroots support.[145]

He thus gradually gathered sweeping evidence from the world political scene to support his pointing out the uses of religious language in political mobilization:

If we look at it from a Marxist point of view, it is a time that "religion = opium of the masses" is still a universal truism for Communist parties who wish to substitute [for religion] another sacred tradition. But take a look at Ghandi's strategies. In India he waged a war against colonialism with the aid of religion. Or [consider] what the Vietnamese Buddhists did in helping the Viet Cong; or what is happening in the European confusion with the participation of the left wing of the [Christian] church [in politics] or what went on in Algeria to get rid of the French; or what happened in our own country during the Tobacco Revolt, the Constitutional period, in nationalization [of oil], and in June 1963.[146]

It was precisely in recognition of such great revolutionary potentials in religion that, despite his great admiration for Khalil Maleki, Al-e Ahmad was gradually drifting away from him:

The other [cause of disagreement between Maleki and me] is the importance I have found for the clerics as a subject of study in the political conditions of the society we live in. Maleki tells me, "You have become an Akhond," or else he says, "You have become an anarchist" or things of that sort.[147]

The Intellectuals and the Clerics

Al-e Ahmad further rehistoricized his detection of revolutionary potentials in Shi'ism. In retrospect, he considered two major social forces as instrumental in the course of the Constitutional Revolution: the intellectuals and the clerics. He also thought the generation of 1920–1940 was chiefly responsible for depleting the revolutionary vigor of these two forces through "Zoroastrianism, Ferdowsiism, Kasraviism, and Bahaiism."[148] These were frivolous, but conspiratorially planned according to Al-e Ahmad, distractions through which the revolutionary power of the alliance between the traditionally sensitive intellectuals and the clerics was uselessly exhausted. Al-e Ahmad's admiration for Mosaddeq, in fact, is precisely in terms that identify him as a politician in touch with realities of his cultural context, which are also the terms in which the Tudeh Party was bound to be defeated. In Al-e Ahmad's view, Mosaddeq was decent enough not to blame his political failure on "the scarcity of instruments, insufficient cadre, and unfavorable conditions for leadership,"[149] an obvious reference to such excuses by the leaders of the Tudeh Party. Consequently, Al-e Ahmad saw Khomeini's June 1963 uprising as further support for his thesis that in order to move the Iranian masses to revolutionary engagement, they ought to be addressed in the religious language most immediate to them: a repoliticized Shi'ism.

Al-e Ahmad's great admiration for Khalil Maleki, of whom he once said, "in social issues he is my master, and that of many other contemporary intellectuals,"[150] was expressed precisely in terms of his having modified socialism to local exegencies. He admired Maleki for having taken "strength from this very soil" and having breathed "in this very climate."[151] He credited Maleki for being a "turning point in [changing] Stalinist communism to democratic socialism."[152] Because of his sensitivities to local factors and his willingness to modify grand theoretical schemes to particular cultural exegencies, Maleki, according to Al-e Ahmad, was able "to break with Stalinism before Tito, say what Khrushchev said before the Twentieth Communist party congress, and foretell the Sino-Soviet conflict long before it happened."[153]

Al-e Ahmad's careful and accurate observation of the Iranian political scene, after almost three decades of being active in it, was that

you can only be effective in politics, or in the affairs of a society, when you have weighed the degree of receptivity or tolerance of that society vis-à-vis your ideas. And in order to achieve this measure, you will have to have known that society, its traditions, history, the factors instrumental in making its collective belief, forces that mobilize its masses in the streets, and then its silence, its sitting silently at home.[154]

In "On the Intellectuals," Al-e Ahmad would reassert his earlier conviction that the loss of Iranian identity and alienation from the potential revolutionary uses that Islam can be put into was essentially a "Western colonial scheme":

the onslaught of Colonialism is not merely to plunder the raw mineral material and human powers . . . from the colonies. It also devastates the language, the customs, the music, the ethics, and the religion of the colonized lands.[155]

And then he would sarcastically ask: "But is it fair for the Iranian intellectual to be an accomplice to colonialists instead of confronting them on all fronts?"[156] The Iranian secular intellectuals, in Al-e Ahmad's estimation, concurred with "The Western" colonialists in denying the contemporary relevance and modern applicability of Islam—as either a formative or a transformative political force.

Al-e Ahmad had a particular conception of "the intellectuals" as a social grouping. Although he did not think they shared all the attributes of the group, he still considered the clerics and the military personnel among the intellectuals, wondered why his European sources did not realize this, and thus finally decided that the omission was due to the secular and democratic nature of "The Western" perspectives.[157] The reason he includes these two social groupings among the intellectuals has to do with what he called "social readership"[158] in his definition of "the intellectual." The importance of his inclusion of the clerics in particular among the intellectuals is the expansion of an otherwise exclusively secular intelligentsia to include those who institutionally operate in a religious frame of reference. This would, in turn, open the society at large to the political and ideological implications of the clerical group.

In order to demonstrate the supremacy and higher legitimacy of religious symbols over the secular frames of political reference, Al-e Ahmad pointed out a crucial fact of his immediate history. In his poignant comparisons of the religious and political authority, he observed that while people paid their religious taxes willingly and voluntarily, the governmental taxes still had to be forcefully exacted from them.[159] He also made a crucial distinction between the political authority, embodied in the army, which was totally dependent on the state apparatus, and the religious authority, institutionalized in the clerical order, which was directly connected to the society.[160] This distinction between state and society had scarcely been considered by any contemporary observer of modern Iranian history. With a remarkably clear and precise description, Al-e Ahmad attributed political authority to the clericals without the slightest awareness of the juridical and doctrinal issues involved:

Because in the context of the Shiʻi faith, the clerics claim political authority on behalf of the [Twelfth] Infallible Imam, that is to say, [because] they principally and by way of deputyship constitute a kind of competition for the political authority, we have occasionally witnessed violent oppositions, or even revolts, launched by the clerics against the powers that be.[161]

This assessment of the clericals' political authority was formulated through a specifically historical, as opposed to doctrinal, reading of Shi'ism.

In reading Al-e Ahmad's "On the Intellectuals" we should not be distracted by his occasionally inconsistent logic, where he once considers the clericals and the military officers as intellectuals[162] and then later as two distinct groups different from the intellectuals.[163] What we should pay attention to is his observation that in the post-Constitutional period the role of the military as the legitimating force of the political authority has increased, while at the same time the clericals have lost their propensity to command the ideological obedience of their constituency.[164] Al-e Ahmad's essential problem in his conceptualization of the "intellectuals" was his inability to distinguish between the social functions of a class and the individual capabilities, such as erudition, of its constituent members. Thus he considered the army officers as intellectuals, despite his repeated recognition[165] that they could not but collectively defend the status quo. But despite such inconsistencies, "On the Intellectuals" is Al-e Ahmad's most sweeping condemnation of all sorts of secular ideologies and a simultaneous affirmation of the positive role religion can and should play in politics.

The Legacy of Jalal Al-e Ahmad

Al-e Ahmad's significance in the course and outcome of the Islamic Revolution of 1979 can scarcely be overemphasized. Sayyid Ali Khamenei, the present "leader" of the Islamic Republic, has called Jalal Al-e Ahmad, playing on the meaning of his name, "the majesty of the men of letters" and "the man who . . . stood at the summit of the literature of resistance."[166] Remote as he has been from the actual scene of Iranian intellectual life of the 1950s and 1960s, even Mohamammad Ali Jamalzadeh, the founding father of modern Persian fiction, has pointed out that

there is no doubt that [Al-e Ahmad] has had a considerable role in preparing the groundwork for the national uprising, and we all have to consider ourselves indebted to his determination, valor, and sufferings.[167]

Al-e Ahmad's disciples are quick to point out, in opposing his Marxist critics, the accuracy of his ideas about the religious texture of the Iranian society. "The victory of the Revolution," one of these disciples attests,

is a reason for the accuracy and extraordinarily precise coordination of Jalal [Al-e Ahmad]'s theory with the people's class roots, as well as with their aspirations in movements and revolutions.[168]

Al-e Ahmad has been called "the greatest artist of our time" or even "a huge trailer, an eighteen-wheeler Mack."[169] Although it is very difficult to assess the exact number of editions through which Al-e Ahmad's books have been circulated, perhaps one statement by a follower of his is not too unrealistic:

after so many legal and illegal printings of Jalal [Al-e Ahmad]'s works, still every one of his books is reprinted at least once every year. And this is a testimony to the persistent and ever larger popularity of his writings.[170]

The same follower also points out the innumerable translations, anthologies, and selections of Al-e Ahmad's works that appear every year. There are also books, stories, poems (some posthumously composed for Al-e Ahmad) that appear every year.[171]

Al-e Ahmad was a turning point in the development of modern revolutionary discourse in Iran. He acutely realized the futility of an overtly secular language in reaching a politically significant audience. His years of affinity with the Tudeh Party had convinced him that a more direct, intimate, and indigenous language is needed before a mass audience, capable of moving a revolutionary machinery, is reached. Al-e Ahmad's revolutionary discourse thus emerged from an essentially secular context and gradually plunged deeper into a religious semantics. His affiliations first with the concocted rationalism of Ahmad Kasravi and then with the imported socialism of the Tudeh Party gave him ample opportunity to realize the futility and political inefficiency of secular ideologies. His *Westoxication* was a serious attempt to find a political discourse that relates effectively the stated ideological objectives of a revolutionary movement to the Iranian audience.

Beyond, or perhaps in conjunction with, his indispensable contribution to the making of "the Islamic Ideology," Al-e Ahmad's primary and singular achievement as a writer was to wed politics to literature. He wrote fictions highly sensitive to political issues. He offered guidelines of how literature should "confront" life. But for a political literature to become viable and legitimate, the most crucial factor is securing a sustained audience. Al-e Ahmad thus favored a relocation of artistic patronage from the court to "the people." But at the same time he realized what was inherent in this transition. Whereas in former days all a poet had to do was secure the patronage of a king, nowadays poets were addressing "the people," but without having any institutional recognition from that vast abstraction. The result was a total confusion of what constituted the audience in most of his contemporary poetry. Al-e Ahmad could only leave the paradox at that dead end.

Al-e Ahmad was surprisingly, for his generation of intellectuals, sensitive to common mythologies. Of the suicide of Takhti, a world-champion wrestler who according to public legend was believed to have been killed by the government or one of the Shah's brothers or SAVAK (there were variations in the urban legend), he observed:

let's see whether this popular legend making is not a kind of defense mechanism for the ordinary man in the street in order to protect his frightened honor in the face of the dominant tyranny, and thus remain hopeful?[172]

By attending the immediate and far-reaching efficacy of such legend-making proclivities among his contemporaries, Al-e Ahmad inevitably became a legend himself. The cultural hero of a whole generation of political consciousness, Al-e Ahmad became a phenomenon. That is perhaps less the inevitable outcome of who he actually was or what he actually achieved than perhaps, more important, who he was turned into posthumously. If upon his death a man manages to have as many devout diehards—who think he was the greatest thing to have ever happened in the Iranian intellectual history—as staunch enemies—who think he was an absolute nobody—he has undoubtedly secured a niche for himself in the annals of his time. On the fortieth day of Al-e Ahmad's death, there was a religious ceremony in the mosque of Molla Hashem in Mashhad, which both his widow, Simin Daneshvar, and his brother, Shams Al-e Ahmad, attended. That this traditional day of mourning and remembrance was held in a mosque in Mashhad, the religious capital of the Shiʻi Iran and that his widow and brother attended this gathering are telling factors of how Jalal Al-e Ahmad's lasting significance must be seen primarily in a religious context. On this occasion, one of Al-e Ahmad's diehards issued a staunch and harsh warning against his Marxist critics: "Against his enemies, we shall defend Jalal with all means, resolutely, and with utmost vigor."[173]

The trajectory of Jalal Al-e Ahmad's biography demonstrates the remarkable passage through which he reached the perhaps inevitable conclusion of a greater affinity for the innate religious traits of his received and contemporary political culture. He began his life in a tightly religious family. He grew up under the compelling spell of a clerical father who, besieged by the universal secular trends of his age, could only demand from his household a more obedient adherence to principles he held sacred. Al-e Ahmad's childhood and early education were thus spent with a deep inculcation of a religiously mandated ethical rectitude that would necessarily put him at odds with an increasing number of his cohorts attracted to the secular lure of the imported alternatives to religious truths and sentiments.

At Dar al-Fonun, Al-e Ahmad received a secular education devised and mandated by the regime of a secular autocrat determined to give a "modern" look to his nation. As he continued to adhere to as much of his religious tenets as his hostile environment would permit, Al-e Ahmad was gradually, but ever so persistently, affected by the new ideals and sentiments to which he was exposed at a nonseminarian learning center. Having abandoned the course of scholastic learning in Najaf and upon his graduation from high school, he was attracted to the positivistic and severely anticlerical ideas of Ahmad Kasravi. It is rather difficult to imagine how Al-e Ahmad could cope with such harsh anticlericalism given his own immediate background. The fact remains, however, that Kasravi acted as a springboard for Al-e Ahmad to jump right into the Tudeh Party. Kasravi's positivism distanced Al-e Ahmad considerably from his religious upbringing. He could have easily been attracted to Kasravi's brand of propagating a rational society devoid of all sentimentalism and superstition. From that crucial step into Kasravi's concocted social positivism, Al-e Ahmad took the next logical step and adopted the crudely imported socialism of the Tudeh Party.

The Tudeh Party gave Al-e Ahmad ample opportunity to shed all but a semblance of his religiosity. At the same time, his tenure as a member of the Tudeh Party provided him with the most cherished chance to devote himself wholeheartedly to the supreme ideals of a socialist paradise. The early 1940s were years of high hopes and great expectations for the newly secularized intellectuals like Al-e Ahmad who thought themselves on the verge of a cataclysmic entrance into the promised land. With the failure of the Tudeh Party to achieve, in any meaningful degree, its stated and hidden agenda of political acculturation in Iran, Al-e Ahmad was severely disillusioned with his involvement with the Party. The disillusion was not severe enough, however, to disrupt Al-e Ahmad's still committed belief in organized political activity under a patently secular ideology. Thus, upon his resignation from the Tudeh Party, he followed through a number of successive political activities, such as the Third Force, in many of which he was a close associate of Khalil Maleki. The primary character of these post-Tudeh Party activities was a more noticeable distance from ideological dogmatism and a healthier respect for moderate socialist concerns that are more sensitive to specific Iranian exegencies.

But even these diverse and haphazard political activities came to perhaps an inevitable closure. Al-e Ahmad began, in the late 1940s, a long and sustained process of soul searching and a markedly individualistic introspection. His preoccupation with Dostoyevski and Camus, translating them into Persian and being concerned with their ideas, is a suggestive mark of his increasing attention to existentialist individualism, as opposed to the essentialist socialism à la Tudeh Party. But even beyond a therapeutic attention to existentialism, Al-e Ahmad found a number of crucial substitutes, or ideological surrogates, for political activity in literature, in anthropological field trips to remote parts of the country, and in extensive traveling in and out of Iran. These substitutes all functioned to broaden his perception of politics and its innate and substantive relations to the larger context of cultural imperatives.

Three major works came out of this existentialist and individualistic period: *Westoxication, Lost in the Crowd,* and "On the Intellectuals." Each of these texts, in its own particular way, represents a specific aspect of Al-e Ahmad as a maverick intellectual who had reached certain conclusions about the nature and function of politics in his received culture. The significant mark of all three works is their going against the main grain of Al-e Ahmad's secular intellectual cohorts. And he could not have achieved this without first having secured a considerable distance and thus independence from the dominant political sentiments and from the overwhelming organizational urges that marked the ideological needs of his generation. Despite his religious background, Al-e Ahmad's home was with the secular intellectuals. From the center of this secular heartland in Tehran, he launched his ideological *coup d'état,* more in the form of a *coup de gifle,* against it.

Westoxication, the textual delivery of that *coup de gifle,* is a perceptive and totally anticlimactic statement. Al-e Ahmad could deliver that statement only in the solitude of his political thought, against the prevalent trend of "Westernization" in the course of which selective and imaginary aspects of European and/or American perceptions were being transplanted to substitute a monolithic and equally imaginative vision of the Iranian "historical" identity. To be sure, Al-e Ahmad himself had a monolithic and mythic view of "The West" that only mirrored the monolithic and mythical view of "The West" propagated by the secular intellectuals at large, a view that Al-e Ahmad had set out to negate. Thus, he totally appropriated and considerably substantiated the monolithic and imaginative view of "The West" that his secular contemporaries had created as an object of veneration. His uniqueness, however, was in negating and opposing this colonialistic and hegemonic grip that "The West" had over the minds and souls of his contemporaries.

Equally negational and anticlimactic was Al-e Ahmad's hajj pilgrimage and the publication of his subsequent travel notes, *Lost in the Crowd.* No secular intellectual contemporary of Al-e Ahmad made a "hajj pilgrimage" or, even more important, made a public confession of it. It was simply too much of an anachronism for a secular intellectual to stand. But in the solitude and certainty of his political, and perhaps even religious, concerns, Al-e Ahmad made the hajj pilgrimage and made a public statement of it just for the record. Al-e Ahmad could not have made that pilgrimage and would not have made a public statement of it had it not been for the gradual accumulation of an intellectual stamina in the course of his post-Tudeh Party experiences. The net result of his hajj pilgrimage and the political impact of *Lost in the Crowd* was an acute recognition of the revolutionary potential at the Muslim disposal, a recognition that neither Al-e Ahmad's former fellow Tudeh comrades could see nor his post-Tudeh secular intellectual cohorts could grasp.

But ultimately, "On the Intellectuals" articulated beyond any level previously attained the perhaps inevitable conclusion that for massive political mobilization the revolutionary ideologues had to appeal, ever so earnestly, to religious symbols. In the course of achieving this political wisdom, Al-e Ahmad had already been much distanced from the majority of his fellow intellectuals, invincibly ignorant of the power of the old myth and elusively having set upon themselves the stupendous task of creating, validating, and operating new ones. The new illusion, awkward and lacking in its partial grip over the Iranian imagination, was no match for the old and engaging enchantment.

By the time Al-e Ahmad had accumulated his wisdom from the Tudeh Party experience and had assumed the arduous task of individually (as opposed to collectively) seeking an existentialist (as opposed to an essentialist) understanding of his political situation, he reached, primarily through *Lost in the Crowd*, as an intermediary between *Westoxication* and "On the Intellectuals," the metaphysical truth of his political culture. At the height of that metaphysical truth stood the time-honored mores and moralities upon which archetypal modes of obedience, political and otherwise, were registered and articulated. By disposition, or perhaps by the sheer exhaustion of his energies, Al-e Ahmad could only point towards the critical path upon which ancient religions meet the exacting demands of contemporary politics. The actual articulation and pronouncement of that critical path remained for others—Shari'ati and Motahhari chief among them—to achieve.

Jalal Al-e Ahmad

What's in a name? Affection. An affection that breeds authority. "Jalal Al-e Ahmad" was a name. But it became a phenomenon that defined, in acceptance or denial, a generation. He was more "Al-e Ahmad" than "Jalal." "Jalal" was more intimate and immediate, fearfully near the center, with no necessary distance. His wife would call him "Jalal." "My husband Jalal" was the title she gave to a personal narrative about him. "Al-e Ahmad," however, was the name by which the rest of the world would know and address him. A ring of affection, masses of inarticulate sentiments, gathered around the name "Al-e Ahmad." "Have you read Al-e Ahmad's letter to Jamalzadeh?" For *Westoxication* you need not have even said "Al-e Ahmad." "Did you know that Americans have translated *Gharbzadegi*, and that they read it in their universities?" The same for *The School Principal*, or any other work of Al-e Ahmad, fiction or otherwise. For others you needed to have said them together, the author and the book: Hedayat's *Buf-e Kur*, Bozorg Alavi's *Chashm-ha-yash*, Sadeq Chubak's *Tangsir*, etc. But not for him. For Al-e Ahmad the mere titles contained all the necessary references. "SAVAK has confiscated *Zan-e Ziyadi* again." But even in unspoken reference, "Al-e Ahmad" was always there, affectionately, warmly, self-assuredly. You may have a classmate in high school or college who was his nephew or niece or something. "Really?" You became more attentive. Yes. "My father was with him when he went to Mecca. He remembers him lying down on the ground and writing his notes." You would be eternally impressed. There was a (prophetic) ring to the name, an almost contagious sanctity to all the political matters it touched. It stood there, "Al-e Ahmad," somewhere, towering in the collective imagination of your generation, as a flag, a sign, a signal, inviting you to discontent. More than anything else, it was familiar, homely, cozy, endearing. He knew all the right and the "in" things to know: Sartre, French cheese, Existentialism, new poetry, Bordeaux wine, European cinema, remote Iranian villages, obscure East European writers. What he knew was the "in" thing to know. Read your Al-e Ahmad and you were in; you knew the most essential vocabularies of the topnotch political activists on your campus. A generation of political fantasy spoke his words, regurgitated his ideas, quoted his passages, came to intellectual puberty with his essays, travelogues, and short stories. "Al-e Ahmad" provided the comfortable margin—between religion and politics, sanctity and modernity. He was not just a name. It was a state of mind for a generation. When a Marxist critic came out of the closet and criticized Al-e Ahmad openly, in the course of a public lecture, you felt nauseated, a sacred realm of your personal identity violated. If Al-e Ahmad was wrong, what would remain? Who else could you trust? You might as well become an anarchist, a pessimist, a born-again Muslim, or something. "Al-e Ahmad" was not just a man whose books you had read, whose fantasies you had shared, whose enchantments you had cherished. "Al-e Ahmad" was the key symbolic passage through which you had passed on your way from childhood to youth to a false sense of political maturity. He made that passage from childhood to youth brutally short, shallow, and permanently premature, and yet its memory so everlasting, eternally sweet. It was precisely for its shortness, shallowness, and prematurity that the brutal passage kept its sentimental grip on you. Sentimentality saturated the name "Al-e Ahmad" even years after you had graduated from his short, shallow, and premature grip on you. You rarely attained this graduation before your high school diploma. For most younger intellectuals the grip would commence the day after graduation from high school or as late as the following hot and melting summer days. By the time you took your university entrance examination (this is the 1970s generation), you better have had your minimum dosage of "Al-e Ahmad" or else. If you were accepted into a university, a 10 percent chance for this generation of hopeful and nervous applicants, your ID would not have been issued, as it were, or if issued, confiscated, if you had not read, cherished, and been mesmerized by every single word Al-e Ahmad had written. So much the better if you could quote him verbatim, or at least had an uncle who was a classmate of Al-e Ahmad at Dar al-Fonum or a cousin who had his autograph. "Al-e Ahmad" was much more than just a name. It was the dominant insignia on your university matriculation card. Years, decades, after you had been cured of your passage through "Al-e Ahmad" you would still look at the last pages of your personal copies of his books, see your childish signatures and the dates you first finished reading those books, and count the number of ways in which that extremely sincere and extremely narrow and extremely distant text has affected your most lasting patterns of personal and public demeanors. You would look at the date— some April day, 1972, reads one perhaps—and relive the unencumbered affections, the uncontrolled sentimentalities, of a generation of young intellectuals who, in sharing "Al-e Ahmad" as a supreme symbol of collective illusion, quietly and in innocent dreams forecasted the precise and the vague terms of a coming revolution, particulars of a more enduring enchantment.

Full of Convictions

"As for my 'lack of convictions,' " responded Gustave Flaubert to George Sand's letter, "alas! I am only too full of convictions. I burst with suppressed anger and indignation. But my ideal of art demands that the artist show none of this, and that he appears in his work no more than God in nature."[174] Al-e Ahmad was full of convictions—changing but always consummate convictions. He knew not of the truth of Flaubert's dictum of eliminating himself from his art, his convictions from his claims to political truths. His art became altogether secondary, truth merely tangential, when the primary cause of politics presented itself. But the literary appeal of his art, full of convictions and guidelines, expanded the boundaries of his ideological claims deep into the moral and emotional sentiments of his ever-larger constituency. That gave the would-be "Islamic Ideology" a free highway to the political commitments of otherwise mute atheists. "The suppressed anger and indignation" were meant to be sublimated in Al-e Ahmad the artist; and yet they were crystallized into the premises of "the Islamic Ideology." Al-e Ahmad did not live to see the fruits of the seeds he scattered on the fertile imagination of his revolutionary generation. How the taste of these belated fruits would have appealed to his palate, delicate but with no constant memory, should always remain the subject of idle but illuminative speculation.

CHAPTER 2

Ali Shari'ati: The Islamic Ideologue Par Excellence

"One of the remarkable facts of his intellectual history during this period," says a biographer of Jonathan Edwards (1703–1758), the great theologian of American puritanism, "is that, despite a very stormy propensity to theological innovation, he seems almost completely untouched by the questions of ministerial authority."[1] There is always something of a contradiction in the very terms of "theological innovation." Theology, as our historically received knowledge of God and as a hermeneutically sealed claim to monolithic interpretation of it, has something in it of the "eternal yesterday," as Weber called it. The atemporal omnipresence of God and the sanctity of the "eternal yesterday" when His knowledge was construed make all present and future "innovations" dubitable propositions. But at the same time, "ministerial authority" always seeks to institutionalize a reading of the received theology that is most compatible with the political exegencies of the status quo. The result of this theological paradox—remaining true to the received charismatic spontaneity of a vision of God or lending a legitimating hand to the powers that be—is an ideological bifurcation: "Theological innovation" is always congenial to critical engagements in matters of politics; "ministerial authority" is often inclined to sustain its own legitimacy via its institutional recognition by the political establishment. In the course of every major revolutionary movement, whether theological in New England or ideological in Iran, there is a major area of contention between "theological innovation," which wants to break loose from the inhibiting doctrinal fetters, and the "ministerial authority," which fears for its exclusive professional claims on possibilities of public salvation. The result never fails to be tumultuous.

From One to the Other

"But I am totally at a loss," Al-e Ahmad exclaimed once towards the end of his life, "why this new generation ... still has fixed its hopes on the previous one? And why it refuses to understand that we no longer are capable of doing anything?"[2] An otherwise acute and perceptive observer of his contemporary political scene, Al-e Ahmad failed to see the heroes of the new generation coming. He could not have fully imagined that right before his eyes Ali Shari'ati (1933–1977) would extend the implications of what he had merely sensed and suggested much beyond his own expectations or abilities. Al-e Ahmad and Shari'ati actually met in Mashhad in 1968, a year before Al-e Ahmad's sudden death. But the significance of their historical meeting, remarkable as it is, is pale and passing compared to their ideological rendez-vous.

Ali Shari'ati: a Phenomenon

How exactly does one man manage to capture the revolutionary imagination of an entire generation? Where exactly is the source of ideological energy one draws from to launch a cataclysmic movement? That Shari'ati energized the Iranian political culture, or at least a significant component of it, beyond anything known in its modern history is, more than anything else, an indication of a deep conviction on his own part, the conviction that he had a vision. Perhaps it is beyond the realm of inquiry for a student of political culture to seek the intellectual and spiritual sources that form and inform this conviction of a man that he has a vision. Perhaps an illusive image, perhaps something in the constitution of one's moral disposition, perhaps a piece of poetry, who knows, perhaps a deep and unlettered nostalgia for a promised utopia that once so deceptively, ever so deceptively, reveals itself to a man. Perhaps. We all live on the margins of possibilities. But what we can see is only the appearance, the external, the visible, which is thus also the invisible, the internal, the content. That is the only way we know how to know and how to judge: by and through the external. There is, undoubtedly, something in Shari'ati's external, the legacy of his writings, the power of his imagination, that betrays a deep and desperate conviction, a panoramic vision, a certain kind of certitude as to what precisely the end is—where the path, who the guide, when the time —and why all this is worth fighting for.

Assuming a voice that can address such a committed vision, the visionary finds all historical accuracy, logical consistency, and breadth of erudition superfluous and irrelevant. Shari'ati's discourse would be totally mutilated, reduced to rhetorical gibberish, were it to be dissected into its matters of fact. Shariʿati was an ideologue, first and foremost. One would be totally misled to treat him as a historian, a philosopher, a sociologist, an Islamicist, or any other such brand of quiet limitations imposed or adopted for addressing the specific course of mundane realities.

Shariʿati wished to change, not interpret; lead, not argue; move, not convince; achieve, not rationalize. To do this he assumed a compelling ahistorical language, a language that would naturally and convincingly make Ayn al-Quddat Hamadani, a twelfth-century Persian mystic, his "brother," who writes—actually writes—an introduction to one of Shariʿati's books first published in 1970. By quoting a long paragraph at the beginning of *Kavir (Desert)* (1970) and calling it an "Introduction" by "my brother" Ayn al-Quddat Hamadani, Shariʿati assumes such a universal language that when he, Shariʿati himself, talks, history talks. Not having the authorial voice of God behind his tone, as did the clerics, Shariʿati settled, as he saw it more fit, for the perhaps equally compelling voice of history: not "history" as the cumulative measures of actual shared experiences, but "history" as the ideological reconstruction of a revolutionary "self" around which every other experience is forced to redefine itself.

To achieve this ahistorical voice, Shariʿati reaches out for the most sincere moments of his thoughts, his silence, and his solitude. Dividing his writings into three broad categories—(1) Societal *(ijtimaʿiyyat)*, (2) Islamic *(Islamiyyat)*, and (3) Deserta *(Kaviriyyat)*—he confessed, "what only the people like are the Societal; what both I and the people like are the Islamic, and that which makes me happy . . . [are] the deserta."[3] What was closest to Shariʿati's heart, obviously, were the writings he called Deserta. He had a cryptomythical notion of the desert. He thought the desert is where you go to do your ritual ablution (the image he sublimated was sands for drops of water) before you reach your truth. From Deserta to Islamica to Societal there seems to be a line, as it were, from Shariʿati's most sincere sentiments to his most political ambitions.

Despite Shariʿati's professed categorization of his own writings, it is not to the advantage of his ideas to divide them into typologies of purpose. He could only bring the totality of his emotional moments and the immediacy of his political agenda to bear on whatever he presently uttered. Shariʿati entered the Iranian ideological scene more like an unexpected thunder than a forecasted rain, thus giving his writings a certain emotional immediacy, a certain urgency of purpose. To look into Shariʿati's collective writings for a systematized political theory or a thorough definition of what is to be done is a futile task. At best, one has to try to catch those vibrant moments of ideological drive that made this revolutionary thunderbolt roar.

The thunder broke in the desert, in the silence and certitude of a primeval conviction. Shariʿati entered the Iranian urban intellectual scene with a deep distrust for the city and a profound, almost mythical, nostalgia for the desert. He identified whatever was corrupt and degenerating with the city and whatever was pure, true, and beautiful with the desert. He longed for the desert as a fish for the sea. He spoke proudly of his learned ancestors who had come from Faryman, a desert oasis in Khorasan, and who had all chosen to return to the desert to live in solitude and serenity. Despite his profoundest love for his father, Shariʿati seems to blame him tacitly for having been the first in the chain of his ancestry to have decided to stay in the city and find his sanctuary there, in that urban celebration of distraction and mediocrity.[4] Concurrent with his disdain for the city, Shariʿati ridiculed and despised the traditional notions of "history," which he considered nothing but an account of the ruling banalities polished by the urban intellectuals garbed and employed as court scribes and official historians. Shariʿati did not believe for a moment the claim of the modern historians to have redirected their focus from the ruling class onto "the real people." Look, he argued, at the enormous publicity that surrounded the death of President Kennedy. The "real" history was the one conducted and recorded in the desert. The desert, in fact, was "a history in the shape of a geography."[5]

Equally compelling in Shariʿati was a deep, almost sardonic, disdain for formal learning. In a moving recollection of a learning experience he never forgot, Shariʿati described how in his early youth he once asked a well digger to show him how he worked in a *Kariz* (a subterranean canal). That experience, which must have occurred some time during Shariʿati's youth in the mid- to late 1940s, remained the archetypal image of learning for Shariʿati, a learning that teaches "revolution, not information, . . . becoming, not being."[6] That almost magical description of how water gushes through the cold stone from the persistent mastery and hard work of the well digger gave Shariʿati the most vivid similitude of how a revolutionary movement would actually take shape and reach its final goal:

I was deeply entrenched in . . . the awesome [artistry] of the Master [well digger], and the miracle he did with his axe, the beauty of labor, the striving in the dark, and the majesty of the courage to plunge in the depth of the earth; and then meaning—so meaningful a meaning—of searching for water, and the superlative sanctity of digging in the heart of darkness, far from [the surface of] the earth, far from life, to open wells which have been closed down. Suddenly I felt a cool and delicate caressing in between the fingers of my bare feet. Gradually the murmurs, intensifying and expanding every moment, came from everywhere, joining together, becoming one cry, and the cries were raised from all over, joining together, and now turning angry, rebellious, aggressive: Water.[7]

The opposite, but integral, end of Shariʿati's pronounced and emphatic political agenda was his personal agonies in search of an ontological identity that would define and locate him in his self-created and self-sustained history. That Shariʿati consciously struggled with such desperate measures

of self-perception we know through a letter he wrote in 1965 to an un-
named friend. In this letter, Shariᶜati sincerely discussed his penetrating
introversion for a self-definition. He admitted that the "I" who has written
and lectured, preached and led, addressed and been recognized by his
audience, is an "I" that he has successfully projected, but is, in fact, only a
mask, a cover *(hejab)* he insists, that he has put on. He does report jubi-
lantly of a truer and more honest "I" that he has recently discovered. He
describes the birth of this new "self" in him with powerful, somewhat
apocalyptic, conviction.[8] But the most remarkable context of this apocalyptic self-creation is solitude, which Shariᶜati describes as his most reliable
"safe house and . . . solid fortress."[9] "The Prophet used to say," Shariᶜati
paraphrased for his friend, that "I love perfume, women, and praying in
your [mortals'] world." But, continued Shariᶜati with absolute conviction,
"I have chosen solitude. Had it not been for this impeccable convent, this
safe haven, this world . . . would have killed me."[10]

More than anything else, what this ability to retrieve into the safe haven
of solitude gave Shariᶜati was a remarkable ability to control and then
gradually release the fury and conviction that was so intensely accumulated
in him. He was, without a doubt, the most furious revolutionary among
the ideologues of the Islamic Revolution in Iran. There is a vast and deep
reservoir of revolutionary fervor in him matched by no other ideologue.
But by his confessed retrievals to conscious and self-imposed solitude, he
seems to have been able to bring his furious energy under control for
gradual and systematic release. There is a short piece he wrote as an
homage to his late teacher in Paris, the distinguished French scholar Louis
Massignon, in which Shariᶜati insisted on the superiority of *dust-dashtan* (a
more dispassionate love in Persian) over *eshq* (passionate love). While *eshq*
is a blind, rapid, and explosive outburst of emotion exhausting itself as it is
consumed, *dust-dashtan* moves majestically and steadily towards a consciously chosen course of devotion where one's immediate gratifications are
postponed and translated into longer spans of sustained beauty and truth.[11]
With the abstract and removed notion of "the people" as his most glorious
object of love and devotion, Shariᶜati did manage, in the short span of life
that he lived, to offer his love a historical measure of gratification. He
charted his energy, the revolutionary fury he so consciously and decidedly
tapped, with a clear, however tacit, political agenda, all mobilized towards
a massive ideological reconstitution of the status quo. The ultimate target
of this conscious sublimation of raw energy was political, leading to a
tangible social transformation of private pieties into public virtues.

From Kariz to Paris

Shari'ati's revolutionary disposition and his almost irresistible urge to revive and redefine single-handedly Islamic history and dogma into a massive and systematized ideology of revolt is rooted, at least partially, in his experiences as a student in Paris. Although it is not possible, nor is it advisable, to reduce Shari'ati's complex revolutionary disposition to traces of his learning and education, one particular influence seems to be more persuasive and relevant than others. In a short piece, titled "My Masters," that Shari'ati wrote in praise of those who had taught him, the name and almost saintly omnipresence of Louis Massignon is particularly evident. The terms of endearment with which Shari'ati praised and honored his old teacher are almost hagiographic in tone, somewhat magical in mythical properties. As an Islamicist, Massignon was attracted chiefly to Mansur al-Hallaj, the martyred Persian mystic who, for the Catholic scholar, was an obvious historical transfixation of Christ, as is quite evident from the title of his magnum opus, *La Passion d'Hallaj*.[12] Chiefly and most pronouncedly a prophet of social revolution, Shari'ati seems to have had a peculiarly antinomial obsession with Massignon, whose mystical, somewhat ascetic, disposition seems so at odds with Shari'ati's pronounced revolutionary postures. The evident paradox ought to be seen in Shari'ati's restless determination to transform Massignon's ascetic mysticism into a puritanical revolutionary absolutism. The closing link, however, between Shari'ati's fascination with Massignon and his committed political activism seems to be in the long and sincere passages on solitude and sustained and dispassionate love he composes in his Deserta writings. There is something in the mystical and ascetic disposition of Massignon that is most appealing to Shari'ati as an ascetic revolutionary. The power, the sustained fury, of Shari'ati's rhetorical discourse comes in part from this mystical belief in the power of his words, in the magic of the Shi'i collective mythology, in the irresistible charm of his charismatic eloquence, so much so that it is as if the mystical truth of the Sufi masters, the stuff of Massignon's scholarship and erudition, is somehow transfused into the ideological truth of Shari'ati's claim to a political agenda. The ascetic exercises, the self-denunciatory demands, that accompany this mystical conviction are equally congenial to the political promotion of a revolutionary disposition. But perhaps more than anything else, it is the self-imposed solitude that provides the indispensable ingredient of the creative imagination inherent in any formulation of revolutionary myth.[13]

A Word of Caution

Before we go any further, building on these preliminary themes of Shariʿati's revolutionary disposition and message, a word of caution is in order. Central as he has been in the ideological build-up of the Revolution, Shariʿati's significance should not be overrated and overemphasized. Certainly such laudatory epithets as "the outstanding intellectual of the . . . whole of contemporary Iran"[14] or "the main intellectual, even the Fanon, of the Islamic Revolution"[15] are highly hyperbolic. Al-e Ahmad was much more central in Iranian political and literary culture than Shariʿati ever was. Motahhari was infinitely more erudite in matters of Islamics than Shariʿati could have ever been. Shariʿati's ideological contribution to the making of the Iranian Revolution of 1979 ought to be measured and balanced in relation to other prominent figures in this category. His knowledge of the French and Arabic languages and Islamic history and doctrine as well as contemporary European literature, sociological and otherwise, has been greatly exaggerated. Although compared to his clerical contemporaries, like Motahhari, he was more directly aware of European sources, that claim does not get him anywhere near the exalted status to which his devoted admirers elevate him.[16]

   This word of caution is necessary because it is important to have a realistic understanding of these ideologues' grasp of the outside world. As it pertains to their knowledge of "The West," the specifics of their actual knowledge of European and American political and intellectual history is crucial in measuring the range of mythological constructions in which they participated. To complicate this picture even further, these ideologues themselves have become, perhaps inevitably, subjects of massive hagiographical mythology. Altogether our knowledge of Shariʿati's years in Iran, his education in Paris, his teaching at Mashhad University, his lectures at the Hosseyniyyeh Ershad, and his death in London are all shrouded in hagiographical and martyrological fantasy. There is as yet no accurate and reliable biography of Shariʿati. What compounds this highly dubitable composure of his martyrology are equally exaggerated negative statements by his opponents about his character. Charges of illiteracy, charlatanism, and even outright accusations—with no concrete evidence—that he was an agent of SAVAK to offset the power of the clergy abound about Shariʿati. These are natural and perhaps even inevitable symptoms of a highly ideological figure thriving in a martyrological and conspiratorial atmosphere. It is indeed the task of a conscientious biographer to collect these scattered data and construct a relatively reliable and coherent statement about Shariʿati. Before that task is competently achieved, false and fictitious pieces of political urban legends ought to be seriously discounted.

   As unreliable as Shariʿati is in his emerging hagiographies, we can be certain of his popularity with the urban students, achieved mainly through the vast body of writings he has left behind. It is precisely with that body of literature that we ought to limit our understanding of Shari'ati and his contributions to the ideological basis of the Revolution.[17]

A Revolutionary Ideologue

The most serious exponent of the revolutionary uses of faith,[18] a Paris-educated sociologist, the chief ideologue of some of the major political trends in modern Iran as well as other Islamic societies, Ali Shari'ati has been recognized as a theorist who "did the most to prepare the Iranian youth for revolutionary upheaval."[19] It has also been suggested that "events made this Muslim sociologist, shortly after his 1977 death, the ideologist of the revolt."[20] Despite such apparent hyperboles, there is a certain element of truth in identifying Shari'ati with some major revolutionary urges in his immediate political culture. He managed to exemplify what was most central to an entire revolutionary spirit.

Born in 1933 in Khorasan, Ali Shari'ati received his early education in this northeastern province of Iran.[21] Upon graduation, at age nineteen, he became a teacher at an elementary school. When he was twenty-three years old, he entered the Faculty of Letters at Mashhad University. That same year he married a fellow student. In 1960 he received a bachelor's degree in French and Arabic. Then, through a scholarship from the government, he went to Paris to continue his advanced education. There he studied sociology and religious history. In 1965 he returned to Iran, was imprisoned for a short time, and then settled in Mashhad. He began teaching, first at a Mashhad high school and then at Mashhad University. From there he went to Tehran in 1967 and commenced a series of lectures at Hosseyniyyeh Ershad, an institution that attracted many of the religiously minded young intelligentsia. Between 1967 and 1972 he actively preached in Hosseyniyyeh Ershad and attracted a considerable number of followers. In 1972, his activities were interrupted, and he was imprisoned. In 1975, he was released from prison following the intervention of the French and Algerian governments on his behalf. Between 1975 and 1977 his activities were tightly controlled by the Shah's secret police. In May 1977 he was permitted to leave Iran for London, where he died of a heart attack on 19 June of the same year.

Shari'ati was raised in a religious family. His father, though not a cleric, was an active Muslim preacher. Ali Shari'ati grew up in Mashhad, the city in which the Eighth Shi'i Imam is buried and which is, next to Qom, the spiritual capital of Iran and the center of the most intense religious activities. At the age of nineteen, Shari'ati had already begun writing and translating works on political aspects of Shi'i Islam. Following his graduation

from Mashhad University and upon his arrival in Paris, he actively participated in many political movements, particularly in the Algerian liberation
cause. During these formative years he was influenced chiefly by Franz
Fanon and Jean-Paul Sartre, who left a lasting impression on him both
intellectually and politically. Shariʿati translated Fanon's *Wretched of the
Earth* into Persian and is reported to have corresponded with him.[22]

Shiʿism: a Total Party

Upon his return to Iran, Shariʿati was determined to leave a revolutionary
mark on his contemporary history. As a revolutionary ideologue, his most
serious obstacle was the persistent clerical tradition against which, as against
the political order that tacitly sustained it, he was to launch his ideological
movement. Particularly evident from the title and content of one of his
major lectures on Shiʿism, "Shiʿism: A Complete (Political) Party," Ali
Shariʿati considered this branch of Islam as a "revolutionary ideology,"
capable, if properly reconstructed, of mobilizing the masses for specific
political purposes. Signalled by this very title, Shariʿati sought to transform
Shiʿism from what he considered to be a religious tradition with a multiple
set of historical traits and institutions into a political ideology of monolithic
revolutionary proportions. As a student of Marxism, actively supporting
the revolutionary causes of Cuba and Algeria, Shariʿati had been convinced
of the necessity of ideological convictions to augment, or advance, the
"material conditions" of any revolution. He said he disagreed with Franz
Fanon, in this particular regard, that "Third-World" countries should
abandon their religion in order to be ideologically equipped to either defeat
the imperialistic powers or launch a revolution against their government.[23]
On the contrary, he sought to use an already-established "ideology" in the
Islamic world in order to create the necessary political apparatus—party,
slogan, banner, and popular force—to achieve the same revolutionary
ends. As an observer of the political movements in the Islamic world, he
witnessed the failure of radical "Western" ideologies, transplanted from
their native soil, attempting to take root in the political consciousness of
the masses. In his own country, he had witnessed in particular the bloody
consequences of the (Communist) Tudeh Party and its endeavors to transform a deeply religious society into a socialist camp. Thus realizing the
fundamental problem of introducing a secular political ideology into a
religious world and, at the same time, aiming to mobilize the masses for
political ends that the very secular ideology had articulated, Shariʿati sought
to achieve his revolutionary ends through the same ancient tradition that
other secular ideologies considered as the opium of the masses. To achieve
this, he had to reconstruct, single-handedly, the entire history and "ideology" of Islam. Thus, he set upon himself the Herculean task of rewriting

the entire Islamic history, while "discovering" and introducing the "true ideology" of the faith. He titled his major work *Islamshenasi (Islamology): a new and revolutionary reading of the "true Islam."* In this version of Islam, Shariᶜati turned the universality of faith and transformed it into a universal ideology. In his newly reconstructed reading, Islam is the "ideology" of emancipation and liberation with a dominant political goal to achieve for all humanity. For Shariᶜati, as later for Khomeini in a different cast, politics and piety, ideology and faith, are interchangeable, indeed synonymous, the same.

For Shariᶜati Shiᶜism had a built-in mechanism of ideological preparation and political mobilization. The form and structure of this ideology and its concomitant politics were already there, in people's collective imaginations and shared sensibilities. The form had to be stripped of its "traditional" and conservative forces and refurbished with up-to-date revolutionary zeal and semantics. His lifelong achievement was precisely this systematic endeavor of reconstructing a new outfit from some very old fabric.

In order to systematize his revolutionary reading of Islam, Shariᶜati gradually developed an ideology that he liked to call "Alid Shiᶜism," a Shiᶜism identified with the authoritative figure of the first Shiᶜi Imam. "By systematizing the concept of Alid Shiᶜism," it has been rightly suggested,

Shariᶜati attained a double result; he detached himself from the petrified official Islam rejected by idealistic youth, and he brought a new and combative meaning to Shiᶜi concepts. Even prayer in this renovated Islam took on a political meaning, tied to action. This insurrectional meaning of common prayer was particularly developed in the 1978–79 revolution.[24]

To counterbalance, in his political vocabulary, the revolutionary "Alid Shiᶜism," Shariᶜati constituted the conservative "Safavid Shiᶜism," that is, the Shiᶜism identified with the Safavid dynasty (1501–1736), which for the first time established Shiᶜism as the state religion. He identified "Safavid Shiᶜism" with the official version of the faith as propagated under the patronage of the Iranian state in particular, or any other dominant power in general. He subsequently proceeded to conceptualize the main Shiᶜite terminologies and dogmas in a new and revolutionary way. Every religious concept, such as *imamat* and *ismat,* assumed, under the rubric of "Alid Shiᶜism," a revolutionary and combative meaning and significance.[25] In general and as opposed to "Safavid Shiᶜism," "Alid Shiᶜism represents original Islam," Shariᶜati thought, and "is a movement of progress and revolution, with no division between intellectuals and the people—Islam in its progressive and dynamic phase."[26] In the new, Shariᶜati-constructed terminology of Shiᶜism, *imamat,* for example, was not "belief in twelve pure, saintly, extraordinary names," but "pure, honest, revolutionary conduct of the people and the correct foundation of society in terms of con-

science, the expansion and independence of people's judgment."[27] *Ghaybat*
(the Shiʿite belief in the occultation of the Twelfth Imam and the expectation of his return to establish the perfect society) meant "total irresponsibil-
ity; the uselessness of all action under the pretext of the Imam's absence"
in official "Safavid Shiʿism"; whereas in his "Alid Shiʿism" the same doctrine meant the "responsibility of men to decide their destiny, faith, spiritual and social life."[28]

As Shariʿati begins to renarrate his collective history, beyond the limited
access of Al-e Ahmad, the entire corpus of Shiʿi doctrinal legitimacy becomes concomitant with the most compelling realities of Iranian contemporary exegesis. The nature of this reconstructed narrative, as it now
commences to coin the terms of its neologistic discontent, is such that a
forceful constituency of revolutionary hopefuls find the particulars of their
mutant voice in its universal appeal.

In order to legitimize his revolutionary reading of Islam, Shariʿati had to
discredit the traditionally maintained view of this faith in all its diversities.
He thus observed that:

The problem which is now at hand is the thirteen-hundred- year-old complex of the
misery of a people, the intellectual hopelessness of an *umma* [Islamic community],
the metamorphosis and going astray of an emancipating and consciousness-giving
belief, the wasting, passivity and going to sleep of a people with tyranny, ignorance,
and poverty; and that with the most sacred, the most exalted, and the most
progressive belief and eternal divine values that we possess, and that with the
dearest personalities and epic-making figures that each one of them is enough for
the awakening, self-consciousness, movement and freedom of a nation or a people.[29]

In trying to establish legitimacy for his revolutionary version of Islam
among the secular intelligentsia, Shariʿati had to distinguish himself from
the traditional figures of religious authority, that is, from the bona fide
clerics. Early in his lecture on "Shiʿism: A Complete [Political] Party," he
indicates that he is not a philosopher, a historian, a jurist *(faqih)*, an artist,
a writer, a literary figure, or a theologian in a traditional sense. "I am none
of these."[30] These are the traditional figures of authority in any Islamic
society. Since Shariʿati's Islam is a new Islam, he has to create, in himself, a
new prototype of authority: a "Western"-educated, politically conscious
and active revolutionary ideologue of grand social causes. This obviously
necessitated a new reading of Islam to be compatible with the rising expectations of a revolutionary generation. For that purpose, traditional authorities first had to be discarded and discredited. A significant proportion of
Shariʿati's energy was devoted to negating the legitimacy of all such figures
of traditional authority in the fabric of any Islamic society. With a similar
perspective, he also thought traditional ways of learning to be cumbersome,
long, scholastic, boring, and totally outmoded. He imagined an action-

Islam as successor to what he considered to be a merely knowledge-Islam. The new Islam necessitated a new class of teachers in action:

Others admonish us and [give us] guidance, good advice and wise, knowledgeable and rational counsel that "first you should think, study, acquire knowledge, do scientific research, read many books, attend many religious schools, study with many learned professors, learn philosophy, sufism, jurisprudence, doctrine, theology, logic, language, literature, history, theosophy and ethics 'with learned masters,' until you are master of both intellectual and transmitted [knowledge], and after passing through this period (which is not really possible), [then] you enter the second phase, the phase of action, the phase of correction, but [even then] individual action, the correction of self."[31]

The True Islam

This Islam was outmoded and reactionary. Shari'ati consciously believed and propagated the idea that his version of Islam, the "true Islam," the Islam that was there but forgotten or never learned, was different from and opposed to the historically received Islam. Attacking two cardinal tenets of traditional Islam, knowledge and virtuosity, and celebrating the all-too-essential revolutionary attitude, he proclaimed:

O how strange! Notice the difference between these two Islams! The other one postpones enjoining the good and prohibiting the evil [a major tenet of Islam]—social responsibility—to after the completion of the [two attributes of] knowledge and virtuosity; the two stages that in order to reach their perfection even the life of Noah is not enough. And this [Islam] puts the social responsibility of enjoining the good and prohibiting the evil upon the delicate shoulders of a young girl or boy, exactly from the moment that invites them to pray and fast! Praying and fasting, simultaneous with the responsibility of enjoining and prohibiting good and evil social deeds, and also the Holy War.[32]

The demographic composition of the Iranian society increasingly in favor of young and underprivileged students, massively migrating from remote rural areas of the country to poor urban settings, had created a particularly receptive constituency for Shari'ati's revolutionary message. For this rising constituency, the minutiae of Shi'i scholastic debates were as strange and irrelevant as the concocted and hesitant language of the Marxist and Nationalist ideologies. For them, so early in their age of political awareness, a language would speak most eloquently that was at once that of conviction and action, of interpretation and commitment, of trust and enticement, the origin of which is the cradle of their childhood remembrance. Shari'ati met this challenge. For him, as for his constituency, it was necessary to act, and to act quickly,

because in life [we] cannot be in the course of understanding and comprehending the truth through intellectual genius, or inner illumination, or scientific thinking and subjective ratiocination. [Because] it is in becoming that [we] can be. Just as one can only 'understand' a fiery bullet when a fiery bullet hits him, so he can understand a concept precisely when he stands in the current course of the application of that concept. It is in action that truth manifests itself.[33]

As a revolutionary ideology, Shari'ati's, the true, Islam was to mobilize the masses, challenge the authorities that be, compete and fight with other ideologies on their own ground and on their own terms. His Islam was not that of individuals standing vis-à-vis their God, striving for or seeking salvation through the established institutions of religious authorities. His was collective salvation through collective political expression. His repoliticizing Islam was much more than Islam sanctifying politics. Shari'ati's vision of Islam is to transform it, quintessentially, into what it was: a political statement best suited for particular revolutionary objectives—in this or in any other age.

Shari'ati's opposition to Islam in its received, institutionalized, mode was manifested in a number of directions: first, against its intellectual, spiritual, and theological aspects; second, against the operative Islam, particularly its submission to a divine will as a religious doctrine. In opposition, he sought to revitalize Islam in a way best suited for his hidden and manifest revolutionary temperament. For this purpose, he concentrated on a revolutionary reimagination of the household of Ali and Fatimah (the Prophet's daughter). This household has provided the Shi'ite world with two of its most revered martyrs, Ali and Hussayn, who figured prominently in Shari'ati's scheme of "Islamology."

But when someone [such as I], with all of his being and life and belief deeply loves this household [of Ali's], both faithfully and humanistically, and believes that the only way for the freedom of this people [that is, Muslims in general, Iranians in particular] is in genuine return to Ali's school and Fatima's house[hold], then, how can he . . . remain "indifferent"?[34]

Beyond figures of authority, the redoctrination of the faith into a revolutionary direction was equally necessary. Shari'ati severely criticized some of the most fundamental doctrinal positions of Shi'ism whenever they appeared to pose an obstacle to his revolutionary reading of the faith. While Ali and Hussayn constantly appear in his portrayal of a revolutionary way of life, in which one sacrifices one's life for a common cause, Shari'ati severely attacked *taqiyah*, one of the most important characteristics of Shi'i Islam, the meaning and significance of which have been interwoven with the entire history of this faith. In doctrinal terms, it means the religious obligation on the part of the Shi'i believer to conceal his true identity in the face of the danger of persecution and other adversities. It developed particularly under the Umayyads (661–750 C.E.) who persecuted the Shi'ites harshly. As a doctrinal position of Shi'ite Muslims, *taqiyah* appeared to

Shariʿati as a reactionary and outmoded mentality. Discarding such a traditional doctrine of Shiʿism was particularly important if Shariʿati was to secure the loyalty of the young revolutionary intelligentsia who were attracted to "progressive" ideologies. He did manage to give his revolutionary ideology a "progressive" aura. This "progressive" feature, however, had to be balanced carefully with a demonstrated anti-"Western" attitude. He was quite successful in presenting his deepest forms of radical secularism in an anticolonial and anti-"Western" language. Such assumptions as "Shariʿati wished to be a politico-religious thinker in the context of the Third World liberation struggles" or that he "felt acutely the problems of colonialism and neocolonialism, and attacked especially cultural colonization, which alienated people from their roots"[35] testify to the degree of this success. Shariʿati, in his diligent attempt to transform the historical complexity and doctrinal diversity of Islam into a unified political ideology best suited for the modernity of his revolutionary agenda, was, in effect, an avant-garde figure in cultural recolonization. Deeply alienated from, and in a disguised way resentful of, the received and operative core of the Islamic character and culture, while at the same time fascinated by the efficiency of "Western" political ideologies (particularly Marxism), he sought to revolutionize Islam to make it best suitable for competition in an age of conflicting ideologies. Permanent revolution was the ultimate goal that he sought as the most external expression of his innermost beliefs. And it was on that model that he redefined "Islam."

Islam Updated

It is in Shariʿati's attempt towards attaining his revolutionary goals that he reveals his most serious preoccupation with the extremest modes of secularism disguised in heightened religiosity. As a true existentialist, reading his Sartre into Islam, he strives to make man totally responsible for what he is and what he does, completely divorced from any historical, sacred, and securing order. Yet since this school of thought and its modern vocabulary are alien to a Muslim society, he appeals to the Qur'an to seek justification of his position and reads an existentialist understanding into this Qur'anic verse: "Those are a people who have passed away. Theirs is that which they earned, and yours is that which ye earn. And ye will not be asked of that they used to do."[36] Being individually responsible for their historical acts, Shariʿati's audience attends its revolutionary present with a clear vision of the Qur'anic mandate, reread through Shariʿati's existentialist eyes. The human choice is central to this vision of Shariʿati's revolutionary man. In matters of faith, as in matters of revolt, he advocates "the choice of religion and its conscious acceptance, not in imitation of your parents and the elders, but with your own reasoning and understanding."[37] From a revolutionary standpoint, he isolates and atomizes individuals from their institutional context and confronts them with his version of the faith. "Religious individualists," who he believed were under the influence of "Sufi ethics of the East" or "Christian asceticism,"[38] were wrong; right was a "religious collectivism" that he sought to materialize on the basis of existentialized Muslimhood. Separated and segregated from the commands and context of their traditional authority, individuals become "rational creatures" ready to adopt ideological identities. To launch a revolution, Shariʿati needed rational creatures, enchanted with his revolutionary terms of identity, and the post-Muslim intelligentsia received his liberating ideology on precisely such rational grounds.

As a restless and confused generation, the young Iranian intellectuals were in search of an "ideology." Yet, if not immediately rooted in their received collective culture, this generation breathed, whether it consciously liked it or not, in a deeply religious atmosphere. Certain attachments, cultural rituals of personal identities, were too powerful to discard; they provided a strong sense of (revolutionary) purpose in life. The paradox presented itself when being a revolutionary and a Muslim at the same time appeared mutually exclusive. If only there were a way out of the impasse of simultaneously being an enthusiatic revolutionary intellectual and a Muslim. Shariʿati showed a path out of the impasse. "Young Iranian Muslim intellectuals," it has been rightly suggested, "found in Shariʿati a revolutionary Iranian Shiʿi response. No more the crying Husain of the Taʿziyeh, but Husain fighting and dying for a just cause."[39] The combination of contemporary revolutionary zeal with a reconstituted sense of Muslimhood was a masterful device to mobilize this particular segment of the society. Shariʿati realized that he could not mobilize a deeply religious society for any end, particularly political, with a fundamentally secular, materialistic, and atheistic ideology (Marxism). But his attempt to read social and economic schemes and ideals of Marxism (or any other secular ideology) into Islam was by far a more involved adventure with ramifications and extensions far beyond any particular political objective. Shariʿati's Islam is a repoliticized Islam, a metaphysical religious order of things as they are turned upside down into a self-conscious political ideology of things as they should be, and on a par with any other, equally powerful and equally susceptible, ideology.

As the strategical apparatus necessary for updating Islam into a revolutionary ideology, Shariʿati conceived of Shiʿism as a complete party; this he sought to prove through his redefinition of what constituted the *ummah* (the Islamic community). Since *ummah*, according to Shariʿati, is "a society on the move, a society not in place but on the way, towards an objective, having a direction," then we need an *Imam* to lead us toward that objective.[40] Imam and *ummah* are mere instruments of revolutionary mobilization. The complete political apparatus needed to launch a revolution—that is, an ideology and a political party, Imam and *ummah*—was detected and identified in the faith of the majority of the people, with the strongest possible attachment between them and their faith securing the most effective mechanism of mass mobilization. As a revolutionary sociologist, Shariʿati recognized the necessity of this direct and immediate communication with the masses. Making direct reference to the Qurʾan and giving them revolutionary interpretations was a strategy that Shariʿati utilized consistently in order to legitimize his reconstruction of Islam. In reading the Qurʾanic verse 29:69, "As for those who strive in Us, we surely guide them to Our path, and lo! Allah is with the good," he provided the following reading:

"Those who fight in our cause, we will put forward our ways for their salvation and freedom; and no doubt God is with those who do good deeds and do things well." And one of these "ways" is to understand "Alid Shiʿism" as a complete party.[41]

Islam thus updated needs a self-sustaining machinery. Shariʿati gives a detailed definition of what he means by a "complete party," his vision of Shiʿism in modernity. This definition reveals the depth and extent of his revolutionary repoliticization of every aspect of Shiʿism:

"Party," in the general vocabulary of world intellectuals, is basically a unified social organization with a "world view," an "ideology," a "philosophy of history," an "ideal social order," a "class foundation," a "class orientation," a "social leadership," a "political philosophy," a "political orientation," a "tradition," a "slogan," a "strategy," a "tactic of struggle," and . . . a "hope" that wants to change "the status quo" in man, society, people, or a particular class, and establish "the desired status" in its stead; and thus each party has two aspects of affirmation and negation: "Thou shalt," and "Thou shalt not."[42]

As for Shiʿism,

it is the party with all the characteristics and dimensions of an ideal and complete party; it is the party whose objective realization is that "party of God" that the Qurʾan speaks of, and is also responsive to the need of this responsible, intellectual generation in giving [political] consciousness, and mobilizing the masses of the society, in leading their class struggle, in eliminating the difficulties and obstacles in the way of such a struggle, and in realizing the hopes of the disinherited classes.[43]

Following this grand scheme of a complete party, Shariʿati came to the ultimate conclusion that:

finally, after considering all the schools, ideologies, revolutions, movements, sociology, Islamology, historical investigation, research into the causes of cultural decline and intellectual and social deviation, and a more profound recognition of [the Prophet's] family, *Imamat, wilayat, intizar, adl,* and man's legacy in the duration of human history, and after experiences, conflicts, reactions, and the clarification of dark spots and concealments, I have reached this inner principle that: "essentially, Shiʿism is a complete party."[44]

A revolutionary party needs a revolutionary and dynamic view of society, a society in movement towards perfection. This Shariʿati tried to achieve with a dynamic definition of *ummah* as "a society of individuals who think alike, walk along the same path, take their steps together, have similar objectives, are responsible, [and] on the move towards a single, direct, clear, stable, and collective destination."[45] The uniformity and unconditional conformity that Shariʿati envisaged for his ideal state makes it clear that there is a direct and short link between Shiʿism as a complete party and the Shiʿite state as a complete, final, and total society.

A revolutionary ideology, furthermore, necessitates revolutionary heroes to provide the followers with prototypical figures of authority. He recognized Abu Dharr, a close companion of the Prophet, as the first revolutionary socialist who

deeply felt upon his shoulders the heavy weight of social responsibility, the responsibility of changing the governing system of the society and the governing faith of his time.[46]

Abu Dharr would constantly appear in Shariʿati's works as the model revolutionary hero to be closely emulated.

The Challenge of Secularism

Shariʿati faced not just a religious but also a secular audience whom he wished to convert to his brand of Islam. In achieving this, he had to present Shiʿism as a "complete political party" in order to compete with the secular ideologies dominant among the intelligentsia, for example, Marxism. Since Marxism presented a total view of the society, along with its philosophy of history, sociology, anthropology, etc., as well as a total party program for implementing its objectives, Shariʿati's Islam had to meet precisely the same criteria. To justify his brand of Shiʿism to his secular audience, he argued that

Of course, this claim might appear to some irreligious intellectuals a bit difficult to swallow ... how can an intellectual take his ideology from religion? ... Because of the experience of Christianity and imitations from the modern perspective of world intellectuals and seeing what today passes as Islam among us and its social role and human impact, these intellectuals cannot imagine that a party ideology or a completely convincing ideology, can have a religious origin! ... While if religion, particularly Islam and especially the Shiʿite school and perspective, were correctly introduced, it would have been the religious intellectual who would be surprised.[47]

There are many hidden dimensions in Shariʿati's "Islamic ideology" that appeal particularly to revolutionary secular intellectuals. Echoing a Trotskyist ideal, Shari'ati sought to secure the idea of permanent revolution as essentially present in his version of Shi'ism. Here Shari'ati assumes and assimilates into his Shi'ite ideology the two most compelling ideas of evolution and revolution. It was the detection of these traits of thought that attracted many secular intellectuals to Shari'ati's Islam. They viewed his reading of Islam as an ideology of liberation and revolution, disguised for convenience in Islamic garb.

To meet the secular challenge, Shari'ati's antiestablishment (antimonarchical) rhetoric was of particular significance. If the Pahlavi dynasty was too close to criticize directly, there were more distant candidates. Thus Shari'ati attacked the Safavid dynasty for what he considered to be their using Shi'ism as their means of legitimizing their rule by establishing it as the state religion. He believed that

> where Shi'ism is so influential among people and can be the best means of securing the class interest of the ruling class . . . why should they bother to choose another faith for themselves that is abhorred and rejected by the people?[48]

He even compares this to the Roman Empire's accepting Christianity for similar political purposes.[49] He, of course, turned his own observation around and launched the most comprehensive program to utilize Shi'ism for his revolutionary purposes.

On yet a different level of complexity, one of the major challenges to Shari'ati's revolutionary Islam and its potential appeal to secular intellectuals was the contemplative and devotional aspect of this faith. This he sought to alter drastically by redefining Islam as a religion of revolutionary and militant action. Both the contemplative and the devotional dimensions of Islam rendered it politically mute and localized it into sectarian divisions. But the Islam Shari'ati was reconstructing rested on its claims on universality:

> The boundaries of *ummah* are not a geographical demarcation; they are not the fixed barriers of a place; *ummah* is a group in "the way," a way that passes "through" humanity and from the heart of the people, because the boundaries of Islam are extended to wherever that man is, that people are, and what am I saying? The country of Muslims is the whole world, the expansion of existence, and the owner and only presiding power upon this *ummah* is God.[50]

These passages were particularly useful in expanding the applicability of Shari'ati's revolutionary Shi'ism beyond the Iranian boundaries. Being primarily identified with Iran, Shi'ism had to be so universally expanded in its revolutionary usefulness to convince not only post-Muslim Iranian intellectuals but also post-Muslim intellectuals everywhere of its great potential for the mobilization of the masses. This universal ideology was to substitute "The Western" revolutionary ideologies, particularly Marxism, which, in an Islamic context, had lost their dynamism, that is, they were not capable of mobilizing the masses in a revolutionary movement. Shari'ati realized the failure of at least one century of disillusioned Marxism in Muslim societies. He considered Islam as the last and only chance to unite and mobilize people for particular revolutionary objectives.

A Muslim in Modernity

While in Europe, Shari'ati plunged deep into a sea of various and conflicting ideologies: Marxism, Existentialism, Liberalism, etc. He was saturated with ideological tendencies and commitments. He was also exposed to many revolutionary movements, particularly those of Algeria and Cuba, actively participating in demonstrations and meetings in support of these revolutions. During this period he recognized the indispensable role of an ideology for a revolutionary cause. Without an ideology, under whose banner to organize and mobilize the masses, he realized that no revolutionary cause could be pursued and attained. Yet he also recognized, in the light of the Iranian political scene of the twentieth century, the inevitable failure of "Western" ideologies in their original secular form. Consequently, he came to the inevitable conclusion that to mobilize the Muslim masses for any revolutionary cause, a domestic and indigenous ideology had to be sought and formulated. Both strategically and tactically this would be a more effective approach, particularly operative among a predominantly religious constituency. What kind of ideology in an historically Islamic society can be more effective than an "Islamic ideology"? Shari'ati's lifelong task was to formulate such an ideology. "The Islamic ideology" had to be "Islamic" to communicate easily and effectively with the masses, in order to use the vast source of Islamic symbolism, which was capable of mobilizing the masses beyond the limited measures that any secular ideology could achieve. Yet the formulated doctrines had to be called "ideology" in order to detach them from the element of faith that was particularly anachronistic to the post-Muslim intelligentsia who were, in Shari'ati's estimation, to lead this revolution. It was this revolutionary use of faith that Shari'ati sought to implement. He single-handedly strove to transform the devotional, contemplative, mystical, and institutional dimensions of Shi'ism into a total and final political ideology.

Man is in Charge

The totality of that political ideology demanded a particular view of man as the center of the universe. Shari'ati saw man as the active political agent in charge of his destiny. For this he always employed the image of a "God-like" man who is in charge of his fate.[51] Man is born free. Man is born knowing. Man is born creative. It is precisely with such divine attributes that Shari'ati's man takes charge of his history. Breathing with the breath of God,[52] man cannot but be responsible for his own fate. Shari'ati's leading the cause of free will, and thus simultaneously opposing predestination, is the necessary theological stipulation of a political responsibility. But Shari'ati's siding with the theological advocates of free will is rooted in a metaphysics of a divine attribute. If God is free and creator, which He is, then man is politically responsible and ideologically creative. The logic follows inevitably. Doctrinally thus justified, man's free will is the metaphysical cause and source of his political commitment.

The ideological charge was to be directed to immediate revolutionary causes. The specifics of that ideology were always secondary to the goals they were to serve. And here is precisely where Shari'ati picked up where Al-e Ahmad had left off. Shari'ati entered the Iranian political scene upon Al-e Ahmad's well-trodden path. In giving the political discourse of the 1960s and 1970s a religious bent, he took Al-e Ahmad's lead to its logical conclusion. If the ultimate end of a revolutionary discourse were to mobilize and lead the masses, then the more intimately the conceptual and symbolic components of this discourse were related to, and derived from, the existing and valid sets of cultural paradigms, the more effective they would be in their purported objectives. Cultural alienation, epitomized for Al-e Ahmad in "Westoxication," had as its most immediate consequence the inability of the secular intellectuals to communicate effectively with their purported constituency. Beyond a mere repoliticization and reideologization of Islam, Shari'ati sought to redefine, ex nihilio, the Islamic heritage into a comprehensive revolutionary apparatus. His "Islamology," chief among other works, is the most systematic and thorough attempt to reconstitute Islamic doctrinal categories in the service of a deeply revolutionary agenda, an agenda in which the mere toppling of the Pahlavi regime was but a preliminary, merely political, stage. This massive and deep reideologization of Islam was launched simultaneously against two sets of political contenders: the ulama' and the secular intellectuals. Against the ulama''s institutional authority, he wished to rescue "Islam" and redefine it into a revolutionary ideology; against the secular intellectuals' growing claim on the ideological loyalties of the youth, he wished to prove and persuade that it is possible to achieve revolutionary goals through a seemingly archaic and outmoded semiology. The revolutionary specifics of that semiology were the quintessential task of Shari'ati's ideological man to construct and legitimate.

Extending from Al-e Ahmad's call for a local construction of an ideology of revolt from indigenous cultural material, Shari'ati's revolutionary discourse attended immediately to a task Al-e Ahmad was not prepared to meet. "The intellectual atmosphere in our society," Shari'ati observed, "continues to be considerably under the influence of the Western climate."[53] The words could have been written by Al-e Ahmad. With a twist of realism, Shari'ati continued that "cultural and scientific independence from the West is nothing but a distant hope."[54] In every aspect of intellectual and artistic life, Shari'ati diagnosed, Iranians demonstrated two major characteristics:

(1) alienation, or even in some instances "hatred," from "self," from their own religion, culture, worldview, and character; and (2) a deep, obsessive, or even boastful pretension to attachment to the West, and rootless and vulgar modernism.[55]

More than the vulgarity of that "modernism," its very claim to substitute the revolutionary potentials of the religious culture had to be encountered. "The Islamic Ideology," the supreme revolutionary identity of Shari'ati's ideal type, was the road to political (and moral) salvation.

Fatimah Zahra': The Perfect Model of the Revolutionary Woman

With his particular brand of revolutionary language, epitomized in "the Islamic Ideology," Shari'ati reached for the widest possible range of committed intellectuals. But in order to give them tangible and compelling images of revolutionary conduct, he had to have more indigenous historical and mythological references. Women were of particular significance in this revolutionary model-building. Early in 1971, Shari'ati delivered a lecture on the life and character of Fatimah Zahra', the Prophet's daughter, Ali's wife. He later expanded this lecture and published it as *Fatimah Is Fatimah*. Although the lecture was intended for Shari'ati's students at the Hosseyniyyeh Ershad, "many others had attended too."[56] In this lecture Shari'ati wished to offer a reconstructed model of the most cherished female figure in Islamic hagiography for modern Iranian women to follow. He wished specifically to address not those women who had been either lost in the received models of passive virtuous propriety or else absorbed by the imported "Western" images, but those who want "to choose themselves, to build themselves, [and who] need a model."[57]

Although Shari'ati had originally intended to give a report of his involvement with Louis Massignon's work on Fatimah Zahra', very early on he is captivated by the figure of this beloved image and sees it more fit to provide a historical answer to the more compelling question of "how is one to be," rather than lament on Fatimah Zahra' 's miseries or deliver a dull and detailed academic account of the Prophet's daughter.[58]

For the perfect image of an ideal woman, Iranians ought to follow their righteous and valiant ancestry and seek to comprehend the "true" figure of Shi'i Imams, not the figures propagated by the Safavid kings. The answer was in the Alavid Shi'ism, not in the Safavid Shi'ism.[59] "True Shi'ism," which is an extension of Fatimah and Ali's household, is not a sect of Islam, it is "the true Islam."[60] In this ("true") Alavid Shi'ism, as in every other revolutionary movement, the mobilized sentiments "think" with the mind of the intellectual leaders and "love" with the heart of the masses.[61] Crying, a testimony of that heart, is a perfectly legitimate expression of sentiments, "even Régis Debré . . . the fellow combatant of Che Guevara"[62] thought it was a noble gesture. The cause of lamentation in the household of Fatimah Zahra has been the innate nobility, the very salvation, of the collective Iranian (Shi'i) spirit. But both traditional religiosity and modern secularism have neglected these ennobling effects of sacred Shi'i personalities. Both have scorned Shari'ati and his revolutionary cause[63] precisely because he has offered such compelling revolutionary models. He lashes out with anger against the ulama' who have miserably failed to convey to the people the "red" Shi'i history, thus leaving them with a dark recollection of their past. Why should Joan of Arc be so celebrated in France as a figure of liberty and freedom but Zaynab, Fatimah's daughter, be remembered as a figure of misery?[64] If the Shi'i Imams have failed to provide a revolutionary model, if Fatimah Zahra' has failed to lead Iranian women to a virtuous life of political awareness, the clerics are to blame.[65]

Upon this premise, Shari'ati sets his agenda of reconstructing "the true" image of these Shi'i figures of supreme authority, Fatimah Zahra' among them. It is precisely with such reconstructed revolutionary images that Shari'ati sought to battle the evils of his time—moral and political, local and universal. This reconstruction is particularly imperative for women who for centuries could only copy the model of their mothers. In these changing times, women, like men, need new, reconstructed, models of virtuous Shi'i figures, like Fatimah Zahra', to follow. Shari'ati's logic for the necessity of this reconstruction is taken from what he considers the "method" of the Prophet Muhammad. There are three attitudes towards social change in Shari'ati's counting: conservative, revolutionary, and reformist (he actually uses these terms in their French pronunciations). But the Prophet's method in establishing Islam, a model Shari'ati wished to emulate, was "to keep the form of the traditions, but change their content from within in a revolutionary manner."[66] This, in Shari'ati's account, is contrary to the Christian method that refuses to see reality as it is. Islam uses realities to achieve its ideals.[67] Consequently, immorality and psychological complexes abound in Europe and the United States. Openly admitting that he took some of his "theses" from Marxism, Shari'ati criticized the Iranian pseudointellectuals who, having failed to understand Islam, its ideals and realities, as well as Marxism, resort to dogmatic parochialism in their ideology.[68]

Taking full account of realities, Islam charges humanity to reach for the highest ideals. Thusly charged, Shari'ati challenges the image of the "European woman," promiscuous and immoral, that the Iranian high bourgeoisie has constructed and celebrated. He gives ample examples of European women of science and virtuosity whom Iranians ought to know. He accuses "the reactionary traditionalist and the à la mode capitalist"[69] of having created that promiscuous image of European women from James Bond movies and having failed to introduce the other model of European female virtuosity. Shari'ati condemns both "The Westerners" and the Iranian Westoxicated for denying a woman her own last name. She carries either her father's name or her husband's. This is a "Western" practice, a remnant of "the age of slavery,"[70] and the Iranian seculars have adopted it, "because they are stupid."[71] Islamic laws, "the pure Islam, not the present diluted Islam,"[72] regarding women's rights are more humane than French ("Western") laws.[73] Since the Renaissance and particularly in the post-Freudian bourgeois culture, women have been reduced to sexual objects. Before that they were wrapped in a "sacred hallow."[74] But in modern times, the bourgeois life has reduced women, and men, to lowly beings. An occasional accident in the Islamic world, suicide is "a social phenomenon" in "The West."[75] Marriage, too, is a soulless, lifeless social contract in "The West," presided upon by a wretched bureaucrat rather than a spiritual figure. The ultimate result is that women have been turned into sexual objects in "The West."[76] This "Western" problem has now been translated into "Eastern" societies. But whereas the sexual maturity of "The Western" men takes a long time to develop, "Western" women reach this stage early. The result is that "Northern European sociologists and psychiatrists have provided many programs to awaken the young European man's sexual urges with artificial or natural female sexuality." "Eastern" men, however, do not have "this problem" because "they reach sexual maturity before their time." Thus "Eastern" men, and women, need different programs by "Eastern sociologists and psychologists."[77] But "The West," in order to rob "The East" of its primary sources and materials, has developed designs for trapping the "Eastern" youth into sexual promiscuity.[78] To achieve this end, "The West" has equally robbed "The East" of its cultural and historical legacy by deliberately destroying it.[79] In this transaction, Muslim women have lost doubly. While they have been attracted to cheap "Western" glimmers, they have been denied their true Islamic rights in the present "pseudo-Islamic" *(Shebh-e Islami)* societies.[80] Chiefly responsible for this state of affairs is the traditional mold of the society, the failing authority of the ulama', the prevailing malaise of the patriarchal system, and the misrepresentation of the Islamic respect for the status of women in society, family, and marriage. The immediate by-product of this attraction to the cheap "Western" model, not to women's genuine achievements, has been the astronomical increase in the consumption of cosmetics, which is a splendid market for "The Western" goods and a massive occasion for demeaning Muslim women.[81]

Thus stranded between the two opposing and equally demeaning images of the traditional and pseudo-"Western" models, the contemporary Iranian woman needs a third option to emulate. Shariʿati offers Fatimah Zahra', properly reconstructed, as this model. Fatimah, the fourth and youngest daughter of the Prophet, and the Prophet himself are portrayed as the daughter and father who revolutionized the despicable state of women in pre-Islamic Arabia where the best "solution" for having a daughter, better than being in her father's house or that of her husband, was to put her in a grave—alive.[82] Shariʿati sympathetically reconstructs the nobility and dignity with which the Prophet treated his daughter, thus establishing a model for that invincibly patriarchal society with its presumed contempt for daughters. Fatimah's care for her father, in turn, was so loving that she earned the title of "the mother of her father."[83] In the course of Muhammad's prophetic career, through thick and thin, Shariʿati portrays the valiant figure of Fatimah Zahra' as supportive of her father. He reenacts the hardships of Fatimah, her mother Khadijah, and her father Muhammad with such emotion and sentiment that parts of this lecture resemble a play full of dialogue among the chief protagonists.[84] Fatimah is traced through her marriage to Ali and the establishment of their household, its chief properties being "love and poverty."[85] Total devotion to her father's calling, unconditional fidelity to her husband, and everlasting love and care for her children are the supreme virtues with which Shariʿati delivers this portrait of Fatimah Zahra'. The rest of her story is the beautification of an idyllic picture of her household with Ali, their children Hasan and Husayn, and the unending love of the Prophet for these four Supreme Figures of Shiʿi piety. From these happy days of contentment to the difficult times of her father's death, the denial of her husband's right to succeed him, and, ultimately, her bitter death, Fatimah is portrayed as the very epitome of love, devotion, courage, and steadfastness: virtues with which Shariʿati thought the modern Iranian woman ought to attend her revolutionary destiny.

The Responsible Intellectual

Beyond the limited confinements of Iranian women, Shariʿati had more ambitious designs for the revolutionary youth of his generation. For both tactical and strategic reasons, he invested his highest hopes in the Iranian youth. He genuinely believed that the energy of youth is being consciously and conspiratorially diverted towards "sexual freedom"[86] so that the love of Ali and Fatimah's household does not take root in the hearts and minds of the young. To balance that, Shariʿati wished to rekindle this fire with a revolutionary intent. The medium through which this was to be achieved was the Qur'an itself which, although the only document that had not been distorted, was still misinterpreted by people led by all its previous commentators.[87] More specifically, the al-Rūm chapter of the Qur'an reads as if it had been addressed to modern committed intellectuals. This chapter is a clear indication of the archetypal and universal relevance of the Holy Text to contemporary realities.[88]

The apparent meaning of this Qur'anic chapter, that it had predicted a future victory of the Romans over the Persians, should not overshadow its real meaning, which, Shari'ati contended, is the promise of victory that the Prophet proclaims to his small group of persecuted followers.[89] Muhammad delivers this message of hope at a time when the "intellectuals" of his time ridiculed him for his lack of knowledge of the vast complexity of the world surrounding him. There is a marked similarity, Shari'ati noted, between the geopolitical terms of the world then and now. In the evident hostility between the two superpowers of the time (Rome and Persia) and in the utter irrelevance of Arabia in world politics, what could Muhammad's promise of victory mean for Muslims? Shari'ati dismissed some of the received interpretations that the Qur'anic passage, in fact, anticipates and celebrates the victory of the Christian Romans over the (nonbelieving) Zoroastrian Iranians. He argues that both Muhammad and Ali had accepted Zoroastrianism as a monotheistic religion and that, with the coming of Islam, Christianity had been superseded. Besides, the question of trinity had seriously marred Christian monotheism.[90]

In Shari'ati's reading of Surah al-Rum, the Qur'an had anticipated the depletion of power between the two armies of Iran and Byzantium, over whom Muslims shall be the ultimate victors. This promise was given to the Muslims at a time, Shari'ati describes in a joyous and celebratory voice, when the contemporary intellectuals ridiculed Muhammad for his lack of proper knowledge of the real superpowers of the world. Substituting "the intellectuals" for the Qur'anic phrase "most of the people," Shari'ati casts a shadow of ignorance upon the Muslim elite who deny the possibility of an Islamic victory in the modern world against the two superpowers of the day, "The East and The West."[91] Extrapolating on the Qur'anic phrase "a specified period," he introduces "historical determinism" as the chief force on the side of Muslims, then and now, to defeat the two superpowers of "The East and The West," then and now.[92] Based on this Qur'anic promise, delivered then but still valid today, "the tyrannical powers ought to know that their might is dwindling, and the weak that their weakness is turning into strength."[93] As for his self-image in this Qur'anic passage, Shari'ati addressed himself as "O messenger / O liberator / O you who want to mobilize this wretched, poor, and weakened nation which is caught between these two [super]powers!"[94]

Shariʿati's guiding objective in reading Surah al-Rum is to bridge a centuries-old gap between the time of Muhammad, when Iran and Byzantium were the superpowers, and his own time, when the United States and the Soviet Union are their functional equivalents. What was to be encountered and condemned in these two powers was their providing two alternatives to "the Islamic Ideology." Shariʿati repeatedly emphasized in the course of this lecture—with a sarcastic and emphatic tone, rhyming his talk periodically with an "I do not know whether I am speaking of the present time or the seventh century?"—the contemporary relevance of this Qur'anic verse.[95] This all-too-essential bringing together and contracting of history is central to Shariʿati's borrowing credence and legitimacy from the Qur'an for his "Islamic Ideology." As Muhammad's message had anticipated a Muslim victory against all odds and against the superpower of the time, so does Shariʿati's. This created a startling point of comparison and contrast between then and now, lending further support to the notion that the Islamic "Self" stands in sharp contrast to everything else, especially such mythically constructed notions as "The West" or "The East."

Through this short but precise exegesis of Surah al-Rum, Shariʿati achieved two objectives simultaneously: (1) establishing Qur'anic legitimacy for his ideological positioning of Islam vs. "The West" and "The East," and (2) anticipating the victory of Islam, via "the Islamic Ideology," over and against the two superpowers. The primary responsibility of the intellectuals in this entire enterprise is to attend the immediate exegencies of their historical context, translate their received cultural imperatives into ideological commandments, and lead "the People" to a utopia of promised ideals thus collectively imagined.

Islamshenasi: *The Revolutionary Reconstruction of a New Collective Understanding of Islam*

The year 1972 was the year of *Islamshenasi,* or "Islamology," Shariʿati's most ambitious attempt to give Islam a new collectively held (re)definition. The lectures that ultimately composed *Islamshenasi* were delivered from early February to mid-November 1972, to a mass student body at the Hosseyniyyeh Ershad and, more than anything else, made Shariʿati the revolutionary ideologue he gradually became. He delivered these lectures with a sense of urgency, bypassing a preliminary course he had intended to give on the "sociology of religion."[96] Some five years earlier, in the mid-1960s, he had given another course on *Islamshenasi* at Mashhad University, from which lectures another book on the subject was published. But he believed that "in method and in content" these new lectures superseded the old ones.[97]

In the introductory lecture, Shariʿati compared his innovative approach to understanding Islam, or what he called "the Islamic Ideology,"[98] to the modern movement in Persian literature. As the modernist movement had revolutionized the received canons of Persian literature, so too had Shariʿati's reconstruction of Islam with the canonical dogmas of the faith as historically predefined in the Islamic hermeneutic circles. With a shorthand argument, he dismissed "Islamic Sciences," the set of disciplines attending the dogmatic validation of the faith, as accurate but irrelevant in the modern world. He accused Muslim scholars of knowing every aspect of their faith in excruciating detail but of having failed to understand its spirit, just as professors of classical Persian literature had failed to understand modern poetry. What he is about to reveal is the very spirit of Islam: its ideology.

What Shariʿati wanted to argue, though with a twisted tongue so that the scholastic masters in Qom could not hear him properly, was that he could populate a new constituency among "Muslim intellectuals" who were concerned with "the Islamic Ideology" and who would leave "the old sciences for the ulama'."[99] Disqualified as a properly trained Shiʿi jurist and equally disqualified as a bona fide university professor of sociology, Shariʿati shunned and ridiculed both and vied for a self-proscribed revolutionary definition that would attract equally impatient revolutionary followers. To create this constituency and to carve a revolutionary ideology out of the Islamic heritage, he introduced the key term of *maktab* (school of thought = ideology) that later became a central concept in the revolutionary language of the Muslim intelligentsia. This is how Shariʿati defined a *maktab*:

A *maktab* is a harmonious and well-proportioned set of philosophical perspectives, religious beliefs, ethical principals and methods of action which in a relation of cause and effect with each other constitutes an active, meaningful, goal-oriented body which is alive, and which all its various organs are fed by the same blood and are alive by the same spirit.[100]

Thus turned into an overwhelming ideological stance, Islam becomes, from Shariʿati's inception forward, so powerful a revolutionary dictum that the word *maktab,* its semiotic registration, found its way into the very first page of the Constitution of the Islamic Republic and into many other pages too.

Engineered by Shariʿati, there thus emerged from a monotheistic worldview a sociology, a philosophy of history, and an anthropology, all converging on and invalidating the god-terms of a generation of impatient revolutionaries: "the Islamic Ideology." Based on this ideology, both the ideal society and the ideal man are constructed in Shariʿati's revolutionary model.[101] Whereas this emerging Islamic worldview is predicated on absolute monotheism, Shariʿati's sociology, in turn, hinges on the dialectic of a class struggle, as expressed in the hostility between Cain and Abel. His philosophy of history equally presumes valid a linear progression from the period of prophethood to that of Imamat, then to *ghaybah* (occulturation of the last Shi'i Imam, which Shari'ati calls "scientific and responsible democracy"), leading to universal revolution. His anthropology (pre)postulates the validity of an innate dialectic operative between the forces of good (Allah) and evil (Iblis) in man. These three disciplines— sociology, philosophy of history, and anthropology—converge, as they sustain a neo-Manichaen dualism of good and evil, in Shari'ati's conception of Islam as the supreme (meta)ideology of a cosmic order, leading to the establishment of the ideal society or *ummah* and to the characterization of the ideal man as the vicegerent of God on earth.[102]

By the time Shari'ati had reached the third lecture in his *Islamshenasi* course, on Friday, 18 February 1972, criticism of his ideas had reached its zenith. The entire introduction of the third lecture and most of its long footnotes, as well as footnotes to other lectures, are devoted to critical responses, however dismissive, to these criticisms. The chief argument against Shari'ati was a serious questioning of his Shi'i faith. Why, for example, did he defend the cause of the Palestinians who were, after all, Wahabi and Sunni?[103] Shari'ati considered these and similar charges malicious and refused to direct his attention away from his main objective to answer them in any detail.

Monotheism

As the metaphysical foundation of Shari'ati's worldview, upon which he constructs his elaborate *maktab,* monotheism is, in his reading, a (meta)epistemological reconciliation between the forces of diversity and multiplicity, compromised towards a unitary vision of the human experience. Thus *tawhid* or monethism is

the unity between love and intellect, between Beatrice and Virgil, between Avicenna and Abu Said [Abi al-Khayr], between Pascal and Descartes. . . . [It] does not divide man into two poles of love and intellect, intuition and rationality.[104]

This insistence on monetheism has a triple function: First, it underscores Shari'ati's quintessentially Islamic language to quell the visceral tradition- alist opposition directed against him; second, it provides his young Muslim audience with a measure of confidence that the ideological adventure they were engaged in was, in fact, "Islamic"; and third, it suggests a monolithic epistemological foundation upon which he could claim an internally coher- ent ideological argument for radical and revolutionary behavior.

Tawhid, as an epistemological and ontological frame of reference, has yet another significance for Shari'ati, rendered more immediately into polit- ical terms. What he wants to establish with this term is a valid and universal justification for revolutionary ideologies based on compelling religious grounds. Convinced that no revolutionary ideology can mobilize the necessary force of politicized masses without a firm ground in common and enduring religious symbols, Shariᶜati planned to develop his mobilizing message from the bottom up. He resorted to both Marx and Weber to teach his students about infra- and superstructures in society.[105] Society is divided into these two major segments: its economic infrastructure and its related ideological superstructure. While Marx insisted on the primacy of the former, Weber pointed out the causal significance of the latter: "which is to say," Shariᶜati interjected, "each, understood half of the social reality."[106] Putting the two halves together, the argument implies, Shariᶜati understood the complete social reality. But—and here is Shariᶜati's main objective in teaching Marx and Weber to his students at the Hosseyniyyeh Ershad—a class-based and hierarchically structured society is the societal expression of (in Shariᶜati's reading of the Marxist half of the social reality) a polytheistic theology. Based on a monotheistic *(tawhidi)* theology as its ideological infrastructure (Shariᶜati taking the Weberian half), a classless society will be created. Contrary to the Marxist conception that all religions are the opium of the masses, a monotheistic religion, such as Islam, is thus ontologically conducive, more than any other ideological frame of references, to the formation of a classless society.[107]

Beyond its immediate implications for Shariᶜati's universal worldview and for his sociology, *tawhid* has two more conceptual thrusts upon which he constructs his "Islamic Ideology": history and ethics. What *tawhid* means in history is the purposeful movement of men towards the historical realization of the divine destiny.[108] What *tawhid* means in ethics is the validation of humanly attainable divine attributes by virtue of which man is "dealienated."[109] This *tawhid* is constitutionally congenial to the formation of Shariᶜati's revolutionary man, who is neither scholar nor vulgar, but simply politically conscientious.[110] For this revolutionary man there is no private virtue in the absence or denial of the public. The phrase "first rectify yourself, then seek to rectify the society" is "extremely horrible and anti-Islamic."[111] And of course ultimately, for this revolutionary man, "faith is [to be] turned into a conscientious ideology."[112]

This faith-turned-ideology had to be the supreme model of whatever is best in every other (secular) ideology. Single-mindedly, Shariᶜati thought that, at least since his senior year in high school, he had been convinced of his mission to persuade others that Islam in his vision embodied the best of the two worlds: socialism and capitalism, in "The East" and "The West," in materialism and idealism.[113] He saw, grasped, and assimilated the two most compelling worldviews of his time and reread Islam in their terms. His very reason for being, he confessed with Albert Camus in mind, was to revolt against the status quo[114] and to lead his multitude, here though unlike Camus, to the promised land of "the Islamic Ideology." He attended this task with a sense of urgency because he believed his was the last generation with any hope of salvation. "If this generation is lost," Shari'ati feared, "then all [the rest] would be type-cast and [brain]washed."[115] He brushed aside his critics as irresponsible social parasites[116] and declared that the single task of a committed intellectual "in an uninformed and corrupt city . . . [is] to awaken [that] society."[117] For this task of awakening the Muslim masses, the Islamic history had to be reunderstood, as African history was reunderstood by Franz Fanon. The task of this reunderstanding the past in Islam was begun by Jamal al-Din al-Afghani and Muhammad Abduh, the great heroes of Shari'ati.[118] But in Shari'ati's estimation these two great predecessors had made two grave mistakes. While al-Afghani had approached the aristocratic elite to implement his ideas, Muhammad Abduh had tried to persuade the clergy. But, Shari'ati declared, standing on the shoulders of his heroes, "both the political and the clerical elites are part of the ruling class" and thus too conservative[119] to have a reunderstanding of Islamic history and dogma conducive to revolutionary goals. Here, contrary to his heroes, Shari'ati thought you cannot educate the educators. With a convinced revolutionary bend, Shari'ati declared, "we have to begin with the people . . . especially with the young generation and the intellectuals."[120] With the massive abstraction of "The People," with the natural disposition of the young to revolt, with the experiences of al-Afghani and Abduh, and with the overwhelming gift of his rhetorical abilities, Shari'ati sought and, in great measure, succeeded in implanting a relentless seed of revolt in his time. The success of "the Islamic Revolution," pregnant with other events yet to unfold, is just one expression of his will, however posthumously attained.

Classless, Monolithic Society

Tawhid, or the Islamic monotheism that Shari'ati turns into a monolithic sociology of religion, is central in the political implications of his social thought. With a firm insistence on the dialectic of monotheism and polytheism ("the logic and the philosophy specific to the East is dialectic"[121]), Shari'ati challenges sociologists and scholars of religion by defending the Qur'anic position that first there was monotheism and then, out of human corruption, polytheism emerged.[122] Upon this dialectic of detecting an innate, but concealed, monotheism in the diverse manifestations of polytheism, Shari'ati constructs a sociology of theology according to which what Marx called "primitive Socialism" or Durkheim called "mechanical solidarity" was congenial, and thus gave rise to, a kind of archetypal monotheism.[123] As the society is subsequently divided into the oppressor and the oppressed, and as Shari'ati's sociology departs from both Marx's and Durkheim's, man's theological preference is dualism,[124] reflecting, in a subconscious Manichaen cosmology, the oppressor and the oppressed. Following the same line of argument and as the ruling class is divided further into economic, political, and religious groupings, an ontological trinity prevails over man's theological disposition.[125] Thus both dualism and trinitarianism in theology or, even more fundamentally, polytheism in man's religious disposition have been reflections of "historical polytheism,"[126] that is, multiplicity in man's perceptions of race, ethnicity, social status, economic class, etc. Only in a classless society, as the conclusion strongly implies, can true theological monotheism be achieved. Put differently, based only on a truly monotheistic theology can a (just) classless society be attained. In the first conclusion, Shariʿati rejected the legitimacy of the Pahlavi monarchy; in the second, he rejected the claim of secular revolutionaries to ideological, social, and political validity.

Revolutionary Ethics

From a "monotheistic" view of (meta)historical existence there emerges a specific kind of ethics, quite unlike the ordinary understanding of the term. Both the popular and the scholarly perceptions of ethics miss the point, one taking received notions of propriety and the other the highhanded analytical discussions for what "ethics truly is."[127] Ultimately, ethics is the commonly propagated ideals of "the perfect man" who sacrifices his interests (sud) for his values (arzesh). Thus, Shariʿati postulates three indubitable principles upon which his revolutionary ethics rests: (1) self-sacrifice (ithar), (2) a distinction between good and evil (Khayr va shar), and (3) an enjoining and forbidding force external to man himself (amr va nahi).[128] Self-sacrifice, that is, foregoing one's present and private interests for some future public good, is the condito sine qua non of Shariʿati's revolutionary ethics. Combined with this, and as argued by Shariʿati's reading of Sartre,[129] is a personal distinction between good and evil. But taking his ethics one step further than Sartre's, Shariʿati argues for the necessity of a metaphysical force of commandment and prohibition external to the individual to give it its universal measure of success. Both Marxism and Existentialism have failed to answer with certainty man's moral dilemma of confronting an uncertain age of conflicting truths. The Marxist attempt to remain philosophically materialist but ethically idealist[130] is a logical fallacy. Confronting the barrage of successive traps to have man alienated from his historical identity—traps ranging from "superstitious religions" to magic, polytheism, asceticism, machinism, technocracy and bureaucracy, the class system, love, scientism, money, civilization, determinism, society, to materialism, and idealism[131]—there is but one hope. That hope rests on the committed intellectual who bypasses the social barriers thus artificially constructed between "The People" and him and who there and then teaches them the emancipating ethics that defies the status quo and anticipates "the perfect man" in the City of God.

For this theological monotheism and its counterpart, ideological determinism, to have their institutional expression, "the Islamic Ideology" recognizes the annual pilgrimages to Mecca as its supreme symbol.[132] Between the two opposing ideals of individualism and socialism, the hajj pilgrimage objectifies an ideal that supersedes the evils of both these extremes. In this ideal state, the Divine attributes are expostulated in the "I" of the individuals.[133] Realization of these Divine attributes in the "I" of the individuals, as objectified in the hajj ceremonies, precludes the possibility of any sacrifice of one for all or all for one. Opposing this "I," which is the true "I" and entails potential godly virtues, are "I's" fabricated by race, ethnicity, nationality, social class, family, guild, etc., organized conspiratorially to have the realization of these godly virtues thwarted in man. The hajj preempts a host of social and psychological maladies, including cultural and historical alienation, dispersion of individuals into atomized selves, mental stagnation, debilitating alienation from contemporary realities, etc.[134] Against the compelling appeal of false philosophies and misguided ideologies, such as materialism and skepticism, there is "the Islamic Ideology," as objectified in the hajj, providing the only possibility for man's moral, intellectual, and political salvation.

Revolutionary Historiography

Shari'ati's anthropology locates man between history and society,[135] that is, between his initial self-consciousness and his defining social strictures. He perceived the moral formation of this historical and social man as having undergone a fundamental revolution whereby aristocratic virtues have been superseded by popular ones. Even the most fascist regimes and ideologies pretend to have popular postures.[136] Shari'ati traced this moral revolution back to the French Revolution in "The West" and to the appearance of Islam in the seventh century in "The East." Ignorant of this mission of the Qur'an to make historical man conscious of himself, some naive believers had sought to reduce the Qur'anic language to their perception of modern scientific achievements. Following Romain Rolland, Shari'ati perceived history as the archetypal construction of a unique reality upon a heap of historical facts, directed towards a specific ideological objective.[137] This is precisely how he himself acted on the Islamic history: reconstructing a revolutionary edifice based on a host of otherwise benign historical "facts," totally speechless if left to themselves. Rejecting historiographies based on the primacy of events, society, race, or culture, Shari'ati ultimately preferred what he called an existentialist perception of history, according to which history is the science of man's becoming.[138] Man, his very individuality, is the essence of history. Equally rejecting historical determinism, Shariʿati formed the view that sees man as conscious of history and in control of his own destiny.[139]

Shariʿati's Disposition

About to begin his eleventh lecture on *Islamshenasi* on Friday, 5 May 1972, Shariʿati was criticized by one of the students who, on behalf of others, asked him why he attended his classes irregularly and why he was often late.[140] In response Shariʿati confessed that by disposition he was "irregular [in] thought and spirit."[141] He admitted that he had always had difficulty maintaining a disciplined and ordered life and gave an example of his daily schedule, indicative of his innermost disposition:

I was here [in Hosseyniyyeh Ershad] yesterday from one o'clock to seven-eight o'clock in the afternoon. Then I went somewhere and sat on the ground and wrote something which had nothing to do either with my lectures or my speeches or with anything [else] I was writing. Nothing at all! I wrote something and when I raised my head, I saw it was a quarter after four [A.M.] today.[142]

Halfway through his lectures on *Islamshenasi*, Shariʿati was himself thoroughly baffled as to exactly what he was doing and where he was leading his students. At the beginning of his second lecture on Marxism, thirteenth on the subject of *Islamshenasi*, he felt compelled to return once more to the question of sciences that are afflicted by mass appeal. But here Shariʿati himself was totally bewildered. At a point, in fact, he confessed "I don't know what to do,"[143] meaning he had completely lost the purpose, language, and reason of his lectures on Marxism. His apparent dilemma was to choose between teaching just the Marxist philosophy of history in order to compare it, along with other philosophies of history, with the (Shiʿi) Islamic philosophy of history, or else teach Marxism in general to provide a better background for these same objectives. But he ended up teaching nothing in that session of Friday, 19 May 1972. Instead, he continued to grapple with the necessity for science to be socially responsible and yet trivialized in the process of achieving precisely that. At this point, the confusion was so bad that one of the students severely criticized Shariʿati[144] who, in turn, confessed that he could not think or teach systematically[145] and yet insisted that it is better to teach how to think than teach per se. He further contradicted his position on knowledge being socially responsible and thus confused his students by preaching the necessity of teaching Marxism and Existentialism "objectively and scientifically,"[146] and by ridiculing those who profess opinions to him, who was, after all, a professor of "these things," by virtue of their having just read a Persian article on Existentialism.

Shari'ati returned to his podium the following week on Friday, 26 May 1972, still in no mood to decide what to say about Marxism. Instead, he delivered a long lecture on periodical soul-searching and introspection as a necessary pause in the career of all great men.[147] In his own career, Shari'ati revealed that he had constructed a balance between technical specialty and a large-scale sensitivity, whereby he forced himself to read Rumi's *Mathnavi* and the writings of André Gide while studying in Europe. Exactly a week after he had promised to teach his students about the Marxist philosophy of history, Shari'ati publicly began psychoanalyzing himself and his occasional self-introspection, arguing against those who might consider this as irrelevant to the subject matter—"in essence I have no private life."[148] Believing himself to be totally a social man, devoid of any true moment he might call private, Shari'ati attached public virtues to his private recollections of a committed ideological life. Matters private to him, which he, of course, published in the form of "Kavir," were, he thought, philosophy and criticism. But he thought that since he was on a "public" scholarship in France, he should study something that is helpful to the public: thus sociology.

Apparently concerned with, and confused by, a perception of futility in his long and loosely connected lectures, Shari'ati devoted the balance of this session of 26 May to justifying a relationship between "thought" and "action." He wished to argue that "in Shi'ism . . . action is part of the definition of religion."[149] Revolutionary and action-provoking thinking, he argued, was the indispensable prerequisite for collective action that leads to a promised objective. He equally rejected the notion that using a religion as an ideological basis forfeits the source and energy of initiating political action to a metaphysical standstill. He, instead, promised a reading of Shi'ism that places the responsibility of action on the revolutionary man: "Relying on Alid Shi'ism is reliance on the most progressive, the most energetic, and the most active values."[150]

Movement in History: Marxism Reconstructed

Shari'ati, gradually emerging from his confusion, taught his students the varieties of perceptions in historical progression, but always with a view towards a revolutionary interpretation of man's destiny. If Toynbee had said that history moved with a succession of attacks and defenses,[151] Shari'ati added that a religious movement (Islam) could always be kept in its aggressive mode through the active interpretation of its actual content as opposed to holding fast to its presumed outward postures.[152] From Toynbee he sought to learn and teach that Islam at this historical moment had to be revived by throwing out its old habits and recasting its content into a new —always revolutionary—mold.

When Shari'ati came to explain his version of Marxism to his students, he betrayed and utterly negated one of his most essential principals: that true knowledge was only partisan and for "the people." At the outset of his lecture on Marxism, he bitterly complained of the "popularization" of knowledge.[153] He realized, of course, the contradiction in his terms mandating the sovereignty of "the people." To avert it, he went to great lengths in order to argue that "I do not mean to oppose the popularization of science";[154] yet he had to admit, contrary to his wishes, that

when science wants to assume social responsibility, coming out of the framework of the specialists and experts in order to perform its message, being accessible to all, becoming the intellectual and ideological weapon of the masses, it compromises itself, and it becomes afflicted with popularization, reducing its scientific depth and value. Marx and Marxism have had a similar destiny.[155]

Upon this premise, Shari'ati proceeds to portray a multiple picture of Marx, whereby he is believed to have passed through three successive phases: (1) unconditional membership in the received traditions, (2) rebellion against received notions and principles, and (3) resumption of "the true self" and acceptance of "true values."[156] But while the masses are incapable of holding such multiple perceptions of a figure in mind, great thinkers like Marx, Abu al-Ala al-Ma'ari, or even Jalal Al-e Ahmad[157] demonstrate this progression within their character—and thought—formation. There are, Shari'ati concludes, (1) a philosopher Marx (youth), (2) a sociologist Marx (adult), and finally (3) the political activist Marx, which is his ultimate historical message. Shari'ati further psychoanalyzes Marx's antireligious sentiments to his unfulfilled wishes to marry a young girl whom he was denied on religious grounds.[158] At this last political stage, Marx sacrifices scientific precision for ideological objectives. Shari'ati, however, is concerned mainly with Marx the sociologist.

Shari'ati's stipulation of three kinds of Marxism, based on a presumed division in Marx's life as a philosopher, a social scientist, and a political activist, was a convenient mechanism through which he sought to legitimize his attraction to Marx and the "scientific" validity of his own ideas. The way he decoded Marx into these three characters, each had a bearing on the other. In other words, Shari'ati wished to accept and accredit Marx's sociological observations, especially his notion of class struggle, without appearing to share the philosophical foundation of Marx's sociology or to follow the political mandate of a Communist party (à la Tudeh Party). This would facilitate his unequivocal adoption of the Marxist terminology and agenda while giving them an aura of Shi'ism. To put it more accurately, Shari'ati was forced to propagate the compromising proposition that one could be a devout Shiʿi Marxist. Thus Shariʿati's criticism of the Tudeh Party was precisely on Marxist terms. The Tudeh Party, he charged, had introduced "medieval Marxism" in a society characterized chiefly by the "Asiatic mode of production," a society where such specifically European events as the Renaissance, the Reformation, or the Industrial Revolution had not taken place. The Tudeh Party was to blame for such miscalculations and for the fact that they had failed to translate even the all-too-essential "Das Kapital" into Persian.

Shariʿati and Marxism

The notion that Shariʿati had a love-hate relationship with Marxism[159] is based on a misreading of his highly superfluous rhetoric. A close reading of Shariʿati's writings leaves no doubt that his chief frame of reference, his conceptions of history, society, class, state apparatus, economy, culture, his program of political action, his strategies of revolutionary propaganda are all in the classical Marxist tradition. The apparent paradox is just in the matter of translating ideals into strategies. He would superimpose upon this underlying Marxist premise, resisting how they may, the Qurʾanic and other canonical precepts. Attempting a close approximation of his Marxist premise with his Islamic (Shiʿi) language, Shariʿati's success has to be measured in terms of a growing audience, during and after his active career, that was principally and operatively attracted to this ideological hybrid. There is, to be sure, nothing incongruent about the ingenious, though perhaps inevitable, connection that Shariʿati concocted between Marxism and Islam. As an ideologue, he reached for any viable frame of reference at his disposal that was instrumental in mobilizing his growing constituency. But we would lose the entire thrust of Shariʿati's ideological language, the rhyme and reason of his rhetoric, should we assume false ambiguities in his ideological proximity to Marxism. Nor should we take his rhetoric of a "return-to-our-origin" at face value and fail to see its great logistic significance for his particular brand of radical "Islamic Ideology." If Shariʿati appealed to the cause of a return to a mythological national (Shiʿi) origin and to his version of the indigenous culture, it was more than a sentimental longing for a presumed golden age. He knew better. He shrewdly realized, however, as he said in so many words, the source of the failure in secular ideologies to be in their highhanded and alien language. Language is everything, Shariʿati realized, in the forging of a convincing and mobilizing political culture. The indigenous Persian-Shiʿi language, properly charged with strategically crucial ideological notions, would be immensely powerful in potentially mobilizing a sizeable constituency, nostalgic about a past it may or may not have, anxious about a future it could or could not have. Otherwise, Shariʿati's innate resentment towards the historically received and institutionalized Shiʿi culture is patently evident in his deep antagonism towards its chief custodians, the ulama'. By discrediting and by-passing them, and with them the hermeneutic circles of Islamic learning they personify and legitimate, and by appealing directly to his own version of the Iranian Shiʿi past, and to its canonical sources, Shariʿati combined the two most basic elements of mass appeal: a committed radical ideology and a popular charisma of the most sentimental sort.

Immediately related to Shariʿati's relationship to Marxism is the question of his "progressive" reading of the Shiʿi tradition. There is a vast and documentable difference between the epistemological and hermeneutic apparatus of the Shiʿi juridical discourse, of which Shariʿati did not demonstrate the faintest idea, and the ideological and political agenda he explicitly pursued. He was without a doubt the master of his created ideological and rhetorical language. The comparison between Shariʿati and the Shiʿi clerical order as one being "progressive" and the other "conservative"[160] fails to see this fundamental difference, treating them, as it were, on common grounds. It is not just at the level of theological and juridical erudition that it would be ludicrous to elevate Shariʿati to the status of, say, Ayatollahs Borujerdi, Kho'i, or Khomeini. It is precisely this antischolastic trait in Shariʿati's ideas that, under the guise of anticlericalism, appeals to his secular admirers. That for "many young members of the intelligentsia," as it has been rightly suggested, the variety of Shiʿi scholastic discourses sounds like "mumbo-jumbo over esoteric issues"[161] is a clear indication of that vast realm of misconception and ignorance that separates the secular intellectuals and the Shiʿi clerics from each other. By sharing Shariʿati's latent resentment against scholastic learning, the secular intellectuals equally shared his blatant anticlericalism. The most prominent feature of this group of secular intellectuals has been an artificial acquaintance with a variety of imported ideological loyalties and, simultaneously, a deep, rather resentful, apathy for the received intellectual disciplines, particularly the juridical which was both difficult to access and exclusively the prerogative of the clerics. There are a number of intellectual discourses with which Shiʿi scholasticism operates, depending on the theological, philosophical, mystical, or juridical languages historically constructed. It is precisely the last language, the juridical, that the secular intellectuals particularly resent. The "mumbo-jumbo" qualification is a telling indication of the deep apathy that both Shariʿati and his secular admirers share towards a major branch of Shiʿi learning, in fact, its very condito sine qua non. The diverse causes of this allergic reaction to the juridical discourse and its institutional expression among the ulama' is too complicated—and tangential to our purpose here—to be analyzed fully. At least since the Constitutional Revolution—but certainly even earlier—the Shiʿi juridical discourse and its institutional custodians, the ulama', have been on the defensive against the

invading secular discourse which is not only personified in secular intellectuals but, more important, transplanted, like a Trojan horse, into the very
heart of the modern political reconstruction of the Shi'i self-consciousness.

That reconstruction of the old faith had to have all the semiotic signals
of the most compelling (secular) revolutionary ideology: Marxism. A key
word that Shari'ati borrowed from the Marxist literature and became a
prominent feature of his emerging revolutionary discourse, giving it a certain air of factuality, was the epithet "scientific." In response to those
political activists who maintained that too much has been said but nothing
done and that it was time to act, Shari'ati once responded that they have
talked, but not "scientifically." Before assuming any course of action, it
was necessary to talk further, but this time "scientifically." Shari'ati's insistence on the term "scientific" was directed simultaneously at two distinct
audiences: the Shi'i ulama' and the secular intellectuals. Yet for each group,
as Shari'ati knew very well, the word "scientific" *(ilmi)* had two vastly
different meanings. The Shi'i ulama', their very title meaning men of "science," understood this word in the context of the Islamic (juridical) epistemology that divided knowledge into the "intellectual sciences" *(al-ulum
al-aqli)* and the "transmitted sciences" *(al-ulum al-naqli)*. The secular intellectuals understood the term to mean that specific and economic-based
feature of Marxist socialism that distinguished it from idealist or "utopian"
socialism. Shari'ati told the clerics that what they called "scientific" was
not "scientific" any more, as judged by his version of French sociology. At
the same time, he told the secular intellectuals that it was possible to talk
"scientific socialism" but with a local (Shi'i-Persian) language. From the
clerics he wished to appropriate the authority of their juridical voice. To
the secular intellectual he wished to address the voice thus appropriated
but with a language they would deem contemporary and thus authoritative.
Shari'ati's success was with two groups: (1) the seminarian—or else simply
religious-minded—students who wished to retain their faith and yet simultaneously attend their revolutionary political agenda effectively and (2) the
university students who wished to see their essentially Marxist ideals addressed but had failed to concoct an indigenously sensitive language that
would appeal to a politically significant number of constituencies. Shari'ati's
failure was with two groups: (1) those seminarian students who saw through
the veil of his blatant Islamic language a hammer and sickle they did not
particularly like to pick or swing and (2) those university students who
were irresistably irreligious in what they took to be their quintessential
disposition and who would break out in rashes at the slightest suggestion
of a Qur'anic verse, Marxistically sugar-coated or not.

For both groups of his constituency, Shari'ati offered an unabashedly
Marxist view of history that is evident in a short treatise he wrote in which
he tried to argue that the insights Marx had provided in the revolutionary

destiny of the proletariat are used equally by the capitalists and other ruling elites to thwart the course of history.[162] Throughout this discussion he presents the essential lines of a Marxist view of social structure and history without the slightest attempt to disguise them in Islamic garb. He insists that capitalists lure "sociologists, philosophers, scientists, even great Marxologists and socialists"[163] to inform them of the ensuing danger that the proletariat poses for them. In Shari'ati's judgment, the reason the socialist revolution has not happened in Western Europe is precisely this capitalist awareness of the dangers to which Marx had alerted them. Among the chief schemes that capitalists have designed to oppose the formation of a revolutionary proletariat is to prevent the concentration of workers and their residential quarters in one area. Shari'ati further insists that more than absolute poverty, relative deprivation ultimately accounts for the proletariat's assumption of a revolutionary role. He believes that conspicuous consumption is an essentially "Western" phenomenon and that Islam has always suppressed extravagant expenditure or manifestation of wealth.

But in modern capitalism, with its establishment learned from Marx, the crucial factor of relative deprivation has been eliminated by intentionally increasing the level of the workers' conspicuous consumption. By going to the seashore, the movies, the operas, etc., workers are given the chance to assume the appearance of having actually shared in experiences formerly denied them.[164] On a larger international scale, Shari'ati believes that the reason rich countries provide loans to poor countries is to prevent dangerous outcomes of an intolerable level of poverty and also to perpetuate the world market for their consumer products.[165] The result of such precautionary measures is that the apparent differences in public consumption are eliminated so that actual differences in economic production and in class interest are preserved.[166]

Throughout this analysis, Shari'ati uses standard Marxist terminologies to analyze the condition of modern capitalist societies. In this and many other circumstances he adopts and presumes valid the Marxist interpretation of social structure and historical progress.

Marxism Islamicized

But Shari'ati's preoccupation with Marxism went much deeper than a mere adaptation of its language. Islamization of Marxism—or Marxification of Islam—was high on his agenda. In two private conversations and in an unpublished manuscript, Shari'ati went into the fullest extent of his Islamization of Marxism. The texts of these three crucial documents were published posthumously.[167]

In Shari'ati's reading, Islam has been historically appropriated by Muslim petit-bourgeoisie, and thus the ascetic revolutionary spirit congenial to the cause of the downtrodden has been sacrificed.[168] Revolutionary asceticism is not something modern Muslims have learned from Marxists. "It is the Marxists who have just learnt it from Islam."[169] In this particular regard, in fact, Islam was somewhat non-Marxist because the former emphasizes the significance of the individual in history, while the latter denies it.[170] The Islamic position is that unless people do not change in themselves, they will not change their social history.[171] That modern Muslims had forgotten about their own revolutionary past and potentials and were attracted to similar alien concepts was the deepest manifestation of their self-alienation and its concurrent "Westoxication."[172] In the true sense of the term, "asceticism" means "puritanisme revolutionnaire."[173]

Islamization of Marxism is a quintessentially semantic and interpretative enterprise. Shari'ati confided to this group of his close followers that all the negative attributes of "bourgeoisie" are best captured in the Persian "worldliness" (zendegi-ye donyavi). But the problem was that the term "worldliness" had been diluted by a history of misuse.[174] As soon as Shari'ati would talk of "denouncing worldliness," his young audience would think him "a molla."[175] Thus, "I do not talk about religion. Because I am a sociologist, and I talk as a sociologist. For example, what is the spirit of bourgeoisie? [or] what is a bourgeois life?"[176] This, however, is only a strategic maneuver. Because

when I presented bourgeoisie as a dirty, stinking, money-grabbing . . . class, and when I made fighting against this bourgeoisie a self-conscious revolutionary stand, with humanist [proportions] . . . they will listen to me. This [mode of] discourse will influence many people.[177]

Once this objective is attained, Shari'ati plans to substitute the "struggle against bourgeoisie" with "defiance of worldliness" (e'raz-e az donya'), which is an Islamically more accurate and even more universal term.[178] At whatever stage of the dialectical progression of history we are, the feudal or the capitalist mode of production, the term "defiance of worldliness" is applicable to that group of revolutionary ascetics who revolt against the oppressive powers that be.[179]

If from the very beginning I were to say "defiance of worldliness," they cannot understand that I wish to say something new. They would think I am talking like those "denounce-the-world" mollas![180]

It is the function of the revolutionary ascetics, thus defined, to refuse a moment of salvation for those who otherwise spend a lifetime accumulating wealth. He once confronted such a person who had come to listen to him in Mecca: "I am not an akhond who takes some money from you and then constantly pampers you, delivering you like an innocent baby to God, the messenger and the Imam[s]."[181]

A Marxist glance at the Islamic history would reveal the quintessential problem, as Shariʿati saw it:

Do you know what is the source of misery for Islam? It is the formation of, and the dependency of the religion on, this [petit-bourgeoisie] class, establishing [, as they have,] a connection between the seminary and the bazaar. Should Islam be able one day to get rid of this dirty connection, it will, for ever, assume the leadership of humanity; and should this relation continue, Islam has been lost forever. The Islam which is growing nowadays and which has adherents is the Islam with connection between Hajis [he means the merchants who have been to Mecca] and the Mollas.[182] And these two have a [cozy set of] reciprocal relationships with each other. This [the Molla] takes care of the other's [the Haji's] religion, and that [the Haji] takes care of the other's [the Molla's] worldliness. . . . Then in [the process of] such a reciprocal relationship they make a religion for people which is of no use to them.[183]

Shariʿati's visceral contempt for the bourgeoisie leads him directly to a critical rejection of the entire corpus of Shiʿi jurisprudence because of its primary justification of the petit-bourgeoisie. "Look at the Islamic economics! It is the economics of the petit-bourgeoisie!"[184] or even more emphatically, "look at our jurisprudence, it is the jurisprudence of the petit-bourgeoisie."[185]

We have to save Islam from this connection [between the merchants and the clerics]. In my opinion, this is the objective. Except for this commitment, with whatever we keep busying ourselves—good or evil, true or false—we have abandoned our responsibility and our mission.[186]

In the same vein, Shariʿati sharply criticized the Islamic utopian moralism that first advocates and encourages the accumulation of wealth and then admonishes the rich to give handouts to the poor. "The Islamic economic system should be such that he [the capitalist] is not permitted to accumulate wealth."[187] What has given rise to this duplicitous state of affairs is that "they admonish the capitalist on the pulpit, but issue juridical injunctions in his favor."[188] It is this outmoded advocacy of the rich that Shariʿati condemns in Islamic law. Addressing a typical jurist, he exclaimed,

the idiot still does not relent to forbid slavery! A juridical treatise published in 1970 states: "While in a sacred state during masʿa[189] you can buy a slavegirl. That is the degree of his stupidity! During the Saʿi the materialist and atheist Jalal Al-e Ahmad says: "I am going mad. I want to bang my head into the wall to explode." And under the same circumstances, Haji Aqa[190] has seen a beautiful slavegirl, he has been aroused, and he wants to buy her. He asks the Molla,[191] "Can I buy her now?" And he says, "yes you can buy her, and yet you cannot copulate with her while you are in the sacred state.[192] You have to have sex after the Saʿi." The date of publication for this treatise is 1970. This is our jurisprudence. All the capitalist laws of the United States are more advanced than the laws of our jurisprudence.[193]

The economic system Shari'ati saw hidden and yet betrayed in Islam prevented the atrocities that result from the massive accumulation of wealth.[194] Such "infrastructural problems" ought to be addressed. For the economic restructuring of Islam, to prevent boundless accumulation of capital in a few hands, the Islamic society had to adopt aggressive and progressive programs. Collective asceticism was the worst enemy of such programs. Societies ought to be materialistic and productive; individuals mystic and ascetic.[195] If Islam recognizes this, its original message, it will once again raise "the flag of permanent historical revolution."[196] This revolution is founded on a visceral contempt of capitalism and its bourgeois agency:

In our eyes, bourgeoisie is loathesome. It will not just be eliminated. It must be eliminated. This [capitalist system] is to be condemned not just because it is incompatible with the "collective production" in modern industrial systems, but more because it is antihuman. It corrupts the human nature. It transforms all "values" to "interests." It changes the nature to "money," and man, who is the representative of God on earth, . . . to a bloody wolf.[197]

To succeed this capitalist state is the socialist, "as we understand it."[198] This is not merely preferable because "after capitalism, it is inevitable."[199] Socialism is preferable because it emancipates man from the economic and spiritual prison of capitalism and permits him to realize his divine origin.[200] But Shari'ati insists that he is not to be taken for a bona fide full-fledged Marxist:

It is clear in what sense we are not Marxists, and in what sense we are socialists. As a universal and scientific principal, Marx makes economics the infrastructure of man; but we [hold] precisely the opposite [view]. That is why we are the enemy of capitalism and hate bourgeoisie. Our greatest hope in socialism is that in it man, his faith, ideas, and ethical values are not superstructural, are not the manufactured and produced goods of economic infrastructure. They are their own cause. Modes of production do not produce them. They are made between the two hands of "love" and "consciousness." Man chooses, creates, and sustains himself.[201]

Shari'ati's socialism went beyond a mere economic preference of collective ownership of the means of production. "It is a philosophy of life," he liked to call it, quintessentially different from capitalism.[202] Socialism for Shari'ati, as light in Manichaen cosmological dualism, was the course, cause, and end of salvation, delivering man from the dark destiny of capitalism. For this socialism to come about, a whole new set of conceptual categories must be injected into the facile old terminologies. "Monotheism," here, is a worldview, "more scientific than materialism."[203] "Faith" is the cause of human progress.[204] The story of "Adam" is the story of what is true about man[205] and what is essential in his dialectical dualism.[206] Monotheism and polytheism are the expressions of class struggle in human history.[207] *Imamat* and *wilayat* are *not* metaphysical and mystical beliefs and hallucinations, they are elements of revolutionary leadership in Islam.[208] *Shahadat* is the responsibility of keeping the flame of struggle alive in difficult times.[209] *Entezar* is the source of continuity of a revolutionary movement in history.[210] The end result of this, the socialist utopia to be achieved, is *jame'eh-ye bi-tabaqeh-ye towhidi* ("the classless, monotheistic society").[211] For this to be achieved, two preliminary ideological preparations are necessary: (1) a radical criticism of Islam as it has been unfolded historically, particularly in its dependency on the unhealthy relationship between the clergy and the merchant class, and (2) an equally radical updating of the most quintessential truth of Islam with the most recent events in human history. For Shari'ati this "quintessential truth" is in the mission of Islam to deliver man from worldly miseries of greed and domination, and the subsequent realization of a classless, tension-free, and perfectly harmonious theocentricism in history.

Bazgasht: *A Return to Self*

To realize that history, the nostalgic remembrance of a revolutionary spirit casting a long shadow on the "Islamic" past, Shari'ati's repoliticized man ought to be conscious of his particular location in the universe he calls home. In a series of lectures called *Bazgasht (Return)*,[212] Shari'ati argued forcefully for the necessity of a rediscovery of the national psyche before any revolutionary course of action could be taken. The underlying assumption in the necessity of this "self"-realization is an ontological bifurcation between Iran (or Islam) and "The West." These two constitute separate and quintessentially hostile polarities. In order to achieve their "true" Iranian identity, Shari'ati's generation had to combat "The Western" scheme of things. In this battle, it would be ludicrous to attack "The West" with its own ideologies of nationalism or Marxism. Only with an inborn ideology, an ideology rooted in its own political culture, can Iran hope to fight "The West" and, in the process, gain its respect. "The Islamic Ideology" was thus the only possible banner of collective political consciousness under which Iranians could reach for their revolutionary ideals. Should Islam in Iran thus achieve its penultimate victory over "The West," the victory would be not only material but ideological, not only historical but metaphysical, not only sociological but theological, not only normative but moral.

Shari'ati: *A Matter of Conviction*

The morality of that utopian victory demanded a prophetic vision. Shari'ati was the last figure of prophetic vision that Iran produced in its penultimate moment of entering the age of pervasive doubt and meticulous uncertainty. He was convinced. He was convinced, like no one else in his historical vicinity, that he had, in fact and in the fullest extent possible, seen the light. He read, wrote, lectured, and revised his ideas with furious fantasy, such forceful determination, such unparalleled conviction and drive, that he torpedoed his audience into believing his faith and sharing his vision. His schemes were universal, his ideals appealing, his factual mistakes sincere, irrelevant, and almost trivial in the face of that romantic revolution (paving the way for that innocent City of God) he so sincerely and single-mindedly wished for. In this, more than in anything else and more than anyone else, he paved the way for Khomeini's arrival. He and Khomeini were worlds apart: Shariʿati the young composer of freshly dreamt melodies of revolt, Khomeini the old master of unflinching moral austerity in matters public and private. But in that vast and blossoming field of public imagination where logic rises obediently to meet the myth, they coincided in orchestrating a massive ceremony of revolt: Shariʿati prophesying a universal revolt of the glorified masses against the tyranny of ideological multiplicity and Khomeini fulfilling, almost unknowingly, that prophecy.

A New Kind of Vision

"Whatever the explanation," is said of Jonathan Edwards's theological disposition, "the fact is that Edwards's own conversion experience ... involved a genuinely new kind of vision of God's glory in every aspect of the natural world."[213] Substitute "politics" for "nature" and Shariʿati's enduring disposition would be identical to Edwards's. "A genuinely new kind of vision of God's glory" was Shariʿati's moving spirit. That vision was focused on the highest and most compelling God-term of Shariʿati's generation: "The People." Converting the historically received elements of his ancestral piety into the most demanding dictums of public discontent, Shariʿati became the most popular visionary of his age, the most vigorous proselytizer of revolutionary zeal. A committed revolutionary ideologue in the prime of his life, Shariʿati drew from experiences he could only accumulate in his tormented drive for a future that may or may not be, founded on a past that might or might not have been. In that drive he saw "God's glory" in every momentous vision where "The People" met his revolutionary demands. Glory—from God's to "The People's"—transfixed Shariʿati into a permanent niche in his followers' collective imagination. That imagination, supplementing other recollections, was the guiding force of the Revolution Shariʿati all but launched, all but witnessed. But "the new kind of vision" he had was a generation of revolutionaries to share, the particulars of which to institutionalize, the boundaries of which to enlarge, the dreams of which to fulfill, the anxieties of which to endure. Beyond Shari'ati's inborn and acquired limitations, beyond the inherent fetters of "the Islamic Ideology," Shari'ati's followers, acknowledged or de facto, live to test the uncertain future of his self-made illusion, terms of his contagious enchantment.

CHAPTER 3

Morteza Motahhari: The Chief Ideologue of the Islamic Revolution

"From that time onwards," observed the earliest biographer of Saint Thomas Aquinas, "it was his custom always to avoid the sight and company of women—except in case of necessity or utility—as a man avoids snakes."[1] The time was about 1244 when, disenchanted with their brother's decision to become a Dominican friar, Saint Thomas Aquinas' elder brothers kidnapped him while he was resting by a spring in Tuscany, took him to a family castle at Monte San Giovanni, and there pleaded with him not to become a Dominican friar. When every line of reasoning seemed futile, brothers sent a seductive woman to his chamber, assuming the ensuing pleasure would do the trick. Saint Thomas, however, is reported to have jumped to his heels, grabbed a brand from the fire, and chased the woman out of his solitude. That night he had a dream in which angels tied his loins in a symbolic sealing of his Perpetual Chastity. From that time onwards Saint Thomas avoided women—except when necessity dictated otherwise—as others did serpents. Imagine that woman the seductive symbol of "The Western" hegemonic lure, and you have a clue as to what animates the soaring soul of "the Islamic Ideologues." Captivated by the magical spell "The West" exercises over the mind and the soul of the present history, resentful of the non-Islamic—nay, indeed, anti-Islamic—primacy of her hegemonic order, the Muslim ideologues, in their solitude or society, reach for every brand in the fire of their Islamic imagination to chase the seductive wench out of their mind, soul, body, and life. Exorcise that witch! The intensity of chasing, alas, only belies the force of the captivation. The ferocity of reaching for fiery brands only approves the power of "The Western" seduction. The extent to which the external agitations and confused utterances conceal the inner attractions and disquieting anxieties, and the manifested anger reveals the latent longing, differs from one ideologue to another. But the anger and the attraction, the fiery brand and the suppressed longing, are two sides of the same coin: the coin whose currency spells "the Islamic Ideology." No one could do more to deliver this ideology from the very depths of the Islamic sacred history, to render it a legitimate historical updating of the Muslim doctrinal self-understanding, than the Martyred Master Morteza Motahhari.

A Life Committed to Learning and Leading

Morteza Motahhari (1920–1979) secured himself a permanent place in the annals of the Islamic Republic in Iran. He was born on 2 February 1920 in Faryman,[2] a small village some ninety miles from Mashhad, the capital of Khorasan province. Located at the fringes of the vast desert, Faryman gave both Motahhari and Shariʿati a sense of grandiloquence for which they had a predilection. Following his initial studies, Motahhari came to Mashhad, the prestigious center of learning and pilgrimage, to study with the highest authorities in his fields of interest. In 1936 he left Mashhad for Qom. A contributing factor to this decision had been the death of Mirza Mehdi Shahidi Razavi, a prominent master of Islamic philosophy. Early on, Motahhari had demonstrated a particular predilection for Islamic philosophy. But in 1936, as indeed during most periods of Islamic history, the study of philosophy was not a readily available course of education. Next to mysticism, the study of philosophy was severely protested by contemporary juridical masters. By 1937, Motahhari moved to and settled in Qom where the study of philosophy, though not openly condoned, was at least relatively possible.

In the summer of 1941, on the verge of the Allied occupation of Iran, Motahhari leaves the intolerably hot weather of Qom and goes to Isfahan where he studies *Nahj al-Balaghah* with a certain Hajj Mirza Ali Aqa Shirazi Isfahani, a remarkable master of this seminal Shiʿi text and someone Motahhari would always remember with deepest affection. In 1944 Ayatollah Borujerdi moves to Qom, and Motahhari begins a formal course of jurisprudence with him. A year later, in 1945, Motahhari begins to read a seminal philosophical text, Hajj Molla Hadi Sabzevari's *Manzumah,* with Ayatollah Khomeini.

In 1946, as he begins to study Akhond Khorasani's *Kifayah al-Usul,* a juridical text, with Ayatollah Khomeini, Motahhari starts his lifelong commitment to study—in order to refute—Marxism. His exclusive sources of information about Marxism are either the propaganda pamphlets of the Tudeh Party or, at best, the writings of a local Marxist propagator, Taqi Erani. Occasionally, Motahhari would also read a secondary Arabic source on the subject. But on the whole, his knowledge of Marxism—or of any

"Western" school of thought—remains confined to what is available to him in Persian.

In 1949 Motahhari commences his study of the sixteenth-century Shiʿi philosopher Molla Sadra's *al-Asfar al-Arbaʿah* with Ayatollah Khomeini. His classmates in this course include Ayatollah Montazeri, Hajj Aqa Reza Sadr, and Hajj Aqa Mehdi Ha'eri. Of these students, Hajj Aqa Mehdi Ha'eri would later prove to be more talented than the others. Khomeini was particularly attracted to the intellectual potentials of this son of his own former teacher, Ayatollah Ha'eri Yazdi.[3]

In 1950 Motahhari concentrates more vigorously on the study of philosophy. While he continues to read the Persian translations of secondary sources on Marxism—texts such as George Pulizer's *Introduction to Philosophy* (a simplified Marxist view of philosophy intended for the proletariate)—he begins to attend Allamah Tabataba'i's Thursday sessions on "the materialist philosophy." The sources of the latter's ideas about "the materialist philosophy" are equally limited to what is available in secondary materials in Persian and Arabic. These "Thursday sessions" continue from 1950 to 1953 and result in the five-volume *Osul-e Falsafeh va Ravesh-e Realism (Principles of Philosophy and the Realistic Method).*[4] Motahhari would later edit these volumes, add copious notes (more extensive than the text itself), and gradually publish them (1953–1985).[5] As these discussions (refutations) of "the materialist philosophy" continue, Motahhari also studies Avicenna with Allamah Tabataba'i. Among his classmates in these studies were Ayatollahs Montazeri and Beheshti.

By 1951 Motahhari had finished his course of juridical studies in Qom. In 1952 he left Qom, went to Tehran, and began teaching at Marvi School. That same year he married the daughter of a distinguished fellow cleric, Ayatollah Ruhani. In 1954 he began teaching at Tehran University's Department of Theology. By the early 1960s he is actively involved in the organization of the Monthly Religious Society *(Anjoman-e Mahaneh-ye Dini)* and the publication of its organ, "The Monthly Discourse" *(Goftar-e Mah).* During this period he is also involved in annual conferences of Islamic associations that were instrumental in giving him an audience much wider than the religiously minded urban activists in Tehran and Qom. In virtually every major Iranian city or town, these associations were the most widespread informal organizations sponsoring different degrees of Islamic causes and concerns. Among Motahhari's publications during this period are the first (1953) and second (1954) volumes of *The Principles of Philosophy and the Realistic Method,* the first (1960) and second (1964) volumes of *The Stories of the Virtuous,* and *Twenty Discourses* (1964).

Motahhari was briefly incarcerated during Ayatollah Khomeini's June 1963 uprising; and "The Monthly Discourse," to which he regularly contributed, was banned. In 1964 Motahhari's promotion at Tehran University from Lectureship to Assistant Professorship is denied. A year later, in 1965, he is instrumental in establishing Hosseyniyyeh Ershad as a privately founded religious organization devoted to the propagation of the Shi'i cause.

In the late—as in the early—1960s Motahhari was writing vociferously: *The Structure of Women's Rights in Islam* (1966–67), *Man and Destiny* (1966), *The Mutual Services of Iran and Islam* (1967), and *Help from the Unseen in Man's Life* (1969), to name but a few. Perhaps the most important publication of this period is *Causes of Attraction to Materialism* (1969), in which he launches a harsh attack against the Iranian secular intellectuals.

Between June 1963 and the advent of the revolutionary movement in 1977–79, Motahhari was in constant contact with Ayatollah Khomeini, and, in fact, through a religious edict, became his sole representative in Iran in charge of collecting and dispensing religious taxes due to the exiled Ayatollah. At the same time he continued to lecture and write on a variety of religious and social issues. *About the Islamic Revolution* (1979?) was a collection of speeches and interviews that was published posthumously after his assassination on Thursday, May 1, 1979. Khomeini wept publicly at his funeral, calling Motahhari "the fruit of my life."[6]

The Significance of Motahhari

Ayatollah Khomeini was deeply moved and visibly disturbed by Motahhari's assassination. In a public speech, which was one of the rare occasions when he wept openly, Khomeini praised the late Motahhari as a "noble martyr, a distinguished thinker, philosopher, and jurist."[7] He lamented that "I have lost a dear son."[8] Khomeini proclaimed a national day of mourning for Motahhari and personally received many mourners at the Feyziyyah Seminary.

After his assassination, Motahhari's books were the subject of some controversy. In his memorial speech on the first anniversary of Motahhari's death, Khomeini has the following cryptic note:

These days we hear that the enemies of Islam and antirevolutionary groups are determined to prevent, with their anti-Islamic propaganda, our dear university students from learning from the books of this master that we have lost. I urge the students and the committed intellectuals not to let the books of this dear master be neglected by non-Islamic conspiracies.[9]

Whatever this may refer to, Motahhari's writings altogether have been widely distributed and massively read in the course of the revolutionary period. But the appeal of his writings, particularly to the religiously sensitive urban professionals, dates back to the earlier phases of his career. From the early 1950s when he began his extensive commentaries on Allamah

Tabataba'i's *Principles of Philosophy and the Realistic Method,* Motahhari took upon himself the task of confronting the political issues of his time on an ideological and intellectual level of discourse rarely adventured before by a bona fide cleric. The very first words in his "Introduction" to this seminal book are in praise of knowledge,[10] promising to meet the challenge of secular (Marxist) ideologues with full charge.

The Weapon of Philosophy Popularized

Motahhari had deemed it necessary to confront the secular ideas spreading fast in Iran by recharging the publicly docile Islamic philosophical tradition, which he believed was "first in order of significance" among all branches of knowledge.[11] He argued that philosophy was not in any way the prerogative of "The West." He was, in fact, always quick to point out "the decline of philosophy in the West" after Emperor Justinian came to power.[12] The presumption of this "decline of philosophy in the West" was more than a mere reflection of asserting a presumed Islamic superiority, in intellectual matters, over a mythological and deified conception of "The West." The streak of a mild, but pervasive, nationalism in Motahhari always found ways of expressing itself: "What is historically indubitable," he genuinely believed,

is that Ancient Greece, too, owes the origin of its principal achievements to the East. The great scholars of that part of the world repeatedly travelled to the East, learned much from the Eastern scholars, and upon their return, spread them in their own country.[13]

Such highhanded statements stem from a certain ideological conviction, characteristic of almost all the ideologues under consideration here, that both rejected and, by virtue of this very rejection, conceded the archetypal validity of "The West." This ideological inevitability was always at odds with Motahhari's aspirations to an academic discourse. But Motahhari, like other ideologues, lacked that serenity of mind that would humble a scholar away from grandiloquent, but empty, generalizations. His impatience with sustained and long-term projects—and his lack of a first-hand knowledge of non-Islamic intellectual traditions—more often than not led him to make such presumptuous thunders as passing judgment on Mohammad Iqbal's book on Islamic philosophy, considering it "very short and insignificant," while confessing that he had not actually seen it.[14] Considering that Motahhari made this statement while he was still rather young —thirty-one years old—and in no particular rush to deliver a speech or meet any immediate obligation, it becomes evident that, despite his better judgment, an innate rashness was instilled in him, as in all the other revolutionary ideologues, that prevented serious and sustained scholarship in the modern or scholastic tradition he paradoxically disliked. From early in his career he seems to have had an immediate and compelling obligation to meet the challenge of his time in, and with, his own ideological language.

Motahhari's disdain for bona fide scholarly agendas in traditional or modern contexts ought to be seen in two distinct frames of reference: First, by disposition, he was more a simplifier of classical Shi'i learning than a first-rate scholastic mind. In Islamic philosophy, for example, he came nowhere near such eminent contemporaries as Mehdi Ha'eri Yazdi or Sayyid Jalal al-Din Ashtiani in the complexity and richness of their discourse. Second, more than genuinely scholastic or scholarly, it was an ideological agenda—both hidden and manifest—that moved Motahhari. His ideological agenda was targeted essentially towards a collective resuscitation of a general Islamic consciousness that was, as he knew it, on the whole on the defensive. This dual imperative led him to harbor a certain unarticulated but strong (dis)like for the (Islamic) scholastic or (modern) scholarly discourse of his time. Between the scholastic discourse of Sayyid Jalaloddin Ashtiani in philosophy and the modern scholarly discourse of, say, Abdolhossein Zarrinkub in historiography, Motahhari could only muster an ideological discourse more akin to Shari'ati's than to anyone else's. To be sure, Motahhari was much more erudite in Islamic learnings than Shari'ati could ever have been. But still, by choice or disposition, or a combination of both, he remained more a propagator and a proselytizer than a scholastic thinker or a modern scholar.

Motahhari's access to "Western" sources, as he would call them, is exclusively through Persian (and presumably Arabic) translations. His references to Hegel,[15] Bertrand Russell,[16] and David Hume[17] are all through Persian translations of secondary sources about them. To be sure, Motahhari was an extremely cautious, systematic, and meticulous reader of his sources, as is quite evident from the extensive notes that have been found in his personal library.[18] These translations of secondary sources on European philosophers were sometimes by very able and competent translators, such as Hamid Enayat, Ahmad Aram, Amir Hossein Aryanpour, Karim Keshavarz, or Najaf Daryabandari. But still the fact remains that Motahhari's access to European sources was limited, first, to what was translated and, second, to the varying degree of accuracy and competence that these translations enjoyed or suffered.

"To Reveal All the Misconceptions of Materialism"

The establishment and active propagations of the Tudeh Party in the 1940s had given unprecedented momentum to Marxist ideas in Iran. The propaganda literature of the Tudeh Party, disseminating Stalinist socialism, permeated the Iranian ideological scene to the point of reaching the seminarian students in Qom. Reacting to this onslaught of Marxist ideology was all but inevitable. That it assumed philosophical, rather than dogmatic or doctrinal, overtone was chiefly because of Allamah Tabataba'i who wished to attack this atheist ideology at its philosophical foundation. Motahhari was instrumental in getting these philosophical responses organized and later edited, annotated, and published. While Allamah Tabataba'i's language in the original text is highly technical in its philosophical discourse and obviously addressed to the seminarian students in Qom (and only to those who had a philosophical training), Motahhari's footnotes were much more comprehensible and, as such, essentially addressed to the secular intellectuals in Tehran. Thus, while the original text contains scarcely any references to contemporary philosophical sources, Motahhari makes extensive annotations in the footnotes to Persian translations of such sources. Persian, and occasionally Arabic, translations remain the sole source of both Tabataba'i's and Motahhari's ideas about "The Western Philosophy."

In order to legitimize his exclusive reliance on an Iranian propagator of Marxism, Taqi Erani, Motahhari attributed unmeasured credence to his significance:

Dr. Erani has given dialectical materialism an expression much better than [those given] by Marx, Engels, Lenin, etc. Consequently, his philosophical writings are superior to his predecessors.[19]

In making Tabataba'i's medieval (scholastic) language accessible to the secular intellectuals in Tehran, Motahhari expanded heavily on the actual text of *The Principles of Philosophy and the Realistic Method,* which is, in fact, delivered as a bona fide (independent) course on "philosophy" as such. The result, however, is a running dialogue, more in Motahhari's footnotes than in Tabataba'i's original text, with "philosophical materialism." In achieving this objective, Motahhari's footnotes occasionally assume the character of encyclopedic entries, giving full and detailed accounts of the minutiae of Islamic philosophy.

In *The Principles of Philosophy and the Realistic Method* Motahhari thought he had found a level of discourse at which he could confront Marxism without resorting to religious dogmatism. "Among all the things that are sacred to human beings," he stipulated, " 'knowledge' is the only thing which is sacred to every one, regardless of race, school of thought, or ideology."[20] No other form of knowledge is so sweeping and universal (and thus convincing) as philosophy. If the philosophical truth, or falsehood, of a matter has been established, no degree of dogmatic or ideological intensification can make a difference. The history of philosophy, this universal search for a common logical ground, is global: Egyptians, Chinese, Indians, Iranians, Greeks, and Muslims have all contributed to this cumulative endeavor. It is a fallacy to assume the Greeks as the original source of philosophy. They received their sources from "The East."[21] Of the history of Islamic philosophy, particularly its recent developments from the sixteenth century forward, "The West" has remained ignorant. The Iranian secular intellectuals, who receive their sources of aspirations and information exclusively from "The West," have remained equally ignorant of these genuine Islamic developments. This has contributed to their admiration for and blind emulation of "The Western" ideologies.

Motahhari also realized that the gradual translations of "Western" philosophical sources into Persian had created the strong impression that scholastic Islamic philosophy could not have had a meaningful dialogue with modern ideas. Although the contrary would be argued in this book, the possibility of a meaningful dialogue between "The West" and Islamic philosophy would also have the intended consequence of rendering Islam a still viable intellectual (and thus political) force in the modern scheme of things. Motahhari confessed that "party and political propaganda of the new materialist philosophy (dialectical materialism)"[22] had prompted these series of lectures on Islamic philosophy. Philosophical materialism, which Motahhari understood as "the denial of the metaphysics,"[23] has had but a short modern history in the eighteenth and nineteenth centuries. In the twentieth century, it has been "faced with severe defeat."[24] "But," Motahhari interjected, "the materialists themselves try to pretend that materialism has had a long historical record."[25]

Despite certain ambiguities, not all the philosophers who have believed in the primacy of matter can be considered to have denied the existence of "the metaphysics." Upon a scattered body of atheistic statements in the eighteenth and nineteenth centuries, the materialists capitalized on Darwin's biological theories and advanced their own positions. But more than anything else, Marxism has propagated the cause of philosophical materialism.[26] Marx adopted the dialectical method from his teacher, Hegel, and extended it into a materialist conception of the world. With the establishment of International Communism, the propagation of philosophical materialism became concurrent with the political might of this movement. In Iran, Motahhari noted, the Tudeh Party had been advocating these ideas in their party literature. As part of this global movement, local Iranian Marxists have given a certain "scientific" aura of inevitability to their ideology:

The advocates of this school openly claim that one either has to accept divine wisdom, believe in God and deny all sciences, industries, and inventions, or else one has to believe in them and cast the divine wisdom aside!!![27]

Motahhari denied any such relations and claimed that there is no correlation between the materialist philosophy and the efflorescence of experimental sciences in modernity. One can at the same time be a believing Muslim and a full participant in man's scientific achievements.

The principal reason behind the rise of philosophical materialism in "The West" has been "the lack of a strong and robust intellectual, philosophical school which could be compatible with [experimental] sciences." [28] Motahhari ridiculed the prosaic nature of St. Thomas Aquinas' *Summa Theologica* which addressed issues such as "how many angels can sit on the head of a pin." [29] He concluded that "Certainly if divine wisdom [philosophy] had advanced as much in Europe as among the Muslims, so many confusing and anarchical philosophical schools would not have appeared." [30]

It was necessary to tackle the onslaught of philosophical materialism, Motahhari emphasized, not because of the inherent significance of this school of thought but because it had, through the agency of the Tudeh Party, targeted the young people for conversion. They had used their elaborate propaganda machine to claim that this was "the most excellent philosophical system in the world." [31] They had claimed that the time of divine wisdom was over. Such intrusions into the intellectual domain of Islamic scholastic learning had to be challenged philosophically.

Constructing the Argument

The content of *The Principles of Philosophy and the Realistic Method* is organized as an independent course of Islamic philosophy. The text consists of fourteen treatises divided into five volumes. The first volume contains four treatises: (1) What Is Philosophy, (2) Realism and Idealism, (3) Knowledge and Comprehension, and (4) The Value of Perceptions. The second volume contains three treatises: (1) Appearance of Multiplicity in Perceptions, (2) Relative Perceptions, and (3) The Reality and Existence of Things. The third volume contains two treatises: (1) Necessity, Possibility, and Impossibility and (2) Cause and Effect. The fourth volume contains four treatises: (1) Possibility and Actuality: Motion and Time, (2) Createdness and Preexistence, (3) Unity and Multiplicity, and (4) Quidity: Substance and Attribute. The fifth and final volume consists of only one treatise: The God of the Universe and the Universe.

Throughout these five volumes, Motahhari would take "the materialists" to task on a variety of philosophical issues. The following example, from the fourth treatise in the first volume (The Value of Perceptions), is representative of the nature of discourse operative in this book. On the question of the validity of mental perceptions, Motahhari took issue with the "materialist" position that advanced the relative nature of such perceptions. As realities exist in the material world, Motahhari argued,[32] they are either conditional and relative (such as material realities) or permanent (such as motion). Insofar as "truth" is concerned, a term Motahhari understands as "the correspondence of concepts, as mental contents, with [outside] realities," they are permanent. "When we say 'Aristotle was a student of Plato in the fourth century B.C.,' " Motahhari stipulated,

we have expressed one of the changing relations of the constituent factors in nature. Because the apprenticeship of Aristotle with Plato is located in a specific piece of time (the fourth century B.C.). But this truth which has come to our mind is always and permanently valid, and corresponds with its reality. In other words it is always valid that Aristotle was a student of Plato in the fourth century B.C.[33]

Motahhari concludes from this premise that "the materialist" notions of the relativity of truth or the progressive notion of human mental perceptions are quintessentially wrong. Such perceptions are either true (that is, they correspond to outside realities) or false (that is, they do not have such a correspondence). No mere passage of time renders a false true or a true false. Experimental sciences, like medicine, are, of course, not based on absolute certitude simply because they operate within the realm of verifiable experiences. But mathematics and philosophy are sciences of certitude. Motahhari then proceeds to refute, point by point, every position on the relativity of truth as argued by "the materialists."[34]

What Motahhari achieves in such discussions in *The Principles of Philosophy and the Realistic Method* is the active operation of a level of discourse that could be read with a degree of seriousness by Tehran intellectuals not only in the 1950s, when they were originally produced, but also in the 1960s and 1970s, when they would have had a larger urban constituency. But beyond their targeted audience, these footnotes were equally compelling among the seminarian students who were becoming increasingly susceptible to Marxist and materialist ideas. Whether or not Tabataba'i and Motahhari were actually able to convince "the materialists" of the falseness of their ideas, the mere publication of this book, and the mere philosophically engaged language it contained, made a successful case for the viability of the Islamic discourse not only in philosophical and intellectual but, indeed, in political and ideological domains. The hidden agenda of the text is thus more ideological than philosophical, more polemical than scholastic. But the ideological manipulations of genuine philosophical issues were directed primarily against the more important political mandate of combating the increasing appeal of Marxism throughout the 1940s. The confrontations with Marxism itself, however, had a dual edge. Attacking an atheist ideology that denied, ipso facto, the very metaphysical foundations of Islam need not have any more reason than just that. But that secular ideology had the equally troubling potentiality, massively materialized in the 1940s, of substituting Shi'ism as the chief ideology of revolt against the status quo. Robbing militant Shi'ism of both its metaphysical claim to truth and its ideological claim to political mobilization was a challenge of Marxism that Motahhari could not have left unattended.

Motahhari and Shariʿati

Motahhari's attention to (Islamic) philosophical issues as the most serious weapon against his (secular) ideological opponents is in sharp contrast to Shariʿati's refusal to grant any contemporary significance to such issues, and to the fact that he harbored a deep disdain for any such language. This particular difference exemplifies a more crucial issue. The difference of opinion, if not outright hostility, between Shariʿati and Motahhari has long been noticed by students of these two ideologues.[35] In the Spring of 1983 this conflict was widely publicized inside postrevolutionary Iran when the nature of their hostility was debated in a number of books and articles.[36] The former was characterized as an "antitraditional" innovator, and the latter as an advocate of "traditional Islam." Shariʿati's supporters have vehemently denied the validity of such assertions.[37] Defending the cause of "democracy" is no indication that Shariʿati was "Westoxicated" or that he was an instrument of foreigners working against "traditional Islam." While his detractors try to identify him as an essentially Marxist revolutionary, an agent of foreigners, an instrument of freemasonry, etc., his supporters point out the similarities of his ideas to Motahhari's and to those of other religious ideologues. Those who oppose Shariʿati have tried to turn Motahhari into a "traditionalist" who opposed Shariʿati and detected the leftist, or "Westoxicated," underpinning of his ideas. On the other hand, they seek to portray an essentially "traditionalist" picture of Motahhari, closer to the Holy Text and the Prophetic tradition.

The affinity and continuity of Shariʿati's and Motahhari's ideas are self-evident. Their mutual rivalry and hostility, to the degree that they were actual and evident, cannot in any way detract from their ideological affinity. What Shariʿati achieved in revolutionizing the principal doctrinal and symbolic registers of Islam, Motahhari advanced further into the diverse dimensions of Islamic collective consciousness. While the hostility and rivalry between these two great revolutionaries, to the degree that they can be ascertained, can be the subject of historical curiosity and investigation, it is their ideological affinity and continuity that have been more instrumental for the outcome of the Revolution. They may, indeed, have had personal rivalries and animosities. Their ideas may have occasionally appeared as if issued from two diverse political worldviews. But in their respective contributions to the making of "the Islamic Ideology," they are part and parcel of the same revolutionary enterprise.

Stories of the Virtuous

Motahhari attended his indispensable share of making "the Islamic Ideology" possible with creative imagination and single-minded determination.

Nothing, from Islamic philosophy to didactic anecdotes about the Muslim saints, would be spared in this massive orchestration of rhetoric and mythology for the cause of "the Islamic Ideology." In 1960 Motahhari turned his attention to the wealth of stories and anecdotes from the prophetic traditions and other such canonical sources. The immediate impact of these stories was to resuscitate the collective Islamic memory, particularly among the youth.[38] Motahhari's stated purpose in collecting and paraphrasing these stories in a simple language was "to guide, advise, and cleanse the public ethic."[39] The idea of collecting such an anthology of ethical and didactic stories from the Shi'i canonical sources germinated in a meeting of the editorial board of *Enteshar* publishing house,[40] of which Motahhari was a member. The existence of such bona fide but ad hoc organizations that sought to propagate a widespread collective Islamic consciousness can be evaluated only in retrospect. A feeling of grave danger in the face of the engulfing secularism prompted such Islamic organizations to do whatever possible to "save" the public morality.

Motahhari had deliberately intended this collection of ethical anecdotes for the general public.[41] He maintained that while general corruption usually begins with the elite, public reform and ethical cleansing emanated from the masses and reached into the elite. By targeting his audience among the general public, Motahhari wished to educate the intellectual elite as well. With Shari'ati in his voice, he once remarked:

This is a wrong notion held by a number of reformists who, whenever they decide to rectify a problem, target the elite of every social group. . . . Experience has shown that such endeavors . . . are more pretentious propaganda and demogoguery than having a true reformist effect.[42]

For Motahhari public virtues were extensions of the public perception of common religious ethics. Private virtues, that is, matters of personal piety, increasingly lost their raison d'être in his revolutionary agenda. Private virtues—such as ascetic exercises, mystical experiences, or intellectual achievements—were limited to those happy few who knew not the use of arms, or perhaps could not care less for matters of public piety—for them a grave contradiction in terms. But publicly staged virtuosities, particularly when given the proper revolutionary twist, ipso facto, condemned the state-sponsored immoralities, as it were, and anticipated, indeed demanded, a radical response to them. Motahhari's new narration of old stories reached, beyond everything else, for politically active and ideologically alert public participation of the otherwise latent Islamic virtues celebrated in these stories.

In his Introduction to this collection of stories, Motahhari refers to a crucial factor in his writing agenda. He had turned to collecting, translating, and publishing these stories after he had completed the lengthy process of writing commentaries on Allamah Tabataba'i's *Principles of Philosophy and the Realistic Method*. Many had apparently objected to Motahhari's choice of collecting stories after that impressive output. They had considered the collection of these stories a trivial task for a man of his intellectual stature. Motahhari severely admonished such attitudes, defended the cause of writing something that is useful to the public, and considered the intellectual snobbery of his critics as a kind of "social disease."[43] He flatly rejected scholarly interests in obscure matters as useless intellectualism and favored such writings that helped the public at large.

The success of this collection of stories in reaching a wide audience is attested to by the fact that before Motahhari could publish the second volume in 1964, the first volume had already been through its second edition.[44] Motahhari himself gives the following figures in support of the popularity of the two volumes. The second volume was originally published in 10,000 copies, an unusually high number for that time. The first volume had been published in 5,000 copies in its second edition in 1963. Presumably the first edition was also 5,000 in 1960. By 1986 the two volumes had been through seven editions. The seventh edition was published in 1986 in 25,000 copies.[45]

All these numbers ought to be multiplied by at least two because publishers at the time had a propensity for printing more than they actually stated officially, for obvious evasions of the royalty fee. If we consider that many of these volumes were read by more than one person and that many were used by public libraries, mosques, Hosseyniyyehs, and Muslim student associations in colleges and high schools, we have a glimpse of the range of audience that Motahhari could reach through these and similar volumes. But the success and popularity of these stories went beyond the written word. During the month of Ramadan in 1963, these stories began to be broadcast on the National Radio.[46] That they were broadcast during a sacred period when religious consciousness was particularly heightened and when millions of Iranians were glued to their radios in the early hours of the dawn or at dusk immediately transplanted their ethical content into a common lore.

The publication and subsequent broadcast of these stories was an extremely clever enterprise that literally brought home the immediate and long-term impact of Motahhari's ideological discourse. With these stories, Motahhari had effectively surpassed a number of barriers. The originals of these stories were hidden and scattered throughout the canonical texts of the Shi'i sources which are, by and large, in Arabic. Both the Arabic language and the technical apparatus of the canonical texts had rendered them inaccessible to the general public. By extracting them from these sources and translating and paraphrasing them into a simple and readable Persian, Motahhari had immediately reached a wide audience beyond the technical limitations of the Arabic originals. The narrative simplicity, the short and concise context, and the anecdotal discourse of these stories not only rendered them easily comprehensible but also turned them into compelling components of a kind of common folklore. To be sure, these stories were not among the common mythological repertoire of the public. They were, on the whole, the exclusive references of the Shiʿi jurists. However, the more or less familiar character of their narrative, as well as the recurrent appearance of Muhammad, Ali, and other Shiʿi hagiographical figures in them, rendered these simple stories easily accessible to the wider audience. The public broadcasting of these stories on the National Radio, not to mention the even more effective forum of local preachers in every neighborhood, effectively surpassed the literacy barrier and reached an audience beyond the urban literates and deep and far into the Iranian illiterate peasantry. Given the success and popularity of this mode of discourse, it is not difficult to understand why Motahhari had wished, but was unable, to continue these two volumes.[47]

It would be futile to search these stories for concealed clues towards a hidden ideological message or a political agenda. On the whole, they celebrate the virtues of learning,[48] patience,[49] magnanimity,[50] love of one's neighbor,[51] humility,[52] hard work,[53] foresight,[54] benevolence,[55] justice,[56] etc. There does not seem to be any rhyme or reason behind the selection of these stories. Their collective impact, particularly in view of their massive audience, was in the general resuscitation of the Muslim collective consciousness. By sharing these stories, Motahhari's audience, literate and illiterate, urbane and peasant, religiously musical or mute, participated in a carefully reconstructed collective memory. The familiar names of the Qur-'anic prophets and the Shiʿi Imams, as well as the sacred memory of such places as Mecca, Medina, and Kufa, created an atmosphere of comfort and trust. The virtues that were thus celebrated in these stories were reminiscent of a mythical utopia somewhere in the imaginary Shiʿi history. These virtues, identified with Shiʿi Islam and with the sacred figures of its supreme authorities, moved common Muslims beyond their tangible miseries and gave them a sense of honorable self-assurance about their being in time and history. There is also a melodramatic undertone in relating these stories: a nostalgia for public virtues that once presumably held the Muslim community together. The subtextual assumption that these public virtues were now contaminated yearned for a renewal of moral rectitude. These were, of course, all tacit and unspoken and perhaps precisely in that aspect compelling and convincing.

Reconsidering Supreme Religious Authority

No matter how central the propagation of these stories was for the resuscitation of a compelling collective consciousness, still the more seminal issue of supreme religious authority was at the heart of contemporary Shiʿi self-understanding. The borderline of that religious authority with the political is where Motahhari's generation of Muslim ideologues rests its case. When Ayatollah Borujerdi died in March 1961, an immediate gap was felt in Qom as to who was to succeed this supreme juridical figure in the Shiʿi community, and, perhaps more important, how his comprehensive authority was to be legitimated. By late 1962 the intellectual and political implications of this question had caused a group of Shiʿi clerics to address some enduring questions of leadership in the Shiʿi community. Four of the seven concerned clerics who addressed this issue were among the chief ideologues of the future Islamic Revolution in Iran: Morteza Motahhari, Sayyid Mahmud Taleqani, Allamah Tabataba'i, and the only nonclerical member of the group, Mehdi Bazargan. The ideological coming together of these four major ideologues of the Islamic Revolution in one volume some seventeen years before the 1979 Revolution is perhaps the most emphatic indication of their collective ideological affinity. This ideological affinity cannot be overinterpreted. Yet the fact that these seminal ideologues of the Revolution, years before their historical reemergence as leaders of the movement, had been occasioned to address the most serious question facing the Shiʿi community, that is, that of the supreme authority, is in itself a crucial premonition of the shape and posture of events to follow.

In an Introduction written to this collection of essays, in the preparation and publication of which Motahhari was instrumental, the significance of choosing a "source of exemplary conduct," or *marjaʿ-e taqlid*, was particularly emphasized. Between Spring 1961 and Autumn 1962, numerous sessions of "the Islamic Societies" were devoted to examining the issue of supreme religious authority, or *marjaʿiyyat*, in Shiʿism. These "Islamic Societies," which were very active during the few decades before the 1979 Revolution, and the significance of which in the course of the Islamic Revolution still remains to be examined, were scattered throughout Iranian cities. Formed chiefly by young urban professionals (physicians, lawyers, and engineers) and students, these Societies were instrumental in keeping the collective Islamic consciousness alive and responsive to contemporary problems. In this particular instance, they were the principal forces behind an unprecedented collective effort on the part of some key figures in the Qom and Tehran religious establishments to address the essentials of the supreme religious authority.

The death of Ayatollah Borujerdi who, despite his apolitical disposition, had, for years, commanded the loyal obedience of the Shiʿi followers, created an occasion to reconsider the entire notion of supreme authority in Shi'ism. As it was stated explicitly in the Introduction to this collection of essays, the implications of who was to succeed Ayatollah Borujerdi and how his authority was to be legitimated went beyond the mere juridical and doctrinal mandates of safeguarding the moral texture of the Shi'i community.[57] In addition to personal religious obligations, "the social aspect, both religious and political," it was argued, "of marja'iyyat has very important [implications] for the country."[58] It is quite evident from the subtextual argument of this collection of essays that the political limitations Ayatollah Borujerdi had imposed, by virtue of his apolitical disposition, on the position of marja'iyyat were being thoroughly reconsidered. The contemporary necessity to expand the juridical and political boundaries of marja'iyyat, as an institutional foundation for historical Shi'ism, was reproblematized in the following terms:

The question of marja'iyyat ("supreme religious authority") and taqlid ("following the exemplary conduct of a religious authority") . . . is not an established, simple, and undisputed [issue] which like saying one's prayers or paying one's alms can have emphatic textual [sources], without any doubt or disputation, accepted and practiced by all Muslims. Of course, and without a doubt, it [like a tree] has a Qur'anic root, and it has been implanted and attended to by the [Twelve] Infallible Imams, peace be upon them. But in time it has been nourished in the course of the development of the Muslim community, according to the historical needs and necessities of the people. It has thus been persistently developed and expanded until it has reached its present [condition]. [Human] reason and [historical] action have not been inconsequential in its development. From now on, too, through our deeds and thoughts, and according to the problems and difficulties of the day, and with the permission of God, it has to grow taller and bigger branches and leaves, giving ever fresher fruits.[59]

The organizers of this series of published lectures made sure to emphasize that the question of "supreme authority" or "exemplary conduct" was not exclusive to Shi'ism. They pointed out that all "civilized people"[60] in the modern world followed the authority or the exemplary conduct of leading figures in political, commercial, medical, scientific, technical, and other such fields.[61] To support this line of argument further, the organizers of these lectures had hoped to include a paper on "Clericalism (Ruhaniyyat) and Supreme Religious Authority (Marja'iyyat) in Other Religions,"[62] that is, principally in Judaism and Christianity. This particular paper, however, was not finally prepared, and the proceedings were published without such a comparative reference. That its inclusion in this collection was even considered is a clear indication that in the universe of discourse adopted by these authors, the non-Shi'i (Islamic), principally "Western," references were high on their historical and analytical agenda.

Ejtehad *in Islam*

Some three weeks after the death of Ayatollah Borujerdi, Morteza Motahhari delivered a lecture on Friday, 21 April 1961, at the Monthly Religious
Society, in which he addressed the then-current issue of *ejtehad* and *taqlid*.
This speech was subsequently published in *Maktab-e Tashayyoʿ*, a journal
devoted entirely to religious matters. A final draft of this lecture appeared
in the volume published on the occasion of Ayatollah Borujerdi's death,
addressing, as it did, the central question of supreme religious authority in
the Shiʿi community. Motahhari concluded from the public grief that followed Ayatollah Borujerdi's death that religion is quintessential to people
and that "it had to be used properly."[63] In this lecture Motahhari distinguishes the practice of *ejtehad* in Shiʿism from that in Sunnism and asserts
that neither *qiyas* ("analological reasoning") nor *ejtehad-e beh ra'i* ("personal assertion of juridical opinion in contradistinction to those founded
on the Holy Qur'an and the Prophetic traditions"), which were specific
features of Sunni law, are acceptable in Shiʿi jurisprudence. But while the
Sunnis declared the gates of *ejtehad* closed and limited Islamic law to the
four specific orthodox lines of the Hanafi, Shafiʿi, Maliki, and Hanbali
schools, in Shiʿism *ejtehad*, with a significant difference in its implications,
has continued to the present day. In Shiʿism *ejtehad* was not meant to
initiate new laws but to qualify a jurist to *extrapolate* juridical injunctions
from the Qur'an and the traditions. Thus by virtue of having mastered the
necessary technical prerequisite of issuing a juridical edict according to the
specifics of the Qur'an and the Hadith, a jurist can claim to have reached
the status of *ejtehad*.

The Usuli-Akhbari Controversy

Motahhari then launches a severe attack against the theory and practice of
"literalism" (Akhbari) in Shiʿi jurisprudence. This movement, which he
identifies primarily with a certain Molla Amin Astarabadi, had advocated a
literal adherence to the letter of the prophetic and Imami traditions and
had denied the legitimacy of any juridical extrapolation from the canonical
sources. Motahhari reports that when in 1945 he went to visit Ayatollah
Borujerdi in Borujerd he remembers him as having attributed the origin of
the Akhbari movement in Shiʿi jurisprudence to the rise of the ideas of
sense perception *(falsafeh-ye hessi)* in Europe. Motahhari regrets that Ayatollah Borujerdi never pursued this line of argument any further and asserts
that he himself has never seen a source supporting this idea. Yet still he
wishes to give credence to this statement which, after all, had been issued
by the highest juridical authority in the Shiʿi community. Fortunately,

Motahhari asserts, the advocates of the primacy of intellect in juridical extrapolation, the Usulis, succeeded over the Akhbaris through the intellectual brilliance of such legendary jurists as Aqa Vahid Behbahani and Shaykh Morteza Ansari. He complains, however, that although the Akhbari school as a movement has been defeated, its traits are still present in anti-intellectual and dogmatic *(jomud)* tendencies in ethical and social matters.[64] He goes into great detail in refuting and, in fact, ridiculing the strict dogmatism of the Akhbari and, conversely, praises the Usulis as the great champions of attending to the spirit of juridical mandates as received from the Twelve Shi'i Infallibles.

Motahhari is equally critical of blindly following a religious leader, *taqlid*, without properly considering the responsibilities of choosing a righteous leader to follow.[65] He then resorts to a tradition attributed to Imam Ja'far al-Sadiq, according to which obedience is due only to a jurist who "has control over his carnal soul, safeguards his faith, opposes his whims, and obeys the commandments of his God. As for the masses, they are to obey him."[66]

Having established a doctrinal mandate for the necessity of *ejtehad,* and the inevitability of *taqlid,* Motahhari then proceeds to refute, based on a traditional juridical edict, the followership of a deceased religious authority and the necessity of choosing a living exemplary model to emulate.[67] This is necessary because the changing conditions of the world demand a living tradition and its supreme figures of authority. Motahhari extends this juridical doctrine to assert that "if a living *Mojtahed* does not respond to modern problems, what is the difference between following a living and a dead [religious authority]?"[68] Thus the essential feature and primary characteristic of a living religious authority is to attend the historical exegencies of his time. "Essentially," Motahhari emphasized, "the secret of *ejtehad* is to correspond general commandments with new problems as well as with the changing events.[69] He stipulates such extrajuridical factors as "world-view" and "being involved in events of life"[70] as pertinent factors in identifying a bona fide supreme jurist. A jurist who "does not believe in the progress and [gradual] completion of life"[71] cannot be a supreme leader of the Shi'i community.

Motahhari then proceeds to reiterate a revolutionary development in Shi'i law. Attributing the source of this idea to Hajj Shaykh Abdolkarim Ha'eri Yazdi, the supreme juridical leader before Ayatollah Borujerdi, Motahhari suggests that the position of "the source of imitation" ought to be divided into subcategories and that people should follow different authorities in matters of rituals, transactions, and politics.[72] He compares such specializations in juridical learnings to medicine where similar compartmentalization of medical authority has taken place. By injecting the subcategory of "politics" among juridical specializations, an exclusive heading not traditionally found in juridical texts, he advances the cause of establishing a bona fide supreme authority for politically conscious clerics who may not necessarily have a predilection for doctrinal and ritual minutiae.

What Motahhari is striving for here is a fundamental repoliticization of the position of *marja'-e taqlid*. He, as did every other clerical political activist, realized the strategic significance of the position of *marja'-e taqlid*. He knew what a powerful position this would be for possible revolutionary mobilization had the right man been located in that position. By insisting on its necessity, by arguing for the necessity of the masses to follow him, by stipulating the prerequisite of concern with the modern world, and by suggesting a politically conscious individual, Motahhari sought to pave the way for the deep and thorough repoliticization of this supreme juridical position of authority in the Shi'i community.

To be sure, Motahhari argues his case through the necessity of advancing the cause of juridical sciences and the fact that further advancements in these fields require more intense specializations. But the underlying political significance of this suggestion is quite evident here in the early 1960s. The apolitical nature of Ayatollah Borujerdi's tenure as the *marja'-e taqlid* had considerably frustrated the political urges of clerical activists. Now, after his death, the purpose of this collective exercise was to prevent the ascendancy of yet another apolitical supreme figure. Equally necessary, Motahhari insisted, is the cooperation among various experts in such subfields.[73] This cooperation, ipso facto, legitimates all subfields of juridical authority, including its political dimension, and grants them independent claims on the obedience of the Shi'i followers. Should that division of clerical authority actually materialize, and should every subcategory have an independent claim on the total obedience of the followers, the politically minded jurists, at Motahhari's persuasion, would autonomously engage in matters of political concern without any possible conflict of jurisdiction with apolitical jurists and without necessarily having any juridical qualifications.

The Significance of Ayatollah Borujerdi

Motahhari approached the same objective from yet another angle. In discussing the juridical significance of Ayatollah Borujerdi in the history of Shi'i jurisprudence, he severely criticized the prevalence of the narrow concentration on certain numbers of legal texts. Contemporary jurists, Motahhari contended, had altogether abandoned the encyclopedic approach they once had towards a number of related disciplines, including Qur'anic commentaries, Arabic literature, or biographies of great Muslims. In recent history, jurists had increasingly narrowed their exclusive attention on the minutiae of juridical speculation without the slightest attention to even the actual practicality of their theoretical stipulations.[74] In distinguish-

ing Ayatollah Borujerdi's juridical character from such impractical speculations, Motahhari, in effect, questioned their relevance and significance in
the modern world.

Contrary to such narrow and idle concentration on obscure juridical
circumstances, Motahhari recalled the hermeneutic explications of Ayatollah Borujerdi in unpacking the actual historical circumstances of a specific
case. Through such explications, he asserted, the juridical judgments of
Shiʿi Imams assumed entirely different contextual meanings.[75] Other than
such actual historical circumstances, juridical issues lose their legitimate
claims on their contemporary constituencies.

Islamic Unity and Integrity

That contemporary constitutency was not limited to the Shiʿi world. Thus
Motahhari praised Ayatollah Borujerdi for his sustained efforts in bridging
the historical and doctrinal gap between the Sunnis and the Shiʿis. Exasper-
ating these sectarian differences, he recollected Ayatollah Borujerdi as having thought, were vicious political schemes of local and colonial powers.[76]
Closer ties with the Sunni world, which constitutes the majority of Muslims, would not only realize the ideal of a unified Islamic society but would
also dispel a variety of misconceptions that existed about Shiʿism, making
its considerable contributions to Islamic sciences more accessible to non-
Shiʿis. Here Motahhari praised in particular the efforts of Ayatollah Borujerdi in cooperation with the Egyptian grand Muftis Shaykh Abd al-Majid
Salim and then Shaykh Mahmud Shaltut in the institutional context of *Dar
al-Taqrib bayn al-Madhahib al-Islamiyyah* (The Institute for Reconciliation
among the Islamic Sects). Established to advance the cause of interdenomi-
national reconciliations among Muslim sects, this institute was instrumental in achieving certain limited objectives in that direction, including the
official recognition of Shiʿism by Shaykh Shaltut as a bona fide Islamic
"School of Jurisprudence" *(madhhab)*.

Motahhari also praised Ayatollah Borujerdi for his efforts in propagating Islam in Europe and the United States, which he, speaking the deepest
layer of his subconscious, refers to as "the civilized countries."[77] He hap-
pily reported that Ayatollah Borujerdi had sent Shiʿi proselytizers to Germany and the United States. He was about to send a group to England
when he passed away. "Should the innate truths of Islam be revealed to the
truth-seeking, inquisitive, and least prejudiced minds of Europeans," Motahhari conjectured, "they would accept this righteous faith."[78] Muslims
should learn from Christians who, for centuries, have been engaged in
actively propagating their faith.

Ayatollah Borujerdi was equally concerned with the active advancement
of modern sciences and their coordination with religious studies. Motah-

hari approvingly reports that Ayatollah Borujerdi contributed from religious taxes to build modern schools.[79] Motahhari was particularly cognizant of the period when high- and low-ranking clericals were deeply suspicious
and resentful of these modern schools. Disturbed by their increasing secularization, he appreciated the effort of "Islamicizing" them. Making financial contributions to these schools was a crucial and active way of reaching
for that objective.

Ayatollah Borujerdi was also attentive to a crucial question of primary
concern to Motahhari. Controlling and centralizing the financial resources
of the clerical establishment was a substantive achievement of Ayatollah
Borujerdi. He had established a central accounting system in Qom whereby
the collection and distribution of *Sahm-e Imam* from all over the country
was controlled. This system, Motahhari testified, put a stop to much confusion and abuse in the collection and expenditure of religious taxes.[80]
Motahhari was particularly enthusiastic about this organizational reform
in the financial aspects of the juridical system.

Those characteristics that Motahhari praised in Ayatollah Borujerdi
were all reflections of his own primary concerns with the Shi'i religious
establishment. Such critical issues as having wide-ranging religious and
social concerns (instead of being narrow-mindedly preoccupied with obscure juridical hypothesis), seeking to advance the cause of Islamic unification (instead of being trapped in sectarian infighting), propagating Islam in
"The West" (instead of being propagated by Christian or, even worse,
secular European ideologies), advancing the cause of modern education
(instead of being branded as reactionary and anti-intellectual), and ultimately organizing the financial backbone of the clerical class (instead of
wasting and mismanaging this great source of independence from governments) were all among the primary concerns of Motahhari as a leading
ideologue of the Islamic cause. By attributing these endeavors and concerns
to the highest-ranking religious authority in recent Shi'i memory, Motahhari wished to give them the aura of legitimacy and urgency that he thought
they deserved. These concerns, addressed and considered as early as the
early 1960s, clearly indicate that the Shi'i clerical establishment had a deep
and far-reaching agenda of action in order to confront the pressing problems that faced them. Motahhari's physical presence in Tehran at this time
(he wrote his short piece on Ayatollah Borujerdi on 3 April 1961, when he
was teaching at Marvi School in Tehran) gave him a considerable advantage in having a clear and realistic grasp of the growing secular threat that
faced him and his clerical cohorts. From his vantage point, particularly
after he began teaching at Tehran University, he could monitor and try to
control the massive influx of "Western" ideas and assumptions that, as
Motahhari saw them, were quintessentially inimical to Islam and to the
Shi'i clerical establishment.

The Problem with the Clerical Order

As is evident in his assessment of the late Ayatollah Borujerdi, Motahhari clearly recognized that there are reforms and adjustments in the received Islamic traditions that are not initiated directly by the formal clerical order. In one of his contributions to the volume published upon Ayatollah Borujerdi's death, Motahhari emphasized that in fulfilling its historical obligations, the clerical order either had to institute changes on its own accord or else coordinate *(ham-ahangi)* its self-understanding in terms of contemporary historical developments.[81] As he saw it, institutional problems with the clerical order had been noted more than a decade before Ayatollah Borujerdi's death. In his assessment of these persisting problems, he harshly criticized the clerical establishment and its neglect of serious contemporary issues.

The primary cause of malfunction in the clerical order, as Motahhari and his fellow activists saw it, was the way *Sahm-e Imam* was used. In order to show how this had affected the larger clerical system, Motahhari argued that, contrary to the Platonic and Farabian position, ideal societies ought to be organized around correct institutional bases, not mere individual virtues.[82] If ideal societies are organized around principles and institutions that safeguard and maintain a virtuous government, the benevolence of particular leaders becomes merely tangential. Concentrating more specifically on the clerical order, as a community of learned men, Motahhari draws a picture-perfect portrait of seminarian virtues and societies. Compared with modern educational systems, the seminaries are founded on no other principle but scholastic learning and moral virtues. All the successive stages of becoming an *alem* ("a learned religious leader") are thus based on virtue and learning, except the last phase of actually becoming a *marja'-e taqlid* ("an exemplary model of conduct") where, because of such considerations as *Sahm-e Imam*, sometimes all "the [previous] arrangements are disregarded and the law of choosing the most virtuous is no longer enforced."[83]

Motahhari also noted some essential problems in the seminary system. There were no entrance examinations, so everyone, regardless of his intellectual capabilities, was admitted into the ranks of the clerics. Nor were the clerical students guided into disciplines that matched their respective dispositions. All the related disciplines were effectively abandoned for a very narrow concentration on strictly juridical studies. Motahhari also criticized the clerical robe as becoming merely a distinguishing symbol that people wore without necessarily deserving it. On more substantial levels, although they studied Arabic grammar for years, the students still could not speak or write in Arabic. Finally, they were not taught enough logic; and their years of training in futile dialogic disputations made them insensitive to contemporary issues.[84]

But the most serious problem Motahhari wished to address was the question of finance, which had caused grave difficulties for the seminarian system. Motahhari opposed the notion of the clerics having a regular profession, just like anybody else, while they attended their religious training and social guidance.[85] Ideally he would have preferred that the expenditures for the clerical class be met by regular endowments and religious taxes. But, to his regret, half of these resources were misused by ill-fitted and undeserving clerics and the other half were appropriated by the state-controlled "Ministry of Religious Endowments."[86] Thus wasted, this considerable financial source could not be used effectively for financing the seminaries.

Sahm-e Imam is thus seen as the only crucial source of financial support for sustaining the clerical establishment. Motahhari was particularly emphatic about the fact that *Sahm-e Imam* (as part of *Khoms*) was given to religious authorities without the slightest hint of pressure or demand. Devout believers calculated their own religious taxes and delivered them to the religious authority of their choice. These taxes, "from small figures to one hundred thousand, to many hundred thousand Tumans,"[87] constituted the principal source of sustaining the Shi'i clerical establishment. While the budget of the Ministry of Endowment is calculated by the coldest rules of budgetary appropriation, *Sahm-e Imam* is given with utmost love, devotion, and humility.

But, and there is the rub, there has been a reciprocal relationship between receiving the highest portions of the total annual *Sahm-e Imam* and the assumption of the highest positions of authority among the clerics. The more money a high-ranking cleric received as *Sahm-e Imam,* the higher his status among his fellow clerics and, thus by implication, his authority in speaking for the religious establishment as a whole. Whereas in older times for every major or minor city there was a local cleric who received *Sahm-e Imam,* with the modern advancements in communications there emerged a national centralization in collecting such religious taxes, with a few prominent high-ranking clerics receiving money from all over the country.[88] The first person to have assumed such an authority was Mirza Muhammad Hasan Shirazi who used the power he thus collected to launch the famous Tobacco Revolt of 1891.

The most important virtue of having *Sahm-e Imam* as an independent source of income for the clerical order is that it makes the religious authorities independent of the political establishment.

Shi'i authorities do not receive their salary from the government. Their appointments and dismissals are not up to the state officials. That is why their independence is always preserved vis-à-vis governments. They are [in fact] a power next to the political power. They have occasionally posed grave difficulties for governments and kings.[89]

In the years to come this source of income would prove indispensable in the making of the Islamic Revolution.

Avam-Zadegi: *Vulgarization of Religious Authorities*

Despite the crucial advantage that the *Sahm-e Imam* has created for the clerical establishment, particularly in its relationship to the state, it has, at the same time, sustained a debilitating feature that is compromising the high-ranking religious authorities to the "taste and opinion of the masses." [90] "Most of the corruption which exists in the Shiʿi clerics stems from this very point." [91] Here, compared with the Egyptian (Sunni) religious authorities, the Iranian Shiʿi clerics had both an advantage and a disadvantage. The highest-ranking religious authority in Egypt, the head of al-Azhar University, was appointed by the president of the country; this, of course, considerably compromised his political authority. Yet, in his juridical opinions, the Mufti of al-Azhar was quite independent of popular pressures. But in Iran any indication of official governmental approval would guarantee a cleric's downfall. However, the political independence of the Iranian Shiʿi authorities, which has historically been the source of their relative freedom from governmental pressure, has been purchased with the exacting price, in Motahhari's estimation, of yielding to popular pressure in matters of taste and wisdom. [92]

Thus religious authorities (both Sunni and Shiʿi), as Motahhari saw them, were faced with a debilitating dilemma: They were either powerful vis-à-vis the governments yet lacked the freedom of opinion from their mass followers or else weak in front of political authorities and yet free to exercise their independent juridical judgment. The paradox rested on Motahhari's fundamental belief that

usually the masses of the people have faith and belief yet they are ignorant *(jahel)*, corrupt *(monhat)*, and unaware *(bi-khabar)*, and thus they oppose reform. But governments are usually intellectual [*sic*] but tyrannical and unjust. [93]

This unfortunate state of affairs, this reduction of the juridical judgment of the high-ranking clerics to the lowest possible denominator of their constituency, Motahhari chose to call *avam-zadegi*, literally "affliction with the [ignorant] masses." [94] This massive and institutionally guaranteed vulgarization of the religious establishment has rendered them incapable of assuming any "progressive" [95] role in leading the Iranian masses towards just and worthy causes. Such critical concerns as "the just distribution of wealth," "social justice," "universal education," and "national sovereignty," which are quintessentially Islamic, [96] have been ignored completely by religious authorities, Motahhari contended, because the masses were incapable of grasping their Islamic significance.

A poignant point of reference for Motahhari was when Ayatollah Ha'eri, the founder of Qom seminary in the early 1920s, had intended to include the study of European languages and modern sciences in the curriculum of the seminarian students. He had realized that this was necessary if the increasingly secularized young generation was "to be kept for Islam." But much to Ayatollah Ha'eri's dismay, and now to Motahhari's anger, "a group of [ignorant] people from the Tehran Bazaar" went to Qom and officially stated that "the money we give [you] as *Sahm-e Imam* is not for seminarians to learn the language of the infidels. Should this continue, we will not give you *Sahm-e Imam*."[97] Acutely aware of the necessity of reaching the younger generation and checking its increasing distance from Islam, Motahhari recollected such incidents with grave apprehension about the future of the religious establishment and its political, social, and cultural relevance. After Ayatollah Ha'eri, his successor Ayatollah Aqa Sayyid Abolhasan Isfahani refused to have anything to do with any modernization of the seminary curriculum. Because of such a state of affairs, "religious universities" had become "colleges of jurisprudence"; consequently, seminary centers became dead and archaic relics of merely antiquarian interests without the slightest attention to matters of contemporary relevance or significance.

The Necessity of Reform

Something had to be done to alter this sad and debilitating state of affairs. But the solution, as Motahhari saw it, was neither in having the clerical authorities take on mundane trades to make a living nor in having them subjugated to political authorities as governmental employees. "The road to reform," he suggested, "is [only] one thing: to give organization to the existing budget of the clerical order."[98] The existing process of collecting and spending *Sahm-e Imam* left much to be desired. The system Motahhari proposed consisted of the establishment of a "collective fund" to which all religious contributions would be made and from which, under the supervision of "first-ranking clerics," every religious authority would receive a sum "proportionate to the service he provides."[99] Thus the religious establishment would no longer receive the source of its daily sustenance directly from the people and would consequently achieve a certain degree of independence in its juridical judgments:

Should this be done, people would pay their [religious] taxes according to their faith and belief, and yet the rule and domination of the [ignorant] masses will cease, and the religious authorities will be released from their grip.[100]

Equally detrimental to a healthy state of clerical affairs has been the uncontrolled wealth of "certain high-ranking religious authorities,"[101] whom

Motahhari called "clerical look-alikes" and claimed had been "created by governments."[102] They always act on behalf of the powers that be and against the Muslims. He insisted that "cutting the roots of" such corruptions was necessary.[103]

Such guarded references are clear indications that by the early 1960s sharp divisions of loyalties and political alliances had existed in Qom and other religious centers. The Pahlavi state was obviously aware of the clerical power and planned to appropriate it into its internal mechanism of self-legitimation. The oppositional clerics, however, were critically conscious of, and deeply disturbed by, the ideological rift that such "governmental clerics" created. Taking advantage of a new epoch in the Shi'i religious establishment, Motahhari and his colleagues thus tried to give both financial and ideological independence to their rank. This attempt, however, had to be delivered in bona fide juridical language—and for the best benefit of the Muslim community—in order to give it the necessary aura of legitimacy.

In need of reform was also that group of low-ranking clerics who had made a business out of their regular sermons on religious occasions.[104] This group, too, needed to be organized and centrally trained, controlled, and financially secured by the clerical establishment itself. This was the crucial network of petit-clerics who reached deep into the Iranian urban and rural centers. As Motahhari saw and heard them, they were engaged chiefly in vulgarizing the tenets and practices of Shi'ism. They, too, had to be liberated from the "tyrannies of the ignorant masses" and given a "correct program" to propagate. These low-ranking clerics had direct and unmitigated access to the privacy of every household. Had Motahhari's suggested reforms been implemented, "the Islamic Ideology" would have had a network of mass communication infinitely more powerful and far-reaching than the sum total of Iranian national radio and television and the state-controlled newspapers together. Although most of these reforms were not to be implemented, the effective persuasiveness of "the Islamic Ideology" was such as to have recruited the active and unavoidable loyalties of the low-ranking clerics.

Pending the implementation of his proposals, Motahhari suggested that his clerical colleagues had to have jobs that would take a minimum of their time and, at the same time, give them that necessary independence from the (ignorant) masses to make them politically and socially responsive to current affairs. Probably having his own image in mind, Motahhari suggested that his colleagues should assume such independent positions in order to defend Islam "from a free front; and thus prepare the preliminaries of a fundamental reform"[105] that could have, as early as 1962, spelled a revolution for Motahhari, who chose to conclude his ideas of clerical reform with a clear warning to his fellow clerics:

Our great religious authorities should pay attention to the fact that the continuity of the clerics and the [very] existence of Islam in this country is contingent upon their assuming positions of leadership in [some] deep reforms which are nowadays necessary. Today they are standing in front of a half-awakened nation which is more and more coming to its senses. The expectations of this generation from the clerical authorities and from Islam are different from those of the previous generations. . . . If our religious authorities do not move quickly, free themselves from the grip of the [ignorant] masses, organize their forces, and intelligently take charge, a grave danger is posed against them by those so-called reformists who have no interest in religion. . . . Today, this nation is thirsty for reform . . . and tomorrow it would become even thirstier. This is a nation which feels backward compared to other nations and is in a hurry to catch up with them. At the same time, there are many who claim to be reformists, most of them with no interest in religion, and who are preying on the new and rising sentiments of this generation. If Islam and the religious authorities do not respond positively to the needs, demands, and rising expectations of this nation, it would turn to those new *qiblahs*.[106] Just think! Should the reforming fronts be occupied by such people, will the [very] existence of Islam and the religious authorities be endangered or not?![107]

To Think Islamic Thoughts: To Confront "The West"

Beyond the necessity of institutional reforms in the clerical establishment, Motahhari equally attended to the all-too-essential matter of re-Islamicizing the intellectual concerns of his generation. Late in April 1970, he delivered five lectures in Hosseyniyyeh Ershad on the occasion of commemorating the Pakistani Muslim thinker Allamah Mohammad Iqbal (1877–1938). In these lectures, later published under the title *Ehya'-e Tafakkor-e Islami (Revification of Islamic Thought)*, Motahhari seizes the opportunity to launch his harshest attacks on "The West," of which, at this—and indeed at any other time—he had only the most general, vague, mythological, and monolithic notion. "Iqbal who has been to Europe, and who has known Europe," Motahhari declares, "considers the future of Europe very ominous and dangerous."[108] Although there is a remarkable essentialist objectification of "The West" on Motahhari's part, so much so that he feels quite comfortable with such phrases as "Europe says,"[109] he still occasionally offers a moderating voice in the severe "anti-Westernism" of his intellectual contemporaries. This moderation, however, equally contributed to the objectification of "The West" as a monolithic phenomenon, something which stands out there and needs to be confronted. Echoing Iqbal's voice, once heard from both Al-e Ahmad and Shari'ati, too, Motahhari states:

If we only consider the intellectual and scientific aspects of Europe, no matter how close we get [to them] there is no danger for us, because science is science, and the

European science is the continuation of the Islamic science. European culture in terms of European science is the continuation of the Islamic culture.[110]

In such rare moments his more open perception of "The West" leads Motahhari to some severe criticism of the status quo through a sober comparison of the Islamic and "The Western" societies:

If we only criticize the European culture and civilization, and celebrate the Islamic culture ... and [say that] the people of the world should come and follow us, nothing will be achieved. Because if people of the world come and follow us, they will become like us: half-dead.[111]

Of particular importance, however, is Motahhari's principle frame of reference, his point of departure, which is always a monolithic, essentialist, and utterly undifferentiated conception of "The West." His attendance to every aspect of Islamic history and dogma has the explicit or implicit, but always subtextually present, points of reference, directions of address, to "The West." His reading of the Islamic intellectual heritage, the very cast of its language, is always, almost irresistibly, voiced in a tone that takes (the supremacy of) "The Western" point of departure for granted. The more diligently he condemns "The West" and "The Westernized," the more articulate his own paradoxical and negational admiration for and preoccupation with "The West" become.

Motahhari's references to Iqbal in this lecture and elsewhere have a tangential reason to them that ought to be noted. Because he had no direct knowledge of "The West," he always exaggerated the credibility of his secondary sources. Although in his 1953 introduction to Allamah Tabataba'i's *Principles of Philosophy and the Realistic Method*, Motahhari dismissed Iqbal's book on Islamic philosophy as "very minimal and insignificant,"[112] here in 1970 he gave the Pakistani thinker highly debatable credentials as an authority on "The Western" philosophy and culture, acclaiming him as "this informed, alert, and knowledgeable man."[113]

Another tangential reference that Motahhari makes at the very outset, without much relevance to Iqbal, is his belief that such eminent Iranian thinkers as his teacher Allamah Tabataba'i should be recognized and celebrated in their lifetime.[114] Although he does not articulate it in so many words, his unspoken point is that Allamah Tabataba'i was infinitely more important a figure than Iqbal and that the former should be appreciated while still alive. As a former student of Tabataba'i, Motahhari always spoke very fondly and with utmost dignity about his teacher and his works. "I can claim," he declared, "that this [Qur'anic] commentary [that is, Allamah Tabataba'i's *al-Mizan*] ... is the best commentary among both the Sunnis and the Shi'is from early Islamic history to the present time."[115] Such laudatory statements, among other indications, reveal the close level of affiliation that existed between Motahhari and Tabataba'i. The focal point of this affiliation was, of course, their cooperation on the seminal anti-Marxist treatise, *Principles of Philosophy and the Realistic Method*. From this anti-Marxist point of concurrence to a more radical political agenda that would have included Motahhari's more ambitious dreams, there was a short distance Allamah Tabataba'i could not but have covered.

The significance of both Allamah Tabataba'i and Iqbal was to be seen in their successful attempt to provide an alternative Islamic discourse to the rising secular language that by-passed religion in its appeal to a wide constituency. To think Islamic thought, to confront "The West" on its own terms, and to pave the way for a revolutionary encounter with the local agents of "Westernization" were among the chief attractions of the Pakistani reformer. That Iqbal himself looked back at Islamic doctrinal history with poorly adjusted post-Nietzchean eyesight never crossed Motahhari's mind.

Karbala and Islam Remembered

When Motahhari delivered his lectures on Iqbal, the occasion coincided with *Arba'in*, the anniversary of the fortieth day after the martyrdom of Imam al-Husayn, the supreme Shi'i martyr, who was killed in 688 C.E. in Karbala. Motahhari used this occasion to reconstruct and develop some major themes in the Karbala event that he emphasized in the course of this lecture. He, in fact, sounds and reads very much like Ali Shari'ati in their mutual attempt to revive the sense of martyrdom latent in the Karbala event:

[We cannot] separate ourselves from the [Karbala] martyrs when the right moment comes, and yet utter an impossibility: *peace be upon thee O father of Abdullah* [Husayn]! *If we could only be with thee, what great salvation we would have incurred!* Husayn ibn Ali, peace be upon him, says, "Karbala is not only in one day, it always is." [116]

When Motahhari delivered this speech in 1970, almost a decade before the Revolution, it might have appeared as a mere repetition of the obvious. Imam al-Husayn and his tragic martyrdom in Karbala have always been a symbolically charged moment in the Shi'i collective memory. What makes the reference poignantly significant is the actual political context of its delivery. Besieged on two opposing fronts—one the tyrannical monarchy and its "Westernization" agenda, the other the secular intelligentsia and their revolutionary claims on the political loyalties of the youth—Motahhari, among other ideologues of "the Islamic Ideology," firmly believed in his historical responsibility to rescue "Islam" from contemporary negligence—or even irrelevance. By attending to the pressing problems of contemporary politics, European philosophy, issues of women's liberation, and the exigencies of the highly technological age, Motahhari wished to keep "Islam" relevant, alert, and responsive to the most compelling problems of the time. Politics, more than any other issue, and revolutionary ideology, more than any other political imperative, were the primary vistas of this revitalization if Islam were to remain religiously, or otherwise, relevant.

To update Islam with the revolutionary and rationalistic spirit of the age, Motahhari had to take one step further. He had to rid Islam of all apparent signs of misery and passivity. For this reason, he severely admonished his audience for chanting, commiserating, and self-flagellating during the Arba'in.[117] He went so far as to challenge the authenticity of the canonical reports that Imam al-Husayn's household actually came to Karbala on the occasion of his martyrdom.[118]

In principle, Motahhari opposed any mode of identification with the Karbala event that did not simultaneously and immediately create a sense of heroism, sacrifice, and activist commitment to take one's destiny in one's own hands. Here he agreed with Jabir ibn Abdullah al-Ansari, a friend of Imam al-Husayn, who was not killed in Karbala: Those who were not killed in Karbala in person are still martyrs if they truly believe in the martyred Imam and follow his example in valor, sacrifice, and struggle for justice. This would amount to their actually having fought, Motahhari paraphrased al-Ansari as having said, alongside and been martyred with Imam al-Husayn.[119] This is a remarkable extension of the reconstructed sacred history into the contemporary realities of Motahhari's time. The ideal and idyllic state of having fought alongside Imam al-Husayn is historically progressed and symbolically identified, on a one-to-one basis, with fighting for just causes today or any other day. Finding a just cause to fight for, in the immediacy of their historical concerns, could very well be left to people's imagination.

This massive historical transfusion was necessary because, in propagating his "Islamic Ideology," Motahhari had to reconstruct, ipso facto, Islamic history. In this reconstruction, this remembrance of things past as things present, there was no logical or chronological limitation. Even, or perhaps particularly, early Islamic history had to be thus reconstituted. There is no idyllic state to go back to in history; that would be physically impossible. Instead, there are idyllic ideological states, paradigmatic frames of revolutionary reference, and mythologized golden ages to be forged and recaptured:

If we Muslims wish to correct our way of thinking, we have to refer back to our past and to our historical records. The reason is that the origin of these defections might very well be in the past. Of course [these defections] are different [in terms of their historical origin]. Some may be three, four, five, or some even thirteen centuries old. That is to say, they might have appeared from the second Islamic century.[120]

This is a gradual build-up towards the "true Islam." By going directly to the sacred texts and sanctified events and thus effectively by-passing the functional forces of their historically mandated and operative hermeneutic circles, Motahhari, like other ideologues of the Islamic Revolution, construes a "true Islam" that does not yet exist in his time and thus, by implication, ought to be attained. To attain this goal, Islam has to be redefined: "Today we often observe," he insisted, "that conceptions and understandings we have from Islam are not capable of giving life and creating livelihood. Thus necessarily we have to revise these conceptions and understandings."[121] Motahhari leaves no margin for error and spells out precisely what constitutes his redefinition of Islam. Based on a fresh and direct reading of the Qur'an, the Prophetic and the Imamite traditions, he asserts that Islam is "a religion of action."[122] Here he insisted on giving primacy to (political) action over merely metaphysical matters and quiet piety. This primacy of action is diametrically opposed, he insists, to the notion of Islam that preexisted in his time and that he wished to oppose and change:

Islam exists [these are Motahhari's words, but they could very well have been Shari'ati's], but a useless and ineffective Islam. An Islam which can no longer warm, move, or stir; an Islam which can no longer give force, can no longer give perception. Instead, it is like a dead and infested tree which is standing, but lifeless and inanimate. Even if it has leaves, they are stale, miserable and sorrowful.[123]

Historical Islam has experienced a persistent distortion of its innate activist dimension, nay indeed, centrality.[124] Motahhari blames the Umayyads for this distortion.[125] Markedly influenced by the Marxist distinction between "utopian socialism" vs. "scientific socialism," he identified "distorted Islam" as "imaginative" (khial-bafaneh) vs. his reading which he called "realistic" (vaqe'-binaneh).

From the vantage point of this activist reading of the "realistic" Islam, Motahhari harshly criticized the Murji'ite tradition in early Islamic history for its pacifist rejection of the primacy of action.[126] He emphatically accredited the statement attributed to Shi'i Imams that "faith is certitude in heart, confession by tongue, and execution with bodily organs."[127] But despite such guidelines, he complained, the Shi'ites have increasingly been Murji'ified, or pacified, unwilling to fight for what they believe in.[128] Motahhari's activist reading of Islam is linked directly to some key passages in the Qur'an. He goes directly to these passages (8:24, 36:70, and 6:122) in order to substantiate his claims Qur'anically. Contrary to the specification of an activist Islam in these Qur'anic passages, Motahhari complains,

"most of ethical and educational principles in Islam—if not all of them—
have been completely reversed in the minds of the Muslims." [129] It is this
"reversed Islam" that he wishes to set aright.

Equally detrimental to the activist reading of Islam that Motahhari
wishes to propagate was ascetic tendencies that abated the ideological
agenda of the revolutionary cause from a variety of perspectives. While
praising the sense of serenity that is attained by virtue of being content with
what one has, Motahhari severely criticized the kind of asceticism that
emerges from physical and emotional weakness. Celebrating the physical
severity and overwhelming dignity of Ali, he proclaimed, "this is the meaning of ascetism. If you could find the like of it, humanity would be proud.
[Asceticism] is not this feebleness we have, whereby we call our clumsiness,
decrepitude, and immobility 'asceticism'." [130] In his condemnation of an
ascetic life, Motahhari tried to instill a positive attitude towards living,
whereby material wealth is enjoyed, and if abandoned it is only to achieve
higher purposes. [131] A perfect example of leading an ascetic life for higher
purposes, he thought, was the champion of Indian independence, Mahatma
Gandhi. But contrary to this kind of revolutionary necessity, Motahhari's
contemporaries, he charged, were entangled in all kinds of unnecessary
extravaganza. He took himself as an example and, ridiculing the type he
attacked, sarcastically said:

I am a great and famous religious figure. I am a Hojjat al- Islam or an Ayatollah.
Should I go to Mashhad for a pilgrimage or not? If I were to think that, it would
not be so simple for me to go to Mashhad. For example, how should I arrive?
Where should I arrive at? How should people come and pay me a visit. . . . All of a
sudden you'll find out a lifetime has passed and that simplest and most necessary
trip . . . has not been occasioned yet, merely because there are so many conditions
and necessities. [132]

Contrary to this image, Motahhari wishes to give the ascetic example of his
own father who used to "eat an early dinner, go to bed three hours after
the night had set, wake up at least two hours . . . before sunrise, and recite
at least one section of the Qur'an." [133]

While establishing the ideological foundations of this activist reconstruction of Islam, Motahhari was himself an employee of the Iranian government, teaching since 1954 at Tehran University. This posited a problem, if
not among Motahhari's fellow activists, then at least in his own mind. The
problem must have been in his mind when he expressed this apparently
hypothetical juridical question:

Islamic ulama' maintain that [accepting] deputyship from a tyrant is forbidden.
That is to say, if a person accepts a position from a government which is tyrannical,
he has committed a sin, a grave sin indeed. Yet if somebody wants to take a post
from a tyrannical government, but his purpose is to serve, to help those who have

been wronged, this would not only not be a sin, but according to certain [other] ulama' it is a recommended act, and according to certain others it is a mandatory obligation.[134]

This apparently conciliatory, but indeed revolutionary, attitude towards the status quo ought to be understood in view of Motahhari's uncompromising statement that

One of the responsibilities of the Islamic ulama' is that where they face a society in which some eat so much that they explode, and others cannot even get a decent meal, in such conditions it is incumbent upon them to revolt, and to fill this gap, to eliminate this discrepancy.[135]

Based on an actively reconstructed Islam, Motahhari's own self-image was that he now performed the all-too-necessary task of ideological preparation until such time that more drastic measures were to be taken. Until then, two objectives were to be met simultaneously: first all secular ideological alternatives (especially Marxism) had to be discredited, and, second, the legitimacy of the status quo (both cultural and political) had to be undermined. In order to achieve this dual imperative, a radical reconstruction of Islam was necessary, one that would spell the specifics of "the Islamic Ideology."

Authorities and Their Legitimacy

Perhaps the most central component of this ideology was the compelling question of legitimate authority. In 1970 the Hosseyniyyeh Ershad published a book on *Khelafat va Velayat (Caliphate and Authorities)*,[136] in which Motahhari had an article entitled *"Vala'-ha va Velayat-ha"* (*Legitimacies and Authorities*) that was subsequently published separately. This is a particularly significant text because it deals with the question of *velayat* ("guardianship," "authority," or "lordship") at almost the same time that Khomeini was delivering his lectures on the subject in Najaf—both tracts published almost a decade before this key doctrine became the central ideological locus of the Islamic Revolution in Iran.

Motahhari distinguishes between *valayat* (which he takes to mean literally "to help," "to assist," "to be loyal to") and *velayat* (literally "to be in charge of something or somebody"). The cumulative effect of these two terms, which concur in meaning and signification around the figure of Ali, is "affection," "love," and "loyalty" towards a just and legitimate leader and the simultaneous responsibility of this leader towards, and lordship over, his subjects. *Valayat,* as in "obedience," is directed from the led to the leader: in terms of affection and loyalty; *velayat,* as in "responsibility," is directed from the leader to the led: in terms of protection and lordship. The two terms, however, concur, in Motahhari's reading, to constitute the legitimate authority of a Muslim leader. There are two kinds of *velayat*, now taken generically to refer to the latter concurrence: negational and affirmative. "From the Islamic point of view," Motahhari asserts, "on one hand the Muslims are expected to reject a certain kind of *vala'* [that is, communal consensus as to the legtimate authority of a leader], and on the other hand, they are called upon to honor a certain other kind of *vala'* and exert themselves to realize it." [137]

The negational *vala'* prevents Muslims from accepting the authority of a non-Muslim offered to or imposed upon them. [138] Although Islam is a universal and independently valid faith, solidarity among the Muslims is crucial to its political legitimacy. Motahhari refers to the relevant Qur'anic passages in order to argue that Muslims should never yield to affinity for and loyalty to non-Muslim individuals. [139] But he is also at pains to ascertain that this is not incompatible with Islamic universality. As the negational *vala'* separates Muslims from others, affirmative *vala'* brings them together by causing among them a sense of *conscience collective*. Affirmative *vala'* is of two kinds: general and specific. General affirmative *vala'* is applicable to all Muslims. "Muslims in their friendships and kindness to each other," Motahhari quotes a prophetic tradition, "are like a body that, when an organ is in discomfort in it, the other parts console it with fever and insomnia." [140] By this particular kind of *vala'* Muslims in general are brought together through their collective participation in the grace of God. General affirmative *vala'* is the positive relationship among the Muslims based on obeying God and being benevolent to each other. Motahhari warns that the enemies of Islam and Muslims have reversed the functions of the negational and affirmative *vala'* and led them to be more affectionate and loyal to non-Muslims than to each other.

There is also a specific kind of affirmative *vala'* that is the exclusive prerogative of the household of the Prophet. Although Motahhari tries to accommodate the Sunni Muslims into his formulation, specific affirmative *vala'* is an essentially Shi'i devotion to the household of the Prophet in general and to Ali in particular. Motahhari's argument runs through the Qur'anic passage (5: 55) which, according to many commentators, including the staunchly Sunni al-Zamakhshari, Motahhari insists, is revealed about Ali. [141] Thus love, devotion, and loyalty to the household of the Prophet, especially to Ali, is a specific kind of *vala'* unto itself.

Vala'-e mahabbat (or *vala'* of friendship) is the exclusive love and devotion due to the household of the Prophet. This love is emphasized because "it is the premise for other kinds of *vala'*s." [142] It establishes a close tie between the household of the Prophet and those who follow them. *Vala'-e mahabbat* is the joyful obligation of Muslims to love the Prophet and his family. *Vala'-e imamat* (or *vala'* of the rightful successorship of Ali and his descendants after the Prophet), which is contingent upon infallibility, [143] is the prerogative right of the Prophet and after him the Imams to religious leadership. This *vala'* remains the exclusive right of the infallible Imams and is not extended to others except in its reversed meaning, that is, "acceptance of this right" as belonging to the Imams. *Vala'-e ze°amat* (or *vala'* of assuming social responsibility or leadership) is the political and social leadership. The first person to hold this position was the Prophet Muhammad who, according to Motahhari, had three kinds of authority: (1) religious, (2) juridical, and (3) political and social.[144] After the Prophet, this exclusive right was that of his household, through Ali and his children with the Prophet's daughter, Fatimah.

Here Motahhari offers a discussion of the word "Imam" and its various uses which, in light of future developments, is rather important. He clearly concludes that although generally this term has been used both positively and negatively, that is, about both just and unjust rulers,[145] and although in Sunnism it refers to "any person from whom religious doctrines are to be learnt,"[146] the word "Imam" (or "Imams") usually refers to the just and righteous leader and in Shi°i custom *(urf)* it refers to the "righteous and infallible leaders who are only twelve individuals."[147]

Vala'-e tasarrof (or *vala'-e takvini*) refers to a mystical and spiritual authority to which the Imams are entitled and to which their followers are obligated. By such references to *awlia Allah* ("the friends of God") and to *Insan-e Kamel* ("the universal man"),[148] it becomes quite evident that Motahhari's concerns here are essentially mystical and, as such, outside the political realm.

The question of *velayat* is central to any notion of the Islamic government. Motahhari summarized his position on this crucial point:

From the Shi°i point of view, whenever the question of *velayat* is discussed, there are three aspects to it, and in every one of these aspects . . . the word *Imamah* is used. First, from a political perspective, who was the most righteous and the most qualified person to succeed the Prophet in leading Muslims politically and socially . . . ? This perspective at the present time is a historical and doctrinal issue, not a practical one. Second, in explicating the religious injunctions, who is the person to refer to after the Prophet . . . ? The Shi°is believe in the leadership of the [twelve] infallible Imams. This, too, is a doctrinal and not a practical issue. Third, from a spiritual and esoteric point of view, according to the Shi°is, in every given time a universal man *(Insan-e Kamel)* who has unseen sovereignty over man and the universe . . . is always present, and it is because of such qualifications that his name is *hojjat* (proof).[149]

In order to make absolutely sure that this last spiritual figure is not confused with a historical one, Motahhari emphatically asserts:

The purpose of *velayat-e tasarrof* or *velayat-e takvini* is not, as some ignorants have presumed, that a human being among other human beings assumes the position of guardianship, or deputyship over the world in such a way that on behalf of God he would be the mover of the earth and the sky, and the creator, the sustainer, the one who brings to life and who causes death.[150]

He also adds that "there is no doubt that *velayat* of the fourth type is a "mystical question."[151] Moreover, he makes extensive references to Allamah Tabataba'i's writings on the subject.[152] But these references, too, as well as the very nature of his own discourse, are theological and mystical, with effectively no concern for political, historical, or contemporary implications of the discussion. This is particularly evident in Motahhari's assessment of the *velayat* of the fourth *(tasarrof)* kind:

His [the possessor of this *velayat*] aim would not be to acquire power and dominate the world, on the contrary his aim would be precisely the opposite of that, that is, it would be 'baseness,' 'humility,' 'annihilation,' and 'nothingness' in and of itself; and this strange way is the path of absolute obedience.[153]

Finally, he stipulates[154] five stages by which one reaches *velayat-e tasarrof:* (1) control over one's carnal soul, (2) control over one's thought, (3) independence from one's body, (4) control over one's body, and (5) control over the external world. All these stages, and their cumulative result, are again entirely in the spiritual and metahistorical realm and, as such, extensions of Shi'i spirituality into Motahhari's ideological discourse. Their presence in his universe of discourse must be traced back to his years of study with Allamah Tabataba'i, who had instilled in his young student a particular bend for the mystical dimension of Shi'ism.

It is remarkable to see how Motahhari was engaged in questions of *velayat* and *Imamat* at almost exactly the same time that Khomeini was addressing similar issues in Najaf and yet he seems to have been completely unaware of the political uses to which the terms could be put. For Motahhari, it is evident, the matter had a scholastic nature that demanded a similar treatment. Why Motahhari, who was in direct correspondence with Khomeini,[155] chose to refute, so thoroughly and emphatically, any contemporary political relevance or legitimacy in the term, at the same time that Khomeini was establishing *velayat-e faqih* as a cornerstone of his claim to political authority, is not quite clear. To be sure, Motahhari took the term more in its mystical implications, while Khomeini took it more in its juridical context. Yet the timing of this incongruency is remarkable.

Summa Contra Gentiles

Despite its essential incongruency with Khomeini's thesis of *velayat-e faqih,* Motahhari's attention to the centrality of the doctrine of *velayat* in the Shi'i political culture helped to resuscitate yet another set of (all but) forgotten sentiments among his increasing constituency. To fortify that constituency for any future mobilization, Motahhari always felt the pressing need of not giving Marxism a free domain in its Iranian version. Thus as he attended to the doctrinal requalification of "the Islamic Ideology"—the launching pad of the future Islamic Revolution—he saw to it that the greatest rival to its monopoly of political truth, that is, Marxism, was simultaneously discredited. During the 1969–1970 academic year Motahhari was invited by the Muslim Students Association at the Teacher Training College in Tehran to deliver a series of lectures that was later published in 1971 under the title of *The Causes of Attraction to Materialism*. This book was later translated into Arabic and published in Beirut.[156]

The late 1960s and early 1970s were the peak of a new generation of Marxist thought, actions, and sentiment in urban Iran. The guerrilla movement of the Fada'ian-e Khalq was the most emphatic institutional expression of the prevalence of Marxist ideas in Iran. The Shah's government, while doing anything in its power to suppress this movement, officially denied any credence or validity to its existence. But Motahhari, who had always been an acute observer of the Iranian political and ideological scene, could not have remained indifferent to Marxist trends among the Iranian youth. While an effective Islamic movement against the monarchy had been in a dormant state since Khomeini's 1963 uprising, the least the proponents of the Islamic movement could do was to meet the equally challenging task of confronting the Marxist revolutionaries and their materialist conception of history.

On the religious front itself, or that particular orientation of which nearly five years after the June 1963 uprising, the late 1960s were a relatively quiet period in terms of effective political activism. More time was now being devoted to the ideological build-up of the movement. Under these circumstances, Motahhari launched, once again, one of his severest attacks against philosophical materialism, in response to its political power he could rediscover Islam. "Believing in God is healthy," he declared, "and materialism is sickness. . . . The question has to be asked: Why have these people become sick? What factors caused their sickness?"[157]

In order to discredit the Marxist claim to authenticity in their version of (historical) materialism, Motahhari gave a detailed historical account in which he argued that

this kind of thinking [that is, materialism] is nothing new. It should not be presumed that the appearance of this mode of thought is the result of modern industrial and scientific developments. . . . It is among the very ancient [forms] of thought.[158]

Upon this background, he proceeds to give examples of the particular expression of materialism in Islamic intellectual history.[159] His objective in giving this historical account of materialism is to discredit the Marxists' claim that their brand of materialism is rooted in, and thus supported by, modern scientific advances. This claim, Motahhari suggests, "is more a joke than a serious fact." [160] But in giving such historical antecedents to "materialism," he is, in fact, reversing his own earlier assertions (in the early 1950s in *The Principles of Philosophy and the Realistic Method*) that "the materialists were fabricating a history for themselves and that not every philosopher who believed in the primacy of matter was a 'materialist' in the sense of denying the existence of the metaphysics." [161]

Motahhari's primary agenda in this series of lectures was to ascertain a set of diverse factors that were in his judgment instrumental in causing the ideological attraction to (historical) materialism, both in "The West" and in the Islamic societies. Chief and foremost among the factors that led to the intellectuals' attraction to (historical) materialism, he asserted, were "the shortcomings of the religious notions of the [Christian] Church." [162] Here he wished to argue that

whether by proposing insufficient conceptions in theology or through its inhumane behavior towards the masses, especially towards the scientists and the freethinkers, the [Christian] Church has been among the chief factors in the attraction of the Christian world, and indirectly the non-Christian world, to materialism. [163]

Motahhari maintained that the conception of "God" promoted by the Christian Church was too "childish" to be taken seriously by those who were attracted to scientific principles. As a result, the young intellectuals rejected the realm of metaphysics altogether. He also argues, through a secondary reference to August Comte, [164] that the more material causality was discovered in European scientific advancements, the more God was forced to retire to the realm of the unknown and thus gradually to total negation. Motahhari then takes issue with this argument in its logical fallacy and argues that such conceptions of God as the immediate cause of material events are essentially wrong. [165] He also takes issue with August Compte's typology of three distinct periods in human history: (1) meta-physical, (2) philosophical, and (3) scientific, asserting that this typology is "utterly wrong" [166] and that within the Islamic frame of reference all three modes have been simultaneously present: "Thus we have to remind Mr. August Compte and his cohorts that there has been a fourth [that is, Islamic] mode of thought, of which you have been ignorant." [167]

Motahhari also blames the Christian Church for having exerted violence in establishing its doctrines and thus having abated any possibility of freedom of thought in the Christian world. [168] While severely criticizing the Christian Church for curtailing the freedom of thought, he seriously believes that Islam has maintained that religion should be rationally ascertained rather than blindly imitated or, even worse, forcibly imposed. [169]

The second major cause of attraction to (historical) materialism in "The West," according to Motahhari, has to do with "Western" philosophical conceptions and their failure to establish the validity of a metaphysical realm.[170] He makes specific references to Hegel, Spencer, and Kant and their inability, in his judgment, to prove the existence of a prime uncaused Cause. Whereas Hegel could not explain the existence of the primary Cause as a quidity sui generis, Motahhari declared, the Shi'i philosopher Molla Sadra shifted the point of emphasis from quidity *(mahiyyah)* to existence *(wujud)*. Since causality is one of the primary attributes of existence at a certain level, it does not follow that it should hold equally true at a higher level of being.

Motahhari's point, although not articulated in so many words, was to explicate Molla Sadra's innovative proposition in Islamic ontology whereby discrepancies can exist between two levels of existence. In Molla Sadra's postulation of "transubstantial motion" *(al-harakah al-Jawhariyyah)*, ontological parameters of existent things transcend from one level of existence to another.[171] Motahhari added the factor of "deficiency"[172] as the principal reason for anything other than the primary Cause being in need of a Cause. Causality is an indication of a deficiency in the caused. Existent beings, in Molla Sadra's language, complete and sufficient unto themselves, have no need for a cause to be evidently present.

Motahhari then shifts his attention from Hegel to Darwin and argues against the implications of the Darwinian theory of evolution for the religious understanding of man. He believes that Darwinism has simply given "The West" yet another excuse to be attracted to the material conception of this world. Taking issue with David Hume, who questioned the totality and comprehensivity of the world, Motahhari dismisses this as yet another "Western" problematic conducive to the prevalence of (historical) materialism.[173] Refuting Hume's positions on four major issues, he concludes that contrary to this "Western" philosopher's perspective, the world has a perfect order and harmony, decisively mandated.

The third group of conceptions that, because of their insufficiency, have contributed to the propagation of materialism are in sociopolitical categories. Here Motahhari argues that theism has somehow been related in "The West" with political quietism, which has, in turn, led to "the inevitable contingency between the rights of national self-determination and atheism."[174] Quoting from Ali, he maintains that Islam has never propagated the notion of accepting the rule of an unjust ruler.[175] It is perfectly plausible to be both politically radical and religiously positive. Indeed, no other mode of ideological disposition is more conducive to revolutionary attitude, Motahhari believed with Shari'ati in his voice, than being Islamically alert. It is in "The West" that the religious establishment supports the status quo and atheist ideologies espouse revolutionary causes. This is not the case in Islam. On the contrary, it is only Islamically that the status quo can be challenged and revolutionary causes espoused.

These three causes of attraction to materialism, Motahhari argued, are specific to "The West." Three additional causes that are common to both "The West" and Islamic societies[176] complete his diagnosis that materialism as a philosophical mode of antireligiosity is a disease and must be prognosed and treated as such. By arguing for a theism that is both normal and congenial to human nature, Motahhari wished to weaken the intellectual hold of Marxism on the young Iranian activists.

The first of the latter three factors concerns nonexperts in religious matters expressing their ill-informed opinions about complicated theological issues. Because their ideas and expressions are naive and primitive, they fail to convince their intelligent audience, which in turn becomes more inclined to materialist explications:

What a great tragedy it is for the knowledgeable people that those who are neither familiar with the theist school [of thought] nor [acquainted] with the materialist perspective take advantage of the anarchy that exists in the religious propaganda system—particularly among the Shiʿis—and write books against the materialists. [They] fabricate nonsensical [ideas] which are the cause of ridicule and laughter. Obviously such propaganda is to the advantage of materialism.[177]

The cause of Motahhari's criticism was a genre of pious but naive literature, primarily produced in the bazaars of Tehran, Qom, Mashhad, and other urban centers, wherein bizarre "scientific" explanations of miracles, or Qurʾanic antecedents for technological advancements, were offered. Motahhari did not spare such pious endeavors, produced by the good intention of his own clerical colleagues, in his critical appraisal of why Iranian intellectuals were increasingly attracted to materialism.

The second cause of attraction to materialism common to both "Western" and Islamic societies is "ignorant ascetics" who radically denounce the world and man's natural instincts and thus give added ammunition to the materialists.[178] Like the first factor in this category, the "ignorant ascetics" were, in fact, in Motahhari's own rank. He severely criticized these "antisocial" elements in order to demonstrate the positive side of Islam and its full celebration of life.

The corruption of the social and, in turn, spiritual atmosphere is the third common factor conducive to materialism.[179] Attraction to lofty and sublime ideas inherent in a theist culture can be retarded in an atmosphere that denounces and belittles such concerns. With a twist of concealed political criticism, Motahhari accused the status quo, created by a corrupt and illegitimate government, of having caused an atmosphere of pessimism, cynicism, and distrust that renders obsolete any idea of a metaphysical nature. This aspect of Motahhari's writings always gives a positive and exuberant tone to his revolutionary reconstitution of Islam.

Motahhari then concludes that all these factors are historical and that the primary reason for an attraction to materialism in modernity is its rebellious and revolutionary character:

Today the young people are inclined to believe that one is either a theist and conciliatory, seeking comfort, [being] silent and indifferent, or else a materialist and active, rebellious, and an enemy of colonialism, repression and tyranny.[180]

Upon this assessment, Motahhari first admits that "religious concepts in our time are devoid of any [sense of] epic."[181] Then he mobilizes a barrage of Qur'anic verses to argue "is it possible to find more and better epic [than in what these revolutionary verses imply]? In its entirety, the Qur'an is the epic of battle and holy war, of enjoining the good, and of prohibiting the evil."[182] He goes so far as to give a radical reading of *taqiyah,* what has been understood historically as the Shi'i doctrine of "prudent fear," of dissimilitude, of pretending one is not a Shi'i, should that identity prove to be hazardous to one's safety. "*Taqiyah*" Motahhari believed as if with Shari'ati in his mind, means to hit more blows and to receive less."[183] This meaning, however, has been distorted, Motahhari suggests, to mean "escaping from the battlefield and leaving it to the enemy."[184] Such terms as *taqiyah* are to be reconstituted into their "true" revolutionary status if Islam is to replace materialism as a radical political cause. As always, two burning desires animate Motahhari's concerns: combating atheism (Marxism) and launching a revolutionary movement against the status quo. Sometimes it is difficult to discern which one is the primary cause: everything and anything to combat atheism, even espousing a revolutionary movement, or else everything and anything to launch a revolution against the status quo, even (de- and then re)constructing your faith to the level, and in terms, of its closest rival, Marxism.

Motahhari's chief agenda in late 1960s thus appears to be (1) to combat the chief ideological opponent of radical Islam, that is, revolutionary materialism, (2) to accuse the status quo, in both its political and religious components, of complacency for having caused this situation, and, finally, (3) to establish a comprehensive and systematically (only initially recognized in *Causes of Attraction to Materialism* but completed in other places) reconstituted Islam in terms of which revolutionary discourse Muslim youth could at once be radically rebellious against the status quo, like the materialists, and yet remain loyal to their faith and religion, unlike the materialists. This last objective proved to be a much more viable alternative than naked secular radicalism, because the revolutionary reading of Islam not only secures a comfortable, familiar, and indigenous atmosphere for its restless constituency but also registers more quickly and effectively with the political agenda of a mass mobilization. "The Islamic Ideology," in other words, completely remedies the two major problems of the materialist (Marxist) ideology: (1) a sense of discomfort and disconcertion inherent in operating within an alien secular context, which is always anxiety provoking, and (2) a deep cleavage between the imported revolutionary language and its noninitiated locals, on one hand, and the mass political constituency it is supposed to lead to ideological conviction and political action, on the other.

Throughout the *Causes of Attraction to Materialism,* Motahhari persistently demonstrates a reconstructed and monolithic perception of "Islam," one that necessarily does not take note of historical variations and nuances. He categorically states, for example, that in Islam religious doctrines ought to be "ascertained, not emulated or imposed." [185] Here, he completely downplays the doctrinal and theological thrust in the Ash'arite tradition in Islamic theological history, which he himself in other places [186] condemns as severely antirational, dogmatic, and blind. Immediately related to the revolutionary reconstruction of a monolithic Islam was Motahhari's inevitable formation of an essentialist and categorical view of "The West." The first part of the *Causes of Attraction to Materialism,* for example, is devoted entirely to an analysis of "The Western" fault in the emergence of (historical) materialism. Here, in very strong terms, "Western religion," that is, Christianity, "Western philosophy," and "Western social and political factors" are blamed for this "malice." His taking issue with Hegel, for example, on philosophical grounds assumes antagonistic terms, even accusing the German philosopher of "childish thoughts." [187]

A Theory of Government

While Motahhari attended to the translated sources of European ideologies in his attacks against the forces of secularism, in constructing his visions of the utopia to come, he appealed to the authority of the canonical Shi'i texts. In 1972 he finally turned his full attention to *Nahj al-Balaghah,* his interest in which dated back to the summer of 1941 when he left Qom, "in order to escape the heat," [188] and went to Isfahan, where he met with Hajj Mirza Ali Aqa Shirazi Isfahani. Motahhari always spoke very fondly and reverentially of this master of *Nahj al-Balaghah:* "He lived and breathed with *Nahj al-Balaghah;* his soul was concomitant with this book, his pulse reverberating, his heart palpitating, with it." [189] After this short summer with Hajj Mirza Ali Aqa, he returned to Qom and to his juridical studies with Ayatollahs Borujerdi and Khomeini and his philosophical studies with Allamah Tabataba'i. But his interest in and attention to *Nahj al-Balaghah* and its potential for a critical political reading remained intact until the early 1970s when he first delivered a series of five lectures on this book at the Hosseyniyyeh Ershad. [190] These lectures were then gradually published in *Maktab-e Islam,* a journal Motahhari helped to establish. Finally in 1974 he wrote an Introduction to this collection of essays and published them as a book. Since then, *Seyri dar Nahj al-Balaghah (A Reading of Nahj al-Balaghah)* has been published repeatedly. There is also an Arabic translation of it by Muhammad Ali Taskhiri, published in Qom,[191] making it available to a larger potential revolutionary constituency.

The *Nahj al-Balaghah (The Model of Eloquence)* is a collection of sermons attributed to Ali, the first Shiʿi Imam. Next to the Qurʾan, it is the most cherished text of canonical authority for the Shiʿis. Motahhari's objective was to make the *Nahj al-Balaghah*, through a rereading of its latent revolutionary message, pertinent to the realities of his historical immediacy.

The language of *Seyri dar Nahj al-Balaghah*, because of its timing, is very guarded and symbolic. Motahhari had to resort to a metaphorically referential language to continue his active writing in the face of severe governmental control, particularly in the early 1970s when an increase in oil revenues and the Shah's grandiose celebration of 2,500 years of monarchy in Iran had created an artificial sense of self-assurance that, precisely because of its artificiality, was least tolerant of any oppositional voice. Motahhari's future discourse would grow to be much bolder and more emphatic, but the revolutionary thrust of his discourse is quite evident in his early writings as well. A radical reading of a sacred text was a safe and sustained procedure, leading him quietly, but surely, forward in the genesis of a successful political discourse with a strong revolutionary overtone.

In any radical reconstruction of an old faith into a new ideological language, the immediate past must be condemned and the remote idealized history glorified, all in order to render the revolutionary cause far more effective than it would have been otherwise by virtue of its mere factual force. Motahhari's attention to the *Nahj al-Balaghah* in the early 1970s could not have remained uncritical of its having been neglected by previous generations. "We Shiʿites must confess," Motahhari declared, "that more than others we have wronged, or at least been negligent of, the person whom we are honored to follow. . . . We have been unwilling or unable to know Ali." [192] But what is always resistant to such radical and revolutionary rereadings of a faith is precisely that set of common beliefs and practices that perform and sustain the religion at a perfectly mundane and politically benign level. It is precisely those kinds of passive operations of religious consciousness that its political reconstruction must oppose. Those "who imagine," Motahhari declared, "that such [political] problems are tangential, and that only questions such as [ritual] purity and impurity are at the heart of the [Islamic] faith should better reconsider their positions." [193] Here he strikes a common chord with his mentor, Khomeini, who equally condemned apolitical piety.

One of the essential themes that Motahhari develops in his reading of

Nahj al-Balaghah is the question of the legitimacy of an Islamic government. He quotes sermon number 214 of *Nahj al-Balaghah* as the ultimate
statement of Shiʿi Islam on the subject:

Among those rights which God Almighty has made mandatory is the right of the
ruler *(al-wali)* upon his subjects *(al- raʿiyyah)* and the right of the subjects upon the
ruler. This is an obligation which God Almighty has mandated for each [of these
two parties] upon the other. He has established this as a system [beneficial both] for
them [that is, the rulers] and for the glory of their subjects. And the subjects shall
not prosper other than through the prosperity of those who govern [them]; and the
rulers shall not prosper other than through the fortitude of their subjects. Consequently, when the subjects perform their duties towards their ruler, and the ruler
his towards them, righteousness shall be exalted between them, the principles of
faith strengthened, the expressions of justice stable, the traditional conducts in their
proper directions, and with that, peaceful shall be the time, the state perpetual, and
the covetous designs of the enemy disappointed.[194]

All these qualifications of an ideal state are tacitly suggested as nonexistent
in the present state of affairs. But, more important, they point beyond their
absence in the present and promise the revolutionary model to be attained
when the moment is right.

Justice: The Supreme Political Virtue

Through a simultaneous resuscitation of such sentiments and conceptions
of authority in Islam, Motahhari infuses considerable revolutionary force
into his political discourse. He is able to do so during the crucial decade of
the 1970s when the Shah's "modernization" programs are in full swing.
The figure of Ali and the concept of "justice" frequently recur in Motahhari's speeches and books. His concentration on "justice" had an obvious
political ring to it, tacitly but emphatically implying its absence in his
contemporary state apparatus. What distinguished Motahhari's discourse
from that of Al-e Ahmad and Shariʿati was grounding his argument deep
into the received Islamic doctrinal and intellectual traditions. He would, for
example, discuss the centrality of "justice" in Islam through arguments in
historical, theological, philosophical, social, and other contexts, relating
and appropriating everything to the historical exigencies of his time.

    To combat passive resignation to the status quo, Motahhari maintained
that since justice is a sacred responsibility incumbent upon man,[195] one
cannot remain a mere spectator to acts of injustice:

When the society is divided into two classes [*tabaqeh,* a patently Marxist term
Motahhari borrowed and frequently used, apparently unaware of either its sociological definition or its ideological weight] of tyrants and tyrannized—one saturated, ill at ease with overindulgence, and yet another famished, distressed with
hunger, Islam does not permit one to sit idle and be a mere spectator.[196]

Justice, Motahhari proclaimed, cannot be "compromised" or "post-poned."[197]

"Justice" is the principle factor upon which every state should be founded. Here Motahhari extends the question of political legitimacy directly to that of the state. Justice, or any notion thereof, is the principal legitimating factor of any state. To the question "Is justice or magnanimity more virtuous?" Ali is reported to have responded, "Justice," because "justice puts matters in their proper place, while magnanimity deroutes them from their [appropriate] direction."[198] In other words, justice directs the course of human affairs towards normalcy, whereas "magnanimity" perpetuates an abnormalcy that is the distinction and separation between those who have and those who do not. Persistent justice is more crucial for a legitimate state than occasional magnanimity.

Extended from the principle of "justice" as the quintessential pillar of the state, Motahhari considers "government" as merely the "deputy" (vakil), the "trustee" (amin), and the "representative" (nemayandeh) of the people.[199] By using these technical juridical terms, he tacitly questioned the very legitimacy of the Shah's government. The Shah's increasingly authoritarian rule was far removed from any proximity to such (Shi'i) juridical notions of a legitimate government. But at the same time, working through the Nahj al-Balaghah, Motahhari argued for the necessity, and indeed indispensability, of government. "Ali, peace be upon him," Motahhari stated, "repeatedly emphasized the necessity of a strong government. He opposed the Kharijites' position which initially held that the Qur'an is enough and that there is no need for a government."[200] Motahhari also maintained that, in the absence of a righteous government, an unrighteous government is better than none at all: "People have no choice but to be governed by a ruler, good or bad. . . . Such governments would at least prevent anarchy, unlawfulness, and the rule of jungle."[201]

From "state" and "government," Motahhari turns to the impending necessity of a legitimate ruler. With a clear reference to the illegitimacy of the Shah's reign, he maintained that the ruler is merely a custodian (amanat-dar) of the people's trust and not a possessor (malek) of their livelihood.[202] The ruler is meant to be for the service of the people, not vice versa. For this point he makes a reference to a verse of the celebrated Iranian poet Sa'di (1213–1292):

The sheep is not for the shepherd,
The shepherd is to serve the sheep.[203]

He elaborates further on the notion of a leader as a custodian by referring to the Qur'anic passage 4:59, the famous "authority verse" which reads in part, "O ye who believe! Obey Allah, and obey the messenger and those of you who are in authority." By referring to a tradition attributed to Ali,

Motahhari argues that the legitimacy of "those of you who are in authority" is bound to their being in custody of a trust bestowed upon them by
God.[204] It is important to remember that this very Qur'anic passage, which
has the key expression of *ulu al-amr minkum* ("those of you who are in
authority"), was used by Ayatollah Khomeini in his resuscitation of the
notion of *"velayat-e faqih."* Although Ayatollah Khomeini had already
delivered and published his treatise on *"velayat-e faqih"* by the time Motahhari was delivering these lectures in 1972, the latter made no note of
this point and, more important, claimed no exclusive authority for the
juristconsult. The major thrust of his argument throughout the book, and
through a host of references to *Nahj al-Balaghah,* is that (1) the Islamically
recognized ruler is merely a custodian of the divine trust to rule over the
Muslim community and (2) "justice" is the principal legitimating factor of
the ruler-ruled relationship. In the context of this argument, there is no
explicit or implicit reference to Khomeini's lectures in Najaf on the subject.
Motahhari pays no particular hermeneutic attention to the key concept of
vali, nor does he in any direct or indirect way consider the ulama' to be the
exclusive custodians of political authority.

Piety Redefined

Be that as it may, Motahhari's antiestablishment ideological undertone is
quite evident in denying the king legitimacy. But equally important was the
task of countering the illegitimacy of the ruling regime with a legitimate
mode of political activism. One of the chief obstacles that Motahhari tried
to overcome in the early 1970s was a mode of passive piety inimical to that
urgent political activism he wished to engender and propagate. For this
purpose, he tried, among other things, to redefine the notion and practice
of piety *(taqwa')* through a radical hermeneutics, a revolutionary rereading,
of its related passages in the *Nahj al-Balaghah.*[205] Here, he emphatically
opposed the common reading of the term as "abstinence from getting
involved in various things." He considered this a "negational" reading of
the term: "If the spiritual form of *taqwa'* is present in a person," he
stipulated, "he does not have to abandon his surroundings. He can keep
himself pure and free from sin without abandoning his surroundings."[206]
By further emphasizing the prophetic tradition that "there is no asceticism
(ruhbaniyyah) in Islam," Motahhari tried to foster a socially positive,
politically active, and communally gregarious attitude towards life. He
contrasted this with Christian asceticism which he considered particularly
antisocial.[207]

The new activist definition that Motahhari wished to give to asceticism
was based on three principles: (1) man needs spiritual as well as material
satisfaction; (2) man and society are interrelated, and thus one cannot live

comfortably while others do not; and (3) man's spirit has an independent validity, distinct and separate from the body.[208] Based on these principles, he rejects an antisocial and quietist reading of asceticism in favor of an active and conscious participation in social and political matters. He makes a clear distinction here between the positive asceticism of a *zahed* ("ascetic") and the negative asceticism of a *raheb* ("a Christian monk"): The former is social, the latter antisocial; the former assures "social responsibility," the latter does not.[209]

This distinction, which Motahhari made here in an Islamic-Christian dichotomy, was, of course, present within Islam itself. That, in fact, was the very reason why it needed to be tackled and redefined. Redefinition of key concepts in Shi'i Islam was the chief factor in shaping Motahhari's revolutionary discourse:

The word "asceticism" *(zohd)*, despite its supreme humanist meaning, has had an onerous fate, and especially in our time is being tyrannically condemned. Usually distinctions and mistakes, intentionally or otherwise, are made as to the significance of this word. Sometimes it is equated with deception and dishonesty, and is taken at other times as synonymous with monasticism, isolation, and seclusion.[210]

Motahhari severely criticized all such negative readings and wished to give the term the revolutionary meaning compatible with an activist participation in the political responsibilities of the individual:

Movements, rebellions, persistent and hard-headed struggles have only been done by those who in effect have had less fetters. That is to say, they have been, in a way, ascetics. With his ascetic method, Gandhi defeated the British Empire. Ya'qub-e Layth-e Saffar,[211] as he [himself] put it, could do well just with a piece of bread and some onion, and thus could frighten the caliph. In our own time, the Viet Kong [are the same]. The astonishing resistance of the Viet Kong is due to that which in Islam is called "the lightness of one's necessities." A Viet Kong can go on for days in hideouts and continue to fight on a fistful of rice.[212]

The concern with redefining "asceticism" is symptomatic of a politically mandated engagement with reconstituting the key conceptual categories that historically have made Shi'i Islam into what it is. Through a revolutionary hermeneutics, Motahhari singles out the crucial Islamic terms and impregnates them with fresh, poignant, contemporary, and radically revolutionary ideas: "asceticism," "worship," "love," "the world," etc. All these terms and their ordinary and received meanings are constantly redefined and reconstituted with one main objective: the creation and legitimacy of a new collective political consciousness. The political dimensions of this targeted consciousness were uppermost in Motahhari's mind, yet its wider social and cultural dimensions were equally present in his agenda and in those of his ideological cohorts. The key contextual references of this massive semantic reconstruction are always the central and sacred texts of Shi'i Islam: the Qur'an, the prophetic traditions, the Imami traditions, and here, of course, the *Nahj al-Balaghah*. The archetypal texts are held constant and from them "Islam" is created anew. This is how language becomes central in, indeed constitutional to, a revolutionary process. Through the word, the world was recreated, reimagined, resignified.

To make "Islam" viable in a rapidly changing world, Motahhari attended to the radical materialism of his age by persistently arguing for a this-worldly reading of the faith, a reading that relocates Islam in the immediate vicinity of its contemporary history. He thought an entirely other-worldly reading of Islam had been falsely perpetuated.

In the world view of a *zahed* [the "ascetic," with Motahhari's positive and activist reading of it], this and the other world are connected together. This world is the [cultivating] field for the other. . . . What gives order, prosperity, beauty, security, and comfort to this world is to bear other-worldly standards upon it; and what secures the other-worldly bliss is to perform this-worldly responsibilities properly, combined with faith, purity, prosperity, and piety.[213]

But to make this activist Islam possible, positive asceticism, self-sacrifice, and communal sympathy[214] are the chief virtues to be achieved. And these virtues are precisely what Motahhari tried to resuscitate throughout his hermeneutic explication of the *Nahj al-Balaghah*. To lead the masses towards a realization of this goal, he stipulated the responsibility of the ulama':

When the society is divided into two segments, the man of God feels responsible. First and foremost, the man of God's effort is [directed to], as the prince of the Believers, Ali, put it, change the existing situation where the tyrants overstuff themselves while the oppressed go hungry.[215]

Judging from the main thrust of Motahhari's reading of the *Nahj al-Balaghah*, his agenda in the early 1970s seems to include the following threefold objectives: (1) discredit the Shah's regime by tacit yet quite clear references to ideas of justice and legitimate government, (2) formulate a complete "Islamic Ideology" in contradistinction to secular ideologies of his time, and (3) develop a large political constituency that is ideologically charged and ready for a future move. This is not to suggest that as early as 1972 Motahhari could have anticipated the magnitude of the events that would occur at the end of the decade. Yet his commitment in mobilizing a politically active Islamic consciousness could not have been an idle speculative exercise. He was, at the same time, also particularly conscious not to give the secular ideologies a free hand among the young Iranian constituency. Although the radical movement on the left was severely and ruthlessly crushed in the early 1970s, the underground and disguised literature expounding an array of Marxist ideologies was still readily available and massively consumed by the youth.

Motahhari was particularly adamant in his ideological confrontation with any mode of secular thought prevalent in the early 1970s. Against the presumed position of, for example, Existentialism, which he knew only through haphazard translations, rejecting any kind of received moral confinement,[216] Motahhari argued that "servitude to God is a kind of slavery which is the very essence of freedom; it is the only kind of confinement and attachment which is not [tantamount to] being stationary and frozen."[217]

In a remarkable way Motahhari himself identified with Ali. This identification is an amazing indication of how potent and alive hagiographical perceptions operate as active symbols. Motahhari described Ali's initial silence against the first three caliphs as a "majestic silence" and then his revolt against the Kharijites as a "more majestic act."[218] Ali tolerated the benign corruption of the first three caliphs, but revolted severely against the dangerous piety of the Kharijites. So, through a process of historical identification, would Motahhari tolerate, the tacit argument would hold, the Shah's regime and yet fortify "the Islamic Ideology" against the dangerous piety of such radical elements as the Mojahedin-e Khalq or their cohorts.

Thus, through the justification of Ali's inactivity during the reign of the first three caliphs, Motahhari justified his own inactivities. "Ali's silence," he decided, "was a calculated and logical silence, not out of fear and hopelessness."[219] Having clearly himself in mind, Motahhari projected his own image backward to Ali and thus concluded that "it was very easy for him to revolt, and the worst that could happen was that in the absence of friends and comrades he and his family would have been martyred. [But] martyrdom was what Ali wished for."[220] Letting Ali speak for him, and he for Ali, Motahhari declared that "my silence is not because of the fear of death, it is because revolt and martyrdom under these conditions are more harmful to Islam than beneficial."[221]

Islamic Nationalism

The propagation of a revolutionary ideology that was deeply rooted in canonical Islamic sources was targeted, most immediately, to an Iranian audience. This created a certain necessity to cater to the Iranian sense of national identity as distinct from the Arabic. It is rather remarkable to note on Motahhari's part a certain degree of pride in being an Iranian, despite the fact that he adamantly opposed Iranian particularism in favor of Islamic universalism. He is very comfortable, for example, with such phrases as "the finest language of Persian"[222] despite his religiously mandated devotion to Arabic. Clear identification of prominent Iranian Muslims as such was another way of Motahhari's tacit recognition of his national identity. He always liked to refer to prominent luminaries of Arabic prose such as Ibn al-Muqaffaʿ as Persian.[223] Mastery of Arabic prose by Motahhari's fellow Iranian Muslims was a historical reference he always liked to make. To be sure, he harbored no acute chauvinism at the expense of Islam. Quite the contrary, he emphatically articulated the primacy of Islam over Iran. Yet there is something peculiar worth considering in his references to Iranian Muslims of prominence.[224]

When taking issue with those who attribute the philosophical orientation in Shi'ism to the influence of the Iranian elements, Motahhari argues that not all Shi'is were Iranians, and not all Iranians were Shi'is. But in actually delivering his argument, he rhetorically asks, "Were al-Kulayni, Ibn Babuyah, and al-Mazandarani Iranian, or al-Bukhari, al-Sajistani, and al-Nishaburi [who were Sunnis] not Iranian?"[225] The question is, of course, rhetorical; the self-evident answer Motahhari strongly implies is that most of the prominent figures of both the Shi'i and Sunni groups were Iranian. Thus when he refers to Sayyid al-Radi and the Fatimids as examples of non-Persian Shi'is, the references remain more a gesture of benevolent universalism than anything else. His book on *The Mutual Services of Iran and Islam* sets out to demonstrate the liberating effect of Islam on Iranians and yet, in effect, turns out to be a detailed two-volume documentation of prominent Iranians who made Islamic intellectual history possible. Thus appropriating Islam for Iranians, Motahhari's hidden agenda was to oppose the latent but strong traits of anti-Arab (anti-Islamic) sentiments prevalent among certain groups of secular nationalists.

The Efficacy of the Ideological Language

The corollary notion of a sustained national identity, equally conducive to the ideological mobilization, was a permanently present monolithic conception of "The West." To be sure, for someone who had no access to any European language, Motahhari had a remarkably detailed, however essentially flawed, knowledge of European thought. Judging by *A Reading of Nahj al-Balaghah,* Motahhari's understanding of Rousseau and Hobbes is entirely from secondary and translated sources.[226] These translations, no matter how accurately they were rendered from their original languages to Persian, always reflected the captivated mind of Iranians with a figment of their imagination they called "The West." Motahhari could only have translated elements of this captivation to forces of his "Islamic Ideology." He had an irresistible tendency to see "The West" as a monolithic entity, completely negligent of the historical diversities that constitute the European and American experiences. He would feel perfectly comfortable, for example, with such phrases as "the Western theosophy" *(Hekmat-e Elahi-e Gharb),* taking "The West" as a kind of religious entity.[227] Such grand generalizations would usually be occasioned by comparative references to Islamic counterparts. This tendency, of course, had a reciprocal effect, that is, the more monolithic a view of "The West" Motahhari postulated, the more he generalized Islam itself at the expense of the vast diversities that made the Muslim historical experience.

Central to this ideological construction of the injured "Self" and the hostile "Other" is a built-in mechanism for avoiding the detailed minutiae of historical analysis. In his 1974 preface to *A Reading of Nahj al-Balaghah*, Motahhari reiterated a phrase common to most of his works. He apologized to his readers for not having produced a detailed and complete work "due to many preoccupations."[228] These preoccupations are always the pretext to publish material he was still not satisfied with. But the unfulfilled wish to attend carefully to scholarly matters always remains with him: "How sincerely do I wish I could."[229] Throughout his writing career Motahhari apologized to his readers for the insufficiency of what he had produced. This was more than a mere sign of humility. As a serious student of Shi'i jurisprudence and Islamic philosophy, Motahhari knew very well what it took to write something genuine in these traditional discourses. He knew how far afield he was taken from the received mandates of bona fide Islamic discourses. He also knew that the primacy of his ideological and political agenda was much too overwhelming to permit him genuine scholastic maturity as his alter ego would have liked him to undertake. And these are the genuine sentiments behind his repeated apologies for the cursory nature of his discourse. Nonetheless, the primacy of his ideological and political objectives was much stronger and more pronounced to be sacrified for a quiet scholasticism. The result was a paradoxical longing for a scholastic excellence he inadvertently disrelished. The bonfire of his revolutionary spirit needed open air to release a concentrated energy much in need of burning and consuming the anger of living Islamically in a tyrannically secular world.

Islamic Education

To attend that secular world Islamically, Motahhari felt compelled to reeducate his generation. As early as 1972 he clearly saw Islam as a bona fide, indeed the only legitimate, "school" *(maktab)* that had educational, legal, economic, and political "systems" perfectly capable of organizing a society and guiding its individual members to salvation.[230] Within this "school," he maintained, Islam paid simultaneous attention to both the individual and the society.[231] His tacit argument here is, of course, against those who considered Islamic juridical doctrines too totalitarian and archaic in their sweeping coverage of the public and private life.

Motahhari has an interesting theory of education that harbors two essential, and highly critical, assumptions. Following a statement attributed to Ali in *Nahj al-Balaghah* (that is, "There are two kinds of knowledge: an innate knowledge and an acquired knowledge, and the acquired knowledge is of no use when the innate knowledge is not available"), he argues that those who have merely memorized and learned a series of facts and opinions are not sufficient in their position as men of knowledge. They ought to reflect on their learning with their own mental and intellectual abilities so that they can reach for insights beyond their received knowledge: "Among the scholars, I really do not have any regard for those who have seen many teachers, many masters, and consider this the source of their pride."[232]

This position makes two crucial stands quite evident: First, in his hasty and urgent political and ideological agenda, Motahhari obviously had no patience for the prolonged duration of a scholastic curriculum. He had more immediate and compelling ideological and political ends to meet. This much he shared with Shari'ati. The latter had also repeatedly scorned the prolonged regimens of scholastic learning. However, Motahhari, contrary to Shari'ati, had grown straight out of the scholastic system himself and thus knew perfectly well how to couch his ideological and political position in the range of Shi'i canonical terms. He referred to the fact that two of the greatest juridical authorities in modern history, namely, Shaykh Ansari and Ayatollah Borujerdi, had had very little prolonged scholastic learning and had spent relatively short periods of time in learning acquired knowledge (elm-e masnu'i), and yet they had a greater impact on their contemporaries because of their "innate knowledge" (elm-e matbu'). By this "innate knowledge" Motahhari did not mean anything illuminative or mystical but rather the mental capability and opportunity to reflect on what one has learned.[233] The implications of this position are quite evident for Motahhari's own scholastic and intellectual career. He, too, had spent a relatively short period of time in Mashhad and Qom learning the principles of Shi'i jurisprudence and some philosophy. Following his studies in Qom, he went to Tehran and gradually assumed a teaching position at Tehran University. He then launched a sustained and systematic program of lecturing and publishing on various social, cultural, legal, and political issues. Obviously, two simultaneous facts worked towards his gradual adoption of an ideological, rather than scholastic or scholarly, discourse. First he engaged in a hasty and demanding regimen of lecturing and writing; and, second, he did not pursue a full-fledged and prolonged scholastic career, such as staying in Qom or moving on to Najaf. The adoption of this ideological discourse was not only more compatible with Motahhari's intellectual disposition but also more suitable to his political agenda.

The same position on education implies a rational, usuli, approach to not only juridical and educational but also social and political matters. Motahhari takes the concept of ejtehad ("exertion of personal opinion on a juridical issue") from the usuli lexicon and asserts that it really means "innovation" (ebtekar).[234] A true thinker and a bona fide mojtahed is one who breaks with the received and imposing hegemonic paradigms of the ancestry and introduces a whole new model of inquiry. Without having heard of Thomas Kuhn, Motahhari expresses the following judgment in the making of a scientific revolution:

As you see in physics, a scientist comes and introduces a new school. Then all other physicists follow him. It is the same in jurisprudence. There are all these ulama', yet only one of them succeeds in producing a new school. A new school which is also acceptable. Then he brings everybody else's thoughts under the authority of his school, his thoughts. Such a person should be called a true *Mojtahed*.[235]

Through the operation of such rational and *usuli*-based arguments Motahhari implicitly but clearly opens the possibility of ideological rejuvenation in Shi'ism. To be sure, Shari'ati had similar objectives; but he did not have the necessary scholastic erudition to work his logic through the innate Shi'i juridical concepts. He simply ridiculed the scholastic insistence on the necessity of learning prior to action. Thus, whereas Shari'ati succeeded on the eloquent rhetoric of his speeches, Motahhari advanced on more subtle and intellectually persuasive grounds, working his way slowly but surely through the maze of the Shi'i juridical discourse.

In his long didactic speeches on the nature and philosophy of Islamic education, Motahhari chiefly advocated the cause of rationality and the measure of human intellect as a unique divine endowment. He goes into full and elaborate detail, turning to a host of canonical Shi'i texts, to prove that the judgment of the mind and human rationality are the essential and critical forces for facing the problems of the time.

In defending the cause of independent judgment, Motahhari severely criticizes that particular type of Muslim scholar who has merely stuffed his mind with the facts and figures of one branch of religious knowledge or another:

There are some of these ulama', those very learned ulama' that is, who are more learned than intelligent. They are learned in the sense of being thoroughly informed. They are less intelligent[, however,] because they accumulate whatever they see, from everywhere, without any sense of judgment. Then they would repeat all these somewhere else without ever thinking whether what they do is rational or not?[236]

There are two immediate levels of subtextual reference in holding this position. First, having fallen short of a sustained and prolonged career in a given traditional field of study, Motahhari had to locate himself in a niche of hermeneutic authority sui generis. Second, having an immediate ideological and political agenda in mind, he claimed a more radically active role for the human intellect to have it wasted in getting to know, on a deep and serious level, the intricacies of Shi'i learning. Here, again, he comes remarkably near Shari'ati who equally, if not more intensely, rejected the disciplined requirements of a life of serious learning. As with Shari'ati, Motah-hari considered this a waste of time and intelligence. There were simply more crucial and immediate (political) concerns and commitments. How much of this preference is by choice and how much a reflection of one's intellectual capacities is a crucial issue that need not be elaborated here. Scholastic learning, the confidence of a master philosopher, thus remained a distant ideal for Motahhari—a distant ideal he increasingly belittled as he increasingly neared the borders and territory of "the Islamic Ideology."

The Supremacy of Reason Over Tradition

Motahhari's chief concern, however, seems to have been a release from the powerful grip of *taqlid* ("emulation") as a chief Shi'i precept. On the surface it is rather ironic that, as a member of the clerics, Motahhari would so seriously challenge the validity of *taqlid,* according to which Shi'is are expected to follow the exemplary conduct of a religious authority of their choice:

The basis of the Qur'an is on admonishing those who are bound by emulation *(taqlid),* following their ancestors, and without thinking [for a moment] to rid themselves of slavery to rotten opinions which, like a chain, ties their arms and legs. . . . The Qur'an wants to teach us that the measure and criterion ought to be the judgment of the intellect and thought, not merely our doing what our fathers did.[237]

But if we keep in mind that his hidden argument is to secure an ideological leverage for his analytical engagement with many issues outside a tradi-tional juridical discourse, then the apparent irony disappears.

In advocating the cause of intellectual judgment vis-à-vis obedience to received notions of authority, Motahhari openly attacks any claim of legit-imacy by the traditional modes of authority:

One common problem among all people, afflicting all the prophets, is this calamity of emulating one's ancestors, or, as it is said today, "traditionalism" *(sonnat-gara'i).* Confronted by such misguided tendencies, the prophets have awakened people's intellect.[238]

He takes this insistence on the superiority of the intellect one step further and claims a certain aristocracy of the mind and rationality against blind popular obedience:

In Islamic [prophetic and Imami] traditions, it has been emphasized that one should not pay attention to people's judgment. It has been repeatedly asked to [heed] the independence of intellect and that of the mind.[239]

Motahhari's favorite Qur'anic passage, which he quotes in support of his insistence on the priority of rational judgment, is 39:17–18.[240] If this presumed superiority of reason over tradition is true about Islam in general, it is particularly true about Shi'ism. He turns to a contemporary Sunni Arab historian, the Egyptian Ahmad Amin, to argue that there is something particularly rational about Shi'ism:

This man [Ahmad Amin], although known to be an anti-Shi'i, confesses that the Shi'i intellect is a rational intellect, and that in every period the Shi'i intellect has been more rational [than others]. He wants to account for this fact by arguing that the reason the Shi'i intellect is more rational has to do with the fact that they have attended, more [than others], to [Qur'anic] hermeneutics. But the fact of the matter is that the source of this phenomenon is in the Shi'i Imams who, more [than others], invited people towards thinking and rationality.[241]

Motahhari never tires of listing a barrage of prophetic and Imami traditions on the virtues of rationality and judicious reflection: "One hour of thinking is better than a year of prayer," "one hour of thinking is better than sixty years of prayer." "One hour of thinking is better than seventy years of prayer," concluding that "thinking itself is prayer."[242]

Motahhari's prolonged and sustained argument, deeply rooted in the Islamic (Shi'i) canonical sources, for the superior position of rationality and intellectual judgment is not accidental. A logical extension of the Usuli (or the primacy of intellect) victory over the Akhbari (or the primacy of tradition) elements in Shi'i juridical history, this glorification of rationality, however rooted in canonical sources, is the necessary and inevitable preface for engagement in contemporary social issues otherwise external to Shi'i juridical discourse. No one did more than Motahhari in legitimating this updated Shi'i juridical discourse. Shari'ati simply concocted his own modern discourse, totally outside of, and indeed antagonistic to, the Shi'i juridical hermeneutic circle. Before and for many years into the Revolution, Khomeini operated essentially within the limited boundaries of traditional Shi'i juridical discourse, with only minor and rather conservative excursions into the historical exigencies of his time. Taleqani, Bazargan, and others never expounded as persuasively as Motahhari in assimilating a wide range of social, political, ethical, and even literary issues into an updated Shi'i discourse.

Motahhari's valiant attempt to update the Usuli juridical discourse, and with it to rehistoricize Islam, was not limited to reiterating the significance of rationality in discussing human affairs. He specifically tackled issues that were at the heart of the secular contention, stated or presumed, against the religious forces. For example, he made no moral bones about the necessity of (legitimate) violence on a grand social level:

In the society at large the issue is quite clear of course. There the factor of violence is necessary (as opposed to its not being necessary to toilet-train a child). This is for cases where the grown-ups know that they should not do a certain thing, and yet they rebel against rules and regulations. In such circumstances, in order to prevent rebellion, there is no inhibition against the use of violence.[243]

Art and Reason

The necessity of violence is argued with the same stringent rationality as the prohibition of music. Music is forbidden because it dulls the human faculties:

Of course one thing is certain about music *(ghena')*: As for such songs [sic = *avaz*] which cause dullness in the mind *(kheffat-e aql)*, that is to say such songs [sic] which so incite the passions that the intellect is temporarily out of control, which is to say they have the same effect as wine and gambling, obviously their inhibition of such is certain.[244]

Motahhari's statement about the doctrinal position of Shi'ism on music is quite guarded and stated in such a way as to allow for alternative interpretations. On the surface, as is quite evident, Motahhari restates and thus supports the Shi'i doctrinal position of the inhibition of music. Yet even within the context of the surface meaning, he has the "music-dulls-your-mind" note fluted quite highly. This gears his position towards the rational elements. Music is bad not just because Shi'i jurists say so, but because "rationality" says so. This is a supreme rationalization of a key juridical doctrine. Then, in a footnote, he appeals to the authority of a supreme Usuli cleric, Shaykh Ansari, "who had thought so."[245] This at once consolidates Motahhari's legitimate juridical discourse and further invalidates it to the rationally minded by its capital insistence on the primacy of intellect.

But at the same time the carefully phrased "such songs which . . ." qualifies, and thus distinguishes, certain songs that incite one's passion from others. The tacit argument, implied rather strongly, is that certain other songs that are not inciting the passion and thus do not dull the intellect are exempted from the Shi'i injunction. This tacit subtext of Motahhari's formulation of the Shi'i position, again, does two things at once: First, it often leaves the marginal possibility for certain kinds of music to be acceptable; and, second, it does this by appealing to the sound judgment of reason.

Motahhari follows a more or less similar argument in defending the Islamic inhibition of plastic arts:

As for sculptures *(mojassameh-sazi)*, the Islamic prohibition is based on its prohibition of, and opposition to, idolatry. Islam has agreed with such opposition to [plastic arts = idolatry]. Because were the statues of prophets and others to be made, we would have undoubtedly had blatant idolatry today.[246]

It was vital for Motahhari to cater to the artistic expectations of the young generation. He grasped the anti-intellectual and anti-artistic accusations of secular intellectuals against clerical Shiʿism, turned them around, and tried to provide a "rational" explication of the Islamic position. In the process, however, he felt obligated to leave some room for future negotiation. His success in denying the antimodernist accusations of the seculars any measure of credence, however, here remains widely open to debate.

Non-Marxist Revolutionary Ethics

Lest such antimodernist tendencies dull the sharp edge of his revolutionary appeal, Motahhari had to develop, as he shifted the level of discourse to a new gear, a radical code of ethical conduct at once "progressive" and non-Marxist. Motahhari's lifelong commitment seems to have been to confront Marxism at every possible front but particularly at the political and philosophical levels. He guided his anti-Marxist energy infinitely more laboriously than he did anything openly similar against the Pahlavi monarchy. Perhaps one reason why he could write and propagate so profusely during the Pahlavi era was the coalition, in this particular instance, of his anti-Marxist agenda and that of the regime.[247]

On matters of ethics he rejected what he considered to be the self-serving and material reductionism of a Marxist view of ethics and argued for the possibility, obviously realized in Islam, of a humanistic and altruistic exposition of ethical principles that are followed for their inherent good rather than for egotistic purposes.[248] Motahhari then goes one step further and argues that the foundations of any set of ethical principles are based on a revealed religion.[249] Ethics lose their reasons and their force once devoid of metaphysical dimensions and promises: "This much is certain that religion, at least as a kind of guarantee, is necessary for the human ethics."[250] The obvious conclusion is that "with the same ratio that religion and faith have been weakened, it is practically observed that the human being is ethically fallen [as well]."[251]

Following this, Motahhari argues for the absolute essentiality of ethical principles and against ethical relativism.[252] Here again his argument is directed chiefly against the Marxists: "Some people believe that ethics is relative, and that economic developments in particular have constantly changed and continue to change the ethics."[253] He fundamentally rejected such readings of ethical relativism.

In defending the case of ethical absolutism, Motahhari opens an important clause that, translated into political terms, becomes rather crucial. Although to tell a lie is principally wrong, should someone ask "is there a place where theft is permissible?" He would answer "yes, it would happen that it is even obligatory."[254] This opens wide the vast possibility of the presumed validity of an end justifying the undeniable wickedness of the means to attain it. Motahhari does not pursue this line of argument and leaves it, perhaps advisedly, as it is.

His principal argument in his discussion of ethics is that without a religious (metaphysiçal) basis underlying the foundations of ethical mores, no degree of authority is warranted them. Religious doctrines are the condito sine qua non of ethical principles. This argument was launched explicitly against a mode of secular humanism which, in its Iranian version, had a particular color of nationalism about it. The Pahlavi monarchy, and its ideologues, wished, gradually, to concoct a collective national consciousness, with an air of ethical righteousness about it, primarily on "Iranian values" and independent of the clerical stamp of approval. In this secular-humanism-cum-monarchy, the appropriation of religious (Shiʿi) doctrines was kosher insofar as it worked independently of the clerical order.

But the argument that the ethical principles were predicated on religious doctrines was also launched against the liberal and revolutionary ideologies that claimed equal attention to their moral righteousness independent of the religious (and clerical in particular) attachment. The liberal element sought to introduce secular humanism, however mutely and tacitly, as a bona fide alternative to the outmoded religious doctrines and practices. The (nonreligious) revolutionary forces saw in secular humanism the elements of a social cohesion and collective consciousness independent of "the opium of the masses." Of course, the intellectual advocacy of this radical secularism was more selective in what ingredients would constitute this (nonreligious) humanism. They would take Maxim Gorki over Feodor Dostoyevski, André Malraux over Albert Camus, and Ignazio Silone over Luigi Pirandello any time.

Motahhari strongly rejected both of these versions of (oppositional) secular humanism, as well as its monarchical brand. The only bona fide collective consciousness underlying a set of ethical principles that he recognized as legitimate was metaphysical. The notion of "Self," he would argue, is rather limited in a collective consciousness based on secular humanism. That "Self" can be expanded, through a universal faith, to include a family, a clan, or a nation. Any notion of humanity at large is predicated on its ultimate expansion to include Truth, or more precisely God.[255]

Women's Rights

Unless anchored in specific social issues, such concerns with abstract moral principles will have had no political relevance. Motahhari commuted back and forth between the distant doctrinal and the more immediate political frames of reference. The question of women in a modern Islamic society was a crucial political point of contention that needed immediate attention.

Motahhari was one of the few Shiʿi clerics who was particularly sensitive to the question of women and their social status in an Islamic society. In his book on Islamic views of education, he happened to quote a famous prophetic tradition on the necessity of learning: "Seeking knowledge is incumbent upon every Muslim *(muslimin)*."[256] In the original Arabic the word for "Muslim" is masculine singular *(muslim)*. He accepts this version of the tradition as valid and considers the version "seeking knowledge is incumbent upon every Muslim (man) and Muslim (woman)" weak in authenticity. However, he then produces an extraordinary explanation in a footnote,[257] where he argues that the Arabic masculine noun "Muslim" stands for both the masculine and feminine genders.

In fact the masculine case in Arabic is not constructed "especifically" for men. Only when standing vis-à-vis the feminine is the masculine case particular [to men]. Otherwise it is general [to both men and women].[258]

Then he provides the argument that many Qur'anic commands obligating Muslims to various religious requirements are expressed in the masculine case. He maintains that the Qur'anic injunctions could not have been issued just for men; they are meant for both men and women. He concludes that whenever the masculine case is used, except when specifically in contradistinction to the feminine, it is meant for both men and women. This would mean that the prophetic tradition cited has obligated both men and women to pursue knowledge. Although Motahhari does not articulate this question any further in this footnote, the ramification of his argument is quite clear: the Islamically sanctioned necessity of universal education for women, which many Shiʿi authorities had objected to up until the Constitutional Revolution and even later.

Women's Rights in Islam

But the question of women's education points towards the larger issue of women's rights in a modern Islamic society. Motahhari could not have left this crucial matter without an ideologically charged answer. In every corner and niche, Motahhari had to re-Islamicize his contemporary history. Given his ideological disposition, he could not have attended the pressing question of women's rights in modern Muslim societies without engaging in an immediate dialogue with "The West," as he did at the very outset of his collections of essays on the subject.[259] The compelling leprechaun of his and his generation's imagination, "The West," never abandoned Motahhari's excruciating endeavors to render Islam historically revalidated. "Freedom" and "equality," he observed, have been the essential features of all "Western" social movements in modern history, including those that have advanced the individual rights of women. The biologically based natural differences between the two sexes, which are self-evident despite the equally natural claim of women to social and legal equality, have been ignored by the capitalist interests in "The West" to exploit the female labor force.[260] Basing his argument on a passage in a Persian translation of Will Durant's *Pleasures of Philosophy,* Motahhari argued that up until the twentieth century women lacked any human rights in "The West," and that it was through the Industrial Revolution that these rights were gradually granted to them. Politicians joined this crusade for obvious political reasons, and "the twentieth-century youth," that is, young men, pretended to advocate the cause of women's liberation so that they could "postpone their marriage until about when they got to be forty-years old, and perhaps remain a 'bachelor'! forever!!!"[261]

Motahhari contended that the women's liberation movements have alleviated some of their former problems but have also created new ones. Whereas women's problems used to be in the denial of their humanity, their new problems rest on the denial of their femininity.[262] In the United States, Motahhari argues through a Persian translation of an article about working American women, women suffer because they have to handle heavy equipment in factories or complain because, as widows, they are no longer treated to special tax exemptions. Women are the weaker sex, Motahhari contends; they ought to be protected and safeguarded. Their "monthly sickness," among other natural weaknesses,[263] indicates that they are of a different physical disposition. The Qur'an, which is a reflection of Divinity, considers both the human and the feminine rights of women.

Muslim Women in Modern Iran

As Motahhari himself explains in his 1974 introduction, his collection of essays about women was originally published during 1966–67 in a popular weekly magazine, *Zan-e Ruz (The Contemporary Woman),* devoted to women's concerns. In 1966, issues of women's rights were particularly high on the agenda of this journal. When a judge presented a forty-point bill in its pages that would revise the civil law with regard to women's rights, Motahhari was asked to respond. A mechanism was worked out with the journal so that for every article that the judge, Ibrahim Mahdavi Zanjani, wrote in defense of these forty points, Motahhari would write a responding article, and both articles would be published in the same issue. In early December 1966, Motahhari and Mahdavi began to write their counterpoising articles. Six weeks into these publications Mahdavi died of a heart attack. Motahhari, however, continued to write his articles, which totalled thirty-three. He had intended to add to them before publishing the entire series in book form. However, he could not find time to do so and decided to publish what he had. He hoped to organize his notes and publish from them a second volume on the question of women; but these notes have remained unpublished.

In his articles in *Zan-e Ruz,* Motahhari was given an unprecedented opportunity to communicate directly to one of the most secularized segments of the Iranian youth. His previous audience was primarily like-minded Muslim students and their professional parents. But through the weekly podium of *Zan-e Ruz,* he charged full blast against the prevalent secular tendencies of his time and, simultaneously, defended the veracity and contemporary relevance of Islamic laws concerning women in a calm, composed, and, in his tone and manner, convincing language.

He pointed out in these articles that questions of family and women were not unique to Iran, that all societies faced them. He urged Iranians to seek solutions culturally compatible with their history and not simply to ape "The West" in this or any other regard. In any possible revision of family law, compatibility with the Iranian Constitution, which had decreed that no law could be passed that was incompatible with Islam, and with "the religious sentiments of the Iranian society"[264] had to be taken into consideration. Motahhari then proceeds to defend the traditional customs of engagement and marriage. In disagreeing with the proposed modifications, he finds nothing offensive in a man's primary function in proposing to a woman. He then proceeds to defend the temporary marriage as stipulated in Shi'i Islam. Especially under present circumstances, temporary marriage is more advisable before fuller commitments are, or can be, made. Had temporary marriage been a "Western" practice, he charged, it would have been celebrated by secular Iranians as a most progressive idea. Motahhari himself, however, wishes to quote Bertrand Russell's opinion in favor of legalized prostitution.[265]

Islam has fully supported the rights of women. In response to Ali's asking the Prophet's permission to marry his daughter, as Motahhari began to renarrate a piece of the sacred history, the Prophet had said that he would ask his daughter.[266] Motahhari defends the elasticity and compatibility of Islamic laws with the contemporary realities. "As a matter of fact," he interjected, "many foreign [that is, "Western"] scholars and writers have studied Islam and have praised Islamic laws as a set of advanced laws."[267] George Bernard Shaw is one of these foreign observers. Motahhari then issues a sweeping condemnation of "The West" and an equally sweeping defense of "The East" and "Islam." In "Western philosophies" the status of the human species is diminished;[268] and the view of "The West" about human beings is self-contradictory.[269] It is only through the authority of the sacred texts, for example the Qur'an, that the human rights of individuals, men and women, ought to be recognized. But even Plato, whom

Motahhari cites from a Persian translation of the Fifth Book of *The Republic,* had recognized the quantitative, which Motahhari distinguishes from qualitative, differences in men and women's respective physical and mental capabilities.[270] "Thank God I was born a Greek and not a non-Greek," Motahhari quotes Plato, "a free man and not a slave, a man and not a woman."[271]

Motahhari then proceeds to defend the Islamically sanctioned practice of dowry which he considers quite natural given the fact that, because of the hardship of both monthly menstruation and childbearing, women grow weaker than men, and thus need to be financially secure. Moreover, women are "essentially" more prone than men to conspicuous consumption.[272] A more or less similar argument is constructed to support the Qur'anically sanctioned injunction that women should inherit less than men under the Islamic law of inheritance. In response to a skeptic who had asked "why should a poor woman receive one share and a man two," Motahhari paraphrases Imam Ja'far al-Sadiq as having said because she is exempted from military service, because she is exempted from certain collectively mandatory retributions, and because she received a dowry from her husband.[273]

Motahhari comes full-fledged to defend the Islamic right of men to initiate divorce, with one important stipulation. Initiating divorce is the "natural" right of man[274] because if a man ceases to love his wife, the marriage is dead (whereas if a wife stops loving her husband, the marriage is only half-dead),[275] yet divorce can be the delegated right of women. That is, Islam postulates the possibility of a man's granting his wife in their marriage contract the right to initiate a divorce. Under some other circumstances, such as the man's sexual impotence, a woman can also initiate a divorce.[276]

Motahhari considers monogamy "the most natural form of marriage."[277] Any form of polygamy, whether polyandry or polygyny, is an aberration from the norm. Yet while he dismisses polyandry immediately, he goes to great trouble to justify polygyny, which is condoned by Islam. Islam has not invented polygyny, he interjects. The idea is actually a medieval European practice.[278] Islam has, in fact, limited it and brought it under strict control. Motahhari also makes sure to refer to the fact that pre-Islamic Iranians exercised polygyny to an unlimited extent.[279] He offers the following justification for the acceptability of polygyny and the unacceptability of polyandry:

Man wants the woman herself *(shakhs-e zan),* and yet woman wants the heart of man and his self-sacrifices. For man, insofar as he possesses the woman herself, he does not care if he loses her heart. Thus man does not care that in polygyny he loses the heart and the sentiments of the woman. But for woman, the heart and the sentiments of man are essential. If she loses that, she loses everything.[280]

There is an important side step to Motahhari's defense of polygyny which charges grave immorality against "The West." He likes to remind his Westoxicated audience that Bertrand Russell, the great British philosopher, recognized the grave difficulty of having more women in England than men and suggested that unmarried women should simply have children with married men and then have the government pay for raising their children.[281] He then compares the Islamic solution to Russell's and derides the British philosopher for advocating immoral acts. He concludes:

Mr. Russell is concerned that should his suggestion not become legalized, many unmarried women would remain barren *(aqim)*. Yet Mr. Russell knows quite well that the unmarried English women cannot wait for such laws. They have effectively and of their own accord taken the matter into their hands and solved the problems of being without a husband and not having children.[282]

Motahhari then proceeds to give facts and figures, quoted from a Tehran daily newspaper, according to which 10 percent of all British are born illegitimate.[283] "Without waiting for the legalization of Mr. Russell's suggestion," he interjects, "the English nation has solved the problem itself."[284] Having thus characterized the moral consequences of disregarding Islamic injunctions, he proceeds to advocate further his portrayal of "The Western" state of moral degeneration. By legalizing homosexuality, he informs his audience, the British government not only did not follow Russell's advice, but it further decreased the female/male ratio.[285] "At the present time," Motahhari wrote in 1967, "in England polygyny is forbidden but homosexuality is permitted."[286]

Man by nature, according to "the current opinion of Western psychologists and social philosophers,"[287] is polygynous. The possibility of polygyny in the Islamic society has been the chief factor helping monogamy to survive. Had it not been for the possibility of polygyny, men would never have married, because there are always more women than men.[288] "There is no doubt," Motahhari emphasized, "that monogamy is better than polygyny."[289] Yet the possibility of polygyny helps unmarried women get married and that prevents the spread of immoral sexual encounters.[290] The outcry against polygyny is actually a plot on the part of the "twentieth-century man" to rid himself of his responsibilities towards more than one wife, to be bound to only one spouse, and then to engage in all kinds of cheap but abundant sexual activities.[291] Motahhari also emphasizes that there are all kinds of moral, psychological, and practical problems to polygyny. By severely restricting its practice, though, Islam has made a balanced virtue out of a natural and social necessity.

Matters of Modernity: Insurance

Although at the center of the issues of modernity, the problems of women's liberation were not the only pressing matters for a Muslim ideologue to attend to. New ideas and unprecedented issues had to be dealt with effectively and immediately if Islam were to safeguard a measure of relevance and continuity for the present age. Motahhari, scarcely leaving a modern issue Islamically unattended, delivered a series of lectures in 1972–73 about the feasibility of "Insurance" in an Islamic context. These lectures, delivered at the request of "the Islamic Society of Physicians,"[292] were meant to formulate a Shi'i juridical stance vis-à-vis this modern phenomenon for which Muslim physicians knew no established position. During the postrevolutionary period, the nature and organization of banks, insurance companies, and many other such financial institutions became subjects of considerable debate. Motahhari's positions on the matter could not have been ignored. Consequently, his 1972–73 lectures were published in October 1982 alongside edicts on "Insurance" by Ayatollah Khomeini.[293] The publisher made sure to distinguish between these two discourses so as not to suggest any discrepancy of ideas between the two religious leaders.[294]

Motahhari approaches the question of "insurance" in the great Usuli tradition: Although it has no precedence in the Shi'i juridical canon, it can be addressed through the intellectual reasoning (aql) of a Mojtahed.[295] Also as a classical Usuli, he argues that every single form and instance of transaction should not be articulated, a priori, in fiqh. He then resorts to two canonical sources, a Qur'anic verse and a prophetic tradition, according to which Muslims are bound to any kind of transaction they contract insofar as it does not transgress a Qur'anic injunction.[296]

Motahhari's judgment is that an "insurance" transaction is a "correct" (sahih) commercial contract and that it need not have a precise nominal reference in Shi'i juridical sources. All it needs is a "principal" justification, which already exists in abundance. The significance of the Usuli school of jurisprudence in Shi'ism for more recent ideological developments becomes particularly apparent when we consider the appeal of such liberal positions of the clerics to the merchants and the larger bourgeoisie commercial prerogatives.

Motahhari goes so far as to consider "insurance" an "irrevocable transaction" (aqd-e lazem).[297] Having defined the legality (or Islamicity) of insurance on Usuli grounds, he proceeds to give an Akhbari defense of it as well. Here he argues that in practice and effect "insurance" is similar to a "guarantee" (zeman), which is a bona fide and long-established juridical concept in the canonical sources.[298] He concludes, however, that we need not call the transaction "insurance" (biymeh). The term "guarantee" (zeman) will convey the practice and the idea properly. "Insurance" itself is

principally an acceptable and correct commercial transaction.[299] Motahhari dismisses the possibility of "insurance" being construed as a kind of
gamble[300] and argues that it has a "known" purpose[301] and a specified
period of time.[302]

The subtext of his argument for the acceptability of insurance, according
to the principles of Shi'i jurisprudence and particularly as delivered at an
organization of physicians, is that the modernity of such practices as life or
property insurance do not, ipso facto, put them outside a Shi'i juridical
context. But perhaps more important, as Shi'i jurisprudence can be extrapolated to meet the needs of modern legal and commercial necessities, then
by logical extension, Shi'ism itself, which in Motahhari's principal orientation *is* the Shi'i *fiqh,* can be expected to meet the compelling needs of the
modern society at large.

From Insurance to Law and Legitimacy

Towards the end of a second lecture he delivered on "liability" insurance,
someone from the audience follows up on a point Motahhari had discussed
earlier and asks him about the responsibility of a governmental agent who
has been commanded to execute someone. Keeping in mind that these
lectures were given in 1972–73, at the peak of Mohammad Reza Shah's
suppression of political activists, the charged atmosphere of this question
becomes apparent. The questions and answers are worth considering here
in some detail:

Q: It occasionally happens that we know that someone has not committed
a sin. Then suppose someone [else] commands one that "if you do not
execute this person, we shall execute you yourself," or even if such a
threat is not made. Now, what is to be done in such a case?

A: Under no circumstances has the person the right [to execute someone
one knows to be innocent]. As we said, in matters of blood, even
intimidation is not relevant. Even if they tell him, "we kill you yourself," he should not attempt [to execute an innocent person].

Q: Now, how do we formulate the question here? Suppose someone is
working for the judiciary system, that is to say, he has a position in the
executive branch [of the government], and then he executes someone
who has committed a crime and who has been legally condemned to be
executed. Now, is this agent of execution responsible for ascertaining
[whether or not the condemned has actually committed the crime]?

A: In such cases, insofar as the [Shi'i] jurisprudence is concerned, no one
other than a just and qualified religious judge *(mojtahed)* can issue such
an indictment.

Q: What if the person who has issued the indictment is a [civil] judge?

A: Should this agent of execution recognize the person who has issued the indictment as the religious judge, then he can assume the indictment to be righteous. But if he does not recognize him as the religious judge, then he cannot assume the indictment to be righteous. Here, no one can say, God willing, that it is [a] righteous [judgment]. No sir, no such nonsense has any place here.[303]

The implications of Motahhari's position here are radically important. Obviously, and as the editor of Motahhari's text has realized,[304] the civil judges during the reign of the Shah were not recognized as, nor did they have any claim to being, religiously trained or qualified. They were the products of the government's secular education system rather than the outcome of the religious seminaries. By specifying the condition that an agent of execution should know and recognize the judge as a religious judge, Motahhari has practiced what in logic is called ta'liq-e beh mahal, or "stipulating upon the impossible." Since all the judges were civil rather than religious, then all judgments were suspended and thus illegitimate. This tacitly but emphatically questions the validity and legitimacy of the judicial system and, with it, since "justice" is at the root of political legitimacy, the entire political order. Thus the implication of the argument goes beyond the judicial system. Ipso facto, it renders equally illegitimate the political system that has legitimated the authority of the legal system, ex officio. Moreover, the specific example of execution that Motahhari uses explicitly questions the legality of many executions, imprisonments, and persecutions carried out on political grounds. The argument is very subtle and rather tangential; yet its implications could not have escaped its audience.

A further implication of Motahhari's argument is a powerful indictment against the very feasibility of both judicial and political orders located in a civil rather than religious, secular rather than sacred, frame of reference. This would not only be a reference to the existing monarchical system, it would equally challenge any potential judicial and political system on liberal-democratic or radical-revolutionary (both secular) grounds. With one strike, Motahhari scores two blows, one against the existing monarchical system and the other against the competing liberal and radical contentions, with whom he had an equally powerful debate.

Immediately connected to this dual rejection of authority and legitimacy in the established and (secular) oppositional forces was Motahhari's almost open call for rebellion against the status quo. The conclusion was quite evident. If the executors of governmental commands were not sure of the legitimacy of their content, how could they avoid committing a moral transgression other than by defying these commands. Although Motahhari issues this specific edict for the case of a governmental executioner, its implications for other governmental employees were quite evident. This line of argument cannot be carried out too emphatically because, after all, Motahhari himself, when delivering these lectures, was a government employee, teaching at the Tehran University, a state organization. However, the implications of his argument for passive defiance of the status quo and the state authority ought to be recognized.

Equally present in Motahhari's argument is the self-evident and confident call for the exclusive legitimacy of the Shiʿi juridical discourse and legal, and with it political, system. It is remarkable that throughout his argument, Motahhari never refers to the compatibility of "insurance" with the Iranian constitution or civil law. His essential line of argument is a dual comparison between the technical aspects of insurance and its compatibility with various juridical categories in Shiʿi jurisprudence. The subtextual assumption is that the only juridical frame of reference within which such modern issues as "insurance" can be discussed is Shiʿi jurisprudence. And by extension, if Shiʿi jurisprudence is the only legitimate frame of reference, then Shiʿism as such is the only viable basis for legal, political, and social order. The legitimacy of Shiʿism as a universal order of social organization is expressed against the refusal of any legitimacy for either the established constitutional monarchy or the oppositional alternatives assumed by liberal or radical (secular) tendencies.

The Extent of Motahhari's Appeal

Motahhari's lecture on "insurance" for a group of self-organized physicians who had formed a voluntary association makes several important matters quite evident: His regular and persistent engagement with keeping the Islamic juridical discourse present and relevant in social settings beyond the reach of the full-fledged clerics from Qom or Mashhad succeeds far beyond anything any other cleric could have reached. Voluntary professional associations, such as those of physicians, engineers, and teachers, as well as the university, college, and high school students, regularly asked Motahhari to lecture to them about various professional, legal, social, and political issues that confronted them. Muslim student associations, in particular, regularly sought and received his opinions about various issues that mattered to them most. Throughout these speeches Motahhari's increasingly difficult task was to keep the relevance and legitimacy of the Islamic discourse alive in the face of a number of ideological forces that, explicitly or implicitly, challenged the validity and relevance of the religious language. To engage in such discussions, largely caused by the exposure of his audience to alien "Western" ideas, Motahhari had to mobilize his limited intellectual means, particularly exacerbated by his lack of knowledge of any European language, to be able to engage in a dialogue that did not immediately disappoint his physician, engineer, teacher, or student audiences, mostly either educated in "The West" or on their way there. Nothing other than sheer determination accounts for Motahhari's overcoming his limitations and scoring a measure of success with the range of his urban intellectual audiences.

It should be noted that during the years when Ayatollah Khomeini was in exile in Najaf, and thus effectively cut off from the majority of his audience, and during the years of Shari'ati's radicalism, Bazargan's quietism, and Taleqani's imprisonment, it was Motahhari's sustained and active engagement with a variety of social groups that kept the flame of the Shi'i revolutionary discourse blazing with heartwarming relevance. In the face of two antagonistic groups of discourses, which while opposing each other agreed on the irrelevance of the religious language, Motahhari persistently confronted the established monarchical and opposing secular discourses with a language deeply rooted in Islamic sentiments.

It is very difficult, if not impossible, to ascertain which social group was attracted to which one of the Islamic ideologues who offered their revolutionary positions. But without a doubt, among Khomeini, Shari'ati, Taleqani, Bazargan, and Motahhari, the lattermost attracted more of the middle-class, urban professionals, and intellectuals. Khomeini appealed essentially to the seminarians and the bazzaris, Shari'ati to the young urban intellectuals, Bazargan to the older generation of technocrats, and Taleqani to the more religiously minded urban political activists. Motahhari, however, had a wide range of constituency among university professors, high school teachers, students at colleges and high schools, physicians, engineers, bureaucrats, the business sector, and the religiously minded urban intellectuals. This massive orchestration of social groupings and religious sentiments by all these ideologues considerably paved the way for the Islamic Revolution.

Questions and Answers

"It is not the answers which Aquinas gives," they say, "but the questions which he asks, which are the measures of his philosophical gifts."[305] Whatever the range and depth of his philosophical concerns, Motahhari's sweeping attendance upon the ideological currency of Islam made him leave untouched no issue of contemporary relevance. He had very few questions of his own. But he had full answers to every question of his time. His significance cannot, and should not, be judged by some abstract notion of philosophical or intellectual vigor. His primary concern, and the essential factor in his continued significance in the unfolding of the Islamic Revolution, was to renovate and update Islam so as to make it new, make it ideologically competitive, politically forceful, and thus in full revolutionary alert should the right moment come. He did more, and sustained a larger course of ideological discipline, than anyone else to make that revolutionary moment possible. In achieving this goal, no other spirit animated him more powerfully, no other anxiety drove him more forcefully, than that lunar apparition, that figment of his captured imagination, the seductive force, the self-destructive urge, unleashed into a hermetic solitude, that he and his cohorts so irresistibly called "The West."

CHAPTER 4

Sayyid Mahmud Taleqani:
The Father of the Revolution

"We have no security for the future," thought Lord Macauley, reflecting on Sir Thomas More, "against the prevalence of any theological error. . . . When we reflect that Sir Thomas More was ready to die for the doctrine of transubstantiation, we cannot but feel some doubt whether the doctrine of transubstantiation may not triumph over all opposition. . . . A faith which stands that test will stand any test."[1] Few people seem to be ready nowadays to die for the doctrine of transubstantiation—or for any other theologically sublimated doctrine for that matter. In the age of "conflict resolution" and the United Nations, the staunchest dragons are brought to negotiating tables with the most valiant and committed knights. But even today, matters of political conviction are the only stimuli that can induce passions of rage and revolt. Multiply the convincing certitude of political convictions by embattled vestiges of a faith that has historically stood the test of abnegation, and you have some notion of how willing contemporary Muslim ideologues have been to die for the radical figments of their revolutionary imagination. That imagination, whether Sir Thomas More's or Sayyid Mahmud Taleqani's, is not the exclusive territory of matters of doctrine and dogma, if indeed it has ever been. Today more than ever, the ideologues of the Islamic Revolution let the realities of their political imagination redirect their attendance in interpreting the historical unfolding of their faith. That faith, the renarrated text of some old (all-but-forgotten) pieties, is now the final repertoire of Muslim revolutionary self-definition. That "self" is currently defined in a space between the verticality of rehistoricized faith and the horizontality of contemporary political existence, or more closely, between religious conviction repoliticized and political certitude sublimated to heavenly reassurances.

The Mosaic of "The Islamic Ideology"

"The Islamic Ideology," as merely sensed intuitively by Al-e Ahmad, trumpeted rhetorically by Shari'ati, and legitimated doctrinally by Motahhari, needed the all-too-essential Qur'anic justification. Al-e Ahmad, experienced in his long political career, sensed the futility of secular ideologies and began to develop the groundwork for "the Islamic Ideology" without getting close enough to call it by that name. Shari'ati took Al-e Ahmad's lead, became the Islamic ideologue par excellence, and demonstrated the full revolutionary potentials of "the Islamic Ideology." What he lacked, however, in the range and depth of Islamic erudition, Motahhari had in full command. Motahhari gave "the Islamic Ideology" its full Islamic certificate, carrying the ideological neologism deep into the sacred precinct of scholastic learning, from theology to philosophy to mysticism. Yet the full Qur'anic justification of the term—and with the term the ideology, and with the ideology the revolt it trumpeted—was left for Taleqani who gave the quintessential Qur'anic interpretation to the pressing necessity for an Islamic revolution to be carried out in the changed and changing terms of "the Islamic Ideology."

Like Father, Like Son

Sayyid Mahmud Taleqani (1910–1979) was born to a devout religious family. His father, Abolhasan Taleqani, was a prominent cleric who had received a scholastic education in Najaf, where he had studied with, among others, Mirza Hasan Shirazi, the distinguished jurist of the late nineteenth century who was instrumental in the famous Tobacco Revolt of 1891–92. Abolhasan Taleqani, Sayyid Mahmud's father, returned from Iraq in 1899 and began his teaching career in Tehran. Although he, like many other clerics who were also considered descendants of the Prophet (a *Sayyid*), could have made his living through obligatory religious contributions, he chose to pursue a trade. He practiced the useful and precise profession of a watchmaker until his death in 1931. His watchmaking shop also served as a meeting place for political activities.[2]

A friendship that presaged that of the younger Taleqani and Mehdi Bazargan developed between the elder Taleqani and Bazargan's father. They, along with a number of other like-minded clerics and laymen, would meet regularly to discuss various religious issues that faced their nation. Their circle became particularly active in propagating a religious consciousness that they thought was in increasing danger. They published a journal, *Balagh,* in which they sought to respond to the gripping questions of the rising generation of politically active Muslims. Abolhasan Taleqani supported Sayyid Hasan Modarres (1870–1938), one of the most distin-

guished clerical opponents of Reza Shah. A prominent cleric of the constitutional and early Pahlavi periods, Modarres had studied in Isfahan and
Najaf. On his return to Iran he had been reelected a number of times as a
member of the Parliament. In his supporters' eyes, he was a politically
active cleric who successfully combined the commanding concerns of an
active political life with religious fervor and conviction.

The elder Taleqani actively participated in the political movements of
the 1910s and 1920s, a period of rapid change, when Reza Khan engineered a coup, toppled the Qajar dynasty, and gradually managed to crown
himself king. His political activities caused much concern and fear for his
family. As the young Taleqani reminisced later:

My father was a prominent clerical activist. Every morning that he left the house,
we the children and our poor mother feared and trembled until his return. I spent
my childhood years with these fearful, horrifying, tumultuous, and aggravating
scenes.[3]

These early childhood memories haunted Taleqani in the most vigorous
and robust years of his political activities. The indignities and anxieties of
an unjustly injured self—father and son—continued to animate his prolonged and persistent political activities. The feeble figure of his frightened
father, harmed more by the humiliations of political defeat than the actualities of daily hardship, was perhaps the most gripping memory of injustice
and indignity the son so ardently devoted his life to oppose.

Reza Shah, by all accounts, was a frightful sight. The dwarfing of
Taleqani's—or Al-e Ahmad's—father at the sight of Reza Shah "the Great"
would later rise to haunt Reza Shah's son, looking in terror at the growing
sons of his father's enemies.

To Grow Up Under Reza Shah

Taleqani spent his early life under the dictatorial grip of Reza Shah's reign.
He reminisced about his childhood with vivid memories:

Since the early days that I opened my eyes into this society, I saw the people of this
land under the whip and boot of the tyrants. Every evening at home we were
expecting [bad] news, wondering what had happened that day, who had been
arrested, who exiled, who murdered, or what else they had decided for people.[4]

But even under the harshest of all conditions, the life of a young cleric
had to have its established routines. Sayyid Mahmud Taleqani's education
began under his father's tutelage in elementary Persian and Arabic grammar and language and Qur'anic studies. In the early 1930s Taleqani moved
from Tehran to Qom, where the late Ayatollah Shaykh Abdolkarim Ha'eri
had just established a distinguished seminary on a par with that of Najaf.

Taleqani studied there under a number of prominent jurists: Shaykh Abdolkarim Ha'eri, Muhammad Taqi Khawnsari, Hojjat Kuhkamari, and Muhammad Taqi Yazdi. His years as a seminarian in Qom were spent under
the fearful presence of a despotic king determined to give a European look
to his country.

Reza Shah had established a law in 1928 standardizing the dress code
and severely restricting the use of the clerical habit. In 1935 he supple-
mented this law with another, forcing Iranian women out of their traditional veils, whether they liked it or not. Taleqani remembered those days
clearly, with painful memories:

When I was a student in Qom, the people of this country lived under severe
pressure and tyranny. They would fearfully run from each other. People's lives and
dignity, even turbans on the head of the clerics and scarves on women's heads, were
subject to the attack and insult of the agents of despotism. This condition caused
such pain and aggravation for me, the results of which are torments and sicknesses
with which I am afflicted until the end of my days.[5]

Taleqani's pain and aggravation with the reign of Reza Shah, the tortu-
rous traces of which crept into the most sacrosanct sanctum of his revolutionary imagination, were tacitly translated into mute resentment towards
the religious authorities, masters of his own profession, who either condoned or tolerated these deeds. He reached the point of actually questioning the validity and relevance of the entire seminarian system: "In those
days [the 1930s]," he reminisced, "I was thinking to myself: 'Aren't these
accurate discussions in religious codes and regulations for the individual's
actions and prosperity in the society?'"[6] His disillusion with the clerical
establishment led to a total reappraisal of precisely what Islam, by which
he meant Muslim activists, could and should do under the prevailing historical circumstances:

This attitude and self-contradiction of certain religious leaders, these dark conditions, these spiritual agonies, inevitably forced me to study and scrutinize ever more
diligently the holy Qur'an, the revered *Nahj al-Balaghah,* the history and biography
of the noble Prophet and the sacred Imams, peace be upon them. I became acquainted with certain great clerics. Gradually I found myself in unique surroundings, got to know the roots of religion. My heart reassured, I recognized the purpose
and the objective of [my] social responsibility. Then as much as I could, and with
the grace of God, I helped others.[7]

A certain revolutionary savoir faire gradually develops out of these sentiments that animates the young Taleqani's self-perception. The Herculean
attempt to reformulate an Islam more in tune with the historical exigencies
of the time, in contradistinction to received doctrines and institutions of
authority, is a determination Taleqani shared with Shari'ati and other
ideologues of the Islamic movement. His attention to the formative pretexts

of Islam was the necessary groundwork to reinterpret the old faith into a new revolutionary posture.

Taleqani's growing dissatisfaction with the clerical establishment, and what seemed to him a sanctimonious display of useless piety, would be compensated occasionally by those clerics who did resist Reza Shah's tyranny. One such cleric was his old teacher Shaykh Muhammad Taqi Yazdi who had been tortured in prison. When Taleqani visited him in his exile in Shah Abd al-Azim Shrine, south of Tehran, Yazdi showed him his signs of torture and urged him to keep alive the flame of resistance.[8]

From a humiliated biological father to a tortured intellectual father, the paternal weight for revenge was quite heavy on Taleqani. Such distractions aside, Taleqani had to attend to the more compelling requirements of his chosen profession. He completed his formal training in 1939, receiving his *ijazeh* ("religious degree") from Ayatollah Ha'eri, and returned to Tehran to pursue a long career of political activity. In Tehran he began teaching at Sepahsalar Seminary, which was founded by Mirza Hossein Khan Qazvini Sepahsalar (d. 1880), a distinguished Qajar reformist. As Tehran grew in political importance under the Qajar dynasty, an increasing number of religious scholars were attracted to the capital. Sepahsalar Seminary became the capital's equivalent of the two great seats of religious learning in Iran at Mashhad and Qom.

Upon his return to Tehran from Qom, Taleqani founded "The Islamic Institute" *(Kanun-e Islam)*, a religious organization devoted to the political propagation of a revolutionary reading of Islam. The official organ of "The Islamic Institute" was *Danesh-amuz,* a journal devoted to the propagation of the young activists' ideas. One of the chief activities Taleqani pursued assiduously upon his return from Qom was conducting a sustained course of Qur'anic interpretations. This was a particularly acute political choice because of the innate revolutionary uses to which the sacred Text could be put. Taleqani held the fundamental belief, shared by Shari'ati, that the Qur'an had been either completely neglected or totally misinterpreted. He took upon himself the task of reinterpreting the Qur'an as he thought it should be and thus reintroduced the sacred Text to the center of active Muslim political life.

To Meet the Challenge

To a revolutionary imagination, the Qur'an has a robust and salubrious effect. As soon as Taleqani found himself in Tehran, he confronted Reza Shah's policies at every minor or major instant. He is reported to have attacked a policeman who had been trying to unveil a woman forcefully.[9] Reza Shah's forceful policy of taking women out of their traditional veil was one of the major stages in giving Iran an overdose of his brand of "modernism." Artificial and dictatorial as this policy was, in the long run it provided an added impetus for the docile process of public self-awareness among the masses of Iranian women. It was designed and implemented with a minimum of institutional and infrastructural support and, moreover, was executed in the most brutal and grotesque manner. Many women in Tehran and in other parts of the country were effectively barred from public appearance because they refused to abandon their traditional and habitual dress. Young women at the prime of their lives, who would have otherwise continued to live a normal, however limited, social life, refused to come out of their secluded homes until their dying day. The indignities suffered by Iranian women during this period (horrific stories are still told by the older generation of how they would be attacked by police if they had a scarf on their head) would be matched by insults of a different sort, decades later under the Islamic Republic, when the women would be publicly harassed if they did not wear the selfsame scarf.

Taleqani's affiliation with Fada'ian-e Islam also becomes established during this period when Navvab Safavi, a pseudonym for Sayyid Mojtaba' Mir-lowhi, founded this radical organization that promoted and practiced political assassinations as a means of achieving its goals. In 1949 Sayyid Hossein Imami (Kashani), a member of Fada'ian-e Islam, assassinated Abdolhossein Hajir, the court minister. Fada'ian-e Islam was also responsible for the attempted assassination of Prime Minister Razmara in 1951. Later in 1965, Fada'ian-e Islam assassinated Hasan Ali Mansur, the prime minister under whose tenure Ayatollah Khomeini's June 1963 uprising occurred.

These political assassinations were not limited to high-ranking governmental officials; they also extended to ideological forces that bore an anticlerical posture. In 1946 Sayyid Hossein Imami, of Fada'ian-e Islam, assassinated Sayyid Ahmad Kasravi, a social reformist with strong anticlerical sentiments. Taleqani was a close collaborator of Imami who would, for example, find refuge at Taleqani's house after periodic assassinations he masterminded.

Taleqani's activities during this period were not limited to such collaborations. In addition to the Muslim student associations, there were professional organizations such as the "Society of Muslim Engineers" that regularly invited Taleqani to lecture on various Islamic issues. These organizations were negatively disposed towards the rapid course of change they witnessed in their society. They had a pending sense of uncertainty, a feeling that things were falling apart. Changes in the cultural, social, economic, and political scenes were not necessarily good or bad—just troublesome, of a sort that needed a figure of authority to explain their causes and consequences.

During the tumultuous year of 1941, the temporary relief from governmental controls and pressures, brought about by the Allied occupation of Iran and the abdication of Reza Shah, gave rise to many political groupings, chief among which was the establishment of the Tudeh Party. But other, less significant—or at least as they appeared at the time—political formations were also taking shape.

Although he welcomed this period of openness, Taleqani was particularly disturbed by the Tudeh Party and its monopoly of the current ideological agenda. To balance and check that monopoly, he saw no better source than the Qur'an. His attempt to reactivate the Qur'an as a central revolutionary text had coincided with the last few years of Reza Shah's reign. Once securely on the throne, Reza Shah, who had come to power by appeasing the clerical establishment, pursued a harshly anticlerical policy. Taleqani's activism was halted immediately by Reza Shah's police, and he was exiled from Tehran. Upon Reza Shah's abdication in 1941, Taleqani returned to Tehran and resumed his activities, which were centered in the Hedayat Mosque in central Tehran. He would direct his political propagation of a revolutionary reading of "Islam" through this mosque until the end of his life in 1979.

At the Hedayat Mosque, his chief constituency, or at least the audience he targeted, was the young urban students and professionals with an innate political disposition who were, as such, increasingly attracted to non-Islamic, and even anti-Islamic, revolutionary ideologies. Marxism, with the Tudeh Party as its chief ideological and political institution, was the major contending force. All proponents of "the Islamic Ideology" in Iran, from Al-e Ahmad to Bani-Sadr, each in his own way, considered Marxism as a chief ideological competitor in the battle over the active loyalty of the young urbanites. On the whole, the group that would be attracted immediately to Taleqani was the younger generation of essentially religious families with an innate hostility towards an increasingly secular society and the anxieties and confusions it inevitably created. By and large this younger generation was educated in the public schools of Reza Shah's period, yet their family upbringing was more or less religious. Obviously, secondary social institutions under state power would respond more immediately to authoritative forces of change than would such primary institutions as the family. As a result, Taleqani's revolutionary preachings would complement the primary upbringing of the young Muslim Iranians and thus fortify them against secondary social institutions that were forcefully guided towards a rapid and occasionally rather awkward change.

The constituency that perhaps appealed most to Taleqani was the secular intellectuals and activists who were mesmerized by a rainbow of imported ideologies. It is difficult to measure, in any statistically meaningful way, the degree of Taleqani's success in attracting a secular audience. The Tudeh

Party was so vastly successful in polarizing the broad spectrum of secular activists under its red canopy that it is hard to imagine any significant number of born-again Muslims diverting their route from Ferdowsi Avenue, where the headquarters of the Tudeh Party was prominently located, to the hustle and bustle of nearby Istanbul Avenue, where the Hedayat Mosque, Taleqani's headquarters, blended into the local architecture of the neighborhood.

Perhaps one telling example of this generation is Jalal Al-e Ahmad who, despite his religious background, chose to join the Tudeh Party in 1944 rather than seek Taleqani, with whom he even had a family tie, in the Hedayat Mosque. It is perhaps more realistic to assume that the combined forces of the state-sponsored "modernization," championed by Reza Shah, and revolutionary secular ideologies, heralded by the Tudeh Party, went altogether against the spirit of religious activism sponsored by Taleqani and his clerical cohorts.

More than anything else, this emergence of religious activism was in organizational need of institutional propagation. Without widespread institutional dissemination, the revolutionary ideas of Taleqani and other like-minded ideologues would have remained socially insignificant. One of the most important series of religious institutions being formed at this time was "Islamic Societies" that young students and professionals formed on their campuses or in workplaces. These were ad hoc organizations, voluntary associations with a patently Islamic agenda, established by the students and professionals themselves to promote and activate a religious response to a generation of new problems—both moral and political. Taleqani would be invited regularly to these "Islamic Societies" to present lectures on various issues of concern to students and young professionals.

The significance of these encounters between Taleqani and the younger generation cannot be overemphasized. Through such contacts with young students, Taleqani gradually developed an acute sense of *Realpolitik,* devoid of any sentimental attachments to unnecessary pieties, that sharpened his understanding of the revolutionary urges of his time. Through their contacts with Taleqani, the students and professionals gradually recognized the revolutionary uses to which their familiar faith could be put. The result of this self-sustaining dialectic was a mutual legitimation of "the Islamic Ideology."

Through the same contacts with the young students, Taleqani was equally made aware of the prevalence of Marxist sentiments among the intelligentsia and the professionals. Confronting Marxism on ideological and material levels thus became uppermost in Taleqani's growing political agenda. His concern with the political currency of Marxism was not limited to mere ideological opposition to its propagation. He went so far as accompanying

the Iranian army in 1946 to Azarbaijan when, upon the departure of the
Soviet army, Mohammad Reza Shah sought to eliminate the last elements
of resistance in Pishehvari's separatist movement.

Taleqani's concern with the spread of Marxism was matched by a
growing concern with the more international concerns of a Muslim activist.
He was one of the chief proponents of the Palestinian cause in Iran. As
soon as the state of Israel was established in 1948, he launched a comprehensive program of lecturing and writing to support the cause of the
Palestinians, a concern that he would uphold literally until the last days of
his life. In a speech delivered to a group of ambassadors from Islamic
countries in September 1979, he stated that the Palestinian problem was
like a headache in the Islamic body politic.[10]

But despite his broader concerns, Taleqani's primary political agenda
made him an acute observer and a committed activist throughout his life.
He was a close collaborator of Mohammad Mosaddeq and Hajj Sayyid
Abolqasem Kashani in the course of the nationalization of Iranian oil. This
episode, as Al-e Ahmad would later point out, was particularly instrumental in demonstrating how a healthy coalition between the religious and
(liberal) nationalist forces would be conducive to revolutionary mobilization. If the political message was clear and convincing, no other coaltion
could match the mass appeal of "Iranian Shi'ism."

Islamic Economics

The overwhelming and immediate mass appeal of Islam and nationalism
notwithstanding, it was Marxism that established the level and nature of
political discourse in the 1940s and beyond. Taleqani's attention to economics, of all subjects, is itself a reflection of, more than a direct reaction
to, the predominance of Marxist ideas during this period. Because of the
primacy that Marxist historiography and sociology gave to economic factors, Taleqani felt obligated to address "Islamically" the issues thus raised.
The ideological predominance of the secular left throughout the 1940s was
such that even its apparent opponents followed its agenda, used its vocabulary, and, even more important, adopted its state of mind. It is rather
remarkable that while Marxism institutionally failed in Iran, it established
the level and content of ideological discourse within the very spirit and
body of the "Islamic" political consciousness. Thus the agenda of *Islam
and Ownership,* as the very title suggests, was set, perhaps even unconsciously, by the Tudeh Party and its anticapitalist, prosocialist ideas and
programs.

In 1953, in the wake of the CIA-engineered coup against the democrati-
cally elected government of Mohammad Mosaddeq, Taleqani wrote his
famous *Islam and Ownership.* Essentially a critique of both centralized

(socialist) and free market (capitalist) economies, this text is an attempt to validate an economic program extended from the Qur'anic passages and from traditions of the Prophet and the Shi'i Imams.[11] Yet, in the very cast of its adopted discourse, *Islam and Ownership* adopts and "Islamicizes" the patently Marxist terminologies.

Taleqani's stated purpose in *Islam and Ownership* is to give a sustained "Islamic" account of man's economic endeavors. Extending from various Qur'anic passages, he maintains that righteous ownership and the absolute power of expenditure are those of God from which power He can, according to His own Judgment, give to whomever He wants.[12] Following this Divine ownership, earthly ownership is natural and innate to human beings. Codes of law and schools of economic thought have been created to account for this human characteristic. Not only human beings but even animals share this innate urge of possession. Primitive and prehistoric societies, too, have demonstrated this urge to own.[13] There is nothing particularly modern about this urge. It is innate to man.

The urge to possess, however, has grown in history to a point where it has "eradicated the balance and equilibrium and caused class struggles." If that be the case, "can [there] be a final and permanent solution for this problem?"[14] The solution, though, ought to be more in moral and political terms than merely in the economic. What necessitates the moral dimension is a mode of historical evolution in the course of which private ownership has been extended from a mere meeting of one's needs to exploiting others for "greed, envy, competition, and hostility."[15] At crucial points in history when the ever-increasing urge to possess predominates a society and leads it to self-destruction, insightful individuals propose ways to remedy that situation. But because their ideas "are not justified from the origins of faith and conviction, they either lack any impact or have a very transitory effect."[16] The origin of any economic renovation ought to be in man's spiritual disposition. The mere economic or even political ordering of human activities is not enough.

Contrary to "The West," Taleqani contends, "Eastern" societies have suffered less from class struggles because their economic reforms have been rooted historically in religion and spiritual matters. But even in "The West," books like Plato's *Republic* have attempted to instill the picture of a perfect society in people's minds, for it might lead to its actual realization.[17] Figures such as Aristotle, Sir Thomas More, Diderot, Adam Smith, Malthus, and Ricardo have sought to address the question of justice in the economic life of man. Ultimately, the emergence of the labor movements in Europe has been a massive demonstration of a "concentrated and malcontent force."[18] The advent of the Industrial Revolution in Europe and the transition of its economy from a feudal to capitalist stage have been the most recent indicators of economic upheaval. By assessing social conditions in the wake of the Industrial Revolution, Taleqani explains the origin of radical revolutionary ideas. With a patently Marxist twist to his argument, he pays close attention to economic factors in both the rise of the Industrial Revolution and the emergence of revolutionary ideologies compatible with it.

Taleqani's full description of Marxist economics, without any footnotes as to the sources of his information, is a bona fide course in the materialist interpretation of history which he reproduces with remarkable clarity. The only occasion that prompts his criticism is the Marxist conception of religion as secondary to economic matters, which he finds unacceptable.[19]

Contrary to all other, "Western," economic systems stands the Islamic which is "under the shadow of faith and belief." Absolute and uncondi-tional ownership belongs to God. Human beings have God-given rights to make use of their properties. By stipulating the existence of an afterlife in which human worldly affairs are punished or rewarded, Islam has given an open-ended dimension to the entire question of ownership. The result is that class conflicts in Islamic societies have never been as drastic and fundamental as in "The Western" societies.[20]

An essential difference between "The Western" and the Islamic societies is the divine origin of Islamic laws. Laws that are man-made are susceptible to human abuse. Islamic law, however, in both its letter and its spirit, is the guarantor of human economic well-being. This law has had a progressive and accumulative history. That it has not progressed recently is more an indication of the general stagnation that has characterized modern Muslim history. That law is the principle reason that Islamic economics can cater to the essential needs of human beings in a just and equitable manner.[21]

Islamic economics, in Taleqani's construction, is founded on the follow-ing principles. Ownership is relative and limited. Land and other natural resources are neither private nor public property; they are to be used by the Muslim leader for public benefit. The mutually exclusive alternatives of capitalism and collective ownership are indications of tumultuous periods of human history. The more moderate (Islamic) alternative is more conge-nial to normal human conditions. This moderation in Islamic economics has its revolutionary counterparts. The Islamic prohibition against usury, for example, is an indication of the "unprecedented intellectual, social, and economic Islamic revolution."[22] The reason for this has been the unavoid-able consequence of usury, which is the unreasonable accumulation of wealth in certain classes of people. Trade, too, should not lead to an uncontrolled accumulation of wealth. It has to be "limited and confined to the Islamic law."[23] There are proper mechanisms of distribution of wealth in Islam that prevent the unjust concentration of capital.

Formation and accumulation of capital, in Taleqani's paraphrasing of Marx, have been the historical occasion of the creation of economic classes.

Yet formation of classes has been innate to all human societies, from the ancient to the modern. Islam has been a unique egalitarian movement in world history. The time of the Prophet and the caliphate of Ali, in Taleqani's estimation, are supreme examples of ruling a classless society. Beyond these archetypal examples, however, a classless society has never been achieved—in "The West" or "The East." Only through a return to the "true" principles of the Islamic doctrine is there hope for the historical realization of the classless society.

In *Islam and Ownership*, Taleqani adopts the Marxist primacy of economics and provides an Islamic account to that effect. Implementing the predominantly Marxist language of "capital," "class," "means of production," etc., gives Taleqani's discourse a current and contemporary relevance. From his account, Islam emerges as an economic system superior to both capitalism and socialism. Denying neither private property nor (in effect) state-controlled public ownership, Islamic economics strives towards a golden mean that recognizes man's innate economic needs and urges and seeks to control and tame them. It is precisely in this religious taming of man's basic economic activities that Islam is believed to have a superior moral claim on revolutionary allegiance.

Rereading an Old Text

The propagation of a legitimate "Islamic Ideology" was not, nor could it remain, limited to responding to the hegemonic terms of Marxist economics. More immediately, Islamic texts, of distant or immediate origin, had to be resuscitated and reenergized for the same objective. In July 1955 Taleqani edited and annotated Shaykh Muhammad Hossein Na'ini's *Tanbih al-Ummah wa Tanzih al-Millah: Fi Luzum Mashrutiyyah al-Dawlah al-Muntakhibah li-Taqlil al-Zulam ala Afrad al-Ummah (Guidance of the Public and Edification of the Nation: On the Necessity of Representative Constitutional Government in Order to Alleviate Tyranny upon Members of Society)* and published it with an Introduction and extensive commentaries. His intentions in editing and extensively annotating this treatise, long after its political effects had been gathered and scattered, are made clear in his Introduction:

But whatever [in the Constitutional period] is done is done. Today with all those sacrifices and bloodsheds, we have a kind of defective constitution[al government]. But could we not augment it? Do we not have any other solution? Is the constitution[al government] not a kind of excuse for rampant despotism? Did founders of religions and reforms not aim at breaking the power of despotism? Could we not, as much as possible, bring closer this constitution[al government] to the supreme objective of Divine government? [24]

Taleqani's rhetorical question "Do we have no other solution?" is an open invitation to revolt, which he conveyed quite succinctly:

I hope that the vigilant religious leaders as well as the honorable Muslims would carefully consider the issues discussed in this book, open their eyes to the conditions of the Muslim nation, and with unity struggle for the salvation and redemption of Muslims. [I hope] they would no longer tolerate this wretchedness and indignity of Muslims perpetuated by a gang of lecherous hoodlums, [who are] instruments of others.[25]

Such accusations against the political establishment were to preface a text that had once stirred its initial audience to revolutionary action. Both Akhond Muhammad Kazem Khorasani and Abdollah Mazandarani, two prominent Constitutionalist clerics, wrote short prefaces to this book and praised it as a significant contribution in demonstrating the compatibility of a Constitutional government with Islam.[26]

Guidance of the Public and Edification of the Nation was one of the crucial pro-Constitutional treatises written in the wake of the Constitutional Revolution of 1906–1911. Both Na'ini and this book appealed to Taleqani. It was written in an atmosphere of an anti-Absolutist, pro-Constitutional period and had assumed a different but equally relevant significance in the mid-1950s when, with the backing of the American government, Mohammad Reza Shah commenced to thrive on a despotic reign.

The author of this famous tract, Allamah Shaykh Mirza Muhammad Hossein Na'ini (1860–1936), was a prominent Shi'i cleric and a distinguished jurist of the Constitutional and early Pahlavi period who was actively involved in the political events of his time. Born in Na'in, he completed his early education in his birthplace and then moved to Isfahan to pursue his studies. He then travelled to Najaf and studied with the celebrated Mirza-ye Shirazi. He also became closely associated with such pro-Constitutional jurists as Akhond Molla Muhammad Kazem Khorasani, with whom he collaborated in his activities. Na'ini combined a rare and acute interest in jurisprudence with an equally impressive attention to theology and philosophy. During World War I, he joined Mirza Muhammad Taqi Shirazi in opposing the British presence in Iraq. He was also instrumental in boycotting the Iraqi election when that country was under British occupation.

That Taleqani meant to introduce and propagate this book as a kind of manifesto for a potential clerical role in active politics is quite evident from the use of the key word "the Islamic Government" in the following passage:

Although [this book] has been written in order to validate the religious legitimacy of a Constitutional government, its significance lies more in its having mandated the Islamic social and political principles, as well as the blueprint and the overall aims of the Islamic Government.[27]

To speak of "the Islamic government" in 1955, when Mohammad Reza Shah's increasing reliance on American might made him bolder in his dangerous megalomanic self-perceptions, was not only courageous but also indicative of the acute determination of a committed cleric on his political aspirations. This is doubly important because it came at a time when the demise of the Tudeh Party in the post-1953 period had left a deep ideological vacuum for emerging oppositional forces.

In a move towards ideological consolidation of his activist reading of Shi'ism, Taleqani made a crucial statement about the nature and contemporary relevance of Na'ini's book. The move was meant at once to validate a politically active religiosity in Na'ini's model and demand ideological obedience on the part of the masses: "This is a rational [estedlali] and judicially binding [ejtehadi] book for the religious authorities, and an exemplary [taqlidi] mandate for the masses concerning their social responsibilities."[28] The key words in this passage are "rational" (estedlali), "judicially binding" (ejtehadi), and "exemplary" (taqlidi), which must be understood carefully. By appealing, first, to the "rational" (estedlali) foundation of the treatise, Taleqani catered to the increasing demands of imported positivism upon the dogmatic principles of an embattled Islam. Political activists, in other words, need not believe dogmatically in the doctrinal foundations of Islam in order to follow Na'ini's political mandates. But beyond the constituency of secular political activists in Tehran, Taleqani's appeal to the "rational" arguments of the text was more pertinently an indication of its authenticity in an Islamic "intellectual" (as opposed to "traditional") discourse. Taleqani here wished to lend "intellectual" credence to Na'ini's text and thus fortify it within the received categories of a rationalistic discourse in Islam. But by equally appealing, second, to the "judicially binding" (ejtehadi) foundations of Na'ini's text, Taleqani wished to give the content of the book a juridically binding force, equally authoritative upon both the clerical and lay Shi'is. Here he would advance credence from the assertive dimensions of Shi'i jurisprudence to substantiate further the legal authority of Na'ini's text. But ultimately, and third, Taleqani appeals to the "emulative" or "exemplary" (taqlidi) authority of the text that makes it virtually mandatory for all believing Shi'is to consider and obey its contents as religiously sanctioned codes of law.

Having established a de jure legitimacy for the clerics, Taleqani proceeds to give this religiously defined authority a democratic posture: "This takes us to the question of election and popular designation [of religious authorities] according to characteristics which have been articulated."[29] This is a particularly important posture that Taleqani wishes to give to the shape of the political apparatus he envisages for Iran. By 1955, when he wrote this Introduction, the ideals of democracy had long since been propagated. The active presence of the Tudeh Party in the 1940s political scene had underscored certain democratic measures they sought, and partially secured, in order to sow the seeds of their socialist ideals. The catalytic impact of such developments was a heightened attention to the popular and intellectual appeal of the ideals of democracy.

Rescuing the Text From Conservative Clerics

To reread a revolutionary message into Na'ini's text, Taleqani also needed a repoliticized clerical class. Treacheries of the colonial powers, he thought, and their local lackeys had radically depoliticized the Muslim clerics. Taleqani spoke of latent and blatant conspiracies on the part of "The Western" countries against Islam. He also celebrated Egyptians in their struggle against the combined effects of colonialism and Zionism. His praise for active political participation was matched by his disdain for apolitical or politically conservative clerics. Like Shari'ati, Taleqani was severely critical of his fellow clerics who either assisted or condoned the tyrannies perpetrated by the powers that be. He recalled the early years of Reza Shah and how some prominent clerics either assisted him or tolerated his tyrannical rule:

Again, certain people in religious habit have imposed, with passages from the Qur'an and the prophetic traditions, a self-serving man [that is, Reza Shah] upon the people. At the same time, certain others have put their stamp of approval [on them] with silence and conservatism. Then, when [the tyrant] was set on the rule of self-interest, held the reins, trotted and destroyed everything people had, they began to pray and supplicate, asking God for the appearance of the Imam of the Time.[30]

Faced with the increasing tyranny of Reza Shah and the duplicity of certain clerics in supporting him, Taleqani resorted to the originating, and reinterpretable, texts of Shi'i Islam, seeking guidance and inspiration:

This contradictory practice of certain religious leaders, this dark environment, these spiritual maledictions, inevitably forced me to study the most sagacious Qur'anic verses and the most noble book of Nahj al-Balaghah, the biography of the noble Prophet and those of the righteous Imams, peace be upon them.[31]

From these canonical sources, spring aspirations for a new interpretation of Islam, Islam reimagined in the modernity of its history. Taleqani shares a prominent feature with most of the other ideologues of the Islamic Revolution: a propensity for "true Islam" as opposed to the historically experienced Islam. Historical Islam is connected intimately to its intellectual disciplines and diverse religious schisms, both of which Taleqani ideologically repudiates. Stripped of the historically received diversity of its theology, jurisprudence, philosophy, and mysticism, "Islam" becomes readily available to Taleqani's audience as the semantic instrument of an updated political agenda. Sectarian differences levelled, Muslims grow in number as the constituency of a mass revolt. There and then, Muslims are born again in their faith. Thus a new "space" is created for Islam. Somewhere between remembering the distant authority of the past and representing the political reality of the present, "the Islamic Ideology," now engineered by Taleqani, creates a revolutionary "space" for itself. In that "space" the absolute necessity of significantly-being-in-the-world is made possible. Through that possibility, "the Islamic Ideology" passes from the mere promise of what life should be and becomes the principal mandate of what life is.

Faced with the onslaught of European secular ideas of state and government, Taleqani argued, anticipating his contribution to the making of "the Islamic Ideology," Muslim intellectuals have either abandoned their faith altogether and assumed the ideological posture of their choice, or else they have sought to assimilate their ideological preference with a notion of Islam they develop personally. "Those who have faith," Taleqani observed, "try to render Islam compatible with whatever social school they like, and they consider this a service to religion."[32] It is more than a mere paradoxical reversal of judgment that Taleqani himself would later wholeheartedly accept and propagate the severest form of social Darwinism and extend it into a sustained "Islamic" theory of social and historical evolution. Unaware of the theoretical implications of social Darwinism, he persistently propagated an evolutionary notion of history and society. Equally impervious to its theological implications, he would subject universal history to a gradual move towards perfection.

Constructing a Theory of Authority

Determined to fight against the onslaught of patently secular ideologies and with them the tyrannical reign of the Pahlavi regime, Taleqani sincerely opposed a quietist religiosity in which believers secluded themselves in their private pieties and left the external world to the whims and fusillades of absolutist rulers. He asked, "What is the point in heartfelt and sincere belief?"[33] He argued that tyrants and despots have always opposed prophets and religious authorities. If religion and politics were separated—religion for worshippers, politics for citizens—Nimrod would not have thrown Ibrahim into the fire, Pharaoh would not have struggled against Moses, Pontius Pilate would not have ordered Jesus killed, Neron would not have burned the Christians, and the Persian and Roman emperors would not have fought against the call of Islam.[34]

Politics thus part and parcel of religion, Taleqani tacitly develops a short theory of authority that excludes the king and gives supreme political power to the religious figures. This theory commences with granting su-

preme universal authority to God Almighty. This is the first and the highest
state of authority. Because the physical world is a constituent part of the
universe, God Almighty presides over the matters of this world as well.
This is the second state of authority and the temporal aspect of the Divine
Will. The third level of authority is that of the prophets and the Imams
whose "will, thought and inner power are entirely subject to these [Divine]
Commandments." At the third level of authority, Taleqani identifies the
characteristics of the Imam as "he who rules according to the Book [that is,
the Qur'an], believes in the righteous religion [that is, Islam], and circumscribes his soul in the Divine Essence." This kind of leader, he proceeds to
argue, "is called *Vali, Khalifeh, Imam, Amir al-Mu'meniyn,* and not *Malek,
Padeshah, Khodavandegar,* and *Malek al-Reqab.*"³⁵ At this third level,
Taleqani also stipulates the condition of "spiritual infallibility" *(esmat-e
ma'nawi)* as a Shi'i doctrine specifying the Imam.

It is at the fourth level of authority that Taleqani identifies "just religious
scholars" *(ulama'-ye adel)* as those who ought to have social affairs in their
hands. At the third level Taleqani locates kings and rulers negatively on a
par with the prophets and Imams and denies them authority, at the fourth
level he relegates legitimate leadership completely to the religious scholars
—his own rank.

At this stage, Taleqani introduces a crucial turn in his argument that is
instrumental in the future legitimation of the clerical reign:

Thus we Shi'ites believe that caliphs and Imams must have spiritual infallibility. At
the fourth level [after God, the Prophet, and the Imams], the social issues are in the
hands of just and pious religious authorities *(ulama')* who are at once knowledgeable of the primary and secondary principles of religion and subject to the Angel of
Justice.³⁶

There is a necessary twist at the end of this theoretical formulation of
authority. Taleqani must, by definition, appeal to the masses and, at the
same time, to that ideological frame of reference that gives them the right
to show and determine the way. Thus, by the time he lowers the geneology
of authority from God Almighty to the clerical class, he turns the structure
upside down and proclaims that "at this stage it is the people's turn to elect
and designate [their leader], according to the characteristics just indicated."³⁷ But "the characteristics just indicated" have no metaphysical
stipulation for "the people." It is only the ideological stipulation of Taleqani's targeted audience that necessitates a complete and structural reversal
of his hierarchical ordering of authority in order to appeal to, and thus
mobilize, the effective machinery of mass sentiments.

The revolutionary mobilization of the mass sentiments necessarily demands a quintessential reinterpretation of Islam. Taleqani's radical repoliticization of Islam reaches a point where he categorically states that "every

school of thought, every social program and platform that controls the tyrants and circumscribes their will is a step closer to the prophets and Islam."[38] Although he is quick to add that "yet ultimately they are not Islam," he has already gone as far as to include "constitutionalism, democracy, and socialism" as "successive steps" towards an Islamic ideal.

Opposing this radical reading of Islam is, of course, the religious establishment with its vested interest in the status quo. Taleqani openly accused some of his fellow clerics of consciously propagating a quietist and backward-looking brand of Islam. "They consider whatever is old as belonging to religion, and whatever new its opposite."[39] The battle between the old and the new was, in fact, a battle over a guiding spirit of Islam and how it had to be interpreted in the face of grave historical changes. Being merely a custodian of the moral and doctrinal foundations of the religious culture and institutions was not the ultimate ideal of the revolutionaries. Islam had to attend the most immediate political issues of historical exigencies.

It is rather remarkable that as early as 1955 Taleqani openly advocated Shaykh Fazlollah Nuri, the staunch anticonstitutionalist cleric. "The murder of the late Aqa Shaykh Fazlollah Nuri, without trial and at the hand of an Armenian, a shameful mark in the constitutional history, distressed and disillusioned most of the constitutionalist clerics."[40] Nuri could hardly be considered a model of revolutionary conduct. He had opposed the revolutionary movement to restrict the absolutist power of monarchy and considered constitutionalism a foreign product, inimical to Islamic principles. However, his militant defense of Islam and, in turn, his insistence that the government should be based on Islamic principles now appealed to a new generation of activists. To be sure, in its original context, Nuri's version of the Islamic government included monarchy and excluded secular constitutionalism, whereas in the new (Taleqani) version, it excluded both the monarchy and secular ideologies.

Updating a Revolutionary Voice

Taleqani's edition of *Tanbih al-Ummah* is the most systematic attempt to appropriate a political discourse of the Constitutional period, with its inherent limitations on the revolutionary measures it prescribes, and radicalize its contemporary message. For his time, Na'ini was certainly a sharply alert political activist who was now particularly appealing to Taleqani. Na'ini wrote a treatise defending the cause of the constitutional monarchy against absolutism. This was good enough but not ideal. Taleqani sought to capitalize on Na'ini's historical significance and authority and, at the same time, breathe a new revolutionary zest into his words, perhaps beyond the author's intentions. His attraction to Na'ini is part of a larger method of appealing to historical figures and texts of authority. The Qur'an and the *Nahj al-Balaghah* were, of course, the primary texts to explore for potential revolutionary updating. The mythical, and metahistorical, character of Ali was equally yielding to reradicalization. But recent and more readily accessible historical figures such as Na'ini—and texts such as *Tanbih al-Ummah*—were also instrumental in bringing home, as it were, the revolutionary messages Taleqani wished to articulate and inculcate.

Taleqani's method for assimilating and incorporating Na'ini's rather benign liberalism into a radical discourse is through extensive notes and concluding summaries at the end of each chapter which renders the book more representative of Taleqani's ideas than those of Na'ini. Usually Taleqani takes a theoretical or historical lead from Na'ini's text and extends it in his footnotes into ideological domains much beyond what the text could hermeneutically tolerate. A few examples should clarify this method. When Na'ini makes a reference to European scientific achievements as a by-product of a post-Crusade encounter with the Islamic scientific tradition, Taleqani engages in a lengthy discussion of how Europeans first achieved social and political liberty and then scientific and individual advancements:

In the West, first social movements, freedom, and [the rule of] law were launched, then [their] minds were pregnant with science and industry. But in Oriental and Islamic lands, in every corner thieves and bandits came to power by conspiring with nomads and tribes. They commenced a despotic reign, and garbed their cohorts into religious habit. While the former busied themselves with stealing and plundering the Muslims' properties and dignities, the latter recited Qur'anic verses and prophetic traditions for them.[41]

Such indictments against the monarchical and the clerical establishment are nowhere to be found in the original text. Yet Taleqani's ideological and political extrapolation from Na'ini's text flows rather naturally and effortlessly. Taleqani's primary purpose at this stage is to condemn not only the monarchical establishment but also conservative elements in his own clerical order. Looking at Islamic history but clearly referring to his contemporary situation, he asserted that through the coalition of treacherous individuals dividing the religious and political positions between themselves,

the social, legal, and political principles of Islam were buried under voluminous books. Muslims were stripped of their independence and dignity; indignity and servitude became their second nature. . . . People who live under such circumstances cannot conceive of any situation other than what they have. They think they are born to obey and serve the powerful, and they try to rule and be worshipped. Such mentalities are the very cause of all kinds of intellectual, economic, and ethical malice.[42]

But Taleqani focuses his attention primarily on the political establishment. He disqualifies the king from legitimate authority through yet another mechanism. The king is as much subject to the extremities of human passions as everybody else. But being at the peak of political power and having control over the instruments of violence, he can harm others more than ordinary people can. As a result, the natural and legal right to government belongs to a person who is infallible, and God's will dominates him. This supreme figure, by the process of elimination, must come from the religious ranks.

Political Activities

Beyond the tacit implications of such theoretical speculations, more concrete organizational steps were to be taken. After the 1953 coup d'état political activities were quite restricted. Yet in 1957, Taleqani founded the National Resistance Movement *(Nehzat-e Moqavemat-e Melli)*, which was the end result of some earlier political developments in which he was actively involved. After the 1953 coup, the Tudeh Party was officially banned and became effectively nonexistent in the political life of the 1950s. However, the docile existence of various student and professional organizations gained momentum and needed a more sustained program of activity. All these events, moreover, concurred at a time when the official clerical establishment, under the supreme authority of Ayatollah Borujerdi, was pursuing a quietist and apolitical course. During this period Taleqani established the National Resistance Movement, which led to his arrest and imprisonment for a year. Upon his release from prison he returned to political activity, headquartered again at the Hedayat Mosque. In 1960 he delivered a speech at Arg Square in central Tehran to a relatively large crowd. The main thrust of this speech was a criticism of government policies. This was a particularly troublesome event for the government. He was arrested again and imprisoned. Upon his release he joined Mehdi Bazargan and Yadollah Sahabi in founding the Iran Freedom Movement *(Nehzat-e Azadi-e Iran)*. Again he was arrested. He was not released until shortly before the June 1963 uprising led by Ayatollah Khomeini, in which he participated wholeheartedly. He delivered a number of antigovernment speeches in the course of the revolt, among them the famous *Holy War and Martyrdom (Jehad va Shahadat)*.[43]

Upon his arrest after the June 1963 revolt, Taleqani was put on trial. General Qarabaqi presided over the court. Taleqani attended this court with remarkable poise and courage. He would sit cross-legged on a chair, appearing to be dozing off through the sessions and refusing to grant the court the legitimacy to try him. The trial continued for seventy-seven sessions, at the end of which, when asked to make a closing statement, he simply recited verses from the holy Qur'an. He was sentenced to ten years in jail but was released in 1968. During these five years he spent most of his time writing. His most important work, *A Ray from the Qur'an,* an extended commentary on the holy Text, is a product of this period.

A Revolutionary Reading of the Qur'an

Taleqani had a sustained and prolonged interest in revolutionary Qur'anic exegesis. From 1939, when he commenced his teaching tenure in Tehran, until his death in 1979 he ceaselessly sought to propagate his political ideas through the medium of the Qur'anic text. Upon his arrival in Tehran in 1939, he organized sessions of Qur'anic commentary in which a group of young Muslim activists participated. This series of Qur'anic exegeses, which would later be continued and developed into a voluminous project, is Taleqani's chief contribution to the making of "the Islamic Ideology."

The Qur'an was a particularly significant text to start rereading for the further justification of "the Islamic Ideology." Its centrality to the Muslim collective consciousness understood, its extension into an active political agenda was a matter of ideological necessity. The transference of the sacred trust vested in the Qur'anic text onto a contemporary political agenda derived from it was all but self-evident. The transference, easily implemented, was facilitated by the immediate access the Qur'anic passages provided for the collective obedience of still a large population of believers. The nature of many Qur'anic passages is such that their universality of discourse and delivery yields easily to multiple historical interpretations. The symbolic constellation of the Qur'anic universe of fables and stories could, on occasion, be narrowed in on the specific realities that moved Taleqani's audience. The achieved correspondence between the Qur'anic passage and a given historical occasion could only compel the Muslim audience to admire the universality of the Qur'an and, at the same time, the Islamicity of the historical exigencies. Consequently, the specific ideological agenda thus extracted from a correspondence between the Qur'an and worldly events would gradually assume the sanctity of the sacred Text itself.

Late in 1963, Taleqani was moved from his individual cell and taken to compound number 4 of the Qasr prison complex where he came in contact with other prisoners and, at their initiative, started teaching them a course in Qur'anic exegesis. His lecture notes would gradually compose the text of his commentary. His public lectures to his fellow prisoners began with the thirtieth section of the Qur'an, a section he considered instrumental for understanding the entire Text.[44] In 1963, while he was incarcerated in an individual cell in Qasr Prison, Taleqani began to outline the draft of his voluminous Qur'anic exegesis. There, early in 1963, he wrote his commentary on the first section of the Qur'an. By 30 October 1978, when he was released from prison, he had completed his commentaries on the opening chapter of the Qur'an as well as the chapters of al-Baqarah, al-Imran, twenty-two verses of al-Nisa', and the entire thirtieth section of the holy Text.

Taleqani was severely critical of the way the Qur'an had been neglected by his contemporary clerics and thus relegated to a mere ritualistic object:

A book which has been the evidence of our religion and has governed every aspect of [our] life, has [now] merely assumed a sanctifying role, like antiquarian objects and bodies of sorcery. It has been pushed aside from the boundaries of communal life and livelihood and pushed to the frontiers of the world of the dead and the ceremonies of salvation, its tonality that of proclaiming death. [45]

This was totally inimical to a revolutionary application of the sacred Text. The new revolutionary interpretation had to go beyond the historical limitations thus created. Bypassing the hermeneutic circle historically constructed, Taleqani knew perfectly well that to render the Qur'an politically radical, he had to strip it out of its doctrinally developed context:

The kinds of acquired erudition and knowledge that make one proud are at the same time certain veils which prevent [direct] thinking about and seeking guidance from the [Qur'anic] verses. There are many technical terminologies and branches of knowledge which have been utilized to understand the religion as well as the verses of the Most Sagacious Book, and yet they themselves constitute a [set of] veil[s] upon it. [46]

Since early Islamic history, a set of ancillary branches of knowledge has evolved around the Qur'anic Text. Arabic syntax and morphology, the correct reading of the holy Text, the *hadith* literature, biographies of the early Muslim generations, and historical annals are among the essential branches of knowledge that a traditional Qur'anic interpreter needed to command. These branches of knowledge, the established figures and institutions of higher learning that promulgated them, and the complex set of technical terminologies all engendered and gave rise to a highly complex network of technical vocabulary and erudite expertise from the center of which the Qur'anic Text was addressed interpretively. To render the Qur'an politically reactive, Taleqani had to bypass this hermeneutic circle. He needed to release the Qur'an from its confinement among the Muslim intellectual elite and give it a mass audience:

But perspicacious men of knowledge and scholars should direct the rational and philosophical universals of the Qur'an as well as their own erudition towards an understanding of the Qur'an which guides [the people], and should not merely limit it to their own perceptions. [47]

To be able to "guide" the people, the Qur'an had to be rearticulated into a program of action, implicitly or explicitly, depending on the existing political exigencies. The nature of these exigencies was of a dual nature. First,

official censorship obviously prevented an open call for revolution through
an exegesis of the Qur'anic text; but, second, and even more important, a
certain degree of vagueness was logistically necessary to attract a maximum
number of revolutionary constituents. The more general the outlines of a
revolutionary program led through the Qur'an, the more widely the recipient of the ideological message would be spread across Iranian class and
status groupings. The more specific the exact nature of this revolutionary
agency and its outcome, the less attractive it would have been to post- and
lapsed-Muslims. This would have decreased Taleqani's constituency considerably—and thus the origin and extent of vague generalities about the
Qur'anic guidance of the potential revolutionary movement.

Taleqani's attention to the essentially revolutionary function of the Islamic sacred texts was not limited to the Qur'an. He knew that to the Shi'i
mind the mere suggestion of the Qur'an immediately conjures up the *Nahj
al-Balaghah,* a series of sermons attributed to the first Shi'i Imam. Like
Motahhari, Taleqani had a particular passion for the *Nahj al-Balaghah* and
decided to provide a new translation of it into Persian. In 1946 he translated eighty sermons. Taleqani had an additional goal of writing, in collaboration with Ayatollah Mirza Khalil Kamareh'i, his former teacher, a voluminous commentary on the *Nahj al-Balaghah.* This project, however, never
materialized, except for one or two short segments published in 1945.[48]
Taleqani conceded that the *Nahj al-Balaghah,* "after the Qur'an, is a great
Islamic document. Religious sciences ought to be taken, after the Qur'an,
from this book. Sectarian and political differences of Muslims ought to be
solved through this book."[49]

The Mass Appeal of Taleqani's Qur'anic Commentaries

Despite his tangential attention to the *Nahj al-Balaghah,* it is in his Qur-
'anic commentary that Taleqani reached the wide constituency of his revolutionary audience. Among the major ideologues of "the Islamic Ideology,"
he is the only one whose revolutionary discourse, deeply rooted in his
reading of the Qur'an, has been adopted most patently not only by the
organs of the Islamic Republic but also by one of its staunchest enemies,
the Organization of People's Mojahedin.[50] Because of this unique institutional affiliation of his revolutionary discourse, it can be examined in both
its combatant and triumphant phases. His simultaneous, however mutually
exclusive, acceptance by both the Islamic Republic and the People's Mojahedin brings this revolutionary ideologue into the main ideological framework of the Islamic Revolution in Iran. The specifics of that ideological
framework necessitated, by all means, a bona fide Qur'anic justification.
There is a specific mode of Qur'anic exegesis that he deemed appropriate
for developing his revolutionary discourse. But before that specific mode is

analyzed, the more immediate question that must be addressed is the mechanism and operative forces of Qur'anic references in the making of a revolutionary discourse.

Centrality of the Qur'an in Islamic Political Discourse

What is the Qur'an? Its physicality? Its textuality? Its authority? There is something in its textual physicality that no revolutionary discourse can avoid emulating, appealing to the authority of its perennial language. The Text stands there, in the Muslim collective consciousness and unconsciousness, the epitome of the very word of God. The very word of God. That means, even for ex- and lapsed-Muslims who wish to claim otherwise, the central logos of truth—political or any other. No Muslim activist, true to his (or her) profession of changing the world to a more perfect picture of her (or his) own imagination, has escaped the commanding word of his (or her) God—personally interpreted. The very physicality of the Text, as you put it in your pocket or hold it high in reverence on your shelf, is an invitation to obedience, to assimilate it into a personal attendance upon your history. The times are hard, and here is the Word of God. The Arabic original is the archetypal language of all the eternal truth you care to memorize. More than memorization of the Qur'an, it is the Qur'anification of their memory that the Muslims do. The Word of God, physically transfixed, attends the changing reality of every facade of life—political or otherwise, mundane or monumental. Standing before this Text, the rest of the world, stable or revolutionary, has to explain itself. There, precisely, rests the power of the Qur'an, the very physical and textual authority of it. God manifest.

More than anything else, a revolutionary discourse needs conceptual and symbolic legitimacy; it must rest its foundations on a metaphysical authority. It must point, from within itself, to something beyond itself. Whereas in secular and imported ideologies that competed with "the Islamic Ideology" it was an appeal to pseudoscientific claims to political and ideological truth that warranted and thus suggested this sense of legitimacy, in modern religious ideologies, such as Taleqani's, it was through a deliberate and tactful resorting to the sacred semantics of the common religious culture, or to its commonly held mythologies, that the same aura of validity was sought to be engendered. As the single most important source of authority and legitimacy in the historical development of the Islamic rhetorical discourse, political or otherwise, the Qur'an commands the full obedience of the Muslims. Even for the Shiʿites, the primacy of the Qur'an over the Imamate legacy is quite clear in the famous Prophetic tradition: "Verily, I leave you with two pillars: The Book of God and my family, they shall not be separated until they reach the *kawthar* pond."[51] One of the chief sources of legitimacy for the Imams in the pre-*ghaybah* period has been their presumed ability to interpret the hidden meaning of the Qur'an. Equally available to conservative or revolutionary interpretations, the Qur'an has always stood at the center of Muslim historical self-understanding.

The general process of secularization in most Islamic societies has not, in any significant way, diminished the importance of the Qur'an as the supreme sacred Text in the Muslim collective unconsciousness. Whether a devout Muslim who uses the Qur'anic references consciously, or a secularized Muslim, to use a contradiction in terms with perfect correspondence to reality, who presumes the holy verses subconsciously, Iranians, among their coreligionists in other parts of the Islamic world, have the Qur'an as their most common frame of symbolic reference. The presence of the Qur'an in the Muslim collective unconsciousness, no matter how inarticulate, makes them particularly attuned and receptive to doctrinal, ideological, and political messages delivered in and through the sacred discourse. Indeed there is that major segment of the political constituency that has become so radically secularized and so deeply alienated from the Qur'anic discourse that it is, or at least appears to be, deeply antipathetic to anything with the slightest religious bend. However, for the range of political constituencies to which this mode of revolutionary discourse is addressed, the Qur'anic references create an aura of sacred certitude, legitimize a voice of authority, that cannot but lend enduring enforcement to the doctrinal, ideological, and political messages thus conveyed.

The Political Uses of the Qur'an

Use of the Qur'an, in the form of Qur'anic commentaries or otherwise, for patently political purposes has a long tradition in Islamic history. In a variety of ways these commentaries have always played a political role in the Muslim community. Since the days when the soldiers of Mu'awiyah reportedly affixed pages of the Qur'an to their lances and asked for arbitration in their historical battle against Ali (July 657), the sacred Text has been used politically. Once the long and varied history of Qur'anic commentaries proper began, the classical distinction between "Qur'anic exegesis through Prophetic traditions" (*al-tafsir bi al-ma'thur*) and "Qur'anic exegesis through exertion of personal opinion" (*al-tafsir bi al-ra'i*) has been an indication of the attempt to close the legitimate hermeneutic circle that could engage with a certain degree of validity in Qur'anic interpretation. The further division of *al-tafsir bi al-ra'i* into "the acceptable" (*al-mahmud*) and "the unacceptable" (*al-madhmum*) is yet another indication that political and ideological factors have played an important role in the definition of the hermeneutic circle around the Qur'anic text.[52]

The classical Qur'anic commentaries are usually supported by materials that are either within the domains of the Islamic canonical sources, such as the Prophetic traditions, or are necessitated by the very language of the Text, such as Arabic syntax, morphology, or etymology. The most essential external element that Taleqani brings to bear on his Qur'anic exegesis is his sincere attempt to verify his specific ideological reading of the existing political situation by repeated references to the sacred Scripture. This exclusive attention to such political concerns is at the top of his agenda, underscoring any other relevant factor that is instrumental in a typical Qur'anic commentary. Taleqani's exegesis thus leads towards a doctrinally mandated, ideologically alert, and politically sensitive verification of the current social atmosphere, conducive to a revolutionary course of action, through and in terms of the sacred Scripture. But doctrinal, ideological, or political readings of the Qur'an are not an entirely new phenomenon.[53]

A review of the classical Qur'anic exegesis indicates that in every age certain commanding extratextual forces have guided the interpretative discourse of the Muslim commentators. Al-Tabari's (d. 923) *Jami' al-Bayan fi Tafsir al-Qur'an (The Compendium of Discourse on Interpreting the Qur'an)* is, as its title indicates, the first attempt to provide a comprehensive commentary on the Qur'anic passages from a variety of perspectives. However, al-Tabari's exegesis is particularly sensitive in refuting the Mu'tazilite rationalistic readings of the Qur'an. On specific theological controversies, such as *huduth* ("createdness") or *qidam* ("eternality") of the Qur'an, anthropomorphism, *jabr* ("predestination"), *ikhtiyar* ("free will"), Divine justice, etc., he takes issue with the Mu'tazilite positions. With the increasing political overtone of the Mu'tazilite theological position under the Abbasids, doctrinal matters had assumed obvious ideological proportions. Al-Zamakhshari's (d. 1134) *Al-Kashshaf an Haqa'iq al-Tanzil (The Revealer of the Truth of the Revelations)*, on the other hand, was a specifically Mu'tazilite commentary that sought to elucidate their ideologically charged theological positions. The Ash'arite counterpart to al-Zamakhshari's commentary is al-Baydawi's (d. c. 1286) *Anwar al-Tanzil wa Asrar al-Ta'wil (The Lights of Revelations and the Secrets of Interpretations)*. With Fakhr al-Din al-Razi's (d. 1209) *Mafatih al-Ghayb (The Keys to the Hidden)*, the Qur'anic commentaries depart from an essentially theological epistemology and assume a philosophical language.[54]

The theological and philosophical interpretations of the Qur'an are matched by mystically oriented exegesis. Ibn Arabi's (d. 1240) *Futuhat al-Makkiyyah (The Meccan Revelations)* and *Fusus al-Hikam (Bezels of Wisdom)* and Rumi's (d. 1273) *Mathnavi*, although not Qur'anic commentary in the strictest sense of the term, are usually considered among the mystically sensitive readings of the Qur'an. There is also a proper Qur'anic exegesis, in the mystical tradition, attributed to Ibn Arabi that is probably that of his student Abd al-Razzaq al-Kashani (d. c. 1330).[55]

Qur'anic commentaries were also produced along sectarian lines. The Shi'ites have directed their Qur'anic exegesis towards their doctrinal positions.[56] Chief among these are *Tafsir al-Qur'an (Commentary on the Qur'an)* by Ali Ibn Ibrahim al-Qumi (d. 939), *Majma' al-Bayan li-Ulum al-Qur'an (The Compendium of Discourse of Qur'anic Sciences)* by Abu Ali al-Tabarsi (d. c. 1153), and *al-Safi fi Tafsir al-Qur'an (The Discretion on Qur'anic Commentary)* by Muhammad Murtada al-Kashi (d. c. 1505).[57]

The influence of doctrinal, ideological, and political concerns on Qur'anic exegesis is thus not a new or entirely innovative phenomenon. Because of its unique legitimating status as the ultimate Islamic sacred Text, the Qur'an has always been used for such purposes. Even Taleqani's introduction of secular motifs from European scientific and ideological movements has its counterparts in, for example, al-Razi's references to philosophical ideas from the Greek peripatetic tradition. Specific political readings of the Qur'an in Taleqani's exegesis have their origin not only in certain Shi'i commentaries but also in the Kharijites' patently political interpretations of the sacred Text. Thus historically, theological, juridical, philosophical, mystical, and, of course, political considerations have given rise to the most varied forms of Qur'anic exegesis. In modern Islamic history, engagement with the hegemonic primacy of "The West," as a monolithic and mythical entity, has added yet another dimension to the contemporary frames of reference operative in interpreting the sacred Text. But in this phase there is an overwhelming emphasis on social and political concerns, at the expense of other aspects of the Qur'an. In *Tafsir al-Qur'an al-Hakim,* begun by Muhammad Abduh (1849–1905) and continued by his student Rashid Rida (1865–1935), the commentators assume a particularly revisionist and modernist attitude towards such controversial juridical issues as polygamy and the status of women in society.[58] In India, Sir Sayyid Ahmad Khan Hindi (1816–1898) reached for a hasty assimilation of modern sciences into the Qur'anic discourse. With Hasan al-Banna' (1906–1949) and the establishment of "The Muslim Brotherhood," modern Qur'anic interpretation assumed active political momentum.[59]

Taleqani's Qur'anic Commentary: A Critique of All Previous Commentaries

The corpus of Taleqani's Qur'anic commentary, repoliticizing the sacred Text yet one more time in this long tradition, may be divided into two phases: (1) his revolutionary exegesis, written mostly in prison and published as *Partovi az Qur'an (A Ray from the Qur'an)* in 1963 and 1979, and (2) his postrevolutionary commentaries on various Qur'anic passages and in specific political circumstances. His commentary on the first and second chapters of the Qur'an were written by 1963 while he was in prison.

His scattered notes on the third chapter were written after his exile in Zabol and before his reimprisonment, that is, during the 1974–75 period. Before the commentary was completed, he was imprisoned again, and the task of collecting and editing the volume fell to one of his associates, Muhammad Mehdi Ja'fari. This volume was first published while Taleqani was still in prison but was revised and republished following his release in 1978. His postrevolutionary commentaries are themselves of three natures: those he delivered on national television and later published as *With the Qur'an on the Scene,* those he offered on public occasions such as Friday Prayers at Tehran University, and those he gave privately to the members of his immediate family at his house. Of the latter category there are cassette tapes still awaiting transcription and publication. Certain distinctions emerge from these two phases—the pre- and postrevolutionary periods. While the language of the former is concealed, symbolic, and loaded, the latter discourse is clearer and more straightforward, flamboyant, mobilizing, and forceful. The concealed charge of Taleqani's prerevolutionary Qur'anic exegesis is evident, for example, in his invoking curses in Arabic against the ruling regime in a language wrapped in the convocational rhetoric of the Qur'an. "[O God!] Forgive us," Taleqani demanded, "save us and have mercy on us. You are our Master. Make us victorious over the unbelievers, and over the tyrants, and over any obnoxious tyrant who does not believe in the Day of Judgment."[60] To Taleqani's audience, those who could read Arabic, the referents were quite obvious.

As early as 1939, when he was a twenty-eight-year-old novitiate returning to Tehran from Qom, Taleqani had begun to experiment with Qur'anic commentary as a channel for conveying political messages. As he reported later, he met resistance from many traditionally minded scholars.[61] But by 1963 he had thoroughly realized the significance of the Qur'an in a revolutionary political discourse. "For God's sake," he admonished, "let's rescue the Qur'an from the graveyard chanters. . . . This Book is the Book of life, Book of movement, Book of power, Book of guidance, Book of faith."[62]

The political nature of Taleqani's Qur'anic commentary is immediately evident from the location where he produced his manuscript—his prison. The publication of this commentary began in 1963, under the title of *A Ray from the Qur'an.* Taleqani did not consider this an exegesis in the traditional sense of the term *(tafsir),* and instead chose this particular title to allow future validation for his revolutionary discourse. *A Ray from the Qur'an* reached an ever wider audience during his lifetime and after his death.

Taleqani was instrumental in establishing a publishing house, *Enteshar,* that was chiefly responsible for publishing his books. While in prison, he would smuggle out his writings and arrange for their publication through *Enteshar,*[63] making the point perfectly clear that his books should be available cheaply to everyone. Nevertheless, *Enteshar* has complained of "the numerous times" that *A Ray from the Qur'an* has been illegally published and sold.[64] The official and unofficial, legal and illegal, publications of Taleqani's works testify to the extent to which his message successfully reached the multitude of his audience.

Taleqani believed that the traditional apparatus of Qur'anic exegesis had created too many obstacles and "veils" for understanding "the Text itself," making it thus irrelevant to the "human consciousness."[65] Discrediting the traditional apparatus of Qur'anic exegesis was concomitant for Taleqani with establishing an independent authority in leadership for the Qur'an as a Text and for such fresh and direct encounters with it as his own. To claim such authority in leadership was indispensable for any political and revolutionary mobilization. To fortify his claim, Taleqani gave the authority of the Qur'anic text and his exemplary fresh interpretation of it something of a natural inevitability. "As light, air, and daily sustenance are indispensable in the preservation and evolution of a living organ," he surmised, "for the continuity of the spiritual life, and for perfection in all domains of life, guidance is . . . [equally] necessary."[66] That guidance had to come from the Qur'an. But before being able to teach and lead the multitude of its adherents, the Qur'an had to be set free from the concurrent set of historical interpretative devices that had rendered it politically ineffective in modern times.

Having thus liberated the sacred Text from its traditional exegetical apparatus—from its legitimating hermeneutic context—and having established independent authority for the very word of the Text and fresh encounters thereto, Taleqani will have to liberate his audience from the historically established bonds that act as barriers between them and a revolutionary reading. Thus, while he complains that there are "so many terminologies and sciences that have been used in order to understand— and yet have become barriers to—the Most Sagacious Book,"[67] he also adds that "liberated thinking and freedom in action are prerogatives of man"[68] and thus inevitable in any meaningful fresh encounter with the sacred Text, should that Text still be deemed relevant to the realities of the time.

As for that relevance, the very purpose of the Qur'anic revelation, Taleqani believed, has been to eradicate "the tyranny of classes" that has plagued every society. The sacred Text has been instrumental in "destroying the distances among the classes."[69] Where "the ruling classes have put their bloody claws"[70] upon the wretched earth, the Qur'an has offered the masses a divine instrument with which to fight back. To advance this updated reading of the Qur'an, Taleqani postulates man's free will in thinking and acting.[71] Thinking and acting freely are not only "the prerogatives of men," they are mutually interrelated.

Taleqani is harshly critical of the history of Qur'anic exegesis. "New-Muslim Jews and their Ulama' " are responsible for having introduced "fantasies, superstitions, and irrelevant material" as Qur'anic exegesis.[72] Others have interpreted the holy Text "according to their own opinion."[73] The Sufis have resorted to "irrational and illogical interpretations."[74] The philosophers, too, have gone astray. Because of this concerted misreading of Jews, Sufis, philosophers, and others, the Qur'an has been so far misinterpreted to the extent that historically the Muslims have been denied direct and unmitigated access to their sacred Text:

The more such matters as [proper] pronunciation [of the Qur'an], etymology, diacritical notations, [and debate over] theological and philosophical issues have been expanded around the Qur'anic verses, the more Muslim minds were prevented from the general and pervasive guidance of the Qur'an. Like flickering and dim lanthems in a dark and tumultuous desert, if these [branches of] knowledge and learning briefly enlightened their immediate surroundings, they prevented the far-reaching light of the bright stars.[75]

This has done obvious injustice to the Qur'an. In fact, the sacred Text has been whimsically used by "every sect according to their taste and preference, as dictated by the opinions of [the previous] interpreters."[76] The result of this state of affairs has been that "this Book of guidance that, as in the first half-century of Islam, should have governed every dimension of spiritual, ethical, juridical, and political life has been thoroughly cast aside, devoid of the slightest relevance."[77] The immediate consequence of this negligence of the Qur'an has been that it

has assumed the status of [an object with which merely] to sanctify and grace, pushed back from the frontiers of [private] and social life, located at the fringes of the world of the dead, the ceremonies of salvation, the tone [of its recitation] that of proclaiming death.[78]

The world of science imagines the Qur'an obsolete, and people are negligent of the rule of anarchy and immorality should this Book be obliterated. The only way out of this situation, Taleqani suggested, is to cast aside these veils[79] and let the bright light of Qur'anic guidance shine through the minds and hearts of Muslims.[80]

Taleqani's criticisms of traditional Qur'anic exegesis extends beyond the problems he saw in the profuse nature of the branches of knowledge one had to cover before reaching the actual content of the Book. This criticism took exception with the entire epistemological foundation of traditional encounters with the holy Scripture. In opposing the linguistic, mystical, philosophical, and other forms of Qur'anic interpretations, Taleqani proposes that in the Qur'an there is a "vast and all-inclusive" program for life, of which Muslims have been denied any meaningful share.[81] What is hidden here behind "vast and all-inclusive" is an innate belief in the absolute totality of the sacred Text as a program of total social life. Totalitarian tendencies, legitimated by this belief in the total completeness of the Qur'an, are always matched by a concomitant populist agenda. Dispensing with the inevitably elitist nature of the Qur'anic sciences, Taleqani took the Qur'an directly to "The People": the ultimate and indispensable engine of the revolution.

Taleqani's solution for the politically mute separation of the Qur'an from the masses and its concomitant enclosure in the historically formed hermeneutic circle of its exclusive interpreters is to approach the sacred Text directly and without any intrusion by the bodies of learning external to it. For this purpose he had a set of six principles that he would follow in his own exegesis: first, an explication of the etymological roots of the Qur'anic words and expressions; second, an explanation of the specific intentions of the Qur'anic passages; third, an analysis of the psychological and intellectual dimensions of social events, as discussed in the Qur'an; fourth, a consideration of the pre-Islamic (*Jahiliyyah*) atmosphere within which the Qur'an created a new man; fifth, implementation of the intellectual and philosophical universals to understand the Qur'an without reducing the Qur'anic passages to the requirements of such issues; and finally, sixth, references to the related literature in the Prophetic tradition to understand the Qur'anic injunctions.[82]

Establishing his new agenda of political necessities, Taleqani also has to discredit all previous Qur'anic commentaries to legitimate his own. The added element in his agenda is a pervasive and necessary consideration for the revolutionary crowd. Whereas most previous Qur'anic commentaries were limited in their address to that elite hermeneutic community that had mastered all the necessary and preparatory sciences pertaining to the Qur'an, Taleqani specifically denounced such exclusive prerogatives and sought to take the Qur'an directly to "The People." But in taking the sacred Text to the most essential revolutionary machinery, the mobilized mass, he still had to carry in his voice that certain authority that the Qur'an gives to its interpreters.

"In the Name of God, the Merciful, the Compassionate"

Precisely in its universal legitimacy, that is, in its remotest resemblances to the actual historicity of Taleqani's time, the Qur'anic text carries authority. The actual historicity of the holy Text obviously reflected events and concerns of the Prophet's period. But, at the same time, beyond its historical specificity, the Qur'anic text had been universalized by, if nothing else, at least the closed hermeneutic community that had chosen to interpret it. Thus universalized, the Text has been the condito sine qua non of every interpretation of contemporary life. It is precisely in this universality that the Text yields itself to revolutionary—or any other mode of relevant—interpretation. The act of revolutionary interpretation locates the Text, ipso facto, at the heart of contemporary life. That life, in every shade of its mundane (political) realities, gives contemporary significance and meaning to the sacred Text. As such, the Qur'an shall always remain the supreme symbol of legitimation for every major or minor shift in the Muslim collective self-understanding. The changing nature of this self-understanding requires a permanent position for the Qur'an.

But the essential function of the Qur'an, in the context of such changing circumstances, is always to legitimize the political (or any other) discourse propagated through its language and imagery. Immediately related to this general impression of legitimacy that the Qur'anic references create for the political objectives thus propagated is the sense of validity given to the revolutionary discourse once it is brought under the opening phrase of "In the name of God, the Merciful, the Compassionate." Without exception, all of Taleqani's revolutionary statements begin by appealing to this sacred invocation. Obviously there are historical antecedents for this practice; and it is quite normal for a religious writer to begin with this formula. However, the implicit—and thus quite powerful—notions that such Qur'anic references create are crucial. By appealing to the authority of this seminal Qur'anic phrase, a universe of discourse is tacitly engendered and sustained through which the ideologue, the ideology, and the targeted political constituency are all brought together under a sacred canopy.

There is a common literary practice among the Muslim writers that is of some significance here and should be noted. That is the customary practice of beginning a particular discourse with an annunciatory passage that is called technically, in its Persian version, bera'at-e estehlal, literally meaning "the virtuous perspicacity of seeking the moon in the sky at the beginning of the month." This phrase originates in the practice of an expert who ascends to the roof at the beginning of the month and looks in the appropriate direction to mark the first appearance of the moon. The meaning has been extended to include the function of a prefatory passage at the beginning of a discourse, religious or otherwise, that is meant to indicate the author's expertise in using such carefully considered words and expressions, technical terms in their respective contexts, that orient the reader's attention to his ultimate objectives and thus function as a prelude to the main thrust of the discourse.

Through the implicit and thus powerful function of bera'at-e estehlal, the Qur'anic passages quoted at the beginning of Taleqani's revolutionary discourses—particularly the phrase "In the Name of God, the Merciful, the Compassionate"—cast a sacred shadow over the range of doctrinal, ideological, and political objectives that constitute the main thrust of his argument. Taleqani himself was quite conscious of this sanctifying function of this phrase. "The Qur'an," he conjectured,

which is the only Book of the unity [of God] and which is for the final perfection of mankind, begins its verses with the phrase "In the Name of God, the Merciful, the Compassionate" in order to make man understand that all its teachings and injunctions originate in and appear from God and His munificence.[83]

It is precisely this same function that Taleqani creates when the phrase appears at the beginning of his religiously charged political discourse and invites its audience into a holy precinct, now in the form of Taleqani's text or then in the air of his public sermon, in which sacred certitude assures the absolute and final validity of pronouncements thus delivered. The Islam thus reinterpreted within the confines of a compelling suggestion of certitude carries the historical weight of its validity while, at the same time, casting an interpretative shadow on every reality pertinent to the Muslim experience and giving it an inevitable significance for radical political action.

Doctrinal, Ideological, and Political Agendas

The entire revolutionary discourse thus sanctified and legitimated, there is a persistent thrust of hidden and manifest agenda that holds together Taleqani's religious language. On this thrust, Taleqani's revolutionary discourse can be considered as being directed towards three specific but inter-related objectives: (1) doctrinal, (2) ideological, and (3) political. His doctrinal objective is to establish a set of principles according to which a particular worldview, Qur'anically derived in his estimation, is ascertained and rendered legitimate. Immediately related to his doctrinal objective, Taleqani develops an ideological conviction that seeks to depict a reality conducive to, and indeed in need of, a revolutionary course of action. But both the doctrinal and ideological foundations of his Qur'anic exegesis lead to the configuration of a political program that suits, and seeks to direct and alter, the historical exigencies of his time. Circumscribed by doctrinal, ideological, and political parameters of interpretation, these historical exigencies are read into a revolutionary course of action. Action, as opposed to mere confession of faith, becomes the defining factor of "being a Muslim," and consequently there remains nothing of a hermeneutic consequence in between doctrinal, ideological, and political levels of interpretation. Islam becomes synonymous with a revolutionary course of action. Or else nothing. And there precisely lies the power of an exclusive revolutionary reinterpretation of faith.

A Progressive View of Human History

How does Taleqani actually work this systematic program of collective revolutionary action into his Qur'anic exegesis, and what are the mechanisms through which this program assumes an aura of legitimacy?

Chief among Taleqani's doctrinal objectives in his Qur'anic exegesis is the propagatation of a developmental and progressive notion of human history. For this purpose, he once developed an elaborate commentary on the Qur'anic passage (59:24), "All that is in the heavens and the earth magnifies Him; He is the All-mighty, the All-wise." In advancing his reading of this phrase, Taleqani abruptly introduces the element of "movement": *All that is in the heavens and the earth,* everything is in the path of perfection. Everyone tries to relieve himself of "impurities and the carnal soul."[84] This (social-Darwinist) developmental notion of human community that Taleqani expresses in connection with the Qur'anic passages leads his commentary towards the ideological validation of an incremental and progressive philosophy of history according to which man chronologically advances towards perfection. "*Tasbih* ('glorification')," he argues, "is derived from *sibahah* which means to be floating. How can the person who is floating in the stormy sea and the waves of water reach for the safety of the shore?"[85] He answers this rhetorical question by pointing out that the proper strategy for this imaginary person floating in the stormy sea is

to fix his vision on the shore, trust his own power and strength, move his arms and legs systematically toward the goal, and not be afraid of the storm. This is glorification [of God]; it is this floating *(sibahah)* that leads to the safety of the shore.[86]

Two objectives are attained in the course of this Qur'anic commentary: (1) a developmental and progressive course is assumed and propagated for history; and (2) by explicating a hermeneutic etymology of the word *tasbih* and relating it to a notion of movement from a sea of troubles to the safety of a promised land, a patently ideological similitude is created between the text analogue thus provided and the political condition of the time as perceived through this ideology. It has been a rather long way from the actual Qur'anic passage to the final political pronouncement that the existing conditions are stormy and people must struggle to reach for an ideal state. But the movement has been quite implicit and, within its ideological framework, logical.

That the Qur'an should be encountered face to face and afresh and that personified leadership must emanate from the Qur'an to the Qur'anic commentator necessarily concurs with a view that considers society and history in progression, movement, and evolution. There are obvious indications that this evolutionary view of history is adopted from, or at least responds positively to, social Darwinism. However, Taleqani's evolution-

ary semantic is enmeshed so thoroughly in Qur'anic terminology that on
the surface it may appear as a version of "transubstantial motion" *(al-
harakah al-jawhariyyah)* as articulated by the sixteenth-century Shi'i philosopher Sadr al-Muti'allihiyn Akhond Molla Sadra Shirazi (d. 1050).[87] In
the general framework of his "Transcendental Theosophy," Molla Sadra
has articulated a conceptual category of movement known as *al-harakah
al-jawhariyyah.* According to this ontological category, "solid bodies are
liquidated and analyzed into a factor of pure potentiality of movement."[88]
Although "this movement"—as, in fact, the one envisioned for history by
Taleqani—"is unidirectionary and evolutionary," it results, contrary to
Taleqani's, "in even higher forms of existence until material existence
reaches the stage where and when it rises beyond the realm of space-
time."[89]

This notion of "transubstantial motion" has been suggested as underscoring Taleqani's view of historical and societal evolution.[90] There are
indeed certain passages in his commentary that suggest such an adaptation:
"Evolution *(takamol)* emanates from the inner being and from the very
essence of the created beings, and it constitutes a motion in their essence."[91]

A closer reading of Taleqani, however, proves this initial impression
untenable. There are altogether too many references to Darwin, explicit
and implicit and in too many diverse contexts, to make this evolutionary
view of society and history an expression of Molla Sadra's ontology.
Taleqani weaves his evolutionary view of history into the very design of
God's creation. Commenting on the Qur'anic passage 2:30, "Behold, thy
Lord said to the angels: 'I will create a [vicegerent] on earth,' " he maintains that "[God] perfected the world to a point, and caused such an
evolution that his representative [man = *khalifah*] could appear on it."[92]
He goes so far as to accommodate Darwinism into the very fabric of the
Qur'anic doctrines. In fact to augment, and thus validate, the Darwinian
theory of evolution, he suggested an Islamic explanation for the "missing
link" by arguing that

in the intervals of the gradual [Darwinian] evolution, there have been sudden
movements and evolutions. Thus while the theory of evolution, which has much
evidence [in its support], is correct, the scientists are spared the trouble of searching
for the missing link.[93]

Taleqani also radically modified the Qur'anic view of creation to assimilate
it into the Darwinist theory of evolution. At a point in the Qur'an creation
is identified as an expression of the Divine Will (2:22).[94] In describing the
phrase "who hath appointed the earth a resting place for you," he points
out that "after many long phases, [God] prepared and expanded the earth
for everybody. And for many years, before the appearance of man, He

deposited the earth with resources and mines." [95] Similarly, Taleqani sees the essential distinction between "the guided" and "the misguided" in the Qur'anic phrase 2:26, "He misleadeth many thereby, and He guideth many thereby," as that of "a group of people who tend towards evolution, and others who are distracted from this path." [96]

Why should Darwinism or, by implication, social Darwinism be of any interest to Taleqani? Here lie some central features of the contemporary political discourse that deeply engaged him, as well as other Islamic ideologues. He tried to establish an evolutionary and progressive view of history according to which societies always move from a bad to a good and then to a better condition. That this could contradict a famous prophetic tradition, according to which Muhammad had said every successive generation of Muslims after him would be led more and more astray, [97] in no way modified Taleqani's evolutionary and progressive view of history. But the evolutionary perspective, especially when fortified by the theological doctrine of "free will" (as opposed to "predestination"), had immediate political connotations for the status quo: that it was bad and that it had to get better through the agency of active political involvement.

The perfect historical (archetypal) example Taleqani could offer to substantiate this determined course of action was an event in Muhammad's prophetic career. He uses the occasion of the Muslims changing their *qiblah* (direction of prayer) to argue that when a group of people are determined to change the direction of their movement they should not fear death or any hardship in their way: [98]

With a soul envigorated by light and energy, and with a vision penetrating and perceptive, [the Qur'anic encouragement] removes the barrier of the martyrs' death from their path, and removes the word of their death from their tongue. [So that people] consider the martyrs so alive and lofty that their spirit is life-giving and uplifting for the earthly creatures, and that their dead body, unwashed and unshrouded, gives blessings to the wretched, their gravesite the site of pilgrimage for the living hearts, the boiling of their blood giving life to dead bloods. [99]

Free Will, Not Predestination

Propagation of an evolutionary theory of history, mitigated through such celebrations of sacrificial martyrdom of the most noble souls, is essential to Taleqani's political agenda, hidden and manifest. But for this theory to become both intellectually and politically operative, he needs to free man's ontological status from an essential dichotomy in Islamic theology. The historical battle between the theological advocates of "free will" and those of "predestination" will have to be resolved before Taleqani can locate man on his path to gradual and evolutionary perfection. "Free will and choice of action are the exclusive privileges of man," he decided. "It is precisely because of this 'free will' that man's actions [either] possess a positive quality or [deserve] a negative punishment."[100] Because of this "free will," there is a duty set upon man to act responsibly. The good and evil that would come from man's actions are all results of his own choice. Translated into political terms, this would obligate Muslims to assume responsibility and take proper action to change their status quo. The Qur-'anic passage that best conveys, in Taleqani's readings, the notion of man's evolution towards perfection is 1:6: "Show us the straight path," whereby man seeks God's guidance towards the righteous course of action. "The secret," Taleqani reveals, "of essential, substantive, and voluntary motion, as well as the principle of evolution, is precisely this reading for 'the path.' "[101]

The stipulation of such a path of perfection upon which man traverses towards an evolutionary destination creates obvious theological problems in a religion of absolute, omnipotent, and omniscient monotheism. The tacit theological implication of this politically mandated position is that there are finite limitations and presumed imperfections in God Almighty and His created universe. This obviously creates unacceptable theological consequences of which Taleqani himself was quite cognizant and that he tried to eliminate. "The path is not towards a specific and finite goal," Taleqani clarified, "because perfections are infinite and God is beyond every perfection, and man, too, is not limited in his potentials; every limit and finiteness he reaches is the beginning of an infinity."[102]

Despite this subordinate clause, Taleqani still insists that the expression of "[the straight path] is the origin and principle of evolution."[103] In this as in many other instances, the necessity of a political agenda supersedes, or at least partially mutes, the impossibility of a theological position. The necessity of a voluntary, progressive view of history was much too crucial for Taleqani's contemporary agenda to thwart it for a mere theological technicality.

The immediate implication of an evolutionary view of history, again translated into political terms, is the Muslim believer's obligation to alter his surroundings to make righteousness possible. "Man," Taleqani proscribed, "has to change constantly his intellectual and spiritual environment [in order to be] located on the straight path."[104] Because this need and capacity are innate to human beings, the principle of evolution, according to his reading of 11:56—"Not an animal but He doth grasp it by the forelock! Lo! My Lord is on a straight path"—governs "all moving creatures."[105] Perhaps to modify his theological preference for "free will," Taleqani gives this movement towards perfection certain teleological inevitability, a matter-of-fact certitude. The mere reflection upon God's beauty and blessing in this world would compel man to follow his nature and seek the innate perfection God has invested in him by using his Divinely ordained freedom of action and alter his environment for the better, and then for the best.[106]

Upon this path of perfection, according to Taleqani's reading of 2:3 — "Who believe in the Unseen, and establish worship, and spend of that We have bestowed upon them"—the holy Qur'an is the best and most perfect guide for mankind. The subject matter, definition, and ultimate objective of the Qur'an are man and his perfection.[107] But to benefit from the Qur'an, Taleqani stipulates an innate virtuosity in man: "The Qur'an is the Book of guidance for the virtuous."[108] Thusly conditioned, the most essential and common human attributes are transformed into higher virtues once man traverses upon this linear path of perfection. This transubstantiates man's earthly and mundane qualities into higher attributes. Thus when God speaks of "pure companion" in 2:25, "There for them are pure companions," that is not a reference to earthly love, but "if this love moves upon the path of perfection . . . it will reach spiritual beauty which is the same as intellectual perceptions, knowledge, and the understanding of universal and general relations."[109]

The Representative of God on Earth: Another Theory of Political Authority

To traverse this road of perfection and salvation, man must have a particular relationship with God. As indicated in the Qur'anic reference to man's being God's vicegerent on earth, 2:31—"And He taught Adam all the names, then showed them to the angels, saying: Inform Me of the names of these, if ye are truthful"—the relationship between the Creator and His most favored created being is founded on the intellectual capacity He has invested in human beings. "If that be the case," Taleqani stipulated,

then the meaning and the secret of vicegerency of every individual is proportional to the limits of his intelligence and [his] perception of the [Divine] names [whereby he receives his earthly attributes], and the application of that vicegerency.[110]

Upon this reading of man as God's vicegerent on earth, Taleqani establishes the conditions for "the selected vicegerents,"[111] or those among human beings in positions of authority who "know the secret of man['s creation] and advance man's hidden capabilities towards goodness and perfection."[112] Mandated by God and directed by Divine Will, this course of human development can be aided occasionally by Providential interventions.

Thus Taleqani is not very sympathetic to such pseudoscientific explanations of, for example, the parting of the Red Sea as offered by Sir Sayyid Ahmad Khan, the Indian commentator of the Qur'an, and believes in the actuality of such events as guided by those "selected" leaders such as

Moses.[113] The political implication of this doctrinal position is that if God actually intervenes in the affairs of His created beings by designating a selected group of leaders, or vicegerents, then the authority of those Divinely ordained representatives is that much more abiding.

This view of "the selected vicegerents" among human beings as those who are in closer affinity with the Divine intention of creation, which is not a Qur'anic phrase but can certainly be extrapolated from the Text, postulates a political theory of leadership that Taleqani is not at liberty to expostulate in more detail at this time. But the implications are quite clear. If, as he argues, the whole purpose of creation is for man to be guided towards his utmost potentiality, and if the realization of such a goal is contingent upon the degree of his intellectual capabilities to approximate his ontological realities to "Divine Names," and, further, if men can be led only by those who are intellectually more qualified to guide them towards such a realization, then there remains no doubt that the Muslim society thus conceived can be led only by those who are more consciously cognizant of the Divine Names and Attributes, that is, the ulama'. The further and most obvious implication of this theoretical position is that kings, who are not philosophers in the Platonic sense or jurists in Shi'i juridical language, are ipso facto illegitimate rulers.

A Theory of Social Corruption: The Status Quo Delegitimated

Following this theory of political authority, which simultaneously delegitimates the lay king and legitimates the learned cleric, Taleqani reaches a theory of social corruption, based on the Qur'anic passage 2:62,[114] with a remarkable ring of contemporaneity to it. Persistent obedience to the carnal soul leads man astray from the path of perfection as pointed out by the prophets. Thus misguided, man's propensity to commit socially harmful crime is intensified and leads to the creation of a tyrannical ruling class and its military apparatus. The miseries and immoralities will thus be further aggravated. "Under these circumstances," Taleqani warned,

prophets and reformers, as well as their true followers [that is, contemporary religious authorities such as Taleqani himself], who wish to enlighten the minds, untie the chains, and help the wretched, are exiled, imprisoned, and killed as disrupters of orders and enemies of reforms by the power of the rulers and the aid of this very wretched people.[115]

Writing these words and constructing these images in prison prior to his exile to Zabol in the remote southeastern part of the country, Taleqani clearly had his self-image in mind. In another passage[116] he clearly blamed "idols, [pseudo]clerics, and whimsical tyrants" for thwarting the potential capabilities of people, for imprisoning the petit-criminals but "not the actual perpetrators." He anticipates the day when someone would appear "to show the way out, prevent the evildoers from going astray, and, with the light of guidance, lead [people] towards the righteous path."[117]

To Narrow in on Contemporaneity

With these doctrinally based readings of the Qur'an, Taleqani has established that the status quo is corrupt, that the politically conscious ulama' are Divinely in charge of leading people to this- and other-worldly salvation, and that the world is in a perpetual state of progress towards perfection. The most immediate problem that challenges this developmental notion of history, however, is for it to be politically confined—and thus doctrinally limited and ideologically retarded—within a frame of historical particularity. That would render its universal and contemporary relevance untenable. To prevent this doctrine from being limited to its presumed archetypal Qur'anic expression, Taleqani moved to expound its universality on a larger frame of reference. For this purpose, he resorted to the following passage (17:44): "Nothing is, that does not proclaim His praise, but you do not understand their extolling." Here, too, he interjects the element of movement in interpreting the passage:

Everything is glorifying [God] . . . everything is [in] movement. They all release themselves from the very essence of impurity with this movement of consciousness, everyone moves towards Truth and perfection.[118]

Thus universalized, however, this doctrinal reading of the Qur'anic passage becomes too general and too vague to be ideologically effective in moving its audience. Taleqani thus took the next step and connected his doctrinal reading of the Qur'an to a specific ideological context of his constituency. The sermon from which this passage is taken was delivered on 3 August 1979, a time when the National Assembly met to ratify the Islamic Constitution. Here is how Taleqani connects his reading of the Qur'anic passage to the actual historical event:

Today, you brothers and sisters went to the ballot boxes. This human act, this divine act, insofar as the faith and the social responsibility are concerned, is a glorifying (tasbih) movement because it means voting for the most honest, most informed, and most conscientious of all people. Election for what? For the preparation of the constitution, that is to say a law that would be able to cleanse the atmosphere from colonialism, tyranny, repression, injustice, selfishness; and thus prepare the means of developing your potential capabilities.[119]

This ideological framework will now have to be specifically focused on a political event. To become fully operational, the hermeneutic domains of Taleqani's Qur'anic exegesis must necessarily extend from its doctrinal and ideological contexts to specific political objectives. Towards the end of this sermon Taleqani wants to express his support for the Pasdars (the Muslim Militia formed in contradistinction to the regular army) and in particular encourage a unification of all the military forces. He proceeds with the following Qur'anic passage (3:103):

And hold fast, all of you together, to the cable of Allah, and do not separate, and remember Allah's favour unto you: how you were enemies and He made friendship between your hearts so that you became as brothers by His grace.[120]

Within the analogical matrix of this similitude, "the cable of Allah" (habl Allah) becomes the Islamic Revolution and thus an expression of God's grace. The reference to "how you were enemies and He made friendship between your hearts" compares and contrasts the pre- and post-Revolutionary periods and points out that in the course of the Revolution feelings of gemeinschaft naturally intensify. The message thus conveyed, through the very word of God, is "do not separate" and be unified behind the Islamic Revolution. Taleqani leaves no discrepancy for guessing exactly what he means by quoting this Qur'anic passage:

we hope that the army, the Pasdars, the gendarms, the police, all of these forces, in cooperation and unity, will protect both the internal security and the Islamic boundaries.[121]

Thus by carefully weaving the actual political events into the very fabric of the Qur'anic text, Taleqani verifies, as it were, the sacred Scripture through its application to the contemporary historical exigencies and, in turn, sanctifies the political events he wishes to have happened by approximating them to the holy Text. A crucial by-product of this Qur'anification of revolutionary purposes is that it, ipso facto, re-Islamicizes the entire political enterprise thus engendered. By bringing the entire revolutionary movement into the conceptual frame of Qur'anic reference, Taleqani effectively delegitimizes any existing or potential secular claim to the event. The revolution is either Islamic or no revolution at all. The interpretative language of Qur'anic commentary that Taleqani thus creates reestablishes the hermeneutic horizons of (once again) being-in-the-world significantly. The necessity of the revolutionary attendance upon the world stems from the Word of God, the language of the Qur'an. Without that language, as it were, there remains little possibility of revolutionary redefinition of Muslims in the modernity of their collective consciousness, the ontotheocentricity of Islam in its immediate, most significant, history.

Jews, Christians, and Marxists

On the whole, Taleqani retains a highly exegetical language in his pre-Revolutionary interpretation of the Qur'anic passages, leaving much of his ideological message and agenda, though explicit, between the lines. Occasionally, however, his extension of the Qur'anic language to matters of an explicitly contemporary nature becomes pronounced. These pronunciations in the pre-Revolutionary period remain, for obvious reasons, limited to matters that the official censorship would tolerate. Attacking Marxism and its ideological and philosophical bases was one such instance.

In his explication of the Qur'anic passage 2:105,[122] Taleqani identifies "the infidel materialists of this century"[123] as the modern version of the *Jahiliyyah* period, that is, the period of "ignorance" before the Islamic revelation. He also lashes out against Jews and Christians who have permitted their respective faiths to be used for the patently economic and political interests of the colonialists. He condemns in particular the Christian missionaries whose activities are merely, in Taleqani's estimation, a coverup for otherwise patently colonial interests,[124] or conversely, when discussing 2:243,[125] condones the African and Asian fighters against colonialism, who are considered as sacred a group of martyrs as those of the third Shi'i Imam, al-Husayn.[126] He also takes time in a footnote to argue against the logical validity of dialectical materialism.[127]

Such approximations of Qur'anic passages to actual revolutionary circumstances give Taleqani's political discourse a certain claim of contemporary relevance. This was, of course, completely antithetical to the grain of secular thinking that considered anything smacking of religious coloring as outmoded and irrelevant. If Islam, which means the Qur'an constantly reinterpreted, were to be made politically relevant—or indeed inevitable— it had to, ipso facto, be rendered into a legitimate ideological proposition on a whole new set of horizons and plains of operation. To be sure, at this stage Taleqani's concern was entirely political and revolutionary. But should those political and revolutionary purposes be met successfully, the Qur'an thus reinterpreted, the Islam thus updated, would be rendered the quintessential level of cultural, social, and economic discourse. The specifics of "the Islamic Ideology" were always articulated towards that penultimate objective.

Men of Science Too

Reference to such contemporary realities, political and otherwise, has the added function of updating the modern relevance of the holy Text—and with it Islam reinterpreted—in the age of "The Western" hegemonic ascendancy. As the revolutionary movement, in toto, is Qur'anified and thus Islamicized, the Qur'an and with it Islam are rendered subject to the reciprocal verification of the matters of modernity. Like Bazargan, Taleqani is particularly attracted to such occasions when a "Western" observer, particularly a man of science, has become a theist or has inadvertently said something in support of Taleqani's theological (ideological) positions. These occasions, of which Taleqani is informed only through Persian translations of secondary sources, are frequently celebrated in footnotes as tacit, but powerful, indications that even "The Westerners," who, after all, are the primary model of comparison and validity, acknowledge the truth of the Qur'anic discourse, even though they may not know it consciously. If a certain American scientist, "Mr. Morrison, the former head of the New York Academy of Sciences," [128] is reported to have come to the conclusion that there is a God, the occasion calls for a footnote to the Qur'anic passage 2:29.[129] Victor Hugo and *Les Misérables* are brought to bear on 2:179.[130] Maurice Maeterlinck[131] and Dr. Alexis Carrel[132] are frequently cited. "The famous German economist, Dr. Schacht" [133] and Paul Samuelson, "the famous economist," [134] are equally supportive of certain Qur'anic passages. The Egyptian researcher, Dr. Rashad, "who lives in America," [135] Mendel, "the Austrian priest," [136] Lamarck, Darwin,[137] and, of course, Hegel[138] are cited to propose one point or another in support of Taleqani's reading of the Qur'an. Without ever reaching a level of conscious articulation—and there precisely is the power of its grip—"The West" always acts as the ultimate and final arbiter in matters of truth. In premodern readings of the holy Text, attributes of the ultimate and final arbiter in matters of truth were the exclusive prerogative of the Qur'an itself. Subjecting, in effect, the veracity of the sacred Text to historical verification by "Western" authorities thus becomes the most sustained animating force in that moving paradox that is "the Islamic Ideology."

The Power of Interpretation

It is precisely within the confinements of this unfolding paradox that the ultimate direction of Taleqani's revolutionary discourse is charted. Taleqani, among his ideological comrades, felt acutely the historical momentum upon which a revolutionary course of action had to be taken. His philosophy of history, patently Darwinist and evolutionist in its conceptual underpinnings, assumed a theological language extended from the Qur'an, thus giving his political assumptions and ideological suppositions a considerable measure of legitimacy. If, as it has been suggested, the notion of the natural and uninterrupted progress of mankind is "a rationalist corruption of Christian eschatology," [139] then Taleqani was much more indebted to the "Western" ideas that he thought he was opposing than is apparent at first sight. Openly defying Christianity—and with it the secular rationalism that he considered a modern evil of "The West"—and yet unknowingly assuming a watered-down version of "a rationalist corruption of Christian eschatology" as the very truth emanated from the Qur'an, Taleqani demonstrated the degree of hidden, but visceral, identification, negational as it may seem, with the supreme symbolic of his time: "The West."

The theological justification of a rational and progressive view of history further assimilates, and thus neutralizes, the ambiguities of actual historical exigencies into a homogeneous and comprehensible mythology of history wherein all events and all actualities, no matter how essential and pervasive their innate atomized irrationality, are made to make perfect sense and validate a perfect harmony in the cosmic world thus envisioned. The bifurcation, and the gap, between the mythological language of conviction and the actuality of the ambiguous historical realities is sought to be filled and interpreted, in the very tone of Taleqani's discourse, by the sanctity of the Qur'anic text. The autologous and self-evident language of the Qur'an thus lends credence and currency to the mythological construction of the status quo, in whose revolutionary tone, the twisted tongue of its facts-and-fantasies, rebellion against the political and (im)moral order is all but inevitable. This reordering of the moral demand system is effectively reminiscent of the original Islamic revolution, the one that started it all, the Muhammadan charismatic movement. Thus through "the Islamic Ideology" Islam itself is renarrated in the modernity of its history. "Islam itself" is that imaginative constellation of authenticity that exacts obedience from Muslims, as much in the privacy of their peity as in the publicity of their revolt. "The Islamic Ideology" rehistoricized Islam, put it back in "place," from the abstracted sentiments of (all-but-forgotten and) pale truths to ideological convictions of radical contemporaneity, action, obedience.

The mythological notion of progress, ideologized for Taleqani's audience through the Qur'anic language, operates, no matter how deeply in concealment, at a borderline between Darwinism and Marxism. Darwinism biologically postulates and Taleqani theologically assumes the necessity of a developmental course of natural history wherein the survival of the fittest is the final, Qur'anically mandated, truth. Translated from biological to social history, this idea of progress is, as has been demonstrated,[140] connected to tools, whether instrumental or conceptual, that man makes and is, in turn, survived by. Where Marxism postulates the progress of human history on the gradual development of means (tools) of economic production, which could range from an automobile industry to theoretical systems of political economy, it meets with the social antecedents of human progress as a natural necessity, extended from the ideological implications of biological Darwinism. It is precisely at this borderline that Taleqani expostulates his reading of the Qur'an. The reading thus achieved caters, simultaneously, to a mythological build-up of a revolutionary course of action and to a Darwinist-Marxist agenda for the course of human history, with all its ideological and political implications.

Moving along this progressive course of history, Taleqani's revolution-

ary man, safely located in a mythological redefinition of the world, takes
his guidance from the eternal words of God, heeds the authority of "the
selected vicegerents" of God on earth, and advances towards the absolute
realization of the kingdom of heaven on earth—redefined Islamically. Sanctified through the revelatory language of the Qur'an, the mythological
language of the revolutionary man caters to and invests in the most innately
human urges to trust and understand the world. Once extended into the
mundane realities of political life, the sacred language of the Qur'an makes
the world intelligible and trustworthy. In the face of an avalanche of new
and conflicting ideological claims to absolute political truth, the archetypal
language of the Qur'an is nothing short of heaven-sent. The success of
Taleqani's revolutionary language, and with it those of other Islamic ideologues, attended the essential need to know and trust an otherwise inhospitable and inscrutable world, a world turning increasingly "modern" in its
self-perceptive particulars, in its compelling universals. In this language,
familiar terms, resuscitated from an old and archetypal source, were offered
to cope with and thus interpret the cruelty of uncertainty in an incessantly
changing pattern of normalcy. The individual participation in this collective
myth, whether committed by conscious political activists or promised by
subconscious mass participation, is the strategic prerequisite for the revolutionary course of action to commence.

Equally necessary for that grand commencement of convocational sentiments to revolt is the innate human need, contemporary in its ontological
origin, that things ought to get better. Taleqani's preference for "free will"
in a theological debate with "predestination" is thus compatible with his
progressive view of human history. Only determined and willing men can
shape their own history. In conscious control of the ideological means at
their disposal and in full conformity with the revolutionary objectives
Taleqani projects for them, Muslim masses are hereby endowed with a
temporal reflection of an archetypal mandate to mobilize and change their
status quo which is always in a state of flux: better than it has been, worse
than it should be. Thus from the passive pieties of an immobile multitude,
"the Islamic Ideology" recreates the active convictions of a mobilized nation. New blood in very old veins, "the Islamic Ideology" becomes as much
its own paradoxical self-negation as the ruling terms of a new generation
of enchantments. Between the verticality of its remembered past and horizontality of its political present, "the Islamic Ideology" creates a marginal
"space" that would gradually expand to rebecome "Islam itself."

Of central significance in Taleqani's linear conception of progress, in this
historical unfolding of "the Islamic Ideology," is the textual veracity of the
Qur'an and with it the ultimate theological truth of Islam thus reinterpreted. This theological necessity, without which Taleqani would, needless
to say, cease to be a Muslim, cannot entertain, for example, a cyclical

notion of history, whereby Islam would be but one cycle among many—with equal claim to truth. The relativization of Islamic history would be too close to the relativization of Islam itself, however reinterpreted, which would be theologically unacceptable. With the absolute paradigmatic veracity of Islam as a doctrinal postulation and with a linear conception of history, all of humanity—Iranians, Muslims, and others—must simply follow this divine commandment. But on the stern face of concrete reality, where the majority of the world's inhabitants are non-Muslims, if not anti-Muslims, conviction in one's doctrinal stand cannot but turn absolutist and dogmatic, uncompromising and totalitarian. The more the external reality denies legitimacy to being a Muslim, whether by Christian colonialists or atheist Marxists, the sharper the edge of absolute conviction in one's embattled version of ultimate truth.

The cutting edge of such necessarily unexamined convictions hinges on the primacy of human action. Presupposing and Qur'anically arguing for a history set on a linear course of progress sanctifies the human act undertaken in that divinely ordained direction. Thus, every political act committed in this vein is simultaneously a theological testament of salvation. Once set upon a revolutionary course of action, this very political act assumes the proportions of a sacred event. No secular ideology, idealized by any version of secular humanism, could match this astonishing achievement of sanctifying the revolutionary act while, and through, repoliticizing what is the most sacrosanct in a religious culture turned political. But there is a heavy price to pay for such political efficiencies. Taleqani could not have thought through all the inevitable implications of his wholehearted acceptance of a linear conception of progress in history. The necessary implication inherent in this conception of history, that Taleqani's time in the latter part of the twentieth century was "better" than that of the Prophet Muhammad and Ali in the early part of the seventh century is a statement that Taleqani would have rejected as a believing Muslim. But these are precisely the kinds of paradoxical conclusions implicit in a linear conception of historical progress. He would have rejected equally the possibility that in a future progressive stage the very Text of the Qur'an would be rendered obsolete. But if rationality and progress are to govern the measures of attaining truth, as opposed to atemporal and archetypal necessities innate to a sacred Text, that inevitable, equally paradoxical, conclusion is precisely what would follow from Taleqani's conception of linear progress in history.

This absolutist view further assimilates and neutralizes a number of cohabitual aspects of a living culture as well as the possibility that while one dimension is in a state of stagnation or even decay, other dimensions may, in fact, be flourishing and in full fruition.[141] The political corruption that Taleqani witnessed in his time was not necessarily compatible with the comparatively higher level of mass literacy, lower infant mortality rates, a relatively greater recognition of the human rights of the other (female) half of humanity, or a more accurate historical awareness of the Iranian past. Even in specifically Islamic terms, more Iranians knew much more about their religious heritage than ever before. Numerous books and treatises were edited from confused and conflicting manuscripts. A full and accurate picture of the Islamic (Shiʿi) political, social, intellectual, and artistic history was now available for the first time ever to a larger group of readers and interpreters. That these latter developments were more social events of multiple and varied causes and consequences than the tangible results of any monarch's so-called "modernization" policies further testifies that a monolithic view of human history—as collectively, congenially, and simultaneously moving towards a synchronous stage of progress—was more a mythological construction for immediate revolutionary purposes than an indication of actual historical experience.

The necessary mythological constructions of the coming revolution constituted the single most important item on Taleqani's agenda, with Qur'anic commentary as his primary reinterpretative tool. For the ordinary Iranian who does not know Arabic, Taleqani's Qur'anic commentary is doubly convincing. With the stroke of his pen, as it were, Taleqani extracts meaning from a Text that in its sacred Arabic original is incomprehensible and, at the same time, force that Text read contemporary realities and proscribe a revolutionary course of action.

What Taleqani thus achieves is the ultimate Qur'anification of the contemporary memory and history—which itself is a two-edged sword. For a traditional Muslim to have lived through the ambiguities and uncertainties of the actual history, Qur'anic interpretations provided the comfort of locating him in the bosom of a metahistory, divinely ordained and humanly followed. That metahistory had a grand design and purpose the specifics of which were not to be deciphered in the limited lives and visions of mortals. Once through Taleqani's Qur'anic commentary the ambiguities and uncertainties of the experienced history were assimilated into the fabric of the sacred Text, and thus, conversely, the archetypal language of the very Word of God was brought to bear on the contemporary historical exigencies, there occurs a contraction in the Muslim collective consciousness, in their expanded shared memory. The contraction, at one and the same time, verifies the contemporary realities through the Qur'an, and, conversely, verifies the Qur'an, as it were, through its applicability to these realities. But, and there is the rub, with no intervening level of conceptual transference between the sacred Text of the Word of God and the profane actuality of the acts of men, the veracity of the Qur'an is rendered entirely contingent upon the mercy of the historical experience. Traditionally, which is to say legitimately in that historically valid hermeneutic context within which

Muslims have repeatedly recognized themselves, the Qur'an has been valid
not because of but despite its presumed doctrinal correspondence with, or
transference onto, human history. After Taleqani's reading, which by doctrinal definition must be postprophetic, the Qur'an can be valid only if
historically relevant. That relevance, always subject to a linear conception
of progress that Taleqani vehemently expostulated, is permanently vicar-
ious.

Thus, the central twist to Taleqani's reading of the sacred Text is ultimately a hermeneutic paradox. To manifest the hidden intent of the Qur'an,
and then to deliver publicly one reading of that hidden message as both
inevitable and unequivocal, implicitly robs all future, as it does all the past,
readings of equal validity. The sacred and the eternal always synonymous,
once a sacred Text is cut off from its previous and future multiple readings,
a prerogative innate to the archetypal language of the Qur'an, it ceases to
be "sacred." That sacredness, however, is essential for the contemporary
validity of the political discourse Taleqani develops. In the face of an
emerging revolutionary agenda, his doctrinal, ideological, and political
mandates are taken directly from his contemporary historical realities. As a
Muslim political activist, he sought to formulate an ideological frame of
reference for his constituency to follow. The Qur'an came as the most
natural and inevitable source of authority. If the voice of authority latent
in the Qur'an, but inarticulate and politically mute, could be translated
effectively into a doctrinal, ideological, and ultimately political agenda, a
great deal of collective force could be amassed for the revolutionary purpose. For this revolutionary purpose to be viable Islamically, the authoritative voice of the Qur'an ought to be given to a progressive view of the
human condition whereby man—or more accurately for Taleqani, "The
People"—is in charge of history. Choosing "free will" over "predestination," Taleqani charged "The People" with the divinely mandated responsibility for altering the status quo and achieving a better condition. Leading
"The People" out of their actual, relative, and imagined misery towards the
idealized and promised land of liberty and prosperity are "selective vicegerents," that is, those who know the true purpose of creation to be the
realization of an innate potential for growth. After the prophets and Imams, the contemporary, and thus politically relevant, "selective vicegerents"
are those who best know the divine message (the Qur'an): the ulama'. But
because of their knowledge and their innate responsibility to lead "The
People," the ulama' are captured, imprisoned, tortured, and murdered. Yet
this is but a passing stage before the masses are fully informed of their
responsibilities and charged with revolutionary momentum. Opposing and
trying to thwart this momentum are not only the local tyrants and their
repressive organs but also the colonial powers who, through their various
agencies, seek to perpetuate this rule of injustice. Jews and Christians are

merely agents of colonial powers. Marxists are misguided souls who are either direct agents of colonial powers or else manipulated by them. Against all these odds is the veracity of the (revolutionary) Qur'anic message that, verified by the latest statement by ("The Western") men of science, can lead to, and promises to deliver, the kingdom of heaven on earth, Islamically redefined.

The Theological Necessity of Religious Authorities

To lead "The People" to that utopia, Taleqani charged his religious cohorts with the highest level of responsibility. But before assuming this responsibility, the internal organization of the clerical order had to be redefined. Taleqani was among the religious authorities invited to write on the occasion of Ayatollah Borujerdi's death and the vacancy of the position of the supreme Shiʻi juridical leader. He was particularly emphatic about the central significance of the religious authorities for the future of the Islamic faith and argued, rather radically, that after the closure of the cycle of prophethood with Muhammad, *ejtehad* "keeps the light of guidance lit and the line of messengership *(nobovvat)* extant."[142] As he understood it, *ejtehad* here meant the ability to exercise jurisprudentially informed opinions about matters of contemporary relevance. *Nobovvat*, or the cycle of divinely ordained prophethood, consists of three phases according to Taleqani: preliminary, intermediate, and advanced.[143] At the last, advanced, level, and after the preliminary and intermediate periods of introducing and propagating the Divine message, "the gates of *ejtehad* are opened."[144] Borrowing this notion from Sunni Islam, because in Shiʻism the "gates" of *ejtehad* have never been considered closed, Taleqani thus emphasizes the significance of attending to the specific immediacies of the present age. Religions will lose their very raison d'être if they cease to address the most pertinent problems of their time. That is precisely, Taleqani stipulated, why in Shiʻism it is forbidden to follow a dead religious authority. But as the realities of the modern world have grown increasingly complicated, he realized, the keynote in the clerical organization had to be "consultation." Individual exertion of juridical judgment was detrimental to Islam.

There are three possible ways of attending to the quintessential question of supreme religious authority and its relation to its wide constituency: first, that this authority should be delegated to a few high-ranking clerics; second, that it should be left totally disorganized and subject to particular variations; and yet third, that it should be centralized in a committee that works through consultation.[145] Taleqani rejects the first choice and its foundation, which stipulates "the necessity of following the exemplary conduct of the most learned" *(Wojub-e taqlid-e aʻlam)*. That stipulation is,

first, impossible to ascertain and, second, impractical to follow. There are
no Qur'anic verses or prophetic (or Imami) traditions to justify such an
exclusive authority being the prerogative of "the most learned." Probably
with the example of Ayatollah Borujerdi in mind, Taleqani also warned
against "religious despotism,"[146] which sets in when one particular individual in his old age assumes the supreme leadership of the Shi'i believers. He
also believed that "treacherous politics" arrange for "ill-prepared or corrupt" people to surround the Shi'i leader and thus keep him unaware of the
pressing problems of his followers. "Thus," he concluded, "centralization
in issuing [religious] edicts and controlling [the Shi'i community] has neither a juridical reason nor a religious justification nor is it in the best
interests of the Muslim faith and community."[147]

Taleqani equally rejects the second choice of not having any organizational centrality in matters of common concern to all members of the Shi'i
community. There are questions and problems that ought to be addressed
and considered before specific religious edicts are issued on their juridical
status. Because of the prevalence of mass communication in the modern
world, the affairs of the Shi'i community at large ought to be considered by
some form of common consensus among the religious authorities.

Taleqani concluded that the best alternative was to have a central committee of religious authorities who, through consultation and collective
consensus, directs the affairs of the Shi'i community.[148] Now that the
means and mechanism of instant and periodic communication were available, Shi'i authorities had to meet on a regular basis to discuss the common
problems of their collective constituency. This collective consensus, as Taleqani understood it, was not necessarily incompatible with the supreme
authority of one or a select group of high-ranking clerics. But a practical
mechanism had to be established through which lower-ranking clerics, as
well as those in remote parts of the country, could be heard and their
particular concerns considered collectively. Such consultations were, of
course, Qur'anically sanctified too. Taleqani's reading of the key term *ulu
al-amr* in the al-Nisa' chapter of the Qur'an, the famous "authority verse,"[149]
consists of the Infallible Imams first and the religious authorities second.[150]

Taleqani's primary concern in this short treatise is to break the long-
established tradition of having one supreme religious authority whose total
attention was focused strictly on juridical matters. This was obviously
antithetical to having younger, and more politically conscious, clerics express their collective concerns about common political and social issues. By
including lower-ranking religious figures in his proposed committee, Taleqani wished to advance the cause of the more ordinary and politically
consequential issues among the high-ranking ulama'. Undoubtedly, any
measure of "collectivization" of the supreme religious authorities meant

their simultaneous repoliticization. This repoliticization, though, was absolutely inevitable for Taleqani if Islam were to remain a relevant and legitimate force in political, social, and cultural domains.

Legitimacy of a Revolutionary Discourse

Repoliticization of the high-ranking clerical establishment had to be predicated, by historical necessity, on a sustained and legitimate ideological discourse that was close enough to the canonical sources of the faith, and yet distant enough to bargain for the largest possible constitutency. Legitimacy, or the apparition of it, is always at the heart of every rising claim to ideological credence. To carry its message to the hearts and minds of its audience, a revolutionary discourse, more than anything else, needs legitimacy. In his revolutionary discourse, and for his political objectives, Taleqani sought and secured this legitimacy through repeated references to the sacred authority of the holy Scripture. Such doctrinal, ideological, and political uses of the Qur'an have historical roots. However, the crucial question for the future of Taleqani's legacy, and for his continued constituency, is not the proximity of his Qur'anic exegesis to its historical antecedents, nor why, in the age of absolutely conflicting and relatively convincing ideologies, a sacred, archetypal, language still carries authority, nor the fact that, in the course of such ideological readings of the Qur'an, the essential epistemological distinction between a sacred discourse and a revolutionary semantic is assimilated, cross-referenced, and ultimately negated. These are all legitimate questions in frames of reference immune to a revolutionary outburst. For Taleqani's immediate constituency, for those who pay for the trust they invest in a revolutionary enchantment with the flesh and blood of their bodily participation in history, the question is more of a reductionist nature. With the increasing repoliticization of the Qur'anic exegesis, its exclusive historical updating, there appears an inevitable hermeneutic reductionism in the multiple, and perhaps even complementary, modes, shades, varieties, and possibilities of reading the holy Text. The political reading is always the most compelling and the most exclusive. Perhaps beyond the doctrinal belief in its Divine origin, it is the hermeneutic possibility of multiple historical readings that has secured an immortal niche for the Word of God. Against the essential thrust of this possibility, Taleqani's Qur'anic exegesis exemplifies a massive process of reinterpretative reductionism through which a multiple set of Qur'anic readings is gradually substituted by a simple domineering interpretation: the political. Once that domineering political reading, supported by its ideological institutionalization into a state apparatus, opens its totalitarian wings and unfolds its assimilating force, there will scarcely be time or place, permission or prudence, for any alternative reading. If, in the age of conflicting ideologies, relative salvation is in exposition to a healthy variety of claims to absolute truths, what the thunder of "Islamic Ideology" and its brand of Qur'anic exegesis lack most and forbid most severely is that saving sign of allowing for the Ibsenian whisper: "on the other hand."

"The Islamic Ideology" Conceived, and in Need

Al-e Ahmad sensed it, Shari'ati legitimized it, Motahhari gave it its full revolutionary potential, and Taleqani justified it Qur'anically. But "the Islamic Ideology," thus conceived, had to face the most serious challenge to its legitimacy: competing with Marxism. Particularly powerful in its logical and philosophical appeal, Marxism was the most serious ideological force that commanded the increasing loyalty of the revolutionary youth. Particularly institutionalized in informal student organizations in universities, Marxism recognized no alternative to its historical inevitability, to its philosophical validity, or to its ideological appeal. If "the Islamic Ideology" was to have a politically significant share of the youth and their ideological loyalty, it had to turn offensive precisely against the philosophical claim of Marxism to absolute, final, and "scientific" ideological validity. If Marxism was not thus challenged, "the Islamic Ideology" would have remained merely the limited conviction of a religiously musical group of activists. A discourse of an entirely different nature was needed to give it philosophical validity. To prepare and strengthen it for final revolutionary mobilization, "the Islamic Ideology" needed a philosophical confrontation against Marxism. For that consolidation, "the Islamic Ideology," from Al-e Ahmad to Shari'ati, to Motahhari, and even through Taleqani, had to wait.

The Continuity of the Political Life

Taleqani was released from prison in 1968 but barred from political activity. This period lasted for two years. In May 1970 he resumed his campaign against the Shah's reign. He pursued his political activities by organizing a mourning ceremony for Muhammad Reza Sa'idi, who had been murdered by the Shah's police for his political activities in collaboration with Ayatollah Khomeini. Following Taleqani's involvement in organizing Sa'idi's mourning in Qiyasi Mosque in Tehran, he was arrested and imprisoned briefly.

In 1971, three student followers of Taleqani—Mohammad Hanif-Nezhad, Sa'id Mohsen, and Ali Asghar Badi'zadegan—founded the "Organization of People's Guerilla" *(Sazeman-e Mojahedin-e Khalq)*. Taleqani was a prominent clerical supporter of this organization, formed essentially by young lay students and professionals. Because of his active support of this organization, he was arrested and exiled to the frontier town of Zabol near

Afghanistan where he spent three years in exile, far removed from the political activities in Tehran. He returned from Zabol in 1974 and secretly resumed his active support of the Mojahedin-e Khalq Organization. By the time he had returned to Tehran, however, a major break had split the Organization. A patently Marxist branch of *Sazeman-e Mojahedin-e Khalq*, taking advantage of the imprisonment of the more Islamically posed faction, had redefined the ideological posture of the organization in more blatantly Marxist terms. Taleqani opposed this redefinition of the Organization. He was confronted by two chief ideologues of the break—Bahram Aram and Vahid Afrashteh—who reportedly threatened his life if he publicly condemned the reorientation of the Organization. Soon after this, however, Vahid Afrashteh was arrested by SAVAK and subsequently revealed Taleqani's link to the Organization. Taleqani was arrested again and sentenced to ten years in prison. He was released after only four years, on 30 October 1978, in the wake of the Islamic Revolution.[151]

Upon Taleqani's release from the Evin Prison, Ayatollah Khomeini sent him a message from Neauphle-le-Château on 2 November 1978, congratulating him on his long-time struggle against the Shah and calling his release an indication of "the battlement of the Shah's imaginary fortress . . . crumbling."[152] This message was, in fact, an invitation from Khomeini to Taleqani to join the former's ranks in the fragmented shape that the opposition movement would ultimately assume. At issue was Taleqani's support of *Sazeman-e Mojahedin-e Khalq*, of which Ayatollah Khomeini did not particularly approve. Taleqani responded immediately and favorably to Khomeini's gesture and considered his release a result of, after God's grace, the people's revolt under Khomeini's leadership. By this response, dated 8 November 1978,[153] Taleqani tacitly but emphatically acknowledged Ayatollah Khomeini's supreme leadership of the Revolution and confirmed that he would serve under his authority.

It is worth considering that Taleqani was only nine years Khomeini's junior, not young enough to obligate him to the revolutionary leader's juridical superiority. In fact, both Khomeini and Taleqani had been fellow students of Ayatollah Ha'eri as the supreme jurist of their time. Taleqani's acceptance of Khomeini's revolutionary seniority was an ad hoc political choice rather than a necessary juridical requirement. Having said that, however, there is no doubt that Khomeini enjoyed a more prestigious stand among the revolutionary ulama'.

The ink on Taleqani's release form was not yet dried when he resumed his political activities. On 2 December 1978, now encouraged by the mounting opposition to the Shah, he issued a statement denouncing the regime and its use of force against civilians and calling for mourning ceremonies for those martyred during the street demonstrations against the Shah. In this message he openly called for active revolt against the Shah's regime through an institutional repoliticization of religious forces. On 10 December 1978 —an emotionally charged religious day in the Shi'i calendar because it coincided with 9 Moharram 1399—Taleqani led a massive rally in Tehran, at the conclusion of which a twelve-point declaration was ratified calling for the establishment of an Islamic Republic under the supreme authority of Ayatollah Khomeini.

Taleqani's services to the Revolution continued well into its successful course. Early in 1979, following the success of the Revolution, he was sent to calm down resurgences among the Turkamans in Northeastern Iran. He also served as a distinguished member of the Revolutionary Council, formed immediately upon the downfall of the old regime to oversee the transitional period. Initially, in the course of the revolutionary movement, the new constitution was supposed to be drafted by a constitutional assembly. The idea was later abandoned in favor of an Assembly of Experts, comprised chiefly of clerics and/or religiously minded individuals, of which Taleqani was a prominent member.

The peak of Taleqani's popularity was demonstrated when Ayatollah Khomeini appointed him the leader of public prayer *(Imam Jom'eh)*, with thousands rushing to pray behind him. But all did not go well with the old, revolutionary master. On 12 April 1979 two of Taleqani's sons were arrested and taken for interrogation by a revolutionary committee. One of them, Sayyid Mojtaba' Taleqani, was involved in the 1975 ideological secession with the *Sazeman-e Mojahedin-e Khalq*. Taleqani left Tehran for Qom. On 13 April he issued a televised statement in which he reaffirmed his belief in Khomeini's leadership. On 18 April, a week after two of his sons had been arrested, Taleqani met Khomeini in Qom. It has been reported that

This led to certain misrepresentations of his political stance, both in Iran and abroad; it was suggested that he somehow represented an "alternative" to Imam Khomeini, either independently or in collusion with Ayatollah Shari'atmadari. Nothing could be further from the truth.[154]

Whatever the truth might have been, on 1 July Taleqani again found it necessary to reiterate his trust in and obedience to the leadership of Ayatollah Khomeini. In the course of this speech, he conceded that "sometimes I go to Qom to discuss an important political matter, and the newspapers start making a noise; they speculate and write articles under banner headlines. But what takes place is an exchange of views."[155] The code term here is the "exchange of views," which both reveals and conceals Taleqani's growing dissatisfaction with the course of the Revolution. One of the key points of difference appears to have been his support for the *Mojahedin*. It has been claimed categorically that "there can be little doubt, however, that his warm support of them [the *Mojahedin*] ceased even before the triumph of the Islamic Revolution."[156] The truth of this assessment is difficult to ascertain, however. It has also been pointed out that "another misunderstanding concerning Taleqani's role after the establishment of the Islamic Republic is that he was somehow inclined to leftist groups and fanned their participation in the exercise of political power."[157] Such indications, too, may account for Taleqani's ultimate disillusion with the outcome of a revolution he had waited a lifetime to see.

The Chest Pain

At 9:30 P.M. on Sunday, 9 September 1979, Ayatollah Taleqani received the Soviet ambassador to Iran. Their meeting lasted for two and a half hours, during which Taleqani took notes. At about 12:00 midnight he retired to his private quarters and had supper; about half an hour after midnight he went to bed. "Tomorrow I have to go to the Assembly of Experts. I have to go to bed soon," he is reported to have said. He goes to his room, locks himself in, and goes to bed. After half an hour he calls for help, vomits all he had eaten, and complains of chest pain. A warm towel and a hand massage are not helpful. A physician is immediately summoned. But it is too late. At 1:45 A.M. Ayatollah Taleqani dies of a heart attack.[158]

In a short eulogy, a follower shared his grief with millions of others:

The old rebel. The standing cedar. He was our life. Our selves. He was one of those rarities of life. Cure to our eyes. The old rebel was the father to us all. He was our selves. . . . The father was quick. He was strong. He was in truth. The father was a bundle of love. The ecstasy of living. The father was a bridge that connected all roads, all the scattered roads. . . . The father is in our lives. The father shall always be with us. His memory be always dear to us![159]

Father Taleqani

The term of endearment with which millions of Taleqani's supporters identified him was "father." "*Pedar* Taleqani," "Father Taleqani," he was. The question is why, or more important to what end? "*Pedar* Taleqani" conveyed a picture. For millions of followers who had not actually seen or heard Taleqani, it was precisely this combination of a picture—bearded, turbaned, and bespectacled—and a name, "*Pedar* Taleqani," that registered what was to be seen and communicated. Thousands of posters disseminated the sketch of "*Pedar* Taleqani's" kind and caring, slightly baffled yet determined and assured, physiognomy to millions of his followers. "*Pedar* Taleqani" thus became, in that fertile soil of Shi'i collective imagination, the epitome of a father figure, caring and determined, set on delivering his children from common misery. The picture cast an extended gaze upon the expectant aspirations of the youthful crowd who carried it on their heads as the protective talisman against the evils of a collectively homogenized enemy. They chanted *"Pedar* Taleqani" as the rhythmic psalms of an apocalyptic delivery. *"Pedar* Taleqani," the mere invocation of the term assured them of their path, gave them confidence in their march. The gaze from behind the spectacles showed them the way, confided in them the absolute confidence of the committed ideologue. The turbanned, bearded, and bespectacled face was frozen old, as old as ever, as confident as eternity. This was not an ordinary photograph of a man who was born once and died once. This was the gaze and the confidence of a forgotten number of millennia, of shared memories of a distant, yet ever present, father from whose mental image every particular father was ever loved and feared. Love and fear were in every pronouncement of *"Pedar* Taleqani." It was, or it became, the term of initiation into revolutionary youth. Had you yet said it or not: *"Pedar* Taleqani"? Had you yet confessed the supreme love, overpowering fear of having a revolutionary father? The revolutionary father of a whole generation, *"Pedar* Taleqani" was loved and held in awe—in awe of revolutionary acceptance. What is in a name? Authority. The ability to command to march, to move, to mobilize, to face that soldier, to seek that bullet, to fear nothing. That was authority in no need of power. It was implemented instantly, merely by willing it. The legitimacy of millennia of shared sentiments was behind this authority. Call him *"Pedar* Taleqani," and you are part of that collective spirit that has animated centuries of cherished memories. Call him *"Pedar* Taleqani" and you are part of a fraternity that claims the most sacred symbolics of your common culture. The rite of passage from nonexistent individuality to meaningful communal identity rests entirely in claiming Taleqani as your father. A father, more than a father, more in revolutionary zeal than in biology, *"Pedar* Taleqani" claims a generation of revolutionaries as his true offsprings. Biological children are mere physical resemblances; revolutionary offsprings extend you to history, make you live in the most cherished recollections of generations to come, on the authority of generations who have gone. It is on the concurrence of generations past and yet to come that a revolution calls its leader "father."

"See Me Safe Up"

"I pray you, Master Lieutenant," Sir Thomas More is reported to have said, as he ascended the scaffold upon which to be beheaded, "see me safe up, and for my coming down let me shift for myself."[160] The scaffold was so weak it was about to fall. More said this merrily, not in anger, vexation, irony, or even submission. Upon the scaffold, before being beheaded, More was told not to make a lengthy speech. He did not. He merely said that he was God's servant first. Power and politics can wait for ranking second.

"See me safe up," says the man of God. Agencies of power—kings, lieuten-ants, ambassadors, etc.—come and go in the dark of the night, in the heat of the day: transitions that mark history, set the time, keep the record, report to their ministries. In their transition, however, they occasion the man of God in "coming down." Having punctuated history in their radical conservatism or in their revolutionary asceticism, men of God then simply demand in exchange: let the people rise, let the kingdoms fall, and then "let me shift for myself."

CHAPTER 5

Allamah Sayyid Muhammad Hossein Tabataba'i: The Philosophical Dimensions of "the Islamic Ideology"

"M. Proudhon has the misfortune of being peculiarly misunderstood in Europe."[1] One can visibly see the grin on Marx's face when he constructed this memorable introductory paradox in *The Poverty of Philosophy*. "In France, he has the right to be a bad economist, because he is reputed to be a good German philosopher. In Germany, he has the right to be a bad philosopher, because he is reputed to be one of the ablest French economists." Here is the master dialectician at work. How did Marx intend the (false?) paradox to resolve itself? That Proudhon was both a bad philosopher and a bad economist? For that logical postulation to become operative and valid Marx needed a realm of identity, a margin of comfort, a setting for inquiry, between, and distinctly different from, France and Germany. For Germans, who presumably know their philosophy, French economics is a terra incognita, anything goes. For the French, who ought to know their economics, German philosophy is a frightful sight, any name commands authority. German philosophers, Walter Kaufmann once observed, make their reputation on the claim that they are misunderstood by their French interpreters. The same paradox holds true between philosophy and ideology, in France and Germany, in Tehran and Qom, no difference. A good philosopher can be a bad ideologue for secular intellectuals in Tehran who know not the operative language of "the Islamic" philosophy. A good ideologue could be a bad philosopher for scholastic masters in Qom who can read their "Western" sources only in broken translations. So which is which? Only a third territory can decide, somewhere between France and Germany, between the Tehran and the Qom states of our imagination. Scholastic philosophy and modern ideology: One needs an angle of vision, properly distanced from both, yet equally attentive to each, from which to observe the active ingredients of one and the other, particularly when they cohabit and proliferate. The Islamic philosophy, as any other, has a language and a manner. So does the commanding authority of modern secular ideologies. Only the extremities of political circumstances, only vital turning points in a set of shared concerns, can necessitate a cohabitation between these two languages and these two manners. Historically realized, the cohabitation becomes a living testimony, in all its self-contradictions, to the political exegencies of an age.

Born of Tabataba'i in Tabriz

Allamah Muhammad Hossein Tabataba'i (1903–1981) was a native of Tabriz, born into a respectable religious family. He lost his mother when he was five years old and his father when he was eight. From early childhood he was particularly attached to a brother with whom he began their early education in Tabriz. Upon completing the initial stages of their studies in Tabriz, the Tabataba'i brothers went to Najaf for more advanced studies. Allamah Tabataba'i's marriage to the daughter of a prominent cleric afforded him solid domestic serenity as he commenced his serious studies. He spent some ten years in Najaf, studying with the most eminent teachers in Islamic jurisprudence, philosophy, and mysticism. His studies completed, he returned to his native Tabriz and resided in the village of Shah-abad, where he continued his active learning and teaching career for a time. He then moved to Qom where he immediately began to teach philosophy to a group of select students. The death of his brother and then his wife were severe emotional blows that affected him for the rest of his life. In the late 1950s, he began a life-long dialogue with the French orientalist Henri Corbin, which proved to be exceptionally fruitful and stimulating. When Allamah Tabataba'i died in 1981, he left behind a generation of immediate and removed students and a body of work that testifies to the range and depth of his erudition and concerns. The political side of his students and admirers and the ideological dimensions of his writings, all reflections of a moral certainty his biography encoded (an encoding I shall examine in more detail later in this chapter), were crucial in the final making of "the Islamic Ideology."

"The Reason I Have Come to Qom"

"The reason I have come to Qom from Tabriz is to correct the [seminary] students' ideas according to truth."[2] Allamah Tabataba'i's explanation was prompted by Ayatollah Borujerdi's objections to his teaching philosophy in the holy City. In the citadel of Shi'i scholastic learning in Iran there should be no such dubious concerns as "philosophy." How Tabataba'i's further explication, "and to struggle against the unrighteous ideas of the materialists and their cohorts,"[3] would have registered with the Grand Ayatollah is hard to ascertain. We know, however, that he was left alone to go on teaching his philosophy. "Nowadays, every [seminary] student who enters through the city gates of Qom comes with a few suitcases full of doubts and questions."[4] Could further amplifications of Tabataba'i have hinted, at least, to the old juridical master the indispensable services that teaching philosophy would accomplish for the cause and consequences of Islam in Iran? Yet Tabataba'i seems to have had to declare, loudly and openly, his active agenda for the new generation of the Shi'i seminarians: "Nowadays, we have to attend to the students' needs. We have to prepare them properly for struggle against the materialists. We have to teach them the righteous Islamic philosophy."[5]

Philosophy has never cohabited easily with Shi'i (or Sunni) law. Law doctrinally renders dogmatic what revelation merely suggests. It leaves no room for philosophical gesticulation. Philosophy smacks too much of its origin in the (non-Islamic) imaginations of Plato and Aristotle. No al-Farabi, Avicenna, Averoes, or Molla Sadra could Islamicize those pagan imaginations to a jurist's satisfaction. Shi'i (and Sunni) law extends the theological veracity of the Qur'anic revelation into the minutiae of daily Muslim life. The body of that law has no stomach for an inquisitive discourse that, by definition, has to operate in a realm of inquiry, at a level of concern with meaning, the jurist, by definition, has to accept as a priori truth. A history of hostility thus comes to bear on the brief dialogue between Allamah Tabataba'i and Ayatollah Borujerdi. The modernity of the encounter, however, the historicity of its impending political exegencies, had a bittersweet taste. In effect, Allamah Tabataba'i told the Grand Ayatollah of the inability, the historical outdatedness, of the juridical discourse to meet the ideological challenge at hand. "Let me handle this," in effect. Here, as if he said so, both the veracity and the historicity, the truth and the method, of our faith are being questioned. Shi'i law, the doctrinal commands of our faith, can have no relevance when the very foundations of our faith, the revelatory language of our discourse, are being discredited. Only philosophy, with its logical claim on everyone's "value-neutrality" can do the trick. They, our young soldiers in faith, come with bags full of doubts. Let me handle the baggage. This, in effect, was Tabataba'i's thrust. The Grand Ayatollah looked the other way.

The Significance of Allamah Tabataba'i in the Making of the Islamic Revolution

The significance of Tabataba'i in the making of the Islamic Revolution in Iran is fully recognized by his former students. "The Revolution that took. place under the leadership of ... Imam Khomeini," one of these former students reports, "more than anything else was predicated on a cultural background which had already been created in this society."[6] Islam, as newly reinterpreted, had been that necessary cultural background upon which Khomeini had acted. This is particularly the case for "a society which is founded on a school and an ideology, [a society] whose revolution is an ideological revolution."[7] Yet "during the last half century ... all aspects of this society were under the direct or indirect influence of foreigners, and [the country] was being run according to their designs."[8] The colonial ("Western") culture had deeply penetrated the society, so much so that "even Islamic virtues were being taken from the foreigners."[9] To prepare the way for the coming Revolution, "such a grave responsibility had to be carried out by someone who had learned the deepest and widest range of Islamic erudition from the most authentic Islamic sources."[10] The obvious conclusion was: "if in the [entire] Islamic world few people could meet these qualifications ... certainly Allamah Tabataba'i ... would be the first [among them]."[11] Although the unintended consequences of an otherwise deeply scholastic mind, aspects of Allamah Tabataba'i's voluminous writings were instrumental in making possible "the Islamic Ideology" and with it the Islamic Revolution.

Two Battle Fronts

This perhaps unintended consequence needs some explanation. In its ideological battle to assume political ascendancy in Iran, "the Islamic Ideology" inevitably worked in two simultaneous, mutually interrelated, directions: against the political legitimacy of the monarchical regime and, at the same time and with almost the same intensity, against the ideological legitimacy of the competing secular calls for oppositional allegiance. Radical-revolutionary and liberal-democratic ideologies, both secular in their quintessential disposition, sought, with varying degrees of intensity and success, to win the ideological allegiance and political loyalty of the revolutionary forces. Of these two potential rivals, "the Islamic Ideology" took more seriously the radical-revolutionary discourse and organization. Despite its shorter historical duration, this discourse had won greater allegiance, with more enduring political results. This radical-revolutionary discourse—particularly its philosophical bases in materialism, imported with all pomp and ceremony from "The West"—was the chief ideological challenge to "the

Islamic Ideology." Although he never actively engaged himself in a confrontational position against the Pahlavi monarchy and never used the term or paid much attention to the political agenda of "the Islamic Ideology," Allamah Tabataba'i did more than any other individual to foster and strengthen the doctrinal position of the Islamic movement against its chief ideological rivals, the radical-revolutionaries, and particularly against their philosophical foundation in philosophical materialism.

Unintended Consequences

There are still those who would rightly take issue with considering Allamah Tabataba'i an "ideologue" of "the Islamic Ideology." He never used the term in his writings. His political concerns were mainly of an intellectual, rather than practical, nature. His discourse is more philosophical than anything resembling ideological. He certainly lacked anything remotely revolutionary in his disposition. There is no reason to believe that he actually approved of the Islamic Revolution in Iran. In fact, indications are that he might have even disapproved of the event. But more than his personal intellectual disposition and potential political stands, it is, perhaps, the unanticipated consequences of his writings that most concern us here. By establishing a clearly articulated agenda of arguing against the currency and credence of historical materialism and the radical revolutionary discourse that represented it, Allamah Tabataba'i effectively, if tangentially, entered the collective Islamic front that at one and the same time fought the monarchical and the radical (Marxist) claims to political legitimacy. If he did not exactly share the sentiment of openly fighting the established monarchical force—to which effect there are, in fact, some indications we shall examine later—he certainly shared the equally important, and ideologically corollary, sentiment of struggling against the rival radical (Marxist) force.

Tabataba'i's active involvement in patently political concerns of not only Iran but also in the larger Muslim world is perhaps best represented by this startling announcement by Motahhari in the course of one of his public lectures:

This man [that is, Allamah Tabataba'i] is an extremely important and noble character. One of the things he has recently done is in sympathy with [our] Muslim brothers. [This pertains to] our Palestinian brothers, who even the Americans cannot confess to their rights [to a homeland]. His Excellency [Allamah Tabataba'i] has recently opened two or three [bank] accounts with the Bank Melli of Iran, the central branch, Bank Bazargani, the central branch, and Bank Saderat, the bazaar branch. If the gentlemen [in the audience] would like, they can jot down the account numbers. Of course [these accounts] are first in his [Allamah Tabataba'i's] name, and second . . . Ayatollah Sayyid Abolfazl Musavi Zanjani, who too is an extremely important but rather unknown person. . . . And of course in order to have a servant, I, too, am the third of them [those authorized to sign checks from these accounts]. These account[s] have been opened in [our] three names.[12]

If there were any doubts as to the politically active nature of these bank accounts, Motahhari drove the point home with a sarcastic comment:

Of course if all of us Iranians put together our money, perhaps it would not amount to those of two Jews who are sitting in the U.S. and who take all the money of the world through usury and theft.[13]

Teaching Philosophy in Qom

By 1944 Allamah Tabataba'i had been established in Qom. There are reports that he actually provided the architectural plan for rebuilding the Hojatiyyeh School there.[14] His decision to teach philosophy in Qom was particularly anticipated by a group of students interested in the "rational" dimensions of Islamic learning, what is known as *ulum al-aqli*. The renowned master of philosophy, Ayatollah Hajj Mirza Mehdi Ashtiyani, had decided to leave Qom and reside in Tehran. His departure had created a vacuum for matters of philosophical interest.[15] When Tabataba'i began teaching philosophy in Qom, his classes were meant to be private sessions to a number of interested students. But, through word of mouth, close to one hundred students attended his first session.[16] He gradually began to develop his close clique of students to whom he taught not only philosophy but also separately arranged sessions on Qur'anic commentary.

Tabataba'i's arrival in Qom immediately met a deeply felt need among the seminary students. One of his students, Sayyid Izzoddin Zanjani, later recalled how deeply pleased and honored he and his father, a former classmate of Tabataba'i, had been when the Shi'i sage had decided to settle in Qom. Zanjani goes to visit Tabataba'i and asks him to teach a course on Molla Sadra's *al-Asfar*, a seminal text in later Islamic philosophy. Tabataba'i responds that his books and other belongings have not yet been sent from Tabriz, at which point Zanjani offers his own text of *al-Asfar*, from which Tabataba'i begins to teach and in which he makes his marginal commentaries.[17] Tabataba'i's teaching of *al-Asfar* had preceded, and then coincided with, the period when Khomeini taught the same text in Qom. But whereas Khomeini's teaching of philosophy was limited to a group of select students, Tabataba'i is reported[18] to have attracted a wider audience. Moreover, through such works as *The Principles of Philosophy and the Realistic Method*, he tried to address some of the key issues in contemporary European philosophy as he best understood them. Although this address was admittedly hampered by Tabataba'i's limited knowledge of European philosophy, a defect partially remedied later by his long association with Henri Corbin, he still managed to demonstrate to his young readers that it was possible to establish a dialogue with the non-Islamic (and, of course, hegemonic) sources of "The Western" philosophy. Although for the most part *The Principles of Philosophy and the Realistic Method* remains at a tangential and rhetorical level, quintessentially incapable of engaging in any meaningful dialogue with either historical materialism or with "The Western" philosophy, whatever they understood by that, it at least creates the impression that such a dialogue is theoretically possible. This impression was particularly strengthened when the late Allamah began his long association and dialogue with Henri Corbin.

Teaching Avicenna and Molla Sadra in Qom was meant to address the increasing secularism that had apparently reached the very centers of scholastic learnings.[19] The hostility of the Shi'i clerical order, in both Qom and Najaf,[20] had been equally intense when Allamah Tabataba'i began his commentary on Muhammad Baqir Majlesi's compendium of *Bahar al-Anwar*,[21] a canonical source of Shi'i jurisprudence that had been considered too sacred a text to be subjected to philosophical scrutiny. Among the principal issues on which Allamah Tabataba'i had taken Majlesi to task was the latter's objection to the Avicennian doctrine that Divine Knowledge is in terms of universals and not particulars. Since Majlesi's perception of the Divine Omniscience, Tabataba'i had argued, was in terms of an "acquired knowledge" *(ilm-e hosuli)*, he could not have but equally believed in God's mere knowledge of the universals (and not particulars). But if God's knowledge is considered to be "presential" *(hozuri)*, then the two dichotomous categories of universals and particulars become rather irrelevant.[22] Such philosophical speculations, however, were not to be tolerated by the Qom or Najaf juridical establishments.

To Finance a Philosophical Life

Allamah Tabataba'i's source of income is itself another major point where the built-in antagonism, or outright hostility, between the philosophically minded and the juridical establishment becomes evident. Allamah Tabataba'i's main source of income was a piece of land that he and his brother had inherited in their native village of Shah-abad of Tabriz, in the northwestern province of Azarbaijan. "This land," Allamah Tabataba'i is reported to have said,

has been the exclusive property of our family during the past two hundred and seventy years. Cultivating it is the only source of our income. Had it been somehow confiscated, our source of income would have been completely cut off, and we would have been put in a very difficult situation.[23]

Although independently in possession of this land and its income in the Azarbaijan province, Allamah Tabataba'i did not lead a comfortable life.

He is reported to have rented a house in Qom for eighty Tumans a month (approximately ten dollars at the official rate or less than one dollar at the current market rate). Some of his students report that this house was so small that the Allamah could not receive his students at home.[24] He would occasionally engage in philosophical discussions with his students right at his doorstep.[25] The Allamah's nobility of character was such that he would be willing "to work for the wage of three Tumans a day willingly and not ask for money from anyone."[26] He did receive royalties from his publications, and that was a major source of his income. This, however, would not be enough, and for years he was reported to have been in debt.[27] But he would refuse to let his friends and close family help him.

The main question is why Allamah Tabataba'i did not receive his share of the stipend from the *Khoms* ("one fifth"), a religious tax calculated as one-fifth of a Muslim's annual income. Historically, it has been imposed on seven kinds of property: (1) booty, (2) mines, (3) that which has been extracted from the sea, (4) revenues from commerce and cultivation, (5) when a rightful property is mixed with an unrightful property, (6) hidden treasures found underground, and (7) a Muslim land transferred to a *Dhimmi* (a Jew or a Christian). The *Khoms* is usually divided into six parts, three of which are known as *Sahm-e Imam* ("The Share of the Imam"); the other three parts are to be allocated for orphans, the poor, etc. During the occultation of the Twelfth Imam the *Sahm-e Imam* is given to the Shi'i clerics to spend at their discretion. Ordinarily, the high-ranking clerics spend a portion of the *Sahm-e Imam* on the juridical students for their school and boarding expenditures. Customarily, *Sahm-e Imam* is at the disposal of a high-ranking cleric who will supervise its proper distribution to the teachers and students of a seminary. To qualify for such stipends, students must study primarily jurisprudence, and their teachers must teach precisely the same. Occasionally, there is one more qualification for the teachers as well: They must have issued a collection of their edicts *(fatva')* to qualify for a share of the *Sahm-e Imam* from their particular constituency.

Technically, Allamah Tabataba'i did not qualify for the *Sahm-e Imam*. Despite his massive erudition in the Shi'i juridical tradition, he was first and foremost a philosopher, a Qur'anic commentator, and a gnostic. He did not teach *fiqh,* nor had he issued juridical edicts. According to his students, "he deliberately chose to do otherwise, from the very beginning."[28] Out of pride and a sense of superiority beyond entanglement in such mundane matters, he chose not to accept the *Sahm-e Imam*. As his students are quick to point out, this sad state of affairs has caused much discomfort for many eminent Shi'i clerics. Ayatollah Shaykh Javad Belaqi Najafi, Ayatollah Allamah Hajj Shaykh Aqa Bozorg Tehrani, and Allamah Amini are among the most distinguished men of learning in Shi'i scholasticism who suffered greatly from the tribulations of not having a steady income. One of Allamah Tabataba'i's former students, now an eminent scholastic in his own right, asks quite poignantly,

Why should such individuals who spend their lives in certain branches [of knowledge such] as philosophy, gnosticism, theology, Qur'anic exegesis, [prophetic and Imami] traditions, history, biography, etc., despite possessing massive juridical erudition, be in need of a most simple and ordinary living. Why should they have innumerable difficulties to make a living with dignity and honor, while they help Islam, respond to the need of the Muslim community in such [branches of] knowledge, fortify weak fronts, and protect and guard the sanctity of the [Shi'i] school? [29]

Historically, the answer to this question has been that nonjuridical branches of Islamic learning, such as philosophy, medicine, etc., have been carried out by men of knowledge who either have been financed by a court, for example, Avicenna, or else have been independently wealthy, for example, Molla Sadra. In modern Iranian history, too, practitioners of Islamic philosophy such as Sayyid Jalaloddin Ashtiyani, Jalal Homa'i, Morteza Motahhari, and S. H. Nasr have been professors at Tehran or Mashhad universities and thus effectively state employees. But philosophers such as Allamah Tabataba'i, who chose to remain more closely tied to the traditional seats of learning, Qom in this case, fell between two stools, as it were. They did not benefit from a state-sponsored academic setting to engage in their philosophical quests, and yet they, as their ancestors, were not financially protected by the juridical establishment.

A Showdown Between Allamah Tabataba'i and Ayatollah Borujerdi

Allamah Tabataba'i's difficulties in teaching philosophy in Qom were not limited to his own financial problems. Upon his arrival in Qom, and when he began teaching Molla Sadra's *al-Asfar al-Arba'ah*, during which sessions "close to one hundred students attended," the Grand Ayatollah Borujerdi, the highest-ranking Shi'i authority in Iran, ordered the cancellation of stipends for all students who had attended the Allamah's course.[30]

The rest of the story is so marvelously interwoven with Allamah Tabataba'i's character and with the entire culture of Shi'i scholastic learning that I shall report it with his own words:

When I heard the news, I was astounded, wondering what to do. Should the stipend of the students be cut off? What could these poor people do who have come from distant towns? Their only source of income is this stipend. And should I, just because the stipend of the students [has been cut off] stop teaching the [al-] Asfar? [If I do that] their scientific and religious learning will be damaged. I was in this situation of embattlement when one day, in utter discomfort [over this incident], as

I was passing around the heater in my room I glanced upon the Divan of Hafez which was on the heating table. I picked it up and did a bibliomancy to see what I was I to do. Should I abandon teaching the [al-] Asfar, or do otherwise? The ghazal came up:
> I am not that sagacious shrewd who abandons
> the beloved and the goblet. . . .[31]
I wondered what a strange ghazal this is. It indicates that teaching the [al-] Asfar is absolutely necessary, and that ceasing to teach it is tantamount to having committed a sin in the spiritual path.[32]

The incident does not end here. In what follows we observe some of the most fascinating workings of the Shi'i intellectual culture. Allamah Tabataba'i continues to teach his philosophical classes and subsequently receives a message from the Grand Ayatollah Borujerdi who declares that

when we were young in the Isfahan Seminary we used to study the [al-] Asfar with the late Jahangir Khan. But we were a few who did it in secret. We would secretly go to his lessons. As for the open teaching of the [al-] Asfar in an official seminary [setting], that is not appropriate, and it must be stopped.[33]

Ayatollah Borujerdi was not only the highest-ranking Shi'i authority in Iran and one of the few in the world, but, as the Grand Ayatollah, he had brought unprecedented dignity and prestige to the position. He was revered as perhaps no other chief cleric before him. Qom to him was what the Vatican is to the Pope. At the seat and center of his authority, whatever he said was law, particularly at the chief seminary of Shi'i studies, a law guaranteed by much more than tangible authority, a law deemed legitimate by an almost metaphysical conviction on the part of his followers. The Grand Jurist's confession that he, too, had a philosophical bone in his body undoubtedly endeared him to the Allamah. But still his command was to stop teaching al-Asfar.

Yet the power of the Hafez bibliomancy for the Allamah, as an indication of his deeply rooted conviction in the viability of the philosophical discourse, was not to be taken lightly either. "In response I said," Allamah Tabataba'i later reported,

Tell Mr. Borujerdi for me that we, too, have studied such ordinary and official courses as jurisprudence and the principles of jurisprudence. We are perfectly capable of teaching such courses. We have nothing less than those [who teach such courses].[34]

To set the record straight, despite his predisposition to the philosophical discourse and his preference to teach philosophical texts, Allamah Tabataba'i wished to emphasize that he was equally capable of teaching in the more canonical discourse of Shi'i jurisprudence. The expression of this qualification is to dispel any doubt as to his learning in what can arguably be called the practical core of the Shi'i faith. In the scholastic language of Tabataba'i-Borujerdi discourse, the expression of this technical qualification is necessary in order to make his teaching of philosophy a matter of choice, not an effect of certain limitations in his learning.

Allamah Tabataba'i subsequently proceeds to make an argument in defense of his preference to teach philosophy and reveals the heart of his commitment to preserving the doctrinal and intellectual integrity of Shi'ism in the face of the onslaught of Marxism in the modern world:

The reason I have come to Qom from Tabriz is to correct the [seminary] students' ideas according to truth, and to struggle against the unrighteous ideas of the materialists and their cohorts. When His Excellency the Ayatollah [that is, Grand Ayatollah Borujerdi] with a few others secretly attended the [philosophical] sessions of the late Jahangir Khan, the seminary students and most of the people, thanks be to God, were believing [Muslims] with a clear conscience. [At that time] there was no need for open sessions on the [al-] Asfar. But nowadays, every [seminary] student who enters through the city gates of Qom comes with a few suitcases full of doubts and questions. Nowadays, we have to attend to the students' needs. We have to prepare them properly for struggle against the materialists. We have to teach them the righteous Islamic philosophy. I shall not abandon teaching the [al-] Asfar.[35]

This message not only demonstrates a remarkable strength of character on the Allamah's part but also indicates the depth of his conviction as to the nature of the challenge that faced Shi'ism and, more important, the proper method of confronting it.

That Allamah Tabataba'i openly declares his primary reason for having come to Qom from Tabriz as fighting against materialism is a crucial testimony of how seriously the challenge must have appeared at the time. His assessment that "every [seminary] student who enters through the city gates of Qom comes with a few suitcases full of doubts and questions" shows that the (secular) radical ideologies and the materialist philosophy had aimed at the very heart of the Shi'i establishment. The radicalization of the young Shi'i clerics in Qom, their increasing attention to the materialist philosophy, and the inevitable consequence of their losing faith in the veracity of Shi'ism appear, from the Allamah's response to Grand Ayatollah Borujerdi, to have been a real threat. Later when Allamah Tabataba'i wrote his famous disputation against materialism, *The Principles of Philosophy and the Realistic Method,* it is quite easy, from the very language of his delivery, to see that the primary target is the scholastic students in Qom rather than any secular audience in Tehran. It is later, when Motahhari wrote his extensive commentaries to Tabataba'i's text, that the treatise reaches for a wider, less scholastically trained, more secularly minded audience.

But to understand the utmost degree of piety and reverence with which Allamah Tabataba'i as a Shi'i abided by the wishes of the Grand Ayatollah, it is important to note the conclusion of his message. "Despite all this," Allamah Tabataba'i ended his message, "I recognize the Ayatollah as 'the chief religious authority' *(hakem-e shar^c)*. If he commands [me] to stop [teaching] the [al-]*Asfar,* the question assumes a new posture." [36] Recognizing Ayatollah Borujerdi as *hakem-e shar^c,* obvious and inevitable as it seems, was still Allamah Tabataba'i's prerogative. Choosing a *marja^c-e taqlid* or recognizing a given *faqih* as the *hakem-e shar^c* is the prerogative of every Shi'i believer. Having thus recognized Ayatollah Borujerdi as the *hakem-e shar^c,* his wishes are laws to the Allamah, disregarding them tantamount to disregarding the commands of a Living Imam.

It would have been impossible for the Allamah's strong case to be lost on Ayatollah Borujerdi. He, too, lived and taught in Qom. He, too, dealt with the young seminary students. He, too, had witnessed, undoubtedly with dismay, the rapid dissemination of materialist ideas and leftist propaganda in his homeland at large and apparently in Qom in particular. He, too, undoubtedly considered a possible erosion of faith at the heart of Iranian Shi'ism with horror. But he probably thought that the danger had to be faced through a consolidation of the clerical establishment, with a firm grip on the students' doctrinal learning. Yet Allamah Tabataba'i's strong argument in defense of Islamic philosophy as a bastion of the antimaterialist campaign was not lost on Ayatollah Borujerdi. After all, he himself had attended "secret sessions" of the *al-Asfar* under Jahangir Khan in Isfahan.

"After this message," Allamah Tabataba'i finally reports, "Ayatollah Borujerdi never complained anymore, and we taught philosophy from [Avicenna's] *al-Shafa* and [Molla Sadra's] *al-Asfar* and other similar texts for many years." [37] The subsequent relationship between the Allamah and the Grand Ayatollah continued to be warm and cordial. "Whenever the Ayatollah happened to see us, he treated us with utmost respect. One day he lent us as a gift a copy of the Magnanimous Qur'an which was one of the best and most accurate editions [of the holy Text]." [38] That, perhaps, was the Grand Ayatollah's way of recognizing what the Allamah was doing, while reminding him that after all the disputations among the Shi'i scholars, they still believed in the central veracity of the Qur'an, which always had to be kept in their hearts and minds.

Tabataba'i: The Philosopher Par Excellence

Tabataba'i was primarily an Islamic philosopher in the tradition of Avicenna and Molla Sadra. It was precisely in this tradition that he wished to address what he considered to be the quintessential problems of the day. Since Molla Sadra, there had been a concerted effort to formulate a balanced discourse between Shi'i theological dogmas and the principles of peripatetic philosophy, a discourse in harmony with the mystical language. Tabataba'i remained chiefly in the Sadraian tradition of advancing the universal and epistemological unity of all these discourses. For him, the existence of God, as the Supreme ontological necessity of the Islamic metaphysics, is proven essentially through the famous Avicennaian argument, adopted by Molla Sadra, dividing "existence" into (1) the impossible being (that which cannot be), (2) the contingent being (that which exists on the condition of a "necessary being"), and (3) the necessary being (that without which no other thing can be).[39] God, thus logically approached, is identified with the Supreme Necessary Being, or that from whom all contingent beings are emanated. This Necessary Being, which exists in Its Essence, is also Infinite.[40] In other words, no limitation defines its quiddity. Logically, this Necessary Being cannot be but One,[41] and yet everything else is contained in It.[42]

What would an Avicennian argument in philosophical theology, with its innate medieval language, have to do with the pressing problems of modernity? Tabataba'i sought to utilize this philosophy primarily to oppose philosophical materialism as, in his judgment, the most serious front of the invading (secular) ideology.[43] Under the commanding rubric of Islamic philosophy, he believed he had reduced Marxism to logical fallacy.[44] In his understanding of these terms, he identified "realism" with (Islamic) philosophy, and "idealism" with the logical fallacy of Marxism.[45] In this sense, Tabataba'i was, in fact, leveling the charge of Marxism against all religions (including Islam) back to Marxism. As such, he identifies Marxism with misosophy, or opposition to philosophy, and (Islamic) philosophy with the primacy of concern with (actual) existence (and hence his correspondence of "philosophy" with "religion"). (Islamic) philosophy, he contended, was "realistic" because it accepted the reality of existence outside the perception of the human mind, whereas Marxism was "idealist" because it gave the primacy of perception to the human mind.[46]

Between Jurisprudence and Philosophy

Tabataba'i developed an acute understanding of the ideological and political demands of his time. Upon his arrival in Qom, he felt the inadequacy of the scholastic curriculum to arm the young seminarians with the proper conceptual apparatus to meet the challenge of the changing times. "A society that had to face up to other cultures," one of his former students suggested, "protecting its cultural identity in front of the foreigners, proving the validity of its ideology vis-à-vis other ideologies, needed other courses of study in addition to those current at the time."[47] Tabataba'i himself is reported to have said:

When I came to Qom, I examined the curriculum of the seminary and thought about the needs of the Islamic society. I did not see that much correspondence between what was [offered at the seminaries] and those needs. . . . In order to offer and defend its ideas vis-à-vis others, our society needed the power of rational argumentation.[48]

Tabataba'i considered defense of the faith "in the face of doubts directed against Islamic principals by foreign schools of thought"[49] his primary duty in Qom. He began teaching "philosophy, Qur'anic exegesis, and ethics"[50] precisely towards that objective. As his former students are quick to point out "this action of the late Allamah [Tabataba'i] is comparable, in its own way, with the activities that our beloved Imam [Khomeini] under-took in political endeavors."[51] To confront foreign ("Western") ideas, to prepare the ideological foundation of the Revolution, Tabataba'i had to have "a courage similar to that of the Imam [Khomeini] in political mat-ters."[52] The primary difficulty that he had to overcome to teach philosophy in Qom was the historical antagonism between the rational and the tradi-tional branches of the Islamic discourses. Ayatollah Borujerdi's opposition to Tabataba'i's teaching philosophy ought to be seen in this context. Some of Tabataba'i's pious students, for obvious reasons, are reluctant to admit publicly to this particular difficulty.[53] In the post-Revolutionary period, however, it is quite easy for them to point out the continuity of his teach-ings with what Ayatollah Khomeini used to teach before his exile to Najaf.

Philosophy, Religion, and Political Agenda

The traditional bifurcation between the juridical and philosophical dis-courses has always caused the practitioners of Islamic philosophy to be suspected of quintessential irreligiosity. From Avicenna to Molla Sadra, Muslim philosophers have always taken extraordinary measures to have their religious piety made of public record. In the age of "the Islamic Ideology," particularly in its attempt to mobilize mass popular support, common religiosity is of central ideological significance. Allamah Tabata-ba'i's genuine devotion to the Shi'i Imams was an essential part of his piety that became particularly manifest in reminiscences that his former students recorded posthumously. He would forgive a philosophical misconception on the part of his students with grace and humility, according to one of his students,[54] but he would not tolerate the slightest disrespect directed against the Shi'i Imams. He would participate in ceremonies of commiseration and would publicly cry. "When it came to commiseration and eulogy [for the Shi'i Imams]," according to eyewitness reports, "he would put all books and scholastic concerns aside."[55] Immediately related to these genuine demonstrations of public piety, however, was his devotion to teaching philosophy in Qom. His former students testify[56] that upon his recognition of the necessity of teaching philosophy, he abandoned altogether the socially more prestigious task of teaching jurisprudence that would have gradually secured for him the status of *marja'iyyat*.

Between religion and reason Allamah Tabataba'i saw a perfect harmony. Most doctrinal positions of the faith were compatible with rational explanations. Doctrines such as bodily resurrection were to be taken as elements of an entirely different discourse than that of the philosophical.[57] Perhaps the most crucial link that connected Tabataba'i's doctrinal and philosophical dispositions, and thus gave his religiosity and his philosophy a certain degree of realistic contemporaneity, was his love for the poetry of Hafez. He would publicly acknowledge his debt to Hafez for having, with one verse, clarified a complicated philosophical issue for him.[58]

His asceticism and noble simplicity never ceased to amaze Tabataba'i's contemporaries. One of his frequent visitors reports[59] that he once went to see him in Qom. Tabataba'i was about to leave for Mashhad for the summer, and thus his rooms had no carpet. When the Allamah wanted to bring in a carpet for his guest to sit on, the visitor prevented him and took off his aba, put it on the ground, and sat on it. "At this old age," the Allamah is reported to have told his visitor, "you taught me a good lesson."[60]

The Mystical and Philosophical Dimensions of Homo Politicus

With such asceticism and humility, learning combined with piety, Allamah Tabataba'i attended the ideological challenge of his time. He met the demands of his age with more of a metaphysical conviction than a patently political agenda. "We have nothing more important to do," he is reported to have said repeatedly, "than to make ourselves."[61] The temporal and atemporal span within which man is to make himself is from pre- to posteternity. Within this span, the function of the Muslim community, as it circumscribes the Islamic homo politicus, is to facilitate this making of a "self." As the chief agency of making man to realize his "self," Islam and its social claims on institution-building have a categorically moral primacy. The certitude thus attained in matters of spiritual conviction is immediately available to political translation. No other claim to truth, other than that of, and the language thus stipulated in, the Qur'anic revelation, can have a relative claim to validity. Any other such relative claim would ipso facto render the Qur'anic claim equally relative. As the Qur'anic language cannot be rendered or presumed relative, in the view of the absolute claim of Islam to Truth, any political or ideological challenge to Islam would be, mondus nascendi, illegitimate.

Thus disposed, the spiritual sage thinks and writes in terms conducive to a utopian realization of his perceived stages of mystical conviction. "Establishing the foundations of the Utopia"[62] has been particularly noticed among Tabataba'i's chief concerns. This perception of utopia cannot but emerge from, as the assumption of moral authority to delineate its boundaries cannot but reflect, a deep mystical conviction in having realized the Truth in its full and comprehensive totality. It is precisely this mystical conviction of totality and certitude that, when translated into political terms, however tacitly, subconsciously or suggestively, denies the remote possibility of any suggestion of "on the other hand." Denying any such possibility of either mystical or political doubt is the almost doctrinal conviction that "in practical mysticism man reaches a point where his purgatorial eyes will be opened, which is to say he observes people according to their true nature and characteristics."[63] The assumption that such a stage has been ascertained for Tabataba'i is a simultaneous self-reflective indictment of any mode of moral or political stipulation outside the Islamic purview.

There is also the equally compelling conviction that the mystical master has transcended the mundane realities as they are and, although visibly here and present, in effect he is in the Divine Presence.[64] Convinced in that status, matters of this world, political or otherwise, are addressed from such a spiritual height, and with such mystical might, that opposing ideas are merely given alternative times to surrender, not equal chance to challenge. When it is firmly believed that "the person of the mystic is with the people and his heart with God,"[65] all pronouncements of this person are delivered, and expected to be received, with absolute moral conviction, indisputable Divine certitude. At this close vicinity of the Divine authority, the mystic is increasingly believed to have assumed divine attributes, at which stage his pronouncements are bound to emulate the revelatory and inspirational discourse of the Qur'an. The virtual impossibility of any other (alien) discourse to approach this language, political or otherwise, is particularly evident from such phrases as "death to a philosophy the principles of which are not concurrent with the Qur'an and the [prophetic] traditions!"[66] presumably first stated by the sixteenth-century Shi'i philosopher Molla Sadra and then reinvoked in a reminiscence about Allamah Tabataba'i. The political implications of such mystical and philosophical certitude is particularly pronounced when emphasized in contradistinction to "The West." Both Allamah Tabataba'i and Molla Sadra are portrayed as particular indications of Divine will and mercy to have given Muslims a spiritual and intellectual alternative precisely at the moment when "The West was attracting people to itself, that is, to materialism."[67]

Addressing the material world from the height of the spiritual, Tabataba'i sees the social dimensions of Islam as its condito sine qua non. Short of reducing Islam to its social realities, he would consider the Muslim community, in the most universal sense of the term, tantamount to its ultimate claim on truth. As a reflection of Divine justice, social justice assumes a reality beyond the immediacy of its historical exegencies. Because a social life is most natural to man and because Islam is, before anything else, attentive to man's most natural needs, then justice, upon which the only viable form of social organization is possible, becomes concomitant with Islam itself. Realization of this ideal social state is possible only through Divinely ordained theocracies which can oppose injustice and corruption on the deepest and most convincing moral grounds. What follows, logically and immediately, from the Islamic nature of the ideal state thus narrated is the necessity of the knowledge of what is good and evil as particularly prescribed in the faith. The Shi'i doctors of law are the most obvious candidates to perform these duties.

To assume such supreme political responsibilities, more than a mere juridical disposition, a mystical disposition was necessary. Allamah Tabataba'i had a philosophically balanced inclincation towards mysticism. In addition to his regularly scheduled classes in Islamic philosophy and Qur'anic commentary, he held informal sessions on mysticism with his students. On these occasions they would go to a nearby garden and discuss mysticism.[68] Both his mystical and philosophical dispositions were deeply reflected in his Qur'anic commentary. This is evident not only from his voluminous exegesis on the sacred Text, but also from his chief preoccupation with its ethical, mystical, and philosophical allusions. His students report that for some time they had asked him to teach them two of the canonical texts in Islamic mysticism, that is, Qaysari's commentary on Ibn Arabi's *Fusus al-Hikam* and Molla Abd al-Razzaq Kashani's commentary on *Manazil al-Sa'iriyn*. He would agree but procrastinate until the students realized that he preferred to teach through the Qur'an than through any other text.[69]

Of immediate concern to Allamah Tabataba'i was the interaction between the philosophical and mystical discourses: one based on rational argumentations and the logical method, the other on direct experience and perceptive illumination. Between reality, rationally perceived, and the truth, mystically experiened, Tabataba'i sought to find a bona fide and positive line of argument. To teach this argument to his students he used a series of correspondence between Sayyid Ahmad Karbala'i, a prominent gnostic, and Hajj Shaykh Muhammad Hossein Isfahani Company, an eminent philosopher. In the course of their correspondence, the gnostic and the philosopher had discussed the essential oneness of Being, as opposed to the existential experience of multiplicity, from their respective points of view, against the other's position. Apparently Allamah Tabataba'i wrote his own commentaries on some of these letters which have not been published or otherwise made available.[70] But it is quite evident that, following Molla Sadra's example in the Safavid period, he wished to render legitimate the fruitful correspondence between experiential and intellectual perceptions of reality. What is the purpose of resuscitating such old scholastic debates in the face of the secular onslaught? Two levels of relevance and engagement suggest themselves. At one immediate level, particularly through contemporary examples, Tabataba'i gave simultaneous modern relevance to two scholastic discourses that would otherwise appear archaic. But at another, perhaps more important, level, he would appropriate the psychological (corresponding to the mystical) and rational (corresponding to the philosophical) discourses of the secular intellectuals, as imported from "The West," and deny them any exclusive claim to understanding the contemporaneity of the human condition.

A Renaissance Man and His Teacher

It took a particular kind of character to personify these two modes of spiritual and intellectual authorities. Unless the otherwise archaic tone of these scholastic concerns with mysticism and philosophy were, in effect, translated into characteristic features of a living individual, they would have failed to achieve any meaningful level of relevance for contemporary political purposes. Imagine a Renaissance man of medieval learning. Allamah Tabataba'i, true to his title, was one. His mastery of Qur'anic exegesis, philosophical discourse, gnostic tradition, and juridical learning was equally matched by the catholicity of his knowledge of mathematics, astronomy, and literature. But, more than anything else, his authority for his immediate and distant students ought to be seen in the context of the long tradition of Islamic philosophy and the ceremonies of its teaching manners. His illustrious teachers, his devotional reverence for one particular Hajj Mirza Ali Qazi Tabataba'i (1868–1946) who taught him philosophy, among other gestures, sentiments, and ceremonies, made Tabataba'i a living relic of scholastic learning whom his students cherished and sought to emulate:

Our master [Tabataba'i] had much love and devotion for his master, the late Qazi. He truly humbled himself next to his master. In the countenance of the late Qazi he sought a world of majesty, awe, divine mysteries, divine unity, virtues, and spiritual states.[71]

One of his students also remembers[72] how Tabataba'i refused to wear any cologne for years after the death of his master Qazi. These small, but significant, signals of scholastic ethics of the master-disciple relationship commanded such an aura of authority for Tabataba'i's students that they always remember him through such reminiscences with admiration and devotion. Once these features are combined with a kind of Kabalistic mythology (that Tabataba'i and his master Qazi both lived eighty-one years, that both were called "Qazi," etc.), the aura of authority about

Tabataba'i reachs metaphysical dimensions. Such admirations, scholastic as they are in nature, have a strong political ramification. They establish a web of group affiliation that extends beyond the immediate code of learning that attended Tabataba'i's sessions in philosophy and mysticism. This web included students who were then, or would later become, prominent political figures. Their devotion to Allamah Tabataba'i would establish a common bondage that would be translated not merely into abstract philosophical congeniality but, more important, into ideological and political affinity. This, in turn, would not merely give a wide ideological forum to the master's philosophical, mystical, and ethical teachings; it would create, simultaneously, a fraternity of common scholastic experience among the students themselves, the practical effects of which will have immediate political results.

What holds this web of group affiliations together is precisely that constellation of common symbolics of reverence and honor that are transmitted historically. It is also the same constellation of such simple but significant ceremonies of traditional continuity that transform an ordinary man of learning into a historical figure of authority with immediate consequence for his social context. Whether it is accidental or otherwise, that both Allamah Tabataba'i and his master lived for eighty-one years—corresponding to the fact that both the Prophet Muhammad and Ali, for the Shi'is his immediate successor, lived for sixty-three years[73]—constitutes a major segment of a larger mythological apparatus on the basis of which an otherwise ordinary man is elevated to the pantheon of a living culture.

In that pantheon of authority, the descending—and ascending—line of masters and disciples is the chief symbolic representation of the living culture. In Najaf Allamah Tabataba'i was particularly attracted to Hajj Mirza Ali Qazi, who, in his eyes, had combined the awesome learning of a scholastic master with the hermetic piety of a saint. "For five years, I spent my days and nights in the presence of the late Qazi, and I did not waste a moment receiving the munificence of his presence."[74] Qazi was a kind of a maverick. Although a prominent jurist, he would not attend regular *madrasah* for teaching. Instead, he received his students at his residence, where he had regular sessions in jurisprudence and where he also held and led public prayers.[75] When students attended his classes and subsequent public prayers, Qazi would occasionally modify his ritual ascetic practices to conform to their limitations. For example, he would ordinarily say his evening prayers as soon as the sun had set. But some of his students, following an alternative juridical opinion, would ask him to wait until the redness of the sunset had disappeared. Qazi would comply. For a devout Muslim that is the ultimate sign of respect and humility on the part of a teacher for his students.

What Allamah Tabataba'i admired in and learned from his master was that perfect combination of society and solitude that he kept. During the first two ten-days of the month of Ramadan, Qazi would regularly keep his daily classes and participate in public prayers; however, during the third ten-days period he would disappear completely from the scene and could not be found anywhere.[76]

Mirza Ali Qazi was reportedly also a gifted poet and is said to have composed pieces of poetry that Arabs would not believe had come from a Persian.[77] There is even a story of how his poetic gift was put to the test by Hajj Shaykh Abdollah Mamaqani who was an expert in Arabic poetry and who claimed that no matter how masterfully composed, he would be able to tell when an Arabic poem was composed by a Persian. Called to the challenge, Mirza Ali Qazi began reciting an Arabic poem by an Arab. In the middle of the poem he improvised certain lines of his own. Upon completing his recitation, he asked Hajj Shaykh Abdollah Mamaqani which of the verses were by a Persian. The latter could not tell. These stories, true or legendary, are the very stuff of which the clerical group affiliation is constructed. To such shared sets of sentiments, in the range of communal feelings and attitudes they engender historically, is precisely where members of the clerical order come home.

Allamah Tabataba'i's principal teacher in Qur'anic exegesis and in the "science of traditions" (fiqh al-hadith) was also Mirza Ali Qazi. Interpreting Qur'anic verses by other Qur'anic verses and by prophetic and Imami traditions was a method Tabataba'i had learned from his master[78] and would later apply in his own voluminous Qur'anic commentary. This method of interpreting Qur'anic verses would prove a particularly poignant response to the pseudoscientific interpretations of the sacred Text so prevalent in the twentieth-century Muslim exegesis. Rejecting the validity of such artificial approximations of the sacred Text to "The Western" sciences, Tabataba'i would deliver a sustained exegetical argument in support of the Islamicity of the Qur'anic hermeneutic apparatus.

More than his vast learning, Mirza Ali Qazi's ascetic practices, moral rectitude, spiritual presence, and innate propensity towards illuminative perceptions attracted the young and astute Tabataba'i to him.[79] Concomitant with this aura of spiritual presence was an inevitable sense of ethical rectitude that dictated renunciatory demands equally upon the old master and his students, Tabataba'i chief among them. This sense of moral rectitude has an obvious immediate effect on the students' ethical upbringing. But it also has a corollary, perhaps more socially relevant, effect. When scholastic learning is combined with moral righteousness and is situated in a context of rapidly changing moral standards, the conditions are ripe for a presumption of moral superiority over and above the rest of the society which obviously necessitates the assumption of political leadership to force the society out of this presumed moral chaos.

The Brothers Tabataba'i

The assumption of that sense of moral superiority and responsibility is deeply rooted in the hagiographical sanctity, in the biographical encoding of a self-reflective narrative, that surrounds a typical clerical upbringing. The specifics of that upbringing have enduring effects on the social and political implications of being a religious authority. As the narrative of the hagio-biographical account is constructed so is the enduring codification of a moral demand system with potential revolutionary twists and turns.

Allamah Tabataba'i had begun his early education under the guidance of his father, Sayyid Hossein Qazi, who was a student of Mirza Hasan Shirazi, the prominent constitutionalist cleric instrumental in the Tobacco Revolt. As his last name indicates, Allamah Tabataba'i was a double Sayyid, that is, both his parents were putative descendants of the Prophet. On his father's side he traced his ancestry to Imam Hasan; on his mother's side to Imam Hossein.[80] He was born into a highly respectable and learned family in Azarbaijan. He and his mentor, Mirza Ali Qazi, had one and the same distinguished ancestry. The title "Qazi" ("Judge") was given to them when one of their forefathers, a certain Mirza Muhammad Ali Qazi, became the chief justice of Azarbaijan.[81] Allamah Tabataba'i lost his mother when he was five years old, and his father when eight. The Tabataba'is were survived by two sons: Muhammad Hossein and his younger brother Muhammad Hasan.[82]

Allamah Tabataba'i and his younger brother continued their early education in Tabriz under the protective and loving care of a custodian whom their father had appointed. The two brothers had fond memories of their childhood in Tabriz, where they used to go to the hills and mountain slopes surrounding the city, spending their days in writing calligraphy. Eventually the young Tabataba'is go to Najaf to pursue their scholastic studies. The two brothers spend ten years in Najaf, where they not only attended regular courses in jurisprudence and principles of jurisprudence but also studied Islamic theology, philosophy, mysticism, ethics, and, of course, Qur'anic exegesis. They then returned to Tabriz, apparently due to financial problems. Their land and property in Tabriz were reportedly improperly managed, and they had to return to their homeland. They spent ten years in the Shah-abad village of Tabriz, where, along with their scholastic studies, they also cultivated their land.[83]

Following this period, Allamah Tabataba'i goes to Qom and his brother Muhammad Hasan remains in Tabriz where he becomes a prominent and respected cleric.[84] A rather unique quality of this learned cleric was his love and knowledge of music.[85] He reportedly wrote a treatise on the composition and impact of music on the soul. According to Allamah Tabataba'i this was truly a brilliant treatise, and unique in the modern world, innovative and matchless. But after he finished writing the treatise, he was afraid inappropriate people and tyrannical rulers would get hold of it, and then modern illegitimate governments would abuse it. Consequently, he destroyed the treatise completely.[86]

Because this treatise is now reportedly destroyed, the exact nature of Allamah Tabataba'i's references is not quite clear. Given the juridical inhibition of music, a cleric's attention or talent had to be particularly suppressed. More than philosophy and mysticism, music was a severely shunned taboo that had to be denied at all costs.

Such reminiscences and rememberings of things past had a profound impact on things present, anticipating with nostalgic expectations the color of things to come. Here, biographical narrative becomes codified morality, with lasting political implications. An entire generation of radical clerics begin to decode Allamah Tabataba'i's hagio-biographical constructions of moral rectitude, translating them into effective political mottos.

The Primacy of the Rational Method

Beyond music, mysticism, and asceticism, it was the primacy of the rational method that guided Allamah Tabataba'i's ideological attendance on the modern world. Such spiritual dimensions of the scholastic learning created an aura of moral authority that was crucial in its political implications. But to meet the challenge of ideological modernity, a more rational and contemplative disposition was necessary. According to his students, Tabataba'i was, by disposition, a contemplative man. Even the simplest questions would be an occasion for deep deliberations. Once a question was put to him, he would pause in silence for some time and think before giving his response.[87] His students also report that in formulating and presenting a philosophical argument he would meticulously stay clear of illuminative, mystical, and poetic allusions. In such circumstances he would operate strictly within the peripatetic line of philosophic argument. This is quite a significant aspect of Tabataba'i's philosophical disposition, because the practice has been quite pervasive, at least since Molla Sadra's introduction of mystical and (Shi'i) doctrinal considerations in the making of a philosophical argument. The use of poetic and aesthetic references, in making an argument, has, of course, a longer and much more common antecedent in the Persian culture of rhetorics. Here Tabataba'i not only stands in clear distinction with his two great predecessors, that is, Akhond Molla Sadra and Hakim Molla Hadi Sabzevari, but he appeals, through a rather serendipitous coincidence, to the radical elements in modern Iranian political discourse, where a particular disdain for mystical and nonrational forces in the Iranian culture is harbored. Quite significantly, he stays clear of mystical and poetic references precisely to avoid the impression that he is a

Muslim apologist after all. That would have been the final blow to his ambition to construct a level of philosophical discourse that would speak convincingly to secular intellectuals. Only on a common logical ground, he was convinced, could secular ideologies be confronted and challenged. Any rhetorical or doctrinal reference to dogmatic principles, whose veracity was to be taken a priori true, would be self-defeating. Thus, according to one of his students, Allamah Tabataba'i

liked very much to discuss within a given scientific discourse, limiting the discussion to the issue and principles of that [particular] branch of knowledge. Different branches of science should not be mixed together. He was particularly in pain by those who confused philosophy, Qur'anic exegesis, and [Prophetic and Imami] traditions together; those who when come short of rational argument and cannot proceed any farther, they reach for [Prophetic and Imami] traditions, and for Qur'anic exegesis, and thus hoping to establish [the validity of] their argument.[88]

It is precisely with this method that Tabataba'i wrote his classical disputation against philosophical materialism, *Osul-e Falsafeh va Ravesh-e Realism*. That this became a classical statement against the philosophical positions of Iranian Marxists was chiefly because the entire argument is made throughout the voluminous work in rational terms, acceptable or rejectable, Tabataba'i hoped, on precisely those grounds. There are scarcely any references to the Qur'anic or prophetic passages as illustrations of a logical point. This approach, while specifically addressed against the philosophical position of the Iranian Marxists, had the perhaps unintended consequence of not only consolidating the anti-Marxist position of the Islamic activists but also giving their general political agenda a certain aura of logical and philosophical certainty and legitimacy. It is precisely this search for certainty and legitimacy that informs most of Morteza Motahhari's extensive footnotes to Allamah Tabataba'i's long treatise. Footnoting Allamah Tabataba'i's text primarily for the secular intellectuals, Motahhari applied the logical vigor of his teacher's arguments to the ideological validity of the Islamic cause. Once the principal doctrines of historical materialism, the backbone of Marxism, were negated logically, in the combined efforts of Tabataba'i and Motahhari, the ideological fallacy of Marxism, and simultaneously the universal validity of "the Islamic Ideology," would be established irrevocably.

In view of his preference for the exclusive rational method in discussing philosophical issues, it is not surprising to find Allamah Tabataba'i's preference for Molla Mohsen Fayz-e Kashani over Kashani's teacher Molla Sadra, or that of the great master of peripatetic philosophy Avicenna again over the same Molla Sadra.[89] This, of course, does not mean that Tabataba'i did not recognize Molla Sadra's overwhelming contribution to the historical progression of Islamic philosophy. But, by disposition, and per-

haps by his sense of historical necessity in his own time, he preferred to
stay clear of "nonrational" allusions and references in the making of his
cases against what he undoubtedly considered to be the gravest threat to
Islamic epistemology, that is, the philosophical foundations of Marxism.

The point of departure between Molla Sadra and Allamah Tabataba'i
addresses an essential epistemological and sociological difference that distinguishes Shi'ism of the mid-sixteenth century from that of the mid- to late
twentieth century. The difference is significant enough to dwell on briefly.
Epistemologically, Molla Sadra comes at the end of a long and illustrious
philosophical gnostic tradition that he tried to synthesize by bringing it into
harmony with the Shi'i doctrinal positions.[90] Sociologically, Molla Sadra is
the most distinguished achievement of a triumphant and secured Shi'ism as
the state religion of the Safavids. But in the mid- to late twentieth century,
a Shi'i philosophical statement could not have remained irresponsive to
Marxist philosophy and still claim relevance in the contemporary annals of
serious ideas. Moreover, the epistemological challenge thus posed for the
scholastic Shi'i philosophy was coupled with a social state of siege in which
the Shi'i clerics had found themselves. The monarchical state was increasingly distancing itself from its Shi'i basis of legitimacy—thus the overwhelming attention to pre-Islamic Zoroastrian symbols and ceremonies—
and, at the same time, the liberal and radical ideas of patently nonreligious
origin claimed ever larger shares of allegiance from the Iranian middle
class. In such epistemological and sociological circumstances, Allamah Tabataba'i's strict emphasis on the rational and philosophical discourse in the
Shi'i tradition was particularly apt and appropriate. It was geared, as it
were, to the ideological and political needs of Shi'ism in the mid- to late
twentieth century.

Such fundamental changes in the historical and sociological configuration of Islamic philosophy had to be properly addressed and communicated
to the students in scholastic seminaries. Students of Tabataba'i report[91]
that he opposed those scholastics who insisted that seminarians first had to
learn the Prophetic and Imami traditions, among other "transmitted sciences," before they could turn to philosophy. Tabataba'i maintained that
much philosophical issues were involved in these traditions and that without proper training one could not grasp their significance. Even the canonical sources of Shi'ism had to be understood precisely in these terms. One of
Allamah Tabataba'i's remarkable achievements was to give philosophical
credence to canonical sources of Shi'ism. *Nahj al-Balaghah,* for example,
was one such source that every Shi'i cleric deeply honored and tried to
memorize. For the secular intellectuals this was but an obscure text of some
medieval relevance. With one stroke of argument, Tabataba'i wished to
establish three scores: (1) that *Nahj al-Balaghah* was a gold mine of philosophical issues, such as the first reference to the fact that God's oneness is

an essential *(dhati)* and not numerical *(adadi)* proposition[92] (the tacit argument here is that the text ought to be rescued from philosophically illiterate clerics who did not know what exactly it was they tried to memorize); (2) that *Nahj al-Balaghah,* among other canonical sources of Shi'ism, deserved meticulous philosophical attention regardless of one's theological position or the state of faith (this argument was targetted against the equally philosophically illiterate, the secular intellectuals, who could not and thus did not read such texts); and (3) that he broke the thick and otherwise impenetrable wall that separated the secular political activists, who consciously or otherwise considered historical materialism as the logical basis of their ideological position, from the elitist and abstruse religious discourse.

Allamah Tabataba'i's preoccupation with Islamic philosophy, and his concern with the primacy of the rational discourse, was not limited to its immediate political underpinning for the secular intellectuals. That primacy is also evident in an episode involving Muhammad Baqir Majlesi's *Bahar al-Anwar,* an encyclopedia of Shi'i knowledge compiled in the sixteenth century. According to one of his students,[93] Allamah Tabataba'i had great respect and admiration for Majlesi's endeavor in putting together such a compendium of Shi'i doctrinal knowledge. However, he is reported to have had certain reservations about Majlesi's treatment of the question of intellect *(aql).* Tabataba'i had decided to write a commentary on *Bahar al-Anwar,* to be published in conjunction with a new edition of Majlesi's work. His commentary was published up to the sixth volume of the new edition of *Bahar al-Anwar,* when his critical assessment of a passage by Majlesi on "intellect" caused dismay among the Qom juridical establishment, for whom Majlesi and *Bahar al-Anwar* had sacerdotal significance. The publisher, "because of external pressures,"[94] refused to print Tabataba'i's material unless he agreed to modify his opinion on Majlesi's passages.

Although in confrontation with the necessity of fighting against secular ideologies it had come to a sharper contrast, the antagonism and innate hostility, occasionally bordering on the mutual denial of legitimacy, between the juridical and the philosophical discourses in Islamic intellectual history is not something new. It originated in the very formative years of Islam and the introduction of Greek philosophy into the fabric of Muslim intellectual disposition. But in its modern phase, and in the case of Allamah Tabataba'i, the conflict must be seen in the context of the contemporary Iranian ideological composition where Tabataba'i's intentions were obviously directed towards consolidating and legitimizing a level of logical discourse responsive to the spirit of the age. He had to reach a level of intellectual discourse, deeply rooted in Shi'i traditions, with which he could communicate and convince the increasingly secular intellectuals, for whom the Shi'i doctrinal beliefs held no innate authority. But a strong resistance to this endeavor came from apolitical juridical sources who wished, on scholastic grounds, to safeguard the great figures and texts of authority in Shiʿism. The support for Allamah Tabataba'i's endeavors came in part from those scholastics with a philosophical bone in their Shiʿi body or else from those politically active clerics, chiefly Morteza Motahhari, who saw great ideological potentials in Tabataba'i's fortification of the Shiʿi philosophical discourse, particularly vis-à-vis the exclusive Marxist claim on logical consistency.

In response to his juridical opponents, who could not see the compelling significance of strengthening the Shiʿi rational discourse, Allamah Tabataba'i refused to abandon his philosophical mindset. He argued that

in Shiʿism, [Imam] Jaʿfar al-Sadiq [the sixth Shiʿi Imam] is more important than Allamah Majlesi, and should it come to the point that, because of statements and explications of Allamah Majlesi, intellectual and scientific objections would be raised against the Infallibles, peace be upon them, we are not ready to sell those Infallibles to Majlesi. I shall not drop a word from what I consider, in appropriate instances, necessary to write.[95]

Needless to say, the subsequent volumes of *Bahar al-Anwar* were published without Allamah Tabataba'i's commentaries.

The nature of Allamah Tabataba'i's argument against Majlesi in these disputed passages is of some importance here. The argument concerns the definition and centrality of intellect, the leveling of Imami traditions which contain significant philosophical references with other less philosophically oriented traditions, and the possibility of an independent, ontologically consequential, existence for the intellect.[96] Majlesi, obviously strong in the juridical tradition, had relied heavily on the centrality of transmitted knowledge and discounted the relevance, and polarity, of the independent propriety of intellectual endeavors. He had taken all Imami traditions literally, at face value, for mass juridical purposes and had denied philosophers, or their discourse, any measure of significance or legitimacy. Tabataba'i, on the opposing end of the historical bifurcation of the Islamic "intellectual" and "transmitted" discourses, stood for the independent veracity of "intellect" as a divine gift and thus an instrument of rational argument for the existence and validity of many philosophical issues in the received traditions of the Shiʿi Imams, and for the inevitability of logical discourse in any meaningful defense of the Islamic (Shiʿi) doctrines.

One of the principal criticisms that Tabataba'i charged against Majlesi was the latter's refutation of the existence of "the abstract intellect" (*aql-e mojarrad*) as a bona fide source of authority in judgment. The only such source, according to Majlesi, was God, and if there is such a thing as "intellect," then that is the "prophetic light" from which the lights of the Imams had emanated. Obviously Allamah Tabataba'i believed in the cause and the bona fide veracity of "abstract intellect" as a source of authority in judgment, and he refuted Majlesi by arguing that "if realization of an abstract existent being other than God is impossible in the external world, then that impossibility would not be altered by changing a name." Changing an appellation from "the abstract intellect" to "light," "predisposition," etc., does not make a difference in changing the actual condition of permitting such external existents.[97] This, in Tabataba'i's estimation, was an anti-intellectual and unacceptable proposition. He repeatedly argued that positions such as those of Majlesi and his contemporary supporters were tantamount to the dismissive position of *Kafana' kitab Allah* ("the Book of God is enough for us"). Without the slightest doubt about the centrality and significance of the Qur'an and having written a massive voluminous commentary on it as proof, Allamah Tabataba'i also believed in the independent legitimacy of "the abstract intellect" not only in the long Islamic philosophical tradition but now also, as an ideological necessity, in the very viability of Islam as a legitimate claim on contemporary Muslims and their intellectual and ideological disposition.

As Allamah Tabataba'i's students have emphatically pointed out in his defense,[98] what makes his steadfast position in support of philosophy particularly strong is the *ejtehad* tradition in Shi'ism. To be sure, *ejtehad* is a juridical mechanism in Shi'i law whereby legal expostulations are rendered possible and legitimate as long as they involve rational extensions of the canonical sources into the specifics of contemporary realities. Perhaps it is the same intellectual disposition that expresses itself in jurisprudence as *ejtehad* and in more specifically philosophical domains as the independence, centrality, and significance of "the abstract intellect." The fact remains, however, that hostility towards philosophical dispositions has been expressed equally by both Sunni and Shi'i clerics and that the bifurcation between the "intellectual" and the "transmitted" sciences is transectarian. But given the centrality of *ejtehad* in the Shi'i jurisprudence, a more persuasive argument for the significance of the intellect in understanding matters of communal or doctrinal concerns could be made for this branch of Islam.

The Necessity of Comparative Philosophy

Perhaps Allamah Tabataba'i's most significant attempt in the context of modern Iranian intellectual history was his emphasis on the necessity of a comparative understanding of "The Western" philosophy. He believed that because philosophy is based on rational arguments, whatever discrepancy exists between "The Western" and the Islamic schools of philosophy has to be the result of a logical incongruency, thus "we ought to search for the secret of discrepancy between philosophers of East and West."[99] Should this discrepancy be accounted for logically, which Tabataba'i inevitably believed would be in favor of Islamic philosophy, all the ideological force of the "Western" claims to political veracity would be ipso facto rendered illegitimate.

Allamah Tabataba'i's knowledge of "The Western" philosophy, though not altogether extensive or systematic, was relatively more than most of his clerical cohorts. With few exceptions, most notably Mehdi Ha'eri Yazdi who has studied philosophy in Europe, the United States, and Canada, the scholastically trained clerics, even of the philosophical stature of Allamah Tabataba'i, knew very little of what was generically called "The Western" philosophy. But Allamah Tabataba'i's knowledge was perhaps more extensive than that of his cohorts because of his associations with the French Islamicist Henry Corbin who, prior to his attraction to Islamic philosophy, was the translator of Heidegger into French. Through the active and instrumental participation of such interested intermediaries as S. H. Nasr, and Daryush Shaygan, Allamah Tabataba'i and Henri Corbin had extensive and periodic sessions in which aspects of Shi'i philosophical and gnostic ideas were discussed in comparative terms with "The Western" and "The Eastern" philosophies.[100]

Every domain of "The Western" achievements that was attractive to modern Muslims had to have its origin in the specifics of its philosophy. Even in the question of technology, the bugbear of "The Western" ideological hegemony, Tabataba'i believed that all these advancements are reducible to logical and rational components that, by implication, could be repeated and executed by anyone. The tacit argument here is that there is nothing magical about "The Western" technological advancements, and that once the basic and logically discernible formulae of technical instruments are ascertained, anybody, or any society, can achieve what "The West" has attained in applied sciences.[101] There are two edges to Tabataba'i's argument here: First, it is directed against the Westoxicated spirit of his age which presumed that adopting the technological achievements of "The West" was contingent upon a wholesome imitation of "The Western" cultural and ideological postures, and, second, it is directed against the dogmatic doctors of Shi'i law who rejected any independent validity to "the abstract intellect." To make this simultaneous engagement with two opposing political forces ideologically valid, Tabataba'i had to rely on a particular philosophical discourse that, while acceptable to these two heterogenous opponents, would not alienate or antagonize them.

The clerical establishment in Qom was particularly hostile to any philosophical dialogue with "The West." To be sure, the outcome of the Usuli-Akhbari controversy in Shi'i jurisprudence had rendered the Shi'i doctors comparatively more tolerant of philosophical speculations. Whereas the Akhbari faction rejected the exertion of intellect in extrapolating principles from the received traditions, upon which further juridical principles could be built, the Usulis insisted precisely on that. The final victory of the Usuli over the Akhbari faction of Shi'i jurisprudence had given the philosophical discourse, of which Tabataba'i was a prominent advocate, a favorable context. Nonetheless, there was still staunch resistance, if not outright hostility, to the logical extremities of the philosophical discourse, particularly when directed towards a dialogue with "The West."[102]

The Supremacy of the Moral Order

No degree of mere philosophical vigor can create authority in a public figure. What is also needed is morality. A profound manifestation of public piety is the most essential ingredient of a collective imagination creating a myth out of a mere man. Despite the aura of great reverence and scholastic majesty that surrounded him, Allamah Tabataba'i is reported to have been very humble in his behavior.

Just like a schoolboy he would sit on the ground of the school yard. Close to the sunset he would come to the Feyziyyeh School. When the public prayers commenced, like all other students he would say his prayers behind the late Ayatollah Hajj Sayyid Muhammad Taqi Khawnsari.[103]

His students draw a picture of an extremely polite and meticulously observant man. In the words of one of them:

He was so humble, polite, and observant of manners to the utmost degree. I repeatedly told him: "Sir, so much consideration of proper manners by you turns us into impolite people! Please, be more considerate of us!" For close to forty years, no one has ever seen him lay back on a pillow or cushion [in front of his guests]. He would always, when he had guests, sit a bit away from the wall, lower [in his position] to the visiting guest. I was his student and used to go to his house frequently. I wished, out of politeness, to sit lower to him. But it was impossible. He would stand up and say, "Well, then, I will have to sit in the threshold of the door, or go and sit outside the room!"[104]

There are many such instances that his students report, with love and affection, all pointing to the great humility that the Allamah assumed so effortlessly. A close student reports[105] that he repeatedly tried to kiss the Allamah's hand, as a sign of reverence to the old master, but never succeeded. The Allamah would hide his hand behind his aba. The student reminds the master of the famous tradition of Ali, "Whoever has taught me a word has made me his obedient servant," and confesses that kissing the Allamah's hand is more for his own benefit and sanctity. But the Allamah would always refuse in good and benevolent temper, and as for the tradition of Ali, he would say, "we are all the obedient servants to God."[106]

Allamah Tabataba'i's humility was the most striking feature of his moral superiority that left an indelible impression on his students and acquaintances. One of his students reports[107] that for close to forty years he yearned to say his prayers behind the Allamah, that is, with the Allamah leading the prayer. But the Allamah would always humbly and politely refuse.

The two major criteria of seniority in Shi'i scholastic system are learning and age. It is particularly for the students of a scholastic master that his learning and age become symbolically and effectively pronounced. Once despite these criteria, the master refuses to assume the symbols and ceremonies of authority, for example, leading a public prayer or sitting in a room farthest from the door, the very act of refusal creates sometimes unbearable thrusts of love, reverence, and affection for him. There is no conscious calculation of increasing one's reverence here. It just works that way. When a scholastic master is innately, or by ascetic training, inimical to the assumption of symbols and ceremonies of power, by definition he increases proportionately his respect and thus his authority.

This is at the heart of the authority of the high-ranking clerical order not only for their immediate students but, by extension, for others as well. Highly technical juridical discussions are the necessary precondition for a limited number of students to become intellectually attracted to a master. But the root and quintessential basis of the authority of the clerical order ought to be sought in the more tangible plane of personal characteristics. A combination of extensive (juridical) learning and old age, with an indispensable dose of genuine humility, the kind that often moves followers to tears, is the most congenial and natural basis of authority in Shi'ism.

This, at a deeper cultural level, is connected to the central question of *mazlumiyyat* in the Shi'ite political culture. Authority, not to be confused with mere power, is always with the *mazlum,* he who demonstrates *mazlumiyyat.* Who is a *mazlum?* This question is most fundamental to the Shi'i collective memory. A *mazlum* is literally someone who has been wronged, someone who has been subjected to a grave injustice. Imam Hossein, the third Shi'i Imam, is the archetypal epitome of a *mazlum. Hossein-e Mazlum* is the profoundest gesture of communal obedience in Shi'ism. Hossein was martyred thirsty. Each time every single Shi'i drinks a glass of water, the first words coming to his (or her) lips must convey remembrance of the injustice done to *Hossein-e Mazlum.* "O, I would sacrifice my life for thy thirsty lips!" says the Shi'i man, woman, and child every time a sip of water is taken. Beyond the archetypal model of Imam Hossein, *mazlum* has a double meaning: someone who is unassuming, humble, considerate of others, self-effacing; one who, in effect, assumes authority, as it were, by ostensibly rejecting it. Any ostentatious assumption of power is inimical to *mazlumiyyat,* which is at the basis of every authority. The authority thus created is immediately spiritual but invariably extensive in its political dimensions. A single sign of unpretentious humility, and all these implications, and much more, are instantly communicated.

As much as the cleric's humble refusal to assume symbols and ceremonies of power works precisely in the direction of intensifying his authority, the actual assumption of political leadership draws him to the mundane realities of routine politics, which is deadly in diffusing the sacred aura of spiritual superiority that surrounds the religious authorities. Here, power consumes its own authority. The Shi'i clerics, thus, have authority insofar as they lack power. The moment they assume power their authority is in jeopardy.

The refusal to assume the compelling symbols and ceremonies of power can be either congenial to the natural disposition of a religious figure or the acquired virtue of long and arduous ascetic exercises in the mystical (Sufi) tradition. Humility and the refusal to assume any symbol or ceremony of earthly power is an essential feature in Sufi teaching. Allamah Tabataba'i had conducted his own spiritual and ascetic exercises under the mastership and guidance of Sayyid al-Arefiyn Hajj Mirza Ali Qazi, the man for whom he reserved the exclusive title of "the master" and whom he held in utmost respect, reverence, and honor. The connecting link between the high moral achievements of the Sufi masters and their wider circle of admirers has always been poetry. Allamah Tabataba'i composed beautiful lyrical poetry. Although few of his poems have been published, one of Tabataba'i's students has recorded one that testifies to the fluent ease with which he composed poetry in Persian,[108] which was not his mother tongue. Tabataba'i's interest in both theoretical and practical mysticism had distinguished him doubly from his contemporaries and deeply informed his poetry. His rather unusual poetic gift had put him in a category unto himself. One of his most beautiful ghazals begins with the following verses:

Thus I say, and said have I so many times, that
My faith is in loving those who love.
In the faith of love, obedience is intoxication.
Those who are conscious are not among this lot. . . .[109]

There are pieces of his poetry, the very model of beauty and grace, in which he has avoided totally the use of any Arabic word.[110] Such unusual poetic dispositions and occasional, but rather exclusive, attention to "pure Persian" are features of Tabataba'i's intellectual character that are quite unique among his contemporaries.

Tabataba'i on the Qur'an

From philosophy to ethics, that pecular combination of compelling logic and disarming humility, particulars of a religious figure of authority are

assayed. For those particulars to become universals of contemporary ideological force, the addition of the revelatory language of the Qur'an and the
authority it engenders are indispensable. The Qur'an has always been at
the center of religious and political discourses of authority in Islam. Modern articulations of religious and political matters, specifics of creating and
sustaining communal authority, have not, as we saw in the case of Ayatollah Taleqani, been exempted from direct appeal to the sacred Text.

In addition to his monumental *Tafsir al-Mizan*, Allamah Tabataba'i
wrote a book on the significance and centrality of the Qur'an in Islamic
religion and history. *Qur'an Dar Islam (The Qur'an in Islam)* sets out to
articulate the central position of the holy Text in the context of the Islamic
doctrines. A distinguishing factor in Allamah Tabataba'i's understanding
of the Qur'an, which immediately sets him apart from many of his contemporaries, is his insistence that we ought to seek the Qur'anic position vis-à-
vis various issues, and not, reversing the order, the position of various
standings vis-à-vis the Qur'an:

In this discussion and investigation, we have to find answers to this question, "What
does the Qur'an say about this issue?" We should not be asking, "We who have
accepted this or that sect within Islam, what do we say about the Qur'an?"[111]

Coming from a tightly traditional setting of religious learning, Tabataba'i's emphatic recognition of the centrality of the Qur'an was in sharp
contrast to many contemporary Qur'anic commentators who had turned
the holy Text into a battleground of legitimacy for specific ideological
sentiments.

Tabataba'i's agenda in *The Qur'an in Islam* is to insist on the relevance
and centrality of the holy Text for the historical validity and legitimacy of
every human society,[112] for every epoch of the Islamic community, and, by
strong implication, for the modern human (Islamic) society. This is a hidden disputation against the host of ideological systems, particularly institutionalized in nationalism and socialism, that implicitly or explicitly denied
the holy Text any further legitimacy or relevance in the modern age.

In *The Qur'an in Islam,* the universality of the Qur'an is argued through
a set of three interrelated Islamic (Qur'anic) doctrines: Theology, Eschatology, and Prophetology.[113] The Qur'an is universal because God is one and
Omnipotent, and the Qur'anic verses are His very words.[114] The Qur'an is
universal because we shall all return to God at a point and account for our
deeds in this world. The Qur'an is universal because through the intermediary of the prophets, God has mandated the proper role of conduct for us
all. The establishment of the universality of the Qur'an, regardless of time
and space, that it is complete,[115] perpetual,[116] and independent,[117] would
emphasize not only its centrality in mandating the public life, but would
also tacitly legitimate the religious discourse in addressing public issues. In

an age when explicit or implicit references to the doctrinal texts of socialism and nationalism were assuming increasing currency, Allamah Tabataba'i was, in fact, lending support to a religious context of ideological references, like Motahhari and Taleqani who rhymed and reasoned their discourse with Qur'anic references. But even more important, Tabataba'i's argument, that the Qur'an was a universal book[118]—meaning that it was not exclusive to one or two nations—had the significant, perhaps unanticipated, consequence of lending support to the universal claim of the emerging religious discourse espousing revolutionary causes.

Tabataba'i also specified certain features of the Qur'an that make it not immediately accessible to the lay Muslims. That the Qur'an has a hidden meaning[119] or that its verses are divided into "clear" (muhkam) and "allegorical" (mutashabih), or that its injunctions are divided into "abrogative" (nasikh) and "abrogated" (mansukh) render it not immediately accessible to the public. Specifically for the Shi'is, the "allegorical" verses of the Qur'an particularly necessitate and justify the position of the Imams.[120] Although their collective wisdom has made the Qur'an self-contained and self-explanatory, by referring the "allegorical" verses to the "clear" ones,[121] still the fact that the holy Text is interpretable[122] particularly necessitates not only the Shi'i Imams but also the entire class of Qur'anic interpreters.[123] Such "ambiguities," or allegorical references, correspond to a level of interpretation that, by definition, is time-specific. Thus, there is a built-in necessity for historically updating the meaning of the Qur'an: an updating that invariably assumes the dominant political terms of its time.

The principles of Shi'i Qur'anic hermeneutics assume a particular "posture," as Allamah Tabataba'i puts it, in the course of history. Here, first and foremost, the prophetic references to specific Qur'anic passages are crucial for understanding or interpreting the Qur'an. The specific references of the "people of the household" and the Imams about the Qur'an are equally authoritative.[124] Second come those interpretations that quote directly from the prophetic and Imami aural tradition in elucidating the Qur'an. Third are those Shi'i authors who have interpreted the Qur'an from specific Islamic viewpoints, for example, Sayyid al-Razi in his literary interpretation of the Qur'an, Shaykh al-Tusi in his theological reading of the holy Text, Sadr al-Muti'allihiyn Molla Sadra Shirazi in his philosophical elucidations of the sacred Book, or Qadi Maybudi in his mystical hermeneutic of the Qur'anic verses.

Allamah Tabataba'i concludes by arguing that there are three kinds of exegesis: (1) based on one's own knowledge, (2) based on traditions received from the Prophet and the Imams, and (3) based on the Qur'anic and traditional contexts of a given verse.[125] He maintains that "the first procedure is not reliable . . . unless it is combined with the third procedure";[126] "the second procedure has been adopted by the Qur'anic interpreters only [earlier] in Islamic history . . . and nowadays the Akhbaris follow it too." [127] Tabataba'i, as a result, rejects both of these procedures as either "opinionated" [128] or "limited in the face of unlimited problems." [129] His preference, consequently, is for the third procedure, which combines contextual understanding of a Qur'anic verse in reference to other Qur'anic passages with a simultaneous reference to authentic traditions received from the Prophet and the Imams, in conjunction with thinking and deliberating about the verses themselves.

The result of this particular formulation of Qur'anic exegesis is that while the Islamic sacred Text is located at the center of society and the world at large, it is not immediately accessible to the public. By clear implication, the necessity of an intervening group of historically legitimated interpreters is stipulated. To be sure, Allamah Tabataba'i here discusses his concern in a valid historical and Islamic context. However, translated into the context of his contemporary conjuncture of religious and political issues, these formulations lend support and legitimacy to the emerging ideologues who vouch for an overall re-Islamization of the Iranian collective psyche and national polity. Motahhari and Taleqani are immediately brought to mind as beneficiaries of this probably unanticipated consequence of an otherwise bona fide discussion of Qur'anic exegesis.

One of the remarkable features of Allamah Tabataba'i's writings is that he candidly faced the crucial questions that had intellectually engaged his time, irrespective of how seriously they challenged the doctrinal foundations of Islam. This was the direct result of an overwhelming confidence that comes only with a deep and thorough knowledge of various Islamic sciences. His *Principles of Philosophy and the Realistic Method* is the most systematic rebuttal of philosophical materialism (as much as he could realistically understand it) in modern Iranian history. The same attitude is present in *The Qur'an in Islam*, where he takes up the question of "revelations" and "prophecy." Having stated the standard Islamic position that the Qur'an was revealed by God through Archangel Gabriel to Prophet Muhammad in the course of twenty-three years, [130] Tabataba'i then proceeds to formulate two versions of an atheist or agnostic view of the prophetic mission according to which, in the absence of a Supreme Deity, it is Muhammad's own noble or perspicacious character that has constructed an elaborate theology, eschatology, and prophetology to make people conform to his social and political reforms, which promise to lead them to a more just and equitable life. [131] The way Allamah Tabataba'i proceeds with his counterargument is by initially denying the materialists and positivists any claim to authority to engage in metaphysical matters, for their area of speculation is primarily and essentially the physical world as perceived through the organs of sense perception, and not the metaphysical. [132] Having discredited them as authorities in metaphysical matters, as it were, he then articulates the internal logic of the Qur'an on the question of revelation and insists that in a metaphysical discourse it is precisely that logic that ought to be taken seriously.[133] If there is a minimum of logical consistency in this apologia for the traditional Islamic position on "revelation," it was translated into a maximum of ideological legitimacy for the contemporaneity of the Islamic discourse.

A derivative discussion from the question of "revelation" is man's social nature and the necessity of a body of laws to regulate it. Rationality alone is insufficient to regulate man's social life.[134] Man's rationality, while self-regulating, is also self-serving and contradicts man's ability to transcend his historical exigencies or his self-interests and regulate laws that would ensure his social life. This leads Tabataba'i to maintain that man's only salvation is in a social life regulated by metahistorical forces, that is, by Divine law. The metaphysical foundation of the revelatory language renders it immune to human fallacy.

Tabataba'i categorically denies the possibility of grasping the nature of the revelatory language except for a chosen few, such as the prophets themselves.[135] This renders the Qur'anic text itself exclusive to the metaphysical nature of the God-Messenger relationship. However, through the varieties of Qur'anic exegesis, the sacred Text is rendered operative at a mass social level.

The universal presuppositions of Tabataba'i's discourse at once establishes the revelatory language of the Qur'an as valid and pertinent not only in a paradigmatic, epistemological sense, but towards a specific and practical direction. The logical underpinning of Tabataba'i's discourse would immediately render the Qur'an itself socially and politically pertinent in contemporary Muslim life. To what specific directions would others, such as Taleqani or Shari'ati, take this lead, Tabataba'i did not and could not know. He merely defended the universal and epistemological validity of the revelatory language, and more specifically that of the Qur'anic discourse.

The contemporary relevance of the Qur'an in the modern world would immediately necessitate the question of "science," and its particular perceptions in Islam. "Science," that is, the empirical foundations of modern biological and physical knowledge, epitomized the contemporary challenges that the Qur'anic revelatory discourse faced. Tabataba'i's stated agenda here is merely to argue that the Qur'an has a positive attitude towards "science" as such.[136] Moreover, specific branches of knowledge such as "natural sciences, mathematics, philosophy, and sciences pertaining to literature"[137] are considered legitimate pursuits by the Qur'an. There are also certain sciences that are contingent upon the Qur'an itself, such as grammar and linguistics, or the Qur'anic hermeneutics. Jurisprudence and theology are among the sciences that the Qur'an has virtually originated.[138] Located thus at the very center of an entire range of sciences, the Qur'anic revelatory language and content could not be, and was not, hostile to any systematic pursuit of knowledge. The Qur'an would not, of course, share certain possible metaphysical implications of experimental sciences.

Allamah Tabataba'i's discussion of these and other detailed and technical features of the Qur'an,[139] had the immediate purpose of giving a preliminary, yet accurate, overview of the central significance of the sacred Text in the total fabric of the Muslim mind, in its traditional or modern cast. The simple and nontechnical language of this book indicates that it was targeted primarily towards a general public. Perhaps the most important impact of this popular treatise on the Qur'an was a tacit but powerful resuscitation of the Iranian collective Qur'anic memory, an achievement without which other reorganizers of this memory would have had a more difficult time than they did in delivering their ideological message in a Qur'anic language.

Tafsir al-Mizan

The interpretative power of the Qur'an went beyond its mere exposition. Allamah Tabataba'i's interest in Qur'anic commentary goes back to his years in Tabriz where he had begun writing on the sacred Text. His main objective was to demonstrate the innate harmony among the various modes of discourses with which the sacred Text had been understood. Thus, historical and ethical discussions are set next to theological, juridical, philosophical, and mystical readings of the Qur'anic passages.

Tabataba'i's Qur'anic commentary is in twenty volumes in its original Arabic. He began writing it in 1954 and finished it in 1972. During that period, he also taught it to his students in Qom.[140] The most essential guideline followed in this Qur'anic commentary is the principle that "certain parts of the Qur'an are defined by certain other parts." This hermeneutic method, which guarantees that no external factor enters the Qur'anic exegesis, has been one of the principal procedures for assuring that external and changing conditions are not forced onto the Qur'anic passages. Before a certain conclusion is drafted out of a passage, its accuracy is tested by references to other related Qur'anic passages. Tabataba'i's method in Qur'anic commentary is precisely the opposite of that of Taleqani who persistently derived preconceived, politically charged, ideologically underscored, and patently Darwinistic interpretations from the sacred Text. Contrary to Taleqani, Allamah Tabataba'i always remained conscious of the archetypal nature of the Qur'anic discourse. This approach would check any inadvertent tendency to reduce the Qur'an to any given historical exigency. This, of course, does not mean that Allamah Tabataba'i's Qur'anic commentary remained totally indifferent to the pressing problems of the time. His Qur'anic commentary was indeed yet another occasion to challenge the validity of philosophical materialism as a legitimate ideology. Such contemporary concerns are always combined with more dogmatic and doctrinal issues in Tabataba'i's discourse. As a Shi'i, he does not miss any occasion in the course of his commentary to defend and vindicate Ali's cause and his right to immediate successorship after the Prophet. But more than such sectarian concerns, his attempt in this extensive Qur'anic commentary is to bring harmony to the historical hostility between the juridical and philosophical discourses. Not only in his Qur'anic commentary but elsewhere too, he considered this the most crucial challenge that would consolidate the internal vigor of Shi'ism as it faced the adversities of imported ideologies.

Many prominent Shi'i scholars have attested to the significance of *al-Mizan*. Allamah Tabataba'i's students categorically consider it the greatest achievement in the history of Qur'anic commentaries.[141] Imam Musa' Sadr has reported that Muhammad Jawad Mughniyyah, the prominent Lebanese Shi'i scholar, had told him that "since I have received *al-Mizan*, my library has been closed off. On my study desk sits constantly *al-Mizan*."[142] Subtracting for its obvious exaggeration, there is an element of truth in the assessment of one of the Allamah Tabataba'i's former students that "*al-Mizan* commentary was a master key for all cultural and religious malaise in a society moving towards perfection and [towards] preparing the groundwork of the Islamic Revolution."[143]

The Authority Verse

One of the crucial passages in Allamah Tabataba'i's Qur'anic commentary, directly relevant to the formation of "the Islamic Ideology," is what is known as the "authority verse."[144] Based on his understanding of this verse, the supreme physical and metaphysical authority is God first and the Prophet second. The authority of God is universal and, in the Qur'anic language, refers to the obligation of the created beings to obey His revealed laws. The authority of the Prophet, however, is both in presenting the specifics of the Divine law and in implementing them through government *(hokumat)* and juridical execution.[145] It is precisely this latter model of command and obedience, that of the Prophet, that corresponds to a revolutionary self-understanding on the part of the religious authorities. The borderline between the political and the juridical domains of the prophetic authority so thinly indistinguishable, the contemporary religious authority could, should the occasion permit or warrant, expand its juridical authority well into the political.

As for the Qur'anic stipulation of "those of authority among you," Tabataba'i emphasizes that they are not in possession of any (new) revelation beyond the authority of God and his last messenger. But their commands ought to be obeyed as if issued from God or the Prophet. In the context of the Qur'anic passage, obedience to God, his Prophet, and "those of authority among you" is particularly juxtaposed against the ungodly possibility of following civil alternatives. In this capacity, as the third source of supreme authority, after God and the Prophet, *ulu al-amr* ("those of authority among you") can neither bring a new law nor could they deny the validity of those established in the Qur'an and the prophetic traditions.

Obedience to God is unconditional. Muhammad's authority is equally binding. But while God's metaphysical inevitability accounts for His Omnipresence, it is the Prophet's infallibility (which is a human possibility) that assimilates the range and depth of his authority to that of God.[146] Tabataba'i is convinced, and here is the significance of his observations for contemporary Shi'i claims to political agenda, that the same sweeping generalization of God's and Muhammad's authority is equally applicable to the *ulu al-amr*. The question remains, however, whether the prerequisite of infallibility is equally necessary. Tabataba'i initially does not consider the condition of infallibility as absolutely necessary. However, he has two crucial stipulations here. First, if the commandments of the *ulu al-amr* are positively contrary to the doctrinal injunctions of the Qur'an and the *hadith*, then they are not binding. But, second, if they are merely considered to be possibly contrary to the same injunctions, they ought to be followed (even if they may, in fact, be contrary to the Qur'an and the hadith).[147] For the doctrinal consolidation of the first stipulation, Tabataba'i resorts to the prophetic tradition that "there is no obedience to a created being when [his actions are] transgressive to the Creator."[148] For the doctrinal validation of the second stipulation, he resorts to the juridical principle according to which

evident procedures *(toroq-e zaheriyyeh)* are [sufficient and binding] proof for the validity of practical matters *(ahkam-e vaqe'iyyeh)*. And should the referents of those practical matters [later turn out to] be contrary to reality, the veracity of the procedure will compensate for that corruption [that is, for the falseness of the referent matter].[149]

Tabataba'i's reason for the binding power of the *ulu al-amr,* even if their decision may be contrary to the Qur'anic and prophetic injunctions, is what he calls "consideration of what is best for Islam and the Muslims":[150]

At any rate, obedience to the *ulu al-amr* is mandatory, even though they are not infallible and capable of corruption and mistake. But if they commanded [an action that is] positively corrupt, they are not to be obeyed. Should they make a mistake and it became [positively] evident, reference ought to be made to the Qur'an and the [prophetic] tradition. Should it [that is, their mistake] not be [positively] evident, their commands are definitive [that is, they must be obeyed], and their disagreement with the actual—not the apparent—injunctions [of the Qur'an and the Prophet] is not important. Because speaking with one voice and considering what is best for Islam and the Muslims is more important than that [that is, than the possibility of a commandment of the *ulu al-amr* to be in contradiction to the Qur'anic and prophetic injunctions].[151]

Tabataba'i also considers the possibility of assuming the infallibility of the *ulu al-amr* as self-evident, since they are mentioned on a par with the Prophet, whose infallibility is doctrinal to Islam. It is this reading that Tabataba'i favors and advances.

As to the question of *amr*, Tabataba'i believes it refers to both religious and temporal matters.[152]

In a grammatical discussion of *minkum* ("from among you"), he makes a tangential, but crucial, reference to his opposing the reading that assumes the *ulu al-amr* to be just an ordinary person without the prerequisite of infallibility. It is evident from this discussion that he considers the *ulu al-amr* to be exceptional individuals in the category of prophets, with the distinguishing feature of being infallible.[153] *Ulu al-amr* is also a plural noun, which means it refers to many individuals of a common type. Tabataba'i categorically rejects the reading of *ulu al-amr* as referring to just any person in a position of political, social, economic (etc.) authority in a community. Here, on doctrinal grounds, he insists on the distinguishing feature of infallibility. "This verse necessitates the infallibility of the *ulu al-amr*. In this regard, the Qur'anic commentators have no alternative."[154] Infallibility is the adjectival property of individuals, not groups. Thus a group of people in a position of authority, political or otherwise, cannot be assumed to have infallibility as their distinguishing character. Only individuals of a certain type, a type congenial to the prophetic, can have this attribute. Taking issue with Imam Fakhr-e Razi (c.1148–1209), a Sunni commentator, Tabataba'i refuses any assumption of infallibility for any group of individuals except for the Shi'i Imams.[155] If all people in position of political authority, throughout Islamic history, were infallible, asks Tabataba'i rhetorically, then why have there been such great upheavals and injustice? He equally rejects the possibility of reading *ulu al-amr* as kings, monarchs, sultans, etc.[156]

Thus eliminating all possibilities, he concludes emphatically that

the *ulu al-amr* are those individuals in the Islamic community [*ummah*] who are infallible in their sayings, obedience to whom is obligatory, recognition of whom is in need of precise designation on the part of God or his Messenger, and these are only compatible with traditions received from the Imams of the [prophetic] Household who have introduced themselves as *ulu al-amr*.[157]

Even more emphatically he asserts:

As for the reading that the *ulu al-amr* are the [four] rightly guided caliphs [that is, Abu Bakr, Umar, Uthman, and Ali], or princes, or the ulama' [that is, the religious (juridical) authorities] ... there are two answers: First, the verse indicates the infallibility of the *ulu al-amr* and certainly among these classes [that is, the caliphs, the princes, and the ulama'] there are no infallibles except, in the Shi'i belief, Ali, peace be upon him.[158]

Tabataba'i then proceeds to refute all objections that have been made to reading the *ulu al-amr* as principally and exclusively referring to the twelve Shi'i Imams.

Women in Islam

In *al-Mizan*, Allamah Tabataba'i also addressed some of the key issues on the position of women in Islam. Particularly alert to issues of contemporary relevance, he realized the significance of women's rights.[159]

In discussing various chapters of the Qur'an that make reference to women, Allamah Tabataba'i rejected the standard interpretations that women were created from men. Women had an independent creation on a par with that of men. In this respect, he even rejected the validity of a tradition according to which woman had been created from man's rib. Qur'anic passages, he asserted, did not support such an assumption. In defending his principal belief in the categorical equality of men and women, Tabataba'i takes issue with certain ideas in Greek philosophy contrary to this position. His rationalistic argument refuses to recognize the slightest quintessential difference in the created nature of men and women. He admits certain degrees of strength and weakness in their shared qualities, but not in their substantive and essential nature. Since men and women are equal in their quintessential nature, there is no reason for the highest material and intellectual achievements of one sex not to be attained by the other. More emphatically,

Insofar as leading [different] aspects of life is concerned, Islam considers man and woman equal. With regard to the application of [human] will to everything that the human existential being necessitates, they are equal. Consequently, like men, women can independently make decisions, act [accordingly], and own the results of their own endeavors.[160]

Women are distinguished by two exclusive characteristics in their creation: First, the continuity of the human race is subject to their natural constitution, and, second, they are created with a more delicate physical and emotional disposition. This delicacy of disposition has rendered them more congenial to aesthetic and emotional characters. Thus, while men are more "intellectually" oriented, women are more "emotionally" inclined.[161] It has been suggested[162] that Tabataba'i's careful wording of this categorical statement confirms the possibility of both "intellectual" and "emotional" dispositions in men and women. Yet, on the whole, Tabataba'i believes that men tend to realize their intellectual possibilities more than women, and woman tend to be more emotional than men. Men, though, are potentially as capable of overwhelming emotional dispositions as women are of intellectual ones.

From this premise Tabataba'i concludes that the divisions of labor stipulated in Islam require men to excel in activities that demand vigor and mind, and women in those that require love and affection. The man's authority *(qaymumat)* is precisely because of this primacy of the intellectual over emotional faculties. But at the same time, Allamah Tabataba'i insisted that in Islam children bore their relations of identity as much from their father's side as from their mother's.

Marriage is a socially sanctioned contract that recognizes the natural human need for sexual intercourse and procreation. Any other form of sexual contact is unnatural and un-Islamic. Tabataba'i argues for the validity and universal necessity of the rules against incest, the necessity of veiling, permanent and temporary marriage, and polygyny. Man's sexual needs are not satisfied by one permanent marriage. Thus he needs to have access to the possibility of both multiple and temporary marriages. Because man's sexual needs are not satisfied by one permanent marriage, his instinctual urges are better regulated and checked than satisfied haphazardly and illegally. At the same time, Allamah Tabataba'i is harshly critical of the way such Islamic injunctions are practiced. He seems to suggest that having failed to understand the spirit of the Islamic rules of marriage, Muslims have miscarried the letter of their law. Polygyny is not a mandatory law but a possibility in Islam. Islam has commenced its laws of marriage with monogamy. But because there are more women than men and because it is unjust for unmarried women not to enjoy sexual intercourse, Islam has permitted the possibility of one man having more than one legal wife. But certain Muslim men, particularly kings and other men of wealth, have used this possibility as an excuse to give free rein to their lust. About such men, Tabataba'i decreed, "the legality of even one wife is dubious."[163]

Osul-e Falsafeh Va Ravesh-e Realism

To arrange for a kind of philosophical dialogue with the most aggressive of "The Western" philosophies, that is, philosophical materialism, Tabataba'i called for sessions to be held on an immediate and regular basis. Among the students who regularly attended was Morteza Motahhari,[164] who would later collect, edit, and annotate the proceedings of these sessions into what has reached us as the *Osul-e Falsafeh va Ravesh-e Realism (The Principles of Philosophy and the Realistic Method)*. This text became the most authoritative source in the clerical battle against the ideological domination of Marxism. In the course of this battle, Motahhari became the great populizer of Tabataba'i's ideas. By disposition Allamah Tabataba'i was tuned more philosophically than politically. He did have a general and yet accurate perception of what the main challenge of his time was; indeed, he responded to that challenge forcefully. But it remained for Motahhari to translate, in his extensive footnotes and elsewhere, Tabataba'i's scholastic philosophical discourse into a language more immediately responsive to the political and ideological challenges of the time.

Allamah Tabataba'i, as his students have later testified,[165] was convinced that any meaningful confrontation with atheist ideas and materialist ideologies had to be launched from the standpoint of philosophy. Only in philosophy, he was convinced, could theist and atheist advocates find a common logical ground upon which to convince or convert each other. If the veracity of Islam were to be proven on rational, not dogmatic and doctrinal, grounds, then there was no reason to fear the influx of secular ideas.

As one of the principal figures involved in preparing *The Principles of Philosophy and the Realistic Method*, Sayyid Izzoddin Zanjani has later recalled that the efflorescence of Marxist and materialists ideas in Tehran colleges and universities had caused much concern among Tabataba'i's companions in Qom. When his students, including Morteza Motahhari, approached him and asked for a philosophical response to Marxism and materialism, he accepted and they all began by reading Muhammad Ali Foruqi's *Seyr-e Hekmat dar Orupa (The Course of Philosophy in Europe)*, a classic Persian source on the history of European philosophy. They wrote their respective summaries of this source, and Allamah Tabataba'i began to deliver his lectures on philosophical materialism. Initially they met every Thursday night at Zanjani's house; but later they rotated in different houses, discussing one lecture every Thursday.[166]

Tabataba'i and Motahhari

The Principles of Philosophy and the Realistic Method, as it was finally formed by Allamah Tabataba'i's text and Motahhari's extensive commentaries, fulfilled two principal objectives. As Tabataba'i composed the original text, it was addressed primarily to the seminary students in Qom. But the nature of this address was such that it spoke through a highly technical philosophical language. As such, it had a limited audience among the seminary students in Qom who, trained primarily in the juridical discourse, were not intellectually prepared to receive and comprehend this language. Philosophical discourse, by definition, has been an elitist preoccupation in the Islamic intellectual history. Juridical discourse, by contrast and by virtue of its doctrinal and political significance for the larger Muslim community, has had a wider and more pervasive currency. But the history of the philosophical and juridical discourse has not always been peaceful coexistence. More often, the juridical discourse has denied any legitimacy in the philosophical language, in fact accusing its exponents of blasphemous intentions. Such hostilities become particularly acute in a tensely religious city like Qom where grand juridical authorities rightly considered themselves as the besieged custodians of an embattled discourse. Thus we have the record of Grand Ayatollah Borujerdi's having emphatically opposed Allamah Tabataba'i's open teaching of philosophy in Qom.

In his response to Ayatollah Borujerdi, as we noted earlier, Tabataba'i is reported to have said that the young seminary students arrived in Qom "with a suitcase full of doubts." Yet in the actual delivery of his philosophical responses to Marxism and to historical materialism, he could only have distanced himself from the vast majority of such doubtful seminary students and from many others. This is not to minimize the significance of *The Principles of Philosophy and the Realistic Method* as the most serious intellectual challenge to Marxism and materialist philosophy within the Iranian context. But as an intellectual exercise, it had its inherent limitations in reaching a wide audience.

These limitations of Tabataba'i's philosophical discourse were compensated, to a large degree, by Motahhari's extensive unpacking of his thick text. If Tabataba'i's original text was directed at the philosophically musical seminary students in Qom, Motahhari's commentaries were directed principally at the secular intellectuals in Tehran. And while Tabataba'i's philosophical discourse was chiefly directed against historical and philosophical materialism, Motahhari's polemical language was targeted at Marxism and Leninism as the political expressions of the same phenomenon. Of course, in his commentaries Motahhari would clarify specific points of philosophical concern to his secular audience. But principally the function of Motahhari's extensive footnotes is to bridge a rather long and arduous distance between Qom and Tehran, one the seat of the Shi'i claim on continued doctrinal and historical validity, the other the emerging capital of radical, and equally secular, malcontent.

Allamah Tabataba'i and Henri Corbin

To cover the distance between Qom and Tehran, Allamah Tabataba'i gave considerable significance to his discussions with the French Islamicist Henri Corbin, intermediated by S. H. Nasr, Daryush Shaygan, and others. According to his students, Allamah Tabataba'i would travel from Qom to Tehran with "grave difficulties . . . and with regular buses"[167] to meet Corbin and have his regular conversations with him. Corbin himself had gradually been drawn to Shi'ism beyond the call of an Islamicist. Short of conversion to Shi'ism, he reached a level of affiliation and discourse in his writings on Shi'ism that would put him at odds with his bona fide Orientalist colleagues.

Allamah Tabataba'i's acquaintance with Henri Corbin began in 1958 and continued for some twenty years.[168] The former was particularly impressed by the latter's devotion to understanding Shi'ism and, of course, by his putative assertion that "Shi'ism is the only religion among all other world religions which is an active and alive faith. All other religions, without exception, have passed their time and have no active and progressive condition."[169] Their conversations were subsequently collected and published in Persian, Arabic, French, and English.[170]

Tabataba'i's Audience

These translations and their originals began to create a reading public that would give political significance to the Allamah's ideas. Among his reading public Tabataba'i found a small but proportionately significant constituency for his mystico-philosophical reading of Shi'ism. This constituency consisted of urban intellectuals of a particular religious disposition who would normally know a foreign language and be acquainted with aspects of "The Western and Eastern" philosophies. His book on Shi'i Islam, which was first published in English through the efforts of S. H. Nasr, was subsequently rerendered into Persian from English. This translation would even include the English introduction of S. H. Nasr which was specifically addressed to "The Western audiences."[171]

Legitimacy and Authority

As Allamah Tabataba'i commuted back and forth between Tehran and Qom, and as certain Tehran-based intellectuals began to establish links between the minutiae of "The Western and The Eastern" philosophy and mysticism, more politically charged currents were flowing. One of the few authorities asked to address the question of supreme religious position after the death of Ayatollah Borujerdi was Allamah Tabataba'i. His contribution to the volume that was published on this occasion is quite revealing of his particular disposition. In fact, in his short piece on the legitimate authority of the ulama', Tabataba'i came closest to the actual and stated agenda of the Islamic Revolution. The timing of this piece, early in the 1960s, clearly testifies that long before the actual unfolding of the Islamic movement, Tabataba'i had articulated the specifics of an "Islamic government." His students, again, are quick to point out the claim that the Allamah thus has on the Revolution.[172]

Supreme Religious Authority

When, upon the death of Ayatollah Borujerdi early in 1961, the entire question of supreme religious authority was being reconsidered,[173] Allamah Tabataba'i provided a general overview of this central question in Shi'i political history. In Shi'ism, as in Islam in general, Tabataba'i considered the centrality of certain codes of religious conduct as quintessential.[174] These codes of conduct ought to be extrapolated *(estenbat)* from the canonical textual sources, that is, from the Qur'an and the prophetic and Imami traditions. Thus *ejtehad*, or expressing an expert opinion on a matter of religious concern, was defined as "obtaining [a] religious edict *(hokm-e Shar'i)* from the canonical sources through theoretical and rational [arguments]."[175] Because not every Muslim is capable of extracting such rules of conduct from the canonical sources, it is necessary for them to follow the exemplary conduct of a qualified religious authority. This necessity, Tabataba'i stipulates, gives rise to the complementary concept of *ejtehad*, which is *taqlid*, or "imitating the exemplary conduct of a religious authority."[176] This dichotomous oscillation between *ejtehad* and *taqlid* is an expression of the human nature that needs to initiate and follow at the same time. Thus Tabataba'i provides a rational, or what he calls inherently natural, explication of the necessity of *taqlid*. He emphasizes that every individual, Muslim or not, exercises independent judgment, or *ejtehad*, in a minor aspect of his own life and then follows the exemplary conduct of figures of authority, *taqlid*, in most other respects.

Velayat *and* Ze'amat

By virtue of living a social life, man is limited in his freedom of action.[177] As a social being, man oscillates between a public and a private pursuit. To guarantee its continuity, society needs certain supraindividual laws and regulations. Very much on the model of Thomas Hobbs, but without knowing so, Allamah Tabataba'i then postulates the necessity of having a supreme figure of authority whose "intellect and will" are superior to others.[178] By way of comparison, as a child needs a parent, and an orphan a protector, so does a people need a "king or a president":[179]

This status which entitles a person or a position to take charge of others, managing their worldly affairs, . . . we shall call *Velayat*. ([This Arabic term] has a meaning which in Persian we understand from *sarparasti* ["guardianship"]).[180]

Tabataba'i emphasized that he wished to address the question of *velayat*, or supreme political authority thus understood, from a social-philosophical, not a juridical, point of view.[181] Thus understood, *velayat* is innately natural to every human society. Essentially attentive to human nature,

Islam has stipulated the specifics of designating the supreme figure of authority in the Muslim community. The manner of human government thus designated ought to be compatible with the general pattern that governs creation at large and the specific nature that governs man's creation.[182] This has to be a stable and permanent pattern of conduct, leading man to continue to be constitutionally compatible with his environment. Should that compatibility be disturbed, Allamah Tabataba'i argues through various Qur'anic passages, man may very well be destroyed by the very nature of those rules and rhythms he has to recognize and honor.[183]

Velayat, that is, the necessity of providing a society with protective leadership *(sarparasti),* is natural to the human condition, and thus Islam attends to it. The question of the natural necessity of a government is so obvious that no one during the life of Prophet Muhammad even raised the question of whether it was necessary. Its necessity was strongly implied in the very acts of the Prophet and in the Muslims' immediately getting together after his death and seeking to find his successor. Relying on specific Qur'anic passages, Tabataba'i argues for the immutability and timeless validity of the very notion of the Islamic government.[184] "The relation of the position of *velayat* and Islamic government to the religious organization and the Islamic society," he emphasized, "is the same as the relation of the head of a family . . . to the familial organization and members of his household."[185]

There are two sets of laws that this political leader of the Islamic community ought to uphold: the immutables and the changeables. The Qur'anic and prophetic laws are immutable and permanently valid. Based upon this, however, the leader of a Muslim community can extrapolate certain other laws that are equally binding but always changeable and subject to historical progress. Tabataba'i takes issue with those (historical materialists) who argue that societies change and so must the rules and regulations governing them. There are secondary laws, issued by political authorities, that are subject to change. But the very necessity of political leadership for the Islamic community itself is an immutable law.[186]

Against Democracy and Socialism

Tabataba'i proceeds to argue that although there are similarities between the Islamic frame of political reference and democratic principles (because in democracies, too, established constitutional laws and other changeable regulations exist), Islam should not be totally identified with democracy or socialism.[187] The principal difference here is the fact that in Islam laws are established by God, while in other social systems they are created through collective consent.[188] But even in minor and secondary laws, Islam differs from democracy: In democracies the will of the majority rules, whereas in

Islam rules are based on "truth, not the will of the majority."[189] Tabataba'i further emphasized that

In the Islamic society the truth and the real good of Islam and Muslims ought to be done, whether or not they comply with the will of the majority. Of course, in that society of knowledge and virtuosity that Islam educates, the majority would never prefer its whimsical wishes over truth and veracity.[190]

Tabataba'i then sought to fortify, much to the delight of the Muslim activists, this assertion against the unconditional supremacy of "Western democracy" by the failure of such imported notions of government to establish any measure of political prosperity:

It is more than half a century [Tabataba'i said this in 1962] now since we have accepted a democratic government and constitution and thus been considered on a par with the civilized Western nations. [Yet] we can visibly observe how our situation has persistently deteriorated and worsened. From this tree, which for others has been fruitful and bounteous, we do not pick but the fruits of misery and shame.[191]

Tabataba'i immediately adds that the reason for such misery is that the Iranian government does not actually behave on democratic principles but simply pretends to do so. Then he turns the question around and rhetorically asks why is it when they, the high-ranking clerics, say Islam is not being actually practiced they are objected to, but when they admit democracy is not being actually implemented everybody agrees? Thus he suggests that should "true Islam" actually be practiced, it would be equally good, nay indeed better, for the immediate and ultimate prosperity and salvation of the country.

To consolidate further his logical objection to the universal validity and appeal of democracy, Tabataba'i asks, again rhetorically, that if democracy is indeed such a globally legitimate mode of government, why is it that after the First World War many democratic nations turned to Communism?[192] Democracy at best, he contends, has transformed the dictatorship of one individual into the dictatorship of a majority. For him there is no difference between individual and collective despotism:

The tyrannies, transgressions, and arrogance of Alexanders and ghingizes which in the past they perpetrated by force, nowadays the powerful and civilized democracies of the world collectively impose on the weaker nations. . . . Still many instructive scenes from the colonial period are visible in every corner of Eastern countries. These are telling examples of democracy. Still living examples like Algeria, Congo, and Korea are present. Still the logic of the French government (the standard-bearer of freedom in the international parade of justice) is that it considers Algeria its own territory, and [yet] still the logic of the exalted [French] government vis-à-vis the call for justice of the oppressed Algerian is that those are internal problems [of Algeria] and outside the jurisdiction of their power. Still. . . .[193]

Tabataba'i issues a sweeping condemnation against democratic nations. He divides the world into "Western democracies" which rule the rest of the world without any moral reservation, and the "backward democracies," which are the "marked slaves" of the first group.[194] No such system, he contends, especially since it abandons moral mandates (on the pretense that they cannot be legally demanded), can provide a model for the "perfection of humanity."[195]

Communism has no stronger claim to leading humanity to political prosperity. Assuming, as Marxists do, Communism to be the advanced stage of human societies, although the most rudimentary levels have not yet been achieved, is utterly illogical.[196] Reaching for Communism in "backward and even barbaric nations"[197] is incompatible with even the logic Marxism assumes for social progress. Thus, in Iran, among other nations caught up in the illusion of misguided Communism, this ideology has appealed principally to the oppressed people who wish for revenge against the wealthy, without any regard for what happens in the future.

Legitimate Authority

Democracy and Socialism are illusions with which the modern world is afflicted. For Muslim societies in particular, Islam is the answer. Through the organic intermediary of *velayat,* or supreme political authority religiously sanctified, Muslims ought to regulate their political system. Although rules and regulations issued through *velayat* do not have the status of *Shari'ah,* the position itself is religiously mandated by both Qur'anic passages and prophetic practice. The necessity of the Islamic government is so natural and congenial to Islamic doctrines that Tabataba'i asks, rhetorically, how is it possible for a religion to be attentive to the minutiae of daily life and yet leave mute the question of government, "which is the only soul through which a society is alive"?[198] He objects to those Qur'anic commentators who take the key term of *velayat* to mean "friendship" and "support" and insists that all references such as those in the "authority verse"[199] refer to the necessity of the Islamic government. Thus he concludes that *"velayat* is one of the articles of the *Shari'ah* which, like other articles of religious law, has to be permanently operative in the Islamic society."[200]

Tabataba'i considers "the multitude of Muslims," that is, all the Muslims, the active agent responsible for designating who is to occupy this highest political position in an Islamic society. But based upon this initial stipulation, he poses the essential question of who is to assume the supreme political position in the Islamic community. After the Prophet's exemplary leadership, he stipulates, the Shi'is believe that the position of *velayat* has belonged historically to the twelve successive Shi'i Imams. In the absence of

the Twelfth Imam, who is in occultation, Shi'is are not to be left without
Islamic leadership. Among other responsibilities, there are the specifics of
Islamic law that need to be implemented. And they need to be fulfilled by
the Islamic leader occupying the position of *velayat*. Tabataba'i stops short
of actually nominating the *faqih*, or the religious scholar, as the obvious
choice to occupy this position of political authority in the absence of the
Twelfth (Hidden) Imam. He does say that to occupy this position the
person must be learned in Islamic sciences and also pious. Yet he leaves the
question at the following level:

[Does *velayat*] belong to any *faqih*, who, in the case of multiplicity and having more
than one [qualified *faqih*], would have power and influence in proportion to his
[juridical] authority? Or does it [that is, *velayat*] belong to the most learned *faqih*?
These are questions outside the purview of our present discussion, and they ought
to be addressed through the juridical discourse.[201]

Given the tone and substance of this language, Tabataba'i leaves no question that, indeed, he advocates the *velayat-e faqih* (or the juridical claim of
the religious scholar to political authority). This remarkable claim was
made in Qom almost a decade before Ayatollah Khomeini's famous tract
on Islamic government, composed in 1971 in Najaf, was executed more or
less on a similar line of argument.[202]

By stipulating the religious and pious qualifications of this supreme
political figure, Tabataba'i leaves no doubt that he considers the high-
ranking clerics as the essential and natural choice for this position. As he
recognizes no temporal limitations to the applicability and necessity of the
Islamic government, he knows of no specific geographical boundary for its
ultimate implementation in past, present, and future history: "The boundaries of the Islamic society are belief and nothing but belief. [They are]
neither natural nor conventional barriers."[203]

The principal model upon which the supreme Islamic political authority,
or *velayat*, ought to be fashioned is the exemplary leadership of Prophet
Muhammad in early Islamic history. Numerous Qur'anic passages testify
that the exemplary prophetic conduct in leadership was graced and sanctified by Divine approval. No Islamic mode of government can thus ignore
the political mores sanctified through the actual and the putative conduct
of Prophet Muhammad.[204]

Tabataba'i does not elaborate on what precisely constitutes the specifics
of prophetic conduct in political practice. But he does indicate that it
negates any mode of "class privileges,"[205] and that the only criterion of
distinction in Islam is religious piety:

The different social classes, such as the employer and the employee, the master and
the servant, the owner and the worker, the man and the woman are all equal to

each other, and there is no preference of one over the other. It is only God whose greatness ought to be unconditionally obeyed and respected.[206]

All people are equal in the judgment of Islamic law. The secondary Islamic laws, that is, those that are extended by the authority of *velayat* from the primary doctrines of the *Shari'ah*, are to be extrapolated through the process of consultation *(Shura')*.

The Tabataba'i Link

Allamah Tabataba'i's position on the question of supreme political and religious authority makes it abundantly clear that as early as 1962 he provided a thorough justification of "the Islamic government" led by the clerical class. But, perhaps even more important, the philosophical foundation of "the Islamic Ideology" was formed as the immediate consequence of a genuine concern with the massive and forceful influx of philosophical materialism. Marxism, however crude and clumsy in its Iranian articulation, acted as a potent catalyst, sharpening the edge of the Muslim intellectual response. Allamah Tabataba'i met the challenge of this grave ideological imposition with the best that Islamic intellectual history could afford. Signalled by Al-e Ahmad, rhetorically activated by Shari'ati, doctrinally envigorated by Motahhari, and Qur'anically fortified by Taleqani, "the Islamic Ideology," the collectively reconstructed sensibilities of an injured ("Islamic") Self responding actively to the dominant ("Western") Other, received its strongest philosophical support from Allamah Tabataba'i. A more pious, and less intellectually elitist, ingredient was to be added by "Engineer Bazargan" before Bani-Sadr could add an economic veracity to it—and this all as a prerequisite for the revolutionary call of Ayatollah Khomeini to have its choral background.

"At the Same Time . . ."

"Being both German and economist at the same time, we desire to protest against this double error."[207] The "double error," as Marx constructed it, was the German assumption that Proudhon was a bad philosopher and a good economist and the French assumption that he was a good philosopher and a bad economist. "The reader will understand," Marx excused himself, "that in this thankless task we have often had to abandon our criticism of M. Proudhon in order to criticize German philosophy, and at the same time to give some observations on political economy." "German and economist" was Marx's critical realm of inquiry upon which he, the stateless intellectual, delivered his deliberate revolutionary discourse, the paradox of escaping from two concurrent stereotypes. An expositional, analytical, and interpretative discourse has no such critical, no such revolutionary, claims. German philosophy and French political economy converged in Marx's critical theory, which responds positively to the revolutionary conditions of his time. Revolutionary conditions demand revolutionary responses, critical, perhaps even unsuitable, formulations of a discourse that defies the rhyme and logic of the received levels of interpretations. Beyond the mandates of the sacred and indubitable tradition, so called always by those who are on the verge of redefining it, political exegencies of the time have a revolutionary appeal of their own. Deeply as a philosopher, a jurist, or a theologian might be engaged in the demanding confinements of his received logic of interpretation, the temptation to "make it new" [208] is always there. Once released, there is no controlling the intended or unintended consequences of one's adventures in revolutionary interpretation, the terra incognita in which grows the modernity of every truth. There is always that all-too-essential distance, there to be covered by the intensity of an imagination, between the intended text and its interpreted implications beyond any meaningful measure of control. But in history, as in any other social and political construction of reality, only the limited or extended domains of reinterpretation matter. We may have the most private of all concerns in the solitude of our texts today. Tomorrow, they might well be trumpeted into the loudest of all public claims. Who is in charge? Who is to say? Who is the arbiter? History, or the political construction of truth, is a collective myth. It knows no individual—philosopher or economist, philosopher or ideologue.

CHAPTER 6

Mehdi Bazargan: The Devout Engineer

"Tzu-Kung asked about government."[1] This is how Confucius used to pontificate. The parable is everything. "The Master said: 'Enough food, enough weapons, and the confidence of the people.' " Even Marx would agree. Weber too. The economic bases of legitimacy, then the ideological and state built up. Weber would call it "external means" (enough weapons), and "inner Justification" (food for and confidence of the people). But Confucius' progressive dialectics unfolds. "Tzu-Kung said: 'Suppose you definitely had no alternative but to give up one of these three, which would you relinquish first?' The Master said: 'Weapons.' " Clausewitz would disagree, but still the state would be prosperous and legitimate. Yet, the ultimate twist is to come. "Tzu-Kung said: 'Suppose you definitely had no alternative but to give up one of the remaining two, which would you relinquish first?' The Master said: 'Food. From of old death has come to all men, but a people without confidence in its rulers will not stand.' "[2] The cruelty of the Confucian wisdom only reveals the supreme law of politics: legitimacy. Beyond that there is the last wisdom. The endurance of the collective confidence is much more urgent in the survival of a people than having its individuals fed. The confidence between the leader and the led is the supreme political covenant, the trust in which draws from the most sacred pool of common symbolics. Institutions and figures of authority sustain their legitimacy or lose their political truth in proportion to their approximation to or distance from that sacred pool. An old countenance, a kind frequency in voice, perhaps a beard, a pair of glasses, a certain kind of glance, one or two benign jokes: legitimacy always needs to work through the visible and audible conversation of gestures. Who commands the gestures? Where does the conversation lead? Interpreting the symbols, received and reconstituted, is everything.

A Muslim Goes to Paris

Medhi Bazargan (b. 1907) was born in Tehran. His family, originally from Azarbaijan, had moved to Tehran with a wave of other provincials who were increasingly attracted to the capital. His father, Hajj Abbas Qoli Tabrizi, was a devout religious activist who was the head of the Azarbaijani mosque and the community in Tehran. Medhi Bazargan was raised under the immediate care of a father whose senses of religiosity were assaulted by a towering dictator who bypassed everybody's Islamicity to connect a refictionalized version of the "Ancient Persia" to a utopian notion of "the modern Iran."

In 1928, Bazargan was among the first group of Iranian students whom Reza Shah sent to Europe. In addition to learning from the technological manuals, Reza Shah had intended for these students to bring back a proper dosage of the "patriotism" he had detected among the Europeans. Bazargan would later remember Reza Shah having received these students in his palace prior to their departure for France.

You are undoutedly wondering [why] we are sending you to a country whose religion is different from ours. It is a free republic. Yet they are nationalists. You will bring back nationalism, arts, and sciences to Iran.[3]

During the 1920s, as Reza Khan styled himself Reza Shah, the order of the day was "modernization": to orchestrate a massive and thorough reconstitution of the Iranian society—signs, symbols, and ceremonies—so that it would look more like the old tyrant's mental image of "The West." In manners and matters, inseparable in their command, Reza Shah wished to have things European transplanted to Iranian soil. The Turkish experience of Mustafa Kemal was particularly attractive to the Iranian monarch. To change the Iranian manner, he passed a law to have his subjects—men, women, and children—change their outer decorum, trade their turbans for châpeaux, their scarves for hats, their beards for ties, their longer *chadors* for shorter skirts, their grey yesterdays for their colorful tomorrows. This was the law: government down to the wardrobe. To change the Iranian matter, to transubstantiate the very stuff that makes an Iranian, he sought to transplant "The Western" age of technology to Iranian soil. Bazargan was among the emissaries of transmutation who were sent to Europe to facilitate the monarch's wishes.

Students such as Bazargan were taken from (deeply) religious families. Their success was due more to their diligent ethical conduct than to a free-spirited encounter with matters educational: more a disciplined manner than a free-floating spirit. Upon his arrival in Europe, Bazargan is reported to have had a cautious attitude as to exactly what they could achieve. "If in this educational trip," he is reported to have stipulated, "we do not gain anything, we should at least not forfeit our previous capital, [that is,] our religion and our ethics."[4] Although deeply attracted to European and American achievements in technology and although undoubtedly optimistic about their ability to translate this technology into operative forces in their homeland, by disposition this group of religiously musical students was cautious in safeguarding their faith, what they were assured of, in the face of an unknown entity they termed "The Western Technology." The composition of this group, however, should not be assumed to be sternly dogmatic. A fellow student told Bazargan about a friend who had envied their going to a country where beautiful girls could be seen walking the streets without any veil.[5]

Bazargan spent seven years in France, from 1928 to 1935, where he received his degree in engineering. In France, and while he pursued his engineering courses, he underwent what was most common among such religiously alert students who were distanced from their origins for a long period of time. He began to develop a fresh attitude towards, a new interpretative bent on, his faith. This is precisely what would happen a few decades later to Shari‘ati. Beginning with the conscious or unconscious, articulated or mute, premise that they ought to remain firmly attached to their Islamic consciousness, they begin to admire "The Western" achievements in arts and sciences—more the sciences, in their collective experiences, than the arts. They ask themselves, consciously or unconsciously, systematically or haphazardly, questions pertaining to the causes and effects of such achievements. They recognize a heightened state of ideological self-awareness on the part of "The West" that they identify as the source and cause of its achievements. They then look back at their own society where such technological achievements were lacking, a fact they attribute, in turn, to the absence of that heightened state of ideological self-awareness. At this stage they invariably develop a dual conception of their faith. They have no doubt that their faith, Islam, had to function as the medium of their heightened state of ideological self-awareness. In this instance, Islam itself is the root of the conviction. As a universal claim to truth, among other such universal claims, Islam cannot be set aside as a metaphysical matter between man and his Creator. Everything, every change and every continuity, ought to be in the context and in terms of some understanding of Islam. Consequently, one could not, being in Bazargan's position, formulate or adopt an acceptable answer to that state of heightened ideological self-understanding without a necessary and altogether inevitable recourse to Islam. At this stage they inevitably confront the historical Islam—Islam as it has been received and practiced in their immediate community of believers, in the neighborhood of their childhood, in the streets of their youth. At this point, where ideals and realities collide,

Bazargan, like most other transplanted Muslim intelligentsia, develops a dual conception of Islam: Islam as it exists now, which he considers backward and superstitious, and contrary to that there is "The True Islam," which he imagines as socially active and politically progressive.[6]

The Engineer Comes Home

"Active" and "progressive" was thus the collective image of "The True Islam" that Bazargan sought to propagate upon his return from France in 1935, at the height of Reza Shah's dictatorial reign. What welcomes Bazargan when he returns to his homeland is the establishment of the Tehran University (in 1934), where he taught for many years; the construction of the trans-Iranian railway, on which he took frequent trips to southern Iran; and the mandatory unveiling of Iranian women (in 1935), which he could only have opposed. The death of Ayatollah Shaykh Abdolkarim Ha'eri in 1933, while Bazargan was in France, and the gradual ascendancy of Ayatollah Borujerdi as the chief Shi'i jurist commenced several decades of official apolitical leadership in the religious establishment, thus giving Bazargan further leverage in his (lay) brand of Islamic activism.

Upon his arrival in Iran, Bazargan was conscripted, from 1935 to 1937, to perform his military services. When Reza Shah came to power in 1925, Iran lacked what can be properly called a standing army; there were only scattered regiments of Cossacks under the control of foreign mercenaries. Reza Shah was instrumental in creating a modern military service divided into an army, navy, and air force. The security of the villages and small towns was also entrusted to the gendarmerie. Military service became mandatory, and every capable Iranian male had to serve two years in the army.

When he completed his military service, Bazargan began teaching at the School of Engineering at Tehran University, while establishing a private company to earn a living independent of his governmental post. The establishment of Tehran University in 1934 was a remarkable achievement in modern Iranian history with grave consequences not only in education but also in social and political developments. Instrumental in making this historical achievement possible were four eminent Iranian statesmen and academicians: Mohammad Ali Foruqi, Qolam Hossein Rahnema, Isa Sadiq, and Ali Akbar Siasi. Ali Akbar Siasi was one of the first Iranians to receive a doctorate from the Sorbonne in 1931. When he defended his thesis in Paris, the event was so remarkable that the Iranian ambassador to France, Hossein Ala', attended. Siasi's dissertation, *La Perse au Contact de l'Occident*, received widespread recognition in the French and English press, and he was honored by a special award from the French Academy. When he returned to Iran in 1931, news of his remarkable academic achievement preceded him through a dispatch from Hossein Ala'. Ali Asghar Hekmat, the Minister of Education under Reza Shah at the time, summoned Siasi and informed him that "on the auspicious occasion of this victory, I have asked His Majesty [Reza Shah] to permit us to establish a university in Tehran."[7] Hekmat convinced Siasi to take charge of establishing the university. On 4 February 1935, Parliament ratified the bill for the establishment of Tehran University. Some eight years later, on 4 February 1943, Siasi was again equally instrumental in giving Tehran University autonomy from the Ministry of Education.[8] When Bazargan finished his military services and began teaching at the Engineering School at Tehran University in 1937, he had good reason to be grateful to Ali Akbar Siasi, a fellow Iranian student he might very well have known in Paris. His teaching position would put him in touch with the most ideologically alert segment of the political community. He would come to know the latest and most compelling ideological forces that found their way into the Iranian youthful imagination. He would gain a great deal of experience from these formative years as he continued to fortify his Islamic convictions and sentiments and as he witnessed interest in the Marxist ideology growing among the youth on his campus.

In 1940, Bazargan became involved in the maintenance of a great national building, Bank Melli, where his engineering virtuosity was admired by the young Muslims working for him. Encouraged by the responses he received from young Muslims, Bazargan began contributing articles to *Danesh-amuz,* the journal that Sayyid Mahmud Taleqani published from the institute he had established, *Kanun-e Islam,* at Hedayat Mosque. His first article was called "Religion in Europe." With its publication, he began his lifelong collaboration with Ayatollah Taleqani which had an interesting background because it began a generation earlier with their fathers. The elder Bazargan, Hajj Abbas Qoli, and Taleqani's father, Sayyid Abolhasan, collaborated in the 1920s to establish an Islamic institute headquartered in Bazargan's residence. Founded in 1924, this religious organization was meant to proselytize Islam among members of other faiths. The elder Bazargan and Taleqani published a journal too, called *Balagh.*

A Rationalized Mind at Work

In 1945, Bazargan published the revised version of a speech he had delivered at Taleqani's *Kanun-e Islam. Motahharat Dar Islam (Purities in Islam)* was Bazargan's first contribution toward the pseudoscientific rationalization of the Islamic juridical injunctions. These injunctions, derived primarily from the Qur'an and the traditions of the Prophet and the Shi'i Imams, historically had been obeyed or disobeyed not because they conformed to (or deviated from) any set of given scientific validation, but because they were the juridical mandates of a religious state of mind, ranging from hygienic regulations to ritualistic prayers, that were established parameters of identifying with the social manifestations of a sacred order. Taking them, instead, for practical verifications of a pseudoscientific view of the physical world, Bazargan sought to "prove" them scientifically viable. This endeavor, persistent with Bazargan, was symptomatic of a deeper problem. The technological advances made in "The West" were seen as predicated on a scientific worldview, something lacking in Islamic modernity. During his student years in France, Bazargan had come to acknowledge that scientific spirit as the condito sine qua non of the technological age. Consequently, if Islam were to instill such a scientific spirit in its believers, then its own binding commandments had to be proven scientifically. Thus the ritualistic aspects of the faith began to be rationalized scientifically. The language of this pseudoscientific verification of the ritualistic dimensions of the faith was directed towards young Muslim students who shared Bazargan's two essential concerns: (1) conforming to the scientific discourse of the mid-twentieth century and (2) validating the veracity of Islam by demonstrating its compatibility with this pseudoscientific discourse.

Totally oblivious to the fundamental distinction between a credal discourse, that of the Islamic juridical language, and a scientific semantic, Bazargan sought to validate the old faith through the modern lingo. That the very act would level the Shi'i juridical discourse, and with it the universal claim of Islam to truth, with a particular phase in paradigmatic changes in modern scientific discourse did not cross Bazargan's mind, nor could he be alert, given his historical exegencies, to such crucial issues. He had simply been fascinated by the modern scientific magic he had witnessed in France. In all sincerity he sought to vindicate his faith through his thermodynamic engineering. The result of this misplaced piety was the publication of *Purities in Islam* in which he tried to demonstrate that the Islamic rules and regulations concerning bodily and ritualistic hygiene conformed to biochemical and mathematical formulae. This staunch commitment to validate Islam with "scientific" accuracy would remain Bazargan's chief characteristic and principal contribution to the making of "the Islamic Ideology." To recruit the active royalties of as many diverse social groupings as possible, this ideology had to have a comprehensive agenda and a universal appeal. Bazargan's pseudoscientific verification of the faith appealed to a particular segment of this political constituency and thus further propagated the political domains of "the Islamic Ideology."

Islam or Communism

The active annunciation of "the Islamic Ideology" was always in need of institutional advancement. The Muslim Students Association was one of the most serious and dedicated organizations that was actively involved, at least from the late 1940s, in propagating various aspects of the emerging "Islamic Ideology." In 1952, in the heat of the nationalization of oil movement, led by Mohammad Mosaddeq, the Muslim Student Association invited Bazargan to deliver a series of three lectures—"God-Worshipping and Self-Worshipping," "Islam or Communism," and "Eschatology"— which were subsequently collected, edited, and published in 1953, the year of the CIA-sponsored coup against Mosaddeq. In these lectures, Bazargan wishes to argue that worshipping God is in the nature of human experience[9] and has been man's way of opposing his worshipping himself. Self-worship, even when projected and expressed in idolatry, could only have prevented man from historical growth. The gradual formulation of aggregate and complex human societies has been the result of man's God-worshipping tendencies. Science and civilization, prosperity and democracy, are all by-products of man's religious institutions. If today's man witnesses the decline of civilization it is precisely because his God-worshipping tendencies have been dulled by materialism. Modern man thinks, according to Bazargan, that such terms as "honor, patriotism, country, fellow man, ideology, etc." can substitute for religion, but he is wrong. "Man is either a God-worshipper or a self-worshipper."[10]

To the hypothetical question "Can man resign from God-worshipping?" Bazargan answers in the negative by arguing that we cannot lead an ethical life based solely on our conscience. Very soon, he argues, our conscience (independent of a metaphysics) would be countered by our growing rationality.

The higher [our rational] understanding and [sense of] distinction goes up, the weaker will become [our] sentiments and attributes which are based on conscience. Rationality, logic, intelligence, and science will substitute emotion, habit, sentiments, and ethics.[11]

Communism, in Bazargan's perception, is precisely the end result of severe "self-worshipping" or individualism. If one thinks, as Bazargan believes a communist does, that everyone has done him wrong, and they do so because they are rich and powerful, then private property has to be eliminated.[12] He further explains to his young Muslim students that "the expression of dialectical materialism, or [other] philosophical issues and concepts, that are said about the Communist ideology are miscellania that function as the make-up of a bride."[13] With the foundation of ethics on conscience rather than on religion, in Europe the appearance of Communism has been inevitable.

Islam and Communism have quite a number of similarities. "But this similarity," Bazargan stipulates, is like the encounter of two travellers who are travelling in two diametrically opposed directions, one going up, the other going down. Both ideologies *(maslak)* see individuals in perfect equality. But one [Communism] sees them equal in worthlessness and lack of character, and the other [Islam] considers all people creations of one God, holding them in honor like brothers.[14]

While Islam elevates man to the presence of God, Communism lowers him to the miserable existence of a short life on this earth. No higher aspiration is left for those who live under a Communist regime. A Communist society is an aggregate of selfish people.

If you sit next to a selfish person on a bus, you know how much trouble you have. Now imagine if the whole world was full of selfish people. Then what? What a stinking hatred?! What an awesome horror?! What trickery and tyranny?! . . . In short, what a hell!?[15]

Absolute dictatorship is the ultimate end of Communism.[16] "On one side a world of people; on the other side just one person! What servitude?! What baseness?!"[17] If there is equality in Communism it is the equality of jack-asses. The scheme that Communism promises for humanity is "an absolute animal society."[18] The Soviet Union and Eastern Europe were, for many decades, living examples of such conditions.[19]

    The only salvation that exists for humanity, thus threatened by Communism, is a return. Man's return from selfishness to God-worshipping is the only way out of this horrid impasse Communism has offered humanity.[20] To survive, man "has to choose one of the monotheistic religions. [One has to] choose a religion that defeats selfishness in the last barrack of Communism, in the arm of materialism."[21] Among the monotheist religions, Zoroastrianism is obsolete, Judaism has bred materialism, and Christianity is dictated by its church. Islam is the only way out.[22] But which Islam? Not the Islam of Saudi Arabia.[23] But a new, "true," Islam.

The Coup of 1953

Until 1953, Bazargan's political activities were limited to a passive and tacit contribution to the dormant making of "the Islamic Ideology." His deep and faithful friendship with Taleqani would sow the seeds of still deeper and more persuasive political collaborations in the future. Around Bazargan and Taleqani, and centered in *Kanun-e Islam,* would gradually emerge a growing constituency of young followers who would later be instrumental in active political engagements. During the post-1953 period, when the CIA-engineered coup put Mohammad Reza Shah back in power and helped him to establish a brutally repressive regime, Bazargan assumed an increasingly active political role. With a sense of humor distinctively his own, he explained his political activities during this period as follows:

[When] the people in position of responsibility . . . did not perform their duties, nay, they did precisely the opposite of their duties, being all thieves and treacherous, then everyone becomes a Jack of all trades. The university professor too turns into a political rabble-rouser.[24]

Because of his political activities during the postcoup d'état period, Bazargan was arrested and swiftly incarcerated in 1955. While in prison, he wrote a number of books on various aspects of the Islamic faith and their relevance to modern life.

The Thermodynamics of Mehdi Bazargan

In 1956 Bazargan published a book with a rather peculiar title, *Love and Worship: Man's Thermodynamics,* in which he wished to tie together three apparently irrelevant issues: "love," as in the relationship between two human beings, "worship" as in the relationship between man and God, and "thermodynamics." Like almost all the other ideologues of "the Islamic Ideology," Bazargan apologizes to his readers for not having had time to attend to these matters in detail and with accuracy.[25] Confessing that he has personally never been in love or in any other way experienced this emotion,[26] he goes on to theorize about love as a sensation that attracts individuals to objects of satisfaction that stand outside themselves. He wishes to universalize that object from a person to a concept.[27] The same observation is "proven" through a thermodynamic discussion, all with charts and formulae,[28] to reach the conclusion that "the human being has been made to be always in need [of something] and should always remain that way."[29] In order to achieve his objects of desire, material or spiritual, the individual must spend the energy, in thermodynamic terms, that is invested in him.[30] This energy expenditure is regulated internally by such factors as physical activity, sickness, memory, sleep, years of heightened activities, and ultimately death.[31] The same thermodynamic principles are equally applicable to a society and its various organs, particularly its economy.[32] More important, ethics and metaphysics are equally governed by the laws of thermodynamics.

The finale of this book occurs in the last chapter, where Bazargan introduces the question of "worship" and provides a short history of socialism as a social and economic design to regulate man's thermodynamic energies, with a purposeful direction, based on justice and equality. But ultimately, in his judgment, socialism has failed[33] to fulfill man's needs. Returning to the notion of "love," he argues that in the absence of any human-made design to systematize man's thermodynamic functions, it is in man's nature to search for a deeper and more permanent mode of "love," one that gives meaning to life. Here Bazargan believes that man has traversed a historical path of growth through which he has realized higher and more noble stages of "love," leading him, in the process, to the more perfect style of worship.[34] In the passage from all mundane forms of "love" to the highest stage of "obedience," he recognizes no motto more noble than Imam Hossein's assertion that "verily, life is conviction and struggle."[35] This motto leads to the realization of the highest stage of "love":

Thus [man] searches for the Beloved. What kind of Beloved? . . . A Beloved that is worthy of his growth, with His entrance so high and His court so vast that would occupy his services day and night, accepting him in "servitude."[36]

That Beloved is God and the prophets are emissaries who lead obediently to His court.[37]

In another book, *Angizah va Angizandah (Motivation and One Who Motivates)*, Bazargan further develops this idea of "love" as the overriding sentiment that has governed the relationship between Muhammad and God.[38] Discounting the view of "The Western" Orientalists that Muhammad was a social reformer, he argues, by statistically "proving that 97.7 percent of the Qur'anic verses center around God,"[39] that nothing other than mere obedience and love had moved the Prophet to serve his Lord.

Thus, tacitly but emphatically opposing the secular accusation that Islam is a violent faith forcefully imposed on Iranians, Bazargan sought to designate "love" at the center of his faith. But this particular mode of love, contrary to that of Christianity, was life-affirming, and its energy ought to be channelled towards the social and economic production of material life. Bazargan argues this fully armed with his thermodynamic charts and formulae, giving the new reading of the faith a "scientific" validity.

Religion: Conscience Collective

The "scientific" validity was to update Islam to meet the challenge of modernity. In the face of the increasing secularization and technicalization of the larger society, Bazargan wished to remake a religious collective consciousness actively present at the most politically relevant social levels. In a series of two lectures he delivered on 26 and 27 January 1960, on the occasion of the anniversary of the commencement of Prophet Muhammad's mission as the Last Divine Messenger, he reminded his audience of the crucial validity of such religious celebrations in bringing them together. Delivered to the Association of Muslim Engineers and the Muslim Student Association, the sites of these two lectures demonstrate the variety and multiplicity of institutional centers where revolutionary religious discourse found its audience. The "character" and "national identity" of Muslims,

Bazargan argued,[40] depended on such regular celebrations as that of the commencement of the the Prophet's Divine mission. Participation in such collective celebrations brings together "the engineer, the physician, the teacher, the student, the merchant, the worker, the cleric, the army officer; the old and the young, the literate and the illiterate."[41]

One crucial feature of this collective consciousness that Bazargan wants to establish and propagate among his audience is that the ceaseless passage of man towards "perfection" is a divinely mandated inevitability.[42] Only God is Perfect. Imperfection is the prerogative of man. Even man's perceptions of God have gone through an evolutionary process. Such social and political God-terms as "nationalism" and "patriotism" have given way to higher ideals of "liberalism," "capitalism," "socialism," and "Communism."[43] This evolutionary view of the world inevitably necessitates an evolutionary and changeable reading of the faith, rendering it compatible with the realities of a given period.

Bazargan translates this evolutionary theory of human religious and social history into a theory of the universality of the Qur'anic language. Whereas both Judaism and Christianity are specific in how they address given human societies,[44] Islam represents a more rationalized stage of divine revelation whereby man has been addressed in his universal characteristics. From this Bazargan concludes that, contrary to the Orientalists' claim, Islam is not a religion revealed fourteen centuries earlier and thus irrelevant to contemporary realities.[45] Because it represents the highest stage of an evolutionary process in the divine message, the Qur'an represents a perfect paradigmatic model for constructing a human society. Quoting George Bernard Shaw on the flexibility of Islam and on the perspicacious character of the Prophet,[46] Bazargan concludes that, contrary to Judaism and Christianity, Islam (because of its universal initiation of humanity to Truth) can attend to individual human needs while guaranteeing the collective well-being of the society at large. In the end, Bazargan is critical of the established clergy[47] for having concentrated their endeavors exclusively on rules of ritual piety and for leaving the larger social and political issues to scientists. "The Muslim," he contends, "has to struggle against tyranny with his hands and his tongue, and if he cannot do that, then at least deep in his heart be discontent with it."[48]

Political Uses of Religious Rituals: Hajj Pilgrimage

No stone should be left unturned in that struggle against tyranny. Every immediate or tangential aspect of the communal faith had to be reread and repoliticized. Compelled by the utilitarian and economic feasibilities of social programs offered by secular ideologies, Bazargan sought to explain the hajj pilgrimage in such terms. In May 1960 he performed his hajj pilgrimage. When, a few years later, he gave a speech on the significance of the event, he reported to his audience that "the supreme objective [of hajj was to] prepare the international background for universal peace and the creation of a single nation and a single government for humanity."[49] Admitting that universal peace has been the great hope of all major world ideological movements, Bazargan goes on to argue[50] that the same goal has been the chief objective of the Qur'an and that the hajj pilgrimage has been intended as a massive celebration of equality where "the Arab has no privilege over the non-Arab."[51] He clearly advocates the political uses of such occasions as the hajj pilgrimage.

The Shi'i Imams on many occasions took advantage of the hajj pilgrimage and guided the people. It was in Mecca that Imam Hossein refused to acknowledge the authority of Yazid, accepted the invitation of the people from Kufah, and proclaimed to the world his intention to go and fight [against Yazid].[52]

More emphatically, Bazargan proclaimed that "Mecca has repeatedly, before and after Islam, been used to propagate, incite, and mobilize revolutionary movements."[53] Thus, by calling "the House of the People" what is ordinarily called "the House of God," by establishing a utilitarian function for the hajj pilgrimage, and, more important, by emphatically advocating an essential repoliticization of the event, Bazargan wished to bring perhaps the most religiously charged symbolic gathering of Muslims into an active engagement in political consciousness. This would have a dual effect: It would translate the otherwise metaphysical significance of the highest Islamic rituals into utilitarian functions; and then, by affixing a patently political posture to such functions, Bazargan would appeal to his young political constituency. These dual purposes would, in turn, strengthen the position of "the Islamic Ideology" vis-à-vis other (secular) ideologies.

The Freedom Movement of Iran

In 1960, Bazargan joined the Second National Front, formed after the fall of Mosaddeq. However, certain policies and the general antireligious atmosphere of this organization did not particularly appeal to him or a number of other members. In April 1961, Bazargan, Ayatollah Taleqani, and a mutual friend, Yadollah Sahabi, left the Second National Front and established the *Nehzat-e Azadi-ye Iran* (The Freedom Movement of Iran). Because of his involvement in the *Nehzat-e Azadi*, Bazargan was arrested in January 1962 and was imprisoned. He spent his years in prison writing a number of other books, chief among them *Bad va Baran Dar Qur'an (The Wind and Rain in the Qur'an)*, in which he tried to prove that the Qur'an was a divine revelation rather than a human discourse,[54] and *Seyr-e Tahavvol dar Qur'an (The Course of Development in the Qur'an)*[55] of which Shari'ati is reported to have said, "the significance of this book in Qur'anic and Islamic Studies is similar to Newton's discovery of the [law of universal] gravitation in the experimental sciences."[56]

The Freedom Movement[57] was a particular crystallization of the general Islamic thrust in modern Iranian history that began to take shape from the early 1940s, when Reza Shah's abdication created unprecedented circumstances for free political expression. The 1940s was the crucial decade when the formation of left and liberal political and ideological groupings gave catalytic momentum to an equally powerful need for an "Islamic Ideology." From that time forward a series of crucial organizations began to provide institutional momentum to the rising Islamic concerns. Students, engineers, physicians, and teachers started to form professional associations with "the Islamic" as their chief identifying factor. Formation of such social groupings was concurrent with more radical movements, such as the Fada'ian-e Islam, which sought more drastic and immediate solutions to the ideological and political problems they perceived. Assassination of ideological and political opponents was high on the agenda of the Fada'ian-e Islam.

As the founders of "The Freedom Movement" saw themselves, their organization was the institutional expression of the deeply felt need to respond immediately to two simultaneous threats: "the corrupt Western culture" and "the aggressive Marxist culture."[58] In organizing themselves into this revolutionary body, the Muslim activists gave their radical interpretation of Islam as "a combatant, progressive, and forward-looking ideology [maktab] which is responsive to the material and spiritual needs and necessities of a society."[59] Accepting the popularly elected Mosaddeq as their legitimating and exemplary model, they promised to engage in open struggle against the "illegal" activities of the monarch.[60] "Freedom" was high on the agenda of this movement:

What the Iranian nation wants is just one word . . . "Freedom." The Iranian people say that one person does not have the right to govern a nation in an arbitrary and tyrannical way. This word [freedom = azadi] is Persian and easily understandable. This word is not Hebrew that for understanding it you need to hire advisors from Israel. If you know what we mean. . . . We want freedom. We say that the Shah does not have the right to establish law, to install [or] dismiss a government, and everything, minor or major, be done according to his views and will, and yet he be [considered] sinless, unaccountable, with a sacred, even everlasting, position. This is reactionary, this is despotism, this is dictatorship.[61]

The Freedom Movement opposed the Shah's "White Revolution," which it considered yet another plot to rob the Iranians of their national wealth and their cultural identity. It also severely criticized the Shah's suppression of Khomeini's uprising in 1963, calling his army "professional hoodlums."[62] By June 1963, The Freedom Movement had openly called for the violent destruction of the Pahlavi regime: "Down with the Shah's despicable regime. Death to Israel, the Shah's monstrous master! Salutations to the blessed spirit of the shroud-bloodied martyrs of the Iranian people!"[63] In the same month "The Freedom Movement" harshly condemned the imprisonment of Ayatollah Khomeini.

In Iranian history, this is the first time when the exalted position of the supreme deputyship of Imam Ali, peace be upon him, is insulted and the source of exemplary conduct, His Highness Ayatollah Khomeini is kidnapped and imprisoned.[64]

The members of The Freedom Movement were quick to point out that while they were engaged in open rebellion against the Pahlavi regime, the Marxists were effectively silent between 1960 and 1964.[65]

After the June 1963 uprising, the leadership of The Freedom Movement was imprisoned. But as the organization itself entered a period of effective eclipse, a more radical offshoot of it, *Sazeman-e Mojahedin-e Khalq-e Iran*, began to take shape in 1965.[66] It was not until 1977–78 that The Freedom Movement reentered Iranian politics in the wake of the Revolution.[67]

The ideologues of The Freedom Movement themselves divide the history of their activities into three phases.[68] First, from 1960 to early 1965, the active participation of the Movement in the ideological and political preparation of the masses for the Revolution—included in this period was the Movement's involvement in Khomeini's June 1963 uprising. Second, from mid-1965 to mid-1975, the expansion of the Movement's activities into military operations through its radical offshoot, the *Mojahedin-e Khalq*—in this same period Shari'ati's public lectures in Hosseyniyyeh Ershad energize the Islamic consciousness of the youth. Third, from mid-1975 to late 1978, the crucial breakup in the *Mojahedin-e Khalq*, when an openly Marxist-Leninist faction briefly took over—during this period, and as the *Mojahedin-e Khalq* regains its patently Islamic posture, The Freedom Movement saw itself as the custodian of the Islamic revolutionary cause. In mid-1975, the Movement sought Ayatollah Khomeini's blessings in Najaf.[69] Upon Khomeini's arrival in France, The Freedom Movement, with Bazargan and Taleqani at the helm, actively participated in propagating Khomeini's messages by organizing mass demonstrations and by arranging for industrial strikes that ultimately shattered the Pahlavi regime.

Bazargan's Indictment of the Pahlavi Regime

The leading cadre of The Freedom Movement was arrested in the early 1960s, ostensibly because of its opposition to the monarch's "White Revolution." Bazargan and Taleqani, among others, were condemned to ten years imprisonment.

Bazargan turned the occasion of his defense into an opportunity for a resounding statement against the Pahlavi regime. His defense consists of two long speeches. In the first speech, a considerable part of which is a splendid autobiography, he defends The Freedom Movement and its political ideals; in the second, he issues a sweeping condemnation of absolutist monarchy. At the very outset, he assured the court that it was not just the leaders of The Freedom Movement who were being tried, but, conversely, the Pahlavi regime itself was also on trial.[70] He recognizes the ultimate goal of the Movement to be the actual implementation of the Iranian constitution (in which the King's authority was restricted by the Parliament).[71] At this stage he did not deny altogether the constitutional foundation of monarchy. In fact, in justifying the cause of his establishment of The Freedom Movement, he said, "the truth of the origin of the Freedom Movement of Iran" ought to be sought in Reza Shah's advice to Bazargan and his fellow students when they were sent to Europe.[72] In articulating the conditions under which he and his fellow Muslim activists thought of establishing a political party, Bazargan asserted how they had come to the conclusion that they had to form a unified organization to engage in politics and that its ideological foundation had to be Islamic.[73] Summarizing the principles that he, as a leader of The Freedom Movement, believed in, he said: "We are Muslims, Iranians, supporters of the constitution, and followers of Mosaddeq."[74] Bazargan concluded the first part of his defense by emphatically rejecting the accusation that they were antimonarchical. "I have to demonstrate," he stipulated, "why and how I agree with constitutional monarchy for Iran."[75] His statement changes abruptly at this point, and he does not articulate "why and how" he supports constitutional monarchy.[76]

The second part of Bazargan's defense, which was not delivered in court but was printed abroad eight years later,[77] is a sweeping condemnation of despotism. Throughout its long history, absolutist monarchy has been the cause of much misery and insecurity in Iran.[78] Even if we accept the fiction of good and benevolent kings, their actual number is dismal in comparison to tyrannical monarchs. Absolutist monarchy has been the cause of public and personal injustice and has had grave consequences for the moral, social, and even economic well-being of the nation at large. Absolutism in modern history has also been wed to colonialism, facilitating the plunder of the national wealth by foreigners. Contrary to the dominant propaganda, absolutist monarchy has not been the cause of national and cultural continuity in Iran. Rather, art, literature, and ultimately religion have provided such vehicles for historical and cultural continuity.[79]

The only haven and refuge of the Iranian people from absolutism, and the [only] thing which, despite all the injustices, the corruptions, and the plunders of absolutism, has preserved a minimum of energy in us, saving us from being annihilated from the face of the earth, are certainly the spiritual matters and, more specifically, our religion. In the shadow of religion, the Islamic faith, the Iranian people have stood up and reacted against despotism, and have thus attained a haven, as well as a measure of success in security, [political] activity, and salvation.[80]

Bazargan continues to assert that religion has always been a locus of antigovernment activities, a banner under which people have fought for their rights. The clerical order has been the only social grouping resistant to despotic rulers. Shi'ism has found its way into the hearts and minds of people precisely for having championed their righteous cause. Opposing depotism on every front, Islam has initiated its own direct way of helping people in easing their burdens. Schools, public baths, mosques, water fountains, etc.—these have been among the range of public services that Shi'ism has provided.

Beyond its public damages, despotism is equally harmful to the growth and dignity of the individual character. The immediate result of absolutism is the creation and sustenance of a servile character. Corruption, deceit, duplicity, and dishonesty chiefly characterize those who live under a despotic regime.[81] Humanity, decency, and belief in the progress of the human condition all disappear in an absolutist state. Deceit and duplicity are the very foundation of despotism and all social realities about it. Absolutism is "the mother of evil."[82] Despotism leads to such debilitating social and individual malaise because, in effect, it propagates idolatry and polytheism:

The kings or the despots either like Egyptian pharoahs or Japanese emperors explicitly represent themselves as God, or as God's epiphany, or else they do not utter such titles [and yet] officially and effectively claim Divinity.[83]

Bazargan proceeds to enumerate the causes of despotism in Iranian history.[84] The first factor has been the impact of the invading neighbors who, since ancient history, have imposed a rule of violence and despotism whenever they have invaded Iran. The second factor has been the geographic setup of Iran where small pockets of urban settlements are surrounded by inhospitable surroundings, thus creating a physical condition for despotic rulers. The third factor is the almost exclusive reliance of the Iranian economy on agriculture. Neither industry nor commerce but agriculture has been the chief source and organization of the Iranian economy. This has given water exclusive supremacy in Iranian national life. Control over water has been an added factor in the creation and sustenance of despotism in Iran. Thus rooted in such perennial factors, despotism has continued to the present day as the chief organizer of Iranian political life. The Pahlavi regime is the last inheritor of this long legacy of absolutism.

The balance sheet of more than forty years of tumultuous despotism after the Constitution[al Revolution] is approaching a scandalous and shaky end. Suffocated under the pressure of injustice, poverty, and shame, the majority of the people are in search of a liberating path, a leader, and a program.[85]

People's Expectations From Religious Authorities

Where is that path? Who is that leader? What is that program? Bazargan, by disposition, was oriented towards Qom. When in 1962 a group of leading religious authorities gathered to address the crucial question of supreme religious and political leadership, *velayat,* in the Shi'i community after the death of Ayatollah Borujerdi, Medhi Bazargan sought to speak for the multitude of followers and thus remind the Shi'i men of authority of their grave responsibilities.[86] At the very outset, he emphatically reiterates that the boundaries of Islamic law are not limited to matters of personal hygiene and private virtues. There are grave public and communal problems that are equally, if not more, important for the future of the faith and, as such, have always been at the center of juridical attention. "Contrary to Jews, Christians, (and perhaps Buddhists and Zoroastrians)," Bazargan stipulates, in Islam "every aspect and dimension of the material and spiritual life, and the [very] pillar of all hopes, thoughts, and activities of the Muslim society" are regulated by the sacred law.[87] Thus, Bazargan wished to address his ideas not only to "the exemplary sources of authority" *(marja'-e taqlid),* but also to those in positions of leadership *(ze'amat),* to the supreme religious and political authority *(velayat),* and to the clerical class *(ruhaniyyat),* in general.[88]

"The People," as Bazargan designates his highest form of reference, expect a great deal from their religious leaders, much more than they expect from physicians or governmental employees. As time passes, these expectations become higher and higher. Bazargan admits that while religious authorities are the target of greatest expectations from "The People," they receive the least possible material gain. Here he wishes to establish for the ulama' a well-deserved ascetic and altruistic set of qualifications that are particularly congenial to the assumption of universal political authority in the context of the Shi'i juridical culture.

Bazargan begins his discourse on the grave responsibilities of the religious authorities by recalling a meeting with the French Islamicist Henri Corbin, in the course of which he is reported to have said that while both Christianity and Sunni Islam have ceased to address the contemporary realities of modern man, only Shi'ism has the built-in mechanism of attending to the compelling contemporary exigencies. He gives particular credence to this statement. It has been uttered by "a man of knowledge who is neither a Muslim nor an Easterner."[89] The key reason for this privileged position of Shi'ism among the world religions is the doctrinal belief in the occultation of the Twelfth Imam who is believed to bring, in his Second Coming, eternal justice to the world. Bazargan complains, though, that in the contemporary reading of the doctrine, the Shi'is have turned this revolutionary belief into a cause of "disappointment, delegation [of responsibilities], and idleness." [90] If read and practiced properly, Shi'ism provides both an illustrious past and a glorious future. But the key link between the virtuous Imams of the past and the expected Twelfth Imam of the Age is the historical and doctrinal position of the contemporary religious authorities. This fact imposes grave responsibilities upon the clerics who ought to mobilize the best in the Shi'i past, master the immediate exigencies of the present, and actively plan and lead towards a prosperous future. Thus, Bazargan provides an active and involved interpretation of the presumption that the gates of *ejtehad* are closed in Sunni Islam, while they are open in Shi'ism:

> The fact that we pride ourselves vis-à-vis the Sunnis and assert that while they have closed the gates of *ejtehad* ... after the four great *mojtaheds* ... Malik, Abu Hanifah, al-Shafi'i, and Ibn Hanbal, we Shi'is are obliged to follow the most learned living *mojtahed* and have thus kept these gates open, so that our faith is kept fresh and alive, progressing with the changes and developments of the world. This honor and privilege are true only when they correspond with reality. [This would be the case only when] in truth the gates of *ejtehad* are kept open, and the problems and issues of the day, in whatever form and capacity they may be, can enter and exit from it. If the ideas, knowledge, and limits of observation of our *mojtaheds* are kept at the level of the issues of the bygone centuries, what is the use of the changing names and transference of positions from a deceased ayatollah to an accepted [living] one? [In such a case] still the gates of *ejtehad* would be dead closed.[91]

The religious manuals of exemplary conduct *(al-risalah al-amaliyyah)* that are issued by the high-ranking clerical order principally address matters of personal hygiene and private pieties, while leaving larger and more important issues of public concerns beyond and outside their immediate purview. The context of these manuals is strictly limited to matters of concern "some ten or twelve centuries ago in Arabia." [92] In those days the dizzying problems of modernity—commercial, geopolitical, etc.—could not have been addressed. What is particularly pertinent to Shi'ism, as Bazargan momentarily forgets the Iranian history since the Safavid period, is the fact that for centuries this has been the faith of a persecuted minority. As a result, Bazargan concludes, most of its juridical and doctrinal developments have occurred around personal pieties and individual transactions. Political and administrative aspects of the larger community, particularly when Shi'ism is not a minority faith, have been left largely unarticulated. The world is changing rapidly, so must the jurists.[93] "The mentality of three-hundred years ago" is not sufficient anymore. The world is shrinking in size. "Even if we do not want to, the foreigners will not leave us alone and, willy nilly, they will drag us into the larger arena and take us for a ride." [94]

Bazargan suggests that Shi'i jurisprudence ought to emulate the developments in modern sciences and thus change its method of learning and teaching. But more important, it must be divided into subspecialties, "like physics," in order to permit both further advancements in jurisprudence and more direct responses to modern issues. On the authority of Morteza Motahhari, Bazargan reports that even Ayatollah Hajj Shaykh Abdolkarim Ha'eri, the founder of the Qom seminary system, had advocated such subdivisions in Shi'i juridical learning, and thus authority. Should this happen, Bazargan anticipates, once again Muslims will assume ascendency in sciences and learning. "Why should ... Muslims be humiliated and poorly fed by the Christian and infidel world?"[95]

To achieve such glorious things, Shi'ism ought to be revived and repoliticized. It is the great honor of Shi'ism, Bazargan reassures his audience, that throughout its history it has been the standard-bearer of resurrection against injustice and tyranny.[96] The Sunnis, on the other hand, have always put their stamp of approval on every act of injustice, simply because it is issued by a companion of the Prophet. Throughout its history, and particularly in Iran, Shi'ism, as Bazargan saw it now, has insisted that "government has to be combined with legitimacy, justice, and piety; and [that] it should have permission, from the Imam and the *ommat* [that is, the Shi'i community]."[97] "In short," Bazargan reasserts his history of Shi'ism, "for Shi'ism the clerics have been both *marja'* [that is, exemplary model of righteous behavior] and *malja'* [that is, where Shi'is have turned for protection from tyranny]."[98] This independence from political authorities, Bazargan insists, has been maintained even when governments have officially adopted Shi'ism as the state religion:

During the reign of devoted Shi'i dynasties, too, like the Safavids and the Qajars, the religious authorities still kept their independence and superiority vis-à-vis the powers that be. Except for certain religious authorities who were either related to or appointed by the court, and except for the periods of Shah Tahmasp and Shah Abbas who were particularly powerful, other religious figures never obeyed or supported the kings. That which has been practiced in the past is [now] expected [from the religious authorities, to] move vigorously and appropriately now and in future.[99]

Under present circumstances, Bazargan insisted, secular governments have appropriated all the civil and legal rights of their citizens. (He puts it in these general terms but he means Iran.) Thus they should at least leave people alone to decide for themselves who their religious leaders should be. Obviously taking issue with the increasing attempt on the part of the Pahlavi regime to influence the post-Ayatollah Borujerdi developments in religious matters, Bazargan warned the ulama' against being, "God forbid,"[100] used by foreign powers and their local agents. People trust their religious leaders as their last reliable refuge. Religious authorities should not betray that trust.

While Judaism, Bazargan comparatively states, has been the religion of the world and Christianity the faith of the world to come, Islam has combined this- and other-worldly affairs in its doctrinal foundation. A Shi'i "source of exemplary conduct" *(marja'-e taqlid)* ought to be as close to his archetypal models in the prophets and Imams as possible in leading the community towards this ideal state where matters of politics and religion coincide. For this coincidence to be beneficial to the Islamic (Shi'i) community, mere old age should not be a determining factor in choosing a supreme religious leader. "At any rate," Bazargan clarified, "that supreme leader and source of exemplary conduct is our hope and expectation who, even though on a lower scale, like Ali is both a man of knowledge and a man of battlefields."[101] Here Bazargan joined Motahhari and certain other revolutionary ideologues in asking for specialization in juridical learning whereby each jurist is expected to command only certain aspects of jurisprudence.

The ramifications of this suggestion, particularly in the political domain, are worth considering further. On the surface, and as it pertained to matters of juridical learning, the suggestion to specialize in certain fields seemed quite innocuous, if not rather beneficial. The idea, in fact, was much older than these revolutionary ideologues imagined. At least since the nineteenth century such specializations were suggested by certain jurists on primarily juridical and practical grounds.[102] The expansion of the field of juridical studies had been so pervasive that no particular individual could be expected to master every aspect of it. But when advocated by such revolutionary ideologues of "the Islamic Ideology" as Bazargan or Motahhari, the issue assumed new and quintessentially political dimensions. The primarily apolitical tenure of Ayatollah Borujerdi and the essentially conservative and perhaps even promonarchical tenure of Ayatollah Ha'eri Yazdi, both as supreme juridical figures, had demonstrated to these religious ideologues that once one particular juridical figure was invested with such overwhelming and singular authority, combined with the fact that years (rather decades) of learning would inevitably render a jurist effectively apolitical, it was not conducive to expect a revolutionary disposition from them. The living example of such great apolitical figures of religious authority, then and now, were grand ayatollahs such as Ayatollah Kho'i who had spent their lives poring over the minutiae of the Shi'i Shari'ah, with no visible signs of political concern. By advocating the cause of specialization in the fields of juridical studies, the revolutionary ideologues would have created a situation where no one individual would have achieved the high status of learning concomitant with supreme juridical authority over the Shi'i community. Learning breeds authority in Shi'ism. By wishing to equalize and thus level this aristocracy of knowledge, the revolutionary ideologues would have created a situation where no one, by virtue of encyclopedic knowledge (and the sanctity it endowed), would have become a living memory of Shi'i scholasticism, in its very juridical nature accommodating, though never totally congenial, to the powers that be.

While grave issues, Bazargan charged, challenged the fundamentals of the Shi'i doctrinal beliefs, Ayatollah Borujerdi's juridical might was wasted on insignificant and irrelevant questions of ritual piety.[103] Bazargan was grateful that at least such people as Allamah Tabataba'i were in Qom who could address the more critical issues facing the younger generation. He seems to be under the impression that Allamah Tabataba'i's philosophical teachings were advocated in Qom, whereas, in fact, and as we noted earlier, Ayatollah Borujerdi had registered his disapproval of such teachings in his jurisdiction.[104]

"For every manual of exemplary conduct," Bazargan charged the religious authorities, "ten scientific, intellectual, principal, social, economic, and political . . . ought to be written." [105] The religious seminaries, echoing Khomeini's views, Bazargan demanded, ought to be concerned principally with the ethical rectitude of the students. Based only on such well-balanced foundations of ethical virtuosity and ideological dialogues with modernity, Bazargan stipulated, could the religious authorities expect the reverence and obedience of their Shi'i followers.

Bazargan also offers this other, rather drastic, suggestion, advancing the practical and social responsibilities of the religious authorities. Following the exemplary conduct of the Prophet and Ali, the Shi'i religious authorities ought to be engaged in practical and professional jobs. There is nothing wrong with having a practical profession. Both the Qur'an and the Prophetic and Imami traditions have blessed it. It also puts the clerical order in touch with more mundane realities. Equally instrumental in rendering the juridical class more socially relevant would be, in Bazargan's approximation of the Shi'i clerics to Christian missionaries, their active involvement in such public programs as establishing "hospitals, orphanages, high schools, universities, guesthouses, factories, qanats, villages, [etc.]. . . ." [106] As these suggested areas of endeavor would expand the domain of social responsibilities for the clerical order, they would, of course, detract equally from their time and energy exclusively devoted to matters of juridical concerns. Bazargan's suggested program here, whether he knew it consciously or not, would ultimately lead to the effective liquidation of the clerical class as it had been historically developed and established. Systematically distanced from being the professional doctors of law (the Shari'ah) and simultaneously assimilated into the commercial and managerial groupings, the Shi'i jurists would be rendered effectively obsolete as the institutional guardians of the sacred Law. But Bazargan is adamant in his recommendation:

Had our religious leaders done such [practical] things earlier . . . for long now the true Islamic government which is both nationalistic and democratic and divine, would have been established. Without resorting to revolution and bloodletting we would have achieved our rights; and tyranny, corruption, and sin would have been eradicated from the country. It is still not too late, and, as the saying goes, better late than never.[107]

The Wind and the Rain

As the clerics had to be repoliticized, the Qur'an, too, needed some updating. No stone unturned for the revolution to come; no sacred text unreinterpreted. There are one hundred and five times, as Bazargan actually went through the Qur'an and recounted, that God mentions Wind and Rain in the holy Text.[108] This attracted his attention, and he wished "to prove that the particular way the wind and rain, and their related conditions, are mentioned in the Qur'an have a peculiarly accurate correspondence with [modern] meteorological discoveries and with scientific knowledge."[109] Upon this observation, he wishes to conclude that "he who has sent the Qur'an . . . is the same who sends wind and rain."[110] He concludes that no one could have said these things about wind and rain without having a "global" view of the world, and that person, fourteen hundred years ago, was God Himself.[111]

What is the meaning of this? Why should a man concern himself with the number of times wind and rain are mentioned in the Qur'an? Bazargan is writing this book, as he argues himself, for "those who would be attracted to modern science more than before, and [conversely for those] students and intellectuals who would be attracted to the Qur'an."[112] After a short summary of the state of the art in meteorology, all with charts, diagrams, formulae, and maps, he sets out to prove[113] that, point by point, those one hundred and five Qur'anic references to wind and rain correspond to the latest scientific observations in meteorology. Supported by the Qur'an, he wishes to argue that "the source and the manager of that energy [which sustains the world] is 'God.'"[114]

The Wind and the Rain in the Qur'an is the epitome of Bazargan's pseudoscientific contribution to the making of "the Islamic Ideology." For the growing constituency of Muslim intellectuals, that ideology needed a putitative foot in the almost magical kingdom of science. That constituency was, by and large, students and young professionals who had been educated either in American or European universities or even in modern Iranian secular universities. For them there had appeared an increasing and deepening bifurcation between their historically received religiosity and their recently acquired scientific methods and knowledge. A trained engi-

neer by profession and, as a professor at Tehran University, intimately
aware of the young students' disposition, Bazargan recognized this debilitating and, in his judgment, dangerous bifurcation and sought to close it.
The result is this pseudoscientific discourse, this systemic recentering of a
bewildering world on the relentless facticity of a sacred text, delivered with
all seriousness, which must have convinced his constituency, at least partially, of not only the miraculous nature of the Qur'an but, perhaps more
important, of the compatibility of science and religion. That putitative
compatibility, the presumed "validation" of the Qur'an by the latest scientific discoveries, would put "the Islamic Ideology" in the bosom of modern,
and constantly contemporary, time: atemporality of the Word of God
verified by the timely supremacy of the man of science.

The Islamic Ideology: Foundations of the Divine Ideology

As a result of the political circumstances of the post-1963 uprising, Bazargan's writings take on more aggressive momentum, less of science now and
more of ideology. By the mid-1960s the term "Islamic Ideology" had
assumed its commanding position among the rising urban Muslim intellectual elite. When Bazargan was invited to deliver his annual lecture, always
on the occasion of the Prophet's designation as the Divine emissary (Id-e
Mab'ath), to the Association of Muslim Engineers in 1966, he was asked
specifically "to talk about ideology, the Islamic Ideology."[115] The currency
of "the Islamic Ideology" by 1966, some three years after the June 1963
uprising, is an indication of the growing significance of an alternative
revolutionary reading of Islam independent of the juridical discourse centered in Qom. "The Islamic Ideology" thus essentially remained a product
of Tehran where the competing presence of the old religious sentiments and
the emerging agenda of the modern (secular) political forces could have a
fateful rendez-vous.

At the very outset of this lecture, Bazargan confesses that there appears
to be a considerable difference between "ideology" and such a generically
Islamic concept as be'that ("the designation of Prophet Mohammad as the
last divine emissary").[116] He then gives the following definition of "ideology":

Our operative definition of this word is the same current meaning as used by
political·parties and intellectuals; that is to say, that constellation of beliefs, or
philosophical and theoretical school, which is adopted by a person or a group as
the intellectual foundation of their political and party orientation, and as an instrument of evaluation for designating the path and method for social struggle.[117]

Bazargan concludes that this definition of ideology, which is based on a
general understanding of how the term is used by "political parties and

intellectuals," is precisely the purpose of Divine missions as well, because prophets, too, have tried to "give man an ideological and intellectual foundation, and the designation of a path and a method for living."[118] This ideology is not a particularly new phenomenon; and human history has always witnessed man's fundamental need for an ideology. However, there is an element of gradual evolution and perfection in man's search for the good ideology. Quoting Marx (through a Persian translation of an English secondary source on the history of political ideas) on the compatibility of every ideological stage with its corresponding mode of economic production, Bazargan concludes that the Iranian youth "should not merely imitate and be hasty"[119] in adopting radical ideology, because for every stage in the history of a society, according to Marx himself, there is a normal and inevitable ideology. Paraphrasing the Persian translation of his source, Bazargan gives a brief summary of ideologies from ancient Greece to socialism and fascism.[120] "What a long and arduous road!" he marvelled, "has man traversed in his search for the perfect ideology! Whom shall we believe?" he asks. "What ideology should we accept? Under the protection of which school and what government can we find security, prosperity, and blissful existence?"[121]

At the conclusion of his summary of world political ideologies, Bazargan asserts that a number of prescriptions can easily be discarded. Kings and rulers have no Divine origin as their claim to authority; individuals have no absolute or relative preference over societies; states do not follow the medieval practice of following a religious institution; rationalism does not totally cover and command man's political experiences; and utilitarianism cannot be the foundation of any acceptable political ideology.[122] While all these ideological traits are to be "thrown away," there are certain others that are generally acceptable: Centrality of the government and its sovereignty, the rule of the majority, the necessity of an ideology, recognition of natural and human realities (as opposed to merely rational principles), and the necessity of programming and leadership.[123]

Upon the rejection and adoption of these two sets of ideological principles, Bazargan turns to the Qur'anic passage 62:2 in order to elucidate the basic tenets of "the Islamic Ideology."

He it is Who hath sent among the unlettered ones a messenger of their own, to recite unto them His revelations and to make them grow, and to teach them the Scripture and wisdom, though heretofore they were indeed in error manifest.

According to Bazargan's reading of this Qur'anic passage, God's recognition of the necessity of an ideology for formation of a proper human society precedes all other human stipulations. God's command that the Divine emissary ought to be from the people themselves conforms to the principle of the rule of the people. His command that this mission ought to be carried out by reference to His earthly manifestations conforms to the necessity of recognizing natural and human realities. Moreover, this "Divine Ideology" is entrusted with the task of purifying its followers. Persistent teaching and guidance is a concomitant feature of this "Divine Ideology." Before following this ideology, and should they fall short of its requirements, people would be led astray.[124]

Bazargan seems to be quite conscious of the kind of secularist criticism that his brand of "Islamic Ideology" would invite. That religion is a "reactionary" phenomenon, that Islam is a religion that appeared fourteen centuries before and is thus incompatible with modern realities, and that all religions are dogmatic and intolerant of freedom of expression are all charges that he is sure would be leveled against "the Islamic Ideology."[125] Bazargan's answer is that all such charges stem from a Christian view of religion, and that "in Islam, from the very beginning, faith and action have been intertwined, religion and politics . . . have progressed jointly."[126] Politics is integral to Islam. For political struggle, ideology is indispensable. Iranians have been a backward nation. They cannot know and practice "The Western" ideologies better than their originators. Their dignity is at stake to come up with their own ideology and fight their political battle against corruption and foreign domination with intrinsic ideological arms.[127] Using the French word for "totalitarianism,"[128] Bazargan insists that "the Islamic Ideology" ought to be all-inclusive and universal, covering every aspect of life, "security, politics, economics, culture, health, art, thought, opinion"; all these have to come "under the shadow" of "the Islamic Ideology."[129] Consequently, and forever, "the ideal ideology is absolutely the Divine Ideology."[130]

Bazargan's indubitable conviction in the absolute superiority of "the Islamic Ideology" ought to be seen in the process of two simultaneous forces. Bazargan was not only the inheritor of a faith that has constitutionally and doctrinally tried to regulate the minutiae of public and private life; he was, at the very same time, responding positively (although he may have thought otherwise) to the totalitarian claims and tendencies of Marxism to every aspect of social life. Institutionalized in the Tudeh Party, propagated through a range of partisan literature, and followed by thousands of secularized intellectuals, Marxism was gaining ground not just at the expense of private pieties of lapsed-Muslims but also on account of their public (political) commitments. Bazargan was relentlessly charged to reclaim these lost grounds. The more intensely and comprehensively such grounds were lost, the more they needed to be equally reclaimed. Thus "the Islamic Ideology" reached for totalitarian dimensions far beyond the already expanded claim of Islam upon public and private pieties. Marxism provided the added momentum, and the prototypical model, to reach for ever larger shares of individual liberties for the presumed salvation of the public.

There is nothing innately wrong, Bazargan contends, with having a religion as the foundation of an ideology, especially if that religion is Islam, with a doctrinal and constitutional belief in all three mottos of what else but the French Revolution. "Equality, Fraternity, and Liberty" are all essential and existential to the very doctrinal basis of Islam.[131] The remarkable aspect of Bazargan's version of "the Islamic Ideology," however, is that even as he rushes forward to make a claim on the political viability of the term, he can pause and assert that

the essential difficulty is that the Divine Ideology is not the work of man and that we cannot construct it. As you can see, it is very easy to claim [to have constructed a Divine Ideology]. [But] it is precisely such misplaced claims, and false or incomplete Divine Ideology, which is the cause of various differences and quarrels. The Divine Ideology, which is issued from the high court of God Almighty, by definition can only be the work of God and nobody else. That which we fathom and build is just dust in the wind. Except for that case in which He would disclose to one of us aspects of His secrets and hand us His commands. In other words, [only if we claim that] inspiration and revelation are at work.[132]

No other ideologue under our examination has had a similar courage of introspection, that rare gift of "on-the-other-hand" self-doubt that distinguishes a modest access to practical (political) wisdom from a superlative claim to absolute (ideological) truth. To be sure, Bazargan's effective denial of contemporary revelation, which would have been a blasphemy to have thought otherwise, does not prevent him, or any other ideologue, from assuming a prophetic and visionary voice in delivering his ideological statements. In a comparative perspective, however, Bazargan has a firmer foot on the ground of mundane practicality. He does not, for a moment, share either Shari'ati's prophetic zeal or Motahhari's missionary convictions. His salvation is his occasional doubts, his sense of humor, his ability to laugh and doubt, attested to not only by those who have known him but also by his written words. When he was the Dean of the School of Engineering at Tehran University, the school began to accept female students for the first time. Bazargan is reported one day as having been approached by senior students who asked, in jest, whether these female student could start their courses from the fourth year and work their way down to the first, so that the male seniors could have female classmates before they graduated. Bazargan is said to have responded "No! Otherwise I would have them start from the Dean's office!"[133]

"The Islamic Ideology": Bazargan's Manifesto

With saving laughter or with damning conviction, with absolute certainty or with hesitant doubt, the task of "the Islamic Ideology" was pressing and underway. The culmination of Bazargan's share of "the Islamic Ideology" was his open manifesto. He characteristically predicates his manifesto of "the Islamic Ideology" on the doctrinally mandated principle of Divine intervention in human affairs through His prophetic emissaries. Human fallibility can only produce incomplete and false ideologies. Only an ideology based on the actuality of Divine intervention in human affairs can claim any measure of truth. And that necessitates the doctrinal acceptance of prophethood through which agency God speaks to mankind.[134] Following this premise and based on the Qur'anic text, the prophetic and Imami traditions, and his "incomplete intellect,"[135] Bazargan sets out to chart the essential features of his manifesto of "the Islamic Ideology." With the exception of *ijma͑*, or legal consensus among the Shi͑i doctors, the three bases upon which Bazargan wishes to build his version of "the Islamic Ideology" are precisely those that support Shi͑i law. The remarkable historical fact is, however, that in constructing this reading of "the Islamic Ideology," Bazargan did have *ijma͑* with other ideologues who contributed equally to this most revolutionary doctrinal offshoot of the Shi͑i faith. Consequently the conceptual foundations of "the Islamic Ideology" were identical with those of Shi͑i law. Whether accidental or deliberate, this constitutional identification of "the Islamic Ideology" with Shi͑i law (which is the quintessential substance of Shi͑ism) is perhaps Bazargan's most revolutionary contribution to the historical process of legitimizing the chief driving force of the Islamic revolution.

In Bazargan's version of "the Islamic Ideology," man's free will, in this politically mandated theological choice, actively predisposes him to create an ideal state. The primary function of this state is to materialize God's government on earth and help men to realize their Divinely originated virtues.[136] This ideological principle, Bazargan likes to insist, is very similar to the philosophical foundation of many "Western" ideologies, except that it postulates the existence of an Omnipotent God. Emanating from this God, as Bazargan amplifies his "Divine [Islamic] Ideology" further, is the set of laws that guarantee man's salvation. "No one," he insists,

whether the king, or the people, or its [various] classes, either through houses of lords or representatives, or through referenda or such similar mechanisms, has the right to establish law or mandate responsibilities.[137]

This principle, too, once understood as the rule of law (as opposed to one group or another), is compatible with "progressive governments."[138] But to implement these Divinely mandated laws, man has an active role to play in history. Means of production, as Marxists claim, are not the instruments of history. "Law and ideology" have been the cause and course of history and civilization.

That the Muslim community ought to be governed solely by Divine law,

Bazargan stipulates, does not mean that there is no need for an intermediary state apparatus. As Ali responded to the Kharijites' rejection of the necessity of government, "people necessarily need to have a prince *(amir)*, whether good or bad, to collect the taxes, fight the enemy, secure the highways, and protect the weak against the powerful."[139] Upon this Bazargan collects a barrage of Qur'anic, prophetic, and Imamic references in support of the inevitability of government, concluding that in Islam the necessity of state, based on the will of God and the democratic participation of the people, is proscribed religiously.[140] Here, too, Bazargan assures his audience that democracy is not exclusive to Islam, and that once upon a time in Athens this form of government was practiced.

In the Islamic state, thus based on "the Islamic Ideology," the security and prosperity of both the individual and the society are guaranteed. To reach that ideal state, "the Islamic Ideology" does not approve of just any method. The end does not, in this "Divine Ideology," justify the means.[141] Equally essential to this ideology is "freedom," which Bazargan considers "a Divine gift and a key for [human] progress."[142] Equality and justice are eminently present in "the Islamic Ideology." No discrimination based on race, status, or knowledge is tolerated.[143] Women are equal to men, and they should be given a voice in the political administration of the state.

The legitimacy of the Islamic state thus engendered is based on the notion of *velayat,* which Bazargan considers as the delegation of authority from the people to their representatives.[144] To ensure the righteous execution of this delegation, he advocates general political education for the masses.[145] Such public education in social responsibilities, he contends, would prevent corruption in a democracy. In this respect, he takes strong exception to those of his contemporaries who consider Islam essentially antidemocratic. In a long footnote,[146] he totally rejects the ideas of a certain writer who had argued that Islam is an essentially elitist type of meritocracy or gerontocracy.

Although "the Divine Islamic Ideology" guarantees both social and individual security, it is the duty of the individual to place public necessities ahead of personal objectives.[147] Should discrepancies arise between personal and social objectives, Bazargan stipulates the necessity of an arbitrating body *(anjoman-e hall-e ekhtelaf)* that would pass judgment in such issues.[148] Through the righteous intervention of this arbitrating body, both social and individual liberties are secured. The questions of war and peace are also in a state of balance and harmony in "the Islamic Ideology." Whereas "Islam" generally advocates peace and tranquility, Bazargan contends, should the Muslim community be threatened, it, of course, has to defend itself.[149] The Qur'an never commands fighting without immediately calling for moderation and peace.[150]

Following the Marxist prototype, "the Islamic Ideology" is equally attentive to matters of economy.[151] The economic production of life is an essential component of every community, but does not, as some (that is, the Marxists) have contended, take priority over everything else. In "the Islamic Ideology" economic matters are not separable from ethical and religious obligations. As ownership pertains to the question of property, because God Almighty is the actual and ultimate owner of everything, then men have only relative ownership of what is in their temporary possession. But no one should deprive them of any property thusly owned. In "Islam" there is a negative attitude towards poverty and asceticism and a positive attitude towards economic activities. But at the same time, too much accumulation of wealth is condemned. Quoting Taleqani from *Islam and Ownership*, Bazargan divides land ownership into three categories: (1) that which belongs to all Muslims and only the infallible Imams can manage it for the community, (2) that which belongs to the infallible Imam personally, and (3) that which has no ownership and is to be divided to Muslims for their benefit.[152] Usury is prohibited. He who cultivates a piece of land owns it. There is nothing wrong with the accumulation or the active use of capital.[153] Thus, with certain limitations, there is principally nothing wrong with capitalism according to "the Islamic Ideology."[154] But this is not to be seen as a rampant rule for a free market economy. In "the Islamic Ideology" the rights of workers are properly guaranteed and protected. Basing his proposition on two prophetic traditions, Bazargan suggests that, although there was no organized labor during Mohammad's time, "Islam" has always been attentive to the needs of the working class. As it equally attends to the compelling question of the equal distribution of wealth in society, "Islam" is quite unique in proscribing mandatory religious taxation through which accumulated wealth is redistributed.[155]

For the supreme political/religious leader, whom he does not distinguish as two and simply calls, in one figure, an "Imam,"[156] Bazargan stipulates widespread responsibilities. The leader is legitimized to have "vast authorities in granting and confiscating lands and properties, in fixing fees and taxes, and in deciding rights and limitations."[157] Despite such sweeping authorities, Bazargan insists that the rights of individuals are protected in "the Islamic Ideology."

Finally, Bazargan turns to the all-important question of nationalism and identifies two opposite extremes: those who have a racist and ultranationalist tendency, and those who have a cosmopolitan and internationalist disposition. Both extremes are blameworthy. "The Islamic Ideology," Bazargan insists, recognizes its historical mission as a universal religion that, more than any other, has advanced the cause of the brotherhood of mankind.[158] The Qur'an, as the very word of God, is addressed to all humanity and calls all mankind to its Truth and veracity:

Thus the Islamic Ideology is the vastest and most sublime universal and humane way of thinking. In its perspective, such concepts as "nation" and "nationhood," as separating and distinguishing brands, have no significance or meaning.[159]

Yet again, Bazargan insists, "Islam" is such a balanced and all-inclusive faith that does not neglect the more immediate needs of man for intimate group affinities. Thus the love of one's family or country is not in any way forbidden in Islamic universality.[160]

Predominance of the Marxist Discourse

Reading Bazargan, it becomes abundantly and repeatedly clear that the Marxist discourse had successfully and thoroughly established the Iranian political agenda from the 1940s through the 1970s. Virtually every term, concept, and concern with which Bazargan chooses to identify and circumscribe "the Islamic Ideology" is mandated by the tacit, and thus compelling, legitimacy of the Marxist discourse. Beginning with the economic foundations of the society, Bazargan wishes to update Islam with Marxism and provide a one-to-one correspondence to its social and historical agenda. His misplaced attention to the working class and to questions of capitalism and private ownership, as well as his abrupt reference to the question of nationalism vs. internationalism, are all mandated by the Marxist language he thought he was refuting. Sincerely adopting this language, he did not recognize that, while on the surface he appeared to refute Marxism, he, in fact, through the agency of "the Islamic Ideology," was paying tribute to and thus further legitimizing it. He thought he was adopting the language of the Marxists to use against them. But a simple layman in any branch of Islamic learning, he did not, and could not, recognize how drastically he was approximating the faith and the doctrinal complexity of his ancestors to the appeal of the secular ideology. To be sure, the success of this language with Bazargan's chosen audience was quite noticeable. Unaware of the grave doctrinal implications of his Marxist metamorphosis of Islam, both Bazargan and his audience went on believing they had reached a bona fide Islamic response to the model of all secular ideologies: Scientific Socialism.

Freedom in India

Sometime in the mid-1960s Bazargan wrote a book on India. The obvious purpose of this book, as its publisher was quick to point out,[161] was to provide a model for revolutionary conduct in achieving political freedom. The Iranians, particularly "the youth,"[162] had to be taught how other nations have achieved their freedom so that "*inshallah* we would see the day when such sentiments and devotions [to freedom] come to fruition, and [then] our people will progress alongside the free nations of the world."[163] Bazargan was explicit, from the outset, that imitating other nations in what they have done is a bad habit. There are no two completely compatible historical circumstances. There cannot be any nation blindly following another in its path to freedom. A comparative assessment, however, is something that can lead to fruitful conclusions.

From early 1962 Bazargan was imprisoned for his political activities in the Freedom Movement of Iran, during which time he wrote his book on India. At the beginning of the book he has a sarcastic reference to how prison gives people ample time for reading thick books. This period had given him ample time to reflect on a variety of issues, including the various national movements for freedom. Although Iran and India had long been compared and contrasted from a variety of perspectives, Bazargan suggested, social movements for independence and freedom have been excluded from such studies. There are many points of difference between the two nations. Yet they share the two essential features of being backward and "Westoxicated."[164] There are also economic, historical, and racial similarities.[165] Bazargan was particularly attentive to the fact that in India religion was the quintessential foundation of social and political movements. "Gandhi himself" had said so.[166] Upon this premise, Bazargan ventures a tentative theory about the religiosity of "the Aryan race":

It is rather strange that as the Aryan race moves from the East to the West, its religious taste and spiritual power diminish. The Indian civilization and kingship is derived from and assimilated into religious beliefs and inspirations. In Iran the great monotheistic religion of Zoroastrianism emerges, yet at a slightly inferior level, slanted towards practical ethics that are accepted and celebrated by the monarchy. And yet religion and kingship are separate from and independent of each other. When they [= "the Aryans"] reach Asia Minor and Europe, they cease to have a religion of their own, and they have to get it from the Semites.[167]

Bazargan concludes that in Iran and India civilization is derived from and based upon religious and ethical principles. The forms of government engendered by these civilizations are consequently more "gentle" and conducive to peace and prosperity. The Assyrians, the Semites, and the Turks, he expostulates, lack such qualities.[168]

The rest of Bazargan's account of Indian independence is a sympathetic short history of the sacrifices and heroism of this neighboring nation towards freedom. In this account, Bazargan is quite specific about the ideological and political preparations for the revolutionary movement,[169] about the necessity of getting the revolutionary message across to the machinery of the revolution: "The People." When referring to the hegemonic influence

of "The West" in India, he makes a passing reference to how "Westoxication" has afflicted Iranians too. "Having lost their selves to Europeans" is
how he identifies some of his compatriots such as Sayyid Hasan Taqizadeh,
who once said, "from head to toe, the Iranians ought to become Westernized." [170]

Bazargan gives particular attention to the role Muslims played in the
Indian independence movement. But beyond Islam, religion in general was
instrumental in this movement. Bazargan quotes Nehru as having said that
"the revival of nationalism in India, as in other Eastern countries, will
inevitably have to be religious [in nature]." [171] Bazargan found the revolutionary and reformist characters of Sayyid Jamal al-Din al-Afghani and
Muhammad Iqbal particularly timely and praised them for their universal
appeal to all Muslims regardless of their sect.

Bazargan's Atomic Theory of Revolution

Bazargan reserved his highest praises for Gandhi whom he considered a
genius. Gandhi's centrality in the Indian independence movement led Bazargan to some interesting reflections on the nature of revolution. These
reflections, in light of what would later actually happen in the course of the
Iranian Revolution of 1979, have a premonitory aspect to them. "It is easy
to say 'revolution,' " Bazargan suggested. [172] The actuality of the event is
much more complicated. It is much easier to sit down in a room, or deliver
a public lecture, and draw the battle lines of a revolutionary movement
than actually implement it. The main determining factor, he thought, was
the ability of the revolutionary participant to endure hardship and sacrifice.
This is particularly difficult because the outcome of the movement is not,
in any way, guaranteed. "All calculations and predictions may turn out as
ill-conceived." [173] Even long ideological preparations are not enough. "Fiery
speeches, persuasions, and proving the benefits of the movement are not
enough." [174]

Even the material means at the disposal of the revolutionary movement
are not absolutely necessary or, if present, enough. "Should we glance at
the process of the [Indian independence] movement from its very inception,
we see that it never had military power or [other] material instruments at
its disposal." [175]

Thus neither the ideological nor the material instruments are the condito
sine qua non of a revolutionary movement.

"The movement," Indian independence or any other, began by a spiritual and
mental revolution and conviction, with a pure spiritual force. The spiritual and
mental revolution gave rise to action and then social, national, and democratic
ideals emanated from it. It penetrated the hearts and minds of the educated class. It
created leaders and sympathizers. [176]

"Fiery mountains and steel walls" are needed for a revolutionary movement to gain momentum.[177] The Indians, and with them any other nation
seeking liberating ideals,

need a force more powerful than the material military and economic might. [They
need] a source of internal resistance and sustenance, with spiritual majesty, so that
they can carry forward the weight of that initial impetus and lead the country to
success.[178]

Upon such stipulations, Bazargan proceeded to define exactly who could
lead such a revolutionary movement:

A leader ought to enter the battlefield, raising the banner of the movement, who is
the symbol and source of such [spiritual and revolutionary] attributes. Those leaders
whose ultimate significance and influence is to understand or execute revolutionary
ideals among the limited intellectual middle classes, cannot assume mighty and vast
responsibilities.[179]

In the wake of Khomeini's June 1963 uprising and with Taleqani in the
same prison, Bazargan could have had either of these two Muslim revolutionary figures in mind when writing these words about Gandhi.

Looking closely at the experiences of the Indian independence movement, Bazargan developed a number of detailed theoretical positions on
every revolutionary movement. "In national movements," he theorized,
"sometimes a point is reached where the revolution assumes a momentum."[180] At this stage of the revolution, "Every action of the illegitimate
regime, whether mild or militant, serves in strengthening the movement
and advancing it towards victory."[181] The mechanism, as seen through the
revolutionary eyes of Engineer Bazargan, was perfectly logical, with the
laws of nuclear physics in its support:

If the enemy demonstrates mildness and retreats, the people use their front to
advance a few more fronts, and thus they are encouraged and enticed. If [the enemy]
intensifies the harshness and suppression, every person who is jailed or murdered
angers the nation, propagates the innocence, and proves the righteousness of the
movement. [This] would lead to a few new people substituting the eliminated
person and entering the battlefield. . . . This is very much like the atomic nuclear
activation when it enters the chain reaction phase. . . . Very soon all the radioactive
material is activated, and a universal explosion and sudden revolution take place.
The atomic bomb becomes the source of an almost infinite and uncontrollable
energy![182]

Every time Bazargan reaches such theoretical observations, anticipating
what would indeed happen just less than two decades later, a boldface print
appears (which in Bazargan's manuscript was probably underlined, or
written with a different color, or perhaps even boldfaced by writing over
the phrase), issuing a revolutionary staccato:

Every movement and revolution, should it have natural and legal grounds, and launched with good intentions and sacrifice, soon reaches such a phase. People's refusal to tolerate tyranny, their tolerance and resistance vis-à-vis the tyrant, forces the illegitimate and despotic ruler to commit greater suppression and atrocity. [He] would fall into a course of action that would increasingly reveal his pernicious countenance and bloody hands, [which, in turn,] would render more legitimate the righteousness and power of the revolutionaries.[183]

Here is the power of implication at work. Bazargan here writes about (Iran or) India. With remarkable similarity and precision, these prison notes became the blueprint upon which the Iranian Revolution of 1979 was unfolded. The chess game played between the Shah and Khomeini was set on a course such that every move the king made, offering the carrot or raising the stick, advanced him further and further into the corner where he would be checkmated. The bishop used the pawns with merciless accuracy. The crescendos of successive *chellehs* ("the customary mourning, forty days after the death of a person") became the tempo of the game. Whether the king permitted the procession of the mourning pawns or ordered his own to charge, he was painted black into his white corner. By the time he had fled the board, the game was over.

Every revolutionary movement, Bazargan further theorized, has to calculate into its ideological and material build-up the possibility, or indeed the inevitability, of human loss. But compared to what is to be gained this is not such a big sacrifice. Natural disasters, or even traffic accidents, have similar, or more, casualties. Yet they lack this- and other-worldly rewards and honors innate to a revolutionary movement against the rule of tyranny.[184]

To achieve such noble ends, revolutionary movements have a built-in mechanism of momentum and growth. Here Bazargan postulated a theory of decline in "natural phenomena" and a theory of growth in "human achievements."[185] In nature—for example, in human organisms—growth begins rapidly and then diminishes; in human achievements the opposite is true. First, the growth in human achievements, social and otherwise, is at a minimum speed. But gradually, as the growth assumes momentum, later advancements are at greater speed and tenacity. The same rule applies to revolutionary movements:

As soon as a force or a devotion towards a noble aim is engendered in a person or in a society, leading to activities in that direction, advancement is always with [geometrical] progressions and achieving [the goals] inevitable. Human achievements are, indeed . . . incremental, like a grain of wheat that is planted in a rich soil: The grain becomes a cluster, and then every grain in this cluster forms into a new cluster next year, and just like Kawthar goes into infinity. O how I wish in every nation such grains and such movements would blossom! *And From God is Success and Upon Him is Our Trust!*[186]

The revolutionaries' most immediate task is to implant the seeds of grand revolutionary ideals that will gradually take root and come to fruition. When that final fruition would occur could not have been very clear to Bazargan and his comrades in the Shah's prison. But given his captivating dark immediacies, he dreamt very vivid visions of the future.

The Centrality of Religion in the Revolutionary Movement

Bazargan used yet another occasion in the Indian independence movement to argue for the necessity of religion in every revolutionary cause. When he reaches the discussion of religious hostilities in the Indian independence movement, where the Hindu-Muslim animosity seriously challenges the achievement of liberty, he pauses and suggests that the issue be considered from a "higher" point of view.[187] He first concedes that religious beliefs and sentiments can be used for conservative and counterrevolutionary forces. He then suggests two ways of confronting such uses. The first solution, "which is apparently straightforward and logical and is chosen by many intellectuals,"[188] is to eliminate the religious force altogether. This solution would necessitate fighting against religious beliefs and institutions, as the revolution is waged against the colonial and dictatorial forces. The second solution is "the recognition of the significance and influence of the religious factor, which is to say, seeking its help and, if need be, reforming it."[189]

Bazargan condemns secular intellectuals such as Nehru who, despite the fact that they chose not to fight against the religious factor, still remained indifferent to it. He is more emphatic in his condemnation of the later leaders of the Indian independence movement who demonstrated "ingratitude"[190] towards the religious forces that were so instrumental in their success. He then clarifies his position and asserts that leaders such as Nehru should not, of course, have assumed valid "the superstitious"[191] ideas of certain religious forces. Instead, he projects the Iranian and Indian revolutionary circumstances together:

With respect, and conceding the legitimacy of the religious factor, they should have sought the solution from religion itself. They should have seen the cause and nature of the problem in the superstitious nature of certain beliefs and rituals, and in distortions in religious [beliefs]. They should have turned their careful attention to the root of the pain, and to the germ that had caused the illness in the spiritual body of the patient. They should have sought the solution in the presentation of a correct thesis and in the creation and sustenance of living, intellectual religious leaders.[192]

Anybody looking for such a solution among Muslims has an easy task because "Islam, from the beginning, is founded on positive, antislavery, and anti-ignorance social dynamism."[193]

Islam, thus reinterpreted, is a quintessential religion of "The East." "In the East," Bazargan believed, "everything is impossible and everything is possible."[194] The dialectic of this paradox rests not on an archaic notion of how Islam was but on a revolutionary urge of what Islam is or should be. In "The East" everything is impossible "if they wish to launch a deep reform with the materialist tradition, with 'The Western' method, under the pressure of colonialism and despotism, and with imposed and imitative thoughts."[195] Upon the postulation of such an impossiblity, which Bazargan targetted against his secular and "Westoxicated" contemporaries, he knew what was possible. "Yet it is possible," he closed the paradoxical dialectic, "when movements are launched with moral and noble ideals and with spiritual force."[196] If we were to launch, or to understand, the Indian independence movement "based on social, political, military and economic calculations of the West," it would have been a futile task. It was successful, and its comprehension is possible only because "it was predicated upon an ideological revolution, and upon a mental and moral movement," and perhaps more important because "the leadership was in the hand of such [men] as . . . Gandhi."[197] History would bear testimony to Bazargan's extrapolations from the Indian independence movement less than two decades later.

Bazargan does not particularly approve what has happened in India since its independence. They have abandoned their high moral grounds and succumbed to more mundane and material realities. Yet he closes his book on India with a laudatory note and then turns his glance to his compatriots and relates all he wishes to teach through this roundabout way with a remarkably precise and appropriate choice from the Qur'an (2:134): "Those are a people who have passed away. Theirs is that which they earned, and yours is that which ye earn."[198]

To Have Faith: Against All Odds

In the late 1960s, with the increasing secularization of the Iranian intelligentsia (and with them the collective political consciousness), the problem that Bazargan and his like-minded activists seem to have confronted was how to continue to legitimate, along the lines he had articulated about India, the contemporary relevance of a religious language. Recognizing that science secularizes, Bazargan faced the particularly acute and compelling necessity of conforming the religious language to the scientific (technological) discourse. Here he felt compelled to prove the continued validity of believing in Islam. Prefacing Medhi Bazargan's *Lesson in Religiosity*, published in 1965, Ahmad Aram, a distinguished translator and friend, proclaimed:

Discussing religion in the present time, in a way that is compatible with the advancements in scientific knowledge and method, is a task that can no longer be performed by [merely] studying [Arabic] syntax and morphology and things of that sort. What Plato, Aristotle, Avicenna, or Khajah [Nasir al-Din al-Tusi] have said is not enough anymore. It is important to know what Russell, Einstein, Heisenberg, Bergson and others have said in our time.[199]

To reach for a "scientific" validation of his faith, Bazargan constructed an elaborate system of ethical mandates. The foundation of this system rests on the centrality of religion in the human constitution. Religion is natural to man. A society cannot function without a set of sacred beliefs. No matter how technologically advanced a civilization might become, it shall always need a system of metaphysical belief.[200] Man's need for religion is as natural as his biological and emotional needs to love. Beginning with the love of physical gratification and comfort, Bazargan enumerates twelve successively nobler needs that end with the love of God.[201] These twelve phases are then divided into four categories: (1) love of self (wealth, prestige, etc.), (2) love of one's cohorts (family, country, etc.), (3) love of principles (truth, justice, etc.), and (4) love of God.[202] Love of God is the highest, and thus less frequently attained, of all. The more people are preoccupied by lesser loves, those of self, etc., the harder it is for them to attain the more noble and higher loves. Sacrificing lesser obsessions for higher ideals is the ultimate sign of nobility in man. The most complete and satisfying of all devotions is that given to God. The lower states are valuable only to the degree they contribute to man's well-being in his path to achieve the highest. Love and devotion to the highest ideal, God, automatically renders all lower states meaningful. Supreme monotheism, total devotion to God and all that He entails, is the ultimate salvation of man.[203]

There are two kinds of recognition of the highest Ideal: polytheism and monotheism. Because polytheism is the gradual construction of man's material conditions, it fails to meet his metaphysical expectations. But monotheism, which Bazargan identifies with "Islam, Christianity, Judaism, and even Zoroastrianism and Buddhism,"[204] is the archetypal expression of supreme metaphysical reality by specific agencies of Divinity, for example, the Prophets. Muhammad, for authoritative sources of whose life Bazargan refers to no Arabic or Persian sources but instead to European titles he calls "la vie de Mahomet" or "Life of Mohammad" (he actually writes them in the Latin alphabet),[205] was one of such Divine agencies. They had independently waged a moral battle against the prevalent corruption of their times. They had devoted themselves to the highest Ideal and thus unified their followers in one unique moral community. Devoid of any personal interest, and totally devoted to their Divine cause, these prophets had provided their immediate community with such archetypal models of justice and salvation that the more science and civilization advance the more their veracity has become recognized.[206] The moral communities they thus established have persisted in history. Monotheism, eschatology, and personal and social responsibility are the essence of prophetic teachings in this tradition.[207] These are duties and obligations that prophetic teachings establish against the staunchest possible resistance. It is precisely in complying with these metaphysical and moral obligations that human salvation—both personal and social—is attained. Regardless of the metaphysical truth of prophetic teachings, their actual moral imperatives are absolutely indispensable for a conscious civilized living. The regulated life of a civilized individual, regardless of the person's religiosity or the lack thereof, is precisely comparable to the daily regiment of a religious person:

As a matter of fact, the [daily] schedule of a civilized person, obliged to clean and brush, read a newspaper, learn and propagate, earn a living, do military service, participate in elections, etc., is quite similar to the very same ritual bathing, ablution, praying, religiously acceptable trade, defense, holy war, enjoining the good, etc., that we have in Islam.[208]

Having thus originated a civilized model of virtuous living that, in fact, goes against the grain of human disposition, the Prophets' self-understanding was that they are the mouthpiece of a reality superior to themselves.[209]

That God created this world is a self-evident truth, Bazargan insists.[210] Yet there are people who deny this truth. But since religiosity is, ipso facto for Bazargan, in the nature of man, then those who deny it ought to prove their case, not vice versa. There are two sets of reasons for atheism: practical and philosophical.[211] Practically, some people may feel unbearable pressure from the moral obligations of their religion, they may feel its ethical mandates outdated in the modern world, or they may see immoral acts perpetrated by religious authorities. Philosophically, they may consider the idea of God as something remote and incomprehensible, they may reject unbelievable and extraordinary claims of their religious doctrines, they may encounter events and experiences they cannot explain, or they may be attracted to alternative schools of understanding the world.[212] Bazargan sets upon himself the task of proving all these excuses untenable. Islam is not the cause of backwardness. If "The West" is technologically advanced, it is not because "Westerners" are irreligious. Quite the contrary, "on the average they are more interested in, and act according to, their religion than we Muslim Iranians."[213] Backwardness is true, but it is precisely because Iranians have ceased to be good Muslims, not being Muslim. If certain religious leaders are not living up to the proper standards they otherwise preach, in Shi'i Islam they may be denied any obedience and other, more righteous, leaders may be followed. If God cannot be seen visibly, it is because His essence and reality are beyond the limits of ordinary human perceptions. But as in all other forms of knowledge, theology deducts the existence of God from visible and tangible realities—very much like geology where changes and developments on earth are traced back to events millions of years earlier. These arguments all lead to the essentialist position that since everything has a cause, then so must this vast universe. Bazargan also puts up a valiant effort to rationalize such Qur'anically sanctified beliefs as those of creation, revelation, miracle, etc.[214] He genuinely believes in the gradual scientific verification of all religiously held doctrines. Medicine, for example, has proven that drinking is really hazardous to one's health. Fornication and gambling have equally been proven to be socially harmful. Although the question of revelation has not yet been proven scientifically, there are indications for its "seriousness and the possibility of its actuality."[215] As for the creation of the world in a few days: "It is possible that by 'day,' geological periods and phases of universal development are intended."[216]

Questions of theodicy, free will or predestination, etc., are also outside the purview of human comprehension, and thus causes of distractions from a religious worldview. But here, too, Bazargan insists, there may well be explanations for apparently inexplicable phenomena. And as for alternative, man-made, schools of thought that seek to explain the world independent of a God, none is capable of satisfying man's eternal quest for a quintessential explanation of his being.[217]

The Islamic eschatology is the last issue Bazargan valiantly defends in the face of the increased rationalization of his age. All religions, not just Islam, have had a fundamental belief in some form of an afterlife. It has a functional purpose to serve. "If we take the day of judgment away from religious teachings," warns Bazargan, "their value and impact are considerably compromised."[218] As for the skeptics who deny the rational feasibility of the day of judgment, Bazargan responds that if we are unaware of the whereabouts or possibility of something, it does not mean that it does not exist. Just to be on the safe side, we better believe that it actually exists.[219] As for science, although it has not yet proven that there is, in fact, a day of judgment, nor has it proven its impossibility. In the meantime, the actuality of the day of judgment is certain because "the prophets have said so."[220] But even reason points to the possibility of resurrection. Nature is renewed every spring. So can man be renewed at a given interval.[221] There are also recurrent visible signs of renewal and resurrection in the animal, vegetable, and mineral organisms. There are also numerous reports of dead people having been resurrected and brought back to life.[222] "Thus, scientifically and principally," Bazargan concludes, "it is not impossible for a part of the human body, even a very small part, like a fetus, seed, root, or branch, under favorable circumstances to grow and thus recreate precisely the same person, with the same face, physiognomy, characteristics, and memories."[223] Believing in bodily resurrection on the day of judgment is thus a perfectly rational proposition.

Bazargan divides the Islamic acts of religious obligations into three categories: (1) personal responsibilities, (2) responsibility towards the people, and (3) responsibilities towards God.[224] This triple set of responsibilities, defining and locating a Muslim in the community, is obviously inter-related. Referring to a French source on the content of the Qur'an, Bazargan points out the number of Qur'anic passages on matters of social and political concerns to be the highest in comparison to other issues. "Serving the people" is thus the highest and most fundamental common denominator of all these responsibilities.[225] From man to God, there is an ascending ladder that necessitates a sacrifice of personal desires for communal concerns before one reaches the attributes of the Divine Presence. Put differently, only such social and political concerns are noble and trustworthy that direct the communal experiences towards God.[226] In ennobling man's communal concerns and political purposes, Islam leads him away from his mundane personal pursuits and redirects him to publicly beneficial ends.

House of the People

Bazargan could not have completed the cycle of his attendance upon the ideological sedimentation of Islam reinterpreted without turning his attention to the most compelling communal symbolic of the faith. Early in the Spring of 1960, he performed his hajj pilgrimage to Mecca. A year later, in 1961, he published his notes from this trip in the widely circulated journal *Maktab-e Tashayyo'*; eight to nine years later, in 1969, he published a book called *The House of the People* in which he reflected on the social and political significance of the hajj pilgrimage.

In Medina, Bazargan begins to see the important sacred sights and to reminisce about crucial historical events: the rise of Islam like a volcano in the black depth of a dark night, the taking of Imam Hossein's family into captivity, etc.[227] He bitterly criticized the deplorable state of sanitation among the pilgrims. Yet he admired the cleanliness and majestic serenity of the Prophet's mosque. He was particularly impressed with the public prayers that emphatically reminded him of "the majesty and unity of Islam."[228] He then proceeds to make a comparison between the serenity and majesty of the Prophet's mosque and the striking filth of where they resided in Medina. This difference, he thought, was precisely indicative of Islam as it was and as it is now. The mere confessing of being a Muslim is not enough, Bazargan retorted. "Accepting the [Islamic] faith is not the end of responsibilities and activities, [it is] the beginning of a life[-long] program, and the commencement of an intellectual and practical movement, both personal

and social."[229] He blamed his fellow Muslims for merely repeating the
words and phrases of their religiosity without the slightest attention to the
actual "reforming of the world."[230] He objects to the Saudi flag depicting
two swords and the Islamic confession of faith. He believes that while, like
all other great "intellectual revolutions," such as "socialism, communism
. . . and Christianity,"[231] Islam has fought for its ideals, still the physical
force does not represent this faith properly. Islam is not a religion of
violence, he contends. Bazargan is severely critical, particularly of his fellow
Shiʿites:

As for what we Shiʿites do: Should we [continue to] have this shameful and
despicable ethical, civil, social, economic, and political situation vis-à-vis other
nations, is that not a treason, a damage to the truth and veracity of Islam? By
[failing to] give the world ([especially] our own citizens and youth) living and
practical examples [to follow], are we not misleading them [to believe] that being a
Muslim is equal to backwardness and misery?[232]

To advance further his rationalization of hajj for an audience he must
have assumed secular, or at least skeptical, Bazargan decided to change the
name of the pilgrimmage destination, traditionally known as *Khaneh-ye
Khoda* ("The House of God") to *Khaneh-ye Mardom* ("The House of the
People"). Changing to "the People" from "God" was no mere accident. It
reflected the predominant political mood of the time, when, through the
hegemonic order of Marxist discourse, such terms as "The People," "the
masses," etc., had assumed wide currency.

In this book, as in most other things he wrote, Bazargan's universe of
discourse was dictated by the most compelling part of his imagination:
"The West." It was against a "Western" skepticism of what is the significance of a hajj pilgrimage that he sought to defend the contemporary
relevance of this supreme religious act. The ultimate objective of hajj, as he
now saw it, was to suggest the imminent possibility of world peace, through
the formation of one single universal Islamic community. Such universal
organizations as the United Nations are mere suggestions of similar posibil-
ities inherent in this obligatory Islamic practice.

There has been a gradual but persistent growth in the Qur'anic language
and its universal claims on humanity.[233] Bazargan actually charted[234] the
frequency of the word *nas* ("the people") as it appears in the Qur'an, from
the first to the last year of the Prophetic mission. According to this chart,
from beginning to end, the Prophetic mission, as reflected in the Qur'an,
was quintessentially concerned with "The People." Abraham, as the archetypal prophet, Kaʿbah, as the archetypal locus of the Divine Presence, and
"The People," Bazargan asserts, form a sacred triangle in the Qur'an.[235]
Against the Islamic goal of universal humanity, postulated in the archetypal
language of the Qur'an, the non-Islamic world has been divided into reli-

gious and other sectarian factions. Even socialism has not succeeded in establishing a universal humanity. It has simply translated religious factionalism to ideological factionalism.[236] Through its customs and practices, and true to its relentless monotheism, Islam has established clear guidelines and practical instruments by which the universal unity of humankind can be achieved.[237] These ideals notwithstanding, Bazargan alerted his audience to the fact that in the course of Islamic history Muslims themselves have massacred each other on the very premise of the sacred precinct.[238] Thus he advocated the establishment of "an International Islamic Brotherhood Group," pending its more universal composition, to supervise the sacred precinct. "You may silently laugh," he guessed:

In the modern world of science and technology, populated by innumerable people and states with mutually exclusive interests, possessing powerful and strange weapons, with wealth, knowledge, wisdom, and strategems, and in a world that on the whole rotates on might and money, in the face of the mountains of difficulties in the real world, what could be the significance of circumambulating around an old cubical, throwing out a few worn pebbles, and finally shedding the blood of an innocent animal?[239]

It is essentially a symbol, very much like the sign of a dove carrying an olive branch in its beak, that Bazargan sees in the unifying force of the hajj pilgrimage. This had to be universalized so that the Kingdom of Heaven could be materialized on earth.

A Man for the Last Season

Electrified by a full grasp of the increasing secularization of his age, Bazargan's main concern has been to twist and turn his understanding of Islam into that formidable form and shape that would validate his high ideals for the young audience he targeted. Because of his French education, and because he earnestly saw the European and American technology as the chief magnetic force for his young compatriots, Bazargan believed that the only way he could render his version of Islam still relevant was by massively and popularly technologizing it. Thus, if "love" and "obedience" were the forgotten terms of a credal language, he translated them into "thermodynamic" and "steam machine" instrumentalities, constructed and implanted in man to move him towards God. The ultimate result of such wholehearted and sincere efforts lent a necessary helping hand in the making of "the Islamic Ideology." There were students of physics, chemistry, and engineering, as well as young professionals, who were attracted to this particular vestige of "the Islamic Ideology." Perhaps even more than social sciences and humanities, with their persistent streak of Marxism checked by conservative classicists who thought them, hard sciences had the great propensity of leading the young Muslim students astray to the rocky roads of disbelief. Bazargan's brand of Islamic apologia was a particularly welcome signpost for this segment of the potential revolutionary constituency. To be sure, his pseudoscientific religious discourse is more defensive than offensive. He wishes to safeguard in sincere piety grounds he felt were being gradually eroded and lost to the mighty secular language of "The West." The battle, he felt, was lost in "The West," in that Other world that most mattered to and chiefly defined him. But it was still possible to score a limited victory at home, where Bazargan felt he could be more in control of his environment. The Tudeh Party and, to a lesser extent, the National Front were the chief institutional forces that, oddly enough, in conjunction with the tyrannical monarchy itself, represented that outside "Western" world that he wished to curb before it was totally unleashed on what he held sacred in the Iranian society and valid in its long and arduous history.

A Good Man

"Only when good men have instructed the people for seven years," says the Confucian stipulation, "may they take up arms."[240] Confucius would have considered Bazargan a good man, in the most simple, sincere, perfectly unsettling, and benign sort of way. He conveyed more than seven years of revolutionary instructions before his followers could take up arms. "To lead an uninstructed people into battle," again the Confucian wisdom adds, "may be described as throwing them away."[241] Putting "good men" and "battle" together, we may conclude the superior Confucian wisdom of the ethic of violence. There is no escaping violence in politics, especially when it turns revolutionary. "Good men" are the Confucian agencies of sustaining the moral imperatives that render violence legitimate. Cornered by the overpowering force of the secular god-terms that animated his age, Bazargan sought to train, to cause to be born again, a class of revolutionary professionals as professional revolutionaries: soldiers of high moral principles revolting against the injustice they saw and imagined in their world. He is less brutal than his chief enemies; and he is willing, and he has been forced, to pay for his ethic of responsibility. He is more ethical (which is to say he can see the wisdom of laughter and doubt) than his chief revolutionary cohorts; and he has no choice but to be swept away by their more brutal convictions in their more absolute truths. Less certain of his absolutes, his supreme virtue, intuitive rather than acquisitive perhaps, his sign of salvation, is his sense of humor. The possibility of laughter, at self and at all the others, has retarded Bazargan's ascent to supreme political leadership, as it has, at the same time, advanced his claim on the more noble necessity of being human: all-too-clumsily human.

CHAPTER 7

Abolhasan Bani-Sadr:
The Monotheist Economist

"There is also a subsidiary point that, at the present stage of things, it is very much easier socially and politically to influence the rate of investment than to influence the rate of consumption."[1] John Maynard Keynes noted this supposition to Josiah Wedgwood, a fellow director of the Bank of England. When "the present stage of things" is given, economists can only ponder and debate between investment and consumption, inflation and unemployment, deficit and depreciation, or any other two sets of binding variables. "No doubt you can encourage consumption by giving things away right and left. But that will mean that you will have to collect by taxation what people would otherwise save and devote to investment—all of which would be a stiff job in the existing political and social setup."[2] Keynes could continue the dialogical juxtaposition further, insofar as "the existing political and social setup" was to stand the logical and indubitable prerequisite. "Perhaps," Keynes conjectured finally, "you may say that that is a reason for getting rid of the existing political and social setup. But is it clear that expenditure on housing and public utilities is so obviously injurious that one ought to attempt a social revolution in order to get rid of it?"[3] The question rhetorical, the answer was "no" for both Keynes and Josiah Wedgwood as well as for any other director of the Bank of England. For Keynes, social revolutions need more drastic reasons, necessitate more forceful causes, because they lead to more radical changes—beyond the limits of economy. But, and there is the distance, once the balance between the opposing economic forces becomes abstracted into graver ideological convictions, once the mysterious urges to construct a flesh-and-blood rational man, with equally rational choices of economy, wed the obsessive sensibilities to construct a social organization of puritanical economic proportions, and finally, once God is called on to bear witness to the monotheistic veracity of one's economic predispositions, then we have every rhyme and reason lined up for precisely that "social revolution" about which Keynes was so circumspect. Circumspection is the first virtue, or is it vice, revolutionaries choose to discard.

The First President

Sayyid Abolhasan Bani-Sadr was born on Wednesday, 22 March 1933, in the small village of Baghcheh near Hamadan in central Iran. He came from a distinguished religious family. His father, Ayatollah Sayyid Nasrollah Bani-Sadr, was the son of Sadrololama' Hamadani, a prominent Shi'i cleric. Bani-Sadr was raised and educated in modern secular schools in Tehran and Hamadan. In the early 1950s, when Mosaddeq led the nationalization of the oil industry, Bani-Sadr is reported to have been active in his support. At this stage, however, he was not a member of any particular political party. In the late 1950s and early 1960s he attended Ayatollah Taleqani's Qur'anic sessions in the Hedayat mosque. At about the same time, he attended the Faculty of Theology and the Institute of Social Research at Tehran University. He later joined the Faculty of Law where he pursued a degree in Economics. His political activities during his years at Tehran University led to his arrest and imprisonment. He also actively participated in the June 1963 uprising of Ayatollah Khomeini. Soon after, however, he left Iran for France where he spent much of his time studying the social and economic problems of Iran. He was one of the first nonclerical activists to join Ayatollah Khomeini in Neauphle-le-Château, as the revolutionary sage led the last stages of the movement to topple the Pahlavi monarchy.

Cult of the Individual

To be educated in Tehran or Paris during the 1950s and 1960s means to be up-to-date on the latest in the Marxist discourse. To be a "Muslim student," with or without a beard, imposes a double imperative. Islam and Marxism demand equal attention. The ideologues of the Islamic Revolution, always active in "the 60s" of their imagination, attended the forceful conceptual arsenal of secular ideologies and with remarkable tenacity sought to render them operative in viable Islamic terminologies, instruments of a mobilizing force.

Bani-Sadr became a significant contributor to the gradual construction of "the Islamic Ideology" more by disposition of character than by any accident or deliberation. Bani-Sadr's prose and personality are synergetically flat, a mere matter of fact. That is why, perhaps, one of Bani-Sadr's main contributions to the making of the Islamic ideological discourse was a book he wrote on the *Cult of the Individual*, in which he enumerates social, economic, political, military, and cultural factors instrumental in the making of a cult of personality. Lacking Al-e Ahmad's charm, Shari'ati's passion, Motahhari's relentlessness, Taleqani's power of persuasion, Tabataba'i's legendary learning, and, most of all, Bazargan's senses of doubt and humor, Bani-Sadr must have, not by accident, attended to his share of "the Islamic Ideology" with a cool denial of "the cult of the individual." But he put this self-psychological necessity to some ideological use. The remarkable aspect of Bani-Sadr's discourse in his discussion of "the cult of the individual" is his persistent use of Qur'anic passages, particularly those in which Pharaoh appears (for example, al-Mu'minun, 45–47), to formulate an Islamic version of this post-Stalinist notion in the history of Marxism. Bani-Sadr also provides an Islamic explanation of why and how the cults of individuals persist,[4] gives a full account of this historical manifestation of Marxism,[5] indicates its symptoms,[6] and finally discusses the methods of its implementation.[7] In the final section of this book, he provides an argument as to why Islam is essentially opposed and antithetical to the cult of the individual.[8] Here he argues, for example, that there is preference in Islam for "what is said" as opposed to "who has said" it.[9] He concludes that

the Islamic thought rightly organizes the struggle against the cult of the individual and calls it the Greater Jihad. . . . We have to avoid following this cult, which disguises itself in different religions and ideologies.[10]

Cults of the individual can develop only in other religions and ideologies. In "the Islamic Ideology" no such cult shall emerge. The Qur'anic text is explicitly against it. Bani-Sadr's attendance upon the historical and doctrinal construction of "the Islamic Ideology" is perfectly prototypical.

Balances and Equilibria

But at the same time, he has to leave his particular mark. A certain kind of equilibrium, Bani-Sadr maintains, is operative in every kind of theoretical proposition, political or otherwise. This equilibrium is predicated on certain modes of relationships among the constituent forces of every theoretical proposition.[11] There can be three kinds of equilibrium: (1) negative, (2) positive, and (3) simultaneously positive and negative. The negative equilibrium, in relationships such as those between man and man, man and the universe, and man and God, entails no relation of power and tyranny. The end result is always positive and constructive. Islam entails such negative equilibria.[12] Bani-Sadr calls this mode of equilibrium a "unitary (monotheistic) relationship" (rabeteh-ye towhidi) that is unique and essential to Islam.[13] Every kind of relationship not based on towhid (unity, or unity of God) is inimical to man and thus friction-provoking. In Islam every kind of relationship is an extension, an archetypal unfolding, of that between man and God. Because that relationship is based on "negative equilibrium" and no friction, then any other relationship should be established through that of the man-God paradigm. Thus, insofar as social, political, and economic relationships—or any other kind of mundane relationship—are based on that of the man-God paradigm, there is no tyranny, friction, or exploitation. If exploitation is the result of social relationships based on any model other than that of the man-God, then alienation of multiple selves results. By referring to Qur'anic and Hadith sources, Bani-Sadr argues[14] that man is created with an innate disposition towards unity, a relationship of obedience to God that imbues no friction, but sustains infinite positive power. This negative relationship of no friction can also be extended, Bani-Sadr suggests, to the relationship of societies with each other, as envisioned by the first Shi'i Imam, Ali. This is quite unlike those relationships in the modern world that are based on exploitation and "positive equilibrium," namely, two separate units confronting each other with equal forces.[15]

Bani-Sadr's is an explicitly and repeatedly theocentric vision. The only way out of the existing frictions between man and man, man and society, society and society, etc., is to return to the man-God paradigm which is frictionless and negational.[16] He shares the Marxist ideal of the ultimate elimination of classes;[17] however, he does not think this is possible insofar as the relationship—man to man and man to society—is not modeled on the man-God paradigm.

Should we want to move from fictional and mythological solutions to a scientific solution, we will have to accept a system that is regulated on the basis of a relationship with God and thus gives all human beings unlimited possibilities for growth (because in the man-God relationship possibilities are unlimited); and that is precisely the solution that Islam offers.[18]

But Bani-Sadr has to account for certain historical discrepancies. The model that Ali provided in early Islamic history was not successful because of the immediate material conditions of the time, not because the idea was misconceived. If future Islamic revolutions are to be successful, they ought to be modeled on Ali's paradigm, on the elimination of self-identity, and on the active recreation of the man-God relationship in every other kind of relationship.[19]

Bani-Sadr believes in the possibility of a total elimination of dominance, as the most emphatic expression of physical force, in a social relationship. This, in fact, is particularly necessary during the revolutionary period:

The significance of leadership [is] in protecting the revolution, and in preventing it from becoming absorbed into the universal order which is founded on force. If a revolutionary society wishes to proceed on the revolutionary path, it should not return, at any cost, to the relations of dominance. . . . This is the first and most essential step.[20]

Insofar as the international relationships are concerned, the Islamic society thus conceived should participate in the world community only to the degree that it does not entail one group exploiting others.[21]

Once the unitarian (monotheistic) society *(Jame'eh-ye Towhidi)* is thus conceived and attained, it should lead other societies to join in this "light of unity."[22] In mandating how this is to be achieved, Bani-Sadr refers to *jehad* ("holy war") as well as the Book (The Qur'an) and justice as the proper mechanisms for bringing the world community into the classless, unitarian, and rather flat society that he thus imagines and constructs. He does not elaborate on how one should use *jehad* to achieve this end and yet remain within the nonviolent control of his "negative equilibrium" stipulation. But ultimately he believes that unless the basic relationship among individuals—and individuals and society—is not reformulated on a friction-free basis, all reformist movements are but cosmetic gestures that lead nowhere.[23]

There are four aspects to this reformulation of human relationships on the basis of a friction-free model: political, economic, social, and cultural.[24] Politically, the absolute authority is that of God, and thus the historical dominance of the few over the multitude should be eliminated. "Instead, through vicegerency, everyone has the right to leadership over himself and others, to the limits of his ability and potentials."[25] Bani-Sadr is not specific on the precise political implementation of this idea into the framework of a state apparatus. Economically, the ultimate ownership is that of God too, and thus there must exist "the ownership of man through vicegerency *(takhlif)* upon labor"[26] which means the elimination of not only private but even collective ownership.[27] Here, too, Bani-Sadr does not provide details of how such an economic model ought to be implemented. Socially, no relationships, even those between husbands and wives and parents and children,[28] are valid unless they are established through God.[29] Culturally, Bani-Sadr argues for absolute freedom in the adoption of a religious worldview.[30] "Let us not forget," he reminds himself and others, "that even thoughts that have been offered in order to eliminate the relations and properties of power have been turned, at the hands of their administrators, into means of legitimizing despotism."[31]

The critical path that Bani-Sadr wants to show towards this state of perfect harmony is constructed as follows:

The entire course of human history has been spent in trying to be released from religious despotism. The only way for emancipation is that which God Himself put at man's disposal. Other than God, no one has the right to consider his thought of absolute certitude. No one has the right to force himself and others to obey it.[32]

A social relationship thus based on the premise of power and authority necessitates an altogether different kind of homo sociologicus. To Bani-Sadr, when men assume their self-identity as something sui generis and not as an extension of the Divine will, they enter into positive relationships with others, which is always friction-provoking. Once they negate their self and enter into relationships with others through self-denial, as they do with God, then they have a negative and friction-free disposition towards that relationship. Unless the very foundation of a human relationship is based on the denial of dominance, one group succeeds the other in relationships of power.[33] Because "The Western" ideologies that preach the ideal of equality postulate a relationship of obedience and dominance to attain that goal, they will ultimately be nullified by the very relationship they wish to establish.[34] There are ideological movements that harbor both negative and positive relationships, but ultimately they are founded on an affirmative recognition of minds (and thus actions) having an identity separate from God, which leads to a multiplicity of identity.[35] Bani-Sadr proceeds to give a complete table of the three modes of relationships[36] according to which only the "negative or nonexistent equilibrium" leads to man's salvation based on a complete elimination of dominance.

The notion of "negative equilibrium" is Bani-Sadr's neo-Sufist, idealist way of extracting physical force from all modes of a social relationship. "Every state is founded on force." Trotsky's remark at Brest Litovsk was so significant an insight into the nature and organization of political order that Max Weber adopted it into his definition of the state.[37] In his own formulation of the relationship of command and obedience, Weber stipulated two conditions: external means (or physical force) and inner justification (or institutional or individual legitimation). Bani-Sadr's aspiration here is to eliminate altogether the factor of physical force. In this utopian design, constructed out of sheer frustration with the centrality of violence in any ideological claim to political salvation, Bani-Sadr provides a crucial glimpse of his cryptopacifist attitude. This attitude, however, conceals, ever so slightly, a latent hostility towards the opposing ideological claims to political truth. This hostility, the origin and direction of its anger, derives its force from an absolute, neo-Sufist, conviction of having the ultimate and final truth on one's side.

Not just Bani-Sadr but all other exponents of "the Islamic Ideology," with the occasional exception of Bazargan, share the absolute conviction that God is on their side. The Islamic nature of this ideology gave the ideologues that sense of inner certitude that they had, in truth, seen the light. In addition to this innate cause of certitude coming from the Islamic dimension of the ideology, there was also the added element of "scientific" certainty, which the ideologues of "the Islamic Ideology" patently borrowed from Marxism and its exclusive claims to "scientific socialism."

Having both God and Science on their side, the Islamic ideologues attended their historical exigencies with indubitable certitude.

In addition to this generic conviction, Bani-Sadr's pacifist denunciation of violence as the condito sine qua non of all kinds of social relationships has a unique and exclusive claim to political truth. The pacifist denunciation of violence is but a thinly disguised visceral contempt for those who resort to it in the political realization of their ideological bid for power. Having denounced violence, Bani-Sadr then assumes a certain sense of moral superiority that adds proportionately to his indubitable certitude that he has absolute truth on his side. Assumptions of moral absolutism are then constitutionally intolerant of conflicting paths that may even point to their own presumed sacred destination.

Consommation Du Futur

Violent or nonviolent, Bani-Sadr had to discredit, in classical Marxist urge, the economic foundation of the status quo. In March 1974, Bani-Sadr published a collection of essays and documents with Paul Vieille. In *Petrole et Violence (Oil and Violence)*, published under the auspices of the National Front in Paris, the authors sought to expose "the repressive police state" in Iran that with "brute force accompanied by the severest control of information" had created the myth of a "White Revolution."[38] In his contribution to this book, "Développement de la Consommation du Futur et Misère" (The Development of the Consumption of Future and Misery), Bani-Sadr offered an analytical critique of the Shah's economic policies in which he charged the monarch's economic policies of artificial expansion without productive investments in the infrastructure. Economic exploitation, political repression, rampant unemployment, and the misery of the working class, Bani-Sadr charged, were the results of these policies.

Dividing the Iranian economy into state and private segments, Bani-Sadr criticized the thrust of two of the five-year plans—the third (1963–1967) and the fourth (1968–1972)—as ill-defined and serving only the monarch's interests. In his estimation, these budget plans had prevented the natural "circulation" of the Iranian economy.[39] Based on the data taken from the annual reports of the Iranian Central Bank, Bani-Sadr wished to argue that the monarch's state capitalism had essentially benefitted the Shah's army rather than the public services.[40] Whereas the state-sponsored investments in preferred areas had enjoyed steady growth of 13.9 to 48.1 percent between 1966 and 1971, the expenditures on public services had fluctuated between 4.4 and 2.4 percent during the same period.[41] Further dividing the state's expenditures between 1967 and 1970 into three categories of (1) administration, (2) army, and (3) development,[42] Bani-Sadr demonstrates[43] how more than 30 percent of the national budget was spent annually on the Shah's army, police, gendarmerie, and the Secret Police (SAVAK). Massive dependence on imports had further rendered the Iranian economy a subsidiary of the dominant "Western" capitalism,[44] only for the benefit of the rising new bourgeoisie, leaving much of the society unaffected and disinherited. Thus, by selling out the oil, the Iranian monarch was plundering the country's natural resources for the benefit of the dominant "West." Iranians had to become the consumers of goods produced abroad. Exporting their natural resources, importing consumer goods, Iranians had been turned into parasites on the world economy. Through the mechanism of the state budget, the Iranian economy had been interwoven into the world market, but to the detriment of its agriculture, an illusion of industrialization, plundering the natural resources, with a minimum or non-existent level of social services.[45] Bani-Sadr's indictment against the economic mismanagement of the monarchy was that it sold the future of the country cheap by preconsuming the national wealth, all for the follies of a man who has caused "a dominated nation . . . [to be] alienated, plunged into an (un)reality where tomorrow is no better than today, devoid of its place, its intelligence, its physical stamina, where only violence can maintain it."[46]

Oil and Domination

Matters of economic mismanagement were high on Bani-Sadr's manifesto against the Pahlavi regime. The centrality of oil in the Iranian economy was of much concern to the Muslim ideologue who wrote his long treatise on *Naft va Solteh (Oil and Domination)*, a variation on the theme of *Petrole et Violence,* between 1969 and 1974.[47] In this book he is engaged in the belabored argument that an intrinsic relationship exists between the political economy of oil and the sustenance of dictatorship in Iran. The United States has forced the OPEC countries to increase the price of oil, with the stipulation that the surplus revenue thus engendered ought to be deposited in American banks and, in turn, channeled into the American domestic economy.[48] The Shah's government sought to alleviate the domestic fear of the depletion of the oil reserves by publishing fictitious figures showing that for the next thirty years (from the early 1970s) Iran can produce nine million barrels of oil per day.[49] But the impending dangers of an economy based totally on imports, sustaining a massive military machine, and overburdened by an expanded bureaucracy are too grave for the regime to tolerate.[50]

Bani-Sadr's purpose in writing *Oil and Domination* was to demonstrate how a total reliance on oil was detrimental to the Iranian economy but beneficial to "The Western" industrial economies. The illusion of oil revenues should not detract from the more essential fact that the true beneficiaries were "The Western" oil companies and their respective economies.

Bani-Sadr presents his arguments fortified with tables, charts, and diagrams. The book is thoroughly documented with sources in Persian, French,
and English, covering a range of primary and secondary materials of the
contemporary Iranian political economy.

Bani-Sadr commences his discourse on the political economy of oil with
a sense of alarm and danger. He feels something threatens the very existence of the country. Opposing any meaningful unified action is the range
of the ideological battles that exhaust the energy of the revolutionary
activists.[51] The clandestine publication of this book in Iran, Bani-Sadr
contended on 5 June 1978, should not be taken as an indication that such
ideological hostilities have been surpassed. Yet he is optimistic that the
publication of books such as his will pave the path for informed political
action. "The function of science is to demonstrate the strengths and weaknesses and to ascertain the foundations of thought and action of the emerging generation."[52]

From time immemorial, Bani-Sadr remembers, oil has always been central to the Iranian economy. Had the contemporary "era of oil revolution"
not coincided with the Iranian political crisis, this country would have been
"a great economic force in the world."[53] The William Knox Darcy oil
concession early in the twentieth century practically sold out the Iranian
national wealth for the whimsical pursuits of the leading elite. Later, in the
early 1930s, the Anglo-Iranian oil concession was extended for sixty years,
perpetuating the plundering of people's wealth. This extended contract
coincided with a period of rapid growth in "The Western" economy that
has been detrimental to Iranian economic independence and advancement.
After World War II, the Allied forces established "the politics of positive
balance" in Iran, whereby both the capitalist and socialist superpowers
exacted political and economic concessions from Iran. While the functional
fifth columns of the Soviets (the Tudeh Party) and "The West" (the Free-
masons) sought to guarantee the economic interests of their foreign masters, Mosaddeq launched the nationalist movement that advanced the cause
of Iranian political and economic independence and sovereignty. His objective was to establish a "negative balance" whereby neither the capitalist
nor the socialist superpowers would exploit the Iranian natural resources.
But both the ruling regime and the Tudeh Party condemned his policy: the
regime for obvious reasons of self-interest and the Tudeh Party because the
Soviets' interests were denied. Bani-Sadr emphatically asserts that those
who believe in a "positive balance" want to sell Iranian resources to both
superpowers in order to sustain their hold on the government, while those
who believe in a "negative balance" are the true advocates of the people's
rights and the national wealth.

Leading the movement towards the nationalization of the oil industry,
Mosaddeq opened a new chapter in the Iranian struggle for economic and
political independence. Bani-Sadr celebrates Mosaddeq as "the veteran

soldier of the nation"[54] who championed the cause of Iranian liberation from domestic and foreign influences. Despite pressures from the Pahlavi regime and the hostilities of the Tudeh Party, Mosaddeq was able to pass a bill in the Parliament in early 1951 whereby Iranian oil was nationalized. By mid-June 1951, in Bani-Sadr's narrative, the nationalization of oil was put into effect and the British were ordered to hand over the industry.[55] The British and the Americans then conspire to topple the Mosaddeq government and succeed by arranging the CIA-sponsored coup of 1953. Other than the British and the Americans, Bani-Sadr considers the Soviets equally complacent in this coup. He also condemns the Tudeh Party (especially its military arm) for having failed to respond.[56]

After the coup of 1953, as Bani-Sadr narrates the history of the modern Iranian political economy, the policies of the Iranian oil industry are dictated by the interests of "The West."[57] In "The West" the "Seven Sisters," or the seven giant oil companies, emerge as the dominant political and economic forces that determine the fate of the oil-producing countries. The result of all this is the ascendancy of the United States as the supreme political and economic force in the world. The United States, and with it "The West" in general, has attained this political and economic ascendancy at the expense of the people of the oil-producing countries. The creation of OPEC was merely a deceptive device to facilitate this massive plundering of natural resources. The policies of OPEC "have not violated the economic interests of the United States of America."[58] The result of such an inequitable state of affairs is that

The inequality between the owner of the wealth and those who actually use it is increased constantly. What is left is anger, in the flame of its fire the children and the potentialities of oil-producing countries are burned.[59]

The political economy of the Iranian oil industry has necessitated a particular mode of relationship between Iran and "The West." The Iranian oil is increasingly fed into "The Western" manufacturing industry; in turn, Iran has been turned into a massive market for "The Western" consumer goods. The result is a trade balance totally injurious to the Iranian interests. In 1976, Iranians have imported twenty-two times more than what they have exported.[60] The crucial impact of this imbalance has been a complete lack of internal investments in local manufacturing and a decline in Iranian goods and services. The oil economy has grown increasingly independent of the overall Iranian economic growth and, indeed, functions completely against it. Totally sacrificing the integrity of the Iranian local economy, the Pahlavi regime has become a mere instrument for selling the most precious Iranian natural resource for "Western"-produced consumer goods:

Thus totally advantageous to the dominating ["Western"] economy, the oil revenues have been the cause of economic disaster in Iran. . . . Having forfeited the

Iranian economic independence, the ruling regime, which is in charge of implementing such [economic] plannings, has condensed the causes of its existence and continuity in exporting the national wealth and importing industrial goods.[61]

Oil plays a negative role in the domestic Iranian economy because it is geared towards playing a positive role in the world capitalist system. The world has become the universal territory for "The Western" capitalist system to rob the weaker nations of their natural resources.[62] Multinational corporations have effectively divided among themselves capital investments, natural resources, and the world's manpower. Oil is merely another natural resource at their disposal. They are thus in such commanding positions to dictate the expenditures of the weaker nations to coincide with the demands of the world market. At the same time, they force their client states, such as Iran, to substitute the interests of the world capitalist system for their domestic economic priorities. As a result, a consumer economy is forced on any possibility of the locally managed production economy. To secure this arrangement, "The Western" capitalists ought to be in complete control of the world's oil production. Multinational corporations are also in charge of the worldwide distribution of consumer goods so they can maximize their profit and miminize their losses from political turmoil in their client states.[63] The colonial powers, at the same time, annihilate the very physical foundations of an autonomous economy in the countries under their control. All economic initiatives in investment, production, distribution, and marketing are at the exclusive disposal of these dominating forces. The more the oil-producing countries become thus dependent on the world economy of the superpowers, the more they lose their chance for any sense of economic autonomy.

That Bani-Sadr's study of the role of oil in the world economy is the first of its kind, he insisted,[64] is merely an indication of how "The Western" powers prevent the dissemination of these facts among the oil-producing countries. In fact, the oil-producing countries receive only 20 percent of every increase in their prices. The remaining 80 percent goes to the industrial countries.[65] If the oil-producing countries could utilize their oil in their own countries, with only 20 percent of their annual production, they could have precisely the same revenue they do now[66] and would have increased the durability of their oil reserves by five times. The current state of affairs prevents the inclusion of oil in the local economies of the oil-producing countries. With only 5 percent of the current rate of production, these countries could create thousands of jobs in their local productive economies, rather than barely sustaining an exporting oil economy. If such measures were taken, the duration of the Iranian oil reserves could be extended from the current estimate of 20 to 25 years up to 700 to 1,000 years.[67]

A Manifesto on Oil

On 23 March 1973, Bani-Sadr was instrumental in drafting a Manifesto in Paris condemning the Iranian government for its oil contract with a consortium of oil companies.[68] Condemning the blatant plundering of the Iranian natural resources, the manifesto, whose text appears in *Oil and Domination,* called for drastic changes in the political economy of oil. All foreign influence over or ownership of the Iranian oil reserves had to be discontinued.[69] The Iranian national economy had to be reevaluated totally, purchase of military equipment abandoned, and the entire export-import ratio reconsidered. An oil industry had to develop inside Iran so that by 1980 the export of oil would be totally stopped. For this purpose, investment in industrial countries had to be stopped and redirected towards investment in the oil industry inside Iran. The relationship between Iranian oil and the rest of the economy had to be restructured so that each would enhance, not impede, the other. The productivity of oil had to be measured by internal Iranian interests, and not by the industrial superpowers for their immediate concerns. The Iranian work force had to be sustained by an economy in which the production of oil is integrated. Whatever oil revenue is generated has to be spent on economic growth so that the Iranian economy is once and for all liberated from the supremacy of "the dominating centers."[70] In all commercial transactions, oil or otherwise, Iran had to free itself from all political bondage to the domineering powers. It had to enter into commercial transactions only with those countries that were willing to respect its political and economic autonomy. In its monetary system, the Iranian currency should not be so totally dependent on oil revenues and in relation to the American dollar. It needed an independent relationship with major world currencies. Iran had to use oil as a weapon[71] to disturb the existing balance whereby the majority of the world is being exploited by the industrial powers. As first Mosaddeq and then Khomeini had emphasized,[72] this was not a time to stand by idly, when Iranian national prosperity and integrity were at stake.

Preventing a realization of such high hopes is the integral significance of oil in the international economies of the industrial superpowers. Bani-Sadr contends with facts, figures, charts, and tables that if we compare the economic growth of eight "Western" countries (Belgium, France, West Germany, Italy, the Netherlands, Sweden, Great Britain, and the United States) in successive periods (1870–1913, 1913–1950, 1950–1970, and then 1973), we conclude that in the latter two phases unprecedented achievements have occurred. During these periods, "The Western" economy has taken advantage of "the oil revolution" to achieve historical economic growth.[73] One crucial consequence of this has been a massive concentration of capital and expertise in these advanced industrial societies.

A massive byproduct of such enormous concentrations of economic force is the creation of a giant military complex in "The West." Thus, there is an internal mechanism through which Iranian oil is gradually translated into massive capital in "The West."[74]

The illusion of an increase in oil prices is nothing but a deceitful scheme to intensify the depletion of oil reserves in the oil-producing countries and the simultaneous concentration of capital in the industrial societies.[75] Because the production of oil in the United States is 15 times more expensive than in the Middle East and 25 times more expensive than in Iran,[76] it is economically more feasible to exploit these resources in the Middle East. Although there are opportunities for exploration in nuclear[77] and solar[78] energies, the industrial superpowers ("The West") do not invest in such projects until they have depleted all the oil reserves of the nonindustrial countries.[79] Bani-Sadr, in fact, concludes with a more drastic pronouncement on the significance of oil in "The Western" countries:

If the industrial countries were to spend all their gross national product to produce substitute energies for oil, they would still fail to produce as much energy as they would with oil. That is the significance and status of oil in the economic growth of the industrialized countries. For twenty more years, the industrialized countries will be dependent on oil not only for their economic growth but for their very daily existence.[80]

This should alert Iranians, along with all other oppressed people of the oil-producing countries, to wake up and use oil as a weapon against their oppressors.

The oil revenues, which are acquired by selling out the most precious natural resoures of the nation, are not used for further economic growth. Quite the contrary, they are transferred back to the industrialized societies through a variety of mechanisms. The very act of exporting the oil to "The West" is ipso facto a transference of gross capital out of the local economy. In addition, oil companies exact a variety of extortions from the oil-producing countries before and after lucrative contracts. By massive investments in "The Western" countries, a considerable proportion of the oil revenues is redirected back to the industrialized economies. The accumulation of foreign currencies in foreign banks, an increase in reserves of foreign currencies, a massive increase in the imports of goods and services, and purchasing "The Western" military equipment are among the chief channels for returning oil revenues to the industrialized countries.

Bani-Sadr concludes that since the inception of a world industrial economy founded squarely on oil, Iran has lacked a national economic independence. "The West" has dominated and exploited the Iranian natural resources.[81] Exports have been effectively eliminated; and the import of foreign goods and services has been substituted for a healthy program of local production. From transportation systems, roads, economic infrastructures, to customs regulations, "Westernization" of the Iranian banking system, and the creation of a culture of consumption, everything in Iran is tangential to foreign interests. This has had grave consequences not only for the Iranian economy but also for the Iranian national and cultural character. As oil production has thus thwarted any meaningful growth in the Iranian economy, it has, conversely, contributed to an historically unprecedented accumulation of wealth, capital, and expertise in the industrial ("The Western") societies. Explaining such catastrophic impacts of economic mismanagement and outright betrayal—and struggle to reverse this state of affairs—should be high on the revolutionary agenda of all responsible Iranians.[82]

The Ideological Force of the Monotheistic Economics

From the political economy of oil to the specific program of action necessary to realign it with Iranian national interests, the agenda and the language attending to the economics of "the Islamic Ideology" were patently set by the Marxist sociology. That economic matters are at the foundation of political issues informed all the particulars of Bani-Sadr's construction of a revolutionary political economy. Adopting the Marxist language and perception, "the Islamic Ideology" would necessarily seek to articulate its economic claims on legitimacy. Although both Motahhari and Taleqani had attended to a number of economic matters, it was left to Bani-Sadr to address these issues specifically.

Bani-Sadr's attention to economic issues are more matters of the ideological articulation of a political agenda than the theoretical elements of a political economy. He sees aspects of his Islamically derived political economy as a mechanism for world unification, all under the Islamic banner. His conceptions of "the internationalization of land and natural resources," his hopes to "universalize nature on the principles of Islam,"[83] translate the universal claims of "the Islamic Ideology" into the factual elements of a "romantic economics."[84] But despite this romanticism in its language and disposition, the political economy he develops is part of an orchestrated endeavor to vindicate Islam as the supreme model of social, political, and economic order. This concerted effort is waged to combat two foes on two simultaneous fronts: the status quo for its economic inequities and the Marxist alternative for its revolutionary appeal. But these two hidden agenda, in turn, are reflective of the singular theme of apologizing for and validating Shi'ism as a bona fide "ideology."

In Bani-Sadr's political economy, issued from the high altar of "scientific" certitude, God is the owner of everything, the sole and chief proprie-

tor.[85] There is that idyllic stage when, in the absence of the human appropriation of power, God Almighty created and blessed and man used freely
and in bounty. There emerged gradually the artificial centers of power that
appropriated what was otherwise the Divine bounty for all humanity.
Ultimately, it is for this paradisal state that Bani-Sadr's unitarian (monotheistic) economy *(Eqtesad-e Towhidi)* serves as a blueprint. Both in the state
of Divine bliss and in that ideal state of history when *Eqtesad-e Towhidi*
shall reign supreme, only human labor constitutes a valid claim to relative
ownership. Absolute ownership is the prerogative of God Almighty, relative
ownership is the rightful claim of labor.[86] Catering to the Marxist agenda
of secular alternatives, Bani-Sadr appropriates the claims of the proletariat
into the moral imperative of land, as the archetype of property as such, to
belong to the one who works on it. In this and all other related matters, it
is quite evident that for Bani-Sadr issues of political economy are primarily
translations of a more pronounced ideological agenda. "Bani-Sadr tends to
avoid," it has been rightly suggested, "precise formulations and awkward
questions that may weaken the radical tone of his utterances."[87] Primarily
ideological in nature, these radical utterances are meant more to mobilize
their targetted audiences than to chart a realistic economic program.

On the opposite side of the laborer stands the capitalist, of whom Bani-
Sadr has an equally politically mandated perception. Always "more conscious of the ideological aspects of these issues"[88] than their respective
economic complexity, he refuses to acknowledge capital as accumulated
labor. Generated capital, or accumulated wealth, is personified in the merchant capitalist, and labor is personified in the laborer. Approximating
Islamic principles to a socialist political economy, Bani-Sadr always tilts the
capital-labor balance to the advantage of the laborer. But his problem,
which is the cause of many "loopholes and inconsistencies [in his political
economy],"[89] stems from the fact that Islam recognizes the right to private
property. The juridical legitimation of private property in Islam, however,
had to be ideologically superseded if "the Islamic Ideology" were to meet
its Marxist challenge.

Accumulation of wealth, in Bani-Sadr's judgment, is ipso facto wrong.
That there are Imami traditions prohibiting the accumulation of wealth[90]
is more a matter of appropriating an ideological justification that one
assumes by virtue of belief than the rational precision of making any
economic sense. That there are serious challenges to Bani-Sadr's ideological
economics from the point of view of a serious political economy[91] is more
a matter of academic curiosity than of any particular relevance in the
orchestrated myth of the "monotheistic economics." By the same token, to
control and manage effectively the affairs of a "monotheistic economy,"
Bani-Sadr inevitably postulates a total state. This state is in charge of an

equal distribution of income, justice, and the consequent national prosperity. From the idealization of this utopian state it is but a short distance to the articulation of a programmatic manifesto.

Capital As Accumulation of Violence

Bani-Sadr's conception of "monotheistic economics" is an extension of his total, pseudo-Sufi, idealistic rejection of violence as the quintessential factor in defining and persistently characterizing any possibility of the human political collectivity. "Economics," he theorized, "is the science of struggle against scarcity." [92] But the scarcity people ought to struggle against is not natural. God has created enough of everything.[93] Scarcity is a socially created malaise. Economics is the science of struggling against such artificially created scarcity. Extended from this premise, Bani-Sadr argues that capital cannot be considered as the quintessential feature of economic life, with everything else elaborated from it. This is his way of rejecting "capitalism" or the primacy of capital in economic production.

In every institutional human grouping four essential concentrations of violence appear—in economics, capital, in politics, power, in society, social relations based on physical force, and in religion (or ideology), systems of belief that sustain such relations of power—upon which human collectivities are founded. Insofar as "positive balances" exist among such relationships, there is no escaping the relations of domination and exploitation inherent in each domain. To break this cycle we must return to "the natural" [94] state of our being wherein material values are important only to the degree that they are transubstantiated into spiritual values. Economics based on "positive balances" can only lead to the exploitation of a majority by a minority. Economics based on "negative balances" leads humanity to transform its material gains into spiritual virtues. The latter possibility is "the Islamic economics,"

which opens the closed circuit and makes it possible for humanity to regain the spirituality that has been denied it. This economics is the science of struggling against systems that are founded on physical violence, adding scarcity upon scarcity.[95]

Nothing short of a revolutionary breakthrough[96] is Bani-Sadr's intention in his "Monotheistic Economics." Accumulation of capital and the right to property have denied millions of people the most natural right to work and produce. Islam has offered the way that reverses this positive equilibrium to a negative balance of power, whereby human energies are not wasted on balancing opposing forces but are directed towards combating nature.

Throughout history a persistent accumulation of power has occurred in centers of domination, an accumulation that has consistently expanded and multiplied its claim to political and economic obedience. Centers of power are created from innate greed and excessive accumulation of wealth. Inevitably, such centers enter into hostile relationships with each other. Altogether four major attributes are present in every relation of domination:[97] (1) The dominating force always assimilates the features of the dominated subjects; (2) the dominated subject enters an irreversible process of self-disintegration as soon as it begins to cater to the alien needs of the dominating force; (3) a persistent relationship of inequality ties the dominating and the dominated groups together; and (4) the ultimate end of all dominating forces is self-destruction.

There is historical overpresence of the centers of power and their accumulation of raw physical force. Only through the Islamically mandated "negative equilibrium" can we reach for a total negation of the very idea of domination.[98] In the interim, the subjects of an oppressive regime ought to refuse to comply with the slightest mode of legitimacy that perpetuates the system in its claims to justified rulership. The economic concentrations of wealth and capital are the most blatant manifestations of political tyranny. There is a vast and pervasive network of economic exploitation that sustains political domination. Islam is the only salvation that, denying the legitimacy of such oppressive economic exploitations, seeks to institutionalize political and economic justice.[99]

Islam opposes the vast and pervasive accumulation of capital (force) through a number of integral responses to innate human needs. On the four fronts of political, economic, social, and cultural concerns, Islam opposes physical force as the ultimate source of ownership.[100] Recognizing only God as the ultimate proprietor, Islam thus shifts the legitimacy of ownership from physical force to labor, which is the only bona fide reason for ownership. Labor is the very mode of the relationship upon which God has regulated His act of creation. Thus labor should also govern the mode of the relationship between men. Extended from this logic, man's relationship to objects of his creation ought to be determined not by accumulation of capital, but by labor.[101] The primacy of labor in such relationships is indicative of the more compelling truth of the Islamic economics that denies any right of ownership except through that of God. No human agency, individual or collective, shares in God's absolute ownership. However, He delegates ownership based on the publicly beneficial virtues of His created beings.[102] Attribution of supreme and this- and other-worldly ownership is the simultaneous denial of any inherent or inherited property right to human beings. Recognition of this Islamic truth requires a tenacious adherence to political struggle until such time as the "Monotheistic Economics," based on the denial of a positive equilibrium between capital and political power, is realized.

"The Monotheistic Economics" is Bani-Sadr's ideal construction of specific ways in which Islam prevents the accumulation of wealth and its concomitant exploitation of labor. As he understands and interprets it, Islam prevents the formation and growth of independent centers of accumulated power.[103] Instructing the Muslim believers not to succumb to political and economic domination, Islam has sought to instill a rebellious trait in the character of its believers. In addition, Islam has curtailed the greed of the wealthy, while preparing the material and ideological grounds for struggle against political and economic exploitation. Islam has done so in full recognition of the variety of ways in which accumulated centers of power seek to perpetuate their rule of corruption and exploitation. Religiously mandated systems of taxation in Islam such as *Zakat* and *Khoms* are institutional occasions for modifying the growth of economic might in one particular social grouping or another.[104]

Islam, as Bani-Sadr interpreted it, recognizes private ownership only to a limited degree.[105] He has a kind of theological explanation for this. Man is the vicegerent of God on earth. That we know from the Qur'an. However, man has a social and personal identity. His social identity, Bani-Sadr postulates, precedes his personal identity. Thus in the God-society-individual postulation,[106] "as it pertains to certain properties, individual ownership is unacceptable; in certain others, collective ownership [is equally unacceptable]."[107] Bani-Sadr's conception of "society" is not merely that of a Muslim country. He says he has all of humanity in mind.[108] Here a certain functional Imamology enters Bani-Sadr's economic theology. The catalytic factor in the God-society-individual relationship—and the active agency deciding what is to be owned collectively and what privately—is the figure of the "Imam."[109]

Foundations of a Political Theory in Bani-Sadr's Imamology

Who is this "Imam"? And what are his political responsibilities? In the midst of Bani-Sadr's "Monotheistic Economics" there appears to be a latent theory of supreme political leadership in a Shi'i community and in much more than that. His Imamology begins in his theology (with its inherent sociology and anthropology), all located in his economics and centered around the pivotal issue of property.

God is the First, the Last, and the Absolute Owner of everything.[110] Man is God's supreme created being and his vicegerent on earth. The only mode of legitimate ownership is the one considered in relation to the absolute ownership of God. Man can claim private or public ownership only to the degree that it is considered an extension of God's grace and beneficience. Any other mode of ownership, not considered inherently "borrowed" from God, is inevitably founded on force and, as such, leads to alienation.[111] When it comes to the all-too-crucial question of public and private ownership, Bani-Sadr postulates a God-society-individual relationship in which man's public character assumes supremacy over his personal nature. This obviously leads to the primacy of public over private concerns. These public concerns are more of a universal rather than particular (Shiʿi) nature. To decide between the specifics of public and private ownership, Bani-Sadr postulates the necessity of an Imam.[112] But even more important, this Imam functions to render the God-society-individual relationship operative, effective, and legitimate.

As we move from God to society to individual, the right to absolute ownership decreases. Thus God has more claim than society to absolute ownership, and society more than the individual.[113] Individual and society are physical realities with tangible rights and feasibilities of ownership. God, a supreme metaphysical reality, has as His "executive representative" *(nemayandeh-ye ejra'i)* the "Imam," who acts on God's behalf as the supreme claimant to absolute ownership, beneath him standing, in right to ownership, society and then the individual.

Bani-Sadr is also emphatic that what he is now actively engaged in is the economic dimension of the God-society-individual relationship.[114] There are obvious other dimensions to this primordial pattern of authority. The political dimension is the paramount feature of the relationship particularly indicated in the chief characteristics of the Imam as God's "executive representative." Having thus been given the status of God's supreme representaive on earth, the Imam's authority is not limited to any Shiʿi or even Islamic constituency. "Islam," Bani-Sadr emphasized, "is not the prerogative of the Arabs or the Persians. It is, rather, a system for all humanity and, as such, not just for a given period of time, but for all times."[115] The dominion of the Imam's supreme political (and any other) authority, as God's chief mouthpiece, is global and atemporal.

But who is this "Imam" with such vast and pervasive claims to world obedience? As a Shiʿi believer, Bani-Sadr certainly must have envisioned one of the Twelve Infallible figures who succeeded the prophetic authority, according to the doctrinal mandates of the Twelvers. The last of these Twelve, the Hidden and Expected Imam, is the only metahistorical possibility Bani-Sadr could have postulated through all these exercises in economic Imamology. Yet throughout these exercises, he speaks of "the Imam" with such evident matter-of-factness that he scarcely appears to have a doctrinal vision of the Infallible figure in mind. There is no specific, or even vague, reference that would identify "the Imam" in his monotheistic economics with any one of the Twelve Infallibles.

Bani-Sadr is reported to have been the first person to refer to Ayatollah Khomeini as "Imam."[116] This posits the strong possibility of a built-in mechanism of "expectation" *(entezar)*, central to Shiʿi Imamology, in Bani-

Sadr's stipulation of "the Imam" and his functional centrality in his theological economics. What makes this possibility particularly strong is Bani-Sadr's notion of "Monotheistic Economics," an economics that aims at "returning" the human material and spiritual conditions to its divine origin. Multiplicity has rendered humanity asunder. What we need is a return to that primordial state of being when unity and harmony reigned supreme. The Imam, as an agent of the Divine will, is the providential agency that would facilitate this return *(rej'at)*.

This built-in mechanism of "expectation" in Bani-Sadr's theological and Imamological economics is perfectly harmonious with the general spirit of his Shi'i predilections, if not with the specifics of its doctrinal mandates. The figure of the Hidden Imam thus assumes an archetypal meaning beyond and above its (Shi'i) doctrinal identification with a particular metahistorical figure. In this archetypal rendition, the Hidden Imam becomes the supreme legitimizing image of resurgent Islam that can account for any number of historical personifications. Bani-Sadr's grandiloquent appellation of "the Imam" for Ayatollah Khomeini is the most natural, even inevitable, outcome of not merely a reconstituted version of his Shi'i disposition, but, perhaps more important, a theoretical necessity in his "Monotheistic Economics."

Bani-Sadr's "Imam" is the active agent in leading a permanent world revolution. Taking issue with Marxism and its illusion of creating a classless society,[117] Bani-Sadr postulates an Islamic theory of permanent revolution, which he calls "permanent resurrection,"[118] whereby societies, led by Bani-Sadr's "Imam," develop through successive phases of economic (cum political) movements before they reach the goal of "monotheistic economy." The primary objective of this permanent revolution is to oppose and annihilate the concentration of violence and the multiplication of economic exploitation. This revolution knows no territorial or natural boundaries.[119]

The identification of this "Imam" with a figure outside the Twelve Shi'i Infallibles is made possible particularly by Bani-Sadr's extension of the term into active revolutionary engagement. This "Imam" has a central significance in Bani-Sadr's economics, particularly in matters of ownership.[120] He plays a central and continuous role in leading the society to the right path.[121] Bani-Sadr is emphatic that this "Imam" assumes a certain mode of limited responsibilities "before reaching the supreme utopian society of the Imam of the Age,"[122] or the Hidden Imam. The functions of Bani-Sadr's "Imam" are to be implemented in this "long historical purgatory" before the Twelfth Imam appears. He has "relatively absolute"[123] authority over the means of production. The owner of all public properties, the "Imam," as contructed by Bani-Sadr, spends the proceeds of his properties for the public good.[124] This "Imam" should abstain from any exericse of prejudice. "If he be an Arab," stipulated Bani-Sadr, "he cannot give the non-Arab property to Arabs; or if he were a non-Arab [Iranian], consider Iranians over others. And also, differences of religious schools *(madhhab)* could not constitute a reason for prejudice."[125] This latter remark makes it particularly evident that Bani-Sadr does not have a specifically (Shiʿi) doctrinal understanding of the "Imam" because all Shiʿi Imams were Arabs.

Bani-Sadr's "Imam" shall lead all humanity to the perfect Islamic utopia, where all violent multiplicity will have given way to absolute unity and harmony.[126] In this utopia there is but one religion in which all hatred and inequality are eliminated, all knowledge is harmonious, nature is unified, classes are eliminated, the economy is monotheized, leadership is synchronized, leader and society are cross-identified, and perfect universal peace is attained.

The Primacy of the Economics

Thus responding to the Marxist primacy of the economic factor, Bani-Sadr constructs an entire theology, Imamology, sociology, and anthropology around the central questions of labor, means of production, capital, and (private and public) ownership. His economic vocabulary is taken straight from Marxism. Intertwined with Qur'anic passages and other related Islamic insignia, his adaptation of the Marxist economic discourse seeks to combat the ascendency of the secular ideology while propagating the Islamic alternative. But beyond the immediate and projected implications of the "Monotheistic Economics" for "the Islamic Ideology," his formulation creates a vacuum for a supreme spiritual leadership he identifies with "the Imam." His conception of this "Imam" is more than a theological doctrine; it is an economic necessity. Translating Marxist economic reductionism into his brand of "the Islamic Ideology," he gives his "Imam" the centrality of an economic necessity. This "Imam" rises not from the doctrinal foundation of the Twelver Shiʿism, but from the material concreteness of Bani-Sadr's economics. Speaking the voice of God, this "Imam" is omnipotent. Having the entire universe in mind, his politics would be global, his revolution permanent, his time eternal. There are desperate attempts by the liberal side of Bani-Sadr's mind to limit, ever so feebly, the Imam's supremacy of power, the primacy of his will. But with God as his author, the expanse of the universe his realm, eternity his domain, and economics the inevitability of his resurgence, Bani-Sadr's "Imam" knows no sky as his limits, no reason for his logic, no time in his destiny, no territory to his ambition, no limit to the totality of his power.

Modarres: A Revolutionary Model

From the vast abstraction of an updated Shiʿi Imamology, Bani-Sadr's ideological construction of a supreme political figure with innate metaphysical inevitability needed to have a specific historical anchorage, without which, preferably in the remembered vicinity of recent historical memory, the Imamological construction would have lost all its ideological relevance. In the autumn of 1979 Bani-Sadr published a treatise reconstructing, as he did, a revolutionary image out of a clerical radical of a former generation, right in the active memory of his targeted audience.

Beyond the immediacy of history, mythical porportions yield more easily to the remaking of a revolutionary model. This much every ideologue knows.

Sayyid Hasan Modarres (1870–1937) was a prominent clerical activist of the Constitutional and early Pahlavi period. His scholastic education took him from Iran to Iraq, where he studied with the leading doctors of Shiʿi law. He returned to his homeland and taught jurisprudence for a number of years in Isfahan, where he was elected a member of the Iranian parliament. He escaped an assassination attempt in 1926. He was actively involved in the politics of the early Pahlavi period and is believed, by his followers, to have been poisoned in Reza Shah's prison.

Bani-Sadr wrote his book on Modarres in the autumn of 1976, on the occasion of the fiftieth anniversary of "the dark reign of the Pahlavi dynasty." [127] It was dedicated to Ayatollah Khomeini, "who is in exile," and to other revolutionary clerics such as Ayatollah Taleqani. The anonymous publisher of this text testifies in length that Bani-Sadr's original manuscript has been expurgated considerably by the omission of certain tedious passages and the addition of certain necessary historical background. [128]

An Economic, Political, and Natural Survey of Iran

Bani-Sadr prefaces his resuscitation of Modarres's memory with a long survey of Iranian economic, political, and "natural" history. In his economic survey, he maintains that integration into the Islamic empire gave Iran an unprecedented opportunity to become a leading commercial force. Between the ninth and the seventeenth centuries, Bani-Sadr proposed, Iran was a leading economic center at the heart of the Islamic world. [129] From the tenth to the thirteenth centuries, Iran was at the height of its commercial power, a status never achieved before or since. Even after the Mongol invasion of the thirteenth century, Iran continued to prosper economically; however, it was gradually cut off from the rest of the Islamic market. The bazaar, as an independent and thriving commercial center, lubricated the economic machinery; commercial transactions were facilitated by an ad

hoc "monetary" and "banking" system.[130] From the Safavid period onward, Iran was cut off from its "natural" economic network (that is, the
Islamic world) and came under the direct influence of "The Western"
interest and influence.[131] With this economic domination came the overpowering influence of "the domineering Western counter-values"[132] that
gradually robbed Iran of its Islamic culture. As Iran becomes part and
parcel, and a subsidiary, of "The Western" economy, it disintegrates in its
own economic terms and interests. This disintegration of Islamic lands was,
in fact, the true objective of the Crusades.[133] After such a long time, "The
West" was finally able to achieve its medieval designs against Islam. As
economic matters stand now, from labor force to investment capital, monetary policies, commercial transactions, and export-import policies, all are
in the service of "The Western" powers. By exploiting the Iranian oil, these
powers have ruined the healthy growth of the economy. Concomitant with
the disintegration of the Iranian national economy and its subjugation into
the dominant economy of "The West," social groupings have also been
formed that seek to perpetuate the cultural and political hegemony of "the
domineering culture."[134]

There has been a political corollary, Bani-Sadr contends,[135] to this eco-
nomic development. For centuries Iran has been "one of the two or three"
world superpowers.[136] Neither the Alexandrian invasion nor the Arab or
Mongol conquest had affected this political supremacy. It is from the
Safavid period that Iran, in effect, began to lose its global political power.
At present, Iran has lost its "independent existence."[137]

With the advent of the Fatimids, the Abbasids began to lose their dynas-
tic grip, and the influx of the Turkish (the Ghaznavids and the Saljuqids)
dynasties gradually weakened the power of the Islamic world. At the same
time, "The West" assumed enough political and economic might "to dare"[138]
to launch the Crusades. The side effect of this "Western" intrusion was
that the Arabic element of domination was succeeded by the Turkish.

Throughout its ancient and medieval history, the primary spirit of Iran
has been "the internalization of the external,"[139] which means all the
Greek, Arab, Turkish, and Mongolian elements have been Persianized into
a homogeneous cultural identity. Unrivalled cultural achievements, as well
as massive but aborted social movements, were the chief characteristics of
this period. Whenever the central governments were weakened, massive
social movements would ensue. Yet whenever these movements achieved
their immediate political ends, two simultaneous metamorphoses would
drastically change their nature. As the leaders would be drawn into "the
cult of the individual," the content of their ideologies would alter from a
"negative equilibrium" to a "positive equilibrium," from a denial of violence as the core of the political organ to its active confirmation.

When the sword was defeated by the gun and the catapult by the cannon, as Bani-Sadr characterized the defeat of Safavid Iran by the Ottomans at Chaldoran, Iran began to lose its global political power and then commenced a reversal of its long historical constitution, "the externalization of the internal." [140] Whereas before the advent of modern times Iran received every passing element of foreign invasion and assimilated it into its own unique Persian *Geist,* it was now yielding and transforming every aspect of its traditional identity to the specifics of the hegemonic "Western" force. As the Safavids and the Ottomans both perished and disintegrated, "The West" rose in political power and cultural hegemony. From this point onward, Iran is but a pawn in superpower rivalries. Iran begins to lose considerable portions of its territory and, even in what is left, the country is not exactly autonomous and independent. Extremities of foreign influence shape the external and internal policies of the sovereign state.

Bani-Sadr divides the Iranian politicians of the colonial period into three groups: the Russophiles, the Anglophiles, and those who believed in "negative equilibrium" between the colonial powers. [141] The king has never represented the third group. He has been a mere index to the rivalries of the two superpowers of the time.

Bani-Sadr divides the religious force into two opposing groups: one that actively opposes the state and its foreign connections, and the other, which he exclusively identifies with the Baha'is, [142] that supports the government in its internal repressive policies and external submissive relations to "The West." Bani-Sadr is particularly critical of the "internationalistic" attitude of the Baha'is who, in his estimation, effectively advocate subjugation of Iran to foreign powers insofar as it caters to the Baha'i faith. [143]

Bani-Sadr's true champions are the great advocates of the "negative equilibrium." National heroes such as Qa'im Maqam Farahani or Amir Kabir opposed both the superpowers and their disruptive influence in Iranian affairs. [144] But the success of these nationalistic forces was always tangential to the rivalries of the Russian and British colonial powers.

The contradictions resulting from the Russophile, the Anglophile, and the nationalist interactions reach revolutionary proportions in the late nineteenth century. Bani-Sadr believes the influx of "political ideology and cultural forces" into Iran was instigated by "The West" and chiefly facilitated through Freemasonry. [145] The advent of the Russian Revolution drastically weakened the Russophiles' position, and the Anglophiles assumed the upper hand during the post-Constitutional period. This paved the way for the coup d'état that brought Reza Shah to power. [146] It is upon this premise, Bani-Sadr's rendition of Iranian modern history, that he sees the revolutionary significance of Sayyid Hasan Modarres. As Reza Shah becomes the active agent in founding the Iranian state totally on foreign "political, financial, and cultural" grounds and in "the Westernization of Iran to [its] bone marrow," Modarres assumes leadership of the nationalist movement.[147] The result is that the massive subjugation of Iran (in economic, political, social, and cultural terms) to the domineering "Western" system renders totally ineffective the revolutionary movements of figures such as Colonel Muhammad Taqi Khan Pessian, Shaykh Muhammad Kheyabani, Mirza Kuchak Khan Jangali, Sayyid Hasan Modarres, and finally Mohammed Mosaddeq.[148] The fifty years of the Pahlavi dynasty, Bani-Sadr observed in 1976, have been spent entirely on intensifying the domination of "The West."

Bani-Sadr finally gives an ecological and demographic history of Iran, beginning with the emergence of the Iranian plateau from the sea.[149] This is an attempt to measure the mutual effects of political and ecological changes—such as the impact of brutal powers on the physical environment—on each other and the forces of periodic changes in water resources on irrigation and respective economic policies.[150] Particularly important has been the political impact on the environment, to the point where only 4 percent of the total land capable of being cultivated is actually thus utilized. The lack of a reliable and continuous political and economic system has led to a two-to-one ratio between cultivations contingent upon rainfall and those sustained by some type of irrigation system. Altogether three modes of irrigation have characterized the Iranian agricultural history: rivers, rain, and qanats. The qanats played a leading role in agricultural irrigation up until the Mongol invasion in the thirteenth century when the network sustained major damage.[151] From that point onward, Iranian agricultural economics has suffered enormously because, in effect, it has had to rely on seasonal rain.

Bani-Sadr continues to examine the significance of wind,[152] earthquake,[153] national epidemics,[154] droughts,[155] and tribal migrations[156] in the political economy of Iranian history. He proceeds to reiterate Karl Mitfogel's theory of the Asiatic mode of production and "oriental despotism."[157] Here, Bani-Sadr believes, political powers have appropriated and slanted to their advantage the Avestan and the Qur'anic injunctions that water is the common property of all people.[158]

Bani-Sadr concludes that in Iran the vast diffusion of the primary (natural) sources of economic productions has prevented a centralized political and economic administration.[159] The irrigation system was too volatile to cope with rapid and violent political changes. Multiple centers of political power have further aggravated this situation. Both state and oppositional forces have used irrigation systems to consolidate or undo each other's power. In fact, political powers were forced to engage in direct agricultural activities. This plus the fact that the scarcity of natural resources had rendered ineffective any meaningful private property have led to the effective ownership of land by the powers that be. To a considerable degree Bani-Sadr takes issue with Mitfogel's theory of "the Asiatic mode of production and oriental despotism" and maintains that the less powerful the central governments have been, the more prosperous the local economies have become.[160] Nature, in fact, has had a dual role in Iranian society: politically it has curtailed the freedom of the subjects, and economically it has restricted the power of the state.[161] But in effect, Bani-Sadr concedes, farmers have had to trade control over their cultivated land for political protection.[162]

The advent of the colonial period has had a devastating impact on Iranian agriculture. Weak governments, under pressure from the colonial powers, have meant poor irrigation policies, which, in turn, translate into disastrous agricultural results: drought, food shortages, and a proportional increase in the mortality rate. With the discovery of oil and with the transfer of the Iranian economy from the ground level to under the ground, the historical balance between state and society has given way to a more despotic relation where the government's rule over the people is totally unchecked.[163]

In the history of the Iranian political economy, nature has been like a woman.[164] Patriarchal politics has exploited nature and women simultaneously.

The Political Ethics of Modarres

This long historical introduction, Bani-Sadr's rhetorical vision of a necessary ideological antecedent, functions as a prelude to his account of "the political ethics" of Sayyid Hasan Modarres.[165]

At the very outset Bani-Sadr concedes that his purpose in attending to Modarres's historical significance is neither biographical nor historical. What is immediately necessary for "the contemporary generation" is "the more useful and the more noble" cause of preparation for the big battle "against the Pahlavi despotism."[166]

The set of criteria according to which Bani-Sadr thinks a political leader ought to be evaluated includes measures of his persistence, valor, virtue, and the ability to resist compromising with the enemy.[167] Also of importance is the ability to resist the temptations of the cult of the individual. He has to be able to translate the specifics of revolutionary leadership into an effective program of action. His ability to transcend personal concerns is crucial in reaching for the higher aspirations of the revolutionary movement. In mobilizing the masses towards the revolutionary goals, the leader —or what Bani-Sadr quite literally calls an "Imam"—ought to be able to organize a central nucleus of leadership. In addition, Modarres, in Bani-Sadr's reading, was also a great champion of "the negative equilibrium." He wished, safeguarding the interest of the masses, to take Iran out of the positive equilibrium that existed between the superpowers and their internal advocates in Iran.[168]

For Modarres, Bani-Sadr recollects, there is no separating religion from politics. "Our faith is precisely our politics, and our politics precisely our faith," Bani-Sadr quotes Modarres.[169] Iranians ought to reject any kind of positive equilibrium with "The West": "You for yourselves; and we for ourselves."[170] For Modarres, as Bani-Sadr narrates the politics of the old revolutionary sage, "negative equilibrium" was not simply a formula for releasing Iran from international tensions. The principle was "the very essence of religion."[171] It is only through this mechanism that true monotheism can be achieved. A class society, based on a positive (affirmative) distinction between social groupings, is the most vivid indication of a polytheistic underpinning to a people's religiosity.

Bani-Sadr further elaborates, taking the lead from Modarres, that not only in social but in international relationships, too, positive or negative equilibrium may exist.[172] If two nations choose to base their mutual relationship on a total negation of power, theirs is a "negative equilibrium." If they accept the principle of physical force as the deciding factor in their relationship, they are engaged in a "positive equilibrium." The former case leads to a classless and mono-ontologistic state; the latter to a case of permanent dialectical conflict. Unless political activists reorganize, Bani-Sadr stipulates, the tight and mutual connection of the internal and international applicability of the principle of "negative equilibrium," they are bound to fail in implementing their revolutionary goals.

Man, Bani-Sadr proceeds to identify his revolutionary model, ought to recognize himself as God's chief representative (khalifah) on earth. He must resist yielding to any relation of command and obedience. He should neither command nor obey, neither exploit nor be exploited. What is needed is a total, unconditional, and quintessential denial of physical force as the innate and primary factor of political life and much more. From this follows, as Bani-Sadr insists, both a psychology and a historiography in which man is at the center of a bifurcating choice between consenting to or denying the primary rule of violence in politics.[173]

In international relations, Modarres advocated the cause of "negative equilibrium." He opposed both the British and the Russians and fought against the 1919 oil concession that totally disregarded the Iranian interest.[174] He maintained a similar attitude of "negative equilibrium" in domestic political affairs. He always sided with the people and against the repressive measures of Reza Shah.[175] Bani-Sadr likes to recall the anecdotal utterance of Modarres who once asked a droshky driver how much he would charge to take him to Reza Shah's palace. "Three Tumans," the driver said. "Three Tumans?!" Bani-Sadr has Modarres wonder. "No way! Reza Shah is not worth three Tumans."[176] But if Modarres was less successful in domestic affairs than in international concerns, Bani-Sadr contends,[177] it has more to do with forces of opposition to a "negative equilibrium" than to anything else. More important, Bani-Sadr believes, Modarres's failure was due to the lack of a clear program of action in achieving his revolutionary goals. To achieve Bani-Sadr's ethos and praxis of "negative equilibrium" (a total denial of positive exercise of violence), a clear revolutionary program is needed which is "rooted in the very realities and problems of the masses."[178] The program must be "a translation of the negative equilibrium inside and outside the [national] territories."[179]

In his revolutionary strategies, Modarres was defeated more by failing to unify his own ranks than by Reza Shah's power.[180] Instrumental in this defeat, Bani-Sadr suggested, was the devastating impact of the cult of personality that prevents the genuine unification of popular forces. Bani-Sadr tacitly accuses other religious leaders as centers of such cults. In his memory, Modarres lacked any self-centered ambition; he was the epitome of love and respect. Reza Shah epitomized hatred and awe.[181] Modarres' leadership, for which Bani-Sadr again uses the term "Imam,"[182] is the sort that would uplift and ennoble, not the sort that would treat people as sheep. At one point Bani-Sadr does not hesitate to compare Modarres with Ali, the archetypal image of reverence, the most enduring picture of legitimate authority in Shi'i collective memory. As the archetype of revolutionary leadership, Ali was able to develop that all-too-essential nucleus of political mobilization that enables a social movement to achieve its goals.

Although relatively successful in every respect, Modarres had not been able to sustain a pervasive network of leadership, and that, instigated by Reza Shah's police, had effectively retarded his mobilizing abilities.[183] Most important, he had failed to form "a revolutionary and avant garde nucleus" of leadership.[184] Bani-Sadr moves back in his historical memory and argues that Prophet Muhammad and the Shi'i Imams, too, first organized their revolutionary leadership, the network of their immediate followers, before they could achieve their divinely ordained goals. He extends the implications of this failure in Modarres' movement into the entire modern Iranian history and attributes the lack of a mobilizing revolutionary cadre primarily to the persistence of the cult of the individual.[185]

Bani-Sadr proceeds to complement "the historical meaning" of Modarres with certain "criticism"[186] in order to render "the [revolutionary] model . . . flawless."[187] Bani-Sadr's primary objection to his construction of Modarres' memory is his lack of discretion and tact in dealing with his immediate followers.[188] He is quite particular about the necessity of being discrete in matters of political concerns. He severely criticized Modarres for not being very resistant to the temptation of expressing and revealing that which is not to be revealed. This aspect of Modarres' disposition and behavior is not indicative of the negative equilibrium.[189]

He also criticized Modarres for having underestimated Reza Shah's brutality. No enemy, Bani-Sadr recommended, should ever be taken lightly.[190]

Beyond such trivial shortcomings, Bani-Sadr thought, Modarres was the very picture of a revolutionary leader. "His ethical disposition, in toto, were the characteristics of leadership *(imamat)*, and indicative of his political thought and ideology."[191] He was not afraid of death. Quite the contrary, in constant danger, he always acted with astonishing and exemplary courage.[192] His courage and valor went beyond a refusal to be afraid of death. He ventured everything in his possession to achieve his political ends.[193] He was relentless and tireless in pursuing his immediate and distant goals.[194] He denounced wealth and all worldly possessions in the pursuit of his political ideals.[195] He never succumbed to despair or disappointment. He charged forward with flawless optimism.[196] A perfect revolutionary model, to be emulated earnestly for all generations to come, was crafted by the time Bani-Sadr finished his "biography" of Modarres.

The Grand Illusion

For Bani-Sadr, as for the rest of the Muslim ideologues, "The West" was the greatest of all grand illusions in terms of which they gave themselves — or, more accurately, painted themselves into a corner of — a revolutionary self-definition. From the time of the Crusades, so goes the narrative, "The West" has had a design for Islam, or from the time of Alexander the Great for "The East." Economic disintegration and political subjugation were the end results — as well as the primary objectives — of this massively orchestrated plot of "The West" for Islam and the Muslims. The grand illusion crystallized "The West," the sheer intensity of the figment of their imagination, as the Supreme Hostile Other in terms of which, and only in terms of which, the revoltuionary Muslims could give themselves their primary self-definition.

At the heart of Bani-Sadr's conception of the Iranian past and present is an anger. Once upon a time, he thought, every foreign element was Persianized; now every Iranian feature is "Westernized." Instead of its habitual "internalization of the external," Iran was now yielding to the rapid "externalization of [every aspect of its] internals." Persianize the world! Do not "Westernize" Persia! So goes the motto. Anger at the loss of a presumed passed glory is at the heart of Bani-Sadr's grand illusion about "The West" and its presumed cultural homogeneity and hegemony.

A crucial aspect of Bani-Sadr's discourse in his economic and political writings is his sincere attempt to document and footnote his assertions with a substantial bibliographical network in Persian, French, and English. Attending to the mythological reconstruction of the revolutionary image of Modarres is both an end in itself and an excuse. Identification with the metahistorical figure of Modarres for contemporary revolutionary uses carries enough justification to undertake the task of reconstructing the mythical image. But the road to that purposeful reconstruction, which makes revolutionary activity of a religious nature meaningful in contemporary politics, passes through a long, arduous, and ideological rendition of the Iranian economic, political, and even "natural" history. This historical preparation, scholastic and academic as it appears in its footnoted and documented discourse, gives a certain degree of logical inevitability to Bani-Sadr's celebration of Modarres, a certain sense of undisputed legitimacy to the ideological and political messages thus reconstructed and forecommunicated in this text.

A central theme of Bani-Sadr's political discourse, a term he borrows directly from Islamic theology, is *towhid* or monotheism. He not only gave this term to his mode of preferred economics, he also used it in a wider and more diffused sense. He would, for example, say "the unification of efforts" *(towhid-e masaʿi)*[197] where others would say "the sharing of efforts" *(tashrik-e masaʿi)*. *Tashrik,* which means "to share" in a common effort, had a ring of *shirk,* or "polytheism," to it that Bani-Sadr did not like. He imagines a primordial state of monotheistic existence to which all aspects of human activity (economic, social, political, and cultural) ought to return. Although *towhid* in its original theological sense means "monotheism," Bani-Sadr uses it here in the sense of a mono-ontologistic conception of communal existence where everything exists in a state of tension-free harmony.

Closely related to the notion of *towhid* in Bani-Sadr's discourse are the two corollary leitmotivs of "positive" and "negative" equilibrium. Under all acute and experienced political circumstances, a "positive equilibrium" exists where repressive force is confronted, and thus checked, by equally repressive force. This "positive equilibrium" ought to be broken in favor of a "negative equilibrium." What he means by "negative equilibrium" is a total lack of positive forces checking each other out. The primary example of "positive equilibrium" for Bani-Sadr was the active rivalries in Iran between the Russians and the British or between the Soviets and the Americans. He favored a "negative equilibrium" whereby neither of these two opposing powers would be actively present on the Iranian political scene. But from such examples and historical cases he extends "the negative equilibrium" into the quintessential component of his utopian drive towards a mono-ontologistic state of life in which no concentration of tension or violence exploits, dominates, or distorts.

Using the historical case of Modarres, Bani-Sadr in effect provides a pragmatist guide to revolutionary mobilization, leading towards the utopian realization of that perfect state of "negative equilibrium." He emphasizes the necessity of an "organic" relationship between the leader and the masses of his followers. He warns against the formation of the cult of the individual. He articulates the cause of a utopian "negative equilibrium" in the ideological foundations of the mass mobilization. He underscores the significance of a "nucleus" of revolutionary leadership and is emphatic about the necessity of a clear program of action. In reconstructing his historical memory of Modarres, Bani-Sadr in effect uses the occasion to build a practical model of revolutionary mobilization. His discourse has a tinge of metahistorical introspection: learning from past mistakes for future movements. The anecdotal episodes in Modarres' revolutionary career give Bani-Sadr's narrative a homely and commemorative twist, appealing to a wide, and sentimentally musical, range of audience.

In awakening the collective memory of his audience and in reaching for the utopian reconstruction of the ideal state of "negative equilibrium," Bani-Sadr moves freely as far back as the emergence of Muhammad's Prophetic movement. The necessity for forming a revolutionary cadre to lead the movement is affected by the fact, Bani-Sadr draws from his historical memory, that both Muhammad and Ali (the latter plus the other Shi'i Imams) did the same. The legitimizing force of such sacred symbols in a nation's cherished memories is beyond measure. Any measure of ideological and political mobilization thus legitimized is sure to win popular support, paving the way for Bani-Sadr's utopian fantasies.

Bani-Sadr quite naturally used the terms "Imam" and "Imamat" for his ideal-typical reconstruction of a perfect revolutionary leader, the agent for attaining the ideal measure of "negative equilibrium." He does this without the slightest sense of doctrinal contradiction. The ease with which he extends this exclusive Shi'i term to supreme political leadership in modernity is an indication of his primary concerns with the contemporaneity of current concerns. If the term "Imam" carries weight and calls for obedience, and it does both, then it ought to be extended into the immediacies of contemporary Muslim realities, with which to mobilize the charged and latent memories of historical Shi'ism. Thus, just about anyone who attains the public recognition of his political calling can claim the sanctifying title of "Imam." There is nothing inherently exclusive about the term and its implication of infallibility for Ali and eleven of his male descendants. There is, or there is an ideological reconstruction of, a common set of symbolic references in which participation is the accidental prerogative of just about anyone who can reach deep enough to stir the most Shi'ite of all nerves, the most mobilizing of all sentiments, in people's cherished imagination: the very core of their identity.

The principle of "negative equilibrium" thus remains the most essential core of Bani-Sadr's revolutionary energy and ethos. This principle rests on a self-negating paradox, so patently evident that Bani-Sadr could not even see it. His pseudo-Sufi, pacifist ideologization of an ethic of nonviolence, whereby man is supposed to reconstitute his quintessential predilections towards the innate conflicts of self and society, presumes, and yet totally conceals, a violently revolutionary agenda for its realization. For Bani-Sadr's utopia to be materialized, however, for his revolutionary man to cherish and practice the ethos of "negative equilibrium," political movements need to be launched, rivers of blood ought to be shed, and quite nasty crusades of "positive equilibria" will have to be led. Every "Down with this!" and every "Long live that!"—as the necessary prerequisites of Bani-Sadr's utopian "negative equilibrium"—requires quite a healthy dose of "positive equilibrium," of guns and of guerillas, generals, and summary executions, of perished youth, and of deeply drowned ceremonies of innocence. Singing the sweet song of "nonviolence," while violently engaged in a passive-aggressive dance towards its utopian realization, turns the concealed paradox of the radically pacifist ideology, its misplaced and untimely piety, into an enchanting chorale of presumed moral supremacy. I am morally superior because I believe in nonviolence. So goes the argument. At the self- and other-deceptive heights of such grand illusions of moral supremacy stands not the slightest chance, not a mere suggestion, of a humanizing "but," of a noble "doubt," of the ethical primacy of a saving "on the other hand."

The Manifesto of the Islamic Republic

In advance of the Revolution in 1979, Bani-Sadr issued his manifesto of the Islamic Republic according to which he proposed to address and resolve all the existing problems of the country. In this manifesto, written some eight years earlier, in 1971–72, he divided all the major and minor problems facing the Iranian society into four categories—political, economic, social, and cultural—based on which he makes a monolithic distinction between the "political" and the "religious" positions. In this cosmic neo-Manichean bifurcation of reality all good is "religious" and all evil "political." In matters of politics, political power seeks to dominate, whereas religion seeks to oppose and eliminate oppression.[198] The political order is totalitarian and dictatorial, whereas religion is democratic and popular.[199] In economic matters, political power recognizes the ownership of the landlord, whereas religion recognizes only God as the owner of everything.[200] Political power exploits natural resources for its own ends, whereas religion opposes exploitation of natural resources. In social issues, political power perpetuates social stratification, whereas religion recognizes piety as the only distinguishing factor among individuals.[201] Political power turns woman into a sexual commodity, whereas religion struggles to secure her human status.[202] In cultural matters, political power recognizes might as the only basis for legitimacy, whereas religion condemns might and tyranny.[203]

Political power changes its ideology according to its changing needs to survive,[204] whereas religion believes that one ideology should govern all political acts.[205]

The Political, Economic, Social, and Cultural Malaise

Having constructed this coeternal neo-Manichean dichotomy between the forces of good (religious) and evil (political), Bani-Sadr proceeds to diagnose the political, economic, social, and cultural states of Iran and, further, to offer a program of how the problems in such areas will have to be addressed, now that the national struggle was gaining momentum "under the leadership of Khomeini."[206]

The political world, Bani-Sadr believes, is under the control of the multinational corporations. The political regimes are merely facades for the inner workings of the multinational corporations that dictate what economic programs the former ought to follow.[207] There is a coalition between the armies of Israel and Iran under the general command of the Americans. On the home front, the Iranian revolutionaries ought to fight the multinationals and their local mercenaries by "bringing the people into the battlefield, in unity and conformity, under one single and powerful leadership."[208] This would cause the collapse of the regime. But before that would eventually happen, the two superpowers force Iran, among other dependent states, to be but a parasite on their respective political and economic primacies. The Iranian regime lacks legitimacy because it is devoid of national support and can survive only as a necessary bandage to American political and economic interests. One consequence of this superimposition of the state apparatus upon the society has been the total elimination of intermediary institutions, such as guilds, tribes, etc. The resulting totalitarian state thus rules with no built-in mechanisms for control. The establishment of state organizations such as the "Religious Corps" is the most blatant indication of the Iranian monarch's attempt to appropriate and thus nullify the pockets of resistance traditionally located in the religious establishment.[209] Devoid of any inherent local legitimacy, the Shah's government merely functions as the agent of foreign powers. The social effect of this situation has been deep estrangement and alienation among the people.[210] Unless the major segments of the society would unite under the banner of "one thought, as the leading idea, and act accordingly,"[211] no revolution would be possible.

On the economic front, the natural resources of the country are distributed between the two superpowers. Commercial activities are centered outside the Iranian market. Iranian production plans are drawn up based on the interests of the multinational corporations. This has left no room for genuine economic programs. Imports have surpassed exports and, even worse, foreign investors practically own the national wealth. The end result of this mode of international commerce imposed on the Iranian economy is devastating: practically selling oil to pay for consumer goods imported from "The West."[212] The internal economic condition is in no better shape. The American economy and its rate of growth is feeding directly on the ruins of internal economics of countries such as Iran. For the American economy to maintain a sustained rate of growth, massive poverty ought to prevail in Iran.[213] In economic terms, "the White Revolution," declared Bani-Sadr, "means to correspond the Iranian society and natur[al resources] with the Western production, a production that needs an ever-expanding market."[214] To keep up with the rate of this production, determined in "The West," Iran has to spend more than its actual oil income, which means a budget deficit paid by the future oil reserves.[215]

Socially, too, the country is in a state of shambles.[216] There has been massive growth in the state bureaucracy and the army, all at the expense of the transitory oil revenues. The growth of the modern bourgeoisie is equally dependent upon the oil industry. Because these social groupings are formed essentially by factors external to Iranian society, there is a pervasive feeling of alienation disintegrating them from each other. Because of the deliberate state policies, there are wide chasms between the various groups in Iranian society: the upper class from the lower class, city dwellers from peasants, sedentary groups from the tribal clans. Under the iron hand of the Iranian secret police, there is no possibility for voluntary associations that could lead to the creation of some intervening institutions between the state and the individual.[217] But the severest of all these chasms is that between the ruling regime and its limited class base on one side and the multitude of the people on the other. What holds this diffused and scattered society together is a set of what Bani-Sadr calls "cults of mythologies or ideology of religious infidelity."[218] In the absence or eclipse of a "genuine faith," people are attracted to a multiple set of cults: cults of individuals, of wealth, of fame, of sex, of prestige, etc. Bani-Sadr's conception of myths is something contrary to the position held by his adversaries, whom he does not identify. Only domineering and dominated societies are, he conjectured, in need of myth. Independent societies need not survive on myths.[219] The only answer to this state of affairs, in Bani-Sadr's countermythology, is a return to "the Self": "Today Iran is lost. To be revived, it has to regain Islam."[220] Any other ideology is misguided. Bani-Sadr is severely critical of leftist groups who, in ideological association with the Soviet Union or China, refuse to recognize their essential anti-Iranian policies. He lashes out against Stalinist and Marxist leftists who refuse to acknowledge the explicit and implicit help that the Soviet Union and China gave to "The West" during the nationalization of oil movement by refusing to buy oil from Mosaddeq's government at half the market price.[221]

In cultural terms, there is the absolute control of "The West" upon "the fields of thought and action."[222] There has been a massive migration of Iranian intellectuals and scientists to "The West," particularly to the United States, where the overwhelming majority, if not all, of its scientists are non-American.[223] The influx of intellectual and scientific forces from the "dominated countries" to the "domineering countries" has made the latter the primary exporters of cultural and scientific models and paradigms. Independence of judgment in matters domestically cultural, artistic, and scientific is thus withdrawn from non-"Western" societies. The immediate impact of this cultural alienation is a historical break with the past and a deep and pervasive identity crisis. The confusion in cultural identity is best represented in the artificial transplantation of a translating language (French-Persian, for example) that essentially fails to render the essence of an alien intellectual tradition and that equally fails to produce a domestic neologistic language of inquiry. "The result of such relations," Bani-Sadr warned, "is the transformation of the history-making man into the man as the object of history, the constructive man into the destructive man."[224]

"The Westernization" of Iran

Merely reduced to an object of history, Bani-Sadr continued, the Iranians have become the target of a massive process of "Westernization." It is not for the first time that "The West" has attacked Iran culturally. Alexander and his successors, too, tried to Helenize the Iranian culture.[225] The purpose of "The West" in uprooting the local cultures is to rob Iranians of their genuine identity. This lost identity would, in turn, deny Iranians the possibility of creativity on their own terms. There are six principles, in Bani-Sadr's reckoning, that underlie the process of "Westernization" in Iran: first, the assumption that "The Western" culture is the best of all cultures and that it should substitute for all others; second, that for the pervasive "Westernization" of Iran to take place, all ties to the past ought to be severed; third, that Iranians ought to avoid creativity by all means and merely follow "The West"; fourth, that avoiding creativity and merely aping "The West like monkeys" is necessary for its cultural hegemony to persist; fifth, that the totality of the intrinsic non-"Western" cultures ought to be distorted—specific features may survive, but the totality of Islam as "a fortress of resistance"[226] ought to be denied; and, sixth, that the discernible aspects of the intrinsic culture ought to be assimilated into the hegemonic "Western" culture.[227] The end result of these hegemonic principles governing the "Westernized" societies is the creation of "subhu-

402   Abolhasan Bani-Sadr

mans who lack a human dimension and who have a confused identity."[228]
The Pahlavi regime is the mere agent of meeting these objectives. The
regime has thus created an "official man" who is incapable of full human
activity, with no future of his own making.[229]

What Is to Be Done?

Having delivered an ideological statement on the status quo, Bani-Sadr
portrays a utopian image of how things would look like upon the success
of the Islamic Revolution. Point by point, he provides an agenda of action
in political, economic, social, and cultural domains.

To attain its political sovereignty, Iran has to sever its relations with the
superpowers, but only to the degree that such relations are domineering
and subject the country to foreign rule. A "negative equilibrium" has to be
established by denying both superpowers control over Iranian affairs, which,
in all their dimensions, ought to be run domestically. Both the state bureaucracy and the army will have to be freed from the organic influence of "The
Western" domination. All this will have to be achieved under an Islamic
leadership because, "at the present time, the realities necessitate that . . .
unity cannot be achieved other than through Islam."[230] Internally, first the
Pahlavi monarchy has to be overthrown. All foreign connections to the
superpowers will have to be severed so that the state bureaucracy and the
army are cut off from their domineering foreign controllers. Independent
organizations such as mosques and schools ought to be revived as autonomous centers of decision-making. Religion ought to be put back at the very
center of people's struggles to reach "the Supreme Monotheistic Society"
(Jame'eh-ye Barin-e Towhidi).[231] But "religious despotism" will have to be
prevented[232] and ejtehad, the independent judgment by the religious authorities, has to update the social functions and responsibilities of religion.
The army has to be released from its class-based, foreign-controlled fetters,
and its operative network extended into the public. Governmental powers
must be turned over to social responsibilities, particularly in the realm of
politics. Under the leadership of Islam, moving towards "the Supreme
Monotheistic Society," Bani-Sadr proclaims, "there is no reason why we
should not become a role model for the freedom of humanity on a universal
level."[233] When the "Islamic government" thus comes to power, bureaucracy will be controlled, decentralization of power will occur, master-slave
relationships will cease to exist, the ruling groups will fall, the "Monotheistic Society" will be achieved, the country will progress in all directions,
separatist movements will cease to exist and a truly national state will
emerge, the mass communication organs (radio, television, newspapers,
etc.) will all be utilized to promote science and knowledge, society at large
will intellectually grow, and tomorrow, thus foreconstructed, will be a

day of "independence, freedom, prosperity, unity (monotheism), and self-realization."[234]

The basis of the utopian reconstruction is the economic breakup from "The West." All foreign influences in the Iranian economy ought to be cut off. Iranian interests must be of primary concern in economic programs. The government ought to budget programs of national significance and for the overall growth of the economy. International trade must be balanced. For every twelve units of import, Bani-Sadr calculated, there is now only one unit of export. That will have to be balanced. All foreign investments must be terminated. This will all lead to connecting the Iranian economy to those of other countries with similar "cultural backgrounds."[235] Internally, oil will have to cease to be the main national product. Agriculture has to compete in the international market. Economic bureaucracy must be cut to a minimum, and the national services—health, education, etc.—ought to grow proportionately. The state will intervene only to balance the short-comings or overgrowth of the various segments of the national economy. This will lead to an even and just distribution of wealth and to the simulta-neous disappearance of classes in the Iranian society. "The Westernized consumption," Bani-Sadr proscribed, "will have to be turned Iranian and Islamic."[236] The urge to consume, which is a "Western" vice, will be turned to the pious virtue of moderation. The adoption of these economic policies will ultimately affect "The Western" domineering economies to the benefit of all the dominated societies and their national economy. All the present economic disparities will turn to a unitarian (monotheistic) economy to secure prosperity in this life and salvation in the next.[237]

Emancipation from "The West" and the realization of the Islamic Self will lead to a flourishing social renewal. Their economic bases eradicated, the rampant bureaucracy and the foreign-controlled army will be assimi-lated back into the self-realized society. The foreign ties of the nongovern-mental (private) bureaucracy will be severed too. All foreign relations that are detrimental to the national interests will be cut off. At the same time, fundamental changes in the social structure will eliminate all class distinc-tions and create the unitarian (monotheistic) society. Social statuses, how-ever, to the degree they are Islamically proscribed, are encouraged.[238] "The Islamic government," Bani-Sadr stipulated, "is not an absolutist govern-ment. Its purpose is to eliminate the administration [*dowlat*] as a tyrannical and unconditionally dominant force upon the fate of the country."[239] Men and women would be equal parts of a complementary unit, all with Islamic sanctity. Religion and politics, in this world of absolute unity, will become one and the same. Society will be released from its "Western" domineering confusion and will reach its essential unitarian Self. When the state as an instrument of oppression is eliminated, when fear is eradicated from the collective mind of society, all cults and mythologies will cease to exist.

There would be no need for the army or for organs of oppression and suffocation (no secret police). People have called Khomeini an "idol-smasher,"[240] Bani-Sadr emphasized, precisely because they are tired of idols, cults, and myths. In the unitarian (monotheistic) society of Bani-Sadr's imagination, soon to be recognized in the success of the Islamic Revolution, there would be no cult of the individual—or any other cult for that matter. A healthy and constructive society will emerge in which perfect and absolute humanity has the opportunity to grow.[241] The young generation should not, Bani-Sadr warns, miss this historic opportunity to give the world a model of the perfect and final society through a "great revolution."[242]

The hegemonic ascendancy of "The West," Bani-Sadr concludes his fourfold utopian agenda, will be terminated through a great cultural revolution.[243] The grounds of thought and action will become "Self-centered" (Khodi-Kardan). Under the leadership of Islam, this Self-realization will create infinite opportunities for local ingenuity and creativity. Beyond thought and action, production and consumption of economic and social goods will be equally centered on the Iranian Self rather than "The Western" Other. The free passage given to the influx of "Western antivalues" will be stopped. Independence of thought will be restored. Moral corruption, a vice imported from "The West," will cease to plague the Iranian society. What will follow is a harmonious integration of all cultural traits in the society. Unified into a homogeneous culture, Iranians will collectively soar in making their own history.[244] Once separated from the hegemonic "Western" influence, the Iranian culture, in turn, will be thoroughly re-Islamicized. There are six ways through which the culture is re-Islamicized.[245] First, the principles of monotheism, prophethood (as the basis of the Islamic political system), Imamat, Divine justice, and the belief in bodily resurrection ought to be remade as the objectives of the culture. Second, reactionary tendencies in the culture, that is, those forces that prevent forward movement, ought to be eliminated. Third, instead of imitation, which is forced by "The Western" capitalism, creativity will be substituted. Fourth, instead of blind obedience, Iranians, as true Muslims, will lead and create. Fifth, culture will be integrated and unified, not segmented and confused as under the influence of "The West." And sixth, all these previous factors contribute to the final universal integration based upon a "negative equilibrium."[246] The result of this re-Islamization of the culture is that the present confusion in the Iranian national identity will disappear; uncertainty in thought and creativity will be removed; and ultimately people will be rescued from "the imaginary and prefabricated [in "Western" models] world, which is located outside time and space."[247] They will be consciously put upon the permanent parameters of reality. "Let us not get tired of repeating," Bani-Sadr demanded, the point that the cure for the Westoxicated in all domains, especially as pertains to the future, is participation in the grand task of building the unitarian (monotheistic) future; it is in seeking solution upon objective realities. . . . The cure is in a return to realities of the Self, in finding the Self, in opening the way to a future with work, thought, and action like an Imam, a future that [only] the Supreme Monotheistic Society can create.[248]

Ideology and Utopia

There is no more perfect textual example of the Muslim ideologues' simultaneous construction of an absolute evil in the status quo and an absolute good in the revolution to come than Bani-Sadr's *Manifesto of the Islamic Revolution*. Turning his imaginative reconstruction of a perfect "unitarian" future into an instrument for collective action, Bani-Sadr portrays a picture of absolute corruption in the state he wishes to see overthrown. The neo-Manichean construction of these two opposing worlds is crucial to a political discourse that intends to move its constituency to redefine their world and to seek to alter it. It is not for the presence or absence of its intellectual and conceptual accuracy, nor for the brilliance of its delivery, that such manifestos ought to be examined. Acting in their political agenda, revolutionary ideologues have the immediate goal of mobilizing their maximum constituency for a set of political goals. Bani-Sadr, among other committed ideologues, has to show the status quo as worse than it actually is and portray the revolutionary future as much brighter than he can visibly demonstrate. Speaking the language of his revolutionary cohorts, he responds positively to the ideological and utopian needs of his time: an ideological portrayal of the evil that is, and a utopian promise of the good that will be. Without their ideological or utopian reconstructions into mobilizing convictions, facts, a priori, are haphazard indices of counterinterpretations. For Bani-Sadr the random selection of those facts that best serve to portray the Shah's regime as corrupt, obsolete, and just about to fall corresponds, on a one-to-one basis, to an imaginative future that he is in full control of beautifying and glorifying as he likes. The most immediate principle governing the selection and organization of "facts" into ideological or utopian images of present and future is the emerging revolutionary agenda, drawn and drafted a priori. The "facts" come from the contemporary exigencies, the fantasies from "Islam." The ideologues, the Muslim children of their particular historicity, enter into a revolutionary hermeneutic conversation with what they remember as "Islam" and then translate it into "the Islamic Ideology." "The Islamic Ideology" thus becomes the historical dialogue into which fell both the authority of the Muslim ideological voice and the textuality of their "Islam" remembered. The remembrance acted on the borderline between ideology and utopia.

Construction of this ideological/utopian dichotomy also requires a simultaneous reconstitution of the received theological language and its commanding terms of truth. Thus, for Bani-Sadr *towhid* assumes, and through it he wishes to propagate, an entirely new meaning. In the context of Islamic theology, both Sunni and Shiʿi, *towhid* has meant the doctrinal belief in the unity of God—or simply "monotheism." In Bani-Sadr's reconstruction, assimilating backward the Marxist ideal of a classless society, *towhid* becomes that ideal state of political, economic, social, and cultural harmony that, through a "negative balance" among the existing forces of oppression attains the absolute unity (harmony) of existence. Through the same reconstruction of the received theological language, *nobovvat,* which has traditionally meant the belief in the messengership of Prophet Muhammad as the last Divine emissary, comes to mean the principle of an Islamic state as an approximation of the political order to ideals of Divine intervention in human affairs.

The emergence of this new and politically updated language of conviction is inevitable. The son of an Ayatollah in Hamadan, Bani-Sadr would have merely sought to politicize the received notions of juridical Shiʿism had he not moved out of his hometown, the Iranian state of his creative revolutionary imagination. Transplanted into Tehran and Paris and molded by courses he took in economics, he develops a new creative perception of his faith, charged with the political activism of which he is a part. From this emerging group of transplanted intellectual Muslims there gradually develops a new Islam, both essentially and existentially different from that historically experienced by former Muslim intellectuals or that of the urban mercantile class or that of the peasantry. As this colossal redefinition of Islam grows in conception and constituency, so does its ideological currency inside Iran. This is a coming together of the urban professionals, the classical and modern bourgeoisie, and most importantly—the very machinery of the Revolution—the uprooted peasantry at the fringes of the lumpen proletariat. Where the emerging militant Islam and its commencing urban constituency meet, the Paris-educated intellectuals and the crowds of urban malcontents, there is the explosive rendez-vous of the coming revolution.

The construction of this ideology/utopia dichotomy further demonstrates that more important than "facts," economic or otherwise, are historically necessitated perceptions of those facts, cast constructively in public mythologies. The ideological condemnation of the status quo and the utopian celebration of the world to come are simultaneous components of that overriding public mythology that sets the mobilized masses on a revolutionary course of action. "The reality," whatever the measures of its historical realization, simply loses the ground under the commanding and convincing power of the myth. There are always enough facts in every fantasy to substantiate its convincing appeal. Beyond economic realities are political fantasies that ultimately make a revolution. In the collective construction of these fantasies, in the common consumption of the figments of imagination, factors such as relative deprivation are much more important than the absolute, perceptions of "The West" much more compelling than empirical facts about Western Europe and the United States.

Taking charge in giving their fellow countrymen a revolutionary interpretation of the world, Bani-Sadr and his ideological cohorts sought, and to a considerable degree succeeded, to supersede this similar function traditionally performed, since medieval times, by the clergy. That ultimately a bona fide clergy actually led the Revolution is testimony that at still deeper social and psychological levels time-honored mores are more effective than updated ideological innovations. But still the preparatory stages of the Revolution, whether in Paris by Shariʿati and Bani-Sadr or in Tehran by Al-e Ahmad and Bazargan, was ideologically paved by the nonclerical elements. Yet both forces, lay and clerical, coincided in preaching, teaching, and thus redefining the world in such terms that their very ontological assumptions proscribe a revolutionary course of action. The breakdown of the medieval monopoly of the clergy over the possibility of interpreting the world for the rest of the society was, on the whole, damaging to this class. The emergence of (secular) liberal and radical ideologies directly challenged the monopoly of the clergy and their interpretative authority. However, with pseudoclerics such as Bani-Sadr functioning at the heart of the Iranian intelligentsia abroad, a considerable population of the revolutionary constituency was won over from the seculars. At least since the Constitutional Revolution of 1906, although there are earlier signs going back to the early nineteenth century, the intellectual monopoly of the clergy, in interpreting the world and rendering it meaningful, had been seriously jeopardized. The function of Bani-Sadr's generation of pseudoclerics became the salvaging of a measure of legitimacy for the reinterpreted religious cause. But the ideological and utopian discourse thus developed by Bani-Sadr, Shariʿati, Al-e Ahmad, and Bazargan commanded its own constituency, distinct from both the secular language of the modernist intellectuals and the scholastic language of the clergy. The most crucial clue to the epistemological assumption of the pseudoclerical discourse of Bani-Sadr and his cohorts is the politically mandated principle that to interpret the world and to change it at the same time were part and parcel of but one ideological statement. To deliver that statement, the Muslim ideologues dwelled in the torrent, tempest, and whirlwind of their revolutionary passion. They were for real. They saw the world from the mountaintop of absolute and unconditional conviction, from that irreducible latitude of having personally seen the light. Theirs was a tomorrow they had never seen, yet the promise of a yesterday they all-too-vividly remembered. They were for real. Men of conviction and Truth with a "T" so capital in their soul they had no room for any halting alphabet of doubt. They overdid nothing. They saw the world underdone. And saw to fix it right. "Islam" for them was the necessity of now, the promise of tomorrow, the burden of yesterday. They were "Muslim Ideologues," in full contradiction with themselves.

Vague Fears; Unreasoned Hopes

Uncertainty is said to be a built-in certainty, a virtue made out of a human necessity, in John Maynard Keynes's *General Theory*.[249] "[B]eing based on so flimsy a foundation," he thought of economics, "it is subject to sudden and violent changes."[250] Rationality must share the inherited anxieties of any old-fashioned brand of mythology. Beyond rational choices and beyond economic determinants—factors and forces of the material production of life—more hazardous choices claim more compelling urges. Sudden and violent changes in the rational course of economic choice must be predicated on a nucleus of political disposition otherwise mute and waiting. "The practice of calmness and immobility, of certainty and serenity, suddenly breaks down." Keynes's anticipation of revolutionary outbursts in economic measures of choice was on the fringes of spontaneity: "New plans and hopes will, without warning, take charge of human conduct. . . . At all times the vague panic fears and equally vague and unreasoned hopes are not really lulled, and lie but a little way below the surface."[251] Below the surface of economic reasoning moves the infinitely more compelling demon of unexamined ideological convictions—there with mythical proportions. "People did not make a revolution for the price of watermelon," Khomeini is reported to have said. "They did it for Islam."[252] God and all creatures of conviction override the harshest of all economic crises. The metamorphosis of economic theology into the animating terms of political mobilization always necessitates the contingent demons of conviction. Where do the demons lie but in the irresistible urges to redefine, reinterpret, and recreate the world, economic and all else. Vague fears and unreasoned hopes, fears of an imagined enemy, hopes for the next enchantment, are the signs of successive illusions that haunt the imagination, the very insignia of every renewed promise to deliver the next (just-around-the-corner) kingdom of heaven on earth.

CHAPTER 8

Ayatollah Khomeini: The Theologian of Discontent

Prompte et sincere in opere Domini. The Latin motto on Calvin's seal reads, "Promptly and sincerely in the work of the Lord." [1] If Calvin's days long ago demanded such exacting sincerities from a man of God that would make a coward of all lesser mortals, nowadays, in the disenchantments of all (abandoned) god-terms reigning no longer supreme, who else can have the courage of his belated beliefs? Politics is, today as ever, the last bastion of beliefs that once engaged the most private pieties of otherwise perfectly public creatures. Across cultures and centuries, whether in Geneva of the sixteenth century or in Tehran of the twentieth, political terms seem to be the only convincing language to appropriate the public virtues of an otherwise skeptical multitude—knowing not beyond the compelling mandates of bread and dignity. In Geneva or in Tehran, there are no limits to boundaries of political mandates, realms of revolutionary movements, when a Calvin has the power of his theological convictions. The price of politics for one's theology of discontent can be as high as it is exacting. For all his moral convictions, and for all his political rectitude, Calvin of Geneva has endured the fair judgment of history. Other Calvins, of Geneva or of Tehran, can only wait for theirs: "Prejudice and admiration alike have blundered. He was no paragon with the mind of an archangel, nor was he a finished Saint. Nor yet was he a malicious and inhuman tyrant, but, rather, a highly gifted and unreservedly dedicated man, whose moral greatness was marred by serious defects. . . . Something must be allowed to a man harrassed, afflicted, and overwrought as he habitually was." [2]

Early Life and Scholastic Learning

Ruhollah Musavi Khomeini was born on Wednesday, 24 September 1902, in the small village of Khomein some sixty miles south of Tehran. His grandfather, Sayyid Ahmad, had moved from Najaf in Iraq to Khomein and married and settled there. He was survived by two children: a son, Sayyid Mostafa, and a daughter, Sahibeh. Sayyid Mostafa married Hajar, the daughter of a distinguished local cleric. Three sons and three daughters were born to them. Sayyid Ruhollah was the youngest son. Sayyid Mostafa was killed sometime in February 1903, when his youngest son, Ruhollah, was less than six months old. Three women became the primary caretakers of Khomeini throughout his childhood: his mother Hajar, his paternal aunt Sahibeh, and a nurse called Naneh Khavar. Khomeini's aunt Sahibeh is noted as having been a particularly distinguished and strong-willed lady. In 1917, at the age of fifteen, Khomeini lost both his mother and his aunt, at which point his older brother Sayyid Morteza (Ayatollah Pasandideh) took charge of his upbringing.[3]

Khomeini's early education took place in his hometown of Khomein, where he studied under a number of local teachers and seminarians, including his own elder brother Ayatollah Pasandideh. In 1919, at the age of seventeen, he left Khomein for Arak, where he began his preliminary and advanced scholastic studies under the eminent jurist Ayatollah Shaykh Abdolkarim Ha'eri Yazdi. One year later, in 1920, Ayatollah Ha'eri was asked to come to Qom and establish that city's seminary as a leading center of scholastic learning in the Shiʿi world. Khomeini followed his distinguished teacher and continued his advanced studies in Islamic jurisprudence. By 1926 he had completed his studies of the canonical sources of Shiʿi law. When Ayatollah Ha'eri died in 1936, the thirty-four-year-old Khomeini had completed his most advanced studies. Along his juridical studies, he was particularly attracted to ascetic exercises and philosophical learning.[4]

In 1929 Khomeini married the daughter of a distinguished cleric, Hajj Mirza Mohammad Thaqafi-e Tehrani. Two sons and three daughters were born to them. His oldest son, Hajj Sayyid Mostafa, who died in 1978, became a distinguished cleric in his own right. His younger son, Ahmad, became his closest companion during the revolutionary period.[5]

Khomeini began his teaching career in 1928, before he was twenty-seven years old. His primary interest in teaching was in Islamic mysticism and philosophy. He was very selective in his group of students. Although he had taught preliminary courses in Shiʿi jurisprudence throughout the 1930s, it was not until 1944 that he began to teach advanced courses in the canonical sources of Islamic law. His teaching in Islamic philosophy and mysticism was enriched by his long years of apprenticeship with such luminaries as Mirza Ali Akbar Yazdi, who was a student of Molla Hadi Sabzevari (d. 1872), the most distinguished Shiʿi philosopher of the Qajar period. Among his other teachers were Mirza Aqa Javad Maleki Tabrizi (d.

1924), Sayyid Abolhasan Rafi'i Qazvini (d. 1975), and Ayatollah Muhammad Ali Shahabadi.[6]

Khomeini's writings, which cover a wide range of subjects in Shi'i jurisprudence, Islamic philosophy and mysticism, Persian poetry, and political
polemics, began to appear in the late 1920s. Some twenty-five books and
treatises have been identified among his writings.[7] In *Mesbah al-Hedayeh*
(1928), he demonstrated his unique mastery of the gnostic discourse. Many
commentaries have been written on this text. In *Sharh Do'a' al-Sahar*
(1930), he gave a philosophical and mystical interpretation, in Arabic prose
and Persian poetry, to this famous prayer of the sixth Shi'i Imam, Ja'far al-
Sadiq. His *Forty Traditions* includes commentaries on seven prophetic
traditions on intellectual matters and thirty-three on ethical matters. His
Serr al-Salat and *Adab al-Salat* provide mystical interpretations of the
designated rituals in the course of the Muslim prayer. *Kashf al-Asrar* (1944)
was Khomeini's sweeping attack against pseudosecular polemics against
Shi'i beliefs and practices. He also wrote many short and long treatises on
Shi'i jurisprudence, chief among which is *Tahrir al-Wasilah*. His *Towzih
al-Masa'il* is a collection of his edicts on a variety of practical questions for
his juridical constituency.[8]

The Historical Setup

Khomeini's early life and scholastic learning and writing coincided with the
two crucial decades of the 1930s and 1940s and then extended into the
formative decades of the 1950s and 1960s. The 1930s was a decade of
grave political events in Iran. In 1936, Reza Shah ordered Iranian women
unveiled, an event with the greatest symbolic significance for the religious
establishment. The construction of the trans-Iranian railway in 1934 had
signaled the dawn of a new era of technological avalanche that the clerical
order always perceived with certain ambivalent hesitation. Established also
in 1934 was the Tehran University, which, for a long time, constituted the
most patent secular alternative to the traditional madrasah system. As the
brutal murder of the Iranian poet Farrokhi Yazdi (1889–1939) signified,
Reza Shah did not hesitate to punish severely those who dared to challenge
his tyranny. When Sayyid Hasan Modarres died in 1934, Khomeini lost a
clerical model whose political activism he greatly admired. A year later, in
1935, Reza Shah brutally suppressed a popular revolt in Mashhad, an
atrocity that left an indelible mark on Khomeini's political consciousness.
When his principal teacher and mentor, Ayatollah Ha'eri Yazdi, died in
1936, Khomeini was left with a relatively eminent position in the Qom
clerical establishment and a highly charged political consciousness.

The Allied occupation of Iran in 1941 ushered in a new era of exposure to new and renovating forces. On September 16, 1941, the reign of Reza Shah was brought to an abrupt end when he was forced by the Allied forces to pay for his flirtation with Hitler's Germany and abdicate in favor of his young crown prince Mohammad Reza Pahlavi. Before the clerical order could determine precisely its responses to such grave changes, the Tudeh (Communist) Party was established in 1941 with the mightiest material and ideological force in modern Iranian history. This movement posed the most serious organizational and ideological threat to the Shi'i establishment.

That such great luminaries of the clerical order as Ayatollah Ha'eri or Ayatollah Borujerdi found themselves in active or passive support of the Pahlavi state was due in part to their perception of a common ideological foe in the Tudeh Party and all it stood for. When Reza Shah abdicated, Mohammad Reza Shah was a weakly installed head of state barely capable of claiming any authority and held in power chiefly by the collective will of the Allied forces and a series of old and wise politicians. By the end of the decade, he was once the target of an assassination attempt, and his chief minister was killed by a member of the radical Fada'ian-e Islam. Fada'ian-e Islam was also responsible for assassinating Sayyid Ahmad Kasravi on 11 March 1946. Kasravi's anticlerical statements had angered much of the religious establishment. Khomeini's *Kashf al-Asrar* (1944) was partially targetted against Kasravi and his supporters. However, this book was much more than a mere attack against certain anticlerical and anti-Shi'i sentiments and thoughts prevalent at the time. Khomeini used this occasion to criticize the tyrannical conditions created during the reign of Reza Shah. The relative freedom after the Allied occupation and the abdication of Reza Shah gave many people, including Khomeini, the opportunity to air long-held grievances against the oppressive measures of the old tyrant. But clearly evident in *Kashf al-Asrar* is the rising concern about the prevalence of secular ideas and the equally powerful preoccupations with "The West." Two years after Khomeini first published this book, Ayatollah Abolhasan Isfahani died in 1946, and the politically mute Ayatollah Borujerdi succeeded him.

In the late 1940s and throughout the 1950s Ayatollah Borujerdi reigned supreme upon the highest seat of the Shi'i juridical establishment. His apolitical disposition was, in effect, translated into tacit support for the legitimacy of the Pahlavi regime. Throughout the 1950s, and in the shadow of Ayatollah Borujerdi, Khomeini continued to teach juridical, philosophical, and gnostic texts, attracting, as he did, quite a number of students, devotees, and juridical followers. But this was the decade of liberal democracy to test its viability in the Iranian political culture. Mohammad Mosaddeq successfully checked the Shah's unconstitutional urges towards authoritarianism and chased his megalomaniac ambitions out of the country. But in 1953, the CIA-sponsored American coup returned the monarch to Iran.

The post-Mosaddeq Pahlavi regime grew increasingly in its tyrannies, effectively eliminating both the liberal-democratic and the radical-revolutionary alternatives. Its attendance to "the Islamic Ideology" was quite a different matter.

The 1960s was the crucial decade in which Khomeini's political discourse assumed a particularly sharp bend towards revolutionary claims on Iranian political consciousness. To understand that revolutionary discourse is to reach for the most vital nerves of the Islamic Revolution in Iran.

A "Philosopher King"

Although not a "king" in the specific sense of the word and not a "philosopher" according to the established standards of the Islamic discourses, Khomeini's was ultimately the idea of a "philosopher king" in the platonic understanding of the term. As for Plato, "justice" was Khomeini's principal political concern. The Iranians had been wronged. Their just due had to be given to them. This "giving to them" necessitated both leading them through a revolution and remaining in power to secure their this- and other-worldly salvation. With a remarkably Socratic argument, though minus his free spirit and his sense of irony, Khomeini maintained, and honestly believed, that people sometimes do not know what is good for them. Occasional untruth, or the platonic noble lie, is the tacit, yet most emphatic, assumption of a "philosopher king" who knows what is best for his subjects and sees to it that they are "rightly guided" to that end. What doctrinally augmented and ideologically solidified this Platonic assumption on Khomeini's part, with a long historical translation of the platonic ideal into the fabric of Islamic political philosophy, was the notion of "the perfect man" (al-insan al-kamil), whereby, in the mystical tradition, the path to spiritual perfection (rendered into political truth) is guided by a master (or morshed). Superseding the philosophical discourse by the mystical, Khomeini could only benefit from the enduring political implications of such powerful traits in Persian and Islamic intellectual history.

Phases in Khomeini's Ideas

The gradual development of Khomeini's revolutionary career and discourse may be divided into eight distinct phases, from his pre-1963 political engagements to the penultimate victory of the Revolution on 11 February 1979, to the final establishment of the Islamic Republic on 1 April 1979.

The first phase of Khomeini's revolutionary career began with his earliest political concerns, gradually leading to his first serious challenge to the Pahlavi regime. The June 1963 uprising marked the end of a sustained growth in Khomeini's political activities and, at the same time, inaugurated

Ayatollah Khomeini

the beginning of a new, more powerful, phase of his attempt to topple the Iranian monarch. In the revolutionary annals of modern Iranian history, 15 Khordad 1342 (5 June 1963)—which coincided with 12 Muharram 1383 (the most passionately charged month in the Shiʿi calendar)—is recorded as the day on which a premonition of the 1979 Revolution should have given the Pahlavi state the initial sign of its coming problems.

The second phase of Khomeini's revolutionary development began with the massive street demonstrations on his behalf in June 1963 in various cities in Iran. From 4 June 1963 to 4 November 1964, when Khomeini was exiled to Turkey, the Pahlavi state saw one of the most serious challenges to its peacock throne. During those seventeen months the Iranian monarch and Ayatollah Khomeini mobilized all the material, ideological, and symbolic forces at their disposal to challenge each other's legitimacy or even existence. In this first round of their fight, the Iranian monarch emerged victorious and banished the Ayatollah to Turkey and then to Iraq.

The third phase of Khomeini's revolutionary career and discourse commences almost immediately upon his arrival in Turkey on 4 November 1964, continues throughout his active years in Iraq, and enters a new phase on 23 October 1977, when Khomeini's son, Hajj Aqa Mostafa, dies under what the Iranian apocryphal martyrology would later call "suspicious circumstances." While in Iraq, Khomeini would strengthen his ties with his followers inside Iran, develop new ideological and material coalitions with Iranian students abroad, and respond promptly and critically to events inside the country.

The political significance of the death of his son was further intensified in January 1978 by the appearance of a deprecating article written about Khomeini in one of Tehran's daily papers; the fourth phase of his ideological rhetoric then commenced, launching his revolutionary discourse into new directions. This period is brought to a dramatic end on 8 September 1978, "Black Friday," when the Imperial army opened fire on people demonstrating in Zhaleh Square in Tehran. Whatever the exact number of casualties, the compelling image of "Black Friday" marked a serious challenge to the legitimacy of the Pahlavi state. From October 1977 to September 1978, Khomeini mounted a relentless avalanche of attacks against the legitimacy of the Pahlavi state and, at the same time, celebrated the heroic deeds of the "oppressed Iranian masses."

The fifth phase of Khomeini's active and massive orchestration of revolutionary symbolics began on "Black Friday" and reached its most serious climax when he left Iraq for Paris on 6 October 1978. In this fateful month of September 1978, Khomeini took full advantage of the "Black Friday massacre."

From 6 October 1978, when Khomeini arrived in Neauphle-le-Château, to 1 February 1979, when he landed in Mehrabad airport in Tehran,

Khomeini launched, in the sixth phase of his elongated revolutionary career, the most devastating attacks against the ideological and material foundations of the Iranian monarchy. This time, aided by the massive, almost obsessive, coverage of the world media, he attained an audience beyond the measures of his imagination.

The seventh, penultimate, phase of Khomeini's revolutionary momentum occurred between 1 February, his arrival in Tehran, and 11 February 1979, "the ten days of the Morning Twilight," when he destroyed the last trembling remnants of the peacock throne. Through a series of speeches, he forced the shaky government of Shapour Bakhtiar (assassinated in 1991) to crumble and made the last prime minister of the deposed king run for his life.

The eighth and final phase of Khomeini's successful revolutionary movement began on 11 February 1979, when the Revolution attained its goal of toppling the Pahlavi state, and ended on 1 April 1979, when Khomeini outmaneuvered his secular rivals and established, on the ruins of the Pahlavi monarchy, the Islamic Republic, pure and simple.

The Significance of Khomeini's Writings in the Making of the Islamic Revolution

It is hardly possible to exaggerate the significance of Khomeini's declarations and writings in the final making of the Islamic Republic. The hypothetical question of "Would there have been a revolution without Khomeini?" has its pedagogic significance, despite its historical irrelevance. The man and his words are inseparable. If the man and the Revolution are also arguably inseparable, then we have before us the historical momentum invested in his revolutionary logic.

The centrality of Khomeini's writings in the making of the Islamic Revolution is perhaps best captured in an introduction to the official collection of his writings, written by Ali Khamenei, then the President of the Islamic Republic of Iran, now its "leader" and successor to Khomeini. Subtracting the obvious, and perhaps inevitable, hyperbole of Khamenei's introduction, we are still left with a clear testimony of how Khomeini's writings were received and perceived during his long and active years of building a revolutionary rhetoric. "The Islamic Revolution," Khamenei testifies, "was begun presently with the far-reaching and not-to-be silenced cry of Imam Khomeini."[9] Despite the presence and significance of many material conditions paving the way for the Revolution, without the unifying and catalytic voice of the aged revolutionary, there would probably not have been an "Islamic Revolution" as we have come to witness it unfold right before our eyes. The massive orchestration of forces by a police state had made the expression of any mode of political dissent almost impossible.

After the June 1963 uprising, which was effectively crushed, Khomeini's exile, first to Turkey in October 1964 and then to Iraq in November 1965, gave him a golden opportunity to say what others dared not utter.

During the two decades of the 1960s and 1970s, the Shah's ruthless police state, through a paralyzing mobilization of actual and intimidating terror, had increasingly made any form of political expression highly hazardous. During this period, of course, oppositional developments occurred in both ideological and political terms. The secular oppositions either assumed concealed symbolic language in poetry and literary prose or else were channelled through guerrilla attacks against the governmental targets. The result was that no effective political (revolutionary) discourse, in the most common sense of the term, could develop. The two extremities of concealed metaphors in prose or poetry or bullet sounds from machine guns could not be translated effectively into a coherent, sustained, and successful political discourse. But at the same time, the gradual formation of the religious political discourse inside Iran was much more effective. Shari'ati, Motahhari, and Taleqani, among others, each in his own particular way, contributed to the effective formation of a multifarious revolutionary discourse. All these revolutionary ideologues were operating within the context of state-controlled censorship. They could not forcefully and openly present or develop their ideas. The importance and strength of their writings were in their physical presence in Iran. Their weakness was in their inability to speak and write freely. Khomeini, however, wrote and spoke without any significant limitation. With his distance from Iran effectively covered by persistent reports he received from his devout followers inside the country, Khomeini enjoyed the freedom of speech afforded him especially by the hostility between the Iranian and Iraqi governments. As he began to write on specific issues afflicting Muslims in general and Iranian Muslims in particular, he became the spokesman and arbiter of "justice," the single most important concept in both Persian and Islamic political culture. Many indications and occasions of injustice in Iran, and indeed in the Muslim world at large, gave him ample opportunity to call for a reckoning with the tyrannies of the powers that be. As he became the spokesman for the cause of justice, he also assumed the authorial voice of speaking for Islam. His became the voice of authority through which "Islam" spoke. Alternative readings of Islam were either state-sponsored and thus rejected, Orientalist and thus discredited, or equally oppositional but from a slightly different angle, in which case assimilated. A rising banner on the sacred Islamic canopy, Khomeini's became the theological statement of revolt.

One crucial factor in making Khomeini a central figure in modern Iranian history and his writings a major voice in contemporary political discourse is the longevity of his life. Born in 1902, Khomeini was actively present in the major political developments before, during, and after the Pahlavi reign. When Reza Shah came to power in 1927, Khomeini was a twenty-five-year-old cleric already politically conscious and active. Throughout Reza Shah's reign (1927–1941), the Allied occupation of Iran, the change of reign from Reza Shah to his son Mohammad Reza Shah, the tumultuous 1940s, and the massive orchestration of Marxist rhetoric by the Tudeh Party, the Mosaddeq era, the 1953 coup, all through his own ill-fated uprising in June 1963, his exile, the Shah's consolidation of power in the 1970s, and the final destruction of the monarchical machine in the 1978–79 period, through all these stages, Khomeini seems to have been there all along—as if from time immemorial in modern Iranian history. "The Revolution and Imam Khomeini are two inseparable phenomena."[10] Khamenei's assessment could very well be made into a bona fide argument for the possibility of the Revolution.

The charismatic dimensions of his leadership rest on the dialectical growth of a unique relationship between Khomeini and his followers, whose texture and tone go beyond the ordinary authority assumed by a high-ranking Shi'i cleric. An ayatollah does indeed occupy the highest position of religious authority in a Shi'i community. The years of learning, the mystic of devotion, and the concomitant spiritual presence they all inevitably attain give the high-ranking Shi'i authorities a certain air of genuine respect and lasting loyalty. Yet the mode and intensity of devotion afforded Khomeini by his followers, particularly in moments leading to the revolutionary crescendo, drive deeper into the collective consciousness of his mass of followers. He grasped something deeply disturbing, something deeply moving, in the midst of the misery, actual and imaginary, that defined his followers. He turned that mute anger against indignity into an articulate voice of dissent and then, being an ayatollah, put God's stamp of approval on it.

Khomeini's significance—his mere presence, his words—ought to be considered in the context of his interaction with his followers. The unit of analysis must be his words and his followers' reaction to them. Certain events—the Shah granting diplomatic immunity to American diplomats, the Iranian army attacking the Feyziyyeh Seminary, the celebration of the 2,500 years of Persian monarchy, etc.—gave Khomeini ample excuse to air his grievances. These grievances, put into words, would assume canonical revolutionary status and, in turn, cause further actions, either by the Shah's government or by Khomeini's followers—in both cases one leading to the other.

Thus the best unit of analysis that contextualizes Khomeini's significance is "action-verbal response-action." The first action originates in something major or minor on the part of the beleaguered state. The verbal response is Khomeini's ideological statement against that action. And the second round of action would be either retaliatory or compensatory policies on the side of the State or revolutionary demonstrations by Khomeini's followers. It is precisely through this chain of events that Khomeini mobilized the Islamic Revolution and brought it to fruition. And the Islamic Revolution, in turn, elevated him to the highest position of a mythical man, turning him into an (eternal) figure of metahistorical authority. "This was not but by God's grace, and by the grace of the vocal correspondence between the leader (Imam) and the led *(ommat)*."[11] There is in Khamenei's assessment the precise dialectic of reciprocity operative in making both the Revolution and its leader possible.

Khomeini's words began in his presence. And it is this presence that transforms his words into canonical commands for his close associates, as well as his removed followers. "Like Prophets," Khamenei offers in his close similitude, "in his being, [Khomeini] presents to the perspicacious observant, religion, politics, revolution, God, and the people, all at the same time. His revolt brings to mind the revolt of the divine Prophets."[12] Khomeini is seen by his followers as the organizer of the three most essential virtues missing from a monarchical tyranny.[13] First, he has revived a religious consciousness without which men are thought to be trapped in a temporal mendacity; second, he has made it possible to believe again in a metaphysics of Ultimate Salvation, whereby limitations of rationality do not hinder a view of the eternal in man; third, he is considered to have enacted a popular epic, an odyssey of revolt for dignity.

Khamenei also points to three prominent features in Khomeini's writings:[14] First, they are chiefly responsible for having moved the people to revolt; second, they have defined the direction and established the course of the revolutionary movement; third, Khomeini has recorded in these writings the historical unfolding of the Iranian Revolution. The most prominent feature of his writings, responsible in part for the massive response to his revolutionary call, is the simplicity of his prose and pronouncements. When he occasionally delivers a lecture on a juridical or mystical topic, it is quite evident that he is perfectly capable of a sophisticated technical prose. But in most of his writings, he speaks to the most common level of his audience. This makes him almost immediately accessible to a mass audience otherwise barred from political participation. Having reached them by a greatly simplified language, Khomeini gave his increasing audience an all but forgotten sense of dignity, a feeling of self-respect, a possibility of better days, and all that in familiar terms. In an almost fatalistic spirit, the Iranian masses seemed like an immobile heap of dead aspirations, lost causes, and betrayed dreams. Khomeini, simply and calmly, with the authority invested in his voice from time immemorial, breathed confidence into that shapeless body of fragmented selves, gave them dignity, and enabled them to see their forgotten dreams made permissible.

Whatever the exact number of casualties in the course of the Iranian Revolution, there is little doubt that this was a historic confrontation between the power of the spoken word and the might of the loaded machine guns. All Khomeini had at his disposal were his words. The king's military might, however hesitantly he could use it, proved useless next to Khomeini's poignantly spoken few words. As his words kept the flame of the revolutionary cause burning in the hearts of the multitude of his followers, Khomeini appealed equally to the revolutionary corps of a variety of ideological persuasions: the young seminarians in Qom and Mashhad, whether they were radical or conservative; students in American and European universities, whether they were secular or religious; and radical and liberal intellectuals in Tehran, whether they had ideological or practical agendas. Without ever compromising his position on Marxism and Communism, Khomeini was always able to bridge whatever gap, ideological or political, that developed among his religious and secular followers. Between the radical and traditional elements among his religious followers and between the liberal and radical elements among his secular followers, he was always able to strike a chord to the tune of which everyone felt compelled, or at least willing, to respond.

Khomeini never appears explicitly in his speeches and correspondences to claim any power or demand any obedience for his person. Even in *Velayat-e Faqih (The Authority of the Jurist)* he argues theoretically for the authority of the jurist without ever explicitly, or even implicitly, indicating that he personally ought to occupy that position. Throughout his correspondences and speeches, more emphatically, he assumes an advisory voice, one that gives guidance and issues warnings. It is only with unspoken words, unwritten declarations, merely by the assumption of an authorial voice for "what Islam truly is" that Khomeini generates in his audience a compelling obedience, a feeling ever so tacit that he is in charge, and that he is to be listened to.

Khomeini's was a cassette revolution. The number of people who could have actually heard his voice personally during the June 1963 uprising in Qom could not have been more than a few hundred. Once exiled to Najaf, his speeches and lectures were taped, and his fiery and defiant voice, smuggled easily into Iran, reached thousands of people. Student organizations in Europe also had his cassettes mailed to them, broadcasting his revolutionary zeal on European, American, and Canadian campuses.

A sense of expectation seems to have anticipated Khomeini's words in Iran whenever the king or his government was about to indulge in yet another pompous ceremony, engage in yet another totalitarian vanity, or experiment with yet another measure of political tyranny. Although the measure of actual expectation was limited to Khomeini's immediate constituency inside Iran and a smaller contingency of Muslim students abroad, the propagation of his letters, cassette tapes, and pronouncements still reached many diverse groups who would not or could not necessarily come to hear him. While Khomeini's was not exactly a household name, during the pre-revolutionary years enough people knew and anticipated news from him to keep aflame the memory of the June 1963 uprising.

When in the early 1970s an ease in the otherwise hostile Iran-Iraq relations created the opportunity for some Shiʿi Iranians to travel to Najaf for pilgrimage, more widespread news of Khomeini's appearance were circulated. Iranian pilgrims would report back to their friends and relatives that in the sacred precinct of Imam Ali's mausoleum they had seen this tall, extremely handsome, and rather radiant man to whom they were attracted unknowingly. Mesmerized by his appearance, the pilgrims would later recover to inquire who he was. They would, of course, be hesitant to approach and speak to Khomeini for fear of reprisals when they returned to Iran. But they would privately report their memorable encounter to friends and families.

A long history of foreign intervention in the internal affairs of the country, the most recent and the most humiliating of which was the CIA-sponsored coup of 1953, had made Iranians particularly responsive to calls of revolt against indications of external domination. Throughout his revo-lutionary career, Khomeini was always a defiant cry of revolt against foreigners. The term "foreigners" (ajaneb) became an outright label of damnation for the revolutionary master. Perhaps the most crucial historical moment of Khomeini's mass appeal occurred when he condemned the Iranian king for having granted Americans diplomatic immunity in Iran. This was portrayed, in the mass perspective of the public eye, as the greatest affront to Iranian sovereignty. Why should Americans not be subject to Iranian law if they commit a crime? This question and all its implications were driven deep into the Iranian heart by Khomeini's famous "anticapitu-lation" speech. Having failed to respond swiftly and appropriately to such pressing questions, the liberal and leftist forces lost shares of their ideologi-cal legitimacy for masses of the Iranian discontent. Having uttered his defiant words in those momentous days in 1964, Khomeini would reclaim, however tacitly, confidence and obedience from his public in the more necessary days of 1977–79.

Throughout the pre-revolutionary years—the closer to the Revolution the more pronounced—Khomeini used to his advantage two most unsus-pecting symbolic charts: first, the Muslim calendar and, second, what can be called a constructed calendar of martyrdom. These two sets of revolu-tionary chronologies fed on each other's symbolic resources. The lunar Islamic (Shiʿi) calendar is held together by a set of sacred days that, like lampposts, brighten and energize the annual cycle in preset intervals. Many observers have noticed the significance of Muharram, the first month in the

Islamic calendar, particularly for the Shiʿi Muslims. But there are eleven more months to the year, each with its own relative significance. Throughout his years in exile, particularly between 1977 and 1979, Khomeini capitalized heavily on these sacred days, recalling the sacred memory of the occasion of a particular day—an Ashura, an Arbaʿiyn—and sending its energy in specific political directions. During such recollections of historical memories, there occurs, as it were, a contraction of time, a bridging of the chronological gap. Ahistoricity means nothing. Men, women, and children in the streets of Tehran, Shiraz, or Ahwaz see themselves *actually* in the desert of Karbala—vivid in their minds. Memories in such moments are expanded, emotions charged, sentiments of *gemeinschaft* extended beyond the limits of physicality and historicity. The physical pain inflicted in the course of ceremonial and dramaturgical self-flagellation, as well as those atemporal moments of nocturnal vigilance, chanting verses from dusk to dawn, compel and instill a pervasive sense of transhistorical inspiration: a feeling that the sun that shines, the trees that grow, and the water that flows are all parts of the same eternal cosmic order that was as valid and current when Ali was struck, when Hossein was martyred, and when you are physically crossing the street, passing the green light, reaching for a glass of water, or changing your colorful shirt for a black one "commemorating" the death of Imam Hossein.

With every major confrontation between the crowd and the army, no matter how few or how many the casualties, and with its concurrent registration of a cabalistic number of "martyrs," begins a second, this concocted, calendar. A cycle of "fortieth" would be set in motion whereby on the fortieth day of a bloody confrontation there would be, by Khomeini's call, a commemorative demonstration in the course of which further confrontations were bound to have happened; these new casualties, in turn, would be reclaimed forty days later in yet another demonstration. As this cycle perpetuates itself, the clear winner, no matter what the Shah would do, is Khomeini. If demonstrations were to be permitted, an unrealistic postulation given the king's nervous disposition, they would snowball out of control right in front of an American camera crew. If they were to be stopped, confrontations would ensue, bullets would be shot, bodies would fall, and the martyrological calendar would be prolonged.

As Khomeini set the agenda during the final months leading to the Revolution, he also uttered the final words, never before spoken. *Shah bayad beravad.* That "the king must go" was perhaps a possibility in many people's minds. But none was brought to utter the actual words. The umbilical cord to a history of monarchical memory was simply too strong for weaker wills. When Khomeini said, "the king must go," he set a new level of emotional courage, a sharper cut to the revolutionary discourse. Until then the very possibility, if not the inevitability, of the continuation of the king's reign in his son defined the language, limited the horizons, and shortened the range of political possibilities in terms of which the revolutionary momentum could unfold. But when Khomeini made the pronouncement that "the king must go," he suddenly unleashed the deeply suppressed anger of a nation and opened a whole new passage of revolutionary possibility, pushing the momentum he had created into a faster and more furious pace. Khomeini cut the Iranians' umbilical cord to their monarchical history.

Once in Tehran, with Shahpour Bakhtiar still prime minister and the monarchy still there in theory, with one speech Khomeini threw the existing government into utter despair. The most memorable statement in that speech, delivered with devastating force at the Tehran cemetery, was a phrase that would enthrall the young revolutionaries in sheer ecstacy. *Man tu dahan-e in dowlat mizanam!* This was the collective voice of a deeply oppressed, deeply wronged, deeply expectant people: "I will slap this government in the face!"

To realize the thunderous impact of this phrase, we have to have experienced the deep fear and even deeper resentment that the reign of a tyrant persistently accumulates in the hearts and minds of his subjects. A tyrant, particularly when weak and characterless in front of foreigners and yet pompous and presuming with his own people, engenders deep senses of resentment and disgust that surface in every aspect of political engagement — revolutionary or otherwise. The mere presence of the Iranian monarch was an insult to his nation's sense of dignity. He would sit on the edge of the royal sofa, while the Secretary of (the American) State, Henry Kissinger, sat comfortably there. But he would look down at his own nation from the dizzying height of the peacock throne. That he was thrown hard from that height, to die in the deep indignity of an exiled nonentity, was but the historical judgment of a deeply hurt nation. The ecstacy of Khomeini's words, *man tu dahan-e in dowlat mizanam,* can be measured only in terms of the opposing sense of disgust that the rule of tyranny, inflicted by a phony dictator, perpetrates on the collective dignity of a nation.

The King and the Cleric

For all intents and purposes, Ayatollah Khomeini's June 1963 uprising seemed to have been crushed by the Iranian monarch. The massive demonstrations that had erupted in Qom, Tehran, Shiraz, Yazd, Tabriz, Mashhad, and Isfahan subsided almost immediately when Khomeini was exiled to Turkey on 4 November 1964. After spending almost a year in Turkey, the Ayatollah went to Iraq in October 1965 for what appeared to be a permanent exile.[15]

The June 1963 uprising was predicated on a decade of rapid consolidation of power by the Pahlavi state. After the CIA-sponsored coup of 1953, Mohammad Reza Pahlavi returned to his throne still shaken by the Mosaddeq experience. But the successive and increasing American support, as well as the capable premierships of a number of Iranian prime ministers, consolidated the political and administrative foundations of the Pahlavi regime. Mosaddeq's trial and the execution of some of his ardent supporters, such as Hossein Fatimi in 1953, the ruthless suppression of the Tudeh (Communist) Party, and the execution of some of its most loyal members, such as Khosrow Ruzbeh in 1957, established the Pahlavi state as the sole claimant to the Iranian political agenda.

Following the formative period of the 1950s, the 1960s constituted the decade during which the Iranian monarch sat firmly on his peacock throne. Under the guardian care of three successive premiers—Ja'far Sharif Imami, Assadollah Alam, and Amir Abbas Hoveyda—and wholeheartedly sponsored by the Kennedy, Johnson, and Nixon administrations, the Pahlavi state fully commanded the Iranian political scene, except for the brief, but prophetic, uprising of Khomeini in June 1963 and the commencement of urban guerrilla movements, announcing the radical claims of the young Iranian political consciousness.[16]

A number of crucial events occurred in Iran during the fateful year of 1963. On 26 January, the Iranian monarch announced wide-ranging economic changes that would lay the foundation for ambitious, however illfated, programs of reform. Clerical opposition, triggered by certain aspects of these reforms, ensued and led to the Imperial army's attack against the seminary students in Qom on 22 March. On 3 April, Khomeini denounced the Pahlavi regime for its ruthless acts. After a series of verbal attacks exchanged between the Iranian monarch and the Ayatollah, Khomeini was arrested on 5 June. Massive demonstrations erupted throughout the country. On 2 July, Khomeini was released from the prison but placed under house arrest. When Tayyeb and Isma'il Hajj Reza'i, two chief organizers of demonstrations in Tehran, were executed, Mohammad Reza Pahlavi probably felt he had the situation under full control.

When, in October of the next year, 1964, the monarch gave diplomatic immunity to Americans working in Iran, Khomeini's anger was rekindled, leading to his famous "anticapitulation" speech, delivered on 27 October. This speech aroused the monarch's anger; the sixty-two-year-old cleric was expelled from his homeland on 4 November 1964. Ayatollah Khomeini spent the next eleven months—from November 1964 to October 1965—in Turkey before he left for what appeared to be his final exile in Iraq. But the signs of trouble for the Pahlavi state were perfectly clear even while Khomeini was in Turkey. On 10 April 1965 Reza Shamsabadi tried but failed to assassinate the monarch. And then, on 21 January 1966, in the wake of Khomeini's arrival in Iraq, the Iranian prime minister Hasan Ali Mansur was assassinated by the Fada'ian-e Islam Organization.[17]

Despite these troubling indications for the Pahlavi state, the Iranian monarch felt secure enough on his throne to launch an extravagant celebration of the 2,500th anniversary of the Persian monarchy on 15 October 1971. The regime equally met the leftist challenge, executing in 1973 a group of Marxists, chief among them Khosrow Golsorkhi and Keramatollah Daneshian. The 1973 Arab oil embargo, in which Iran did not participate, offered the Pahlavi state historically unprecedented access to petrodollars, giving rise to the megalomaniac dream of creating "the Japan of the Middle East." When President Carter offered his champagne toast to the success of "the island of stability" and its monarch in 1977, Mohammad Reza Pahlavi must have felt quite secure at the peak of his reign on the peacock throne.[18] And thus when Khomeini left Iraq and entered the small suburban village of Neauphle-le-Château on 3 October 1978, the monarch could not have fully grasped the depth of difficulty into which his throne would be cast.

Formation of a Revolutionary Language

Between 1964 and 1977, as the Iranian monarch spent his oil millions on the expensive toys of a modern arsenal, the aged Ayatollah sharpened his pencils and sat cross-legged at his tiny desk to write letters, issue edicts, announce declarations, and dispatch telegrams. Khomeini's pencils and papers proved to be not only massively less expensive but infinitely more effective than the monarch's state-of-the-art military technology.

Between the commencement of his exile in November 1964 and the launching of his final putsch against the Pahlavi state in 1977, Ayatollah Khomeini created, gradually but consistently, unsystematically but coherently, a language of revolt with which he would reclaim the scepter of power from "the King of Kings." In Iraq he gradually developed a revolutionary discourse that, combined with concomitant events in Iran, would lead to his dramatic return and the establishment of the Islamic Republic. Although the roots of this revolutionary discourse go back to the preparatory stages of the June 1963 uprising and although the ultimate making of the Iranian Revolution of 1979 depended on a variety of ideological frames of reference (sacred and secular) other than that of the Ayatollah, this formative period has had a lasting impact on the very constitution of the Islamic Republic.

Most important, the chief ideological statement by Khomeini in this period is the now-famous *Velayat-e Faqih (Authority of the Jurist)*, first published in 1970, in which he outlined the juridical argument for the assumption of political authority by the clerics. The juridical roots of the notion of *velayat-e faqih* are most immediately in the writings of a nine-teenth-century Shi'i jurist, Molla Ahmad Naraqi,[19] with deeper traces in the earlier notions of political and juridical authority in the Safavid period.[20] A more detailed consideration of these notions can also be traced back to the earliest periods of Shi'i history and the conception of its jurisprudence.[21] Of equal importance, though not examined as thoroughly, are the letters and proclamations of Ayatollah Khomeini during the period between 1964 and 1977.[22] In this collection of writings, considered chronologically, the essential features of Khomeini's revolutionary discourse, the language of his revolt, and the terms of his discontent are orchestrated in a relentless attempt to mobilize his growing constituency for the final assault against the Iranian monarch.

From the viewpoint of the public mobilization of collective Shi'i memory, these writings are perhaps even more important than the single statement in the *Velayat-e Faqih*. Whereas the circulation of *Velayat-e Faqih* was rather limited during the pre-Revolutionary period, these letters and proclamations were widely distributed. Whereas the language of the *Velayat-e Faqih* is technically juridical and elitist in tone, the language of these letters is easily comprehended by the majority of Khomeini's supporters. Whereas the authority of *Velayat-e Faqih* was limited to that of a learned juridical treatise, some of these proclamations were in the form of legal edicts thoroughly binding on the followers of the aged Ayatollah. These features of Khomeini's writings and proclamations, written and issued between 1964 and 1977, render them essential for understanding the growth of his revolutionary discourse. While *Velayat-e Faqih* made the calm and deliberate claim for the supreme authority of the jurist in religious and political domains, the letters and proclamations assumed the validity of this authority as self-evident and sought to implement it in practice. If *Velayat-e Faqih* was the de jure argument for Khomeini's authority, his letters and edicts were the de facto extension of theory into action.

A Storm Gathers

It would be a mistake to assume that Ayatollah Khomeini went into exile determined to topple the Iranian monarchy. In a letter to Ayatollah Najafi, dated December 1964, he seems to have submitted to his fate and asserts that "whatever God Almighty has ordained, He would know best. I beg God Almighty for success in compliance with His judgment."[23] Khomeini's revolutionary discourse, instead, had a gradual and rather accidental course of development. He would respond appropriately to specific events that would occur in Iran, and gradually, in the course of his responses, a unique revolutionary discourse would emerge. Events in Iran were the cause and the target of his statements; the Iranian monarch provided many occasions for these statements to be grievous.

The summation of Khomeini's political disposition in the wake of his arrival in Najaf is expressed in a statement about "the responsibilities and duties of presidents and kings of Islamic societies, and those of the ulama'." [24] As he begins this period of his political activities, he has a clear understanding of what constitutes his primary enemy. During this period the most important enemy against which Khomeini believes the forces of Islam ought to be mobilized is "The West," consisting of Jewish and Christian elements. Just like their ancestors during the Prophet's time, the Jews and the Christians conspire against Islam. They resist the righteous cause of Islam to expand into "the four quarters of the globe." [25] The most intolerable symbol of "The Western" tyranny against the Muslims, Khomeini believes, is the state of Israel. Muslims should be united under their "kings, presidents, and shaykhs" against their common enemy, the conspiracy of the Jews and the Christians in the form of "The Western" creation of the state of Israel. He argues that had "the seven hundred million" [26] Muslims been united, the Jews would not have been able to establish their state in Palestine or the Indians dominate Kashmir. [27]

With "The West" as the primary target of Khomeini's revolutionary rhetoric, the next immediate question is how Muslims are to fight this enemy. Here Khomeini offers both the material and the ideological instruments with which "The West" must be confronted. For this purpose he turns to Islam as the chief ideological force that can unite Muslims against their common enemy. It is important to note that throughout his writings during this period—and indeed any other period—he makes no distinction between the Shi'i and the Sunni branches of Islam. Although he operates primarily within a Shi'i juridical discourse, he intentionally stays clear of any sectarian division within Islam. His language has a universally Islamic tone to it. Given that he was living in the Arab world during this period, the overwhelming majority of which is Sunni, and that his political agenda, particularly in relation to the Palestinian question, was beyond the specifics of Iran, it is quite understandable why he diminished the Shi'i particularity of his revolutionary language. The result of acquiring this language was that when his writings were translated into Arabic not only the Arab Shi'is but also the Sunnis could identify with his cause.

Thus united in faith against their common enemy, "The West," all Muslims ought to fight, with Islam as their chief metaphysical force, to regain their lost dignity. Here the primary objective of Khomeini's statement is to pronounce the political dimension of Islam. The subtext of his argument seems to be directed against those who wished to depoliticize the faith. Since he had just been expelled from Iran because of his political engagements, it is conceivable that certain oppositions to his political uses of Islam had been raised by such scholarly minded and apolitical clerics as Ayatollah Kho'i.

In this statement, Khomeini refers to the putative letters of the Prophet Muhammad to the kings and emperors surrounding Arabia, inviting them to join Islam.[28] If the Prophet of Islam translated his religious message into a political agenda, so should his followers, no matter how distant in history. Here, Khomeini makes specific references to Christianity as a religion that is concerned primarily with the personal relationship of individuals with God. "It should not be presumed that Islam is like Christianity: just a spiritual relationship between individuals and God Almighty. Islam has a program for life, . . . [and] for government."[29] Khomeini insists that contrary to a church, which is the site for paying personal tribute to the majesty of God, a mosque is a place for both worship and organizing an army for battle, just as in the time of the Prophet. The patently political activities of the Prophet in establishing Islam in its formative period provide Khomeini with the set of commonly held sacred symbols and memories through an activation of which he legitimates his own insistence on the political charges of Islam. The archetypal memory of Muhammad in the Muslim collective consciousness is the primary source of authority for Khomeini's drive towards the construction of his revolutionary discourse.

But it should not be assumed that at this stage Khomeini claims the political authority inherent in Islam to be a prerogative of the ulama'. He indicates explicitly that "those who bear the utmost responsibility are the Islamic governments, Islamic presidents, Islamic kings."[30] He further adds that "those leaders to whom God Almighty has given leadership are responsible. They have to propagate Islam as it truly is."[31] If there is any doubt that by "leaders" Khomeini means kings and presidents, he eliminates it by insisting that the kings and presidents "must consult with the Islamic ulama' to clarify the truths of Islam for them, and then they [that is, the presidents and the kings] would propagate them in radio and other publications."[32] Or, further confirming this advisory capacity for the ulama', he asserts, "this is so insofar as our political leaders are concerned, as for the other group who are the Islamic ulama' . . ., they too have grave responsibilities."[33] This is a crucial statement in demonstrating the gradual formation of Khomeini's political ideas. It is not until later, particularly in the lectures that were subsequently collected as *Velayat-e Faqih* in 1970, that Khomeini specifically claims political authority for the ulama'.

Having articulated the political aspect of Islam as the chief ideological force with which Muslims can and should defend their rights against "The West," Khomeini insists that the propagation of this political agenda of Islam has first priority. He emphasizes the significance of propaganda to the point of actually identifying Islam as a "commodity" that has to be advertised loudly: "Such a good commodity!" Khomeini exclaimed. "You have access to such a good commodity and yet you cannot introduce it to the world. They ... introduce their Bible. Their propagators have gone all over the world."[34]

To carry out the crucial task of the ideological leadership of the movement, Khomeini sets the necessary ascetic standards of training the revolutionary cadre. He insists on the ethical rectitude of the ulama' which, in his judgment, is as important as their scholastic learning. Both their scholastic learning and their ascetic rectitude are the primary prerequisites for assuming revolutionary leadership. Learning alone is not sufficient; what is needed is also revolutionary asceticism:

There are many people who know the minutiae of the [religious] sciences better than anyone else, and yet God Almighty does not grant them that necessary light. For that they need asceticism, hard labor, and self-denial. Sir! You who have come to join the ranks of this group [of ulama']! You have to practice asceticism. You have to do hard labor. You have to be observant. Put your carnal soul on trial![35]

With such disciplinary asceticism on the agenda, the object of Khomeini's revolutionary discourse could not remain for long either an abstract entity called "The West" or its ancillary power, the state of Israel. Gradually, the focus of his attention is redirected to Iran. After his establishment in Iraq, Khomeini kept a vigilant contact with his colleagues and constituencies inside Iran. In a telegram to Ayatollah Montazeri, sent sometime in 1964 while he was still in Turkey, he assured his long-time associate that "I truly wish I was with them [the clerics], sharing their joy and sorrow. ... As soon as the prohibition [against my coming back to Iran] is lifted, God willing, I shall be with them."[36]

The Question of Insurance: Attending to More Mundane Realities

While becoming increasingly engaged in a campaign of writing letters and building up his wider constituency, Khomeini also took time to address some of the essential, though more mundane, problems facing the community of believers. Such occasions provide further opportunities to see the particular cast of his mind. One of the interesting occasions on which Khomeini's "rational," as opposed to "traditional," bend of mind becomes apparent is in his discussion of the question of "insurance." The "rationality" of Khomeini's approach to this question, as well as to many other similar issues, is a clear indication of his built-in *usuli* approach to matters of modern juridical concern. It is important to keep in mind that this "rationality" is an innate juridical principle in Shi'ism and has nothing to do with the so-called "modernization" or "Westernization." Juridical rationalism *(usuli)* was articulated expressly against juridical literalism or traditionalism *(akhbari)*. Khomeini's juridical preference for the rational approach has far-reaching implications in his political ideas. This should become evident through a brief consideration of his treatment of the question of "insurance."

Like Motahhari, but with less of an engaged juridical language, Ayatollah Khomeini addressed the question of "insurance" as a modern phenomenon and defended its compatibility with Shi'i law. He has specifically addressed the question of insurance at least three times: first, in 1964 during his regular advanced (kharej) classes in fiqh; second, in the passage in his *Tahrir al-Wasilah*, written during his short exile in Turkey; and third, in *Towzih al-Masa'il*.[37] His positive edict, affirming the feasibility of insurance, is based on the same kind of *usuli* argument as that of Motahhari, demonstrating how, like Motahhari, he had a principally rational, rather than traditional (akhbari), juridical attitude. When asked about the feasibility of "insurance," in view of the fact that no such transaction existed during the time of the Prophet, Khomeini responded:

First, some [jurists] have considered it similar to "guarantee" (zemanat), or "guarantee in kind" (zemanat-e beh avaz). Secondly, suppose that [this] transaction has no antecedent. Why should a transaction have an antecedent? Of course in the early Islamic period, most transactions that are carried out today have been in practice. But there is no absolute necessity that the legislator should have stipulated that such and such a transaction is lawful or unlawful. Instead, the legislator has legislated every [kind] of contract and arrangement that could have been drawn between two parties, whether with or without antecedent, unless there is a reason contrary to that [lawful contract].[38]

In response to the further question that, contrary to other kinds of contract, in "insurance" you pay for something you may or may not receive, Khomeini insists on the acceptability of this transaction and maintains that "it is a rational contract. Such contracts are valuable to rational people."[39]

As with Motahhari, the significance of Khomeini's argument is in his principal or rational (usuli) defense of the insurance contract. This otherwise tangential treatment of a juridical question demonstrates the degree to which Khomeini believed in updating and rendering socially responsive the fundamentals of the (Shi'i) Islamic doctrines. Modern realities, Khomeini's extrapolation clearly implies, demand historical verification of Islamic (Shi'i) doctrines by rendering them still valid and operative. "Insurance" is as much a part of contemporary social contracts as political order. No domain of social action, political or otherwise, remains outside the Islamic claim to continued legitimacy and authority.

Connections Are Made

There were more pressing problems at hand than a juridical consideration of the question of insurance. Khomeini had to carry from Turkey to Iraq his wishes to be in Iran. In a letter to Ayatollah Najafi Mar'ashi, dated 25 October 1965, he assures his colleague that although it is a great honor to reside in the holy city of Najaf, he prefers to be in Iran and asks his supporters not to lose hope.[40] In the meantime, he begins to consolidate various oppositional forces that were active inside and outside Iran and were ready to accept his general leadership. Chief among these oppositional forces outside Iran were the Muslim student organizations in Europe, the United States, and Canada. A report had been circulating in Iran to the effect that Ayatollah Khomeini had refused to meet with the representatives of the Muslim Students Association in Europe. Khomeini immediately issued a statement denying such an incident, attributing its circulation to the Pahlavi regime, and asking the students to join him in denying the validity of such reports.[41]

During 1966, Khomeini was unusually quiet. The vicissitude of the relationship between the Iranian and the Iraqi governments, in which Khomeini's presence in Najaf must have been a crucial factor, may have had something to do with this long silence. Such occasional and rare moments of silence are uncharacteristic of Khomeini.

The Putsch Tested

During 1967, some occasions lead us to believe that Khomeini had a sense of getting old and not living to see the downfall of the Pahlavi regime. In a letter to the Muslim students in Europe, dated sometime in 1967, when Khomeini was sixty-five, he wrote, "In these last moments of my life . . . I feel joy and pride . . . to see students of old and modern [schools] cooperate in this sacred Islamic movement."[42] If there is hope, Ayatollah Khomeini seems to invest it in the unification of diverse forces, such as the students in secular modern universities and their counterparts among the seminarians. Khomeini calls for a collaboration, in the spirit of the Islamic cause, between the students of the old and modern colleges. In the 1967 letter to the Muslim students in Europe, he commends the Islamic virtues of the young students abroad, as well as those of their brethren in scholastic schools.[43]

Despite these occasional feelings of old age, and perhaps encouraged by the high-spirited expectations of his young admirers, as early as 1967, some four years after his initial bid for power against the Pahlavi regime, Khomeini seems to have become convinced of the possibility of an all-out revolution. Encouraged by the news of young Muslim students in Europe being politically active and willing to join ranks with their clerical counterparts, he now spoke of a "sacred Islamic movement that, God willing, leads to cutting off the hands of the instruments of foreigners, those who advocate colonialism, and the Westoxicated."[44] He further proceeds to "give myself the good tidings that, God willing, a bright future awaits the oppressed nations."[45] His contacts with Muslim students in Europe was one of the chief sources for keeping the revolutionary cause alive.

With the direction of his revolutionary rhetoric focused on Iran, Khomeini launches, from 1967 onward, a series of denunciations against specific events in his homeland. For example, in his letter to the Muslim students in Europe he bitterly criticizes[46] the so-called "Religious Corps" that the Pahlavi regime had mobilized to assimilate the religious institutions into its state machinery. Subsequently, early in 1967, after four years in exile, Khomeini felt secure and confident enough to write a direct letter to the Iranian prime minister. The incident that prompted this letter was the news that the Iranian monarch was about to coronate himself, a momentous event that he actually carried out with great pomp and ceremony—the Kiani crown on head, the jeweled scepter in hand, all wrapped in the royal cloak—on 26 October 1967, at the Golestan Palace in downtown Tehran. On 16 April 1967, having heard the news of the upcoming coronation, the Ayatollah wrote an angry letter to Prime Minister Hoveyda. Judging from the language of this letter, Khomeini's revolutionary discourse clearly assumes a more direct and determined tone. This letter is the most serious statement, after his exile, in which Khomeini challenges the legitimacy of the Pahlavi state.

Early in the letter, Khomeini states that he has been expelled illegally from the country simply for having opposed giving undue diplomatic immunity to Americans. It is important, however, to note that at this stage he refers to both "the religious law and the constitutional law" to argue for the illegality of his expulsion.[47] This is the same constitutional law that legitimates the monarch. Although he tacitly acknowledges the Iranian constitution, Khomeini proceeds to deliver the most serious challenge to the legitimacy of the Pahlavi regime based on a number of essential charges against the government.

First, there is the massive poverty of the Iranian people. "Everyday, people's poverty and destitution are increased,"[48] he charges. "You keep people in a state of poverty and backwardness in the name of progress."[49] Against the background of this poverty, the monarch's celebration of his coronation is ludicrous and appalling. "The expenses for these [celebrations]," he charges, "are taken with bayonet from the wretched people."[50] Second, there is a general state of bankruptcy among the Iranian merchants. Khomeini attributes this bankruptcy to "the dominance of Israel in economic matters."[51] Third, the economic and political domination of the foreigners has been at the expense of Iranian prosperity. "There is a black market for [the benefit of] the foreigners."[52] While local merchants suffer, foreign capitalists prosper. Fourth, there is a grave danger against Islam. "In the name of Islam," Khomeini warns, "the heaviest blows are struck against the Holy Qur'an and the Divine commandments."[53] Here he particularly attacks the attempt to assimilate the Shi'i clerical order into the state bureaucracy. Fifth, there is not the slightest indication of democracy in the state. "You are incapable of giving freedom, *the traitor is fearful*," he charges. "Denying the freedom of the press and the dictating [of what can or cannot be printed] by the so-called Security Organization [SAVAK] are indications of backwardness."[54]

Khomeini concludes his letter to Prime Minister Hoveyda with a clear ultimatum:

Fear the anger of God! Beware of the wrath of the people! Do not tamper with the commandments of God Almighty, calling it "the progressive religion!" Do not jeopardize the Islamic commandments in the name of the Qur'an! Do not behave so violently with the seminarians, the servants of the people and their culture, in the name of conscripting them as useless soldiers. And finally, do not force the ulama' of this people to take a different course of action with you!

These were not empty threats. Khomeini was now pursuing his campaign against the Pahlavi monarchy with a fuller attention to details. As Khomeini's revolutionary momentum began to take shape and purpose in 1967, one of the immediate questions that obviously faced him was the financial aspect of the movement, directly connected to the whole political economy of mass mobilization against the enemy.

Sometime during 1967 Khomeini is officially asked, *estefta'*, whether those Iranian ulama' who had permission from him to collect the religious taxes, and yet were now supportive of the Pahlavi state, were still in possession of such authority.[55] "Those who have approved of the tyrannical state," he responded in his edict,

or do so now, and thus act contrary to the Sacred Law, should they have any permission from me [to collect religious taxes], it is now nullified. The [Muslim] believers should not pay them religious sums of the *sahm-e Imam*, peace be upon him. *May God protect us against the evils of ourselves!*[56]

The last invocation is the clear indication of Khomeini's anger against those clerics who supported the Pahlavi state. In the same year, and following the same format of a religious edict, Khomeini also declared an economic war against the state of Israel. He emphasized that

helping Israel, whether in the form of selling arms and ammunition or oil, is forbidden and contrary to [the commandments of] Islam. Any connection with Israel and its agents, whether commercial or political, is forbidden and contrary to [the commandments of] Islam.[57]

Ayatollah Khomeini's connection with Iran during 1967 is evident from his correspondence with Hojjat al-Islam Sa'idi, a pro-Khomeini activist who continued his antigovernmental activities after the June 1963 uprising. Educated in Mashhad and Qom seminaries, Sa'idi stayed in Iran after Khomeini's exile, became the public prayer leader in a downtown Tehran mosque, and both directly and through Morteza Motahhari was in contact with the exiled leader. He was subsequently arrested and killed in prison. In a letter dated 29 June 1967, Khomeini writes to Sa'idi to take care of "the sick." He insists that "it is pointless to postpone the treatment any further."[58] Since Sa'idi at the time was quite militant in antigovernment activities, the reference to "the sick" and to "treatment" could very well be some secret communication to political activists who still supported the exiled leader. The active presence of a group of Khomeini supporters at that time is also evident from a later letter to Sa'idi, dated 12 September 1967, in which Khomeini writes,

I believe I have received one letter from your highness that I have not yet responded to. Mr. Montazeri has written, however, that you have said there are a number of letters by you which I have not answered . . .[59]

It is also quite possible that the Iranian secret service intercepted Khomeini's correspondence.

Further Finance: Extended Connections

After he disqualified those ulama' who had not joined ranks with him, Khomeini issued a new edict, dated 24 March 1968, designating Morteza Motahhari, his former student, as his sole representative in collecting the religious taxes. "His highness . . . Mr. Hajj Sheykh Morteza Motahhari . . . is authorized," Khomeini decreed,

to collect the sacred sahm-e Imam, peace be upon him, and to spend half of it in matters beneficial to the advancement of Islam, the propagation of the sacred commandments, and the consolidation of the righteous religion; and to send the other half to me in order to spend in [other] important Islamic centers.[60]

In the same year, Khomeini also authorized the donation of such religious taxes as zakat and sahm-e Imam to be given to factions of the Palestine Liberation Organization.[61] "It is absolutely worthy, nay mandatory, that some necessary portions of such religious sums as zakat and the like be allocated to these [Palestinian] fighters in the path of God."[62] He further stated that

the best way [to proceed] is that the Muslim people of Iran try with whatever is at their disposal to cut their transactions with the local Zionists and their like in Iran . . . leading an economic battle against them.[63]

In yet another religious edict, dated 28 August 1968, Khomeini responded positively to the inquiry of a group of his supporters who had asked whether "religious taxes, such as *zakat,* can be used to arm and train the Muslims [against 'the Jewish infidels']."[64]

Khomeini was as concerned about unifying his forces outside Iran as he was about consolidating his bases inside the country. This he had to do by maintaining his former constituency, opposing the clerics who had not joined ranks with him, and, perhaps most important, winning new members to his cause among the young clerics. In a letter to Morteza Motahhari, written some time in early 1968, Khomeini gives proper instructions as to how the internal forces ought to be kept alert.[65] He seems to be concerned that Motahhari is in Tehran, and Qom is left to other ulama'.

The reason I am concerned about your being away from Qom, and concerned about certain other gentlemen (clerics) whom the seminarians in these anarchical time could benefit from, is precisely for such corruptions [that Motahhari had apparently mentioned in his letter].[66]

Khomeini then concludes with a hopeful sign for the future of a unified clerical stand:

Their Excellencies [the ulama'], thank God, have been admonished [enough] and [thus] changed their path. I hope that people will take heed of this, and that conflict and segmentation will be eliminated or at least subsided.[67]

From the tone of Khomeini's response, it appears that Motahhari had complained of the infiltration of leftist ideas into the seminarian circles. "In a letter that I have just written in response to the confederation of Muslim students in Europe," Khomeini reassures Motahhari,

I have thoroughly explained the principal problems and shown the way. I have emphasized the corruptive [forces] of this misguided ideology [= Marxism?]. . . . Should there be an[other] occasion, I shall [further] explain this in a letter to the Qom seminary. However, admonition alone is not enough. Such diversions ought to be opposed with action.[68]

This could very well be a reference to those high-ranking clerics who advocated the Pahlavi state openly and then were persuaded otherwise by the local supporters of the exiled Ayatollah, or else a reference to the leftist infiltration among the seminarian students, or even to Shariʿati's ideas or to the Mojahedin-e Khalq Organization.

While engaged in these crucial maneuvers against monarchical and leftist infiltrations into the high-ranking clerical orders, Khomeini was equally attentive to those mainline supporters who served his revolutionary cause selflessly. In a short letter dated 3 November 1968, he expresses his deep appreciation of Saʿidi's endeavors despite the fact that "the majority have secluded themselves."[69] In another letter, written sometime during the same year, he demonstrates one of the rare occasions in which he speaks of his deep emotions. "I like people like you so much," the sixty-six-year-old Ayatollah writes to Sa'idi, "that perhaps I am unable to express my deep emotions properly. [It is not but] God Almighty who has graced you with His favours to serve the faith." [70] In a later letter to Sa'idi, dated 5 November 1968, [71] Khomeini makes a cryptic reference that could be an indication of a widespread propaganda network established in the Iranian mosques. "As for the mosques," he writes to Sa'idi,

I have already been informed. It has even been reported that [something or some-body?] has been designated for the Sayyid Azizollah Mosque. But I am not sure of the accuracy of the report. The point is, however, that no front should be easily abandoned. [72]

That Sa'idi, the recipient of this letter, is killed by the Shah's police some-time later in 1970 could be an added indication that there were under-ground movements, organized through the local mosques as early as 1968, to mobilize pro-Khomeini support should the proper occasion manifest itself.

There is, however, a reference in this letter, again, to old age. "I am spending the last moments of my life," writes the sixty-six-year-old Khom-eini, "and I worry about the general and specific conditions of the scholastic centers." [73] This pessimistic reference, however, should not be overinter-preted. Khomeini's general attitude during 1968 is quite optimistic and determined. At sixty-six, he, of course, could have felt old, but not so much as to lose hope. He gives encouragement to Sa'idi that "you the young generation should not be disappointed. With determination and resolution, be prepared to serve at the right moment!" [74]

In the same letter of 5 November 1968, Khomeini seems to oppose some extreme factions of his followers: "With such extremisms on their part, and such laxities on our part, I do not know what will ultimately happen." [75] More than anything else, he is dismayed with those among the ulama' who have not joined him in his revolt. He complains of "duplicity at home," [76] meaning at the Qom seminary. He reminds Sa'idi of the lost historical opportunities.

Our most righteous ancestors, may they rest in peace, lost a golden opportunity when the wicked ancestor [of the Shah, namely Reza Shah] left. There were other lost opportunities too, until the present calamities appeared. As long as this wicked tree is implanted, there is no hope. [77]

Moments of Disappointment

The periodic negative ring to Khomeini's voice continues well into 1969. Almost a year after this letter to Sa'idi, sometime in November or December 1969, he wrote to Mohammad Reza Hakimi, a devout follower, "I am spending the last days of my life, and yet unfortunately could not do anything for the beloved Islam and the Muslims."[78] In the same letter, moved by a poem that M. Azarm, an Iranian poet, had composed for him, he admits, "the spirit of disappointment and resignation, which has been injected by the colonialists in the people and even in their Muslim leaders, prevents them from doing something."[79] Disappointed in his old age, Khomeini hopes that "the younger generation" will lead the cause.

Indictment of the Left; Ultimatum to the King

Such momentary pauses were not to last. The year 1970 produced yet another fierce ultimatum to the Pahlavi regime. Khomeini's denunciation was brought on by the murder of Hojjat al-Islam Sa'idi.

The year had started on a pessimistic note for Khomeini. The same sentiments of "I am spending the last days of my life" and the hope that the younger generation will assume the responsibility are expressed in a letter to Muslim students in Europe, dated 1 January 1970.[80] On 31 May 1970, Khomeini wrote a letter to Muslim students in Europe, expressing his appreciation of their attempt to understand and propagate "the true Islam" and accusing the European Islamicists and Orientalists of having distorted Islam. Concentrating on "buildings and paintings" of Islam and giving credence to the illegitimate rule of the Umayyads and the Abbasids, and by doing so having "kept the true countenance of Islam behind these veils,"[81] the Orientalists have falsified the true message of Islam. By using the key term gharbzadeh, (Westoxicated), Khomeini also criticizes those nominal Muslims who have been misguided by "Western propaganda." He urges his student followers "to wake [them] up."[82]

In May 1970, Mohammad Reza Sa'idi, who had been in close contact with Khomeini, was arrested in Iran and killed in prison. On the occasion of his death, which coincided with the Pahlavi regime's striking lucrative commercial contracts with foreign capitalists, Ayatollah Khomeini sent a telegram to his followers in Iran, dated sometime in late July or early August 1970, in which he attacked both leftist and rightist forces, the Soviet Union and the United States, for plundering the national wealth of the Iranian masses. He openly declared that the continuation of the Pahlavi state spelled poverty and destitution for the Iranian masses, humility and bankruptcy for the Iranian merchants, yet lucrative deals for the foreign capitalists.[83] He challenged the legitimacy of the members of the Iranian parliament and appealed to "impartial international authorities" to intervene and prevent the execution of such illegal contracts.[84] He openly declared void and invalid any kind of commercial contract between the Iranian government and foreign companies. Among his growing constituency, he appeals in particular to the religious and political leaders and the seminarian and university students.[85]

By The Authority Vested in Me

Haphazard and occasional responses to the specific events inside Iran would not have accumulated into a forceful political pressure unless accompanied by a deliberate reflection on the nature of political authority in (Shi'i) Islam. By far, the most significant event of 1970 was the series of nineteen lectures soon to be known as *Velayat-e Faqih (The Authority of the Jurist)* delivered over the course of nineteen days, from 21 January to 8 February 1970. Since then a number of official and clandestine editions of these lectures have appeared under three different titles: (1) *The Islamic Government,* (2) *Authority of the Jurist,* and (3) *A Letter from Imam Musavi Kashef al-Qita'.*[86] But all three titles refer to this series of lectures. These lectures were delivered and the subsequent volumes were published in Persian, Khomeini's native tongue.

The Arabic rendition of the Persian original does not appear until 1979, some ten years after its original publication and in the wake of the Iranian Revolution. In the publisher's preface to this version there are repeated references to the fact that these lectures were delivered ten years earlier. The assumption that these lectures were delivered or published in Arabic is false.[87] A comparison of the Persian and Arabic texts clearly shows that the Arabic version is an abridged translation of the Persian, and not vice versa.[88] Whereas the Persian text is in the normal diction and fluency of Khomeini's other writings, the Arabic text is verbatim and artificial. A comparison of this Arabic translation with *Sharh Do'a' al-Sahar,*[89] a treatise Khomeini did write in Arabic, further testifies that the text of this Arabic translation is not Khomeini's.

The Arabic version of *Velayat-e Faqih* is a condensation and a paraphrasing of the original Persian. However, occasional phrases are added to the Arabic translation that do no exist in the original Persian. One such key addition is to the sentence on page 172 of the Persian text where, in a reference to Molla Ahmad Naraqi, Khomeini maintains that the jurists have precisely the same privileges as the Prophet.[90] In the Arabic translation, the following subordinate clause is added: "with the exception of such privileges by which he [that is, the Prophet] is [uniquely] distinguished."[91]

The assumption that the original lectures were given in Arabic is further discredited by the fact that in the original text all Arabic phrases, such as the Qur'anic passages, the Prophetic hadiths, or excerpts from the *Nahj al-Balaghah* are immediately translated and explicated in Persian. If the original delivery were in Arabic, the Persian explication would be both redundant and ludicrous.

Upon the publication of the first edition of *Velayat-e Faqih,* as Khomeini himself testifies,[92] the Iranian embassy in Iraq sought to thwart its circulation. But apparently it was unable to do so, and the book was made widely available. Its publication in Iran was facilitated by its clandestine distribution under one of the alternate titles noted above, "A Letter from Imam Musavi Kashif al-Qita'." These editions usually contain another treatise of Khomeini's, *The Greater Holy War,* as a supplement. Although printed unprofessionally, hurriedly, and on very cheap paper, these editions offer eye-catching subtitles, provocative Qur'anic passages, and a laudatory statement by the unknown "publisher" on Khomeini's great revolutionary merits. The date of this introduction by "the publisher" is Dhi al-Hajjah 1392, which corresponds to sometime between 6 January and 3 February 1973. This indicates that as early as three years after its original delivery in early 1970, *Velayat-e Faqih* was widely available in Iran. The typography of these Iranian versions also differs from the one published in Iraq. The typography of the Iraqi version has certain indications in its alphabet that show the printing house in Iraq did not have access to all the Persian letters. Although the letters "P" and "G" are represented properly in the actual text, there is no exact reproduction of the Persian "Y," and the Arabic "Y," with two dots under the letter, is substituted. One crucial exception is the key footnote to the Qur'anic passage 4:59, the famous "authority verse," quoted to support the argument for the political authority of the religious figures such as Khomeini. In this footnote, pages 27–28, the three exclusively Persian letters "CH," "G," and "P" are approximated to their closest Arabic equivalents, that is, "J," "K," and "B," respectively. The Arabic "Y" is also used for the Persian "Y." This may indicate that the footnote was a later addition to the text, printed by a different printing house (probably in a rush) where the Persian letters were not available or the publisher was in too much of a hurry to secure them from other sources.

Velayat-e Faqih is delivered from an essentially juridical point of departure. It identifies the concept of *velayat-e faqih* as one of "the topics discussed in jurisprudence [*fiqh*] in religious seminaries."[93] That its discussion has been neglected in recent times, Khomeini charges, is precisely because of its political nature, antithetical to the powers that be. Oblivion of the political implications of *velayat-e faqih,* as a contemporary reality, is deeply rooted in the Jewish propaganda against Islam, Khomeini recalls, and its contemporary counterpart in the colonial designs against the faith. Since the Crusades, the colonial powers realized how important Islam has been in unifying Muslims, and now they seek to obliterate it to dominate the Muslims more effectively. Through a variety of agents, chief among them the Orientalists, the colonial powers have sought to eradicate the revolutionary and political nature of Islam. The result is that not only the masses but even the educated Muslims have been led to believe that Islam is a "deficient faith."[94] Islam, in Khomeini's definition, was 99 percent more concerned with society and politics than with matters of ritual purity and personal ethics. It is incumbent upon Khomeini's students to propagate the true nature of Islam and show that Islam is not like Christianity, "the nominal not the actual," limited to "a few commandments concerning the relation between God and the people."[95] On the contrary,

> when there was nothing in the West and its inhabitants lived in barbarity, and America was the land of half-barbarian Indians . . . and Iran and Byzantium were under the rule of tyranny . . . God Almighty, through the noble Prophet (God's benedictions be upon him), sent such laws that one is amazed by their majesty.[96]

Islamic laws, Khomeini declared, are "progressive, complete, and all-inclusive." But following the designs of the foreigners, certain members of the clergy have played in their hands and propagated an apolitical reading of Islam.

Constitutionalism was a design of the British, Khomeini declared, implemented in Iran through their local agents.[97] The result was a constitution more in tune with Belgian, French, English, and American laws than compatible with Islam. Islam does not recognize monarchy. The Prophet sent letters to the Persian and Roman kings admonishing them and inviting them to embrace Islam. Imam Hossein fought against Yazid and his monarchical claims. The result of this anti-Islamic constitution is injustice for the Muslims, whose rights the present civil law cannot secure.[98] The civil law is selective in its punishment. It executes a heroin dealer but refuses to ban alcoholic beverages, just "because the West does the same."[99] These, Khomeini decided, are all indications of a massive conspiracy designed by "The West" against Islam to rob Muslims of their most effective arm against the colonial powers. Helping the colonial interests of "The West" are their local agents who have been fascinated by the technical achievements of Europe and the United States. "As soon as they go to the moon, for example," Khomeini warned, the "Westoxicated" locals "imagine they have to abandon their [Islamic] laws. [But] what has going to the moon got to do with the Islamic laws?"[100] Conquer the universe how "The West" may, Khomeini reassured his students, they are incapable of solving their moral and social problems. To cure their moral malaise, "The West" has to turn to Islam.

Contrary to the propagandas of "The Western" colonialist, Khomeini charges, Islam is not merely an embodiment of ethical and legal injunctions. It has equally specified the necessity of the executive branch to complement the legislative.[101] Khomeini appropriates modern terms such as "the executive" and "the legislative" branches of the government into his otherwise (Shi'i) juridical parlance as if such conceptualizations of power were innate to the Islamic political discourse. The executive aspect of Islam, Khomeini proceeds to argue, is necessitated both doctrinally and as indicated by the exemplary conduct of the Prophet. Doctrinally, the Qur'an has mandated the necessity of obedience to God, the Prophet, and "those of authority among you." As indicated by the exemplary conduct of the Prophet, he too (in Shi'ite understanding) designated his successor. From these two sources emerges the Shi'i doctrinal necessity of *velayat*, or successorship to the authority of Muhammad, as the executive power of the Islamic political order. Translating the executive aspect of the Islamic political order into "Islamic government" as such, Khomeini extends the (Shi'i) doctrinal mandates of his version of the faith to the most immediate ideological agenda of his time: questioning the monarchy. "To fight towards the establishment of the Islamic government," Khomeini decreed, "is the logical conclusion of the belief in *velayat*." [102]

Khomeini charges his students with moral encouragement against two principal enemies: the "Westoxicated" secular intellectuals, who are the local agents of the colonialists, and the colonialists themselves. While the secular intellectuals import the barrage of their "Western" ideologies and with them intimidate the clergy, the colonialists propagate the false notion that in Islam religion and politics are separate and thus rob the religious authorities of their historical responsibility. [103] Should, as "The West" wishes, Islam be limited to mandating rules and regulations for ritual routines, no one would challenge the plunder of the colonialists. "You can pray as much as you want," Khomeini poignantly reminded his apolitical students and colleagues, "they [the 'Western' colonialists] want your oil. They would not bother with your prayer. They want our natural resources. They want our country to be the market for their goods." [104]

Muhammad: The Chief Executive

For a religious order to be operative in a society, Khomeini decreed, it needs more than merely the legislative doctrine; it also needs the executive force. [105] Muhammad was not only instrumental in bringing the Islamic law, he was also its first executor. He "cut off hands, chopped off limbs, stoned adulterers to death." [106] Upon his death, he had designated a caliph, in Khomeini's Shi'i judgment, to do precisely the same. Execution of the Divine will is part and parcel of its legislation. To execute the legislated Divine will, beyond His last emissary (Muhammad), God has designated "those in authority among you." These are primarily the Twelve Infallible Shi'i Imams. After them, their function as the interpreters of the Divine law, its execution, and the propagation of its validity falls upon the "just jurists." [107] Khomeini considered himself a "just jurist."

The exemplary conduct of the Prophet makes it obligatory for the successive religious authorities to assume active political power. Execution of the Islamic laws was not limited to the Prophet's time. Their atemporal validity makes it necessary for contemporary religious authorities (like Khomeini) to assume political power and seek to implement them on a permanent basis. Thus both doctrinally (the mandate of *Shar^c*) and logically (the mandate of *aql*) the clerics are entitled to political authority. In a profoundly sarcastic tone, Khomeini rhetorically asked:

> One thousand and a few hundred years have passed since the Lesser Occultation. One hundred thousand more years may pass and conditions may not permit that His Holiness [the Twelfth Imam] come back. Should during this period the Islamic laws remain idle? Could anyone do just as he pleases? [But] that is anarchy. Were the laws for the expression, propagation, and execution of which the Prophet of Islam suffered limited to only a short period of time? Did God limit the execution of His laws to only two hundred years? Did He let go of everything after the Lesser Occultation?[108]

It is in the very nature of the Islamic laws to cover every aspect of Muslim life—public and private, political and personal. From cradle to grave, Islam has rules and regulations about everything and the Islamic government ought to be established at a most comprehensive level. The elaborate rules and regulations controlling the financial, territorial, and legal aspects of a Muslim society are clear testimonies that the government of a Muslim people should be Islamic.

Revolution is Mandatory

Under these circumstances there is no way to remain a believing Muslim without revolting against the status quo. Except for the reign of Ali, Khomeini considers all postprophetic governments as un-Islamic, from the reign of the Umayyads to the present.[109] To restore the true Islamic rule, as modelled on those of Muhammad and Ali, to oppose the Satanic reign of nonbelieving rulers, and to prepare a social condition congenial to the ethical virtuosity of Muslims, there is no way but to revolt and "abolish the corrupt and corrupting governments."[110] To return the previous ideal unity to the Muslims and prevent the tyrannical anti-Islamic governments from jeopardizing this unity, the establishment of an Islamic government is absolutely necessary. The colonialists have dominated the colonialized world by dividing it into a small minority of tyrants and a large majority of tyrannized. Islam cannot accept this and necessitates the establishment of a righteous government to prevent it.[111]

A Cascade of Arguments

Khomeini thus brings together a number of arguments for the necessity, indeed the religious obligation, of establishing an Islamic government. Logically, God could not have meant the execution of His laws for only a short period of time. In the absence of the Hidden Imam, Islamic laws ought to be equally binding, and for their execution a religious authority like Khomeini must be in control. Doctrinally, the Qur'an has commanded that beyond the Prophet and (for Shi'ites) the Imams, people of religious authority, in Khomeini's reading of "those of authority among you," ought to be in control. The exemplary conduct of the Prophet himself and that of Ali are equally binding in necessitating an "Islamic government." The very nature of Qur'anic commandments and the received traditions of the Prophet and the Imams necessitates an all-inclusive "Islamic government." Further verifying the Qur'anic passage designating "those of authority among you" is the tradition attributed to the Eighth Shi'i Imam, al-Rida, which is equally emphatic in the necessity of an Islamic government so that Muslims act according to the Divine mandates.[112]

Khomeini further advances these doctrinal arguments with a political translation of a mystical notion of the innate "incompleteness" of man and his need for guidance towards perfection. "People are deficient," he decreed, "and they need to be perfected."[113] "The perfect man" *(Insan-e Kamel)*, as a mystical notion stipulating the ideal-typical striving of man towards total identification with all the Divine attributes, is here translated into political terms necessitating the active operation of an "Islamic government" leading people towards their own perfection. To implement this objective and other tasks of the "Islamic government," *Vali-ye amr* (The Person of Authority) is the central political figure. This *Vali-ye amr* is none other than "a ruler who is the agent of the perpetuation and operation of Islamic law and order."[114] In the absence of such a central, commanding figure, Iranians have been subjected to "alien laws and foreign cultures," leading to the creation of "Westoxicated people."[115]

Theocracy Defined: Characteristics of the Islamic Government

"Islamic Government," Khomeini declared, "is like no other government."[116] It is not absolutist. It is constitutional,

of course not constitutional in the regular sense of the term in which ratification of laws is contingent upon the [approval of the] majority of the people. It is constitutional [conditional] in the sense that those who govern are subject to a set of conditions in their reign that are specified in the Qur'an and the traditions of the most noble Prophet, God's benedictions be upon him.[117]

"The Islamic government," Khomeini concludes, "is the rule of the Divine law upon people."[118] Consequently, there is no legislative body in the "Islamic government." There are only "planning bodies" whereby the Divine Law is administered into different social programs. Since all people have already accepted Islam, the Divine laws are more democratic than those of a republic or of a constitutional monarchy where the members of parliament claim to represent the people, whereas they actually legislate whatever they want and impose it on all the people as laws.[119] From the Prophet himself, to all his legitimate successors, to "those of authority" at the present time—all are executioners of the Divine Law. Thus the "Islamic government" is the rule of the Divine Law.

Because the "Islamic government" is the rule of virtuous models like the Prophet and the Imams, there is no corrupt ruling class wasting the nation's resources. The vast bureaucracy that the monarchy has created is wasteful. Under the "Islamic government" just one "Qadi with two or three agents, a pen and an ink box" can take care of a city.[120]

The supreme figure of authority in the "Islamic government" is qualified by virtue of two characteristics: knowledge of the Divine Law and justice.[121] Any other kind of knowledge, sacred or secular, is irrelevant. By virtue of the knowledge of the Divine Law, "the jurists have authority upon the rulers."[122] Then Khomeini takes one step further and, with the Socratic voice in his tone and an Islamicized version of the philosopher/king in his mind, emphatically declares:

If rulers are Muslims they ought to obey the jurists. They have to ask the jurists about the [Islamic] laws and regulations, and then act accordingly. Thus the true rulers are the jurists themselves, and the government ought to be officially given to them, not to those who because of their ignorance of the [Divine] law have to obey the jurists.[123]

Next to knowledge of the Divine Law, the Islamic ruler has to be just in order to be in a position to execute religious mandates. Both of these qualifications "are present in many contemporary jurists. If they cooperate, they can establish the general righteous government in the world."[124] The obvious conclusion is that in the absence of the Hidden Imam:

should a meritorious person who has both of these qualifications emerge and establish a government, he has the same authority (velayat) in ruling the society as that of the Prophet, and it is incumbent upon all the people to obey him.[125]

As he formulated this revolutionary Shi‘i position about government, there is little doubt that Khomeini saw himself as this qualified person. He further explained that although the spiritual virtues of the Prophet and Ali were superior to those of anyone else, the political authority of the jurist is no less than theirs.[126] Khomeini is quite careful not to offend the doctrinal sanctity of Prophet Muhammad and Ali's characters and insists that the jurist's position, spiritually, is, of course, inferior. But politically he is on a par with them. This is not so much a privilege for the jurist as it is a responsibility. The jurist's responsibility towards a nation is like that of a guardian over an underage individual.[127] The assumption of such authority is no one's but "the jurist of the time" *(faqih-e asr)*, a term with a remarkable assonance with *vali-ye asr*, exclusively reserved for the Twelfth (Hidden) Imam.

Khomeini has equal circumspection for his fellow jurists. Although the authority *(velayat)* of Muhammad and Ali was "absolute" in their respective times, the contemporary jurist has no such claim to his fellow clerics. To assume this responsibility is absolutely mandatory *(vajeb-e aiyni)* for those jurists who can do so and "relatively mandatory" *(vajeb-e kefa'i)*, if they cannot.[128] But Khomeini insists that the jurist's assumption of political authority as "absolutely mandatory" on his part is not concomitant with his (doctrinally unacceptable) assumptions of some "spiritual" status as those of the Imams or the Prophet.

The Teleology of the Islamic Government

The ultimate purpose of assuming the supreme political authority is to establish a reign of justice.[129] Government is but an instrument to guide people to their potential perfection. As for the jurist, assumption of power is a responsibility, not a prestigious position. The position is sanctified for the jurist by the prophetic tradition, transmitted through Ali, according to which Muhammad is reported to have blessed his "successors" *(khulafa')* three times. The Prophet has further identified his successors as "those who come after me, relate my traditions and my exemplary conduct, so that people will learn them after me."[130] Through a meticulous hermeneutic explication of this hadith, Khomeini concludes that these "successors" are none other than the "just jurists."[131] There is another tradition, this one attributed to Imam Musa ibn al-Ja'far, the Seventh Shi'i Imam, according to which the jurists are considered to be "the fortress of Islam."[132] This is no mere formalism, Khomeini contends. The jurists cannot simply attend to the ritual obligations of the Shi'i believers and leave these grave responsibilities to others, who are not qualified to perform them anyway.

The next tradition Khomeini quotes, through Molla Ahmad Naraqi,[133] identifies the jurists as "the trusted associates" *(omana')* of the Prophet.[134] Since the Prophet's function was to execute the Divine commandments, then the jurists, too, as those to whom the Prophet entrusted his legacy, are entitled to the same authority.[135] More specifically, the function of judgment on matters of dispute among Muslims, Khomeini argues through a tradition attributed to Imam Ali,[136] and another tradition attributed to Imam Ja'far al-Sadiq,[137] is specifically that of the jurists. Although some jurists, Khomeini concludes, have disagreed with Naraqi and Na'ini's position on the general authority of the jurists over all aspects of Muslim life, all agree that legal judgment is exclusively that of the clergy.[138] The inevitable conclusion is that

The jurist is the deputy *(wasy)* of the most noble Prophet, God's benedictions be upon him, and in the period of Occultation, he is the leader of the Muslims, the supreme figure of authority in the nation. He has to be the judge; and nobody other than him has the right to judge and prosecute.[139]

Extrapolating from a tradition attributed to the Twelfth (Hidden) Imam, Khomeini argues that in the absence of the last Shi'i Imam, the jurists are of central authority in matters pertaining to the community.[140] It is on this authority that Khomeini asks the Iranian monarch, "Why did you spend the people's money on [your] coronation and on all those celebrations?"[141] Driving these rhetorical questions further home, Khomeini altogether challenges, through two traditions twice attributed to Imam al-Sadiq,[142] the Sixth Shi'i Imam, the legal validity of injunctions issued by nonreligious courts,[143] and, in turn, the very legitimacy of the political order that validates a civil juridical system. In matters both juridical specifically and political in general, the only legitimate authorities to turn to, according to Khomeini's reading of this tradition, are the religious jurists by virtue of their knowledge of the Divine Law and proof of their personal justice.[144] This designation of authority is not limited to the time of the Infallible Imams and is always atemporally valid.[145]

Khomeini then proceeds to quote, after Naraqi, a Prophetic tradition[146] and a tradition of Imam Ja'far al-Sadiq[147] according to which "the jurists are the inheritors of the Prophet." After an extended hermeneutic explication of the phrase "the jurists are the inheritors of the Prophet,"[148] he concludes that the jurists are the Prophet's successors and are in charge of the "Islamic government."[149] To substantiate this further, he quotes Naraqi's version of a tradition according to which jurists are said to have the same authority as the prophets of Israel, for whom Khomeini designates political authority.[150] There are other traditions according to which Muhammad is believed to have said that "In the Day of Judgment, I shall be proud of the ulama' of my people, they are like prophets before me,"[151] or that "the matters and injunctions are in the hands of the ulama'."[152] The ultimate conclusion of these and other traditions is that to be true to their faith, Muslims ought to engage in "armed struggle"[153] to have an "Islamic government" established.

Upon these readings of the traditions congenial to a politically conscious and active participation in a revolutionary movement, Khomeini turns to one of the essential tenets of Shi'ism, again accentuating its political tone. "Enjoining the good and forbidding the evil" is a mandatory obligation of all Muslims. Should they obey it fully, Khomeini contends, "the tyrants and their agents could not confiscate people's property."[154] He admonishes his fellow clerics for having limited the implications of this doctrine to petty crimes in their vicinity and having forgotten the larger, greater in ferocity, and more vicious political crimes. He encourages them not to be afraid of the powers that be. "They are extremely fearful," he assures his students and follwers, "they retreat very fast." [155] To compel his audience to assume this responsibility, Khomeini's leitmotif throughout *Velayat-e Faqih* is that the canonical commandments of the Shi'i sacred sources are universally and atemporally valid. "Every ruler, every vizier, every governor, every jurist" is subject to Islamic doctrines mandated by these texts. [156]

Khomeini concludes his doctrinal exposition of *velayat-e faqih* by insisting that it is a self-evident Shi'i precept, supported by the Qur'an and by the traditions of the Prophet and the Imams, as well as by a logical consideration of these sacred sources (in addition to their doctrinal authority). [157] Among the previous jurists who have supported the idea, Khomeini refers to Mirza Muhammad Taqi Shirazi and his edict against the use of tobacco during the Tobacco Revolt, to Kashif al-Qita', and to Molla Ahmad Naraqi. [158]

A Blueprint for Action

Khomeini proceeds to draw a general course of action that ought to be taken in order for the "Islamic government" to be established. Propaganda, he insists, is the chief mechanism of action at the revolutionaries' disposal. "You have neither a country nor an army," he reminds his supporters in Iraq, "but propaganda is possible." [159] Next to propaganda is training the revolutionary cadre. [160] Training is essential to combat the Jewish design to rule the world and the attempt of the Orientalists to distort the true Islam. [161] Students of secular universities in Iran and abroad ought to be told of the true revolutionary Islam. Public gatherings such as Friday prayers and pilgrimages to Mecca ought to be recognized for their political dimensions. [162] An "ashura' " has to be created through active political participation. There is a long struggle ahead, Khomeini anticipated in 1970, "no one in his right mind expects that our propaganda and training will soon lead to the establishment of the Islamic Government." [163] But programming is essential in any revolutionary movement. Of central significance is the massive politicization of the religious seminaries and an all-out war against the educational, political, and ideological hegemony of "The Western" colonialism. Clerical look-alikes ought to be severely admonished. If they are not thusly rectified, "then they will be dealt with differently." [164] The religious seminaries must be cleared of elements who are not active in this all-out war against tyranny. All the "court clerics" ought to be banished. But ultimately the revolutionary clerics must discipline themselves spiritually in order to lead the cause against the tyrannical regimes.

"God Almighty!" Khomeini pleads, "Cut off the hand of tyrants from the Muslim lands! Cut off the root of those who betray Islam and the Islamic countries!"[165]

By What Authority?

Velayat-e Faqih is the masterful construction of a relentless argument, supported by the most sacred canonical sources of Shiʿi Islam, for the absolute necessity of the "Islamic government" led by the religious authorities. In it, Khomeini proceeds from a very simple premise: It was the Divine will to establish a just and sacred community on earth, for which purpose He sent His last emissary, the Prophet Muhammad. Upon the death of the Prophet, the future of the Islamic community, thus Divinely established, could not have been left to chance or reversal to ungodly rule. Thus the doctrinal position of Shiʿis on the designation of Twelve Infallible Imams perpetuates that Divine will. But in the absence of the Twelfth (Hidden) Imam, neither God Almighty nor the Sacred Text He revealed permits the rule of injustice, or tolerates a reversal to ungodly rule. Before the Twelfth Imam physically reappears, Khomeini, based on the phrase, "those of authority among you" in the Qur'anic passage, charges the ulama', who are just and most knowledgeable of the Divine will, with actual command over the political authority of the Muslim community. All other authorities, such as that of a monarch, not thus defined are illegitimate and opposition to them religiously mandatory.

Voicing the First Battle Cries

Beyond the (successful) formulation of the doctrine of *velayat-e faqih* in 1970, in early 1971 Khomeini summarized his chief ideological positions in a message he sent to the hajj pilgrims. In this message, dated 8 February 1971, Khomeini made one of his most convincing appeals to repoliticize the hajj pilgrimage, to which he had already hinted in the *Velayat-e Faqih*:

It is incumbent upon you, the beloved Muslims . . . to take advantage of this opportunity and try to find a solution . . . for the Muslim problems. . . . You ought to be united in your thoughts and in your determinations towards independence and the uprooting of the cancer of colonialism.[166]

In the same letter he addressed the Palestinian issue and charged that the persistence of this humiliating sore on the Islamic body politics is due to disagreement and hostility among the Muslims themselves. He blames the leaders of the Muslim countries for such counterproductive animosities. He then turns to a number of dissenting voices among the Muslims themselves, particularly in reaction to Shiʿi-Sunni hostility, and suggests that these are all plots of the colonial powers to divide the Muslim ranks to facilitate their own rule.[167]

The central focus of Khomeini's hajj message is the illegitimacy of the Iranian government. He directs his charge against the Pahlavi regime via a reference to the friendly and cooperative relations between the Iranian and Israeli governments.[168] By this reference, he appeals particularly to the humiliation of the Arabs and recruits their sentiment, if not their active support, for his cause.

Having addressed the Muslim pilgrims in general, Khomeini then turns to Iranians in particular. Through a remarkable synthesis of diverse political forces, he makes a sweeping statement against the legitimacy of the Pahlavi state:

The foreigners have complete immunity in this country. And yet the ulama', the men of knowledge, the high school teachers, and other groups are not protected from any tyranny. The respectable merchants are all going bankrupt, one after the other. The tyranny and repression of the ruling regime is strangling this oppressed nation. Repression, incarceration, and medieval torture rule freely. In the name of the "Literacy Corps" and the "Health Corps" and other such illusive terms, the wicked goals of colonialism, as well as the dispersion of immorality into the heart of villages and towns, are in full sway.[169]

Khomeini's last powerful strike is at the heart of the mass misery in the background of the stupendous extravaganza of various national celebrations of the Pahlavi glory:

This shameful and bloody "White Revolution," as they call it, that in one day annihilated some fifteen thousand Muslims, as is known, with tanks and machine guns, has caused more misery for the nation. The livelihoods of the captive peasants and farmers have worsened. Now in many cities and most of the villages there are no physicians, no hospitals, no drugs. There are no traces of public baths, no drinking water, no schools. According to some newspapers, in certain villages people take their innocent hungry children to graze on grass. And yet the tyrannical regime spends hundreds of millions of Tumans from the national treasury for shameful celebrations: The birthday party of this or that, the celebration of the twenty-fifth year of [the Pahlavi] monarchy, the celebration of [the Shah's] coronation, and, worst of all, this diabolic celebration of Two Thousand Five Hundredth anniversary of monarchy that only God knows what calamity for the people and what source of bribery and extortion for the instruments of colonialism it entails. Had the stupendous budget for such despicable events been spent on feeding the empty stomachs and providing a living for the miserable, some of our calamity would have been alleviated.[170]

At the end of his message, Khomeini seeks the help of all Muslims in assisting him to "cut the root of colonialism and the colonialists" in the Islamic world.[171]

While Khomeini's concern was directed at Iran via a mass repoliticization of the universal Muslim gathering at Mecca, the first signs of Iraq turning into an inhospitable environment for the Ayatollah and his activities became evident in 1971. Sometime during that year Khomeini wrote a letter to the Iraqi president pleading for the cause of Iranians living in that country.[172]

But Khomeini was not to be distracted by such events. His active and systematic contact with his supporters becomes evident from the prompt responses he writes to their regular correspondence. For example, he received a letter from the Muslim students in Europe on Monday, 26 April 1971, which corresponded in that year with 30 Safar 1391. In the Muslim (Shi'i) lunar calendar, the end of Safar is a particularly sacred period. The twentieth of Safar commemorates both the anniversary of the death of the Prophet Muhammad and the martyrdom of Imam Reza, the Eighth Shi'i Imam. The combination of these sacred days makes the thirtieth of the month a particularly reserved moment for a devout Shi'i, too sacred, perhaps, to be engaged in such mundane matters as routine correspondence. Yet on the very day that he receives the letter, Khomeini sits down to write a rather long response, outlining the course of action he thinks they ought to take. He again begins with the leitmotif of his getting old and not having seen his wishes come true. But, again, he expresses hope and optimism for the promising unification of the secular university students and the students of seminaries. In the same vein, he demonstrates his particular responsiveness to the ideological sensitivity of the students in secular universities. In inviting them to join ranks with their brothers among the seminarians, he urges them to "understand the corruption of the present culture, . . . and God willing throw away the [colonial] culture and replace it with the Islamic-humanistic [*Islami-Insani*] culture."[173] The key term here is "Islamic-humanistic," where the hyphenated "-humanistic," an alien term in Khomeini's juridical discourse, is, in fact, a concession and a signal, however inadvertent, that the contribution of the secular liberals will be recognized in the final composition of the revolutionary movement. Of course, the concession is made at the most tacit level. There is nothing essentially wrong with hyphenating the "Islamic" with the "humanistic." But the Persian neologism *"insani"* in this context is a clear reference to "secular humanism" that, consciously or unconsciously, Khomeini's hyphenating the "Islamic" acknowledges. Yet, it is quite evident, even at this early stage, that Khomeini has a noncompromising attitude toward leftist tendencies. He emphatically asserts that

if the young generation . . . understood . . . the goals of the Islamic government . . . the foundation of tyrannical and colonial states, as well as the misguided Communist schools and their like, would automatically crumble;[174]

or "should the Islamic government . . . come to power, the very foundation of leftist diversions will be blown away." [175]

The composition of these Muslim students who studied in Europe and in the United States and who were attracted to Ayatollah Khomeini, regularly corresponding with him and receiving his revolutionary messages, is also of some significance in the future making of the Revolution. In their letters to Khomeini, repeated references occur to two major characterizing aspects: First, they insist on being identified as "Muslim students"; and second they have an "annual meeting—the Persian language group" to distinguish them from other, non-Iranian, Muslim students. Given that during the 1960s and 1970s there was a pervasive process of secularization among the Iranian students abroad, in the course of which both Islam and the Persian language were beginning to lose their historical grip on their identity, the former more than the latter, this repeated emphasis on Islam and the Persian language demonstrates a deliberate and conscious effort to remain isolated from "The Western" transformative forces and contexts. They had, of course, physically moved to European and American cities. They were bright young students who studied mostly physics, chemistry, mathematics, engineering, and computer science. But the minimum language requirement to study in these disciplines meant that they could go to Paris, London, or Cambridge (Massachusetts) and spend four to eight years earning their degrees without any significant modification in their received and perceived notions of history, religion, or politics. Their deliberate seclusion behind the protective, however vaguely constructed, walls of "Muslim" and "Persian-speaking" inevitably spelled an innate suspicion of anything alien (particularly "Western") and an equally compelling propensity to respond positively to signals and symbols of traditional authority. A religiously minded student, seventeen or eighteen when transplanted to a European or American university campus, with a petrified and estranged constitution and no inquisitive mind beyond the call of scholastic duty, who could just barely cope with the boisterous noise of an erupting "Western" youth movement, and who had neither the capacity to evaluate independently nor the spirit to experiment freely, would generally be attracted to distant calls of a familiar voice. Khomeini was that distant call. He spoke with that familiar voice.

For their secular-minded compatriots, these religiously minded students were something of an antiquarian oddity. The separation between the two types originated in Iran where decades of secularization had created an urban bourgeoisie, liberal or left in its ideological disposition, vis-à-vis the traditional (bazaar) bourgeoisie. Although exceptions could be found, children of the modern (comprador) bourgeoisie had a greater propensity to be secular in their ideological disposition. Dividing the political loyalties of these secular students were left and liberal ideas. Confronting them on both constitutional and ideological dispositions were children of the traditional (bazaar) bourgeoisie who were born and bred with a stronger dosage of Shi'i sentimentalities. While the secular students would be automatically attracted to left and liberal political groupings, the religiously oriented would gather around their politically resensitized public pieties. Friday prayers were the most public form of their gatherings. Such gatherings were not necessarily political in nature. They were, in effect, a transplanted similitude of nostalgic memories about their home. Yet it was precisely such communities of faith and fidelity that responded positively to Khomeini's call for revolution.

Comparing Good and Evil: Ali and Mohammad Reza

Back in Iran, the preparation for the international celebration of the 2,500 anniversary of the Persian monarchy, highlighted in Persepolis on 15 October 1971, was underway and gave Khomeini the most striking opportunity to lash out against the Pahlavi state. In a statement dated 27 May 1971, Khomeini updated his revolutionary message to the Iranian public. He addressed his message first and foremost to his clerical colleagues. "Under certain circumstances," he declared, "I feel obligated to remind Your Excellencies of the Muslims' predicament. Perchance Your Excellencies, too, would feel obligated. Perchance, you too would do your share to help your Muslim brothers."[176] The stupendous extravaganza of Pahlavi vanity in these celebrations was the occasion that Khomeini thought would incite the moral indignation of his apolitical colleagues. He proceeds to deliver a poignant admonition against "the carnal soul," which he considers the chief barrier preventing the historical realization of a "truly Islamic government under Ali" or afterwards. The reference to the hazards of following the carnal soul could not be lost on Khomeini's clerical colleagues who had chosen to support or at least with their silence condone, and thus give their active or passive blessings to, the Pahlavi monarchy. In this statement Khomeini deliberately sets the agenda for reconstructing a historical image for "the Islamic government." Throughout Islamic history, after the period of the Prophet himself, he considers the short caliphate of Ali (656–661) as the only ideal state when "Islam as it truly is"[177] manifested itself. The most prominent feature of this short-lived but ideal state, which renders it an archetypal model for all legitimate modes of political order, is "justice." Ali's justice as a binding virtue is best demonstrated in the purposeful ascetic exercises that he willingly endured. The admiration with which Khomeini speaks of Ali, his ascetic exercises, and the ideal Islamic state he created and ruled leaves no doubt as to how Khomeini sees himself in the mirror of Shi'i collective memory. Ali, according to Khomeini's recollection of his ideal image, was such a person that when he came to power, his life, while a ruler, was more meager than those of us [clerics], of you seminarians, or those of these shopkeepers and greengrocers. A piece of barley bread which was so hard that . . . towards the end of his blessed life he could not break it with his hand. He would break it with his knee and would eat it [moistened] with water. That was the Islamic government.[178]

Such renunciatory demands put upon oneself, particularly when amplified in a Shiʿi context, are at the heart of the legitimacy that justifies a ruler and his reign. "I am afraid," Khomeini paraphrases Ali as having said, "that someone in my kingdom [sic = he means 'dominion'] would go hungry. . . . How can I go to bed with a full stomach, while even one of my subjects is hungry."[179] Justice, that no ruler should go to bed with a full stomach while his subjects are awake hungry, is the basis of legitimacy. Injustice, that a ruler should spend millions of dollars on flagrant pomposity while millions of his subjects live in destitution, was the most serious challenge to the legitimacy of a ruler. With such a powerful orchestration of historical imageries, the Iranian monarch was in deep trouble explaining himself to Khomeini's self-understanding and the virtuous images of Ali he provoked.

In a truly remarkable passage, Khomeini argues that the tragedy of Ali's rule coming to an abrupt end is even greater than that of the Karbala, when Ali's son Hossein and his supporters were massacred by Yazid's army on 10 October 680. Then with a deliberate pun on "celebration," he declares that if one has to celebrate anything in this world, it should be the short rule of justice under Ali. Against the reconstruction of such historical and mythical images the Iranian monarch did not have the slightest possibility of a convincing counterimage. In this universe of discourse, increasingly assuming revolutionary ascendancy, Cyrus the Great did not mean a thing.

Under the "Islamic government" there is also "the Islamic law" that Khomeini begins to propagate as a legitimate term in his political lexicon. Contrary to the non-Muslims, by which he also meant to include the ex-Muslims, the post-Muslims, and the lapsed-Muslims, who in Khomeini's sight thrived on an insatiable appetite for lust and debauchery, the true followers of Ali had but one simple source of legitimate sustenance, validated by "the Islamic law." Such moral extrapolations would later become the cornerstone of Khomeini's ethical codification of the revolutionary period. Beyond the immediacies of his revolutionary agenda in the early 1970s stood, somewhere remote in the horizons of Khomeini's agitated imagination, the vague but compelling image of a Republic of Justice and Austerity he wished would reign one day supreme in the four corners of the world.

As for the more immediate realities conducive to the revolutionary cause, Khomeini strikes hard at the sheer stupidity of the "2,500 Celebration" on two fronts. First, despite the massive poverty that Khomeini's supporters have written to him about from all over Iran, "millions of Tumans are spent on the celebration of monarchy"; and, second, while Israel is "the enemy of Islam and currently at war against Islam,"[180] Israeli experts are organizing the celebration. Based on these two principal grounds, Khomeini categorically challenges the entire monarchical history and, with it, denies legitimacy to the very notion of the Persian monarchy which, he decreed, "from the day it started to this very day has been the shame of history."[181] He refers to tyrannical kings, Reza Shah (reigned 1925–1941), Aqa Muhammad Khan Qajar (reigned 1794–1796), Nader Shah (reigned 1735–1747) and asks what there is to celebrate about the murdering and plundering of these rulers. Balancing the image, he refers back to the rule of Ali—the rule of humility, asceticism, and justice—that puts Mohammad Reza Shah's celebration to shame and renders his reign utterly illegitimate.

Khomeini lashes out against his apolitical clerical colleagues, too. He questions the relevance and validity of their quiet pursuit of jurisprudence while the Shah sells Iranian oil to Israel which, in turn, has endangered the Muslims' very existence. He urges the ulama' to send telegrams prohibiting the king from such shameful acts. But he immediately reminds himself that "how could such a thing happen? I would be very grateful if they did not object to my objections."[182] Responding angrily to those apolitical clerics who had maintained that religious authorities should not interfere in politics, Khomeini asks rhetorically were not Prophet Muhammad and Ali religious leaders? He insists that interfering in politics is the responsibility and duty of the clerics should they be true to their calling. Assuming total historical responsibility in fighting against injustice, he argues that from the very beginning religious figures have opposed monarchical tyranny. "God Almighty," speaks Khomeini from Qur'anic memory, "sends Moses to annihilate this king [Pharaoh]."[183] There is no excuse for sitting idly, wasting the Muslim money they receive as various religious taxes, and not lifting a finger to help them fight against their misery. His followers should have courage. Victory is not such a far-fetched ideal. "Should we stay alive, we will do something. Do not make any mistake [assuming this government invincible]!"[184] This was in May 1971, some eight years before the Revolution.

Some Preliminary Preparations

Khomeini calls for two specific courses of action at this stage: first, that people engage in passive resistance, and, second, that all Iranian clerics express their disapproval of these celebrations. He assures the clerics that the government cannot imprison or kill them all.

If they could get rid of us, they would have killed me. It is not to their advantage. But I wish it were to their advantage. What do I want this life for?! Death to this life of mine! Do they think I am enjoying this life?![185]

Turning to the international attention that the celebrations were attracting, he calls on his clerical colleagues to write letters, "a stamp is not that expensive,"[186] to political figures in various Muslim countries prohibiting them from participating in a celebration the Israelis are organizing.

After the news of the "2,500 Celebration," the establishment of the "Religious Corps" was another occasion to incite Khomeini's wrath in 1971. This time he knew perfectly well the hidden dangers should the government successfully appropriate the religious institutions. On 12 November 1971, he sent a message vehemently denouncing the formation of the "Religious Corps" and branded it yet another plot by the colonial powers and their agents to subvert the sacred authority of the Muslim clerics. He saw the formation of the "Religious Corps" as an attempt on the part of the Pahlavi state to appropriate the Islamic medium of legitimacy away from its historical institutional basis in the clerical class. Khomeini, of course, would not tolerate this for a moment. The political authority was in no position to appropriate from the religious establishment its historical claim to safeguarding the Islamic doctrines. Quite the contrary, it has been the religious authorities, Khomeini remembered, who have safeguarded the territorial integrity of the state in times of crisis, as the Tobacco Revolt and the Constitutional Revolution clearly demonstrate. Khomeini calls on all members of the clerical class, regardless of their internal conflict, to unite against the formation of this corps and particularly attend to remote villages and towns to which this new plot of the state was targeted.[187]

Five days after his statement on the "Religious Corps," on 17 November 1971, Khomeini issued a religious edict that has two crucial references. He had received an *estefta'* asking him about the juridical feasibility of spending portions of religious taxes for the families of political prisoners. He responds that one-third of the *sahm-e Imam* may be used to provide for the families of those Muslim activists who had been imprisoned or killed.[188] Significant as this edict is in financing, in effect, the oppositional movement, it is more important as the causal explanation for the juridical feasibility of such an allocation of religious taxes, because it is in this explanation that we see a truly revolutionary reading of an otherwise prosaic Shi'i ethical doctrine.

One of the seven "minor" *(foru')* doctrines of Shi'ism is "enjoining the good and forbidding the evil" *(al-amr bi'l-ma'ruf wa'l-nahy an'l-munkar)*. The doctrine commands the Shi'i Muslims to encourage people to do the right thing and prohibits them from committing forbidden acts. Although this is a "mandatory" *(vajeb)* doctrine, it is in the category of "sufficiently mandatory" or "relatively mandatory" *(Vajeb-e Kefa'i)*, which means once one Muslim, or one group of Muslims, depending on the nature of "enjoining" and "forbidding," has fulfilled it, other Muslims are relieved of the duty. Shahid Thani (1505–1557), one of the chief theoreticians of Shiʿi jurisprudence, in *Sharh-e Lumʿah,* one of the canonical sources of Shiʿi law, identifies five major requisites for fulfilling this obligation: (1) the person who does the enjoining and the prohibiting ought to be knowledgeable of what is good and what is forbidden; (2) the person who is being thus admonished is persistent on doing otherwise; (3) the person who does the enjoining and the prohibiting is safe from personal damage and injury; (4) there is the possibility that the act of enjoining and prohibiting would, in fact, be effective; and (5) the act of enjoining and prohibiting ought to begin with guidance and admonition and, if that is not effective, then harsher measures are to be taken.[189]

Both in the *estefta'* sent to Ayatollah Khomeini and in the edict he issued in response, the juridical obligation of "enjoining the good and forbidding the evil" is cited as the doctrinal justification for such extreme political activities that have resulted in the incarceration or death of Muslim activists. In Khomeini's reading of this otherwise ethical doctrine, aggressive political actions by lay Shiʿi activists against an illegitimate state on the authority of a "source of exemplary conduct" *(marjaʿ-e taqlid)* are rendered mandatory. The juridical mechanism of this logical conclusion is impeccable. On the authority of Ayatollah Khomeini, as a supreme *marjaʿ-e taqlid,* his personal followers could enjoin the good and prohibit the forbidden in any realm, including politics, with perfect juridical justification. Translated into lay terms, this means that Ayatollah Khomeini's followers were doctrinally and legally bound, in the context of Shiʿi dogma and jurisprudence, to engage in active political struggle against a government they considered both illegitimate and the propagator of forbidden acts. It is precisely this doctrinal explanation that justifies Khomeini's allocation of money from the *sahm-e Imam* for the families of those imprisoned or killed by virtue of having obeyed this juridical injunction. The legal and doctrinal argument of the edict is flawless.

The significance of this revolutionary reading of the doctrine of "enjoining the good and forbidding the evil" cannot be overemphasized. With the existence and active operation of such simple doctrinal mechanisms, Khomeini's simultaneous construction of the *velayat-e faqih* argument, as the chief ideological justification of his revolutionary movement, is almost superfluous.

Some ten days later, on 27 November 1971, Khomeini was on the verge of leaving Iraq for Lebanon. The status of the Iranian community in Iraq was always subject to the fluctuation in the relationship between the governments of Iran and Iraq. Tension between the two governments had grown when Iraq suspected Iran's involvement in a countercoup against the Ba'th government. This led to the expulsion of an Iranian diplomat from Iraq on 22 January 1970. Iranian citizens were also subject to suspicion and harassment. Mass expulsions of Iranians were ordered by the Iraqi authorities. Khomeini was deeply distressed by the expulsion of the Iranians. "Under the present circumstances, I think my presence here is unnecessary. I shall send my passport to the proper authorities tomorrow, asking for an exit visa." [190] Much to the emotional distress of his audience, Khomeini declared that he wished to move to Lebanon and, "like the other Two Martyrs [Shahid-e Awwal (d. 1384) and Shahid-e Thani (1505–1557)], we too be blessed [with martyrdom]." [191] This movement, however, was not to materialize. Although it is not quite clear how and why Khomeini changed his mind, there were indications that Muslim student organizations, or perhaps their Iraqi members, had intervened on his behalf. [192]

Toward the end of 1971, Khomeini seems to have become resigned to remaining in Najaf while most of the Iranian community was expelled from Iraq. In a speech delivered on 23 December 1971, he encourages his student supporters not to lose hope. He reminds them that the Prophet Muhammad, too, had tactical setbacks when he was in Mecca. Khomeini contributes this problem to conflict among the two respective governments. He instructs his students to continue their studies, attend to the purification of their souls by asceticism, and more than anything else, seek to serve Islam, which is much more important than simply "learning a few words and concepts." [193] From the content of Khomeini's speech, it is quite evident that there were Iranian seminarians studying with him in Iraq who were subjected to deportation. He assures them that "God willing, we shall meet again here. Even if I, spending the last days of my life, may not be with you, you will come together here." [194] With a subtle but compelling messianic undertone, Khomeini assures his followers that the hostile governments cannot oppress the seminaries, and that the Muslims, particularly the Shi'ites, will support them. He particularly appeals to non-Iranian seminarians—the Afghanis, the Pakistanis, the Iraqis, etc.—and expects them to stay and not to lose the battlefront. In a mysterious reference he asserts, "of course my departure is due to certain considerations that many may not know. But other gentlemen [clerics] ought to stay and should not leave the battlefront vacant." [195] He is not specific as to precisely what these "certain considerations" are. He concludes with a reference to the recurring theme of "the victory of the oppressed" and reminds his Shi'i students that after all his tyrannies, Mu'awiyah is so obscure a figure now that nobody knows where his grave is. He expresses hope that the Iranians will support the "more than one hundred thousand refugees who have been expelled from Iraq." [196]

Undoubtedly, this massive expulsion of Iranians from Iraq, instigated by the outbreak of hostilities between the Iraqi and Iranian governments in 1971, damaged Khomeini's growing constituency in Najaf. However, the transference of many of his student supporters from Iraq to Iran consolidated his active representation inside Iran. He recommends to his students "to give my regards to the Iranian brothers, and tell them he begs you to be helpful . . . to their expelled Iranian brothers." [197]

A Determined Revolutionary Survives the Mass Expulsion of His Supporters

During the first half of 1972, Khomeini seems to have remained silently observant of the effect of this mass Iranian expulsion from Iraq. The first time we hear from him is in a letter, dated 13 July 1972, in response to a group of Muslim students in the United States and Canada in which he is particularly emphatic about the inhibition of mixing Islam with "deviant and misguiding schools which have emanated from the human mind." [198] This could very well be a reference to the emerging forms of "Islamic Socialism" à la the Mojahedin-e Khalq Organization, which undoubtedly had a mass appeal to Muslim students abroad. In this letter Khomeini equally condemns both "the Left and the Right" plots against the unique promise of Islam for this-worldly and other-worldly salvation. He attacks both the United States and the Soviet Union for having conspired against Islam. He considers the creation of Israel a manifestation of this conspiracy between "The East" and "The West" to annihilate Islam and the Muslims. [199]

Here, in the middle of 1972, there is no ambiguity that Khomeini's ultimate goal is to establish "the Islamic government." He asks for the active support of Muslim students to help him achieve this end and provides them with tactical and strategic guidance as to how to engage in propaganda warfare against the Pahlavi regime. [200]

On 11 September 1972 Khomeini sent a message to "the honorable people of Iran, especially Their Excellencies the clerics, the men of knowledge, the seminarians, God Almighty help them all." [201] Specifically attacking actions on the part of the Pahlavi state such as the conscription of the clerics, the attack against the seminaries, and the imprisonment, exile, and murder of opponents, Khomeini once again declared the Iranian government illegal and a puppet of the colonial powers. The appearance of such new terms as "neocolonialism," "developing country," and "the state-controlled press" indicates that Khomeini's political vocabulary is being expanded gradually beyond his ordinary juridical discourse. What is precisely the source of this expansion, what material he reads or whom he consults is difficult to ascertain. He obviously reads the Iranian newspapers. What other sources were at his disposal is subject to future biographical studies. Among his reading material, there seems to be the Shah's *Mission for My Country*,[202] which he ridicules, accusing the Iranian monarch of having no other mission but

to suppress the students ... annihilate the seminaries, imprison and torture the ulama', entrust the sacred [precepts] of the nation to Israel ... give the control of what is left of the country's wealth to foreign investors, propagate adultery ... give [diplomatic] immunity to foreign advisors ... expand the neocolonial culture to the farthest reaches of the country.[203]

Khomeini concludes this message with a strong appeal to three broad groups of Iranians. First, he calls on the Iranian masses and asks them to "disobey the unjust laws as much as you can." Second, he urges clerics and seminarians to "study jurisprudence, cleanse your ethics, and enlighten and guide the oppressed nation [of Iran]." And finally, and most important, he obligates the soldiers in the Iranian army, whom he refers to as "the soldiers of the Hidden Imam, may God Almighty hasten His Appearance," to

stay firm in their military trainings, so that like Moses, peace be upon him, who was raised in the bosom of the Pharaoh and then annihilated the foundation of his tyranny, you too, on the day that the conditions permit, under the command of a righteous authority, can cut off the hands of these evils and uproot this corruption and injustice.[204]

The last we hear of Khomeini in 1972 is a statement, dated 11 October, on the occasion of the commencement of the holy month of Ramadan 1392.[205] With a passing reference to those who, in pursuing their colonial and anti-Islamic goals, occasionally even use Islam itself, a probable reference to leftist tendencies with Islamic postures, he turns the sharp point of his discourse towards the Palestinian question. Throughout his years in exile, Khomeini was an active, perhaps even a pioneering, supporter of the Palestinian cause. He clearly and without the slightest hesitation in his language permitted Shi'i religious taxes to be spent actively on training Palestinian fighters and supporting Palestinian refugees. In this statement he openly declared:

Today it is incumbent upon all Muslims in general and upon the Arab governments and administrations in particular—to safeguard their own independence—to commit themselves to support and assist this valiant group. They should not spare any effort in arming, feeding, and supplying material for these fighters. It is also incumbent upon the valiant fighters [themselves] to trust in God, be bound by the teachings of the Qur'an, and with steadfastness and determination persist in their sacred objective.[206]

"The Greater Battle"

Khomeini's political objectives, both immediate and distant, stemmed from an inner conviction and determination, whose specific nature is worth considering further. In late 1972, in the course of a public lecture in Najaf, he confessed that his knowledge of what was happening in Iran was rather limited.[207] Actively engaged in constructing his revolutionary discourse, he left the task of propagating his ideas to his students and followers in Iran. The numbers of these followers in the mid-1960s to mid-1970s should not be exaggerated. At best, this support was more intense in Qom, in Tehran Bazaar, and perhaps in old commercial centers of certain other large cities. The bond between the aged Ayatollah and his militant constituency throughout these trying years will have to be understood in deeper terms of a shared mystical conviction, operative at the most sublimated levels of subconsciousness. The revolutionary contraction of public and private ethics involves the social particulars of the mystical universe of shared sentiments that became operative between the aged Ayatollah and his distant followers. This distance itself, this physical invisibility, became an archetypal expression of something enduring in the Shi'i political culture. Since his exile in the early 1960s, Khomeini was both absent from and present in the Iranian political scene. He was nowhere to be seen visibly, to be sought out personally, yet his voice and presence were perfectly audible and visible among his constituency. Through that dual paradox is precisely how the Shi'i collective memory remembers its last figure of cosmic authority—the Hidden Imam. The identification need not have been final, absolute, total, or articulate. Mental pictures of communal and doctrinal origin, on one hand, and social and political realities, on the other, have a way of finding each other out.

Towards the end of 1972, Khomeini wrote his famous treatise on "the Greater Jehad." According to a famous prophetic tradition, battle against the carnal soul, a necessity, is a harder task than fighting the enemies of Islam. In his extended exegesis on this tradition, Khomeini charged the cutting edge of his ethical criticism particularly against his fellow clerics:

> The ordinary people never let themselves have any claim to being an Imam, or a Mehdi, a prophet, or a divinity. It is the corrupt clergy that corrupts the world, *Once the clergy is corrupted, the world is corrupted.*[208]

Moral rectitude combined with the necessary knowledge of jurisprudence are the elementary prerequisites of leading an ascetic revolutionary cause towards a just moral society. Only through personal ascetic exercises, combatting the evils of the carnal soul, can men achieve the necessary moral authority to lead a nation. True to the essentials of his juridical profession, Khomeini stated that

If you want to be a useful and consequential member for Islam and for the society, lead a nation towards Islam, and defend the foundations of Islam, you ought to consolidate your [knowledge of] jurisprudence, and become an expert in it.[209]

But in addition to this indispensable achievement, and particularly for his present students, Khomeini anticipated future responsibilities of grave consequences, which necessitated unprecedented attention to moral rectitude. Yet he was not a man who dreamt minor dreams or envisioned limited roads. Ethical and juridical preparations were for higher and more ambitious purposes:

When you enter the seminary, more than anything else you ought to reform yourself . . . so that when you leave and . . . assume the leadership of a group of people in a city or in a neighborhood, people can benefit from your deeds. . . . Now that you are free, if you are negligent of your ethical purification and reform, when the society turns to you, you cannot reform yourself.[210]

The voice of moral rectitude thus heard and sustained reaches far beyond Khomeini's immediate clerical constituency. Perhaps his greatest moral strength came from having waged, in his mind and in his body, ethical warfare against vices of all sorts, demanding virtues in both public and private domains. As a jurist, he had, of course, a canonical belief in scholastic learning. But in this address to his fellow seminarians, he admonished them for having been inadvertent in their ethical purification while attending their scholastic studies:

Concomitant with learning the scholastic issues, the seminarians equally need to learn and to teach themselves ethical concerns and spiritual matters. They need ethical guides, masters of spiritual virtues, sessions of advice and guidance.[211]

From Private to Public Virtues

Khomeini goes so far as to consider technical scholastic learning merely a preliminary agenda for the more essential objective of ethical purification.[212] In his writings public and private virtues assume supremacy over the technical virtuosity of scholastic learning.

The first group Khomeini admonishes for ethical self-purification is the clergy. He instills in them a deep sense of responsibility towards society and warns them not merely against transgressive *(moharramat)* acts, but even against remissive occasions *(mobah)*: "When you leave the scholastic center, you are expected to be [ethically] purified and rectified, so that you can guide the people . . . you have grave responsibilities."[213] Khomeini was quite sensitive to the dwindling status of the clergy in the Iranian society, which even bordered occasionally on ridicule. Demanding the highest manifestation of public virtues from the clergy, Khomeini warned them:

If a greengrocer committed a transgression, people say "that particular greengrocer is a transgressor." If a druggist committed a vice, people say "that particular druggist is an evildoer." But if a clergyman did something wrong, they won't say "that particular clergyman is misguided." They would say "the clergy are bad!"[214]

Khomeini's actively political view of the clergy and his belief that they have a leadership responsibility towards the masses led him to expect the highest standards of ethical conduct from them: "The [ethical] responsibilities of the clergy are very demanding and much more than other people."[215] There is a direct relationship between the public and private virtues of a clergyman and those of the society:

If a clergyman is misguided, he may misguide a nation and lead them to corruption; if a clergyman is [ethically] purified, living up to Islamic ethics and customs, he would purify and guide the society.[216]

In advancing the issue of private and public virtues, Khomeini faced not only the obvious rarity of profound scholastic achievements, which created a presumptuous position for the clergy, but certain notions of public decorum and propriety valid among the seminarians as well. One such notion was that distinguished scholars would not deliver sermons from the pulpit. Thus, being a *manbari,* a clergyman who delivered moral speeches from the pulpit, was associated with a lower rank cleric, unbecoming of a distinguished scholar. Khomeini condemned this tacit but obviously elitist code of propriety severely. Invoking the greatest code of Shi'i collective memory, he observed:

Nowadays in certain seminaries going to the pulpit and delivering ethical admonitions is considered rather shameful! Do they not know that His Holiness Ali, peace be upon him, went to the pulpit, admonishing the people, informing and guiding them, and keeping them alert. Other Imams did the same.[217]

A necessary, perhaps inevitable, component of Khomeini's collective rejuvenation of public virtues was a latent xenophobia usually expressed in the conspiratorial "certain hidden hands"[218] or "certain secret elements."[219] Like most active, or passive, participants in Iranian politics, Khomeini believed foreigners were always secretly plotting against Iranian interests. Reaching the extremities of Anglophobic dimensions, such conspiratorial theories of Iranian history would ordinarily lead to refusing direct and unmitigated responsibilities for Iranians in their national history. In Khomeini's case, he does manage to keep an active political assertiveness in conjunction with his conspiratorial suspicion of foreigners.

In articulating public virtues, Khomeini sometimes uses frames of reference completely out of the Shi'i doctrinal context. In referring to Ali's virtues as a model, for example, he is reported to have fought against "tyranny, injustice, and class interest."[220] The Marxist notion of "class interest" enters his terminology without the slightest self-consciousness. To be sure, the occurrence of such terms in his discourse is relatively limited. To the degree that he used such terms, he appealed, whether he knew it or not, to a range of secular political activists who were particularly responsive to standard Marxist terminologies. Khomeini does not appear to recognize such terms as "class interest" as patently Marxist in their origin. But, in effect, he assimilates a large and active political community, presumably secular in its self-perceptions, into his redefinition of public virtues. The larger the ideological and ethical domains of this political constituency, as defined by Khomeini, the more effective a revolutionary instrument it would be when occasions for such instrumentalities arise.

Bridging the domains of private and public virtues, revolutionary asceticism was the chief attribute Khomeini celebrated for the clerics.[221] He referred,[222] for example, to a report he had read according to which the annual budget for the Vatican to send a priest to Washington equals the annual budget of an entire Shi'i seminary. This meager living, he agreed, obligated the clerics to abandon their petty competitions and concentrate on their moral purification. Such comparative imageries performed a dual function. Christianity and "The West" approximated each other; the opulence of each was identified as a corrupt and corrupting feature. Simultaneously identifying poverty with Shi'ism and Shi'i seminarians would ensure a great source of political and spiritual legitimacy. Asceticism and voluntary poverty breed authority. The prophetic tradition that "my poverty is my pride" is the quintessential legitimating force of both ascetic exercises and their concomitant, however tacit, political claims to authority. If a man has renounced worldly comfort, so the unspoken logic would read, his calls for political and revolutionary actions ought to be, ipso facto, altruistic and, in the Shi'i context, Divinely ordained.

Not to think him an antiquarian ascetic who works primarily through outdated symbols, preaching old virtues to a changing generation, we ought to observe Khomeini using modern imageries in driving a point home. In the world to come, he promised, we will witness our deeds performed in this world, "as if our life is being filmed, to be shown in that world."[223] Or during the month of Ramadan, when satanic forces are in chains, one should not be "like a watch that has been wound by Satan . . . and automatically goes on doing evil deeds contrary to Islamic injunctions."[224]

The tone of Khomeini's speech on ethical conduct, which was delivered towards the end of the month of Sha'ban, before the beginning of the holy (fasting) month of Ramadan, is a clear indication of a religious leader, set on a revolutionary course of action, putting his own house in order. He wants the clergy under his instructions to be the perfect examples of ethical conduct so that they would function as the best exemplars of moral behavior in a show of force against a regime he considered deeply and irreversibly rotten. At the same time, the subtext of Khomeini's treatise clearly indicates that he is extremely angry with the petty internal fighting among the clerics. He constantly warns his own rank against back-biting, libel, malicious intents, hatred, envy, and cynicism.[225] Here he severely criticized the artificial and insignificant barriers in the path towards the political unification of the clergy as a potential revolutionary force. The subjects of his admonitions at this point were not merely the limited audience who attended his lectures in Najaf. Obviously, the tape machine that recorded his lectures reminded him of the larger political constituency in Iran that needed his fiery remarks.

A Revolutionary Reading of "Infallibility"

In his articulation of public and private virtues, Khomeini gives a new definition of "infallibility" *(esmat)* that is revolutionary not only in the canonical doctrines of Shi'ism but also in its implications for the nature of contemporary political authority. As a doctrinal foundation of Shi'ism, *esmat* is exclusive to the Twelve Imams, who are Divinely prevented from committing any sin. Khomeini redefines *esmat* to mean "nothing other than perfect faith."[226] He reconstructs the canonical definition of *esmat:* "The meaning of the *esmat* of prophets and saints *(awlia')* is not that, for example, Gabriel holds their hand [and guides them]. (If Gabriel held Shimr's hand too, he would of course not commit a sin)."[227] Upon this reunderstanding of *esmat,* Khomeini emphatically asserts that "infallibility is borne by faith. If one has faith in God, and if one sees God with the eyes of his heart, like sun, it would be impossible for him to commit a sin."[228] His argument is that "in front of an armed powerful [master], infallibility is attained."[229] That is, when one constantly sees himself in the presence of God, one is bound to avoid sinful acts. This argument is extended to account for the infallibility of the Shi'i Imams: "The [Shi'i] infallibles [the Twelve Imams], peace be upon them, after having been created from a pure substance, they constantly saw themselves in the presence . . . of God Almighty through asceticism, acquisition of illumination, and virtuous dispositions."[230] The subtext of the argument, quite obviously, is that anyone who sees himself in the constant presence of God, through such acquisitive virtues as asceticism, would be infallible.

At this stage, Khomeini shifts the level of discourse to a mystical dimension that immediately suggests his own infallibility. The shift from a theological/Imamological to a mystical discourse is meticulous and rather remarkable in its logical consistency.

Khomeini had established that through acquisitive virtues such as asceticism, and the illumination that ensues, anyone can achieve infallibility. But it is by virtue of putting men in the constant presence of God that asceticism and illumination can lead to infallibility. By the time the trilateral signals of asceticism, illumination, and the constant presence of God are invoked, we are already translated into a mystical discourse. Khomeini then takes this lead and, by invoking other ancillary mystical signals, guarantees the possibility of infallibility for a mystic who is not one of the Twelve Imams. This is how he transforms his language from, technically speaking, a theological to a mystical discourse:

The Infallibles . . . see themselves *(moshahedeh)* in the presence of God Almighty. They have faith in the meaning of "there is no divinity but Allah," that everything and everyone except God is perishable and cannot have a role in man's destiny: "Everything will perish save His countenance" [The Qur'an, 28:88]. If man has certitude *(yaqin)* and faith *(iman)* that the manifest and the latent worlds are [both at] the presence of His Majesty, and that Truth Almighty is omniscient and omnipresent, in the Presence of Truth, and in the bounty of His favors, it would be impossible for him to commit a sin. In front of a child who distinguishes [between good and evil], one does not commit a sin, would not appear naked, how can he appear naked [that is, commit a sin] in front of the Truth Almighty, in the Majesty of His Presence?![231]

Such key mystical notions as "the presence of God in everything" and "there is nothing in existence but God," which are immediately related to the Sufi notion of *wahdat al-wujud* as particularly expounded by Muhy al-Din Ibn Arabi,[232] provide Khomeini with an accessible leverage to seek his way out of the Imamological impossibility of infallibility for a Shiʿi cleric who obviously is not, nor has any claim to being, one of the Twelve Imams. Khomeini's infallibility is thus argued by a crucial and strategic shift in the level of discourse from an Imamological to a mystical language. Crucial in making this shift in polemical discourse possible are the collective writings of Muhy al-Din Ibn Arabi and Sadr al-Moteʾallehiyn Molla Sadra Shirazi,[233] of which texts Khomeini was a distinguished teacher for many years. Ibn Arabi had strongly argued for the primacy of an archetypal manifestation of historical *awlia'* (friends of God) whose criteria of recognition were established on a wide range of mystical exercises and their concomitant experiences. By wedding Ibn Arabi's mystical discourse to the rigorous canonical langue of the Shiʿi doctrines, and by then subjecting the two to the overriding scrutiny of a deeply philosophical mind, Molla Sadra had (successfully) demonstrated the feasibility of a gnostic, a philosophical, and a dogmatic concurrence of a "transcendental" view of the Divine Unity. Upon this strong Sadraian tradition, Khomeini constructs his revolutionary possibility of claiming "infallibility" for a Shiʿi cleric, and that *within* the doctrinal confinements of the faith.

Immediately related to the question of infallibility, as now established for Khomeini, is who, accordingly, constitutes a figure of authority. In the same passage that dealt with the question of infallibility are three crucial references to figures of authority. These references are particularly important because of their casual occurrence. Quite subconsciously, Khomeini makes the following three references to the supreme figures of authority in Islam: (1) *anbia'* and *awlia'* are believed to be the exclusive figures endowed with infallibility;[234] (2) God, prophets, *awlia'*, and the angels are considered the target of animosity by those who love this world, as opposed to the other;[235] and (3) God and *awlia'* are again considered the object of animosity by those who have lost their faith.[236] The crucial point is that Imams, the Twelve supreme canonical figures of Shi'i authority, have been systematically excluded from this constructed hierarchy of command and obedience, particularly as the authority of these Shi'i Imams is derived from their infallibility. The shift of discourse that carefully establishes infallibility for Khomeini as one of the *awlia'*, as opposed to one of the Imams, is here further substantiated by putting the category of *awlia'* next to the Prophets, under God, and bypassing the Shi'i Imamological stipulation.

The established hierarchy of these seminal figures of authority is important. In his casual, and thus subconsciously revealing, references to these figures, Khomeini has virtually eliminated the categorical necessity, and the intermediary function, of the Shi'i Imams, established God as the Supreme Figure of authority, under whose authority those of the prophets and *awlia'* are, on equal standing, legitimated. Below both prophets and *awlia'* stand the angels. But this has a long tradition in various Islamic discourses that goes back to the famous passage in the second chapter of the Qur'an (2:30).[237]

To be sure, Khomeini's shift of discourse and his bypassing the categorical necessity of Imams as figures of authority are done in a perfectly bona fide mystical language. Within the context of the mystical discourse, in which he operates, it is the *velayat* aspect of the Imams that becomes relevant, not their *imamat*. In other words, it is as *awlia'*, and not as Imams, that Ali and his eleven descendants figure in the hierarchy of authority that Khomeini reconstructs here. Khomeini has been able, by a remarkable and rather revolutionary shift of discourse, to secure the all-important attribute of infallibility for himself as a member of the *awlia'* by eliminating the simultaneous theological and Imamological problems of violating the immanent expectation of the Mahdi.

Khomeini never claimed to be the Twelfth Imam. Nor has anyone serious among his companions suggested that. The root of his authority, and the honorific title of Imam attributed to him, will have to be understood on a continuum between the notion of *velayat-e faqih* and the range of deeply felt communal reverence offered him voluntarily. If we consider carefully the interplay between the two terms of *vali* and *Imam*, we should get to the heart of Khomeini's claim to legitimate authority, as well as to the theological, juridical, mystical, and Imamological roots of this claim.

From Ethics to Politics

The cumulative effect of *Jehad-e Akbar* is a forceful call for a revolutionary and politically committed reconstitution of the clerical order. In an emotional appeal to his fellow clerics, the then seventy-year-old Khomeini warned that

I am spending the last few days of my life. Sooner or later I shall not be among you anymore. But I predict a dark future and black days for you. Should you not rectify yourselves, prepare yourselves, discipline your studies and lives, God forbid, you would be condemned to annihilation in the future.[238]

Very clearly, Khomeini drew the lines where the battle was to be fought. On his side would stand the militant clergy. The seminarians would be readied for combat. Agents of colonialism were all conspiring against them; the clerics had to be alert.[239] To combat the enemies, Khomeini spoke for the militant clergy: "I have to be an armed Muslim soldier, and be ready to sacrifice myself for Islam. I have to work for Islam, until I am annihilated."[240]

This is a critical reconstitution of what *Jehad-e Akbar* has meant historically. In the prophetic tradition, it was meant to balance *Jehad-e Asghar* (the lesser holy war). Khomeini's reading of *Jehad-e Akbar* totally repoliticizes the fighting against the carnal soul and redirects its moral energy against the "external" enemy of the faith. Here, he redefines the notion of *Jehad-e Akbar* from the mystical discourse, where it has meant to balance the exclusive preoccupation with worldly affairs, political or otherwise. Khomeini takes this concept from its mystical context, carries its obvious spiritual weight, imbues it with massive political content, compounds it with such strong emotional, prophetic, and millenarian appeals as "I shall not be among you, but . . . ," and thus launches the doctrinal notion with tremendous cultural and political force.

Khomeini's severe admonitions of the Shi'i clergy in 1972 are an astounding indication of the terrible disciplinary disarray they must have been in at the time. These admonitions resemble, indeed, the self-disciplinary measures of a revolutionary leader who seeks to have his camp in order before a battle. To be sure, Khomeini's ardent criticism of the clergy in Najaf was in no way unique or peculiar. We witness more or less similar criticisms by some leading scholastic figures inside Iran, with or without a revolutionary disposition.[241]

The Old Man and the Sea of Troubles

In 1973, Khomeini further consolidated his ties with his followers inside and outside Iran, hammered harder at the atrocities of the Pahlavi regime, and thus gave more evidence of the illegitimacy of the state. But more emphatically than ever, he bitterly attacked those members of the clerical order who had not joined him and were, in fact, actively or passively supporting the Pahlavi state. In early 1973, it was quite evident to Khomeini that the Iranian government was in a massive process of appropriating the religious institutions. His letter of 15 March 1973 to Muslim students in Europe, the United States, and Canada, taking note of this fact, was thus targeted more for internal consumption in Iran.

By exploiting the propaganda possibilities at its disposal—radio, television, newspapers, and its various ministries—the Pahlavi regime, charged Ayatollah Khomeini, was acting on behalf of the colonial powers to destroy Islam in the name of Islam. Whether in organizing Islamic conferences, publishing new editions of the Qur'an, establishing the Ministry of Religious Endowments, forming the "Religious Corps," or "any other deceptive title," the ultimate purpose of the government was to "confiscate the Islamic circles, control and check the religious ceremonies, and infiltrate the seminaries."[242]

Assisting the Iranian monarch and his colonial masters in attaining these goals were a "bunch of misguided pseudoclerics who were directly or indirectly in the service of the tyrannical regime"[243] and who, Khomeini commanded, had to be expelled from the seminaries. "If the fabricated clerics and the dishonorable ulama' look-alikes were to disappear from the society, so that they could not deceive the people," Khomeini promised, "the tyrannical regime will never be able to implement the wicked designs of the colonialists."[244] He was so enraged by the possibility of the Shi'i institutions and figures of authority being appropriated and assimilated by the state that no more than a month after this letter to the Muslim students abroad, he sent a message directly to Iran, dated sometime in late March or early April 1973, in which he reiterated his suspicion that the Pahlavi state was actively determined to obliterate the historical independence of the Shi'i ulama':

Today there are vast and pervasive designs in operation . . ., designs with the implementation of which they want, in their rotten imagination, to turn all grand ayatollahs, distinguished scholars, and honorable orators into worthless and insignificant governmental employees.[245]

In the same statement, Khomeini is appalled by the news that the Iranian king is purchasing "two billion dollars" in arms and spare parts from the United States, in addition to other purchases from "the colonialist English." He accuses the Iranian monarch of going mad towards the end of his life. "I am concerned about Islam and the Muslims from the psychological maladies that afflict these thugs in their old age."[246]

At the end of this letter, Khomeini, for the first time since his exile in

November 1964, calls for open defiance by the clerics. Prohibiting the Iranian masses from going to mosques and other religious gatherings organized by the Ministry of the Religious Endowments, he calls on his clerical followers, "should conditions permit, to strike and not go to mosques and pulpits for a limited time."[247] He equally commands his mass of followers to support these clerics should they decide to strike.

In a simultaneous letter to his "dear young seminarian and university students, the merchants, the peasants, and other groups," dated 25 March 1973, Khomeini's tone of voice has a particularly sharp edge. He calls on his young supporters to "throw out these shameless oilmongers and their despicable agents from the country like garbage."[248] He again expresses hope for their doing what he may not live to see. As a final and crucial blow to the legitimacy of the Iranian monarch, he refers to the Iranian youth as "the dear ones in the country of Amir al-Mu'menin [Ali]." The country belonged to the first Shi'i Imam, not to the last Persian king, as the Iranian soldiers were the army of the last, Hidden, Shi'i Imam, not the instruments of "the First Person of the Kingdom."

The second anniversary of the "2,500 Celebration" in 1973 coincided with the Arab-Israeli war. Khomeini did not miss the dark irony of the Iranian monarch celebrating his royal lineage when Muslims were fighting against Israel. In a statement to the Iranian people, dated Friday, 14 September 1973, he bitterly condemned the Iranian monarch and his support for Israel and called on Iranian clerics to force the monarch to join other Muslim countries in attacking Israel. He urged the Iranian masses—openly, clearly, and loudly—to "oppose the interests of the United States and Israel in Iran, attack them even to the point of destruction."[249] He called on Iranian Shi'is to counterbalance the help of the Iranian Jewish community to Israel by establishing and contributing to funds for Palestinians and others who fight against Israel.[250] In a separate statement, issued on 7 November 1973, Khomeini addressed all the Muslim countries and nations, asking for their help in the Palestinian cause. He encouraged the Arab oil embargo against the governments that support Israel and asked for "material and spiritual support . . . blood, medicine, arms, and food"[251] to be sent to the fighting Muslims.

Signs of Silence

The year 1974 was the occasion for yet another long pause when the exiled revolutionary master remained secluded with his private assessments of what was to be done. The strained relationship between the Iranian and the Iraqi governments, which almost resulted in war, the mass expulsion of many Iranians from Iraq, accompanied by some prominent clerics, may have been the external causes for Khomeini's yearlong silence. Perhaps advisedly, he did not wish to issue hostile proclamations against the monarch of his native land while his host country publicly opposed him.

The "Resurrection Party" Resurrects Khomeini's Wrath

But Khomeini's silence did not last long. On 12 March 1975 he issued a rather long edict in response to an *estefta'* by a group of his followers about the "Resurrection Party."

In March 1975 the farce theatricality of a dual-party system, which gave a thinly disguised posture of political civility to the Iranian monarch's reign by brute force, came to an abrupt end when Mohammad Reza Pahlavi considered it more efficacious to have one all-embracing political party that would extend his authoritarian rule deep into totalitarian dimensions. Reminiscent of the National Socialist Party in the 1930s Germany, the Resurrection Party, *Hezb-e Rastakhiz*, was to include all Iranians from all walks of life in all their political and civil aspirations. The monarch's argument, put very explicitly, was that you either believed in the ideals of modern Iran designed by His Imperial Majesty or you did not. If you did, you would join the party; if you did not, you would leave the country. Joining the Resurrection Party became the subject of serious fear and concern for ordinary Iranians. For Iranians with a religious bent, or for those with serious sympathy for Ayatollah Khomeini, it was a matter of ideological and religious principle. Khomeini's supporters lost no time in officially asking for his edict in the matter, nor did he lose any time in emphatically issuing his opinion and thus emerging from more than a yearlong silence.

"In the Name of God, the Merciful, the Compassionate," Khomeini's statement began ever so officially, ever so emphatically. "Because this party is opposed to Islam and to the Muslim nation of Iran, participating in it is forbidden and [tantamount to] helping the oppression and destitution of Muslims."[252] This was, of course, a religious commandment obligating believing Shi'is to abstain from becoming members of the Resurrection Party. However, the declaration that followed this inhibition was even more crucial in drawing the battlelines between the megalomaniac monarch and the angry Ayatollah. "Opposing it," Khomeini decreed about the Resurrection Party, "is one of the clearest cases of 'forbidding the evil [act].'"[253] This made active opposition to the latest, most politically ambitious, wishes of the Iranian monarch more than just an ideological conviction—it rendered it a mandatory religious obligation. Khomeini turned the formation of this party around and made it into the most emphatic mark of the failure of the monarch's so-called "king and the people revolution." "If this so-called revolution was by the king and the people," he asked rhetorically, "then what is the need for this mandatory party?"[254]

Khomeini challenges the validity of this party on constitutional grounds and on "international principles."[255] He enumerates the number of ways in which the monarch has violated the Iranian constitution. But lest he would appear to approve the Iranian constitution, according to which the ceremonial position of the king is legitimated, he takes one last step and charges that "the rotten monarchical system is Islamically annulled."[256] By having sold the Iranian national wealth and honor to foreign, particularly American, interests and having failed to provide the Iranian masses with a decent standard of living, the Iranian monarch, Khomeini charged, has lost all basis of his legitimacy. It is thus all too conceivable for Khomeini to call, now that with the mandatory establishment of a totalitarian party, the king has confessed his failure to secure his legitimacy, for "this rotten regime to change, God willing."[257]

Towards the end of his statement, Khomeini calls on his fellow clerics, seminarians and university students, merchants, workers, and peasants to defy the wishes of the monarch and refuse to join the Resurrection Party. Although he appears to ask merely for "passive resistance,"[258] he does, for the first time since his exile, promise that "the regime is about to fall."[259] He assures his followers that "victory is yours"[260] and warns them not to be fooled by the duplicity of the government that while it "disregards the Qur'anic commandments, publishes [the Holy Book] itself."[261]

Khomeini concludes this statement with the first allusion, since his 1964 exile, to his wishes to return to Iran and lead the movement against the Pahlavi state:

Secluded here in my exile, I am in agony for the miseries of the Iranian nation. How I wish I could be with them in these trying times, cooperating with them closely in these sacred struggles to save Islam and Iran. I beseech God Almighty to cut off the hands of the foreigners and their agents.[262]

Some four months later, on 11 July 1975, Khomeini followed up his March statement with yet another signal of the coming Revolution. "The news from Iran, though the cause of utmost sorrow and sadness, is [also] the cause of hope and the shining promise of victory."[263] On Saturday, 7 June 1975, some three months after his initial statement on the Resurrection Party, on the occasion of the twelfth anniversary of the June 1963 uprising, there had apparently been a demonstration in Qom with some reported casualties.[264] Khomeini commended his followers for having defied the monarch's sham political party, declared the Pahlavi state "reactionary" and "medieval,"[265] and once again expressed fear that the mad Iranian monarch might take drastic measures out of desperation and because of psychological defects.[266] Feelings of "these last days of my life"[267] still persist in Khomeini.

Towards the end of August, Khomeini's hopes for a revolutionary movement seem to be quite high. In a letter to the confederation of Muslim student associations in Europe, dated 25 August 1975, he speaks of "good tidings . . . which strengthen the hope for a near future."[268] He is optimistic that the close association between the old and the new, the seminarians and the university students, will lead to tangible results. He charges the Muslim students to do their best from their vantage point.[269]

Khomeini's optimism is extended well into the next month. On Wednesday, 24 September 1975, he responds to a letter from the Muslim student associations in the United States and Canada. Again he expresses hope for the "commencement of the people's awakening,"[270] of the shameful defeat of the king and his party, and of the desperate measures of the regime that now during the month of Ramadan was broadcasting religious programs from the radio (24 September of that year coincided with 17 Ramadan, two days before one of the most sacred days of the month, 19 Ramadan, when Ali was struck by Ibn Muljam's sword in 41 A.H./661 C.E.).

Taming the Excitement

For some reason, the revolutionary excitement apparent in Khomeini's writings during 1975 disappears in 1976. Except for two instances, he is not heard from. And in these two instances the color of his optimism has faded.

Early in 1976 Khomeini arranged for some financial aspects of the revolutionary momentum. In an edict issued in response to an *estefta'*, dated 21 February 1976 (which coincided with 20 Safar 1396, the Arba'in, the fortieth day after the martyrdom of Imam Hossein, a sacred date in the Shi'i calendar), Khomeini permitted the use of portions of the religious taxes due to him to be spent on "the printing and publication of political-Islamic books which express the Islamic truths and the opinions of the grand religious authorities on opposing and fighting the tyrants."[271]

We next hear of Khomeini some seven months later, in a statement issued on Saturday, 25 September 1976, on the occasion of *Id-e Fetr*, 30 Ramadan 1396, the last day in the holy month of Ramadan. The only significant reference in this statement is to the news of the Iranian monarch's latest wishes to change the Iranian calendar, an event that demanded Khomeini's full attention.

For most of its Islamic period, Iran has regulated its history with the common Islamic calendar, which is lunar and begins with the migration of the Prophet Muhammad from Mecca to Medina on 24 September 622 C.E. In modern Iranian history, however, two other calendars have been commonly used as well. First is the Iranian calendar, which, contrary to the Islamic, is solar, with pre-Islamic Persian names for its twelve months and which, like the Islamic, commences with the same migration of the Prophet. Second is the common Gregorian calendar which, with increasing contact between Iran and the world's commercial and political organizations, became inevitable. Thus, on a normal day Iranians thought of themselves as living their lives in three concurrent chronological universes: the Iranian, the Islamic, and "The Western." Which day of which month of which year an Iranian would reckon a particular Monday was perhaps the most symbolic gesture of his or her self-perceived identity. The more religiously oriented were sensitive and alert to the passage of time in lunar terms, with Arabic names of the months, hallowed and venerable, charted and sanctified by the regular intervals of sacred days, months, periods. The more nationalistically oriented Iranians counted the days of their lives in solar terms, with archaic but much too dear Persian names of the months, all culminating in the single most important day on the calendar, the celebration of the national new year, *Nowruz,* on the vernal equinox, 1 Farvardin (21 March) of every year. But when in "The Western" mood of their assumed identity, the "modern" state of their mind, Iranians were equally, if not increasingly more, sensitive to the passage of the Occidental time, to the 1 January when the post-Muslim regulars of uptown nightclubs left no available seat for the local Armenians, to 14 July when the Francophiles stormed the Bastilles of their imagination, to 25 December when the misplaced American-educated elite sat around their Christmas trees opening boxes of their nostalgic youth from New York or San Francisco.

As yet another measure of his attempt to shift the cultural basis of his legitimacy from Islamic to Iranian symbolics, the monarch decided to alter this arrangement. He wished for the Iranian calendar, the one particularly dear to the nationalists, to begin not with the migration of the Prophet Muhammad from Mecca to Medina, but, instead, to commence with the presumed date of the coronation of Cyrus the Great, the assumed royal progenitor with whom the man identified. Thus, instead of 1,353 years after the migration of the Prophet from Mecca to Medina, the year was, in fact, the Iranians were informed one morning, 2,535 years after the coronation of Cyrus the Great. By some happy accident, or perhaps through some ingenious calculations, the last two digits of the year, 35, were also the number of years that His Imperial Majesty was in power.

Khomeini in Najaf did not like these numbers or the idea behind them. He considered them the clear indications of the anti-Islamic designs of the regime and forbade Iranians from using the new calendar.[272]

The Final Pre-Revolutionary Statement

What rekindled Khomeini's revolutionary zeal in 1977 were events in Lebanon, not in Iran. His first official announcement in 1977 was in reference to the Palestinian predicament in Lebanon.

His close proximity to events in Lebanon had made Khomeini particularly sensitive to the fate of the Palestinians and the Muslim community in general in that country. The indirect intervention of Syria in the Lebanese civil war in January 1976 led to a more active role for this country in the internal affairs of Lebanon. The abortive coup d'état of General Aziz al-Ahdab in March 1976 led to the full-fledged Syrian invasion in June 1976. The Palestinian opposition, the Syrian second offensive in September 1976, and the formation of the Lebanese Front and the Lebanese Forces all made 1976 one of the fiercest and bloodiest years in the history of the civil war in that country.

In a statement publicized on 22 January 1977, Khomeini refers to the temporary halt in hostility in Lebanon. This must be a reference to the Riyad and Cairo agreements that briefly ended the Lebanese civil war in October 1976. The principal point of this statement is to draw attention to the miserable survivors of the Lebanese civil war—women and children in particular. Repeatedly emphasizing the procedure of this help to be "respectful and honorable," lest the recipients be offended, Khomeini calls on all Muslims, particularly Iranians, to organize material assistance for the Lebanese victims. He permits portions of monies from religious taxes due to him to be spent on this endeavor.[273]

Later that year, Khomeini's attention was redirected to a principal ideologue of "the Islamic Ideology," a man who did his best, however inadvertently, to prepare the state of psychological expectation for Khomeini's coming. On 19 June 1977, Ali Shariʿati died in London of a heart attack. This resulted in many letters to Ayatollah Khomeini from Muslim students abroad, expressing their condolences. Sometime in July, Khomeini sent a letter to Ibrahim Yazdi, a leader of the Iranian Muslim Students Association in the United States and a future participant in the Revolution, acknowledging the sympathies expressed in these letters. His actual reference to Ali Shariʿati in this letter is terse, rather dismissive, and even unattentive. "Many telegrams have been received from associations of Muslim students and other respected brothers in Europe and the United States on the [occasion of the] death of Dr. Ali Shariʿati."[274] That is the only time Khomeini actually refers to Shariʿati's name. He does not say anything else about him, his significance, or his contributions to the Islamic cause. He demonstrates no appreciation of Shariʿati's role in Islamicizing a significant portion of the contemporary political culture. Even more significant, towards the end of the letter he severely criticizes "mysterious elements who wish to create divisions among Muslim associations."[275] He accuses these forces of being agents of foreigners and orders them expelled from the Muslim associations. He commands his student followers to gather around "the flag of Islam which is the only banner of unity."[276]

It is possible to assume that Khomeini was not particularly attracted to Shariʿati's version of a reconstructed Islamic consciousness. It is quite possible that he suspected Shariʿati and his followers of Marxist tendencies. Some members of the Muslim student associations abroad were indeed attracted to Shariʿati's ideas. This might have created certain tensions or even factionalism in the student body. "Agents of foreigners" is usually Khomeini's key word for Communists, in his judgment agents of the Soviet Union. At any rate, the lack of a record of written communication between Khomeini and Shariʿati during the crucial decades of the 1960s and the 1970s and a comparison between Khomeini's affection for Hojjat al-Islam Saʿidi and his genuine sadness at his death and a complete lack of sentiment at Shariʿati's death suggest that Khomeini was probably suspicious of the whole Hosseyniyyeh Ershad movement as later dominated by the Paris-educated sociologist. The cleavage that critically alienated Shariʿati and Motahhari from each other, in light of the close ties between Motahhari and Khomeini, may further confirm this possibility.

What is certain, however, is the growing suspicion, in fact outright condemnation, of Islamic activists with Marxist tendencies, or, what would amount to the same ideological hybrid, Marxists with Islamic postures. Some time in July or August 1977, Khomeini receives a letter from his supporters inside Iran asking him to clarify his position on

certain ["Communists, followers of Marx, and those who have been diverted from Ali's, peace be upon him, status of *velayat*"] who unfortunately introduce themselves as related to you, and as your followers.[277]

This could be either a specific reference to the Mojahedin-e Khalq Organization or a generic reference to them, all supporters of Shariʿati, and any one else who would fit the description.

Khomeini denounces such leftist tendencies with one of his strongest key terms, reserved for Communists. "It is quite possible," he surmised poignantly, "that groups engaged in anti-Islamic and antireligious activities in Iran, under various names and with different methods, are political organizations created by foreigners in order to weaken Islam, the sacred Shiʿi religion, and the exalted position of the clerics."[278] Even more emphatically, he identified these groups as those engaged "in creating misguided parties, connected [to foreign powers], and groups apparently Islamic but in truth hostile to it."[279]

Khomeini condemns the local agents of the foreign powers, "whether leftist or rightist," and considers the claim of his being connected to such leftist groups as one of their many stratagems. Foreigners, as enemies of Islam, he contends, have recognized the righteous cause of the Muslim clerics and have historically tried to suppress it through a variety of political means:

Sometimes through the empowering of their wicked agents upon the Muslim countries; sometimes through creation and propagation of such false religions as Babism, Bahaism, and Wahabism; and sometime through misguided parties.[280]

To leave no room for misinterpretation, he emphatically proclaimed:

I hate and despise these treacherous groups, whether Communist, or Marxist, or those diverted from the Shi'i religion. . . . I consider them traitors to the country, to Islam, and to the [Shi'i] faith.[281]

At the end of this statement, Khomeini makes two references that could gather in the figure of Ayatollah Taleqani. First, he admonishes that

it is necessary for those who belong to the clerical [class], and who defend Islam and the [Shi'i] faith, to stay away from these corrupting groups. They are to defend the exalted position of the clerics, avoid diversion and dispute, and with alertness dispel the stratagems of the foreigners.[282]

Taleqani was the chief clerical figure who actively supported the Mojahedin. Second, Khomeini commands that "the respected writers and thinkers ought to refrain seriously from interpreting and explicating the Magnanimous Qur'an and the Islamic commandments according to their personal opinion."[283] Taleqani, as we have noted,[284] was the author of the multivolume *Partovi az Qur'an,* which offered a markedly modern and pronouncedly evolutionist reading of the Holy Text.

Although pending further concrete evidence it is incorrect to assume any particular bend in the mode of the relationship between Ayatollah Khomeini and such figures as Ali Shari'ati and Ayatollah Taleqani, it is quite evident from these past two documents that by disposition Khomeini did not particularly trust the kinds of rival ideological reconstitutions that updated Islam in the 1960s and 1970s.

The last we hear from Khomeini before the death of his son on Monday, 23 October 1978, is a comprehensive statement to his students in Najaf, dated Wednesday, 28 September 1977. The opening section reveals one of the rarest moments of humor in his written records. He reports that after his lecture on "forceful appropriation" *(ghasb)* the day before, one of his students had reminded him that he had covered that topic in a previous lecture.

This is not unusual from the likes of me. When one grows old and age conquers him, all one's powers weaken. As one's physical powers grow weak when one becomes an old man, so does one's mental and spiritual strength, as well as one's power and spirit to express one's obedience [to God].[285]

One other remarkable moment in this speech is when Khomeini contemplates the nature of man—whom he calls "the very essence of the universe"[286]—consisting of three simultaneous states of mineral, animal, and sublime existence. Here is a rare glimpse of Khomeini as his more serious students remember him teaching mysticism in Qom. His reference to these hierarchical states of man is an allusion to an elaborate tradition in Islamic mysticism best captured in the following verses of Rumi:

> I died to the inorganic state and became endowed with growth, and (then) I died to (vegetable) growth and attained to the animal.

> I died to the animality and became Adam (man): why, then, should I fear? When I become less by dying?

> At the next remove I shall die to man, that I may soar and lift up my head amongst the angels;

> And I must escape even from (the state of) the angel: *everything is perishing except His Face.*

> Once more I shall be sacrificed and die to the angel: I shall become that which enters not into the imagination.

> Then I shall become nonexistence: nonexistence saith to me (in tunes loud), as an organ, *Verily, unto Him shall we return.*[287]

Khomeini then links this hierarchical conception of man's spiritual growth to the ancillary notion of "the Perfect Man,"[288] according to which there is an archetypal model of perfection towards which ordinary man ought to strive.

The idea of "the Perfect Man" has a long and elaborate tradition in Islamic mysticism. One of the chief theoreticians of the concept is Aziz al-Din al-Nasafi who, in his *al-Insan al-Kamil,*[289] gives an elaborate description of how, through ascetic and spiritual exercises, man achieves the highest potentials that are divinely entrusted to him. To help attain this state of perfection, Islam has its own political agenda, Khomeini argues, which is essentially different from man-made schools of political order. "Secular governments . . . are only concerned with the social order."[290] In these secular modes of political order, he believes, insofar as one is socially harmless, the government will leave him alone.

What he wants to do in the privacy of his home, drinking wine, . . . gambling, or other such dirty deeds, the government has nothing to do with him. Only if he comes out screaming, then he would be prosecuted, because that disturbs the peace.[291]

But this, Khomeini contends, is the way secular governments work.

Islam and divine governments are not like that. These [governments] have commandments for everybody, everywhere, at any place, in any condition. If a person were to commit an immoral dirty deed right next to his house, Islamic governments have business with him.[292]

The business of Islam with man is not limited, Khomeini assures his students, to merely political matters.

[Islam] has rules for every person, even before birth, before his marriage, until his marriage, pregnancy, birth, until upbringing of the child, the education of the adult, until puberty, youth, until old age, until death, into the grave, and beyond the grave. [The Islamic rules] do not come to an end simply [because the person] is put into the grave. . . . That is just the beginning.[293]

To put it very simply, "the Islamic rules are not limited just to this world, and they are not limited just to the other world."[294] When translated into political terms, the idea of "the perfect man," perfectly harmless in its mystical context, necessitates a total, final, and absolutely unconditional program of moral and ideological righteousness upon which Islam, as a social and metaphysical order, teaches, regulates, guides, and controls every conceivable move and manner of a Muslim individual, from before-the-cradle to after-the-grave, in this and in the world to come, from pre- to posteternity.

Next in Khomeini's agenda in this long lecture is a clear admonition of the kinds of Qur'anic exegesis pioneered by Ayatollah Taleqani. After a preliminary discussion of the modes of Qur'anic commentary, which he divides into two categories of philosophical and gnostic, at one end, and theological and juridical, at the other, Khomeini turns to "some writers . . . [who] are turning all spiritual matters to material ones."[295] He makes sure to refer to "these writers" as "good Muslims who serve [the people]" and who "write very well."[296] But he admonishes them for having gone to the extreme opposite of those who merely emphasize the other-worldly and spiritual aspects of the Qur'an. With the following passage, he makes an explicit indictment of this "material" mode of Qur'anic exegesis:

Now that materialism has become so powerfully predominant in the world, and there is much glitter in the world . . . there are many who are particularly attached to this world. Consequently, a group of people have now come forward who maintain that the ultimate principle of all Islamic rules is to create social justice, that social classes are [to be] eliminated, and that there is nothing more to Islam.[297]

The description fits Taleqani's reading of the Qur'an in his *Partovi az Qur'an*. Khomeini, without naming Taleqani, assures him that although he likes him, he thinks he is mistaken in such readings.[298] This kind of Qur'anic exegesis, Khomeini contends, merely attends to verses that support one's opinion and leaves others uninterpreted.[299] The philosophers and mystics, too, made the same mistake, but from the other extreme point, transforming every aspect of the Qur'an, Khomeini charges, into spiritual matters.

In making such conclusive statements about the nature of Qur'anic exegesis, Khomeini assumes an authorial and definitive voice for Islam. "It may be said that Islam began incognito, and it is still incognito. From the beginning until now, Islam has been incognito. Nobody has known Islam."[300] By merely saying so, Khomeini's becomes the definitive voice of Islam—Islam as such, "Islam as it truly is."

Khomeini then wishes to mediate between an apparent schism in Iran between the supporters of a radical (socialist) reading of Islam, represented by Ayatollah Taleqani, Ali Shari'ati, and the Mojahedin-e Khalq Organization, and a more traditionally normative Islam, perhaps represented in the ideas of the politically mute clerics. Khomeini condemns both kinds of extremism, one insisting on the religious dimension of Islam, the other on the political. Islam is at once religious and political; one has to be Muslim in thought and in action.[301]

The last word of advice that Khomeini issues is for such divisions to be set aside. In view of the atrocities and immoralities that the Pahlavi regime has perpetrated, the last of which in the form of an art festival in Shiraz, "the staging of the sexual intercourse, the act itself!"[302] the concerted energy of all parties, regardless of their particular interpretation of what Islam is, will be needed for days to come. "Should, God willing, this regime fall," Khomeini anticipated, "people will celebrate. You do not know how wonderful that celebration would be!"[303]

In an undated letter to the Muslim students in the United States and Canada, Khomeini refers to "internal and external" conditions that have made the situation ready for a final putsch against the regime. He calls on Muslim students to put pressure on the Carter administration to withdraw its support of "the illegal and servile Pahlavi regime."[304] "From God Almighty I seek the success and victory of all Muslims in implementing the enlightened Qur'anic and Islamic commandments. Peace and benedictions of God Almighty, and His beneficence be upon you all!"[305]

Khomeini in Iraq: An Assessment

Khomeini cannot be assumed to have had a warlike appointment, let alone a revolutionary agenda, when his initial challenge of the Pahlavi state was chased out of his immediate constituency in Qom. But once stationed in Najaf, one of the most sacred precincts in the Shi'i imaginative geography, he was in full command of the most cherished collective memories of his faith. For his part, the Iranian monarch should not have thought Khomeini made of stuff so flat and dull as to resume his scholastic pursuits quietly. Assuming that, and under the spell of a persistent orchestration of common Shi'i memory launched against him from Najaf, aggravated by being deeply entrenched in his megalomaniac pomposity, the king could not but fall from public grace, which is tantamount, but not necessarily equal, to a fall in deed.

Lest the passage of idle time would qualify the spark and compromise the fire of his wrath, Khomeini kept a vigilant watch on events in Iran and an even more vigilant persistence in creating a revolutionary discourse, a collective myth of mass movement, that would become the political machinery upon which he would ride back home.

Beginning with an uncertain standing and a dubious future, Khomeini gradually focused on "The West" as the primary target of his wrath and as the ultimate cause of the Muslim misery, the fight against which he felt compelled to lead. To project the common cause of all Muslims against "The West," he totally underplayed the deep historical animosity between the Shi'ites and the Sunnites. His physical presence in the Arab world, his deep concerns with the plight of the Palestinians, and his intention to address the Islamic world at large, prevented any particular identification with the exclusionary Shi'i cause. Although the tone of his language remained essentially Shi'i juridical, he appealed to all Muslims throughout the Islamic world.[306]

Perhaps the most crucial challenge Khomeini faced in the mid-1960s, energizing his emerging political agenda, was the powerful grip of secular —both liberal and radical—ideologies to which an increasing number of Muslim, or ex-Muslim, intellectuals were attracted. By this time, Iranian intellectuals and political activists in particular had experienced some two centuries of (secular) liberal, as well as close to a century of radical, ideologies. The increasing migration of Iranian students to Europe and the United States had actually intensified this process of secularization, whether in a liberal or a radical direction. Khomeini recognized the challenge and set out to meet it almost immediately upon his arrival in Najaf. He maintained a close watch on and a vigilant contact with the student associations in Europe and the United States and thus indirectly curtailed their secular urges.[307]

To present the Muslim political activists with a viable alternative to the glaring secular ideologies, the most important item on Khomeini's agenda was to repoliticize Islam to the fullest degree of modern possibilities. Islam, from its very inception, had a built-in political dimension that has been revived and rearticulated throughout its history. Khomeini's task, which he met successfully, was to strike a tangible and convincing reciprocity between the contemporary political exigencies and the doctrinal and symbolic repertoire of the Islamic collective consciousness. That challenge successfully met, he was able to supersede the secular alternatives to his brand of repoliticized Islam to an ideologically significant degree. What helped him to achieve his objectives was the persistent and conscious uses of ideological propaganda with which he charged his young followers.[308]

Khomeini appealed to his young followers perhaps more for his stubborn resistance to tyranny than for the specifics of his ideological positions. Many professedly secular, even Marxist, students testify to their attraction to Khomeini's single-minded perseverence against the Iranian monarch. His stubborn disposition was perhaps nowhere better demonstrated than in his pronounced asceticism. Always austere and astringent in his appearance, he personified the utmost of his ascetic preachings to his students. He never failed to urge his student followers to purify their souls, abstain from luxuries, refrain from excesses, and totally devote themselves to the revolutionary cause. One explanation for this perhaps excessive, almost compulsive, concern with purity, cleanliness, and asceticism, might be an unconscious personification of precisely the opposite of what is loathed in the enemy. Since the enemy, whether it is personified in the Shah or symbolized in "The West," is always identified with excess, defilement, conspicuous consumption, overindulgence, and extravagance, the accuser conspicuously, however unconsciously, distances himself from such attributes by assuming precisely their opposites.[309]

A similar explanation may account for Khomeini's repeated, almost ritual, references to his mortality—that he does not have much longer to live. Repeated and almost irresistible references to his own mortality may be another conscious effort at distancing himself from the pompous representations of immortality chiefly behind the monarch's chronic celebrations of his grandeur.[310] Perhaps unconsciously personifying precisely the opposites of what he loathed in his archenemy, Khomeini sincerely projected an austere and ascetic image that would unfailingly command the respect and even devotion of his young admirers.

The genuine portrayal of a revolutionary ascetic thus personified, Khomeini's focal point of anger could not for long remain on a vast abstraction called "The West." An absolute personified good necessitates an absolute personified evil. As he projected the Iranian monarch as the archvillain, and to focus his attention more specifically on Iran, Khomeini further consolidated his forces within the clerical establishment in the country and expanded his active constituency to include the all-too-important group of young Muslim students in Europe and the United States. Whether these students remained in their host countries or returned to Iran, their collective correspondence with Khomeini became a crucial aspect of their coming to political consciousness, in turn effectively translated into active propaganda for the Ayatollah's cause.

Among his student supporters, Khomeini recognized the difference between those in secular universities in Europe and the United States and those in religious seminaries in Iran and Iraq. The students in the secular universities, usually in "hard sciences," must have had a religious bent to their political activism before they were ideologically committed to Khomeini. But a vast difference in their curricular training was translated into a difference of perspective in their political agenda. Khomeini successfully bridged the gap between these two types of students. However that bridging might have been temporarily constructed and subject to future ideological disjunction, it worked as designed for the common cause of opposing the Iranian monarch.

With a variety of forces thus ideologically mobilized, Khomeini did not miss any opportunity to attack the Iranian monarch. The monarch did provide him with many occasions for public outcry. But when Khomeini attacked the extravagant expenditure on the king's coronation, the celebration of 2,500 years of the Persian monarchy, or the establishment of "The Religious Corps," he did not merely question the wisdom behind these pompous or politically motivated gestures. He took these occasions one step further and, through them, challenged the legitimacy of the Pahlavi state.[311]

The language of this challenge often assumed the juridical discourse of a religious edict *(fatva')*. This was the language with which Khomeini was most comfortable. The juridical nature of these *fatva*'s not only provided a bona fide ideological medium to challenge the legitimacy of the Pahlavi state, it also entitled Khomeini to direct the financial resources at his disposal for specifically revolutionary purposes. "The share of the Imam," as this particular religious tax is known, was stipulated in juridical terms with Khomeini as the judge of how it could be spent appropriately. He used this financial source not only to organize his forces inside Iran, but also to finance aspects of the Palestine Liberation Organization with whose cause he intimately identified.

On the home front, in order to organize a unified stand, Khomeini met a number of challenges simultaneously. Through the agency of Ayatollah Morteza Motahhari he unified the hard core of his immediate supporters. The active intermediary role played by Motahhari, linking Khomeini and his supporters between 1964 and 1977, is evident from the edict according to which Khomeini appointed him the sole representative to collect the religious taxes due to him. Motahhari was also instrumental in combatting what he reported to Khomeini as the infiltration of Marxist ideas into the seminary circles. As Motahhari took charge of the larger ideological issues, Khomeini organized his mass support at the local mosque level through such clerics as Hojjat al-Islam Saʿidi. He took two other crucial steps towards an ideological consolidation of his forces. First, he criticized and thus curtailed more radical tendencies among the clerical groups; second, he charged the more tacitly liberal elements by branding them "Westoxicated," a term that he most probably learned from Jalal Al-e Ahmad's famous essay on the subject.[312] Although the arrangement of this diverse set of crucial moves cannot be attributed to a calculated master design, their collective effect was to consolidate the clerical forces behind the recognized leadership of Ayatollah Khomeini.

While attacking the radicalization of Islam into a socialist ideology à la Shariʿati, while severely confronting the infiltration of Marxist notions into the clerical rank, and while opposing the radical political uses of the Qurʾanic text à la Taleqani, Khomeini himself repoliticized aspects of the Shiʿi doctrines within the legitimate confinements of his juridical discourse. Perhaps the most important doctrine, other than the *velayat-e faqih,* which was extensively repoliticized, was the principle of "enjoining the good and forbidding the evil." Although primarily an ethical—not a political—doctrine, the ideological extension of the term into broader social jurisdictions was carried out quietly and without the slightest doctrinal difficulty. What facilitated this smooth transition from ethical to political domains was perhaps some characteristic feature in the historical divisions in Islamic philosophy. Divided into theoretical and pragmatic, the Islamic philosophical discourse has attended to ethical and political matters as related topics in the domain of practical philosophy.[313]

But philosophical matters are elitist concerns; they can persuade only the theoretically minded, who are not always politically responsive. Perhaps more important for the transition of ethical concerns to political matters in the public perception, where a revolution works itself out, is the collective mythology that holds them, and with them their shared hagiological history, together. The working of common symbols that bind a community of believers together is always on a borderline between myth and reality. It is precisely the dialectic of the two that gives revolutionary momentum to an otherwise mute public mythology. All that is needed for that mute myth to narrate and articulate itself at some time is just a word, a mere word, only a word.

Imam Khomeini

"Imam"—the mere word—is an invitation to obedience. More: It is a command to believe. Take it or leave it, it says. Defying all doctrinal problematics, the term "Imam" rings of infallibility and of immortality in a Shiʿi ear. It approximates the man to the sacred vicinity of the Twelve Infallibles, the Immortals of the Shiʿi attendance upon metahistory. Its designation and collective approval are the revolutionary recognition of a thankful crowd which, in want of this- or other-worldly rewards, can only bestow epithets of immortality—the Great, the Immortal, the Infallible, the Imam. In giving such recognitions, the crowd can only retrieve the terms most sacred to its shared imagination. There is scarcely any term more sacred than "Imam" in the cherished remembrance of a Shiʿi mind. They have had it somehow exclusively for Ali, that very archetype of "the Perfect

Man." And then for a particular line of his Infallible descendants, chief among them, in moments of Shiʿi collective anxiety, Imam Hossein. One utterance of "Imam Hossein" and you are set on a plane of self-sacrifice, transfixed onto a state of metahistoricity, that denies legitimacy or relevance to time, place, pain, propriety, or law. Subtract the term "Imam" from any one of the sacred Infallibles and something cosmic is missing in the universe. Add it to Khomeini, or any other man, and you have extended your absolute obedience to the uppermost, deepest, level of your piety, humility, devotion. There stands the man. The Imam. But not just any man. The model of revolutionary righteousness. The abstraction of whatever is sacrosanct. Khomeini earns the thankful recognition of "Imam" from an ecstatic crowd which, in moments of its self-effacement, invests every ounce of its collectivity (and all its forgotten individualities) in the man who would deliver the earthly experience of the sublime. "Imam Khomeini," in defiance of all historical or doctrinal prohibitions that may dictate otherwise, demands, indeed exacts, obedience with the combined force of facts and fantasies. You utter it, "Imam Khomeini," obediently, and you are in. "In" is that fantastic realm of mythical operations where time stands still and place is irrelevant. "Imam Khomeini," thusly shaped and thusly termed, becomes the key instrument of deliverance, unlocking, as it does, the most irresistible treasure houses of the possibilities of personhood, of being, of being-significantly-in-the-world. Without that key, the magic of a mere utterance, the access to the jealously guarded realm of historical identity, you, as an individual, are left desparately characterless, nameless, faceless —a man (or woman) but not a person, a person without persona, a mask with no marks, a walking embodiment of contradictions, lacking all senses of unity, comprehension, direction, purpose. There you stand: Not a Shiʿi, not an Iranian, not a revolutionary, not even "a participant observer." Merely a bundle of misdirected sentiments, your particular individuality atomized into particles of fragmented fears and anxieties, hopes and confusions. Standing united and wholesome before you is an army of public rage, mobilized myth, moving in floods of anger and conviction, an avalanche of demonstrations, meetings, gatherings, prayers, all in a row, bending and bowing to truth manifest. You either join them, "Imam Khomeini" loudly bursting in your voice, and you are, or else you hesitate, a moment of doubt, and then you are not. Physical or metaphysical, actual or figurative: In truth you are made or broken in your confession or denial of only one word, a mere word, just a word, of the "Imam" in "Imam Khomeini."

The End

There is the myth manifest. In just one word. The rest of the myth is now part and parcel of Iranian history. The history of the Revolution itself, the

sacred decade that Iran lived under Khomeini, very much like Geneva under
Calvin, is yet to be told, narrated in one way or another. But the story of
the man himself, and of his revolutionary ideas (put succinctly into action),
holds its own fascination, from beginning to end. "The goblet of poison"
Khomeini drank in August 1988,[314] by accepting United Nations resolution
536 and effectively paving the way for a peace treaty with Iraq, was so
effective that, given his strong spiritual stamina, it killed the old revolutionary sage in less than a year. Khomeini knew no defeat, understood no
compromise, forgave no enemy. He kicked his archenemy out of Iran and
made him die in indignity and humiliation, the death of a dethroned and
exiled king. He humiliated President Carter, who had dared to raise his
champagne glass to the Great King, out of office. He ridiculed both superpowers and dared them to touch his regime. Then he turned his anger
against a nobody: Saddam Hossein. Eight years of intense attacks, hundreds
of thousands killed on both sides, billions of dollars in damages, and
Rafsanjani convinced the old master they could not win the war, they could
not oust and humiliate Saddam. The old man was not made of all misdirected nerves. He knew the limits of reason—defied them, but knew them.
Failing to defy the limits of Rafsanjani's reason, failing to humiliate yet
another enemy, Khomeini drank from the poisonous goblet in August 1988
and in less than a year, in June 1989, rested his case with history. Anger
and wrath move through the thickest of all bloods, the hardest of all veins;
but restful resignation, having no more battle to fight, no more enemies to
humiliate, is a call for the angel of mercy. In peace or in discontent, we
shall never know, Khomeini joined history, the collective imagination of his
first and future followers, having shed, as he did, the very last drop of his
anger.

Conclusion: Dimensions of "The Islamic Ideology"

We have come a long way, unpacking the revolutionary minds and sentiments of these chief ideologues of the Islamic Revolution in Iran. Here, in conclusion, I wish to pick up some of the theoretical threads intentionally left loose at the end of my Introduction. I wish to pull these threads together tightly and bring them to the conclusion of a memorable knot.

Regular Intervals

"Thus there is something eternal in religion," concluded Durkheim after an exhaustive examination of one particular case. That "something," he believed, "is destined to survive all the particular symbols in which religious thought has successfully enveloped itself."[1] That which in a religious language corresponds to something eternal in man is the key operative mechanism of revolutionary revivals, seeking, as it does, to reach beyond the particular ephemeralities of life. But religion, as Durkheim taught us, can only live a symbolic life. The ever-changing succession of symbolic forms in which a particular religion, let alone the religious *Geist* as such, manifests and registers itself has been the most compelling single thrust of human history. It is precisely that thrust that justifies Durkheim's sweeping generalization:

There can be no society which does not feel the need of upholding and reaffirming at regular intervals the collective sentiments and the collective ideas which make its unity and its personality.[2]

How often these "regular intervals" actually occur differs from society to society, from religion to religion, from one collective sentiment to another, depending on where each society and religion stands on that all-too-essential continuum of mobilizing certitude and debilitating doubt. But perhaps more important, reaffirmation of collective sentiments and ideas often operate at two—short-term and long-term—levels of "regular intervals": There are the usual, cyclical, and periodic intervals that annually regulate and attune the religion and society; and there are the longer intervals when a procrastinated period of dormant routinization screams for a charismatic renewal. From Christ to Muhammad, from Calvin to Khomeini, history, mothering them all, divides her attention between the routinized certitude of established collective sentiments and the charismatic glory of reconstructing them through a revolutionary redefinition—the terms of the new enchantment. The unity and personality of a moral community, those forces that constitute its measure of historical substance and metahistorical identity, are thus always at stake when a cataclysmic charismatic movement holds history at bay until it redefines its future self-understanding.

Any dormant moment of contemporaneity may dull the wit as to the power of such recurring symbolics. Durkheim blamed this systemic inability to see the charismatic restlessness behind the surface of redundant ceremonials on "a stage of transition and moral mediocrity"[3] in his own time. He regreted, it seems, that

the great things of the past which filled our fathers with enthusiasm do not excite the same ardour in us, either because they have come into common usage to such an extent that we are unconscious of them, or else because they no longer answer to our actual aspirations.[4]

Durkheim, like Weber, underestimated the power of reinterpretations, in variety and multiplicity. Consider the eight ideologues we have examined here and then look at the Iranian Revolution of 1979. Fathers are resuscitated in their children, born again with energy and zest. Common usage can be rendered obsolete; new blood, thin and shining, may overflow old veins, strong in the texture of their orientation. Old sentiments may be made to answer to the most compelling issues of modernity. Old sentiments establish the conviction, and the new messages mobilize the mass revolts. For Durkheim's regret that "as yet there is nothing to replace them"[5] there need not be a completely new religious message. Every reinterpretation can update the old symbolics to perfect modernity.

"In a word," Durkheim summarized his moral judgment of the modernity, "the old gods are growing old or already dead, and others are not yet born."[6] Consider "the Islamic Revolution" in Iran and you see how old god-terms of authority may be given new, second, or third chances to command innermost obedience. "It is life itself," Durkheim chastized Compte's artificial attempt at culture-building religiosity, "and not a dead past which can produce a living cult."[7] As life unfolds, it is experienced with old, or what Weber called "the unimaginably ancient recognition"[8] of, enchantments. To produce "a living cult," master manipulators of the dead or dying symbolics can do wonders. New forms for old contents, new contents for old forms, the paradox of living forces in dying convictions, "the Islamic Ideology" reached deeper than any perfectly old or perfectly new ideological enchantment for mass mobilization. Modern Iranian history testifies to it.

This much Durkheim knew. His prophetic soul:

But this state of incertitude and confused agitation cannot last forever. A day will come when our societies will know again these hours of creative effervescence, in the sense of which new ideas arise and new formulae are found which serve for a while as a guide to a humanity.[9]

There is the innate, even constitutional, human need for permanent reenchantment. Durkheim locates the agency of such permanent revolutions in "society" because for him that is where the perpetual source of man's myth-making urge lies. What would the direction of "creative effervescence" be other than towards a constant and radical upgrading of the most essential symbolics of a religious culture with whatever realities that be? "New ideas and new formulae," as in the case of "the Islamic Ideology," are but the ideological (cum institutional) expressions of the rejuvenated forces of man's symbolic remembrances that resurrect with compelling might to reclaim any lost territory in human conviction. Speaking of the "end of ideology"[10] or the "end of history"[11] is neglecting the most essential truth about man's myth-making inescapability. The brilliance of Durkheim's prophetic vision lies in the truth of his insight that

when these hours [of creative effervesence] shall have been passed through once, men will spontaneously feel the need of reliving them from time to time in thought, that is to say, of keeping alive their memory by means of celebrations which regularly reproduce their fruits.[12]

A look at the Iranian post-revolutionary calendar demonstrates the power of remembrance through which archetypal memories are reawakened. In pre-revolutionary calendar, the Shi'i year was divided into cyclical episodes of remembering the initial charismatic effervescence of the originating force of Shi'ism in Islamic history. The birth of Prophet Muhammad, the day he nominated Ali as his successor, the day Ali was assassinated, the day Imam Hossein was killed, the day the Twelfth Imam was born, etc.: all the celebratory confirmations of Shi'is in their received and glorified collective memory. Added in post-revolutionary Iranian calendar is a set of yet another, renewed, collective remembrance of the updated charismatic effervesence. The June 1963 uprising, the day Khomeini returned, the ten days of "the morning twilight" when the Islamic Revolution dawned, etc.: all the collective registrations of just one moment of creative effervescence that has spelled the terms of the new enchantment—to last until the next.

Attending the content, not just the form, of symbolic effervescence, Durkheim knew of the secular renditions of such otherwise sacred prerogatives. "[T]he French Revolution," he noted," established a whole cycle of holidays to keep the principles with which it was inspired in a state of perpetual youth." [13] "A state of perpetual youth" may, indeed, be too much to ask for any set of historically realized constellation of symbolics. Adoptability, to be able to speak the changing languages of time and history, is the key operative force of every symbolic constellation of command and obedience. But Durkheim can account for every transitory period in symbolic history. "If this institution," namely "a whole cycle of holidays," Durkheim stipulated, "quickly fell away, it was because the revolutionary faith lasted but a moment, and deception and discouragements rapidly succeeded the first moments of enthusiasm." [14] Every revolutionary faith lasts "but a moment." Disenchantment with the revolutionary cause is almost cooriginal with the very moment of enchantment. Every revolution in symbolic terms of obedience is, or breeds, its own undoing. Two weeks or fifteen centuries, symbolic systematizations of obedience could not care less about the historicity of their manifestations. Perpetually renovated in collective memories, sacred symbolics use history as they discard it.

"There are no gospels which are immortals, but neither is there any realm for believing that humanity is incapable of inventing new ones." [15] Old gospels, too, now the terms of our "conservative" dispositions, were once invented in a creative moment of effervescence. History may exhaust the particular relevance of a gospel in the exigencies of her contemporaneity. But for Durkheim, or any other social constructionist theorist of the supreme forces of the human condition, the mere collectivity, the sheer communal presence, of the person breeds new symbolic imperatives to match the changing conditions.

Durkheim's dismissiveness in tracing the forms and contents of future symbolics of authority is a mere theoretical pause.

As to the question of what symbols this new faith will express itself with, whether they will resemble those of the past or not, and whether or not they will be more adequate for the reality which they seek to translate, that is something which surpasses the human faculty of foresight and which does not appertain to the principal question. [16]

We can follow the Durkheimian lead and take a few more steps. The new faith will have to have elements of the old—in signs, symbols, and ceremonies of its authority. Every translation of confused and unintelligible realities into the symbolic orchestration of meaning and confidence will cater to new facts with reinterpreted old sentiments. That in this process, when new forces feed into old fantasies, when new illusions resuscitate old enchantments, new and unprecedented paradigmatic patterns of command

and obedience emerge is self-evident. Beyond and through the symbolics, religious orchestrations of the highest order are intended to interpret the world and render it meaningful and trustworthy. "[A] system of ideas," Durkheim stated, "whose object is to explain the world."[17] In that explanation, it is self-evident that older languages have cozier claims on obedience and belief. If its dramaturgical thrust is targeted towards action, and its cosmology towards thought, as Durkheim distinguished them, then man's historical and existential self-definition is always circumscribed between new experiences and old perceptions, between the theoreticality of social action and its metaphysical justification. As religious conviction "enriches and organizes"[18] the historical life, certain amounts of investments are made for future dividends.

The Permanent Force of Discontent

These scattered and sacred dividends are collected and cashed in revolutionary moments of collective remembrance of things past. Here, beyond its material causes, the ideological, mythical, and theological dimensions of a revolution give communal expressions to man's most moving precept: Discontent. A deeply rooted desire to change, to alter, to modify, to transgress, and ultimately to become another seems to lurk beneath every veneer of calm civility that the status quo demands and rewards. Permanent revolution is simply the political expression of a more abiding truth, which is permanent change in one's self-understanding. Here, on this borderline, the conservative, the liberal, and the revolutionary all concur. Reenacting "Islam Itself," "the Islamic Ideology" is the historical case of the hermeneutic conversation between the authority of the ideological interpreter and the legitimacy of the remembered text—all to (redefine) man's quintessential discontent with merely being-in-the-world. The "text" in the Islamic case is much more than the Qur'an and the Hadith, etc. It is that palaverous constellation of symbolics and sensibilities, figures and figurations of authority, that at every historical conjunction its believers obediently call "Islam," or, as in the modernity of its manifestation, "the Islamic Ideology." That term of disenchantment registers the radicality of contemporary Muslim's bewildering discontent.

This radical desire for permanent change is itself a more mundane expression of an even more abiding truth, which is the irresistible longing for permanent rebirth—man's defiance of death. The ecstasy, conscious or sublimated, of the primary birth, and the permanent awareness of its inevitable counterpart, forces man to reexperience (or wish to reexperience) that primordial moment of coming-into-being. Coming-into-a-new-being, thoroughly redefined by a fundamental change in one's communal self and identity, is what a social revolution promises. The delivery is immaterial.

Only the promise counts. The political success or failure of a revolution is not only a contradiction in terms but, more important, an irrelevant question. In the sense of a renewal of the primary birth, a revolution is at once a success and a failure: The revolutionary experience succeeds in simulating the primordial birth by promising a renewal of the communal self, and it fails the moment the provisional government calls for peace and prosperity.

Reenacting creation and renewal, claiming back prerogatives once upon a time invested in gods and demons, is the ultimate driving force of the modern revolutionary spirit. The rest is simply the minutiae and the detail for the historian to fill in. But as historians search and collect the data of the last revolutionary episode and as the provisional government seeks recognition and legitimacy, the revolutionary spirit, the endless quest for reenacting the primordial act of creation, dreams of the promises of the next revolution to come. The historical repetition of such promises of renewal, despite all failures, despite all illusions, and despite all disenchantments, is man's metaphysical denial of his mortality. Now that the world, and our life in it, is permanently finite, let us create a semblance of infinity in the repetition of our personal and communal selves, in our endless striving for change, in our all-out ideological, mythical, and theological justifications of revolution.

Ideology thus gives political expression to a visceral denial, and yet at the same time the negational acceptance, of mortality. In highfalutin ideological denials, we take the received notions of proprieties and shake them for political renewals—the most socially explicit semblance of immortality. Mythology translates the ideological articulation of denial into a vast repertoire of symbolic inferences where they can hope for a more enduring validity and permanence. Signs and symbols outline the signified and the symbolized. The cult of Khomeini feeds on fertile Persian imagination beyond the finality of the revolutionary sage. Theology, ultimately, approximates the denial of mortality to the vicinity of the Everlasting, to god-terms of our permanently religious culture. Beyond these god-terms, our received notions of infinity and permanence, we cannot conceive of any immortality in the face of the penultimate fear. Here our permanently religious culture draws the final line. Theology is the supreme language of the religious culture with which we attend even our most secular ambitions. Without this metatheoretical language the political rhetoric will always lack that necessary zest, that appealing charm, that illusion of truth. We know no other language that so thoroughly expresses our innermost fears, our uppermost hopes. Thus, theology is the most natural language of our most visceral discontent, the language of all revolutions. From that permanence—past, present, and future—there is no escape.

Articulation of a Theology

Where does the dialectic of permanent enchantment and almost immediate disenchantment lie? How do ideologies rise and die? The answer lies in the historical vicinity of every ideological attendance upon the world. The historicity of every ideology, its mere matter-of-factness, is both its source of energy *and* its undoing. The Islamic Revolution in Iran gives ample evidence, in its very ideological foundations, to that effect.

Given the theocentric nature of every theology, the theology of discontent, too, needs its anthropocentric articulation, the historicity of its metaphysics. Every definition of God is the simultaneous articulation of man. "The Islamic Ideology" and *velayat-e faqih* (the authority of the jurist) developed as two distinct ideological and doctrinal frameworks within the received Islamic (Shi'i) discourse, both directed at this theological articulation of locating God, man, and society on a historical continuum. These two ideological constructions coincided in and bracketed the Islamic Revolution. In retrospect, and insofar as the Revolution was the inevitable culmination of a rising spirit of discontent, "the Islamic Ideology" and *velayat-e faqih* were, while separate in their doctrinal assumptions and course of development, interrelated and politically complementary. Moved towards a revolutionary utopian solution to the real and perceived problems of their day, the operatives within the Islamic discourse either responded to the onslaught of contemporary secular ideologies and concocted "the Islamic Ideology" or else remained chiefly loyal to the Shi'i juridical discourse and resuscitated the *velayat-e faqih*. The two revolutionary statements appealed to two different social groupings: "the Islamic Ideology" primarily to the young urban professionals and students, still practically comfortable within an Islamic frame of self-reference and yet attracted to effective "Western" ideological forces; and *velayat-e faqih* to the activist seminarian students in Qom and Najaf or any other centers of heightened religious sentiments.

The doctrinal and ideological roots of these two components of the revolutionary Islamic discourse, the supreme symbolics of the creative effervescence in revolutionary religiosity, are directly related to their political constituency. While *velayat-e faqih* is an innately Shi'i juridical notion, "the Islamic Ideology" is the ideological radicalism of European origin creolized into an Islamic hybrid. "The Islamic Ideology," as distinct from both "Islam" (in its religious sense) and "Ideology" (in its secular sense), is thus the Muslim secret admiration, deeply disguised as total negation, for "the West" and its enchanting forces. "The Islamic Ideology" and *velayat-e faqih* have developed separately, and they shall have different fates as they experience their post-mortem revolutionary experiences. The responses and reactions to *velayat-e faqih* shall essentially and most seriously come from within the hermetic seal of the Shi'i jurists themselves. The nonclerical lay responses and dismissals of *velayat-e faqih* lack any legitimate mode of discourse to be taken seriously. In this regard, the silence of an Ayatollah Kho'i is infinitely more important than volumes of misguided arguments by lay critics. But "the Islamic Ideology" carries the forces of its own self-contradiction, the terms of its own disenchantment as in all other ideologies, within itself. Too much assimilation into the grand schemata of the total secular ideologies, particularly socialism, shall prove indigestible to the organisms of the Islamic bodies that swallow revolutionary precepts. The historicity of every ideology, the course of its energy, is also its own undoing.

"The Islamic Ideology" and *velayat-e faqih* cannot doctrinally converge, despite the fact that they can always combine their forces politically. There is a doctrinal antipathy between these two revolutionary precepts. Khomeini could not understand Shar'ati's language; he would equally dismiss much of what Motahhari comfortably brought under the rubric of "the Islamic Ideology." Al-e Ahmad celebrated Khomeini's revolutionary vigor, but the scholastic language of *velayat-e faqih* would have been too thick for him to swallow.

There is another basic and far-reaching difference between "the Islamic Ideology" and *velayat-e faqih*: While both have responded to the revolutionary needs of their day, they represent two diametrically opposed modes of response to the threat of the unknown. "The West," the mighty "West," has always remained a mysterious source of force for the Islamic world. Some have responded to this force, coming from "The Western" side of Muslim imagination, by attempting to assimilate what they had perceived "The West," the source of mystery, to be. They garbed this perception in Islamic language and called it "the Islamic Ideology." But there is also a more, perhaps, natural response in the face of the unknown: a retreat back to the comfortable and familiar language, "the house of being." Khomeini extracted the specifics of this return to the innately known, familiar, trustworthy, and meaningful from the Shi'i juridical legacy, one of the most pervasive and institutionalized modes of authority in Iranian history, even before the Safavids established it as part and parcel of the national psyche. An appeal to the new, "the Islamic Ideology," and a retreat to the old, *velayat-e faqih,* while both reactions in the face of the unknown, while both reconstructed convictions from scattered pieces of memory, and while both complementary for a brief political moment, shall always and innately remain diametrically opposed.

Pulled apart by the forces of their countercontradiction, equally dismembered by the innate tensions of their own self-contradictions, "the Islamic Ideology" and *velayat-e faqih,* as the two most compelling ideological terms of the Islamic Revolution, gradually witness the power of their historical necessity turning against their own relevance. The historicity of these two ideological updatings of Islam, the power of their immediate enchantment, thus breeds their own undoing.

History of a Success

Whatever the future may hold for "the Islamic Ideology" and *velayat-e faqih,* the immediate historical origin of the re-Islamicized political discourse in modernity will have lasting effects. The continuing effects of the future generations' remembrance of "Islam," the ceaseless production of new and more powerful terms of reenchantment, can only follow a similar course of development as the present ones. How "the Islamic Ideology" and *velayat-e faqih* came about tells us much about the universal mechanism of constantly rendering the world reenchanted. In this regard, modern Iranian history has much to teach.

The final supremacy and the effective mastery of the Islamic discourse over and above its secular competitors shall always remain a central point of contention among the students of the Revolution. Al-e Ahmad, however, should remain the key figure in any understanding of how the Islamic discourse was to succeed and supersede all other (secular) alternatives. And one good point of departure to reach for the political validity of the Islamic discourse, and the centrality of Al-e Ahmad's recognition of Islam as a political force, is the pre-Constitutional period.

By the 1800s, the Islamic discourse, political and otherwise, was the chief, nay the sole, semantic apparatus within which social concerns could have been articulated. To be sure, strong Iranian influences were instrumental in the general conceptual apparatus of Islamic political culture.[19] At least since the Abbasid Revolution in the mid-eighth century, the considerable influx of Persian administrative skills and theories of government infiltrated into Islamic social thought and political action.[20] But regardless of this particular Persian inflection, or one might also add Greek influence in its constitutional formation, the Islamic political discourse, Sunni or Shiʻi, effectively dominated the collective perception of political realities.[21]

From the early 1800s onward, ideological forces of European origin—whether radical or liberal in composition—began to find their way into various circles of Iranian intellectuals. Here the key role was played by the Qajar prince, Abbas Mirza, who sent the first group of Iranian students to England.[22] Although there are at least two significant precedents to it, Mirza Saleh Shirazi's *Safarnameh* is a seminal text in bringing secular ideas, chiefly liberal rather than radical, to Iran.[23] Shirazi, one of the five students Abbas Mirza sent to England, began the long and fascinating process of introducing European secular ideologies to Iranian political self-consciousness.

The Tobacco Revolt of 1889 was the first testing ground for both the Islamic *and* the secular revolutionary discourses to have measured their respective ideological holds on their constituencies. Despite the fact that ultimately it was Ayatollah Shirazi's *fatva'* that forced Naser al-Din Shah to abrogate the tobacco concession, the fact still remains that liberal-democratic ideals already preached by Mirza Saleh Shirazi and others were equally instrumental in this uprising. In a remarkable way the Revolution of 1979 was a playback of the Tobacco Revolt, when liberal-democratic, and to a lesser degree radical revolutionary, ideas contributed considerably to the ideological preparation of the uprising, and yet it was ultimately a religious push by a cleric that won the day.

The Constitutional Revolution of 1906 was the next historical testing ground of the viability of these two modes of revolutionary discourse—the newly emerging secular and the traditionally rooted Islamic. In one word, the final victory of the Constitutionalists and the hanging of their chief clerical opponent, Shaykh Fazlollah Nuri, demonstrate the supremacy, at least in immediate historical exigencies, of the liberal-democratic and the radical-revolutionary discourses over and above the Islamic. Thus, while the Islamic discourse won the day during the Tobacco Revolt, it was a combination of liberal and radical (secular) ideas, in conjunction with certain voices among the clerical order, that succeeded the religious discourse, in the strict sense of the term, in the wake and conclusion of the Constitutional Revolution. This is not to underestimate the significance, and perhaps even the centrality, of the Shi'i clerical force in the making of the Constitutional Revolution. But the dominant discourse that emerged from the Constitutional period, and which was institutionalized in the Iranian constitution of 1906, owed more to Mirza Saleh Shirazi and Mirza Aqa Khan Kermani, as two prominent ideologues of the liberal and radical (both secular) causes, than it did to the juridical language of the Shi'i authorities, including that of the supporters of the Revolution.[24]

From the post-Constitutional period onward, the Islamic discourse, or at least its essentially juridical language, was considerably overshadowed by (secular) liberal and radical ideas. The establishment of the Tudeh Party in 1941 can be considered the chief institutional achievement of the radical discourse triumphant in its post-Constitutional period. Through the widespread translation and propagation of Marxist literature and through the tireless efforts of such ideologues as Taqi Erani, the radical discourse was successful in establishing an important niche for its claims on contemporary political realities. During the 1940s the radical discourse left its widest and most persuasive impression on the modern Iranian political culture.

The early 1950s, when Mosaddeq gradually came to power, witnessed a wide currency for liberal-democratic ideals. For the first time in modern Iranian history "the government of the law," so dearly cherished by the early exponents of liberal democracy, became remotely possible. But the 1953 coup, through which the Tudeh Party was banned and Mosaddeq's government dismantled, put an effective end to the institutional expressions of both radical-revolutionary and liberal-democratic ideas. "The Mother of Parliaments" and the children of Thomas Jefferson denied an entire nation the remote possibility of a democracy.

During the post-1953 period, the radical discourse was effectively aborted. To be sure, even in its heyday in the 1940s, the radical discourse had little bona fide intellectual vigor. The reason for the poverty of radical ideology in Iran has to be sought, ironically, in the very existence and mode of operation of the Tudeh Party. Odd as it sounds, the fact is that the Tudeh Party was the chief institutional barrier, the single most important force, against a vigorous and critical development of the radical discourse in Iran. This radical discourse was infinitely more vigorous and varied during the pre-Tudeh period, in the writings of Mirza Aqa Khan Kermani in the wake of the Constitutional Revolution, than after the establishment of the de facto Communist Party of Iran. By dictating a medieval code of ideological dogmatism, the Tudeh Party perpetuated an almost theoretically illiterate party line and thus prevented the possibility of any genuine and serious development of Iranian radical ideas. The Iranian radical intellectuals were effectively banned from direct and multidimensional contact with European intellectual radicalism and, as a result, a typical member of the intelligentsia knew less about contemporary radical thought in Europe than Mirza Aqa Khan Kermani, for example, knew nearly half a century earlier. Malignant ideological slavery to Soviet bureaucratic Marxism effectively put an end to a healthy pursuit of intellectual radicalism by secular Iranian intellectuals. Odd as it sounds, more than the clerical establishment and infinitely more effective than the Pahlavi brutal censorship, the Tudeh Party itself aborted the Iranian secular radicalism, perhaps beyond repair, and thus prevented its healthy course of development. Blind party obedience and doubly blind slavery to Soviet bureaucratic colonialism turned potential radical intellectuals into agents of Stalinist totalitarianism. When potential revolutionary ideologues marched and demonstrated under the protection of Soviet soldiers and their bayonets, the growth and legitimacy of the radical ideologues was perhaps irrevocably discredited in Iran.

The fate of the liberal-democratic ideals fared no better. The vigorous and valiant attempt of Iranian secular intellectuals from the early 1800s onward was ultimately vested in Mohammad Mosaddeq and the faintly composed ideological posture of the National Front. Thus, in the face of the critical and fateful moment, Mosaddeq's liberal movement was afflicted with grave misconceptions of *Realpolitik,* internal confusion and disarray, pitiful demagoguery, and, worst of all, a total lack of vision as to what posture they wished to cast for the Iranian collective identity. The liberal-democratic movement was rendered effectively docile in the post-Mosaddeq era when a nervous autocrat simply refused to tolerate the slightest sign of political resistance to his megalomanic perceptions of power politics.

While both the radical and liberal discourses, as well as their institutional expressions in the Tudeh and Mosaddeq phenomena, respectively, were thus being aborted and discredited, the Islamic discourse assumed, slowly but surely, increased legitimacy and constituency. In its dual course of development, "the Islamic Ideology" and *velayat-e faqih,* the Islamic discourse found sufficient energy and momentum to launch a revolution unprecedented in its full dimensions in the long and languishing history of Iran. The king's massive war machine pitifully crumbled under a mere orchestration of words. The trembling but assertive voice of Khomeini, the gentle but emphatic voice of Motahhari, the fluent and fiery voice of Shari'ati, etc., orchestrated a symphonic Hallelujah of words—symbols charged with fear, hope, ecstacy, and revolt—no war machine could resist.

There is no inevitability in matters of history. Things can go anywhere —but perhaps with a logic, however a posteriori derived. If there is any legitimacy in branding the Iranian Revolution of 1979 "Islamic" it must inevitably be because more Iranians, and more in Iranians, were touched and moved by words of patently or latently Islamic resonance than by any other. And that is reason enough to call it "the Islamic Revolution." Other claims to it, verifiable as they might be, are merely academic. The Islamicity of the Revolution ultimately rests on its theological language. The theology of discontent, calling God on one's side when drafting a political agenda, is but one, yet crucial, element in the mythology of revolt. Once set on an active revolutionary course, the mythology of revolt breeds in every facet of an old and pervasive political culture. The older a culture—the more diversified its manifestations in religious dogmas, poetic traditions, literary texts, emotive modes, etc.—the more energized and powerful the reactivation of the myth of revolt. Construction of a collective revolutionary myth need not be a conscious and deliberate act. Pieces of the mythological puzzle can come together accidentally by a combination of factors—internal and external to a given political culture.

Revolutionary Uses of Religion

However concomitant, in Durkheimian understanding, religion and society might be, the central question of modernity still remains: Why should a revolutionary movement in our time use religion as its principal mode of mobilization? Identification of such terms as "a crisis of modernization"[25] or as "a postmodern"[26] phenomenon simply begs the question. More sober attempts have been made in accounting for "When ... Revolutionary Movements Use Religion."[27] When there is "a preponderantly religious world view among revolutionary classes," such a usage of religious ideas is believed to be inevitable.[28] In the Iranian case, at least a segment of the revolutionary leadership derived its primary source of symbolic and doctrinal mobilization from Islam. It cannot be claimed that all revolutionary classes shared a religious world view, in the strict sense of the term. But as the revolutionary movement unfolded, an increasing number of patently Islamic symbols came to identify the nature and define the direction of the revolutionary movement.

It has also been suggested that if a particular theology is at variance with the existing social order, then there is a greater propensity for the revolutionary movement to assume a religious voice.[29] The position of Shiʿism vis-à-vis political authority is a matter of considerable debate.[30] It may be argued, however, that no mode of political authority is ever completely independent of justification to religious authorities.[31] Through both the resuscitation of the *velayat-e faqih* doctrine and the coinage of "the Islamic Ideology," Shiʿism was reconstructed in such revolutionary terms that would challenge the legitimacy of the existing political order. Thus, in terms of a revolutionary reconstruction, Shiʿism was redefined into an ideological stance vis-à-vis the status quo. Even if we assume Shiʿism as doctrinally apolitical, an assumption challenged by its doctrine and history, in its contemporary reformulation it has had clear claims on political leadership.

If the clergy is closely associated with the revolutionary classes, it has been stipulated,[32] then the ensuing revolution may be presumed to have a religious overtone. Heightened in its modern political aspirations, the Shiʿi clergy, at least since the Tobacco Revolt of the late nineteenth century and the Constitutional Revolution of the early twentieth, have had a strong propensity towards revolutionary mobilization. By gradually assuming the supreme political, if not the total ideological, monopoly of leadership of the revolutionary movement, the Shiʿi clergy gave a distinct religious character to the Iranian Revolution. This assumption of supreme leadership was obviously predicated on the decades of ideological preparations that preceded the Revolution itself.

That the revolutionary classes might be united in a single religion has been considered a contributing factor in religious symbols and ideas leading a movement to success.[33] Given the significant contribution of secular intellectuals to the making of the Iranian Revolution of 1979, we cannot categorize all revolutionary classes into one religion. However, since the overwhelming majority of the Iranian revolutionaries were born Shiʿis, in a very loose and general sense they may be assumed to have belonged to one faith. Although consciously left and liberal revolutionaries would not have considered themselves religious in a specific sense of the term, their collective participation in their received political culture would still make them receptive, even though subconsciously, to religious sentiments.

It has been observed that should the revolutionary classes profess a religion different from that of the dominant class, the ensuing revolution might assume a religious coloring.[34] In the Iranian case, this particular observation cannot be assumed as applicable. Both the ruling regime and the leading oppositional force openly claimed to be Shi'i Muslims. In fact, one might argue that between the Pahlavi regime and the Islamic movement opposing it an ideological battle emerged as to which was more Islamic. The monarch and his family did not spare a photo opportunity to demonstrate their religious piety. In fact, there are reasons to believe that the king himself was a rather pious believer, in his own particular way. But here, as in everything else about the ideological construction of a revolutionary discourse, it is crucial to remember that Khomeini, as the leading spokesman of the Revolution, increasingly branded the monarch as an impious brute with loose moralities. This reenactment of the classical Manichean encounter between the forces of good and evil was, in fact, instrumental in the gradual formation of a strong moral dimension in the texture of "the Islamic Ideology."

Perhaps the most applicable clause to the Iranian case about the possibilities of a revolutionary movement assuming a religious posture is in the postulation that "alternative organizational structures [are] not available."[35] Although there had been at least two centuries of (secular) liberal democratic and at least one century of radical revolutionary discourses in Iran prior to the outbreak of the 1979 Revolution, due to repressive measures adopted by the Qajar and Pahlavi dynasties, successful institutions of democratic expressions did not emerge in full formation. Both the Tudeh Party and the National Front of Mohammad Mosaddeq were the most widespread expressions of secular alternatives that commanded considerable force in modern Iranian politics. But both these movements, and their related ideological discourses, were severely crushed by the authoritarian measures necessary to secure the tyrannical monarchy. Freedom of political organizations was stipulated in the Constitution of 1906 but effectively denied by both Pahlavi monarchs. In the absence of any meaningful (secular) political organization to give active and legitimate expression to ideological aspirations of different classes, "the Islamic Ideology" became the most effective discourse for expressing such proclivities. But beyond the mere construction of an effective and communicable language, "the Islamic Ideology" also became the institutional organ of a vast network of professional and student voluntary associations, of mosques and other religious centers, and, most crucially, of the hierarchical structure of the Shi'i clerical order. Although not every member of this order actively participated in this institutional revolt against the legitimacy of the Pahlavi state, a considerable proportion, enough to render them politically significant, did use their unique position for patently political purposes.

The Genesis of "The Islamic Ideology"

But even the political and ideological compatibilities between religious sentiments and their revolutionary uses cannot fully explain the contextual forces that drive a political culture towards its most common and compelling denominators. The power of remembrance that begins to reconstruct a political culture in terms of its most sacred memories needs to have more energetic historical resources, more compelling encounters with its immediate exigencies. The act of de(just immediately to re)totalizing "Islam," through an act of ideological reconstruction code-named "the Islamic Ideology," opens up the old faith for newer probings.

In its claim to orthodoxy, unless the enchantment is to be reinterpreted, "the Islamic Ideology" reconstructs both the "Islamic" and the "Ideology." It reconstructs the "Islamic" from the medieval memory of its past remembrance, under which the most varied forms of secular ("Western") claims to political salvation are to be propagated. It reconstructs the "Ideology" by denying any possibility of being judged or joined, praised or condemned, on comparative grounds. "The Islamic Ideology" has, as it were, God on its side, which makes it impossible to approach that Supreme political art: the compromise. Reconstructing both the "Islamic" and the "Ideology," from the received orthodoxy of these two commanding terms, "the Islamic Ideology" derives its force from an illusion, socially constructed and massively sustained, that has resulted from the historical exigencies of trying to mobilize a maximum of popular force to achieve an optimum of political ends in the shortest possible span of time. Having failed to mobilize enough material force to topple the old regime and sustain its revolutionary grip over the new order, secular ideologies gave ground, however unwillingly, to the compelling illusion of "the Islamic Ideology." This ideology has its material roots in the Text of its authority: the Qur'an reinterpreted. Through the (un)written words of the Qur'an, "Islam" is always made contemporaneous with the applicability of its historical reunderstanding. The predilection of these Muslim ideologues with the Qur'anic exegesis, even beyond what Tabataba'i achieved, has to do with the effective translatability of the textual authority of "tradition" into the contemporary authority of the ideological voice. That voice, coming from the deepest memories of Islamic collective remembrance, has its inescapable historicity.

"The Islamic Ideology" was born in modern history, as a perhaps inevitable offspring of an unwanted marriage between "Islam and the West." Thus juxtaposed, "Islam and the West," the very duality of it, is more a figment of the imagination, compelling though in its apparition, than having any claim on historical veracity. As cultural constructs, both "Islam and the West" feed on the universal need to create a "Self," as an "Other" is being simultaneously given birth to.[36] As "The West" created "the Orient" to complete its "Self"-imagination, Muslims, in collaboration with their European and American counterparts, invented "The West" for precisely the same purpose. While in "The West," "The West" was the self-congratulatory pronouncement of all things good and admirable, for Muslims it became the symbolic construction of corrupted excellence, an object of discrete adoration and manifest hatred.

As Muslims, Europeans, and Americans chased each other in their figments of collective imagination, in their mythical construction of "Islam and the West," in their social construction of "Self" and the "Other," the Islamic political agenda was increasingly redefined in new and compelling terms of a hybrid origin and destination. The world was changing fast, and at the peak of world cultural hegemony stood "The West": a force that its sheer self-conscious indifference demands to be reckoned with. "The West" became an imaginative geography from which radical ideologies spread to conquer the world, Islam and all. Upon the world stage: exit old pieties of collective virtues, enter alien ideas of magical spells—from necktie to neurosis, from hat to hegemony, from Marxism to mini-skirt, from narcissism to nuclear plant. The discrete charm of "The Western" bourgeoisie began to act on the Islamic bazaars, as on the felicitous enchantment of the intellectuals. The old order, kings and clerics at the top, begins to lose legitimacy. As kings and clerics try to modify their respective roles in such radical encounters as the Constitutional Revolution of 1906, a third mighty force, the secular left, enters the scene, denying them both any measure of contemporary relevance. Declaring kings and clerics outmoded, the secular (imported) ideological force begins to coin new terms of obedience, frame new pictures of paradise, claim higher charges on political truth, and win larger shares of ideological constituencies.

A negational ménage à trois takes shape: the kings, the clerics, and the secular radicals. Any two could coinspire against the third: kings and clerics against secular radicals, clerics and secular radicals against the kings, but rarely kings and secular radicals against the clerics. In the Constitution of 1906, there were kings and clericals on one side and clericals and secular radicals on the other. The secular radicals and their side of the clerics won the day. After seven decades of several rearrangements, finally, in the Islamic Revolution of 1979, the clericals and the secular radicals coinspired against the king and won the game. Then the clerics kicked the secular radicals out of political relevance and, with them, their ideological currency.

How did the modern clerics, or Islam updated, win the day? As the secular radicals began to engage the kings and bypass the clerics, the clerics saw their future enemies in their present allies. They saw in the secular radicals a rival against a monopoly of political truth launched to dethrone the kings who had an increasing claim on a monopoly of evil. Out of the clerics emerged a subclass that sought to update the Islamic political discourse. That, they thought, was the key to a larger constituency of massive mobilization. The old language of the clerics and certainly the language of the court were too outmoded, given "The Western" scheme of things, to confront the secular radicals and their claim to "scientific" validity. To oppose that claim, and at the same time to oppose the kings, the clerical sentiments had to be articulated in precisely the secular radical parlance. Thus emerged the greatest and the most far-reaching ideological hybrid in Islamic history: "the Islamic Ideology."

"The Islamic Ideology" had to adopt the terms of the secular radicals and the very cast of their mind to compete effectively with the rapid expansion of vast illusions substituting new god-terms in place of the outmoded ones. The adoption of the new (secular) language inevitably changed "Islam" as it, or rather its interpreters, tried to cope with the perils and promises of the new age. But the old interpreters of the faith had as much claim on it as the new ones. Legitimacy was up for grabs: one community of interpreters against another. Hermeneutic politics made all the difference. Whereas the old interpreters were increasingly chased into the solitude of their scholastic hair-splitting, the new semioticians of revolt claimed every symbolic aspect of the faith for their expanding revolutionary workshop. Adopting the new language also had the added illusion of speaking to a more global concern: no more feeble sectarian infighting. The new interpreters reached for an "Islamic" consensus against "The West," the World Power-monger. The secular radicals had proved, in vast territories like Russia and China, the universality of their claim to political truth. Couple that claim with the Islamic inherent enchantment with universality, and no other illusion even comes close in its conviction of having actually seen the light.

Adopting the secular language, whatever its impact on the internal legitimacy of Islam as a universal faith, had the tangible and desired effect of empowering "the Islamic Ideology" to combat blatantly secular ideologies on their own terms. The secular ideological forces, nationalism and socialism in particular, were narrowing in on patently Islamic territories. Every day and with every generation, younger hearts and mightier minds were being lost to secular ideologies. Islam caught in its scholastic tongue was incapable of voicing even its anger, let alone its challenge, against the infidelities of the age. But "the Islamic Ideology" untied its Islamic tongue, learned the new language—from the alphabet to the semiotics of the revolutionary age. Against the common enemy of the Pahlavi regime, "the

Islamic Ideology" had to compete with secular ideologies and their glaring promises to substitute a convincing version of paradise on earth for the atrocities of the status quo. The power "the Islamic Ideology" acquired by assimilating the secular language went beyond anything at the disposal of "traditional Islam," or even of blatant secularism. By combining the power of both "traditional Islam" and the secular ideologies, "the Islamic Ideology" reached for, and appropriated, the most politically decisive segment of obedient loyalty.

Whatever the process of its formation, the primary target of "the Islamic Ideology" was not its rival secular ideologies. The state and its "Westernized" despotism are what most animated "the Islamic Ideology." The most immediate impact of adopting the secular discourse in opposing the despotic regime was that the monarchical establishment, the "Westernized" accused, could not use the "reactionary" line against its religious opponents. "The Islamic Ideology" saw and portrayed the Pahlavi regime as the epitome of corrupt despotism. At the top of the state apparatus stood the king, corrupt to the marrow of his bone in the reactivated Islamic collective imagination. In turn, the misguided course of the regime had resulted in deep and pervasive corruption in the rest of the society. Designating themselves as the contemporary custodians of the moral community they called "Islamic Iran," the Muslim ideologues assumed responsibility for eradicating the primary threat to the very fabric of that morality. Against the state, the Islamic ideologues spoke not just with ideological conviction and political certitude but, more important, with moral indignation. That indignation, ipso facto, rendered the Pahlavi regime illegitimate. Passively silent or brutally repressive, the Pahlavi regime could only fall in public grace in the face of such delegitimating voices. The regime could not level the charges of anarchy or instruments of foreigners against the Islamic ideologues, as it did against the secular ones. "The Islamic Ideology" spoke from the high moral ground to which the Pahlavi state had no access, and from which it had no escape.

On that high moral ground "the Islamic Ideology" assumed a reality sui generis. The power of its conception was such that not everyone who contributed to its making was fully conscious of his participation in a revolutionary redefinition of Islam. Of course Shari'ati, Motahhari, Taleqani, Bazargan, and Bani-Sadr used the term and meant by it a massive orchestration of Islamic symbols for specific political purposes. Yet Al-e Ahmad, Tabataba'i, and even Khomeini contributed effectively to the making of "the Islamic Ideology" without ever articulating it in so many words. As they operated in their literary, philosophical, and juridical universes of discourse, respectively, they inadvertently lent political, conceptual, and historical validity to the legitimate operation of their construct. Thus metamorphosed into an independent organism, "the Islamic Ideology" was coined, "christened," and tested in the rhapsody of a successful and complete revolutionary ritual.

Through that ritual, "the Islam Itself," was renarrated. That "Islam" was thus rehistoricized gives us a factual, historically evident, clue as to the working of Islam in the entirety of its remembered history, not just now in Iran, ever since its primary conception in seventh-century (C.E.) Arabia. As their ancestors in a history they cannot forget, as their contemporaries in other parts of the Muslim world, the Islamic ideologues in Iran became the architects of a revolutionary edifice reconstructed from the ancient relics of a citadel that may or may not, could or could not, have once existed in anything but the collective imagination of a people. Between that may or may not, that could or could not, the uncertainty of fact-and-fantasy, dwells the unending paradox of being-Islamically-in-the-modern-world. Through the collective texts of these ideologues, Islam was reimagined and revealed. At the center of this revolutionary hermeneutics stood the Qur'an, the authority Text of any historicity for the Islamic metaphysics. And extended from it were the most distant revolutionary interpretations that any text could ever sustain. From center to periphery, from the Text to its most varied interpretations, the Muslim ideologues claimed not just the political but the moral high ground.

The Revolutionary Function of An Ideology

To divide and rule the world from that high moral ground, every ideologue needs to have a symbolic correspondence with the particulars of his constituency. The vast and overwhelming confusion of those particulars cries for order and significance. "The Islamic Ideology," as any other, receives its mobilizing energy from the inner voices of conviction that want the world to be meaningful and trustworthy. The multiple function of ideology, Islamic or otherwise, has secured a continued presence for such subjective constructions of reality that extend the boundaries of imagination beyond the immediate limits of material life. Marx's identification of the distortive function of ideology became the cornerstone of a larger scheme in the textual construction, and the simultaneous politicization, of the proletariat.[37] Divesting considerably the term of its political overcharge, Mannheim coupled "ideology" with "utopia" to argue for the inevitable social foundations of every claim to political truth.[38] The formative effects of both "ideology" and its functional equivalent "utopia" became the central concerns of Mannheim's sociology of knowledge. Weber saw the great legitimating function that ideologies perform in mobilizing the relevant collective sentiments.[39] Extended from such legitimizing functions, Clifford Geertz has unpacked the integrative function of ideology as a collective cultural artifact.[40] But strongly present in the distortive, formative, integrative, and legitimating functions of ideology is the potential revolutionary alternative that can break loose from any structural-functional compromise it might have been wont to. The revolutionary function of ideology is deeply rooted in the alternative, and historically constructed, tasks it has invariably performed. The key to such multiple, and equally accessible, historical alternatives, whether structural-functional or radical-revolutionary, is the repertoire of common symbolics, the power of remembrance, from which ideology, as a cultural construct, draws its formative units and mobilizing energy. That repertoire of common symbolics, that power of remembrance, is not a static artifact. It moves, develops, shrinks, and expands with history. But it always remains attached to the most sacred, the most perennial, notions of good and evil, of right and wrong, the permitted and the forbidden in a culture. At the heavy and exacting price of anxiety-provoking fears and tribulations, the moral demand system,[41] always tacitly underlying this repertoire of common symbolics, ensures not only an integrative but also a disintegrative, not only a functional but also a revolutionary, not only a legitimating but also a delegitimating, not only a formative but also a reformative function of ideology. The revolutionary function of ideology is cohabitant with its other formative forces.

The revolutionary function of "the Islamic Ideology" received its impetus as well as its driving force from dormant common mythologies deeply rooted in the Iranian collective memory. This ideology was constructed, by a range of committed architects, out of materials sacred to the Iranian Shi'i self-consciousness. The nature of this ideological construction was such that it connected the most immediate political concerns of the day to the subjective constitution of the Iranian mind. Pre-Islamic archeologists of this collective mind may argue, in fact, for more archaic layers in this same site. Cultural paradigms, or patterns of legitimate thought and action, quintessential to the Iranian collective psyche became resuscitated and reconstituted in this fascinating episode in archeological ideology. Reach for the remotest layer of common conviction to construct the highest contemporary claim to political truth!

The cultural paradigms thus selected and rendered relevant in contemporary politics then acted as energized agencies of mass communication between the ideologues (archeological architects) and their growing constituency. At the center of competing claims on the massive machinery of the revolutionary movement lies the ability of the communicators to mobilize the greatest number of symbols sacred to the greatest number of people. There is a formula for any revolution. In this almost arithmetic of revolutionary mobilization, competing ideologies of rival camps can calculate the measure of their successes or failures on precisely this number of common and easily communicable cultural paradigms the revolutionaries share with their constituencies.

Neither the symbolic origin nor the revolutionary possibilities of an "Islamic Ideology" thus conceived has any limitation other than those imposed by their constituent forces. Given the possibilities of such formative forces, the revolutionary ideology can go in any number of political directions—liberal or conservative. Once the initial hook is made, more a function of sentiment than reason, the lead of the ideological movement can be twisted and turned in any number of directions. Despite their cultural origins and their social constructions of reality, revolutionary ideologues have an energy sui generis. Measures of actual political success have their added momentum for the continuity and direction of the rest of the social movement. The distance, otherwise known as "heresy," such ideological offspring may take from their fathering dogmas may ultimately alienate a number of disenchanted parents. But the number of enchanted children the newly constructed ideology fathers in its own right can far outnumber the number of disenchanted (grand)fathers it leaves behind. There is a family feud that can confuse a culture as it reconstitutes itself. Scholastic minutiae of misrepresentation, quietly aired by disenchanted grandfathers, are whispers compared to the loud clamor of revolutionary change, screamed by less cautious grandchildren. It is precisely at this juncture that the structural-functional forces of ideology yield rather obediently to the young and raw energy of the new rebellious interpretation. As the hermeneutic circle around the old and conservative scholasticism digresses more narrowly into a niche of antiquarian anxiety, the rising interpretation, the theology of discontent, claims larger and larger spheres of political obedience. The sky is the limit. The traditional hermeneutics having painted itself into a corner of contemporary irrelevance, the rival (secular) ideologies in their permanent goose chase *à la recherche d'une conscience collective*, "the Islamic Ideology," updated and newly improved, conquers the hearts and commands the minds of the largest popular body on the move.

Towards a Triumphalist Theory of the Islamic Revolution in Iran

Having rendered its rival alternatives irrelevant at the crucial moment of revolutionary mobilization, "the Islamic Ideology" is the key conceptual force for gaining insight into the moving spirit of the Revolution itself.

The ideological anticipation of the revolution has an innate propensity towards the stipulation of moral imperatives as articulated in a metaphysical frame of inevitability. The veracity of such a metaphysics is so self-evident that it is always assumed and rarely addressed. The moral conviction of "the Islamic Ideology" leads the direction of a theoretical statement about the Islamic Revolution towards the ethical imperatives that both the ideology and the Revolution so strongly imply. Renunciatory demands are self-imposed on part of these ideologues, particularly in the case of Khomeini, in order to denounce the ideological opposition not on merely political but, more important, on moral grounds. The central idea of "justice," so universal throughout the Islamic and Iranian political culture, is integral to this moral obligation to change the shape of a communal order in which "injustice" is perceived to reign supreme. The immediate effect of assuming such high moral grounds is a deeply rooted communal solidarity in the course of the revolutionary movement where every activist believes himself or herself to serve the cause of nothing less than absolute and universal justice. The organizational translations of such communal solidarities based on high moral convictions have far-reaching implications for the continuity and perseverance of the revolutionary movement. When a movement and its leaders believe God Almighty is fighting on their side, the forces of group solidarity thus engendered are, however temporarily, overwhelming. Moral certitude sanctifies political convictions.

In the shrinking dimensions of the global village where a fisherman's boat in the Persian Gulf can have an effect on the stock of Chrysler in Detroit, and where combined structural forces, material or ideological, can have immediate impacts on a social movement in a "remote part of the world," the public sympathy of the international spectators can become a mighty weapon. Social movements with a universal claim on high moral primacies can invariably count on such forceful opinions. Perhaps the single most important theme in the mobilizing rhetoric of "the Islamic Ideology" was its insistence on the dichotomous battle between "justice," on the side of the revolutionaries, and "injustice," on the part of the established regime. *Zolm,* Persian and Arabic for injustice, was the primary accusation against the monarch and his tyrannical rule. Why should millions of Iranians suffer subhuman material conditions while "the king of all kings" spent billions of dollars of their wealth on stupendous extravaganzas? Why? Having no legitimate answer to such questions, the Shah's government was ipso facto rendered illegitimate. This illegitimacy pronounced on moral, not primarily political, grounds, the language of revolt then inevitably assumes an ethical posture that, in effect, renders any alternative invalid. Such a moral consolidation of revolutionary forces thus engages its enemies not only at the level of the established order but also at the level of its ideological competitors: the secular revolutionaries—radical or liberal.

As the moral conviction of the revolutionary movement, aided by God Almighty Himself, consolidates its ideological and material forces, there is also a simultaneous demoralizing effect on the state apparatus, the constituent members of which, from the king to his footmen, begin to lose confidence and hope in their own abilities or even legitimacy. The crucial factor of the military force, which acts on the side of the state on administrative grounds of legitimacy, is either rendered ineffective or even won over to the side of the revolutionaries precisely on moral grounds. In his last speech in Neauple-le-Château, before leaving for Tehran in February 1979, Khomeini reminded the army officers that they were, in effect, "servants" of American advisors, while he wanted to liberate and make them "masters."[42] Such highly loaded moral terms, combined with the strong possibility of soldiers actually having members of their own families in the crowd, as well as the international condemnation when soldiers were shown on television firing at defenseless demonstrators, all contributed to the pervasive demoralization of the state apparatus and its own sense of legitimacy. The more the revolutionary force assumes the high moral ground, the more the state is rendered immoral and thus illegitimate. The casualties of public demonstrations or industrial strikes, rendered "martyrs" immediately, became the supreme symbolics of the legitimacy and morality of the revolutionary movement and, simultaneously, of the illegitimacy and immorality of the king and his monarchy. If the revolutionaries were willing to put their lives where their minds and moralities were, there could be no higher order of ethical primacy in any other alternative ideological claim to political truth, whether in the state apparatus or among the rival revolutionaries.

Morally charged with a visceral condemnation of its political opponents, the ideological foundation of the Islamic Revolution was deeply moved and forcefully animated by a repulsive rejection of "The West." Mythologized into a monolythic entity, "The West" became the epitome of moral corruption, of ethical bankruptcy, of illegitimate domination of the world, and of plundering the wealth and the dignity of other sovereign nations. "The West" was the cause of all ills, the mother of all corruptions, the condition of all despair, the father of all tyrannies. Projected backward into medieval and ancient history, "The West" came to finalize centuries of its confrontation with "Islam," with "The East," all concocted in the fertile imagination of not just Muslims but Americans and Europeans too, "The Westerners." From Alexander to Napoleon, a vast diversity of historical and cultural realities came to be homogenized into "The West." As Muslims thus homogenized the intolerable diversity of world history into an easy fabrication of "The West" vs. "The East," Europeans and Americans promoted the same fantasy, albeit with a Self-raising/Other-lowering conception of "The West." As Europeans and Americans began to fabricate a notion of "The West" consisting of such diverse and even hostile elements as the civilizations of Athens, Rome, and Jerusalem, the Muslims bought the fabricated idea and yet invested in it such equally diverse and opposing realities as a Macedonian general and a Roman crusader. As Europeans and Americans congratulated themselves by claiming Socrates and St. Paul, Christ and Marx, Michelangelo and Mussolini, even Hitler and Walter Benjamin, without the slightest sense of self-contradiction, the Muslims returned the fabrication by raising diverse and unrelated brutalities in human history and code-naming it "The West." Trapped in their figments of imagination, in their selective power of remembrance, in particular manifestations of their innate need to construct their "Self" even as they formed their "Other," Muslims, as well as Europeans and Americans, coined, validated, and thus perpetuated "Islam and the West" or "The East and the West" as the most dangerous terms of their confrontation, their mutual disenchantments. Diffuse and contradictory realities were subsumed under comfortable but dangerous rubrics of hostile imagination.

As Muslims bought the fabricated notion of "The West," as they failed, just as the Europeans and Americans did, to see and confront the troubling diversities of universal world history, they epitomized the construction as the supreme symbol of the wicked adversary. Against all historical realities, Muslims began to understand and project themselves as an injured "Self" tyrannized and colonialized by a supreme hostile "Other." "Islam" the unjustly wronged "Self," "The West" the supreme hostile "Other." "The West," now the story began to gain currency, has defeated, dominated, and humiliated "Islam" in modern times. But this has not always been the case. In previous instances, during the medieval and ancient periods, "Islam" had defeated "The West." The world is this theatrical operation between the forces of good ("Islam" or "the East") and evil ("The West"). We have defeated them once or twice; they have defeated us once or twice. Now we live in times of their victory. But revolt. One last victory over "The West" at any cost.[43] A deeply triumphant culture, "Islam" comes to be seen, by its contemporary architects, as the last bastion of yet another victory of good over evil. Manichean to the marrow of its bones, such a triumphalist view of two magical forces of good and evil has deeply, pervasively, and to the fullest extent of shared sentiments animated contemporary Muslim self-understanding. Revolts and revolutions, whether charged against actual and imaginary colonial powers or against "their local lackeys," are but specific and minor skirmishes in the more universal, the more enduring battle, between the eternal forces of good and evil. Manichean to its deepest convictions, such triumphalist vindication of two cultural constructs, "Islam and the West," perpetuates figments of fertile shared imagination into absolute terms of moral and political convictions, all delivered in an essentialist language of ideological mobilization.

Further intensifying the triumphalist urge of the postcolonial Muslim discourse was the quintessential ethos of Islam as a warrior faith. No turning the other cheek here, if anywhere at all. Triumphant and domineering from its very inception, the time of its birth, Islam came to fruition and self-construction with an absolute sense of self-certainty. For that faith to become subjugated, in its believers' obedience, to corrupt infidelity was tantamount to metaphysical and theological delegitimation. If defeated politically, then it was irrelevant theologically, invalid metaphysically, and fallacious doctrinally. The institutionalized version of Muhammad's initial charismatic truth, Islam will have to be validated perpetually. Denying validity to Muslims, by rendering them politically subordinate, is the verisimilitude of the institutionalized and the original charismatic claim to veracity proven fallacious. For a triumphalist faith, political verification and theological legitimacy go hand in hand. The world divided into the realm of Islam *(dar al-Islam)* and that of anti-Islam *(dar al-harb)*, political subjugation of the former to the latter, shakes the metaphysical veracity of the triumphalist faith to its very foundation.

Opposing the Iranian monarchy is negating "The West." Negating "The West" is reclaiming the political cum theological veracity of Islam: the source of all Muslim identity.

In this triumphalist theory of the Islamic Revolution, not just in Iran but anywhere, the moral charge of "the Islamic Ideology" is seen as the single most important symptom of "Islam and the West," whether separately or taken together. "One last victory over 'The West' at all costs" becomes the chief driving force that animates the movement, the supreme moral conviction that is instrumental in strategic success, whether in Iran or anywhere else. With a deep sense of *ressentiment* towards the means of domination at "The Western" disposal, Muslims loudly denounce the destructive forces of modernity while secretly wishing they had exclusive, or at least equal, access to them. Whether manifested in brutal acts of terrorism or in servile attitudes of assimilation, the deformative force of this *ressentiment* is the most blinding magical spell of the postcolonial legacy, the very stuff of which resentful revolutions are made.

The Terms of the Islamic Revolution

The terms of the Islamic Revolution, the language of its theocentric revolt, whether in Persian, Arabic, English, or whatever, bespeak, however convolutively, the spirit and the orientation that have animated its most compelling driving force. For a revolutionary movement, there is no escaping the originating terms of its initial claims on political truth.

In its most compelling terms of conviction, "the Islamic Ideology," and the revolution it begot, was deeply moved by, as it has been perhaps permanently trapped in, the postcolonial Islamic political culture. The demons of colonialism and neocolonialism had so deeply penetrated Muslim body-politics, they are not to be exorcised so easily. Neocolonialism, actual and perceived, was, in fact, a purgatorial construction to perpetuate the feelings and sentiments of colonialism beyond its logical and inherent limitations. The historicity of colonialism exhausted, neo- and postcolonialism are terms of perpetuation with which modern Muslims have articulated

their most elementary forms of political thought and behavior. The postcolonial culture has thus robbed the Muslim intellectuals of any possibility of
coming to terms with their own history on their own terms, with the power
and profusion of their own fantasies and facts, their own intelligence and
stupidities. This "Other-centered" culture of defining everything, from skirt
to eschatology, in terms of "The West" has denied the successive generations of Muslims unmitigated access to terms of their own enchantments.
The "Other"-centrism of Muslim radicals has led them wholeheartedly to
the illusion of the efficacy of violence, the most brutal fact of all politics, in
attending the modernity of their existence. No culture of narcissism here.
Politics stripped to its most naked truth, a claim on the monopoly of the
(legitimate) use of physical force, has stirred the most active nerves in
Muslim self-consciousness. That "Self"-consciousness is not but a reflection, a degenerative negational convolution, one among many, about the
most compelling "Other" in their universe of discourse, in the very metaphysics of their identity: "The West."

The "Other-centered" culture of Muslim modernity has become the
most compelling force of their contemporary history. In the profoundest
metaphysical sense, nothing was, unless defined by patently "Western," or
what they perceived to be "Western," in the scheme of things. Alienation,
in the deepest and most degenerative sense of the term, opened its wide and
far-reaching wings upon the Muslim mind—body and soul. The Muslim
"Self" was consequently denied, even as it was tacitly portrayed in negational terms to "The Western" hegemony. That "Self" is permanently
severed from the roots of its own historical identity and is being totally and
pervasively reconstructed out of a mere response, the brutal illusion of an
echo, to the overpowering presence of "The West" as the supreme construction of the "Other" in the modern Muslim collective imagination.
More than a "Muslim," you are either a "pro-" or an "anti-Western"
entity.

Trapped in its postcolonial culture, with "The West" as the exclusive
hegemonic force of universal evil, the collective *ressentiment* of Muslim
radicals conceals as much negationally expressed admiration as it reveals
positively expressed denunciation. "The West" has come, the argument
goes, and robbed us of our wealth and political choice. We have been
denied our political preferences through successive, brutal, and amoral
interventions. The immediate and the distant aims of all "Islamic" ideological constructions are to regain this actual and imaginary loss of sovereignty. The boundaries of this sovereignty are not limited to territorial
claims, to land and political administration. Religion and culture, art and
literature, character and morality: Everything has been through a pervasive
metamorphosis of "Westernization," approximation to a nonentity, changing into something which is not. To regain political independence is utterly

meaningless, if indeed at all attainable, if not coupled with a genuine recapturing of cultural identity of the Islamic *Geist,* the remembrance of the Islamic history minus "The West." But, and there is the rub, the actual and imagined colonial experience is so powerful that in the postcolonial recuperation all terms of cultural self-definitions, including the religious self-understanding, are delivered and articulated in precisely "The Western" scheme of things, arrangements of priorities as presumed to be held by "The West." No imaginary construct, no mere figment of a collective imagination, has ever proven to be so brutally domineering, so violently dehumanizing, than "The West" to Muslims—the act of their own creation, the figment of their own imagination.

As "The West" became this inevitable "Other" in whose actual and presumed terms every Muslim particular, from turban to theology, had to be redefined, the Islamic "Self," if having any reality sui generis, oscillated between a presumed past and an imagined future. Either a fictionalized view of glorious past or an idealized panorama of an equally elusive future have circumscribed the dual possibility of defining a "Self" for the Muslim collective identity. The present "Self," if there, is miserable and unacceptable—there to be changed, revolted against, redefined, reconstructed. Resting on a degenerative present and caught between an imaginative glorious past and an elusive revolutionary future, the Muslim self-consciousness is trapped in a social psychology of momentary accreditation. No memory of a historically verifiable past, no direct perception of present realities, and no realistic expectation of days to come, the Muslim individual and collective consciousness needs to feed on every spare moment to prove its existential legitimacy, its very reason for being.

The Muslim entrapment into the postcolonial rhetoric has not been limited to religiously minded revolutionary ideologues. Secular intellectuals, proponents of socialism and nationalism are equally caught by the feverish addiction to "The Western" cause, affirmative or negative. Even beyond every mode of oppositional force, religious or secular, the established regimes have also chosen to give their self-definition in the same postcolonial discourse. In recognizing a figment of their collective imagination, "The West," as the supreme hegemonic force in their cultural and political universe, kings, clerics, and intellectuals share a common fascination, a grand response to a universal illusion, and join in a compelling enchantment. As kings, clerics, and intellectuals rebel, or seem to rebel, against "The West," in their innermost convictions they pay fullhearted homage to its command of a hegemonic world domination, to its monopoly of a metaphysical might. Standing in awe in front of "The West," the lapsed-Muslims look at their self-delegated glory.

This collective enchantment with "The West," most acute in moments of rebellious agitation, characterized the quintessential features of the pre-revolutionary decades in Iran, leading to and engulfing the cataclysmic event itself. The enchantment was fully articulated in the ideological discourses that paved the way for the Revolution and thus the overpowering presence of "The West" in all these writings. "The West," concocted in the collective imagination of these ideologues, became the essential catalyst that defined the terms and articulated the nature of the revolutionary movement to come. When the Revolution did come, it could only politically unfold the textual sources of its origin and authority. The visceral contempt against "The West," the symbolic identification of the United States with "the Great Satan," even as they concealed the latent ambivalence of the Muslim *ressentiment,* immediately revealed the heightened anxieties of a triumphalist sentiment believed to have reached the zenith of its enchantment.

The enchantment with "The West," the terrible illusion of a global plot against the Islamic cause, has continued well into the post-revolutionary period, into the consolidation of the clerical order, into the very language of the Islamic constitution, into the hostage crisis, into the costly and catastrophic war with Iraq, and thus deep into the minds and hearts of the children of the Revolution. After Khomeini's death, the illusion continues. The total fascination with, the irresistible fixation on, "The West" seems to have no end in sight. No alternative "Other" seems to be able to substitute "The West" as the magical touchstone of contemporary Islamic self-understanding.

Thus in the collected mythology of "the Islamic Ideology" we witness the relentless construction of a revolutionary edifice within which political action begins to make sense far beyond the immediate vicinities of politics. Man is lost outside a frame of four-cornered certitude that begins to make sense of the word the moment it has exorcised all its contradictions, uncertainties, doubts, alternatives. Serenity and certitude begin to set in, even under the most revolutionary of all circumstances, when a collected mythology has arranged for a politically significant constituency. People may trade, under one set of historical circumstances or another, one myth for another, this illusion for the next. Permanent, however, is the relentless need to be perpetually enchanted with a possibility of being—meaningfully and significantly—in-the-world. But while mobilizing and signifying, "the Islamic Ideology," at the same time, became the great and convincing negation of man's inescapable historicity, a flight into the labyrinth of being-in-the-world vicariously, tangentially, parasitically, a mere footnote—however elongated—to "The West." A helpless entrapment in "The Western" state of imagination, "the Islamic Ideology" became the concocted remembrance of an (un)real haven, the illusion of a power that never was, never is, never will be. His immediate and unmitigated historicity denied, the modern Muslim became a contradiction in terms, a walking paradox—ill-equipped to reach for the modernity of his existence, unable to let go of the antiquity of his imagination. That imagination, de-, re-, and de-, reconstructed constantly, is relentless, fueled by daily doses of humiliation and denial. The ambiguity is polished and refurbished so that it looks like the real thing, the actuality of being-in-the-world. From Darwin to Freud, Marx to Sartre, everything could be Qur'anified, Islamicized, domesticized, familiarized into one ancient verse or another. History, apparition of events, is assimilated backwards, into the remotest corners of a relentless remembrance. The absolutism of reality too confusing to handle, too debilitating to face, "the Islamic Ideology," became the grandest of all illusions, swiftest of all enchantments, whereby the modern Muslim sought and secured yet another temporary, though always appearing to be permanent, house for being, occasion for repose, control of the deepest and most enduring anxieties.

Beyond the Limitations of "the Islamic Ideology"

How is historicity possible—the actuality of being-in-the-world without the mitigating comfort or cruelty of an illusion?

No "Self" can define itself, individually or collectively, without a simultaneous significant "Other." "Islam and the West," as the mutual cross-construction of Muslims and Euro-Americans, continues to haunt the imagination of both. Euro-Americans are trapped in this as much as Muslims.

For postcolonial Muslims a turning point can occur only when another "Other" is gradually constructed: an "Other" quintessentially different from "The West." But what could be an alternative to "The West" after so many generations of collective consolidations of the idea by Muslims and Euro-Americans alike? How can "The West," as the most convincing figment of Muslim imagination, be discarded, deconstructed, detotalized into the fragmented countersentiments that make it? Here we confront the thick walls of mythological constructs, such as "The West," which are so deeply interwoven with the human psyche that they refuse to crumble under rational scrutiny. No realistic perception of Europe and the United States, in their confused and heterogenous actuality, may hope to substitute "The West" for Muslims. The detailed actuality and the minutiae of experienced historicity are simply too distractive to hold an imaginative and mythological hold on the Muslim or any other mind. (The same is true for Euro-Americans who cannot substitute a realistic detail of Muslim realities for their "Islam" and "Muslims." But given the crucial relation of power, this is not as damaging to Euro-Americans as it is to Muslims.) The transitory and confusing nature of Euro-American realities, the persistent refusal of their factual realities to be categorized into a monolithic entity, cannot substitute the comfortable certitude of such imaginative constructs as "The

West." Muslims, just as Americans and Europeans, are too comfortable with this most recent, most compelling, artifact of their collective imagination.

Muslims, the alternative of looking to their "East" for a substitute "Other" has already proven futile and irrelevant. For a time, India, and its Gandhi, Japan and its technological marvels, and China and its historical continuity against the intrusion of "The West" seemed to constitute some alternative to the primacy of "The Western" state of Muslim imagination. But those were, and are, too distant realities, with no immediate history of territorial hostility such as the Crusades or even the state of Israel, to register a responsive chord in Muslim self-perceptions. More important, vis-à-vis "The West," Iran and all other parts of the "non-Western" world are part of "The East." Muslims cannot project aspects of their own self-perception as an "Other." In the imaginative geography thus created, whereby on the Rubik's Cube of world divisions Japan, Israel, and South Africa are construed as part of "The West," India or China could not register agitated memories or mesmerizing illusions in any significant way.

There can be no "Self" without an "Other." "The East" cannot substitute "The West" as the Muslim significant "Other." And, more important, no human community can continue in history without a persistent engagement in "Self"- and "Other"-definition. It is precisely through such continuous and historically alert "Self"- and "Other"-definitions that nations find and refind their collective identity. The facticity of the daily minutiae can never be a substitute for the grand illusions that imaginative perceptions of "Self" and "Other" create and sustain.

The fate of the Muslim societies, Iran included, and the mechanism of collective identity it necessitates cannot be considered in isolation from the rest of the world. The global village is now in a state of a permanent weekend—Friday, Saturday, or Sunday bazaar. Everything is now out for haggle. Historical changes in what used to be the Soviet Union and what continues to be Europe, the ascendancy of Japan as a super economic power, the reunification of Germany—all these megahistorical events have drastically altered the cold-war geography of sentiments and imagination. The United States has been permanently denied its supreme hostile "Other": the Soviet Union. Saddam could not last for long. "The Western" and "The Eastern" Europe are reverting back to more traditional borderlines of multiplicity, of alliance, and of hostility. The world is changing, and quickly. If not by a stubborn deliberation, the postcolonial rhetoric should crumble under the weight of such colossal events. If this opportunity is lost, nobody knows when the modern Islamic political culture can rid itself of its nineteenth-century hang-ups. New and more ferocious world powers are coming of age. If Muslims continue with their postcolonial rhetoric, they would outdate even further an already outdated language of political self-deprecation. Operations "desert" this, and operations "desert" that, can only aggregate further the brutal antiquity of that language.

But how fast, how realistically fast, can a political culture, deeply rooted as it is in the most convincing symbolic apparatus of a religious community, respond to the realities of its surroundings, of diverse origin, nature, and destination? How quickly, if ever, can the changing realities, the reconstructed exegencies, of the global village, enter this old and tired house and rearrange the furniture, redesign the setup, relocate the entrance, and reconstruct the seating arrangement, the basic build-up of identity, destiny, and purpose? How is this refurbished house to be peopled? How are these people to dwell in their existential self-definition? In what particular terms? With what specific sentiments?

Heidegger's dictum reigns supreme. "Language is the house of being." It is within that house that all and every rearrangement, redefinition of identity, of "Self" and, of "Other" takes place. Any change in the constitutional build-up of "Self" and of "Other" must necessarily be through the received languages of self-perception. Getting to know a language, as a prerequisite for reconstructing a new identity, is sometimes an impossible necessity. Being a Shiʿite (or a Muslim), or an Iranian (or an Arab or an Indian, a Pakistani, a Malai, etc.), or once a superpower, or once colonized, are all among the inevitable terms of the language with which Muslims define themselves. Such terms of encampment, such enchantments with communal identities, stereotypes that chase realities, have their inherent paradoxes. There are limitations that they abstract, even as fields of dream they cultivate. They construct symbolic mechanisms of continuity even as they raise walls of discommunications. They build homes of security and trust even as they imagine deserts of anxiety and doubt. For their members, escape them as they may, such instrumentalities of collective identity and behavior are not museum pieces of foreign curiosities. Artifacts of archaeological fieldwork for Others, they are, in fact, elements of daily sustenance—cultural, social, economic, and psychological terms of being-in-the-world. Exotic oddities at the gravesites of an ancient civilization for occasional or professional visitors, these are the very living stuff of which sentiments of collective behavior—angers and anxieties, hopes and hallucinations—are made. Any alteration, any collective reconstitution of identity and reason for being will have to be made precisely through these scattered houses of being, apartments of identity.

Here we face our most frightful question: How much of the future is predetermined by these pasts and presents? Can a symbolic collectivity, a nation, a political culture, rid itself, in any measure of certitude and success, of its pasts and presents, of its paradigmatic patterns of command and obedience? For such paradigms of authority symbols are everything. Revolutionary ideologies, illusions of grandiloquent change, are merely active mobilizations of these symbols, a heated conversation of their gestures. But even symbols, in the majesty of their semiotic authority, need historical verifications. They need shared sentiments, endured memories, to render them further legitimate. To become operative historically, symbols need geographical unfoldings. But once operative, subliminally or blatantly, they scarcely abandon their grip. They rarely just let go. They have a built-in power of self-perpetuating themselves. You can deny them during the day, they haunt your dreams during the night. You can emigrate from your homeland, they follow you to California.

To oppose them, where does one begin? How does one seek to negate and nullify the illusion of an omnipotent "West" manipulating the destiny of a whole people? How does one confront any powerful construction of one's own collective consciousness, supported, perpetually, by that very "Other" you have helped the world to imagine? Two kinds of antidotes can act against such illusions of an omnipotent "West" or against any other persistent construction of collective imagination. Either actual and detailed experiences with Euro-American realities—from the streets of New York to Sicilian villages—can begin to interact with other realities of the global perspective and thus give rise to alternative symbolics and references, or else natively constructed symbols may begin to search the world for historical verification. Detailed exposition to heterogenous realities of the Euro-American historical and contemporary experiences, through whatever immediate or distant channels possible, could have the effect of confronting monolythic stereotypes persisting in the Muslim mind. If such realities, particularly in their existential, nonessentialist, diversity, can reach beyond the built-in binoculars of cultural stereotypes—and that is a big "if"—they may gradually succeed in eradicating the unconditional sway that monolythic constructs such as "The West," as a supreme demonic "Other," hold. Conceivably such an ideal exposure to existential realities of the Euro-American experiences, such collective deconstruction of "The Western" edifice, would, ipso facto, create other, equally compelling, generalizations about them. Whether or not such alternative constructs are beneficial or injurious to Muslim, or Euro-American, interests is an entirely unforeseen proposition. But any course of events that would release contemporary Muslims from the spell of a monolythic omnipotence of "The West" is bound to untie this debilitating knot of cultural obsession.

The alternative scenario would be the formation of substitute categorical constructs about the Muslim "Self" from the specifics of their own historical and doctrinal realities. A "Self" without an "Other"? Such an ideal, and positive, formation would, in turn, supersede the postcolonial discourse and necessitate a new language of encounter with the physical realities of Euro-American, or any other, origin. The origin and constructive mechanism of such alternative self-understandings, which inevitably involve a simultaneous deconstruction of the last two centuries, would testify that the local soil of the so-called "Islamic" lands are not limited to Islamic influences. Two centuries of persistent exposure to secular—radical and liberal—ideologies have left their mark permanently on the collective consciousness of ex-, lapsed-, post-, and now for all effective purposes non-Muslims. Such realities cannot be denied or ignored. Any reconstruction of a collective self-understanding will have to have not only Islamic but patently non- or even anti-Islamic realities in mind. Disregarding such long exposures to secular ideas is as dangerous and foolhardy as neglecting the reality of Islam as perhaps the most compelling and regenerative cultural force in modern Muslim self-consciousness, ex-, lapsed-, post-, or any other kind. A self-consciousness thus constructed on the basis of a wide range of postcolonial realities, as opposed to sentiments, could lead to surpassing the postcolonial grip on the Muslim mind and the beginning of a new era in its unfolding history. What further facilitates such reconstructions of "Self" and then "Other" are actual cultural and linguistic diversities in the Islamic world. In the Iranian case, the distinct cultural and linguistic dimensions of being an "Iranian" in addition to being a "Muslim" can help in the gradual construction of a more realistic perception of the Iranian "Self." Add to that two centuries of exposure to radical and liberal ideas of European origin and you have the primary material of a new mythological construct that would, ideally again, relieve the present tension between a presumed Muslim "Self" and an equally fictitious "Western Other." The experiences of the Muslim ideologues we have examined in this book clearly testify that it is quite possible to delve deep into the shared sentiments of a people and emerge with buckets full of a convincing construction of a hostile confrontation between a "Self" and an "Other." If that is possible, then so is its deconstruction.

That any such future deconstructive construct, if realistically attainable, would be equally mythological, equally based on a communal illusion, equally celebrating yet another enchantment, is self-evident. Man is invincibly mythological. If there is any reason to believe in the possibility of a future reconstruction of the Muslim "Self"- and "Other"-perception, it is precisely in such mythological constructions being dethroned by a set of different constructs. The notion that at collective, or even individual, levels of sublimated generalities we can substitute concrete realities, whatever they are, for products of excited collective imagination is sociologically and psychologically too naive to be taken seriously. But what is possible, and historically verifiable, is the gradual formation of one set of constructive and life-affirming myths to replace a set of destructive and life-negating imaginings.

Political authorities are the primary architects of such a quintessential reconstruction of Muslim, or any other, political culture, and historical imagination is the condito sine qua non of its accomplishment. But can any politician, Muslim or otherwise, be accused of "historical imagination" nowadays? Democratization of the political process, actual or feigned, leads political authorities into inevitable compatability with, in fact taking ideological advantage of, the existing patterns of command and obedience, the old habits of complacency. The mode of political leadership destined for the future of Muslim countries can only follow a traditional, a rational-legal (constitutional), or a charismatic modality. The traditional mode of leadership inevitably rests on mores sanctified since time immemorial. Those are precisely the terms of persistent entrapment in the habitual discourse of command and obedience. Rational-legal leadership will have to be predicated on constitutional forms of legitimacy achieved through revolutionary or anticolonial movements. These constitutions, too, are textual constructions and legitimations of unexamined sentimentalities about the Muslim past, present, and future, about the glorified Islamic "Self" and generalized non-Islamic "Others." The only frame of reference, it seems, of a bona fide emancipating discourse rests on the possibility of a universal charismatic leadership. But even here, the stipulation of a "gift of grace," even in its Weberian secularization of the original Christian doctrine, renders the mode of leadership particularly attentive to, if not the letter then at least the spirit of, the established levels and legitimacies of political discourse. Be that as it may, it is in the nature of the charismatic leadership to defy "what is written" by the crucial stipulation of "but I say unto thee." The future of the Muslim political culture rests precisely on this "but" which opens a vast plethora of possibilities to alternative symbolics of "Self"- and "Other"-perceptions. Whether the thrust of such a deliberate future construction should, or would, be in a factual-symbolic or symbolic-factual direction remains to be seen, anticipated, or simply wished for.

Such a wishful imagination has always had its historical agency. When we reach the realm of the symbolics, the constituents of the political culture, we are led inevitably to the very architects of collective imagination—the intellectuals. Could the intellectuals have the key? They are the custodians of the sacred, of the most enduring, lore, whether or not they know or like it. Historical imagination is invariably the prerogative of the intellectuals, the ability to manipulate the cultural symbols beyond their remote sacred magnitude or beneath their immediate operative forces. But the contemporary Muslim intellectuals—lapsed, ex-, post-, or whatever—seem to have more personal axes to grind, more satanic verses to exorcise, more aesthetic techniques to experiment with, more literary landmarks to achieve, more prizes to win, recognitions to receive—sometimes at terrible costs. In the increasingly narcissistic subculture of Muslim intellectuals, inside and outside their homelands, lost in imagined countries, where can we locate a class of visionaries with historical imagination? But here, on a more compelling note, Muslim intellectuals have been forced to exit their customary hermetic seal and face global realities in their original, not the translated, terms. This, challenging as it is for the present generation, would create a level of discourse beyond the parochial preoccupations of Muslim self-deception. Muslim intellectuals—ex-, lapsed, post-, or otherwise—will sooner or later have to begin to deconstruct their essentialist views of "The West." Vast and pervasive historical changes in Europe and in what used to be the Soviet Union are rendering obsolete the entire geopolitical rhetoric. These events will have to have their effects on the mental and intellectual disposition of the Muslim intellectuals, rooted in their own lands or else transplanted abroad in their imagined countries. Such fresh and compelling realities entice historical imaginations of intellectuals—the institutional manipulators of cultural symbolics. There is no way to ascertain what the precise direction of such a future reconstruction of "Muslim" identity would be, how the compelling freshness of contemporary events would lead these architects of Islamic self-imagination to rearrange their historical memory. The undeniable fact remains, however, that the already elongated and overextended postcolonial discourse cannot continue to justify and sustain itself in the face of grave and immediate contradictions the world over.

With the verticality of every moral and aesthetic order leveled, where would visionary intellectuals, if any existed, locate themselves or others? Where would the place be that a Muslim intellectual could call home? Where is the corner on which a homeless mind could address, in moments of some sincerity, the compelling issues of Muslim (post)modernity, of the Islamic past, of the necessity of a reconstructed "Self" and "Other," of a permanent and final disengagement with the postcolonial discourse? Lacking that confident corner, we stand, mere individuals, upon a heap of old, scattered, useless and yet dangerous memories. Whether they control us or we them is the key criterion to any meaningful future. That future, it seems to me now, can be meaningful only in terms of our particular individualities, in plural, rather than our communal identities. That particular individuality, too, standing at the crossroads of existential realities that vary from one to another, can only construct an imaginative geography. But in that construction the individual, as opposed to any meaningful form of collectivity, at least has a wider, a less elusively susceptible, range of existential possibilities. In an otherwise impossible culture, limited possibilities are our only sign of salvation. But as I write the very last word "salvation," I realize how limited, how linguistically and thus ontologically paradoxical, we are, I am, in the finest and most irreducible moments of our, of my, individualities, individuality.

With that line we reach the end of our road. Here revolutionary myth ends and individual limitations begin. Here is one limited possibility: Beyond the immediacy and compelling inevitability of the revolutionary myth lies a larger claim on the span and stamina of our altogether too much intellectualizing about the historicity of the event itself. This is a matter of faith, a language of symbols. By the time an Umberto Ecco has constructed a science of semiology for us—and certainly in a shorter span of time than it takes the master semiotician to write a best-seller novel out of his semiotic mind—dozens of images and hundreds of mental notes have been communicated and registered. Hundreds of thousands of flyers have disseminated revolutionary signals to millions of souls before a single sentence is constructed to reflect accurately what occurs in a symbolic language, in the colorful labyrinth of a semiotic mind. To understand how symbols operate, how convictions move, how history leads, how memory commands, and how the language of faith stirs, angers, mobilizes, leads, and succeeds, we mere mortals, the academic intellectuals, have to know our inherent limitations, drop our pen, and let the masters of the symbolic tongue, practitioners of the magical discourse, speak.

"Mr Dedalus Laughed

loudly and lay back in his chair while uncle Charles swayed his head to and fro.

"Dante looked terribly angry and repeated while they laughed?

"—Very nice! Ha! Very nice! . . . .

"Mr Dedalus gave a snort of contempt.

"—Ah, John, he said. It is true for them. We are an unfortunate priest-ridden race and always were and always will be till the end of the chapter.

"Uncle Charles shook his head, saying:

"—A bad business! A bad business!

"Mr Dedalus repeated:

"—A priestridden Godforsaken race!

"He pointed to the portrait of his grandfather on the wall to his right.

"—Do you see that old chap up there, John? he said. He was a good Irishman when there was no money in the job. He was condemned to death as a whiteboy. But he had a saying about our clerical friends, that he would never let one of them put his two feet under his mahogany.

"Dante broke in angrily:

"—If we are a priestridden race we ought to be proud of it! They are the apple of God's eye. *Touch them not,* says Christ, *for they are the apple of My eye.*

"—And can we not love our country then? asked Mr Casey. Are we not to follow the man that was born to lead us?

"—A traitor to his country! replied Dante. A traitor, an adulterer! The priests were right to abandon him. The priests were always the true friends of Ireland.

"—Were they, faith? said Mr Casey.

"He threw his fist on the table and, frowning angrily, protruded one finger after another.

"—Didn't the bishops of Ireland betray us in the time of the union when bishop Lanigan presented an address of loyalty to the Marquess Cornwallis? Didn't the bishops and priests sell the aspirations of their country in 1929 in return for catholic emancipation? Didn't they denounce the fenian movement from the pulpit and in the confessionbox? And didn't they dishonour the ashes of Terence Bellew MacManus?

"His face was glowing with anger and Stephen felt the glow rise to his own cheek as the spoken words thrilled him. Mr Dedalus uttered a guffaw of coarse scorn.

"—O, by God, he cried, I forgot little old Paul Cullen! Another apple of God's eye!

"Dante bent across the table and cried to Mr Casey:

"—Right! Right! They were always right! God and morality and religion come first.

"Mrs Dedalus, seeing her excitement, said to her:

"—Mrs Riordan, don't excite yourself answering them.

"—God and religion before everything! Dante cried. God and religion before the world!

"Mr Casey raised his clenched fist and brought it down on the table with a crash.

"—Very well, then, he shouted hoarsely, if it comes to that, no God for Ireland!

"—John! John! cried Mr Dedalus, seizing his guest by the coatsleeve.

"Dante stared across the table, her cheeks shaking. Mr Casey struggled up from his chair and bent across the table towards her, scraping the air from before his eyes with one hand as though he were tearing aside a cobweb.

"—No God for Ireland! he cried. We have had too much God in Ireland. Away with God!

"—Blasphemer! Devil! screamed Dante, starting to her feet and almost spitting in his face.

"Uncle Charles and Mr Dedalus pulled Mr Casey back into his chair again, talking to him from both sides reasonably. He stared before him out of his dark flaming eyes, repeating:

"—Away with God, I say!

"Dante shoved her chair violently aside and left the table, upsetting her napkinring which rolled slowly along the carpet and came to rest against the foot of an easychair. Mrs Dedalus rose quickly and followed her towards the door. At the door Dante turned round violently and shouted down the room, her cheeks flushed and quivering with rage:

"—Devil out of hell! We won! We crushed him to death! Fiend!

"The door slammed behind her.

"Mr Casey, freeing his arms from his holders, suddenly bowed his head on his hands with a sob of pain.

"—Poor Parnell! he cried loudly. My dead king!

"He sobbed loudly and bitterly.

"Stephen, raising his terrorstricken face, saw that his father's eyes were full of tears. . . ."[44]

"[It pained him that he did not know well what politics meant and that he did not know where the universe ended. He felt small and weak. Who was right then?]"[45]

"MacMahoon took another sip, and said, 'This is the end of Mina's story. Say, "Well done," Yusof. What a story I've made from a few fabricated and real things you repeated from your twins. You said the people in your city are born poets. You can see that the people of Ireland are the same.' And he became silent."[46]

Notes

Bibliographical references in the following notes are only to the last names of the authors and the titles. Full references to all sources are in the Bibliography in alphabetical order.

Introduction

1. Quoted in Schama, *Citizens,* p. xiii.
2. For a full theoretical discussion of this approach, see the advancement of Quentin Skinner's argument and some critical assessments of it in Tully (ed.), *Meaning and Context.* Particularly relevant is Skinner's "Motives, Intentions and Interpretations of Texts," pp. 68–78.
3. For a full discussion of these three processes, see Berger, *The Sacred Canopy,* pp. 3–28.
4. See Berger's chapter on "The Process of Secularization," in Berger, *The Sacred Canopy,* pp. 105–125.
5. See Boyce, *Zoroastrianism,* pp. 20–21. An insightful discussion of the pre-Islamic ethos of Persian conceptions of political authority is to be found in Amir Arjomand, *The Shadow of God and the Hidden Imam,* pp. 85–100.
6. For a full discussion of the post-Muhammadan unfolding of the question of authority, see my *Authority in Islam.* Equally important, yet entirely different from my perspective, is Crone and Hind, *God's Caliph.*
7. For a discussion of the image of kingly authority, see Inlow, *Shahanshah,* passim.
8. See Boyce, *Zoroastrianism,* p. 25.
9. Ulmstead, *History of the Persian Empire,* p. 125; and Cook, *The Persian Empire,* pp. 58–66.
10. For a discussion of this argument, see Frankfurt, *Kingship and the Gods,* passim.
11. For a full discussion of these developments, see my *Authority in Islam,* passim.
12. For the most authoritative account of these developments in a historical and

analytical context, see Amir Arjomand's *The Shadow of God and the Hidden Imam*.

13. "Inner justification" and "external means" are the two most basic pillars of any mode of legitimate authority as typologized by Max Weber. For a short account of the statement, see Weber, "Politics as a Vocation," in Weber, *From Max Weber*, pp. 77–128. For the original German version of this seminal essay, see Weber, *Gesammelte Politische Schriften*, pp. 505–560. For fuller accounts of Weber's typologies, see his *Wirtschaft und Gesellschaft*, Kapitel III, "Die Typen der Herrschaft," pp. 122–176. For the English translation of this text, see Weber, *Economy and Society*, Roth and Wittich (eds.), chapter III, "The Types of Legitimate Domination," pp. 212–301. For the difficulty of translating the word *Herrschaft* into English, see Mommsen, *The Age of Bureaucracy*, pp. 72–94. Further on the problem of authority, see Bierstedt, *Power and Progress*, pp. 242–259.

14. For various discussions of the origins and development of *velayat-e faqih* as a juridical and political category, see Enayat, "Iran: Khumayni's Concept of the 'Guardianship of the Jurisconsult,' " in Piscatori (ed.), *Islam in the Political Process*, pp. 160–180; and Bayat, "The Iranian Revolution of 1978–1979: Fundamentalist or Modern?" For the most reliable translation of Khomeini's treatise on *velayat-e faqih*, see Khomeini, *Islam and Revolution*. For a discussion of Mulla Ahmad Naraqi's ideas on *velayat-e faqih*, as an antecedent of Khomeini's thoughts, see my "Early Propagation of *Wilayat-i Faqih* and Mulla Ahmad Naraqi," in Nasr, Dabashi, and Nasr (eds.), *Expectation of the Millennium*, pp. 287–300. For a full discussion of the question of just ruler in Shiʿism that can provide a background to this issue, see Sachedina, *The Just Ruler in Shiʿite Islam*. This is not a totally reliable source. See a critical review of it in Modarressi, "The Just Ruler or the Guardian Jurist: An Attempt to Link Two Different Shiʿite Concepts."

15. For a full account of the Mahdistic tendency in Shiʿism, see Sachedina, *Islamic Messianism*.

16. Particularly significant in this regard are the ideas of Muhammad Jawad Mughniyah. For a full discussion of his ideas, see Göbel, *Moderne schiitische politik und Staatsidee*, pp. 65–139. For a sample of the conflicting views on the juridical and political authorities of the Shiʿi religious figures, see Algar, "The Oppositional Role of the Ulama in Twentieth Century Iran," in Keddie (ed.), *Scholars, Saints, and Sufis*; Floor, "The Revolutionary Character of the Iranian Ulama: Wishful Thinking or Reality?" in Keddie (ed.), *Religion and Politics in Iran*, pp. 73–97; Eliash, "Some Misconceptions Regarding the Juridical Status of the Iranian Ulama"; Eliash, "The Ithna Ashari-Shiʿi Juridic Theory of Political and Legal Authority."

17. For a discussion of Molla Ahmad Naraqi's ideas, see my "Early Propagation of *Wilayat-i Faqih* and Mulla Ahmad Naraqi," in Nasr, Dabashi, and Nasr (eds.), *Expectation of the Millennium*, pp. 287–300.

18. See Naraqi, *Awa'id al-Ayyam*, p. 186.

19. For a full account of Khomeini's formulation of *velayat-e faqih*, see Algar's translation of "The Islamic Government," in Khomeini, *Islam and Revolution*, pp. 25–166.

20. See Montazeri, *Dirasat fi Vilayah al-Faqih: Fiqh al-Dawlah al-Islamiyyah*.

21. For a full critical discussion of "the *absolute velayat-e faqih*," see Anony-

mous, *Velayat-e Motlaqeh-ye Faqih.* See also Keddie, "The Roots of the Ulama's Power in Modern Iran," in Keddie (ed.), *Scholars, Saints, and Sufis,* pp. 211–229.

22. For a full discussion of the significance of nationalism, democracy, and socialism in modern Islamic political thought, see Enayat, *Modern Islamic Political Thought.* For some additional reflections on Enayat's text, see my review essay, "The Revolutions of Our Time: Religious Politics in Modernity," pp. 673–676.

23. For an insightful discussion of the interaction between secular ideologies and the Islamic heritage, see Binder, *Islamic Liberalism.*

24. Enayat, *Modern Islamic Political Thought,* p. 111.

25. For a full discussion of the problems of nationalism in Iran, see Cottam, *Nationalism in Iran.* See also Katouzian, "Nationalist Trends in Iran, 1921–1926."

26. For the latest research on Mosaddeq, see Mosaddeq, *Musaddiq's Memoirs,* and Katouzian, *Musaddiq and the Struggle for Power in Iran.*

27. On this and related issues, see Sanjabi's recollections in his memoir, *Omid-ha va Na-Omidi-ha: Khaterat-e Siasi.*

28. On some of these contradictions, see Enayat's discussion in his *Modern Islamic Political Thought,* pp. 126 ff. See also Cottam's observations in *Nationalism in Iran,* passim.

29. On points of divergence and convergence between Islam and socialism, see Enayat, *Modern Islamic Political Thought,* passim; Rodinson, *Marxism and the Muslim World;* and the same author's *Islam and Capitalism.*

30. On the history of the rise of radical movements in Iran, see Zabih, *The Communist Movement in Iran.* For an excellent account of the multiplicity of political discourses in modern Iran, see Kazemi, *Politics and Culture in Iran.* The varieties of political languages that Kazemi discusses here have been instrumental in the expansion of what Said Amir Arjomand has called "the expansion of the political society." See [Amir] Arjomand, "The Causes and Significance of the Iranian Revolution," p. 43.

31. For the most authoritative account of the *Mojahedin-e Khalq* Organization, see Abrahamian, *Radical Islam.*

32. For a preliminary treatment of this aspect of "The Islamic Ideology," see my "The Islamic Ideology: The Perils and Promises of a Neologism," in Amir Ahmadi and Parvin (eds.), *Post-Revolutionary Iran,* pp. 11–22.

33. For insightful comments on the significance of this aspect of Al-e Ahmad's ideas, see the appropriate passages in Mottahedeh, *The Mantle of the Prophet,* particularly pp. 293 ff.

34. For a discussion of these aspects of Shari'ati's ideas, see my "Ali Shari'ati's Islam: Revolutionary Uses of Faith in a Post-Traditional Society," pp. 203–222.

35. For a discussion of Shari'ati's ideas on, and as influenced by, Marxism, see his *Jahat-giri-ye Tabaqati-e Islam.* This particular volume of Shari'ati's collected work is rather difficult to locate. I am grateful to Ervand Abrahamian for giving me a copy of the book.

36. See Alavi, *Panjah-o Seh Nafar.*

37. See Khameh'i, *Khaterat-e Anvar-e Khameh'i.*

38. Khameh'i, *Khaterat,* pp. 14–28.

39. Khameh'i, *Khaterat,* pp. 31–35.

40. Khameh'i, *Khaterat*, passim.

41. See Abrahamian, *Iran between Two Revolutions*, pp. 484–485.

42. For one such collection of poetry, see Kho'i, *Siahkal*.

43. See Ricoeur, *Lectures on Ideology and Utopia*, p. 17.

44. See Weber, "Politics as a Vocation," in Weber, *From Max Weber*, p. 78.

45. See Ayatollah Khomeini's speech upon his arrival in Tehran at the Behesht-e Zahra' Cemetery in his collected letters and declarations, *Sahifeh-ye Nur*, vol. 4, pp. 281–287.

46. See Ricoeur, *Lectures on Ideology and Utopia*, p. 14.

47. See Marx and Engels, *The German Ideology*, p. 47.

48. Marx and Engels, *The German Ideology*, p. 47.

49. Marx and Engels, *The German Ideology*, p. 47.

50. See Althusser, *For Marx*, p. 232, or as quoted and discussed in Ricoeur, *Lectures on Ideology and Utopia*, p. 137.

51. See Ricoeur, *Lectures on Ideology and Utopia*, p. 137.

52. Ricoeur, *Lectures on Ideology and Utopia*, p. 137.

53. Ricoeur, *Lectures on Ideology and Utopia*, p. 137.

54. See Weber, "Politics as a Vocation," in Weber, *From Max Weber*, p. 78.

55. Weber, "Politics as a Vocation," in Weber, *From Max Weber*, p. 78.

56. See Weber, "Politics as a Vocation," in Weber, *From Max Weber*, pp. 78–79.

57. See Habermas, *Legitimation Crisis*, p. 97.

58. Habermas, *Legitimation Crisis*, p. 97.

59. Habermas, *Legitimation Crisis*, p. 97.

60. See Geertz, "Ideology as a Cultural System," in Geertz, *The Interpretation of Cultures*, p. 229.

61. Geertz, "Ideology as a Cultural System," in Geertz, *The Interpretation of Cultures*, p. 229.

62. Geertz, "Ideology as a Cultural System," in Geertz, *The Interpretation of Cultures*, p. 229.

63. The statement is by J. C. Droysen in his *Outline of the Principles of History*, pp. 45–46, or as quoted and discussed in Mannheim, *Ideology and Utopia*, p. 199.

64. See Ricoeur, *Lectures on Ideology and Utopia*, p. 314.

65. On the making of this dialectic, see my "The Islamic Ideology: The Perils and Promises of a Neologism," in Amir Ahmadi and Parvin (eds.), *Post-Revolutionary Iran*, passim.

66. See Skinner, *The Foundations of Modern Political Thought*, vol. 1, p. xi.

67. See Merton, "The Sociology of Knowledge," in Merton, *Social Theory and Social Structure*, pp. 514–515.

68. For the entire discussion, see Mannheim, "The Nature and Scope of the Sociology of Knowledge," in Mannheim, *Ideology and Utopia*, pp. 264–311.

69. Mannheim, "The Nature and Scope of the Sociology of Knowledge," in Mannheim, *Ideology and Utopia*, p. 266 ff.

70. See Mead, *Mind, Self, and Society*, pp. 152–164 and 173–178. See also Hughes, "What Other?" in Hughes, *The Sociological Eye*, pp. 348–354. For a pioneering study of "self" in its religious context, see Schlossmann, *Persona und ΠΡΟΣΩΠΟΝ*, particularly the historical discussion of "Geschichte des Wortes

Persona," pp. 11–21. Schlossmann's discussion is resumed and expanded with a more sociological bent by Mauss in "A Category of the Human Mind: The Notion of Person, the Notion of 'Self,' " in Mauss, *Sociology and Psychology,* pp. 57–94. Hughes's "Work and Self," in Hughes, *The Sociological Eye,* pp. 338–347, also has some other reflections on the relation between the formation of Self and its environmental context.

71. See Geertz, "Art as a Cultural System," in Geertz, *Local Knowledge,* p. 97.

72. For a discussion of this phrase of Ezra Pound on the necessity of modernity, see Bradbury, *The Modern World,* p. 3 ff.

73. See Shils, "The Intellectuals and the Powers: Some Perspectives for Comparative Analysis," in Rieff (ed.), *On Intellectuals,* p. 26.

74. Shils, "The Intellectuals and the Powers," in Rieff (ed.), *On Intellectuals,* p. 26.

75. Shils, "The Intellectuals and the Powers," in Rieff (ed.), *On Intellectuals,* p. 26.

76. See Bell, *The End of Ideology,* p. 393.

77. Bell, *The End of Ideology,* p. 400.

78. Bell, *The End of Ideology,* p. 402.

79. Bell, *The End of Ideology,* p. 405.

80. See Fukuyama, "The End of History?" p. 3. Fukuyama is categorically dismissive of any universal significance for Islam: "In the contemporary world only Islam has offered a theocratic state as a political alternative to both liberalism and communism. But the doctrine has little appeal for non-Muslims; and it is hard to believe that the movement will take on any universal significance" (p. 14). Compare this with the defensive pronouncement of Claude Levi-Strauss about Islam made some four years earlier in Grisoni (comp. and ed.), "Levi-Strauss en 33 Mots," p. 26: "Islam: Une religion que je connais mal. J'ajouterai pourtant que nous sommes aujourd'hui les protagonistes d'un phénomène assez parodoxal de l'histoire, auquel l'Islam me semble mêlé. . . . J'ai commencé à refléchir à un moment au notre culture agressait d'autres cultures dont je me suis alors fait le défenseur et le témoin. Maintenant, j'ai l'impression que le movement s'est inversé et que notre culture est sur la défensive vis-à-vis de menaces extérieures, parmi lesquelles figure probablement l'explosion Islamic. Du coup je me sens fermement et ethnologiquement défenseur de ma culture."

81. See Bloom, *The Closing of the American Mind;* for a critical examination of Allan Bloom's arguments, see Stone (ed.), *Essays on the Closing of the American Mind.*

82. See "Responses to Fukuyama," in Fukuyama, "The End of History?" p. 19.

83. See Weber, "Science as a Vocation," in Weber, *From Max Weber,* pp. 129–156, especially pp. 155–156.

84. See Eagleton, *The Ideology of the Aesthetic,* p. 95.

85. See Rieff, *Fellow Teachers,* p. 71. For a new edition of this text with a new Introduction, see Rieff, *Fellow Teachers: Of Culture and Its Second Death.* See also Ferrarotti, "The Paradox of the Sacred," and Elliott, "Biological Roots of Violence."

86. Rieff, *Fellow Teachers: Of Culture and Its Second Death,* p. 102.

87. See Parsons, *Essays in Sociological Theory Pure and Applied,* p. 153.

88. See Schutz, "Max Scheller's Epistemology and Ethics: I," pp. 307–309.

89. Schutz, "Max Scheller's Epistemology and Ethics: I," p. 308.

90. Schutz, "Max Scheller's Epistemology and Ethics: I," p. 308.

91. Schutz, "Max Scheller's Epistemology and Ethics: I," p. 308.

92. See Weber, "Science as a Vocation," in Weber, *From Max Weber*, p. 155. See also Wrong, *Power*, pp. 60–64.

93. Weber, "Science as a Vocation," in Weber, *From Max Weber*, p. 155.

94. Weber, "Science as a Vocation," in Weber, *From Max Weber*, p. 155.

95. Weber, "Science as a Vocation," in Weber, *From Max Weber*, p. 155.

96. Weber, "Science as a Vocation," in Weber, *From Max Weber*, p. 155. For a discussion of the oscillation between rationalization and myth in Weber's own thoughts, see Mommsen, *The Political and Social Theory of Max Weber*, pp. 133–144.

97. Weber, "Science as a Vocation," in Weber, *From Max Weber*, p. 155.

98. Weber, "Science as a Vocation," in Weber, *From Max Weber*, p. 155.

99. Weber, "Science as a Vocation," in Weber, *From Max Weber*, p. 155.

100. Weber, "Science as a Vocation," in Weber, *From Max Weber*, p. 155.

1. Jalal Al-e Ahmad

1. For the text of George Sand's letter to Gustave Flaubert, see Ellmann and Feidelson (eds.), *The Modern Tradition*, pp. 312–15.

2. Ellmann and Feidelson (eds.), *The Modern Tradition*, pp. 312–313.

3. Al-e Ahmad, *By the Pen*, p. 115. I have modified Ghanoonparvar's translation slightly.

4. There is no biography of Al-e Ahmad. Scattered materials do exist; and Michael Hillmann is in the process of writing a biography. A short autobiographical sketch is to be found in Al-e Ahmad, "Masalan Sharh-e Ahvalat," in Tabrizi (ed.), *Jalal Al-e Ahmad*, pp. 62–68. For a translation of this piece, see Al-e Ahmad, *Iranian Society: An Anthology of Writings*, pp. 14–19. Equally informative is Daneshvar, "Shohar-e Man Jalal." For an excellent short account of Al-e Ahmad's life and dilemmas, see Hillmann, *Iranian Culture*, pp. 119–144.

5. For a useful discussion of Iran in the 1920s, see Knapp, "1921–1941: The Period of Riza Shah," in Lenczowski (ed.), *Iran under the Pahlavis*, pp. 23–51.

6. See Jamalzadeh's letter to Zamani-nia in Zamani-nia (ed.), *Farhang-e Jalal Al-e Ahmad*, p. 20. This "Encyclopaedia" of Al-e Ahmad's writings, thematically organized, is an extremely useful research tool from which I have made frequent quotations.

7. For a general review of Reza Shah's reign and his policies and politics, see Alamuti, *Iran dar Asr-i Pahlavi*, vol. 1.

8. See Al-e Ahmad, *Gharbzadegi*.

9. This is the general consensus from my interviews with a number of his classmates at the *Dar al-Fonun*.

10. This is also from my interviews with some of his classmates.

11. For a representative sample of Ahmad Kasravi's ideas, see his *Sarnevesht-e Iran Cheh Khahad Bud?* and *Emruz Chareh Chist?*

12. This is an observation I have heard from a number of former Tudeh Party members as well as several former Kasravites.

13. For a discussion of the rise of communism in Iran, see Zabih, *The Communist Movement in Iran*.

14. For a useful discussion of the emergence of new ideas in this period, see Adamiyyat, *Fekr-e Demokrasi-e Ejtemaʿi dar Nehzat-e Mashrutiyyat-e Iran*. For the ideas of a particularly significant intellectual, see Adamiyyat, *Andisheh-ha-ye Mirza Aqa Khan-e Kermani*.

15. See Zabih, *The Communist Movement in Iran*, pp. 71–122.

16. Zabih, *The Communist Movement in Iran*, pp. 98–107.

17. Zabih, *The Communist Movement in Iran*, p. 106.

18. Some former members of the Tudeh Party report that Maleki was resentful that he had not advanced to the top echelon of the party. Nonetheless, this should not detract from his ideological divergence from the mainline orthodoxy of the party's policies. For a discussion of Maleki's relationship to the Tudeh Party, see Katouzian, *Musaddiq and the Struggle for Power in Iran*, pp. 95 ff. Equally informative is Katouzian (ed.), *Khaterat-e Siasi-ye Khalil Maleki*.

19. Al-e Ahmad, *Yek Chah va Do Chaleh*, pp. 23–27; and as quoted in Zamani-nia (ed.), *Farhang-e Jalal Al-e Ahmad*, pp. 138–139. There are those members of the Tudeh Party who, of course, do not concur on Al-e Ahmad's version of the story of this break with the party. For yet another view of the event, see Khameh'i, *Panjah Nafar va Seh Nafar*, passim.

20. Who wishes to remain anonymous.

21. Al-e Ahmad, *Dar Khedmat va Khianat-e Roshanfekran*, p. 344; and as quoted in Zamani-nia (ed.), *Farhang-e Jalal Al-e Ahamd*, p. 109.

22. Al-e Ahmad, *Dar Khedmat va Khianat-e Roshanfekran*, pp. 343–344; and Zamani-nia (ed.), *Farhang-e Jalal Al-e Ahmad*, pp. 135–136.

23. For representative views of Parviz Natel Khanlari, the editor of *Sokhan*, on modern Persian literature, see his *Haftad Sokhan*, vol. 1.

24. See Daneshvar, "Shohar-e Man Jalal," p. 7.

25. See Kianush, "Al-e Ahmad dar Dastan-ha-ye Kutahash," in Dehbashi (ed.), *Yadnameh-ye Jalal Al-e Ahmad*, pp. 440–472. Ali Dehbashi's dedication to Al-e Ahmad's legacy has been instrumental in collecting and editing otherwise scattered pieces on his writings. His *Yadnameh-ye Jalal Al-e Ahmad* has been very useful in my readings on Al-e Ahmad.

26. Kianush, "Al-e Ahmad dar Dastan-ha-ye Kutahash," in Dehbashi (ed.), *Yadnameh-ye Jalal Al-e Ahmad*, p. 449.

27. Kianush, "Al-e Ahmad dar Dastan-ha-ye Kutahash," in Dehbashi (ed.), *Yadnameh-ye Jalal Al-e Ahmad*, pp. 446–456.

28. Al-e Ahmad, *Nefrin-e Zamin*, p. 81; and Zamani-nia (ed.), *Farhang-e Jalal Al-e Ahmad*, p. 66.

29. Al-e Ahmad, *Nefrin-e Zamin*, p. 59; and Zamani-nia (ed.), *Farhang-e Jalal Al-e Ahmad*, pp. 192–193.

30. Al-e Ahmad, *Nefrin-e Zamin*, p. 59; and Zamani-nia (ed.), *Farhang-e Jalal Al-e Ahmad*, pp. 192–193.

31. Al-e Ahmad, *Arzyabi-ye Shetab-zadeh*, pp. 243–244; and Zamani-nia (ed.),

Farhang-e Jalal Al-e Ahmad, p. 192. For a sample of Al-e Ahmad's social criticism, see his "What Are the University and Education Doing?"

32. Al-e Ahmad, *Nefrin-e Zamin*, p. 86; and Zamani-nia (ed.), *Farhang-e Jalal Al-e Ahmad*, pp. 197–198.

33. Al-e Ahmad, *Sargozasht-e Kandu-ha'*, p. 54; and Zamani-nia (ed.), *Farhang-e Jalal Al-e Ahmad*, p. 67.

34. Al-e Ahmad, *Sargozasht-e Kandu-ha'*, pp. 56–88; and Zamani-nia (ed.), *Farhang-e Jalal Al-e Ahmad*, pp. 120–121.

35. Al-e Ahmad, *Nun Va al-Qalam*, p. 160; and Zamani-nia (ed.), *Farhang-e Jalal Al-e Ahmad*, pp. 69–70.

36. Al-e Ahmad, *Nun Va al-Qalam*, p. 195; and Zamani-nia (ed.), *Farhang-e Jalal Al-e Ahmad*, p. 77.

37. For a representative sample of his style of writing, see Khabiri, "Dar Iqlim-e Nathr-e Jalal Al-e Ahmad," in Tabrizi (ed.), *Jalal Al-e Ahmad*, pp. 83–96. For a historical perspective, see Heydari, "Az Monsha'at-e Qa'im Maqam ta Khasi dar Miqat," in Dehbashi (ed.), *Yadnameh-ye Jalal Al-e Ahmad*, pp. 517–526. For a more general discussion of the significance of language in modern Iranian society, see Beeman, *Language, Status, and Power in Iran*. My reservations about this text are expressed in my review of it in *Iranian Studies*.

38. See Kianush, "Al-e Ahmad dar Dastan-ha-ye Kutahash," in Dehbashi (ed.), *Yadnameh-ye Jalal Al-e Ahmad*, especially pp. 463–477. For other sympathetic views on Al-e Ahmad's fiction, see Ali Asghar Zarrabi's interview with Simin Daneshvar, "Jalal: Bozorgtarin Qesseh-nevis-e Imruz," in Tabrizi (ed.), *Jalal Al-e Ahmad*, pp. 73–82. For samples of Al-e Ahmad's fiction, see his "The Mobilization of Iran," which includes a good biographical note by Michael C. Hillmann, and "The Cursing of the Land: A Plot Summary."

39. Gide, *Bazgasht-e Az Shoravi*, pp. 11–12; and Zamani-nia (ed.), *Farhang-e Jalal Al-e Ahmad*, pp. 194–195.

40. Gide, *Bazgasht-e Az Shoravi*, p. 10; and Zamani-nia (ed.), *Farhang-e Jalal Al-e Ahmad*, pp. 195–196.

41. Al-e Ahmad, *Kharg*, p. 11.

42. Al-e Ahmad, *Kharg*, p. 11.

43. Al-e Ahmad, *Tat-nishin-ha-yi Boluk-e Zahra'*, p. 14.

44. Al-e Ahmad, *Kharg*, p. 12.

45. Al-e Ahmad, *Kharg*, p. 14.

46. Al-e Ahmad, *Urazan*, p. 6.

47. Al-e Ahmad, *Urazan*, p. 1 of the English preface.

48. Al-e Ahmad, *Urazan*, p. 8.

49. Al-e Ahmad, *Dar Khedmat va Khianat-e Roshanfekran*, pp. 362–363; and Zamani-nia (ed.), *Farhang-e Jalal Al-e Ahmad*, p. 115.

50. Al-e Ahmad, *Kar-nameh-ye Seh Saleh*, pp. 200–201; and Zamani-nia (ed.), *Farhang-e Jalal Al-e Ahmad*, p. 194.

51. Al-e Ahmad, *Kar-nameh-ye Seh Saleh*, p. 89; and Zamani-nia (ed.), *Farhang-e Jalal Al-e Ahmad*, p. 178.

52. Al-e Ahmad, *Kar-nameh-ye Seh Saleh*, p. 182; and Zamani-nia (ed.), *Farhang-e Jalal Al-e Ahmad*, pp. 224–225.

53. Al-e Ahmad, *Kar-nameh-ye Seh Saleh*, p. 183; and Zamani-nia (ed.), *Far-hang-e Jalal Al-e Ahmad*, p. 225.

54. Al-e Ahmad, *Seh Maqaleh-ye Digar*, p. 22.

55. Al-e Ahmad, *Seh Maqaleh-ye Digar*, p. 55.

56. Al-e Ahmad, *Seh Maqaleh-ye Digar*, pp. 13–14.

57. Al-e Ahmad, *Seh Maqaleh-ye Digar*, p. 13.

58. Al-e Ahmad, *Kar-nameh-ye Seh Saleh*, pp. 93–94.

59. Al-e Ahmad, *Kar-nameh-ye Seh Saleh*, p. 74.

60. Al-e Ahmad, *Kar-nameh-ye Seh Saleh*, p. 159.

61. See Shams Al-e Ahmad's Introduction to Al-e Ahmad, *Safar beh Velayat-e Isra'il*, p. 10.

62. See Al-e Ahmad's references to that effect in *Dar Khedmat va Khianat-e Roshanfekran*, pp. 366–367.

63. See Shams Al-e Ahmad's Introduction to Al-e Ahmad, *Safar beh Velayat-e Isra'il*, p. 11.

64. Shams Al-e Ahmad's Introduction to Al-e Ahmad, *Safar beh Velayat-e Isra'il*, p. 11.

65. Al-e Ahmad, *Sangi bar Guri*, p. 37.

66. See Shams Al-e Ahmad's Introduction to Al-e Ahmad, *Safar beh Velayat-e Isra'il*, p. 11.

67. Shams Al-e Ahmad's Introduction to Al-e Ahmad, *Safar beh Velayat-e Isra'il*, p. 14. For a sympathetic reading of Al-e Ahmad's travels, see Kazim Sadat-e Oshkuri, "Siahat-nameh-ye Za'eri az Rusta'," in Tabrizi (ed.), *Jalal Al-e Ahmad*, pp. 27–30.

68. Shams Al-e Ahmad's Introduction to Al-e Ahmad, *Safar beh Velayat-e Isra'il*, pp. 15–16.

69. Shams Al-e Ahmad's Introduction to Al-e Ahmad, *Safar beh Velayat-e Isra'il*, p. 36.

70. Shams Al-e Ahmad's Introduction to Al-e Ahmad, *Safar beh Velayat-e Isra'il*, p. 37.

71. Shams Al-e Ahmad's Introduction to Al-e Ahmad, *Safar beh Velayat-e Isra'il*, p. 39.

72. Shams Al-e Ahmad's Introduction to Al-e Ahmad, *Safar beh Velayat-e Isra'il*, pp. 40–43.

73. Al-e Ahmad, *Safar beh Velayat-e Isra'il*, p. 50.

74. Al-e Ahmad, *Safar beh Velayat-e Isra'il*, p. 52.

75. Al-e Ahmad, *Safar beh Velayat-e Isra'il*, p. 57. For a good review of Al-e Ahmad's travel literature, see Naser Vothuqi's "Az Urazan ta Kharg," in Dehbashi (ed.), *Yadnameh-ye Jalal Al-e Ahmad*, pp. 473–489.

76. Al-e Ahmad, *Safar beh Velayat-e Isra'il*, p. 58.

77. Al-e Ahmad, *Safar beh Velayat-e Isra'il*, pp. 62–63.

78. Al-e Ahmad, *Safar beh Velayat-e Isra'il*, p. 84.

79. Al-e Ahmad, *Safar beh Velayat-e Isra'il*, p. 90.

80. Al-e Ahmad, *Safar beh Velayat-e Isra'il*, p. 92.

81. Al-e Ahmad, *Safar beh Velayat-e Isra'il*, p. 92.

82. Al-e Ahmad, *Safar beh Velayat-e Isra'il*, p. 93.

83. Al-e Ahmad, *Safar beh Velayat-e Isra'il*, p. 11. See Al-e Ahmad, *Khasi dar Miqat*. This book has been translated into English; see Al-e Ahmad, *Lost in the Crowd*.

84. Al-e Ahmad, *Khasi dar Miqat*, pp. 84–85.

85. See Shams Al-e Ahmad's Introduction to Al-e Ahmad, *Safar beh Velayat-e Isra'il*, p. 12.

86. Shams Al-e Ahmad's Introduction to Al-e Ahmad, *Safar beh Velayat-e Isra'il*, p. 12. Unpublished also are Al-e Ahmad's diaries which are with his wife, Simin Daneshvar. Some of his writings are also said, by his brother Shams, to have been stolen by SAVAK, the Iranian Secret Police. This, however, cannot be otherwise verified. See Shams Al-e Ahmad's Introduction to Al-e Ahmad, *Safar beh Velayat-e Isra'il*, pp. 12–13.

87. Shams Al-e Ahmad's Introduction to Al-e Ahmad, *Safar beh Velayat-e Isra'il*, p. 13.

88. Hanibal Ilkhas pays Al-e Ahmad one of his highest compliments: "This son of an Akhond knew wine better than a Parisian." See Hanibal Ilkhas, "Hichkas Jayash ra por Nakhahad Kard," in Tabrizi (ed.), *Jalal Al-e Ahmad*, p. 51.

89. Al-e Ahmad, *Gharbzadegi*, pp. 11–12. For a pioneering critique of Al-e Ahmad's views of "Gharbzadegi," see Daryush Ashuri, "Negahi beh Gharbzadeqi va Mabani-ye Nazari-ye An," in Dehbashi (ed.), *Yadnameh-ye Jalal Al-e Ahmad*, pp. 490–513.

90. Al-e Ahmad, *Gharbzadegi*, p. 15.

91. Al-e Ahmad, *Gharbzadegi*, p. 15. Ernst Jünger, essayist and writer, was a contemporary of Martin Heidegger. *Obur az Khat* was the Persian translation of Jünger's *Über die Linie*. Heidegger's *The Question of Being*, translated by Kluback and Wilde, was written in response to Jünger's *Über die Linie*. See Neske and Kettering (eds.), *Martin Heidegger and National Socialism*, pp. 17–18, 110, 119, 142, 180, 191, 249, and 266. Jünger's *Der Arbeiter Herrschaft und Gestalt*, published in 1932, was a crucial contribution to existentialism. Both in this book and in *Über die Linie*, Jünger considers man as the victim of technology. In part, this issue was Al-e Ahmad's concern in *Gharbzadegi*. On the occasion of Jünger's sixtieth birthday, Heidegger wrote him a long letter and titled it, "Über 'die Linie.'" This letter is one of the best expositions of Heidegger's criticism of technology. For the German text of this letter and its English translation, see *The Question of Being*.

92. Al-e Ahmad, *Gharbzadegi*, p. 16.

93. Al-e Ahmad, *Gharbzadegi*, p. 17. For a sympathic reading of *Gharbzadegi*, see Bahram Rezayen, "Gharbzadegi: Marthiyyeh-ye Jahan-e Chapavol Shodeh," in Tabrizi (ed.), *Jalal Al-e Ahmad*, pp. 69–72.

94. Al-e Ahmad, *Gharbzadegi*, p. 17.

95. Al-e Ahmad, *Gharbzadegi*, p. 16.

96. Al-e Ahmad, *Gharbzadegi*, p. 17.

97. Al-e Ahmad, *Gharbzadegi*, p. 18. For another critical perspective on *Gharbzadegi*, see Isma'il Nuri-Ala', "Ma'na-ye Ejtema'i-Siasi-ye Gharbzadegi," in Dehbashi (ed.), *Yadnameh-ye Jalal Al-e Ahmad*, pp. 527–537.

98. Al-e Ahmad, *Gharbzadegi*, p. 22.

99. Al-e Ahmad, *Gharbzadegi*, p. 23.

100. Al-e Ahmad, *Gharbzadegi*, pp. 17–18.

101. Al-e Ahmad, *Gharbzadegi*, p. 21.

102. Al-e Ahmad, *Gharbzadegi*, pp. 21–22.

103. Al-e Ahmad, *Gharbzadegi*, pp. 168–169.

104. This is a reference to a quatrain of the medieval Persian poet Omar Khayyam (c.1048–1131). The following is Fitzgerald's close approximation:

Think, in this battered Caravanserai
Whose Doorways are alternate Night and Day,
How sultan after sultan with his pomp
Abode his Hour or two, and went his way.

See Khayyam, *Rubaiyat of Omar Khayyam*, p. 48.

105. Al-e Ahmad, *Gharbzadegi*, p. 87.

106. Al-e Ahmad, *Gharbzadegi*, p. 117.

107. For a partisan review of such charges against Al-e Ahmad, and a spirited response to them, see Mostafa' Zamani-nia's Introduction to Zamani-nia (ed.), *Farhang-e Jalal Al-e Ahmad*, pp. 26–27.

108. Mostafa' Zamani-nia's Introduction to Zamani-nia (ed.), *Farhang-e Jalal Al-e Ahmad*, p. 27.

109. Mostafa' Zamani-nia's Introduction to Zamani-nia (ed.), *Farhang-e Jalal Al-e Ahmad*, p. 31.

110. *Keyhan* newspaper, 4 Shahrivar 1358/26 August 1979, p. 5.

111. *Keyhan* newspaper, 4 Shahrivar 1358/26 August 1979, p. 5.

112. *Keyhan* newspaper, 4 Shahrivar 1358/26 August 1979, p. 5.

113. Al-e Ahmad, *Gharbzadegi*, p. 142, footnote.

114. Again see Mostafa' Zamani-nia's Introduction to Zamani-nia (ed.), *Farhang-e Jalal Al-e Ahmad*, p. 107.

115. Al-e Ahmad, *Dar Khedmat va Khianat-e Roshanfekran*, pp. 327–328; and Zamani-nia (ed.), *Farhang-e Jalal Al-e Ahmad*, p. 55.

116. Zamani-nia (ed.), *Farhang-e Jalal Al-e Ahmad*, pp. 55–56.

117. Zamani-nia (ed.), *Farhang-e Jalal Al-e Ahmad*, pp. 43–44.

118. Zamani-nia (ed.), *Farhang-e Jalal Al-e Ahmad*, p. 45.

119. See Weber, "Politics as a Vocation," in Weber, *From Max Weber*, p. 78.

120. Similar ideas are present in Al-e Ahmad, *Kar-nameh-ye Seh Saleh*, for example, p. 140; also in Zamani-nia (ed.), *Farhang-e Jalal Al-e Ahmad*, pp. 54–55.

121. Al-e Ahmad, *Kar-nameh-ye Seh Saleh*, and Zamani-nia (ed.), *Farhang-e Jalal Al-e Ahmad*, pp. 54–55.

122. Al-e Ahmad, *Gharbzadegi*, p. 28.

123. Al-e Ahmad, *Gharbzadegi*, pp. 53–54.

124. Al-e Ahmad, *Gharbzadegi*, p. 78.

125. Al-e Ahmad, *Gharbzadegi*, p. 137.

126. Al-e Ahmad, *Gharbzadegi*, p. 104.

127. Al-e Ahmad, *Gharbzadegi*, p. 111.

128. Al-e Ahmad's reference, in *Gharbzadegi*, p. 111, footnote, is to René Grousset, *La Face de l'Asie*, p. 132.

129. Al-e Ahmad, *Gharbzadegi*, p. 111, footnote.

130. Al-e Ahmad, *Kar-nameh-ye Seh Saleh*, p. 164; and Zamani-nia (ed.), *Farhang-e Jalal Al-e Ahmad*, p. 171.

534 1. Jalal Al-e Ahmad

131. Al-e Ahmad, *Gharbzadegi*, p. 110.

132. See Al-e Ahmad's letter to Amir Pishdad and his note to this effect in Dehbashi (ed.), *Nameh-ha-ye Jalal Al-e Ahmad*, pp. 203–204.

133. See Al-e Ahmad, *Dar Khedmat va Khianat-e Roshanfekran*, vol. 1, p. 16.

134. Al-e Ahmad, *Dar Khedmat va Khianat-e Roshanfekran*, vol. 1, p. 16.

135. I have heard this from the regular members of those luncheon meetings.

136. Al-e Ahmad, *Dar Khedmat va Khianat-e Roshanfekran*, vol. 2, pp. 149–150.

137. Al-e Ahmad, *Dar Khedmat va Khianat-e Roshanfekran*, vol. 2, pp. 320–321; and Zamani-nia (ed.), *Farhang-e Jalal Al-e Ahmad*, p. 101.

138. Zamani-nia (ed.), *Farhang-e Jalal Al-e Ahmad*, p. 103.

139. Zamani-nia (ed.), *Farhang-e Jalal Al-e Ahmad*, p. 108.

140. Zamani-nia (ed.), *Farhang-e Jalal Al-e Ahmad*, p. 108.

141. Zamani-nia (ed.), *Farhang-e Jalal Al-e Ahmad*, p. 108.

142. Zamani-nia (ed.), *Farhang-e Jalal Al-e Ahmad*, pp. 108–109.

143. Zamani-nia (ed.), *Farhang-e Jalal Al-e Ahmad*, p. 109.

144. Zamani-nia (ed.), *Farhang-e Jalal Al-e Ahmad*, p. 110. For an insightful discussion of Al-e Ahmad's position on religion, see Mottahedeh, *The Mantle of the Prophet*, pp. 299–305. Incidentally, I think Mottahedeh's translation of "Euromania" for "Gharbzadegi" leaves much of the weight of "Gharb"—which is "West" not "Europe"—behind. The construction of "The West" as a monolythic "Other," quintessentially different from the historical experiences of "Europe," is central to the ideological disposition of Al-e Ahmad and all other Muslim ideologues in modernity. While I am on the subject of Mottahedeh's book, let me also say that I think *The Mantle of the Prophet* is the single most successful text on modern Iranian intellectual history, a theme all but abandoned by modern Iranian scholarship. For some enduring theoretical observations on the subject of intellectual history, see Hughes, *Consciousness and Society*, pp. 3–32. For a critical assessment of *The Mantle of the Prophet*, see Sadri and Sadri, "*The Mantle of the Prophet*: A Critical Postscript."

145. Zamani-nia (ed.), *Farhang-e Jalal Al-e Ahmad*, p. 112.

146. Zamani-nia (ed.), *Farhang-e Jalal Al-e Ahmad*, p. 198.

147. Zamani-nia (ed.), *Farhang-e Jalal Al-e Ahmad*, p. 147.

148. Al-e Ahmad, *Dar Khedmat va Khianat-e Roshanfekran*, vol. 2, pp. 154–160.

149. Al-e Ahmad, *Dar Khedmat va Khianat-e Roshanfekran*, vol. 2, pp. 369–370; and Zamani-nia (ed.), *Farhang-e Jalal Al-e Ahmad*, p. 127.

150. Zamani-nia (ed.), *Farhang-e Jalal Al-e Ahmad*, p. 135.

151. Zamani-nia (ed.), *Farhang-e Jalal Al-e Ahmad*, p. 136.

152. Zamani-nia (ed.), *Farhang-e Jalal Al-e Ahmad*, p. 136.

153. Zamani-nia (ed.), *Farhang-e Jalal Al-e Ahmad*, p. 135.

154. Zamani-nia (ed.), *Farhang-e Jalal Al-e Ahmad*, p. 173.

155. Zamani-nia (ed.), *Farhang-e Jalal Al-e Ahmad*, p. 180; compare also with Al-e Ahmad, *Kar-nameh-ye Seh Saleh*, p. 89.

156. Al-e Ahmad, *Dar Khedmat va Khianat-e Roshanfekran*, p. 52; and Zamani-nia (ed.), *Farhang-e Jalal Al-e Ahmad*, p. 180.

157. Al-e Ahmad, *Dar Khedmat va Khianat-e Roshanfekran*, vol. 2, p. 9.

158. Al-e Ahmad, *Dar Khedmat va Khianat-e Roshanfekran*, vol. 2, p. 10.

159. Al-e Ahmad, *Dar Khedmat va Khianat-e Roshanfekran*, vol. 2, p. 11.

160. Al-e Ahmad, *Dar Khedmat va Khianat-e Roshanfekran*, vol. 2, p. 12.

161. Al-e Ahmad, *Dar Khedmat va Khianat-e Roshanfekran*, vol. 2, p. 13.

162. Al-e Ahmad, *Dar Khedmat va Khianat-e Roshanfekran*, vol. 2, pp. 9–10.

163. Al-e Ahmad, *Dar Khedmat va Khianat-e Roshanfekran*, vol. 2, p. 16.

164. Al-e Ahmad, *Dar Khedmat va Khianat-e Roshanfekran*, vol. 2, p. 16.

165. Al-e Ahmad, *Dar Khedmat va Khianat-e Roshanfekran*, vol. 2, p. 20.

166. As quoted in Shams Al-e Ahmad's Introduction to Al-e Ahmad, *Safar beh Velayat-e Isra'il*, p. 36.

167. See Jamalzadeh's letter to Mostafa' Zamani-nia in Zamani-nia (ed.), *Farhang-e Jalal Al-e Ahmad*, p. 23.

168. Zamani-nia (ed.), *Farhang-e Jalal Al-e Ahmad*, p. 26.

169. See Tehrani, "Chehel Ruz Gozasht," in Dehbashi (ed.), *Yadnameh-ye Jalal Al-e Ahmad*, p. 73.

170. See Mostafa' Zamani-nia's Introduction to Zamani-nia (ed.), *Farhang-e Jalal Al-e Ahmad*, p. 37.

171. For a representative collection of poems composed for him after his death, see Dehbashi (ed.), *Yadnameh-ye Jalal Al-e Ahmad*, pp. 695–736. Included in these poems is Ahmad Shamlu's famous "Sorud bara-ye Mard-e Roshan keh beh Sayeh Raft," pp. 722–724. When this poem was first published, it was commonly believed that it was composed for Al-e Ahmad. In the first edition of Shamlu's *Shekoftan dar Meh*, published in 1349/1970, this poem, pp. 29–32, is not dedicated to Al-e Ahmad. When Shamlu published his *Collected Works* in (then West) Germany, he felt obligated to include the following note to this poem:

The publication of this poem occurred sometime after the death of Jalal Al-e Ahmad. There was a rumor that it was composed in his memory. The conditions were such that not only I could not deny it but they indeed prompted me to acknowledge it. But the truth is that I have never been in agreement with him. . . .

The publication of Ahmad Shamlu's *Collected Works* in 1368/1989 and in Europe is the contextual evidence that many of Al-e Ahmad's former (secular) friends reflected their frustrations with the outcome of the Islamic Revolution back on Al-e Ahmad whom they, rightly, considered a forerunner in reconstruction of Islamic sentiments for revolutionary purposes.

172. As quoted from *Arash*, Number 18, in Zamani-nia (ed.), *Farhang-e Jalal Al-e Ahmad*, p. 140.

173. Tehrani, "Chehel Ruz Gozasht," in Dehbashi (ed.), *Yadnameh-ye Jalal Al-e Ahmad*, p. 77.

174. For the text of Gustave Flaubert's letter to George Sand, see Ellmann and Feidelson (eds.), *The Modern Tradition*, pp. 316–317.

2. Ali Shari'ati

1. Ahlstrom, *A Religious History of the American People*, vol. 1, p. 367.

2. Al-e Ahmad, *Dar Khedmat va Khianat-e Roshanfekran*, p. 398; and Zamani-nia (ed.), *Farhang-e Jalal Al-e Ahmad*, p. 199.

3. Shariʿati, *Kavir*, p. ix. For a series of brilliant reconstructions of Shariʿati's ideas, see Fischer and Abedi, *Debating Muslims*, et passim.

4. Shariʿati, *Kavir*, pp. 2–29.

5. Shariʿati, *Kavir*, p. 18.

6. Shariʿati, *Kavir*, p. 33.

7. Shariʿati, *Kavir*, p. 38. Equally eloquent is Shariʿati's remembrance of Imam Hossein's cosmic revolutionary character. See his "Hossein: Vareth-e Adam," in Shariʿati, *Hossein: Vareth-e Adam*, pp. 1–108.

8. Shariʿati, *Kavir*, p. 56.

9. Shariʿati, *Kavir*, p. 46.

10. Shariʿati, *Kavir*, p. 46.

11. Shariʿati, *Kavir*, pp. 59–76.

12. Translated by Herbert Mason; see Massignon, *The Passion of al-Hallaj*.

13. For an excellent study of solitude and creative imagination, see Storr, *Solitude*. For an appreciation of this neomystical dimension of Shariʿati, read his "Niayesh" in his *Niayesh*, pp. 91–124. Equally important is his *Ziba-tarin Ruh-e Parastandeh*, pp. 125–179. See also his "Irfan, Barabari, Azadi," in Shariʿati, *Khodi-sazi-ha-ye Enqelabi*, pp. 59–90; see also his *Hobut dar Kavir*.

14. Abrahamian, *Iran between Two Revolutions*, p. 464.

15. Abrahamian, *Iran between Two Revolutions*, p. 466.

16. See, for example, the introductory material to Shariʿati, *Man and Islam*, pp. vii–xxi.

17. For a typical hagiographical sketch, see the Introduction to Shariʿati, *On the Sociology of Islam*, pp. 11–38. This book, however, does contain a selection of excellent translations of Shariʿati's writings.

18. For a concise theoretical treatment of the extent and ramifications of the therapeutic and revolutionary uses of faith in modernity, see Rieff, *Triumph of the Therapeutic*.

19. Keddie, *Roots of Revolution*, p. 215.

20. Keddie, *Roots of Revolution*, p. 215.

21. There is no biography of Shariʿati in English. The existing Persian sources need considerable critical judgment in using them. See Keddie, *Roots of Revolution*, p. 294, note 50.

22. For a complete list of Shariʿati's works, see his bibliography prepared by Y. Richard in *Abstracta Iranica*, 1 and 2, and as quoted in Keddie, *Roots of Revolution*, p. 295, note 51. English translations of Shariʿati are scarce, sporadic, and confusing. Hamid Algar has translated some of his works into English. See particularly *On the Sociology of Islam* and *On Marxism and Other Western Fallacies*. Shariʿati's *Hajj* has also been translated into English by A. Behzadnia and N. Kenny. Hosseyniyyeh Ershad, the institution at which Shariʿati lectured, has published some English translations of his speeches as well. None of these translations is to be totally trusted, however. Reference should always be to Shariʿati's original lectures transcribed into books.

23. See Abrahamian, *Iran between Two Revolutions*, p. 465, for a good discussion of this point.

24. Keddie, *Roots of Revolution*, p. 220. See also Shariʿati, *Tashayyoʿ-e Alavi va Tashayyoʿ-e Safavi*, especially pp. 196–251. Compare these passages also with

Shari'ati, *Madhhab alayh-e Madhhab*. His *Jame'eh-shenasi-ye Adyan* is also full of such conservative and revolutionary comparisons of religion. See also his *Tarikh va Shenakht-e Adyan*.

25. Keddie has covered this aspect of Shari'ati's thought extensively. See Keddie, *Roots of Revolution*, pp. 218–20.

26. Keddie, *Roots of Revolution*, pp. 217–18.

27. Keddie, *Roots of Revolution*, p. 218.

28. Keddie, *Roots of Revolution*, p. 220.

29. Shari'ati, *Shi'ah*, p. 9.

30. Shari'ati, *Shi'ah*, p. 9.

31. Shari'ati, *Shi'ah*, pp. 23–24.

32. Shari'ati, *Shi'ah*, p. 28.

33. Shari'ati, *Shi'ah*, p. 19.

34. Shari'ati, *Shi'ah*, pp. 14–15. Ali and Hossein were not the only figures whom Shari'ati sought to reinterpret in a revolutionary spirit. Abu Dharr al-Ghifari was equally central to his reconstruction of Muslim revolutionaries. See Shari'ati, *Abu Dharr*. But the most compelling archetype was, of course, that of the Prophet Muhammad. See a perfectly revolutionary reconstruction of Muhammad in Medina in Shari'ati, *Az Hejrat ta Vafat*. His *Sima-ye Muhammad* is equally important. Salman the Persian occupied a particularly compelling position. See Shari'ati's translation of Massignon's *Salman-e Pak*. A memorable statement on Ali is to be found in his *Ali: Maktab, Vahdat, Edalat,* and on Hossein in *Hossein: Vareth-e Adam.*

35. Keddie, *Roots of Revolution*, p. 217.

36. Pickthall (trans.), *The Glorious Koran*, 2:134. For other examples of Shari'ati's modern reinterpretations of Islam, see his *Shahadat, Mi'ad ba Ibrahim,* and *Hajj*.

37. Shari'ati, *Shi'ah*, p. 27.

38. Shari'ati, *Shi'ah*, p. 28.

39. Keddie, *Roots of Revolution*, p. 223.

40. Shari'ati, *Shi'ah*, p. 42.

41. Shari'ati, *Shi'ah*, p. 16.

42. Shari'ati, *Shi'ah*, p. 16.

43. Shari'ati, *Shi'ah*, p. 16.

44. Shari'ati, *Shi'ah*, p. 16.

45. Shari'ati, *Shi'ah*, p. 42.

46. As quoted in Keddie, *Roots of Revolution*, p. 221.

47. Shari'ati, *Shi'ah*, p. 147.

48. Shari'ati, *Shi'ah*, pp. 57–58.

49. Keddie, *Roots of Revolution*, p. 217.

50. Keddie, *Roots of Revolution*, p. 217.

51. For a full discussion of Shari'ati's conception of man, see his tenth lecture in *Islamshenasi*, vol. 2, pp. 3–40.

52. Shari'ati, *Islamshenasi*, vol. 2, p. 6.

53. Shari'ati, *Cheh bayad Kard?* p. 34.

54. Shari'ati, *Cheh bayad Kard?* p. 34.

55. Shari'ati, *Cheh bayad Kard?* p. 35.

56. Shari'ati, *Fatemeh Fatemeh Ast*, p. iii.

57. Shariʿati, *Fatemeh Fatemeh Ast,* p. iv.

58. Shariʿati, *Fatemeh Fatemeh Ast,* p. 2.

59. Shariʿati, *Fatemeh Fatemeh Ast,* p. 8.

60. Shariʿati, *Fatemeh Fatemeh Ast,* pp. 8–9. For other ideas of Shariʿati on women, see his "Entezar-e Asr-e Hazer az Zan-e Mosalman," in Shariʿati, *Zan,* pp. 207–240.

61. Shariʿati, *Fatemeh Fatemeh Ast,* p. 12.

62. Shariʿati, *Fatemeh Fatemeh Ast,* p. 14.

63. Shariʿati, *Fatemeh Fatemeh Ast,* pp. 18–19, continuation of footnote 1 starting on p. 17.

64. Shariʿati, *Fatemeh Fatemeh Ast,* p. 21.

65. Shariʿati, *Fatemeh Fatemeh Ast,* p. 30.

66. Shariʿati, *Fatemeh Fatemeh Ast,* p. 40.

67. Shariʿati, *Fatemeh Fatemeh Ast,* p. 42.

68. Shariʿati, *Fatemeh Fatemeh Ast,* pp. 45–46.

69. Shariʿati, *Fatemeh Fatemeh Ast,* p. 59. For Shariʿati's view on veiling, see his "Hejab," in Shariʿati, *Zan,* pp. 261–284.

70. Shariʿati, *Fatemeh Fatemeh Ast,* p. 60.

71. Shariʿati, *Fatemeh Fatemeh Ast,* p. 61.

72. Shariʿati, *Fatemeh Fatemeh Ast,* p. 61.

73. Shariʿati, *Fatemeh Fatemeh Ast,* p. 61.

74. Shariʿati, *Fatemeh Fatemeh Ast,* p. 64.

75. Shariʿati, *Fatemeh Fatemeh Ast,* pp. 67–68.

76. Shariʿati, *Fatemeh Fatemeh Ast,* pp. 73–74.

77. Shariʿati, *Fatemeh Fatemeh Ast,* p. 74.

78. Shariʿati, *Fatemeh Fatemeh Ast,* p. 75.

79. Shariʿati, *Fatemeh Fatemeh Ast,* p. 76.

80. Shariʿati, *Fatemeh Fatemeh Ast,* p. 77.

81. Shariʿati, *Fatemeh Fatemeh Ast,* p. 89. For an extension of similar ideas, see Shariʿati, "Seminar-e Zan," in Shariʿati, *Zan,* pp. 241–258. In the course of Shariʿati's speech at this "conference" someone in his audience interrupts his talk and refers to modern "Western" culture as a contemporary case of pre-Islamic "ignorance" (*jahiliyyah*). Shariʿati agrees. See the footnote on p. 243.

82. Shariʿati, *Fatemeh Fatemeh Ast,* p. 91.

83. Shariʿati, *Fatemeh Fatemeh Ast,* p. 105.

84. Shariʿati, *Fatemeh Fatemeh Ast,* p. 114.

85. Shariʿati, *Fatemeh Fatemeh Ast,* p. 121. For other related ideas of Shariʿati about women, see his "Entezar-e Asr-e Hazer az Zan-e Mosalman," "Seminar-e Zan," and "Hejab," all published in Shariʿati, *Zan,* pp. 207–283. For a major address to parents and their revolutionary responsibilities, see his *Pedar, Madar, Ma Mottahamim.*

86. Shariʿati, *Payam-e Omiyd beh Roshanfekr-e Masʿul,* p. 2.

87. Shariʿati, *Payam-e Omiyd beh Roshanfekr-e Masʿul,* p. 3.

88. Shariʿati, *Payam-e Omiyd beh Roshanfekr-e Masʿul,* p. 6.

89. Shariʿati, *Payam-e Omiyd beh Roshanfekr-e Masʿul,* p. 13.

90. Shariʿati, *Payam-e Omiyd beh Roshanfekr-e Masʿul,* p. 28.

91. Shariʿati, *Payam-e Omiyd beh Roshanfekr-e Masʿul,* p. 35.

92. Shariʿati, *Payam-e Omiyd beh Roshanfekr-e Masʿul*, p. 36.

93. Shariʿati, *Payam-e Omiyd beh Roshanfekr-e Masʿul*, p. 38. For a further discussion of the centrality of "oppression" in human history and the Abrahamic mission to oppose it, see Shariʿati, *Miʿad ba Ibrahim*, pp. 38–61.

94. Shariʿati, *Payam-e Omiyd beh Roshanfekr-e Masʿul*, p. 43.

95. Shariʿati, *Payam-e Omiyd beh Roshanfekr-e Masʿul*, pp. 21, 37, and 43. For other reflections on the nature and function of intellectuals, see Shariʿati, "Barkhi pishtazan-e 'Bazgasht-e beh Khishtan' dar Jahan-e Sevvom" and "Talaqqi-ye Madhhab az did-e Roshanfekr-e Vaqeʿ-biyn va Roshanfekr-e Moqalled," in Shariʿati, *Vizheh-gi-ha-ye Qorun-e Jadid*, pp. 409–423 and 459–461, respectively.

96. Shariʿati, *Islamshenasi*, vol. 1, p. 4.

97. Shariʿati, *Islamshenasi*, vol. 1, p. 4.

98. Shariʿati, *Islamshenasi*, vol. 1, p. 8.

99. Shariʿati, *Islamshenasi*, vol. 1, p. 11.

100. Shariʿati, *Islamshenasi*, vol. 1, p. 11.

101. Shariʿati, *Islamshenasi*, vol. 1, p. 14, fig. 1.

102. Shariʿati, *Islamshenasi*, vol. 1, p. 15, fig. 2.

103. Shariʿati, *Islamshenasi*, vol. 1, p. 88, footnote 1, which starts on p. 83.

104. Shariʿati, *Islamshenasi*, vol. 1, p. 106.

105. Shariʿati, *Islamshenasi*, vol. 1, pp. 118–134.

106. Shariʿati, *Islamshenasi*, vol. 1, p. 126. For other ideas of Shariʿati on the sociology of religion, see his *Jameʿeh-shenasi-ye Adyan*. Particularly significant in his construction of "The West" is his discussion of "The Spirit and Perspective of the West," pp. 127–163.

107. Shariʿati, *Islamshenasi*, vol. 1, p. 135.

108. Shariʿati, *Islamshenasi*, vol. 1, p. 141.

109. Shariʿati, *Islamshenasi*, vol. 1, p. 149.

110. Shariʿati, *Islamshenasi*, vol. 1, p. 169.

111. Shariʿati, *Islamshenasi*, vol. 1, p. 168.

112. Shariʿati, *Islamshenasi*, vol. 1, p. 167.

113. Shariʿati, *Islamshenasi*, vol. 1, p. 178. For some of Shariʿati's best statements about "the Islamic Ideology," see his *Jahan-bini va Ideology*, especially pp. 94–100.

114. Shariʿati, *Islamshenasi*, vol. 1, pp. 180–181.

115. Shariʿati, *Islamshenasi*, vol. 1, p. 182.

116. Shariʿati, *Islamshenasi*, vol. 1, p. 188.

117. Shariʿati, *Islamshenasi*, vol. 1, p. 188.

118. Shariʿati, *Islamshenasi*, vol. 1, p. 197.

119. Shariʿati, *Islamshenasi*, vol. 1, p. 198. For Shariʿati's more extensive discussion of the nature of modern Islamic movements, see his *Bazgasht*, especially pp. 3–33, 35–44, 81–90, and 94–100.

120. Shariʿati, *Islamshenasi*, vol. 1, p. 200.

121. Shariʿati, *Islamshenasi*, vol. 1, p. 209.

122. Shariʿati, *Islamshenasi*, vol. 1, p. 209.

123. Shariʿati, *Islamshenasi*, vol. 1, p. 222.

124. Shariʿati, *Islamshenasi*, vol. 1, p. 223.

125. Shariʿati, *Islamshenasi*, vol. 1, p. 224. The cultivation of these ideas and

their relevance for the future mobilization of Shiᶜi political sentiments by Khomeini were not lost on the revolutionary participants themselves. For a particularly significant linkage between the ideas of Shariᶜati and Khomeini, see Aram, *Bot-Shekani va Jedal-e Kheyr va Shar: Az Ibrahim ta Khomeini,* pp. 61–118.

126. Shariᶜati, *Islamshenasi,* vol. 1, p. 232.
127. Shariᶜati, *Islamshenasi,* vol. 1, p. 237.
128. Shariᶜati, *Islamshenasi,* vol. 1, pp. 245–256.
129. Shariᶜati, *Islamshenasi,* vol. 1, pp. 254–255.
130. Shariᶜati, *Islamshenasi,* vol. 1, p. 258.
131. Shariᶜati, *Islamshenasi,* vol. 1, pp. 267–292. For a fuller discussion of religion and its various social and psychological functions, see Shariᶜati, *Tarikh va Shenakht-e Adyan.*
132. Shariᶜati, *Islamshenasi,* vol. 1, p. 305.
133. Shariᶜati, *Islamshenasi,* vol. 1, p. 317.
134. Shariᶜati, *Islamshenasi,* vol. 1, p. 326.
135. Shariᶜati, *Islamshenasi,* vol. 2, p. 4.
136. Shariᶜati, *Islamshenasi,* vol. 2, p. 10.
137. Shariᶜati, *Islamshenasi,* vol. 2, p. 29.
138. Shariᶜati, *Islamshenasi,* vol. 2, p. 35. For another version of Shariᶜati's view on history, see his "Binesh-e Tarikh-e Shiᶜah," in Shariᶜati, *Hossein: Vareth-e Adam,* pp. 229–252.
139. Shariᶜati, *Islamshenasi,* vol. 2, p. 40.
140. Shariᶜati, *Islamshenasi,* vol. 2, p. 42.
141. Shariᶜati, *Islamshenasi,* vol. 2, p. 43.
142. Shariᶜati, *Islamshenasi,* vol. 2, p. 45, footnote 1.
143. Shariᶜati, *Islamshenasi,* vol. 2, p. 106.
144. Shariᶜati, *Islamshenasi,* vol. 2, p. 123.
145. Shariᶜati, *Islamshenasi,* vol. 2, p. 123.
146. Shariᶜati, *Islamshenasi,* vol. 2, p. 123.
147. Shariᶜati, *Islamshenasi,* vol. 2, pp. 112–113.
148. Shariᶜati, *Islamshenasi,* vol. 2, p. 151.
149. Shariᶜati, *Islamshenasi,* vol. 2, p. 155.
150. Shariᶜati, *Islamshenasi,* vol. 2, p. 175. For a revolutionary reading of the Shiᶜi doctrine of "Expectation," see Shariᶜati, "Entezar, Madhhab-e Eᶜteraz," in Shariᶜati, *Hossein: Vareth-e Adam,* pp. 253–304.
151. Shariᶜati, *Islamshenasi,* vol. 2, p. 47.
152. Shariᶜati, *Islamshenasi,* vol. 2, pp. 57 and 65.
153. Shariᶜati, *Islamshenasi,* vol. 2, p. 75.
154. Shariᶜati, *Islamshenasi,* vol. 2, p. 76.
155. Shariᶜati, *Islamshenasi,* vol. 2, p. 76.
156. Shariᶜati, *Islamshenasi,* vol. 2, p. 79.
157. Shariᶜati, *Islamshenasi,* vol. 2, p. 81.
158. Shariᶜati, *Islamshenasi,* vol. 2, pp. 90–91.
159. Abrahamian, *Iran between Two Revolutions,* p. 467.
160. Abrahamian, *Iran between Two Revolutions,* p. 471.
161. Abrahamian, *Iran between Two Revolutions,* p. 473.
162. Shariᶜati, *Beh Sar-e Aql Amadan-e Sarmayeh-dari,* pp. 2–3.

163. Shari'ati, *Beh Sar-e Aql Amadan-e Sarmayeh-dari*, p. 7.

164. Shari'ati, *Beh Sar-e Aql Amadan-e Sarmayeh-dari*, p. 20.

165. Shari'ati, *Beh Sar-e Aql Amadan-e Sarmayeh-dari*, p. 23.

166. Shari'ati, *Beh Sar-e Aql Amadan-e Sarmayeh-dari*, p. 28. For other uses of Marxism by Shari'ati, see his *Insan, Marxism, Islam* and *Agar Pope va Marx Nabudand*. See also the second volume of *Tarikh-e Tamaddon* which contains a classical Marxist interpretation of society, history, and culture.

167. Shari'ati, *Jahat-giri-ye Tabaqati-ye Islam*. See note 35 to the Introduction.

168. Shari'ati, *Jahat-giri-ye Tabaqati-ye Islam*, p. 1.

169. Shari'ati, *Jahat-giri-ye Tabaqati-ye Islam*, p. 2.

170. Shari'ati, *Jahat-giri-ye Tabaqati-ye Islam*, p. 2.

171. Shari'ati, *Jahat-giri-ye Tabaqati-ye Islam*, p. 3.

172. Shari'ati, *Jahat-giri-ye Tabaqati-ye Islam*, p. 6.

173. Shari'ati, *Jahat-giri-ye Tabaqati-ye Islam*, p. 8.

174. Shari'ati, *Jahat-giri-ye Tabaqati-ye Islam*, p. 9.

175. Shari'ati, *Jahat-giri-ye Tabaqati-ye Islam*, p. 12. Here "Molla" has a derogatory connotation.

176. Shari'ati, *Jahat-giri-ye Tabaqati-ye Islam*, p. 9.

177. Shari'ati, *Jahat-giri-ye Tabaqati-ye Islam*, p. 10.

178. Shari'ati, *Jahat-giri-ye Tabaqati-ye Islam*, p. 10.

179. Shari'ati, *Jahat-giri-ye Tabaqati-ye Islam*, p. 11.

180. Shari'ati, *Jahat-giri-ye Tabaqati-ye Islam*, p. 12.

181. Shari'ati, *Jahat-giri-ye Tabaqati-ye Islam*, p. 12. Here "akhond" has a negative connotation.

182. "Haji" is the respected title given to a Muslim who has performed his hajj pilgrimage. But here Shari'ati uses it with a sarcastic, derogatory connotation, referring primarily to the wealthy bazaar merchants. "Molla," too, has a sarcastic, negative meaning here.

183. Shari'ati, *Jahat-giri-ye Tabaqati-ye Islam*, p. 36.

184. Shari'ati, *Jahat-giri-ye Tabaqati-ye Islam*, p. 36.

185. Shari'ati, *Jahat-giri-ye Tabaqati-ye Islam*, p. 36.

186. Shari'ati, *Jahat-giri-ye Tabaqati-ye Islam*, p. 36.

187. Shari'ati, *Jahat-giri-ye Tabaqati-ye Islam*, p. 37.

188. Shari'ati, *Jahat-giri-ye Tabaqati-ye Islam*, p. 37.

189. Mas'a, or "place of running," during the Muslim hajj pilgrimage "is a relatively wide street and one of the principal markets of the city [Mecca]. It starts at a small, paved platform approached by some steps—the hills of as-Safa. Here the pilgrim turns to the Ka'ba, which is not visible from this point, and says a prayer. He then descends the Mas'a, which passes around the southeastern corner of the *Haram*." See Von Grunebaum, *Muhammadan Festivals*, p. 30.

190. "Hajj Aqa," literally "Mr. Haji," is used here sarcastically to refer to the Muslim pilgrim.

191. Again, "Molla" is used sarcastically.

192. That is, in *ihram*, the ritual state of having been dressed in "a garment that consists of two unsewn and preferably white sheets." See Von Grunebaum, *Muhammadan Festivals*, p. 26.

193. Shari'ati, *Jahat-giri-ye Tabaqati-ye Islam*, pp. 37–38.

194. Shariʿati, *Jahat-giri-ye Tabaqati-ye Islam*, p. 38.

195. Shariʿati, *Jahat-giri-ye Tabaqati-ye Islam*, p. 44.

196. Shariʿati, *Jahat-giri-ye Tabaqati-ye Islam*, p. 65.

197. Shariʿati, *Jahat-giri-ye Tabaqati-ye Islam*, p. 78.

198. Shariʿati, *Jahat-giri-ye Tabaqati-ye Islam*, p. 79. For Shariʿati's further thoughts on Marxism (as well as on capitalism and existentialism), see his *Insan, Marxism, Islam,* especially pp. 28–41. His discussion of "Insan dar Tazad-e Marxism va Madhhab," pp. 42–80, is equally important.

199. Shariʿati, *Jahat-giri-ye Tabaqati-ye Islam*, p. 79.

200. Shariʿati, *Jahat-giri-ye Tabaqati-ye Islam*, p. 79.

201. Shariʿati, *Jahat-giri-ye Tabaqati-ye Islam*, p. 79.

202. Shariʿati, *Jahat-giri-ye Tabaqati-ye Islam*, p. 80.

203. Shariʿati, *Jahat-giri-ye Tabaqati-ye Islam*, p. 82.

204. Shariʿati, *Jahat-giri-ye Tabaqati-ye Islam*, p. 82.

205. Shariʿati, *Jahat-giri-ye Tabaqati-ye Islam*, p. 82.

206. Shariʿati, *Jahat-giri-ye Tabaqati-ye Islam*, pp. 82–83.

207. Shariʿati, *Jahat-giri-ye Tabaqati-ye Islam*, p. 83. Compare these ideas of Shariʿati with those expressed in Shariʿati, *Bazgasht,* pp. 78–81 and 164–173.

208. Shariʿati, *Jahat-giri-ye Tabaqati-ye Islam*, p. 83.

209. Shariʿati, *Jahat-giri-ye Tabaqati-ye Islam*, p. 83.

210. Shariʿati, *Jahat-giri-ye Tabaqati-ye Islam*, p. 83.

211. Shariʿati, *Jahat-giri-ye Tabaqati-ye Islam*, p. 83.

212. See his "Bazgasht beh Khiyshtan" and "Bazgasht beh Kodam Khiysh," in Shariʿati, *Bazgasht,* pp. 3–33 and 35–401, respectively.

213. Ahlstrom, *A Religious History of the American People,* pp. 367–368.

3. Morteza Motahhari

1. Kenny, *Aquinas,* p. 2.

2. For some preliminary biographical sketches of Morteza Motahhari see Khorasani, "Seyri dar Zendegi-ye Ilmi va Enqelabi-ye Ostad-e Shahid Morteza Motahhari," in Sorush (ed.), *Yadnameh-ye Ostad-e Shahid Morteza Motahhari,* pp. 317–380. A useful bibliographical reference is Anonymous (ed.), *Seyri dar Athar-e Ostad-e Shahid Motahhari.*

3. For these and additional biographical data, see the Introduction to the eighth edition of Motahhari, *Elal-e Gerayesh beh Maddi-gari,* pp. 5–52. For a series of brilliant reconstructed narratives on Motahhari's ideas, see Fischer and Abedi, *Debating Muslims,* passim.

4. See Tabataba'i, *Osul-e Falsafeh va Ravesh-e Realism.* For additional information on Motahhari's contribution to these five volumes, see Sorush (ed.), *Yadnameh-ye Ostad-e Shahid Morteza Motahhari,* p. 535.

5. See, for example, Motahhari's Introduction to the Fourth Treatise of the first volumes of Tabataba'i, *Osul-e Falsafeh va Ravesh-e Realism,* pp. 94–129.

6. See the text of Khomeini's speeches on Motahhari's death and his picture while weeping in Sorush (ed.), *Yadnameh-ye Ostad-e Shahid Morteza Motahhari,* pp. 3–9.

7. Sorush (ed.), *Yadnameh-ye Ostad-e Shahid Morteza Motahhari,* p. 3.

8. Sorush (ed.), *Yadnameh-ye Ostad-e Shahid Morteza Motahhari*, p. 3.

9. Sorush (ed.), *Yadnameh-ye Ostad-e Shahid Morteza Motahhari*, p. 30.

10. See Motahhari's Introduction to the first volume of Tabataba'i, *Osul-e Falsafeh va Ravesh-e Realism*, p. iii.

11. Motahhari's Introduction to the first volume of Tabataba'i, *Osul-e Falsafeh va Ravesh-e Realism*, p. iv.

12. Motahhari's Introduction to the first volume of Tabataba'i, *Osul-e Falsafeh va Ravesh-e Realism*, pp. iv-v.

13. Motahhari's Introduction to the first volume of Tabataba'i, *Osul-e Falsafeh va Ravesh-e Realism*, p. v.

14. Motahhari's Introduction to the first volume of Tabataba'i, *Osul-e Falsafeh va Ravesh-e Realism*, p. viii.

15. Motahhari, *Elal-e Gerayesh beh Maddi-gari*, p. 107.

16. Motahhari, *Elal-e Gerayesh beh Maddi-gari*, p. 160.

17. Motahhari, *Elal-e Gerayesh beh Maddi-gari*, p. 175.

18. See Sorush (ed.), *Yadnameh-ye Ostad-e Shahid Morteza Motahhari*, pp. 437–534.

19. See Motahhari's Introduction to Tabatabata'i, *Osul-e Falsafeh va Ravesh-e Realism*, vol. 1, p. 19.

20. Tabataba'i, *Osul-e Falsafeh va Ravesh-e Realism*, vol. 1, p. B.

21. Tabataba'i, *Osul-e Falsafeh va Ravesh-e Realism*, vol. 1, p. H.

22. Tabataba'i, *Osul-e Falsafeh va Ravesh-e Realism*, vol. 1, p. YV.

23. Tabataba'i, *Osul-e Falsafeh va Ravesh-e Realism*, vol. 1, p. KA.

24. Tabataba'i, *Osul-e Falsafeh va Ravesh-e Realism*, vol. 1, p. K. Motahhari's concern with "The Western" philosophy in general and with philosophical materialists in particular is also evident in philosophical discussions he held in his own residence later when he moved to Tehran. In these gatherings "professors of the Western philosophy" from Tehran University participated. See Motahhari, *Sharh-e Manzumeh*, vol. 1, p. 6.

25. Tabataba'i, *Osul-e Falsafeh va Ravesh-e Realism*, vol. 1, p. K.

26. Tabataba'i, *Osul-e Falsafeh va Ravesh-e Realism*, vol. 1, p. KV. For an insightful discussion of Motahhari's own philosophical positions and their significance in the prerevolutionary period, see the chapter on Motahhari in Davari Ardakani, "Defaᶜ-e az Falsafeh," in Anonymous (ed.), *Yadnameh-ye Allamah Tabataba'i*, pp. 69–124.

27. Tabataba'i, *Osul-e Falsafeh va Ravesh-e Realism*, vol. 1, p. KH.

28. Tabataba'i, *Osul-e Falsafeh va Ravesh-e Realism*, vol. 1, p. KT.

29. Tabataba'i, *Osul-e Falsafeh va Ravesh-e Realism*, vol. 1, p. L.

30. Tabataba'i, *Osul-e Falsafeh va Ravesh-e Realism*, vol. 1, p. LA.

31. Tabataba'i, *Osul-e Falsafeh va Ravesh-e Realism*, vol. 1, p. LA.

32. Tabataba'i, *Osul-e Falsafeh va Ravesh-e Realism*, vol. 1, p. 100 ff.

33. Tabataba'i, *Osul-e Falsafeh va Ravesh-e Realism*, vol. 1, p. 103.

34. Tabataba'i, *Osul-e Falsafeh va Ravesh-e Realism*, vol. 1, p. 137 ff.

35. For an excellent comparative assessment of Motahhari and Shariᶜati, see Sorush, *Roshanfekri va Dindari*, especially pp. 40 ff.

36. For an English account of these rivalries, see Algar's Introduction to Motahhari, *Fundamentals of Islamic Thought*, p. 16 ff.

37. For another account of these rivalries, see Akhavi, *Religion and Politics in Contemporary Iran*, p. 144 ff.

38. Motahhari, *Dastan-e Rastan*, vol. 1, p. Nine.

39. Motahhari, *Dastan-e Rastan*, vol. 1, p. Ten.

40. Motahhari, *Dastan-e Rastan*, vol. 1, p. Ten.

41. Motahhari, *Dastan-e Rastan*, vol. 1, p. Fourteen.

42. Motahhari, *Dastan-e Rastan*, vol. 1, p. Fifteen.

43. Motahhari, *Dastan-e Rastan*, vol. 1, p. Seventeen.

44. Motahhari, *Dastan-e Rastan*, vol. 2, p. Nine.

45. Motahhari, *Dastan-e Rastan*, vol. 2, p. Nine.

46. Motahhari, *Dastan-e Rastan*, vol. 2, p. Ten.

47. Motahhari, *Dastan-e Rastan*, vol. 2, p. Eleven. Other than in these stories, Motahhari was in other ways attentive to the religious and ideological implications of literature. See, for example, his taking strong exception to a materialist reading of Hafez in *Tamasha-gah-e Raz*, particularly pp. 41–50 and 85–103.

48. Motahhari, *Dastan-e Rastan*, vol. 1, p. 1.

49. Motahhari, *Dastan-e Rastan*, vol. 1, p. 22.

50. Motahhari, *Dastan-e Rastan*, vol. 1, p. 58.

51. Motahhari, *Dastan-e Rastan*, vol. 1, p. 88.

52. Motahhari, *Dastan-e Rastan*, vol. 1, p. 110.

53. Motahhari, *Dastan-e Rastan*, vol. 1, p. 192.

54. Motahhari, *Dastan-e Rastan*, vol. 2, p. 22.

55. Motahhari, *Dastan-e Rastan*, vol. 2, p. 89.

56. Motahhari, *Dastan-e Rastan*, vol. 2, p. 221.

57. Anonymous (ed.), *Bahthi dar Bareh-ye Marja'iyyat va Ruhaniyyat*, p. 5. This is an extremely significant text in which a number of leading Muslim ideologues are brought together to reflect on the nature of supreme authority. For a general account of this text, see Lambton, "A Reconsideration of the Position of the *Marja' al-taqlid* and the Religious Institution."

58. Anonymous (ed.), *Bahthi dar Bareh-ye Marja'iyyat va Ruhaniyyat*, p. 5.

59. Anonymous (ed.), *Bahthi dar Bareh-ye Marja'iyyat va Ruhaniyyat*, pp. 6–7.

60. Anonymous (ed.), *Bahthi dar Bareh-ye Marja'iyyat va Ruhaniyyat*, p. 3.

61. Anonymous (ed.), *Bahthi dar Bareh-ye Marja'iyyat va Ruhaniyyat*, p. 3.

62. Anonymous (ed.), *Bahthi dar Bareh-ye Marja'iyyat va Ruhaniyyat*, p. 9.

63. Anonymous (ed.), *Bahthi dar Bareh-ye Marja'iyyat va Ruhaniyyat*, p. 36.

64. Anonymous (ed.), *Bahthi dar Bareh-ye Marja'iyyat va Ruhaniyyat*, p. 46.

65. Anonymous (ed.), *Bahthi dar Bareh-ye Marja'iyyat va Ruhaniyyat*, p. 50.

66. Anonymous (ed.), *Bahthi dar Bareh-ye Marja'iyyat va Ruhaniyyat*, p. 55. Motahhari further explores the political responsibilities of the religious authorities in a remarkable reconstruction of Islamic social movements in modern times. See Motahhari, *Nehzat-ha-ye Islami dar Sad Saleh-ye Akhir*. For another assessment of the same period, yet with a post-revolutionary slant, see Mojtahed-e Shabastari, "Diyanat va Siyasat."

67. Anonymous (ed.), *Bahthi dar Bareh-ye Marja'iyyat va Ruhaniyyat*, pp. 56–57.

68. Anonymous (ed.), *Bahthi dar Bareh-ye Marja'iyyat va Ruhaniyyat*, p. 57.

69. Anonymous (ed.), *Bahthi dar Bareh-ye Marjaʿiyyat va Ruhaniyyat*, p. 58.
70. Anonymous (ed.), *Bahthi dar Bareh-ye Marjaʿiyyat va Ruhaniyyat*, p. 58.
71. Anonymous (ed.), *Bahthi dar Bareh-ye Marjaʿiyyat va Ruhaniyyat*, p. 60.
72. Anonymous (ed.), *Bahthi dar Bareh-ye Marjaʿiyyat va Ruhaniyyat*, p. 61.
73. Anonymous (ed.), *Bahthi dar Bareh-ye Marjaʿiyyat va Ruhaniyyat*, p. 63.
74. Anonymous (ed.), *Bahthi dar Bareh-ye Marjaʿiyyat va Ruhaniyyat*, p. 239.
75. Anonymous (ed.), *Bahthi dar Bareh-ye Marjaʿiyyat va Ruhaniyyat*, p. 241.
76. Anonymous (ed.), *Bahthi dar Bareh-ye Marjaʿiyyat va Ruhaniyyat*, p. 243.
77. Anonymous (ed.), *Bahthi dar Bareh-ye Marjaʿiyyat va Ruhaniyyat*, p. 245.
Read these comments with the severe critical assessment levelled against Bazargan for his "Westoxicated" understanding of Islam in Soltani, *Khat-e Sazesh*, pp. 129–161.
78. Anonymous (ed.), *Bahthi dar Bareh-ye Marjaʿiyyat va Ruhaniyyat*, p. 245.
79. Anonymous (ed.), *Bahthi dar Bareh-ye Marjaʿiyyat va Ruhaniyyat*, p. 246.
80. Anonymous (ed.), *Bahthi dar Bareh-ye Marjaʿiyyat va Ruhaniyyat*, p. 248.
81. Anonymous (ed.), *Bahthi dar Bareh-ye Marjaʿiyyat va Ruhaniyyat*, pp. 165–166. This idea is to be revisited and expanded in Motahhari's postrevolutionary reflections on the nature and function of the Islamic Revolution. See Motahhari, *Goftari dar Bareh-ye Jomhuri-ye Islami*, and Motahhari, *Piramun-e Enqelab-e Islami*.
82. Anonymous (ed.), *Bahthi dar Bareh-ye Marjaʿiyyat va Ruhaniyyat*, p. 169.
83. Anonymous (ed.), *Bahthi dar Bareh-ye Marjaʿiyyat va Ruhaniyyat*, p. 174.
84. Anonymous (ed.), *Bahthi dar Bareh-ye Marjaʿiyyat va Ruhaniyyat*, p. 176.
85. Anonymous (ed.), *Bahthi dar Bareh-ye Marjaʿiyyat va Ruhaniyyat*, p. 177.
86. Anonymous (ed.), *Bahthi dar Bareh-ye Marjaʿiyyat va Ruhaniyyat*, pp. 178–179.
87. Anonymous (ed.), *Bahthi dar Bareh-ye Marjaʿiyyat va Ruhaniyyat*, p. 180. Further on the political implications of "Sahm-e Imam," see Fischer and Abedi, *Debating Muslims*, pp. 125–128.
88. Anonymous (ed.), *Bahthi dar Bareh-ye Marjaʿiyyat va Ruhaniyyat*, pp. 180–181.
89. Anonymous (ed.), *Bahthi dar Bareh-ye Marjaʿiyyat va Ruhaniyyat*, p. 181.
90. Anonymous (ed.), *Bahthi dar Bareh-ye Marjaʿiyyat va Ruhaniyyat*, p. 182.
91. Anonymous (ed.), *Bahthi dar Bareh-ye Marjaʿiyyat va Ruhaniyyat*, p. 182.
92. Anonymous (ed.), *Bahthi dar Bareh-ye Marjaʿiyyat va Ruhaniyyat*, pp. 182–183.
93. Anonymous (ed.), *Bahthi dar Bareh-ye Marjaʿiyyat va Ruhaniyyat*, p. 183.
94. Anonymous (ed.), *Bahthi dar Bareh-ye Marjaʿiyyat va Ruhaniyyat*, p. 184.
95. Anonymous (ed.), *Bahthi dar Bareh-ye Marjaʿiyyat va Ruhaniyyat*, p. 184.
96. Anonymous (ed.), *Bahthi dar Bareh-ye Marjaʿiyyat va Ruhaniyyat*, p. 195.
97. Anonymous (ed.), *Bahthi dar Bareh-ye Marjaʿiyyat va Ruhaniyyat*, pp. 187–188. The constitution of the Islamic Republic is now a testimony to the success of the argument for updating the Islamic doctrines. See *Qanun-e Asasi-ye Jomhuri-ye Islami-ye Iran*.
98. Anonymous (ed.), *Bahthi dar Bareh-ye Marjaʿiyyat va Ruhaniyyat*, p. 189.
99. Anonymous (ed.), *Bahthi dar Bareh-ye Marjaʿiyyat va Ruhaniyyat*, p. 190.
100. Anonymous (ed.), *Bahthi dar Bareh-ye Marjaʿiyyat va Ruhaniyyat*, p. 190.

101. Anonymous (ed.), *Bahthi dar Bareh-ye Marja'iyyat va Ruhaniyyat*, p. 194.
102. Anonymous (ed.), *Bahthi dar Bareh-ye Marja'iyyat va Ruhaniyyat*, p. 194.
103. Anonymous (ed.), *Bahthi dar Bareh-ye Marja'iyyat va Ruhaniyyat*, p. 194.
104. Anonymous (ed.), *Bahthi dar Bareh-ye Marja'iyyat va Ruhaniyyat*, p. 196.
105. Anonymous (ed.), *Bahthi dar Bareh-ye Marja'iyyat va Ruhaniyyat*, p. 197.
106. *Qiblah* means direction of prayer, which, for a Muslim, is towards Mecca. Here Motahhari's reference is to an expansion of this direction to include new points of attraction in people's loyalties, for example, towards "The West."
107. Anonymous (ed.), *Bahthi dar Bareh-ye Marja'iyyat va Ruhaniyyat*, pp. 197–198.
108. Motahhari, *Ehya'-ye Tafkkor-e Islami*, as an appendix to his *Haq va Batel*, pp. 70–712. All references here are to this edition of *Ehya'-ye Tafkkor-e Islami*. There are other versions of this text, published separately.
109. Motahhari, *Ehya'-ye Tafkkor-e Islami*, p. 74.
110. Motahhari, *Ehya'-ye Tafkkor-e Islami*, p. 72.
111. Motahhari, *Ehya'-ye Tafkkor-e Islami*, p. 79.
112. See Motahhari's Introduction to Tabataba'i, *Osul-e Falsafeh va Ravesh-e Realism*, vol. 1, p. H.
113. Motahhari, *Ehya'-ye Tafkkor-e Islami*, p. 73.
114. Motahhari, *Ehya'-ye Tafkkor-e Islami*, p. 86.
115. Motahhari, *Ehya'-ye Tafkkor-e Islami*, p. 86.
116. Motahhari, *Ehya'-ye Tafkkor-e Islami*, p. 89.
117. Motahhari, *Ehya'-ye Tafkkor-e Islami*, p. 90.
118. Motahhari, *Ehya'-ye Tafkkor-e Islami*, p. 90.
119. Motahhari, *Ehya'-ye Tafkkor-e Islami*, pp. 91–92.
120. Motahhari, *Ehya'-ye Tafkkor-e Islami*, pp. 94–95.
121. Motahhari, *Ehya'-ye Tafkkor-e Islami*, p. 136. For a particularly mobilizing perspective on the religious (that is, Islamic) understanding of "this world" *(donya')*, see Motahhari, "Nazar-e Din dar bareh-ye Donya'," in Motahhari, *Bist Goftar*, pp. 200–213. Equally important in its reconstruction of an "Islamic" perspective on science is "Nazar-e Islam dar bareh-ye Ilm," pp. 214–224 of the same book.
122. Motahhari, *Ehya'-ye Tafkkor-e Islami*, p. 95.
123. Motahhari, *Ehya'-ye Tafkkor-e Islami*, p. 78.
124. Motahhari, *Ehya'-ye Tafkkor-e Islami*, p. 96.
125. Motahhari, *Ehya'-ye Tafkkor-e Islami*, p. 97.
126. Motahhari, *Ehya'-ye Tafkkor-e Islami*, p. 97. The Murji'ites were an early Islamic sect who believed, contrary to the Kharijites, that by merely committing a sin a Muslim does not, ipso facto, become an infidel. This doctrinal position in turn led to a rather pacificistic orientation in their politics. For further details, see A. J. Wensinck, "al-Murdji'a," in Gibb and Kramers (eds.), *Shorter Encyclopaedia of Islam*.
127. Motahhari, *Ehya'-ye Tafkkor-e Islami*, p. 98.
128. Motahhari, *Ehya'-ye Tafkkor-e Islami*, p. 99.
129. Motahhari, *Ehya'-ye Tafkkor-e Islami*, p. 123.
130. Motahhari, *Ehya'-ye Tafkkor-e Islami*, p. 131.
131. Motahhari, *Ehya'-ye Tafkkor-e Islami*, p. 154.

132. Motahhari, *Ehya'-ye Tafkkor-e Islami*, p. 164.

133. Motahhari, *Ehya'-ye Tafkkor-e Islami*, p. 173.

134. Motahhari, *Ehya'-ye Tafkkor-e Islami*, p. 127.

135. Motahhari, *Ehya'-ye Tafkkor-e Islami*, p. 159.

136. See Sorush (ed.), *Yadnameh-ye Ostad-e Shahid Morteza Motahhari*, p. 537.

137. Motahhari, *Vala'-ha va Velayat-ha*, p. 5.

138. Motahhari, *Vala'-ha va Velayat-ha*, p. 6.

139. Motahhari, *Vala'-ha va Velayat-ha*, p. 10.

140. Motahhari, *Vala'-ha va Velayat-ha*, p. 15.

141. Motahhari, *Vala'-ha va Velayat-ha*, p. 18.

142. Motahhari, *Vala'-ha va Velayat-ha*, p. 22.

143. Motahhari, *Vala'-ha va Velayat-ha*, p. 29.

144. Motahhari, *Vala'-ha va Velayat-ha*, pp. 33–34.

145. Motahhari, *Vala'-ha va Velayat-ha*, pp. 35–36. Equally significant in understanding Motahhari's position on supreme religious and political activity is his extensive discussions in Motahhari, *Imamat va Rahbari*, particularly, pp. 23–34, 46–60, and 67–84.

146. Motahhari, *Vala'-ha va Velayat-ha*, p. 34.

147. Motahhari, *Vala'-ha va Velayat-ha*, p. 36.

148. Motahhari, *Vala'-ha va Velayat-ha*, p. 37. For a classical treatise on the notion of *Insan-e Kamel*, see Nasafi, *Kitab al-Insan al-Kamil*; for a reading of this text, see my "The Sufi Doctrine of 'The Perfect Man' and a View of the Hierarchical Structure of Islamic Culture."

149. Motahhari, *Vala'-ha va Velayat-ha*, p. 38.

150. Motahhari, *Vala'-ha va Velayat-ha*, p. 38.

151. Motahhari, *Vala'-ha va Velayat-ha*, p. 42.

152. Motahhari, *Vala'-ha va Velayat-ha*, pp. 48–50.

153. Motahhari, *Vala'-ha va Velayat-ha*, p. 52.

154. Motahhari, *Vala'-ha va Velayat-ha*, pp. 53–64.

155. See, for example, Khomeini's letter to Motahhari, dated 4 Farvardin 1347 (Sunday, 24 March 1968), and another letter of roughly the same period in Khomeini, *Sahifeh-ye Nur*, vol. 1, pp. 142–143. The first of these two letters authorizes Motahhari to collect religious taxes on Khomeini's behalf; the second is a reflection of Khomeini's and Motahhari's concern·about the infiltration of "undesirable elements" in the ranks of seminarian students in Qom.

156. See Sorush (ed.), *Yadnameh-ye Ostad-e Shahid Morteza Motahhari*, p. 538.

157. Motahhari, *Elal-e Gerayesh beh Maddi-gari*, p. 58.

158. Motahhari, *Elal-e Gerayesh beh Maddi-gari*, p. 60.

159. Motahhari, *Elal-e Gerayesh beh Maddi-gari*, pp. 61–63.

160. Motahhari, *Elal-e Gerayesh beh Maddi-gari*, p. 64.

161. See Motahhari's Introduction to Tabataba'i, *Osul-e Falsafeh va Ravesh-e Realism*, vol. 1, pp. K-KA.

162. Motahhari, *Elal-e Gerayesh beh Maddi-gari*, p. 69 ff.

163. Motahhari, *Elal-e Gerayesh beh Maddi-gari*, p. 71.

164. Motahhari, *Elal-e Gerayesh beh Maddi-gari*, p. 75.

165. Motahhari, *Elal-e Gerayesh beh Maddi-gari*, p. 79.

166. Motahhari, *Elal-e Gerayesh beh Maddi-gari*, p. 84.

167. Motahhari, *Elal-e Gerayesh beh Maddi-gari*, p.84.

168. Motahhari, *Elal-e Gerayesh beh Maddi-gari*, p. 85.

169. Motahhari, *Elal-e Gerayesh beh Maddi-gari*, p. 85.

170. Motahhari, *Elal-e Gerayesh beh Maddi-gari*, p. 95.

171. For a thorough and authoritative exploration of Molla Sadra's philosophy, see Ashtiani, *Sharh-e Hal va Ara'-e Falsafi-ye Molla Sadra*. For an introductory English account, see Rahman, *The Philosophy of Mulla Sadra*.

172. Motahhari, *Elal-e Gerayesh beh Maddi-gari*, pp. 123–124.

173. Motahhari, *Elal-e Gerayesh beh Maddi-gari*, pp. 174–197.

174. Motahhari, *Elal-e Gerayesh beh Maddi-gari*, p. 202.

175. Motahhari, *Elal-e Gerayesh beh Maddi-gari*, pp. 203–204.

176. Motahhari, *Elal-e Gerayesh beh Maddi-gari*, p. 205.

177. Motahhari, *Elal-e Gerayesh beh Maddi-gari*, p. 212.

178. Motahhari, *Elal-e Gerayesh beh Maddi-gari*, p. 218.

179. Motahhari, *Elal-e Gerayesh beh Maddi-gari*, p. 226. For other similar criticism on historical and philosophical materialism, see Motahhari, *Naqdi bar Marxism*, pp. 57–124.

180. Motahhari, *Elal-e Gerayesh beh Maddi-gari*, p. 238.

181. Motahhari, *Elal-e Gerayesh beh Maddi-gari*, p. 239.

182. Motahhari, *Elal-e Gerayesh beh Maddi-gari*, p. 243.

183. Motahhari, *Elal-e Gerayesh beh Maddi-gari*, p. 245.

184. Motahhari, *Elal-e Gerayesh beh Maddi-gari*, pp. 245–246.

185. Motahhari, *Elal-e Gerayesh beh Maddi-gari*, p. 85.

186. Such as in Motahhari, *Seyri dar Nahj al-Balaghah*, pp. 45 or 50.

187. Motahhari, *Elal-e Gerayesh beh Maddi-gari*, p. 102.

188. Motahhari, *Seyri dar Nahj al-Balaghah*, p. viii.

189. Motahhari, *Seyri dar Nahj al-Balaghah*, p. x.

190. See Sorush (ed.), *Yadnameh-ye Ostad-e Shahid Morteza Motahhari*, p. 538.

191. Sorush (ed.), *Yadnameh-ye Ostad-e Shahid Morteza Motahhari*, p. 538, footnote 2.

192. Motahhari, *Seyri dar Nahj al-Balaghah*, p. 38.

193. Motahhari, *Seyri dar Nahj al-Balaghah*, p. 102.

194. The original Arabic quoted in Motahhari, *Seyri dar Nahj al-Balaghah*, p. 107.

195. Motahhari, *Seyri dar Nahj al-Balaghah*, p. 114.

196. Motahhari, *Seyri dar Nahj al-Balaghah*, p. 115.

197. Motahhari, *Seyri dar Nahj al-Balaghah*, pp. 115–116.

198. Motahhari, *Seyri dar Nahj al-Balaghah*, pp. 110–111.

199. Motahhari, *Seyri dar Nahj al-Balaghah*, pp. 118–119.

200. Motahhari, *Seyri dar Nahj al-Balaghah*, p. 104. For a discussion of the difference between the Shi'ite and the Kharijite conceptions of authority, see my *Authority in Islam*.

201. Motahhari, *Seyri dar Nahj al-Balaghah*, p. 105.

202. Motahhari, *Seyri dar Nahj al-Balaghah*, p. 127.

203. Motahhari, *Seyri dar Nahj al-Balaghah*, p. 128.

204. Motahhari, *Seyri dar Nahj al-Balaghah*, pp. 130–131. For a fuller discussion of the "Authority Verse" in the Qur'an, see the relevant sections in the chapter on Allamah Tabataba'i in this book.

205. Motahhari, *Seyri dar Nahj al-Balaghah*, pp. 200 ff.

206. Motahhari, *Seyri dar Nahj al-Balaghah*, p. 202.

207. Motahhari, *Seyri dar Nahj al-Balaghah*, p. 214.

208. Motahhari, *Seyri dar Nahj al-Balaghah*, pp. 218–219.

209. Motahhari, *Seyri dar Nahj al-Balaghah*, pp. 221–222.

210. Motahhari, *Seyri dar Nahj al-Balaghah*, p. 250.

211. Ya'qub-e Leyth-e Saffar (d. 878), the founder of the Saffarids, an autonomous Persian dynasty early in Islamic history, is famous for his legendary encounter with the Abbasid caliph.

212. Motahhari, *Seyri dar Nahj al-Balaghah*, p. 236.

213. Motahhari, *Seyri dar Nahj al-Balaghah*, pp. 222–223.

214. Motahhari, *Seyri dar Nahj al-Balaghah*, pp. 223–230.

215. Motahhari, *Seyri dar Nahj al-Balaghah*, p. 226.

216. Motahhari, *Seyri dar Nahj al-Balaghah*, pp. 290–291.

217. Motahhari, *Seyri dar Nahj al-Balaghah*, p. 292.

218. Motahhari, *Seyri dar Nahj al-Balaghah*, p. 183. For other revolutionary reconstructions of the figure of Ali, see Motahhari, *Jazebeh va Dafe'eh-ye Ali*, pp. 35–104 and 107–178.

219. Motahhari, *Seyri dar Nahj al-Balaghah*, p. 176.

220. Motahhari, *Seyri dar Nahj al-Balaghah*, p. 176.

221. Motahhari, *Seyri dar Nahj al-Balaghah*, p. 177.

222. Motahhari, *Seyri dar Nahj al-Balaghah*, p. 192.

223. Motahhari, *Seyri dar Nahj al-Balaghah*, p. 11.

224. A particularly significant text in which Motahhari's repeated references to the Iranian origin of Muslim luminaries are evident is his *Khadamat-e Motaqabel-e Islam va Iran*. The relationship between Islam and Iran was (and is) a particularly thorny one. Where was the basis of one's primary loyalty? In Islam or in Iran? Were they to be treated as polar opposites or as complementary identities? Beyond the questions of identity, the issue also had a political dimension to it. Muslim ideologues did not wish to have their "nationalist" credentials questioned by the more secularly oriented nationalists. For extremely important post-revolutionary reflections on precisely this theme, with particular reference to Motahhari, see Anonymous, "Dar Yadman-e Mo'allem-e Andishidan." In this article the editors of a leading doctrinal journal of the Islamic Republic have asked some leading ideologues to reflect on the significance of Motahhari's *Khadamat-e Motaqabel-e Islam va Iran* and also to express their own opinions on the subject. Abdolkarim Sorush, for example, provides an eloquent exposition of Motahhari's text wherein he argues that the hostile dichotomy constructed between Iran and Islam was a false one. Virtue and goodness, he argues, know no boundary. Then he extends this argument from "Arabs" to "The West." Not everything that has come from "The West" is bad either. He concludes with a truth of Rumi that, "Should the Sun rise from The West / Yet 'tis Sun and nothing else." See Anonymous, "Dar Yadman-e Mo'allem-e Andishidan," p. 8.

225. Motahhari, *Seyri dar Nahj al-Balaghah*, pp. 42–43.
226. Motahhari, *Seyri dar Nahj al-Balaghah*, pp. 121–122.
227. Motahhari, *Seyri dar Nahj al-Balaghah*, p. 76.
228. Motahhari, *Seyri dar Nahj al-Balaghah*, p. xv.
229. Motahhari, *Seyri dar Nahj al-Balaghah*, p. xv.
230. Motahhari, *Ta'lim va Tarbiyat dar Islam*, p. 1.
231. Motahhari, *Ta'lim va Tarbiyat dar Islam*, pp. 1–2.
232. Motahhari, *Ta'lim va Tarbiyat dar Islam*, p. 6.
233. Motahhari, *Ta'lim va Tarbiyat dar Islam*, p. 6.
234. Motahhari, *Ta'lim va Tarbiyat dar Islam*, p. 8.
235. Motahhari, *Ta'lim va Tarbiyat dar Islam*, pp. 8–9.
236. Motahhari, *Ta'lim va Tarbiyat dar Islam*, p. 19.
237. Motahhari, *Ta'lim va Tarbiyat dar Islam*, p. 25. For Motahhari's celebration of "logic" and "philosophy" in Islamic history, see Motahhari, *Ashna'i ba' Olum-e Islami: Manteq va Falsafeh*.
238. Motahhari, *Ta'lim va Tarbiyat dar Islam*, p. 26.
239. Motahhari, *Ta'lim va Tarbiyat dar Islam*, p. 29.
240. Motahhari, *Ta'lim va Tarbiyat dar Islam*, p. 182. This is the Qur'anic passage (39: 17–18):

17. And those who put away false gods lest they should worship them and turn to Allah in repentence, for them there are glad tidings. Therefore give good tidings (o Muhammad) to my bondmen.
18. Who hear advice and follow the best thereof. Such are those whom Allah guideth, and such are men of understanding.

241. Motahhari, *Ta'lim va Tarbiyat dar Islam*, p. 184.
242. Motahhari, *Ta'lim va Tarbiyat dar Islam*, pp. 238–239.
243. Motahhari, *Ta'lim va Tarbiyat dar Islam*, pp. 37–38.
244. Motahhari, *Ta'lim va Tarbiyat dar Islam*, p. 45.
245. Motahhari, *Ta'lim va Tarbiyat dar Islam*, p. 45, footnote 8.
246. Motahhari, *Ta'lim va Tarbiyat dar Islam*, p. 46.
247. During 1976 and 1977, Motahhari organized a group of interested individuals in Qom and for about forty-five sessions delivered a series of critical lectures on Marxism. These were posthumously collected and published as *Naqdi bar Marxism*.
248. Motahhari, *Ta'lim va Tarbiyat dar Islam*, pp. 67–68.
249. Motahhari, *Ta'lim va Tarbiyat dar Islam*, p. 78.
250. Motahhari, *Ta'lim va Tarbiyat dar Islam*, p. 78.
251. Motahhari, *Ta'lim va Tarbiyat dar Islam*, p. 79.
252. Motahhari, *Ta'lim va Tarbiyat dar Islam*, p. 79.
253. Motahhari, *Ta'lim va Tarbiyat dar Islam*, p. 79.
254. Motahhari, *Ta'lim va Tarbiyat dar Islam*, p. 109.
255. Motahhari, *Ta'lim va Tarbiyat dar Islam*, p. 165.
256. Motahhari, *Ta'lim va Tarbiyat dar Islam*, p. 11.
257. Motahhari, *Ta'lim va Tarbiyat dar Islam*, pp. 11–12, footnote 13.
258. Motahhari, *Ta'lim va Tarbiyat dar Islam*, p. 11.
259. Motahhari, *Nezam-e Hoquq-e Zan dar Islam*, p. xiv.

260. Motahhari, *Nezam-e Hoquq-e Zan dar Islam*, p. xix.
261. Motahhari, *Nezam-e Hoquq-e Zan dar Islam*, pp. xx-xxi. All exclamation marks are in Motahhari's text.
262. Motahhari, *Nezam-e Hoquq-e Zan dar Islam*, p. xxi.
263. Motahhari, *Nezam-e Hoquq-e Zan dar Islam*, p. xxii. For other views of Motahhari on women, and particularly on sexual relationships, see Motahhari, *Akhlaq-e Jensi dar Islam va Jahan-e Gharb*. As evident from the title, this is yet another textual construction of "Islam and The West" as two monolithic entities.
264. Motahhari, *Nezam-e Hoquq-e Zan dar Islam*, p. 7.
265. Motahhari, *Nezam-e Hoquq-e Zan dar Islam*, p. 29.
266. Motahhari, *Nezam-e Hoquq-e Zan dar Islam*, p. 58.
267. Motahhari, *Nezam-e Hoquq-e Zan dar Islam*, p. 74.
268. Motahhari, *Nezam-e Hoquq-e Zan dar Islam*, p. 128.
269. Motahhari, *Nezam-e Hoquq-e Zan dar Islam*, p. 141. For the ethical foundation of Motahhari's argument here, see his discussion of ethics in Motahhari, *Islam va Moqtaziat-e Zaman*, vol. 1, pp. 339–352.
270. Motahhari, *Nezam-e Hoquq-e Zan dar Islam*, pp. 170–171.
271. Motahhari, *Nezam-e Hoquq-e Zan dar Islam*, p. 171.
272. Motahhari, *Nezam-e Hoquq-e Zan dar Islam*, p. 233.
273. Motahhari, *Nezam-e Hoquq-e Zan dar Islam*, p. 253–254.
274. Motahhari, *Nezam-e Hoquq-e Zan dar Islam*, p. 312.
275. Motahhari, *Nezam-e Hoquq-e Zan dar Islam*, pp. 283–284.
276. Motahhari, *Nezam-e Hoquq-e Zan dar Islam*, pp. 326–327.
277. Motahhari, *Nezam-e Hoquq-e Zan dar Islam*, p. 331.
278. Motahhari, *Nezam-e Hoquq-e Zan dar Islam*, p. 340.
279. Motahhari, *Nezam-e Hoquq-e Zan dar Islam*, pp. 340–341.
280. Motahhari, *Nezam-e Hoquq-e Zan dar Islam*, p. 350. See also Motahhari, *Akhlaq-e Jensi dar Islam va Jahan-e Gharb*, pp. 69–78.
281. Motahhari, *Nezam-e Hoquq-e Zan dar Islam*, p. 381.
282. Motahhari, *Nezam-e Hoquq-e Zan dar Islam*, pp. 382–383.
283. Motahhari, *Nezam-e Hoquq-e Zan dar Islam*, p. 383.
284. Motahhari, *Nezam-e Hoquq-e Zan dar Islam*, p. 383.
285. Motahhari, *Nezam-e Hoquq-e Zan dar Islam*, pp. 382–384. For other reflections on Russell's ideas on sexual relations, see Motahhari, *Akhlaq-e Jensi dar Islam va Jahan-e Gharb*, pp. 23–25 and 84–91.
286. Motahhari, *Nezam-e Hoquq-e Zan dar Islam*, p. 384.
287. Motahhari, *Nezam-e Hoquq-e Zan dar Islam*, p. 386.
288. Motahhari, *Nezam-e Hoquq-e Zan dar Islam*, p. 390.
289. Motahhari, *Nezam-e Hoquq-e Zan dar Islam*, p. 391.
290. Motahhari, *Nezam-e Hoquq-e Zan dar Islam*, p. 392.
291. Motahhari, *Nezam-e Hoquq-e Zan dar Islam*, p. 392.
292. Motahhari, *Bar-rasi-ye Feqhi-e Mas'aleh-ye Bimeh*, p. 9.
293. Motahhari, *Bar-rasi-ye Feqhi-e Mas'aleh-ye Bimeh*, p. 12.
294. Motahhari, *Bar-rasi-ye Feqhi-e Mas'aleh-ye Bimeh*, p. 12.
295. Motahhari, *Bar-rasi-ye Feqhi-e Mas'aleh-ye Bimeh*, pp. 14–15.
296. Motahhari, *Bar-rasi-ye Feqhi-e Mas'aleh-ye Bimeh*, pp. 18–19.
297. Motahhari, *Bar-rasi-ye Feqhi-e Mas'aleh-ye Bimeh*, p. 22.

298. Motahhari, *Bar-rasi-ye Feqhi-e Mas'aleh-ye Bimeh*, p. 22.

299. Motahhari, *Bar-rasi-ye Feqhi-e Mas'aleh-ye Bimeh*, p. 26. Motahhari's "rationalist" *(usuli)*, as opposed to "literalist" *(akhbari)*, approach in his discussion of "insurance" is important also because of its further implications for his contemporary repoliticization of Islam, which needs, as its ideological requisite, the supremacy of "logic" over "tradition."

300. Motahhari, *Bar-rasi-ye Feqhi-e Mas'aleh-ye Bimeh*, p. 27.

301. Motahhari, *Bar-rasi-ye Feqhi-e Mas'aleh-ye Bimeh*, pp. 27–28.

302. Motahhari, *Bar-rasi-ye Feqhi-e Mas'aleh-ye Bimeh*, pp. 28–29.

303. Motahhari, *Bar-rasi-ye Feqhi-e Mas'aleh-ye Bimeh*, pp. 70–71.

304. Motahhari, *Bar-rasi-ye Feqhi-e Mas'aleh-ye Bimeh*, p. 71, footnote 1.

305. See Kenny, *Aquinas*, p. 81. The statement is Wittgenstein's about Aquinas.

4. Sayyid Mahmud Taleqani

1. Lord Macauly's remarks on Sir Thomas More are quoted in Kenny, *Thomas More*, p. 3.

2. There is no biography of Ayatollah Taleqani available. A collection of good primary data about his life and activities is to be found in Anonymous, *Yadnameh-ye Abu Dharr-e Zaman;* Afrasiabi (ed.), *Pedar Taleqani dar Zendan;* a special commemorative issue of the daily newspaper *Keyhan* (13 September 1979); Taleqani, *Partovi az Qur'an*, vol. III, pp. 468–472; and Deldam, *Rehlat ya Shahadat.* For a short biographical account in English, see Taleqani, *Society and Economics in Islam*, pp. 9–18. For various phases of Taleqani's relations with the Mojahedin, see Abrahamian, *Radical Islam*, passim.

3. From Taleqani's introduction to Na'ini, *Tanbih al-Ummah wa Tanzih al-Millah*, as quoted in Ja'fari (trans. and ed.), *Nehzat-e Bidar-gari dar Jahan-e Islam*, pp. 145–146.

4. Taleqani's introduction to Na'ini, *Tanbih al-Ummah va Tanzih al-Millah*, as quoted in Ja'fari (trans. and ed.), *Nehzat-e Bidar-gari dar Jahan-e Islam*, p. 145.

5. Taleqani's introduction to Na'ini, *Tanbih al-Ummah va Tanzih al-Millah*, as quoted in Ja'fari (trans. and ed.), *Nehzat-e Bidar-gari dar Jahan-e Islam*, p. 146.

6. Taleqani's introduction to Na'ini, *Tanbih al-Ummah va Tanzih al-Millah*, as quoted in Ja'fari (trans. and ed.), *Nehzat-e Bidar-gari dar Jahan-e Islam*, p. 146.

7. Taleqani's introduction to Na'ini, *Tanbih al-Ummah va Tanzih al-Millah*, as quoted in Ja'fari (trans. and ed.), *Nehzat-e Bidar-gari dar Jahan-e Islam*, p. 146.

8. Taleqani's introduction to Na'ini, *Tanbih al-Ummah va Tanzih al-Millah*, as quoted in Ja'fari (trans. and ed.), *Nehzat-e Bidar-gari dar Jahan-e Islam*, p. 147. For a useful discussion of the centrality of the Qur'anic exegesis in Taleqani's politics, see Chehabi, *Iranian Politics and Religious Modernism*, pp. 50–51.

9. Taleqani's introduction to Na'ini, *Tanbih al-Ummah va Tanzih al-Millah*, as quoted in Ja'fari (trans. and ed.), *Nehzat-e Bidar-gari dar Jahan-e Islam*, p. 147.

10. Taleqani's introduction to Na'ini, *Tanbih al-Ummah va Tanzih al-Millah*, as quoted in Ja'fari (trans. and ed.), *Nehzat-e Bidar-gari dar Jahan-e Islam*, p. 150.

11. Taleqani, *Islam va Malekiyyat*. All my references are to this original Persian text. For a good English translation, see Taleqani, *Islam and Ownership*. A

shorter English version appeared in Taleqani, *Society and Economics in Islam*, pp. 23–72.

12. Taleqani, *Islam va Malekiyyat*, p. 5.

13. Taleqani, *Islam va Malekiyyat*, pp. 8–9.

14. Taleqani, *Islam va Malekiyyat*, p. 9. For a discussion of Taleqani's ideas on economics, see the introductory material to Taleqani, *Islam and Ownership*, pp. vii-xviii. See also Abrahamian, *Radical Islam*, pp. 62–83.

15. Taleqani, *Islam va Malekiyyat*, p. 10.

16. Taleqani, *Islam va Malekiyyat*, p. 13.

17. Taleqani, *Islam va Malekiyyat*, p. 16.

18. Taleqani, *Islam va Malekiyyat*, p. 38.

19. Taleqani, *Islam va Malekiyyat*, pp. 58–59.

20. Taleqani, *Islam va Malekiyyat*, p. 127.

21. Taleqani, *Islam va Malekiyyat*, p. 142.

22. Taleqani, *Islam va Malekiyyat*, p. 177. See also Chehabi, *Iranian Politics and Religious Modernism*, pp. 61–62.

23. Taleqani, *Islam va Malekiyyat*, p. 197.

24. Taleqani's introduction to Na'ini, *Tanbih al-Ummah va Tanzih al-Millah*, p. 14.

25. Taleqani's introduction to Na'ini, *Tanbih al-Ummah va Tanzih al-Millah*, p. 18.

26. Taleqani's introduction to Na'ini, *Tanbih al-Ummah va Tanzih al-Millah*, p. 1.

27. Taleqani's introduction to Na'ini, *Tanbih al-Ummah va Tanzih al-Millah*, p. 18.

28. Taleqani's introduction to Na'ini, *Tanbih al-Ummah va Tanzih al-Millah*, p. 15.

29. Taleqani's introduction to Na'ini, *Tanbih al-Ummah va Tanzih al-Millah*, p. 9. See also Chehabi, *Iranian Politics and Religious Modernism*, p. 60.

30. Taleqani's introduction to Na'ini, *Tanbih al-Ummah va Tanzih al-Millah*, pp. 5–6.

31. Taleqani's introduction to Na'ini, *Tanbih al-Ummah va Tanzih al-Millah*, p. 6.

32. Taleqani's introduction to Na'ini, *Tanbih al-Ummah va Tanzih al-Millah*, p. 4.

33. Taleqani's introduction to Na'ini, *Tanbih al-Ummah va Tanzih al-Millah*, p. 7.

34. Taleqani's introduction to Na'ini, *Tanbih al-Ummah va Tanzih al-Millah*, p. 7.

35. Taleqani's introduction to Na'ini, *Tanbih al-Ummah va Tanzih al-Millah*, p. 9.

36. Taleqani's introduction to Na'ini, *Tanbih al-Ummah va Tanzih al-Millah*, p. 9.

37. Taleqani's introduction to Na'ini, *Tanbih al-Ummah va Tanzih al-Millah*, p. 9.

38. Taleqani's introduction to Na'ini, *Tanbih al-Ummah va Tanzih al-Millah*, p. 10.

39. Taleqani's introduction to Na'ini, *Tanbih al-Ummah va Tanzih al-Millah*, p. 14.

40. Taleqani's introduction to Na'ini, *Tanbih al-Ummah va Tanzih al-Millah*, p. 17. See also Chehabi, *Iranian Politics and Religious Modernism*, pp. 42–43. For a representative treatise of Shaykh Fazlollah Nuri, see my translation of "The Book of Admonition to the Heedless and Guidance for the Ignorant," in Said Amir Arjomand (ed.), *Authority and Political Culture in Shi'ism*, pp. 354–68.

41. Taleqani's introduction to Na'ini, *Tanbih al-Ummah va Tanzih al-Millah*, pp. 2–3 of Na'ini's text.

42. Taleqani's introduction to Na'ini, *Tanbih al-Ummah va Tanzih al-Millah*, p. 3.

43. For an English translation of this speech, see Taleqani, "Jihad and Shahadat," in Abedi and Legenhausen (trans. and eds.), *Jihad and Shahadat*, pp. 47–80. There is another English version of this speech in Taleqani, *Society and Economics in Islam*, pp. 73–109. For a full account of the Iran Freedom Movement, see Chehabi, *Iranian Politics and Religious Modernism*.

44. Ja'fari (trans. and ed.), *Nehzat-e Bidar-gari dar Jahan-e Islam*, p. 154.

45. Taleqani, *Partovi az Qur'an*, vol I, p. 13.

46. Taleqani, *Partovi az Qur'an*, vol. I, p. 16.

47. Taleqani, *Partovi az Qur'an*, vol. II, p. 18.

48. Ja'fari (trans. and ed.), *Nehzat-e Bidar-gari dar Jahan-e Islam*, p. 149.

49. Ja'fari (trans. and ed.), *Nehzat-e Bidar-gari dar Jahan-e Islam*, p. 149.

50. For an assessment of the significance of Taleqani for the Mojahedin Organization, see Abrahamian, *Radical Islam*, pp. 193–197.

51. For various versions of this hadith, known as *hadith al-thaqalayn*, see al-Harrani, *Tuhaf al-Uqul*, p. 32; Qomi, *Safinah al-Bahar*, p. 132; and al-Nasa'i, *Khasa'is al-Imam Amir al-Mu'minim*, p. 150.

52. For a detailed study of the various modes of Qur'anic commentary, see Shahatah, *Ta'rikh al-Qur'an wa al-Tafsir*.

53. Nor are such contemporary political readings peculiar to Taleqani. In the modern Arab world there is a long and thriving history for such Qur'anic commentaries. See al-Jadili, *Nazarat Hadithah fi al-Tafsir*, for a discussion of these commentaries. Khorramshahi, in *Tafsir va Tafasir-e Jadid*, pays more attention to commentaries in Persian.

54. For selected passages from these and other classical commentaries, see Gätje, *The Qur'an and Its Exegesis*. For a thorough discussion of the differences among these modes of commentaries, see al-Dhahabi, *al-Tafsir wa al-Mufassirun*.

55. See Shahatah, *Ta'rikh al-Qur'an wa al-Tafsir*, pp. 148–183.

56. For a thorough bio-bibliographical study of Shi'i Quranic commentators, see Mazlumi, *Tafsir-e Shi'eh*.

57. For a critical discussion of these sources, see Shahatah, *Ta'rikh al-Qur'an wa al-Tafsir*, pp. 184–196.

58. Shahatah, *Ta'rikh al-Qur'an wa al-Tafsir*, pp. 120–146.

59. For a critical review of these and similar exegeses, see al-Dhababi, *al-Ittijahat al-Munharifah fi Tafsir al-Qur'an al-Karim*.

60. Taleqani, *Partovi az Qur'an*, vol II, p. 283.

61. Taleqani, *Do Shahid-e Ershad*, as quoted in Khorramshahi, *Tafsir va Tafasir-e Jadid*, pp. 39–40.

62. Taleqani, *Hedayat-e Qur'an*, as quoted in Khorramshahi, *Tafsir va Tafasir-e Jadid*, pp. 38–39.

63. Taleqani, *Partovi az Qur'an*, vol III, p. v.

64. Taleqani, *Partovi az Qur'an*, vol. III, p. vi.

65. Taleqani, *Partovi az Qur'an*, vol. I, p. 16.

66. Taleqani, *Partovi az Qur'an*, vol. I, p. 3.

67. Taleqani, *Partovi az Qur'an*, vol. I, p. 16. In a comparative context it is important to note that Al-e Ahmad knew of Taleqani's Qur'anic commentaries and their political significance. See Al-e Ahmad's letter to Amir Pishdad in Dehbashi (ed.), *Nameh-ha-ye Jalal Al-e Ahmad*, p. 286.

68. Taleqani, *Partovi az Qur'an*, vol. I, p. 4.

69. Taleqani, *Partovi az Qur'an*, vol. I, p. 2.

70. Taleqani, *Partovi az Qur'an*, vol. I, p. 2.

71. Taleqani, *Partovi az Qur'an*, vol. I, p. 4.

72. Taleqani, *Partovi az Qur'an*, vol. I, p. 10.

73. Taleqani, *Partovi az Qur'an*, vol. I, pp. 10–11.

74. Taleqani, *Partovi az Qur'an*, vol. I, p. 11.

75. Taleqani, *Partovi az Qur'an*, vol. I, p. 11.

76. Taleqani, *Partovi az Qur'an*, vol. I, p. 12.

77. Taleqani, *Partovi az Qur'an*, vol. I, p. 13.

78. Taleqani, *Partovi az Qur'an*, vol. I, p. 13. See also Khorramshahi, *Tafsir va Tafasir-e Jadid*, pp. 137–144.

79. Taleqani, *Partovi az Qur'an*, vol. I, p. 16.

80. Taleqani, *Partovi az Qur'an*, vol. I, p. 17.

81. Taleqani, *Partovi az Qur'an*, vol. I, p. 11.

82. Taleqani, *Partovi az Qur'an*, vol. I, p. 18.

83. Taleqani, *Partovi az Qur'an*, vol. I, p. 24.

84. Taleqani, *Majmu'eh Goftar-e Pedar Taleqani*, p. 17.

85. Taleqani, *Majmu'eh Goftar-e Pedar Taleqani*, p. 17. The origin of resorting to etymological and grammatical investigations to elucidate a Qur'anic passage goes back to the time of Abd Allah ibn Abbas, the Prophet's cousin, who is traditionally considered the originator of Qur'anic commentary. Having been admonished for this practice, Ibn Abbas resorted to pre-Islamic Arabic poetry for elucidating specific words. Ibn Abbas' limitation within the Qur'anic context for its exegesis and the specific inhibition against using non-Qur'anic, for example, Jewish and Christian, sources indicate the theological necessity of having the Qur'an govern, and not be governed by, historical exigencies. But resorting to etymological explication of key words in the Qur'anic passage is not a new phenomenon, and has its origin both in historical references to Ibn Abbas and in such prominent commentators as al-Zamakhshari. For a brief discussion of these and related issues, see Bell and Watt, *Introduction to the Qur'an*, pp. 167–172.

86. Taleqani, *Majmu'eh Goftar-e Pedar Taleqani*, p. 17.

87. For a short account of Molla Sadra's life and thought, see Nasr, *Sadr al-Din Shirazi & His Transcendent Theosophy*. For a thorough examination of his philo-

sophical positions, see Mishkat al-Dini, *Nazari beh Falsafeh-ye Sadr al-Din Shirazi*. Molla Sadra's principal philosophical positions are best represented in his *al-Sha-wahid al-Rububiyyah fi Manahij al-Sulukiyyah*. Molla Sadra himself has a Qur'anic commentary in line with the transcendental philosophy; see his *Asrar al-Ayat*. For a capable translation of one of Molla Sadra's chief treatises, *Hikmah al-Arshiyyah*, see Molla Sadra, *The Wisdom of the Throne*. For a discussion of Molla Sadra's social thoughts, see my "A View of Mulla Sadra's Social Thoughts: Social Order in a Sacred Order," pp. 407–428.

88. Rahman, *The Philosophy of Mulla Sadra*, p. 94.
89. Rahman, *The Philosophy of Mulla Sadra*, p. 94.
90. Khorramshahi, *Tafsir va Tafasir-e Jadid*, p. 145.
91. Taleqani, *Partovi az Qur'an*, vol I, p. 35.
92. Taleqani, *Partovi az Qur'an*, vol I, p. 113.
93. Taleqani, *Partovi az Qur'an*, vol I, p. 113.
94. The Qur'an, 2:22, "Who hath appointed the earth a resting-place for you, and the sky a canopy; and causeth water to pour down from the sky, thereby producing fruits as food for you. And do not set up rivals to Allah when ye know (better)." All Qur'anic passages are from Pickthall (trans.), *The Glorious Koran*.
95. Taleqani, *Partovi az Qur'an*, vol I, p. 87.
96. Taleqani, *Partovi az Qur'an*, vol I, p. 103.
97. "Allah's Apostle said, 'the best of my followers are those living in my generation, and then those who will follow them, and then those who will follow the latter. . . . There will come after you people who will bear witness without being asked to do so, and will be treacherous and untrustworthy, and who will vow, and never fulfill their vows." Anonymous (ed.), *Sahih al-Bukhari: Arabic-English*, vol. 5, p. 2.
98. Taleqani, *Partovi az Qur'an*, vol II, p. 24.
99. Taleqani, *Partovi az Qur'an*, vol II, p. 24.
100. Taleqani, *Partovi az Qur'an*, vol II, p. 29.
101. Taleqani, *Partovi az Qur'an*, vol I, p. 33.
102. Taleqani, *Partovi az Qur'an*, vol I, p. 33.
103. Taleqani, *Partovi az Qur'an*, vol I, p. 34.
104. Taleqani, *Partovi az Qur'an*, vol I, p. 36.
105. Taleqani, *Partovi az Qur'an*, vol I, p. 37. Taleqani's text says verse number 2:60, but it is actually 2:56.
106. Taleqani, *Partovi az Qur'an*, vol I, p. 43.
107. Taleqani, *Partovi az Qur'an*, vol I, p. 52.
108. Taleqani, *Partovi az Qur'an*, vol I, p. 52.
109. Taleqani, *Partovi az Qur'an*, vol I, p. 98.
110. Taleqani, *Partovi az Qur'an*, vol I, p. 118.
111. Taleqani, *Partovi az Qur'an*, vol I, p. 118.
112. Taleqani, *Partovi az Qur'an*, vol I, p. 118.
113. Taleqani, *Partovi az Qur'an*, vol I, p. 155.
114. The Qur'an, 2:62, "Lo! those who believe (in that which is revealed unto thee, Muhammad), and those who are Jews, and Christians, and Sabaeans—whoever

believeth in Allah and the Last Day and doeth right—surely their reward is with their Lord, and there shall no fear come upon them neither shall they grieve."

115. Taleqani, *Partovi az Qur'an*, vol I, p. 180.

116. Taleqani, *Partovi az Qur'an*, vol I, p. 197.

117. Taleqani, *Partovi az Qur'an*, vol I, p. 198.

118. Taleqani, *Majmu'eh Goftar-e Pedar Taleqani*, p. 17.

119. Taleqani, *Majmu'eh Goftar-e Pedar Taleqani*, p. 18.

120. Taleqani, *Majmu'eh Goftar-e Pedar Taleqani*, p. 22.

121. Taleqani, *Majmu'eh Goftar-e Pedar Taleqani*, p. 22.

122. The Qur'an, 2:105 "Neither those who disbelieve among the People of the Scripture nor the idolators love that there should be sent down unto you any good thing from your Lord. But Allah chooseth for His mercy whom He will, and Allah is of Infinite Bounty."

123. Taleqani, *Partovi az Qur'an*, vol I, p. 259.

124. Taleqani, *Partovi az Qur'an*, vol I, pp. 259–261.

125. The Qur'an, 2:243, "Bethink these (O Muhammad) of those of old, who went forth from their habitations in their thousands, fearing death, and Allah said unto them: Die, and then He brought them back to life. Lo! Allah is a Lord of Kindness to mankind, but most of mankind give not thanks."

126. Taleqani, *Partovi az Qur'an*, vol II, p. 173.

127. Taleqani, *Partovi az Qur'an*, vol II, p. 175.

128. Taleqani, *Partovi az Qur'an*, vol I, p. 105.

129. The Qur'an, 2:29, "He it is Who created for you all that is in the earth. Then turned He to the heaven, and fashioned it as seven heavens. And He is knower of all things."

130. The Qur'an, 2:179, "And there is life for you in retaliation, O men of understanding, that ye may ward off (evil)."

131. Taleqani, *Partovi az Qur'an*, vol II, p. 69.

132. Taleqani, *Partovi az Qur'an*, vol II, pp. 70 and 72.

133. Taleqani, *Partovi az Qur'an*, vol II, p. 263.

134. Taleqani, *Partovi az Qur'an*, vol II, p. 264.

135. Taleqani, *Partovi az Qur'an*, vol III, p. 9.

136. Taleqani, *Partovi az Qur'an*, vol III, p. 98.

137. Taleqani, *Partovi az Qur'an*, vol III, p. 104.

138. Taleqani, *Partovi az Qur'an*, vol III, pp. 137 and 201.

139. Ricoeur, *History and Truth*, p. 81.

140. Ricoeur, *History and Truth*, p. 82.

141. For a full discussion of such diverse possibilities, see Ricoeur, *History and Truth*, p. 89 ff.

142. See Anonymous (ed.), *Bahthi dar Bareh-ye Marja'iyyat va Ruhaniyyat*, p. 202; the footnote is continued from p. 201.

143. Anonymous (ed.), *Bahthi dar Bareh-ye Marja'iyyat va Ruhaniyyat*, p. 202.

144. Anonymous (ed.), *Bahthi dar Bareh-ye Marja'iyyat va Ruhaniyyat*, p. 202.

145. Anonymous (ed.), *Bahthi dar Bareh-ye Marja'iyyat va Ruhaniyyat*, p. 203.

146. Anonymous (ed.), *Bahthi dar Bareh-ye Marja'iyyat va Ruhaniyyat*, p. 207.

147. Anonymous (ed.), *Bahthi dar Bareh-ye Marja'iyyat va Ruhaniyyat*, p. 207.

148. Anonymous (ed.), *Bahthi dar Bareh-ye Marja'iyyat va Ruhaniyyat*, pp. 207–208.

149. See the relevant sections on the "Authority Verse" in Allamah Tabataba'i's chapter in this book.

150. Anonyous (ed.), *Bahthi dar Bareh-ye Marja'iyyat va Ruhaniyyat*, p. 209.

151. For the details of these events, see Abrahamian, *Radical Islam*, pp. 145–169.

152. As quoted in Algar's Introduction to Taleqani, *Society and Economics in Islam*, p. 14.

153. Algar's Introduction to Taleqani, *Society and Economics in Islam*, p. 14.

154. This is Algar's assessment; see Algar's Introduction to Taleqani, *Society and Economics in Islam*, p. 15.

155. Quoted in Taleqani, *Society and Economics in Islam*, p. 146.

156. This is Algar's assessment; see Algar's Introduction to Taleqani, *Society and Economics in Islam*, p. 17.

157. Again, Algar's assessment; see Algar's Introduction to Taleqani, *Society and Economics in Islam*, p. 16.

158. The details of this account are taken from the daily newspaper *Keyhan*, 10 September 1979, p. 2.

159. *Keyhan*, 10 September 1979, p. 2.

160. As quoted in Kenny, *Thomas More*, pp. 89–90.

5. Allamah Sayyid Muhammad Hossein Tabataba'i

1. See Marx, *The Poverty of Philosophy*, p. 29.

2. See Hosseini-ye Tehrani (ed.), *Mehr-e Taban*, p. 62.

3. Hosseini-ye Tehrani (ed.), *Mehr-e Taban*, p. 62.

4. Hosseini-ye Tehrani (ed.), *Mehr-e Taban*, p. 62.

5. Hosseini-ye Tehrani (ed.), *Mehr-e Taban*, p. 62.

6. See Mesbah, "Naqsh-e Allamah Tabataba'i dar Ma'aref-e Islami," in Anonymous (ed.), *Yadnameh-ye Allamah Tabataba'i*, p. 194.

7. Mesbah, "Naqsh-e Allamah Tabataba'i dar Ma'arif-i Islami," in Anonymous (ed.), *Yadnamah-ye Allamah Tabataba'i*, p. 94.

8. Mesbah, "Naqsh-e Allamah Tabataba'i dar Ma'arif-i Islami," in Anonymous (ed.), *Yadnamah-ye Allamah Tabataba'i*, pp. 194–195.

9. Mesbah, "Naqsh-e Allamah Tabataba'i dar Ma'aref-i Islami," in Anonymous (ed.), *Yadnamah-ye Allamah Tabataba'i*, p. 195.

10. Mesbah, "Naqsh-e Allamah Tabataba'i dar Ma'aref-i Islami," in Anonymous (ed.), *Yadnamah-ye Allamah Tabataba'i*, p. 195.

11. Mesbah, "Naqsh-e Allamah Tabataba'i dar Ma'aref-i Islami," in Anonymous (ed.), *Yadnameh-ye Allamah Tabataba'i*, p. 195.

12. See Motahhari, *Ehya'-ye Tafakkor-e Islami*, p. 88.

13. Motahhari, *Ehya'-ye Tafakkor-e Islami*, p. 88.

14. Hosseini-ye Tehrani (ed.), *Mehr-e Taban*, p. 8.

15. Hosseini-ye Tehrani (ed.), *Mehr-e Taban*, p. 8.

16. Hosseini-ye Tehrani (ed.), *Mehr-e Taban*, p. 9.

17. See Zanjani, "Allamah Tabataba'i: Jame'-e Hekmat va Shari'at," p. 1.

18. See Sobhani, "Maqam-e Elmi va Farhangi-ye Allamah Tabataba'i," p. 5.

19. See Zanjani, "Allamah Tabataba'i: Jameᶜ-e Hekmat Va Shariᶜat," p. 3.

20. Zanjani, "Allamah Tabataba'i: Jameᶜ-e Hekmat Va Shariᶜat," p. 3.

21. Zanjani, "Allamah Tabataba'i: Jameᶜ-e Hekmat Va Shariᶜat," p. 3.

22. See Dynani, "Allamah Tabataba'i va Nazar-e Motekalleman dar bareh-ye Elm-e Khodavand beh Joz'iyyat," p. 9.

23. See Hosseini-ye Tehrani (ed.), *Mehr-e Tababan*, p. 57.

24. See Mesbah, "Naqsh-e Allamah Tabataba'i dar Maᶜaref-i Islami," in Anonymous (ed.), *Yadnameh-ye Allamah Tabataba'i*, p. 198.

25. Mesbah, "Naqsh-e Allamah Tabataba'i dar Maᶜaref-i Islami," in Anonymous (ed.), *Yadnameh-ye Allamah Tabataba'i*, p. 198.

26. Mesbah, "Naqsh-e Allamah Tabataba'i dar Maᶜaref-i Islami," in Anonymous (ed.), *Yadnameh-ye Allamah Tabataba'i*, pp. 198–199.

27. Mesbah, "Naqsh-e Allamah Tabataba'i dar Maᶜaref-i Islami," in Anonymous (ed.), *Yadnameh-ye Allamah Tabataba'i*, p. 199.

28. See Hosseini-ye Tehrani (ed.), *Mehr-e Taban*, p. 57.

29. Hosseini-ye Tehrani (ed.), *Mehr-e Taban*, p. 58.

30. Hosseini-ye Tehrani (ed.), *Mehr-e Taban*, p. 60.

31. I dare not translate the rest of the *ghazal*. Translating a *ghazal* of Hafez makes more a mockery of the translator than it conveys a minimum of what the *ghazal* signifies in its multiple and rather uncontrollable layers of meaning and signification. The rest of the *ghazal*, as indeed its opening verse, indicates that one should not hesitate to do what is right for fear of disapproval by others, however powerful they might be.

32. See Hosseini-ye Tehrani (ed.), *Mehr-e Taban*, pp. 60–61.

33. Hosseini-ye Tehrani (ed.), *Mehr-e Taban*, pp. 61–62.

34. Hosseini-ye Tehrani (ed.), *Mehr-e Taban*, p. 62.

35. Hosseini-ye Tehrani (ed.), *Mehr-e Taban*, p. 62. The infiltration of Marxist ideas into the heartland of Shiᶜi scholastic learning and piety was not limited to Qom. When in 1957 Elizabeth Fernea visited Karbala, she reports that "the pilgrims brought hashish, spices, copper and rugs to trade in Karbala; they managed also to bring smallpox and cholera, and agents disguised as pilgrims brought in Marxist leaflets." See Fernea, *Guests of the Sheik*, p. 218.

36. Hosseini-ye Tehrani (ed.), *Mehr-e Taban*, p. 62. For an insightful postrevolutionary reflection on the significance of philosophy in the prerevolutionary period, see Ardakani, "Defaᶜ-e az Falsafeh," in Anonymous (ed.), *Yadnameh-ye Allamah Tabataba'i*.

37. Hosseini-ye Tehrani (ed.), *Mehr-e Taban*, p. 62.

38. Hosseini-ye Tehrani (ed.), *Mehr-e Taban*, p. 62.

39. See Tabataba'i, "Maqalah fi al-Tawhid," in Anonymous (ed.), *Yadnameh-ye Allamah Tabataba'i*, pp. 22–26.

40. Tabataba'i, "Maqalah fi al-Tawhid," in Anonymous (ed.), *Yadnameh-ye Allamah Tabataba'i*, p. 23.

41. Tabataba'i, "Maqalah fi al-Tawhid," in Anonymous (ed.), *Yadnameh-ye Allamah Tabataba'i*, p. 24.

42. Tabataba'i, "Maqalah fi al-Tawhid," in Anonymous (ed.), *Yadnameh-ye Allamah Tabataba'i*, p. 24.

43. See Ardakani, "Defaᶜ-e az Falsafeh," in Anonymous (ed.), *Yadnameh-ye Allamah Tabataba'i*, pp. 29–56.

44. Ardakani, "Defaᶜ-e az Falsafeh," in Anonymous (ed.), *Yadnameh-ye Allamah Tabataba'i*, p. 43.

45. Ardakani, "Defaᶜ-e az Falsafeh," in Anonymous (ed.), *Yadnameh-ye Allamah Tabataba'i*, p. 44.

46. See Jaᶜfari, "Falsafeh-ye Gharb az Did-gah-e Allamah Ostad Sayyid Muhammad Hossein Tabataba'i Qaddasa Sirrahu," in Anonymous (ed.), *Yadnameh-ye Allamah Tabataba'i*, pp. 57–86, especially p. 80.

47. See Mesbah, "Naqsh-e Allamah Tabataba'i dar Maᶜaref-i Islami," in Anonymous (ed.), *Yadnameh-ye Allamah Tabataba'i*, p. 196.

48. Mesbah, "Naqsh-e Allamah Tabataba'i dar Maᶜaref-i Islami," in Anonymous (ed.), *Yadnameh-ye Allamah Tabataba'i*, p. 196.

49. Mesbah, "Naqsh-e Allamah Tabataba'i dar Maᶜaref-i Islami," in Anonymous (ed.), *Yadnameh-ye Allamah Tabataba'i*, p. 197.

50. Mesbah, "Naqsh-e Allamah Tabataba'i dar Maᶜaref-i Islami," in Anonymous (ed.), *Yadnameh-ye Allamah Tabataba'i*, p. 197.

51. Mesbah, "Naqsh-e Allamah Tabataba'i dar Maᶜaref-i Islami," in Anonymous (ed.), *Yadnameh-ye Allamah Tabataba'i*, p. 197.

52. Mesbah, "Naqsh-e Allamah Tabataba'i dar Maᶜaref-i Islami," in Anonymous (ed.), *Yadnameh-ye Allamah Tabataba'i*, p. 197.

53. Muhammad Taqi Mesbah, for example, writes, "I am not at liberty to relate and explain all these difficulties [that Allamah Tabataba'i faced]." Mesbah, "Naqsh-e Allamah Tabataba'i dar Maᶜaref-i Islami," in Anonymous (ed.), *Yadnameh-ye Allamah Tabataba'i*, p. 197.

54. See Ahmadi, "Akhlaq-e Allamah va yek Bahth-e Falsafi," in Anonymous (ed.), *Yadnameh-ye Allamah Tabataba'i*, pp. 169–186, especially p. 173.

55. Ahmadi, "Akhlaq-e Allamah va yek Bahth-e Falsafi," in Anonymous (ed.), *Yadnameh-ye Allamah Tabataba'i*, p. 173.

56. Ahmadi, "Akhlaq-e Allamah va yek Bahth-e Falsafi," in Anonymous (ed.), *Yadnameh-ye Allamah Tabataba'i*, p. 173.

57. Ahmadi, "Akhlaq-e Allamah va yek Bahth-e Falsafi," in Anonymous (ed.), *Yadnameh-ye Allamah Tabataba'i*, p. 175.

58. Ahmadi, "Akhlaq-e Allamah va yek Bahth-e Falsafi," in Anonymous (ed.), *Yadnameh-ye Allamah Tabataba'i*, p. 176.

59. See Jaᶜfari, "Falsafeh-ye Gharb az Did-gah-e Allamah Ostad Sayyid Muhammad Hossein Tabataba'i Qaddasa Sirrahu," in Anonymous (ed.), *Yadnameh-ye Allamah Tabataba'i*, p. 60.

60. Jaᶜfari, "Falsafeh-ye Gharb az Did-gah-e Allamah Ostad Sayyid Muhammad Hossein Tabataba'i Qaddasa Sirrahu," in Anonymous (ed.), *Yadnameh-ye Allamah Tabataba'i*, p. 60.

61. See Amoli, "Allamah Tabataba'i dar Manzarah-ye Erfan-e Nazari va Amali," p. 3.

62. Amoli, "Allamah Tabataba'i dar Manzareh-ye Erfan-e Nazari va Amali," p. 6.

63. Amoli, "Allamah Tabataba'i dar Manzareh-ye Erfan-e Nazari va Amali," p. 6.

64. Amoli, "Allamah Tabataba'i dar Manzareh-ye Erfan-e Nazari va Amali," p. 8.

65. Amoli, "Allamah Tabataba'i dar Manzareh-ye Erfan-e Nazari va Amali," p. 8.

66. Amoli, "Allamah Tabataba'i dar Manzareh-ye Erfan-e Nazari va Amali," p. 9. See also Allamah Tabataba'i's ideas on the nature of religious beliefs in Tabataba'i, *Islamic Teachings,* pp. 43–66.

67. Amoli, "Allamah Tabataba'i dar Manzareh-ye Erfan-e Nazari va Amali," p. 11.

68. Amoli, "Allamah Tabataba'i dar Manzareh-ye Erfan-e Nazari va Amali," p. 11.

69. Amoli, "Allamah Tabataba'i dar Manzareh-ye Erfan-e Nazari va Amali," p. 11.

70. Amoli, "Allamah Tabataba'i dar Manzareh-ye Erfan-e Nazari va Amali," pp. 11–12.

71. Hosseini-ye Tehrani (ed.), *Mehr-e Taban,* p. 15.

72. Hosseini-ye Tehrani (ed.), *Mehr-e Taban,* p. 15.

73. Hosseini-ye Tehrani (ed.), *Mehr-e Taban,* p. 16.

74. Hosseini-ye Tehrani (ed.), *Mehr-e Taban,* p. 16.

75. Hosseini-ye Tehrani (ed.), *Mehr-e Taban,* p. 16.

76. Hosseini-ye Tehrani (ed.), *Mehr-e Taban,* p. 17.

77. Hosseini-ye Tehrani (ed.), *Mehr-e Taban,* p. 17. Allamah Tabataba'i himself was also a gifted poet. See an example of his *ghazals* on p. 56 of the same book.

78. Hosseini-ye Tehrani (ed.), *Mehr-e Taban,* p. 17.

79. Hosseini-ye Tehrani (ed.), *Mehr-e Taban,* p. 17.

80. Hosseini-ye Tehrani (ed.), *Mehr-e Taban,* p. 20.

81. Hosseini-ye Tehrani (ed.), *Mehr-e Taban,* p. 21.

82. Hosseini-ye Tehrani (ed.), *Mehr-e Taban,* p. 21.

83. Hosseini-ye Tehrani (ed.), *Mehr-e Taban,* p. 23. For a full discussion of the significance of Allamah Tabataba'i's philosophical positions during the prerevolutionary period, see the chapter on Tabataba'i in Ardakani, *Defaᶜ-e az Falsafeh,* pp. 9–69.

84. Hosseini-ye Tehrani (ed.), *Mehr-e Taban,* p. 23. For a brief autobiographical sketch in English, see Tabataba'i, *Islamic Teachings,* pp. 13–18.

85. Hosseini-ye Tehrani (ed.), *Mehr-e Taban,* p. 23.

86. Hosseini-ye Tehrani (ed.), *Mehr-e Taban,* p. 24.

87. Hosseini-ye Tehrani (ed.), *Mehr-e Taban,* pp. 25–26.

88. Hosseini-ye Tehrani (ed.), *Mehr-e Taban,* p. 26.

89. Hosseini-ye Tehrani (ed.), *Mehr-e Taban,* pp. 26–27.

90. For a discussion of this aspect of Molla Sadra's significance, see Ashtiani's Introduction to his edition of Molla Sadra, *al-Shawahid al-Rububiyyah fi al-Manahij al-Sulukiyyah* or Nasr, *Sadr al-Din Shirazi & His Transcendent Theosophy.*

91. Hosseini-ye Tehrani (ed.), *Mehr-e Taban,* p. 28.

92. Hosseini-ye Tehrani (ed.), *Mehr-e Taban,* pp. 29–35.

93. Hosseini-ye Tehrani (ed.), *Mehr-e Taban,* p. 36.

94. Hosseini-ye Tehrani (ed.), *Mehr-e Taban,* p. 36.

95. Hosseini-ye Tehrani (ed.), *Mehr-e Taban,* p. 36. As a prominent example of

Allamah Tabataba'i's preference for the primacy of the philosophical discourse, see Tabataba'i, *Nahayah al-Hikmah*.

96. Hosseini-ye Tehrani (ed.), *Mehr-e Taban*, pp. 36–38.

97. Hosseini-ye Tehrani (ed.), *Mehr-e Taban*, p. 39.

98. Hosseini-ye Tehrani (ed.), *Mehr-e Taban*, p. 39.

99. Hosseini-ye Tehrani (ed.), *Mehr-e Taban*, p. 39.

100. Parts of these interviews and discussions were later published in Tabataba'i, *Shi'ah*. I have the details of these sessions from various interviews with S. H. Nasr.

101. Hosseini-ye Tehrani (ed.), *Mehr-e Taban*, p. 40.

102. See, for example, Tabataba'i's response to a critic at the end of another version of his dialogues with Henri Corbin in Tabataba'i, *Zohur-e Shi'ah*, pp. 124–144.

103. Hosseini-ye Tehrani (ed.), *Mehr-e Taban*, pp. 50–51.

104. Hosseini-ye Tehrani (ed.), *Mehr-e Taban*, p. 51.

105. Hosseini-ye Tehrani (ed.), *Mehr-e Taban*, pp. 63–64.

106. Hosseini-ye Tehrani (ed.), *Mehr-e Taban*, pp. 63–64.

107. Hosseini-ye Tehrani (ed.), *Mehr-e Taban*, pp. 51–52.

108. Hosseini-ye Tehrani (ed.), *Mehr-e Taban*, p. 56.

109. For the text of this *ghazal*, see Tabataba'i, "Kish-e Mehr," p. 4. This *ghazal* was also sung by the eminent Iranian singer Shahram Nazeri to the music of Jalil Andalibi, C&G Audio & Video Recording and Duplicating, Inc., 1987.

110. See Sobhani, "Maqam-e Elmi va Farhangi-ye Allamah Tabataba'i," p. 7.

111. Tabataba'i, *Qur'an dar Islam*, p. 4. Equally significant on Allamah Tabataba'i's views of the Qur'an is his *Tarikh-e Qur'an*, which, in fact, is a collection of essays extracted from the more voluminous *al-Mizan*. It is noteworthy that the editor of Tabataba'i's *Tarikh-e Qur'an*, Muhammad Ali Lesani-ye Fesharaki, points out that the expression "Tarikh-e Qur'an" ("The History of Qur'an") is an Orientalistic construction imposed on the science of Qur'anic studies. He insists that "in reconstructing the Islamic culture" such imported terms ought to be avoided. Yet he proceeds to use the term not only in the text but as the very title of the compilation. See the editor's introductory remarks in *Tarikh-e Qur'an*, p. 6.

112. Tabataba'i, *Qur'an dar Islam*, pp. 5–18.

113. Tabataba'i, *Qur'an dar Islam*, p. 17.

114. Tabataba'i, *Qur'an dar Islam*, p. 18.

115. Tabataba'i, *Qur'an dar Islam*, p. 24.

116. Tabataba'i, *Qur'an dar Islam*, p. 25.

117. Tabataba'i, *Qur'an dar Islam*, p. 27.

118. Tabataba'i, *Qur'an dar Islam*, p. 22.

119. Tabataba'i, *Qur'an dar Islam*, p. 30.

120. Tabataba'i, *Qur'an dar Islam*, p. 41. For a short statement about the significance of the Qur'an for Allamah Tabataba'i, see Tabataba'i, *Islamic Teachings*, pp. 97–106.

121. Tabataba'i, *Qur'an dar Islam*, pp. 44–46.

122. Tabataba'i, *Qur'an dar Islam*, pp. 47–59.

123. Tabataba'i, *Qur'an dar Islam*, p. 63.

124. Tabataba'i, *Qur'an dar Islam*, p. 70.

125. Tabataba'i, *Qur'an dar Islam*, p. 76.
126. Tabataba'i, *Qur'an dar Islam*, p. 77.
127. Tabataba'i, *Qur'an dar Islam*, p. 77.
128. Tabataba'i, *Qur'an dar Islam*, p. 77.
129. Tabataba'i, *Qur'an dar Islam*, p. 77.
130. Tabataba'i, *Qur'an dar Islam*, p. 90. For Allamah Tabataba'i's position on the relationship between the Prophet and the Qur'an, see Tabataba'i, *Shi'ite Islam*, pp. 153–156.
131. Tabataba'i, *Qur'an dar Islam*, pp. 91–93.
132. Tabataba'i, *Qur'an dar Islam*, p. 94.
133. Tabataba'i, *Qur'an dar Islam*, pp. 94–109.
134. Tabataba'i, *Qur'an dar Islam*, p. 115.
135. Tabataba'i, *Qur'an dar Islam*, p. 128.
136. Tabataba'i, *Qur'an dar Islam*, p. 132.
137. Tabataba'i, *Qur'an dar Islam*, p. 134.
138. Tabataba'i, *Qur'an dar Islam*, p. 137.
139. Tabataba'i, *Qur'an dar Islam*, pp. 141–187.
140. For the details of these circumstances, see Hosseini-ye Tehrani (ed.), *Mehr-e Taban*, p. 41.
141. Hosseini-ye Tehrani (ed.), *Mehr-e Taban*, p. 44.
142. Hosseini-ye Tehrani (ed.), *Mehr-e Taban*, p. 44.
143. See Mesbah, "Naqsh-e Allamah Tabataba'i dar Ma'aref-i Islami," in Anonymous (ed.), *Yadnameh-ye Allamah Tabataba'i*, pp. 200–201.
144. Here is the full text of the "Authority Verse" in the Qur'an, 4: 59 (in Pickthall's translation):

O ye who believe! Obey Allah, and obey the messenger and those of you who are in authority; and if ye have a dispute concerning any matter, refer it to Allah and the messenger if ye are (in truth) believers in Allah and the Last Day. That is better and more seemly in the end.

145. See Tabataba'i, *Tafsir al-Mizan*, vol. 8, p. 237. For a different reading of the significance of this verse, see Amir Arjomand, *The Turban for the Crown*, pp. 177–183.
146. Tabataba'i, *Tafsir al-Mizan*, vol. 8, p. 240. Zamakhshari (d.528/1133), in his *al-Kashshaf an Haqa'iq Ghawamiz al-Tanzil*, considers "those of authority among you" to refer to "the just rulers" (umara' al-haqq) because God and his messenger do not order people to obey "the unjust rulers" (umara' al-jawr). (See Zamakhshari, *al-Kashshaf an Haqa'iq Ghawamiz al-Tanzil*, al-Juz' al-awwal, p. 524.) However, Al-Tabarsi, a prominent Shi'i commentator of the sixth Muslim (twelfth C.E.) century on the authority of al-Baqir and al-Sadiq, the Fifth and the Sixth Shi'i Imams, considers "those of authority among you" to be referring to the Shi'i Imams, who have to be obeyed absolutely and as a matter of principle *(bi al-itlaq)* and on the same par with the authority of God and his messenger. He further adds that "it is not permissible that God would obligate obedience to any person absolutely and as a matter of principle except for those whose infallability is established." (See al-Tabarsi, *Majma' al-Bayan fi Tafsir al-Qur'an*, al-Juz' al-Thal-ith, p. 100.)
147. Tabataba'i, *Tafsir al-Mizan*, p. 240. Further on the political significance of

Allamah Tabataba'i's Qur'anic commentary, see Sahbi, "Falsafeh-ye Siasi az Did-gah-e Allamah Tabataba'i."

148. Tabataba'i, *Tafsir al-Mizan*, p. 240.
149. Tabataba'i, *Tafsir al-Mizan*, p. 241.
150. Tabataba'i, *Tafsir al-Mizan*, p. 241.
151. Tabataba'i, *Tafsir al-Mizan*, p. 241.
152. Tabataba'i, *Tafsir al-Mizan*, p. 242.
153. Tabataba'i, *Tafsir al-Mizan*, p. 242.
154. Tabataba'i, *Tafsir al-Mizan*, p. 243.
155. Tabataba'i, *Tafsir al-Mizan*, pp. 247–248.
156. Tabataba'i, *Tafsir al-Mizan*, p. 250.
157. Tabataba'i, *Tafsir al-Mizan*, pp. 250–251.
158. Tabataba'i, *Tafsir al-Mizan*, p. 251.
159. See Soltani, "Sima-ye Zan dar 'al-Mizan,' " p. 14. This is an excellent analysis of Allamah Tabataba'i's position on women in Islam.
160. Soltani, "Sima-ye Zan dar 'al-Mizan,' " p. 15.
161. Soltani, "Sima-ye Zan dar 'al-Mizan,' " p. 15.
162. Soltani, "Sima-ye Zan dar 'al-Mizan,' " p. 15.
163. Soltani, "Sima-ye Zan dar 'al-Mizan,' " p. 16.
164. See Hosseini-ye Tehrani (ed.), *Mehr-e Taban*, p. 40.
165. See Zanjani, "Allamah Tabataba'i: Jame'-e Hekmat va Shari'at," p. 3.
166. Zanjani, "Allamah Tabataba'i: Jame'-e Hekmat va Shari'at," p. 2.
167. Hosseini-ye Tehrani (ed.), *Mehr-e Taban*, p. 46.
168. For an informative account of Corbin's presence in the Iranian philosoph-ical scene, see Daryush Shaygan, "Seyr va Soluk-e Corbin: Az Heidegger ta Sohre-vardi."
169. Hosseini-ye Tehrani (ed.), *Mehr-e Taban*, p. 47.
170. See Tabataba'i, *Zohur-e Shi'ah*.
171. See S. N. Nasr's Preface to Tabataba'i, *Shi'ite Islam*, pp. 3–28.
172. See Mesbah, "Naqsh-e Allamah Tabataba'i dar Ma'aref-i Islami," in Anonymous (ed.), *Yadnameh-ye Allamah Tabataba'i*, p. 201.
173. In the form of a book, Anonymous (ed.), *Bahthi dar Bareh-ye Marja'iyyat va Ruhaniyyat*, in which Taleqani, Motahhari, Bazargan, Allamah Tabataba'i, and many others reflected on the nature of juridical authority.
174. Anonymous (ed.), *Bahthi dar Bareh-ye Marja'iyyat va Ruhaniyyat*, p. 14.
175. Anonymous (ed.), *Bahthi dar Bareh-ye Marja'iyyat va Ruhaniyyat*, p. 16.
176. Anonymous (ed.), *Bahthi dar Bareh-ye Marja'iyyat va Ruhaniyyat*, p. 17.
177. Anonymous (ed.), *Bahthi dar Bareh-ye Marja'iyyat va Ruhaniyyat*, pp. 71–72.
178. Anonymous (ed.), *Bahthi dar Bareh-ye Marja'iyyat va Ruhaniyyat*, p. 74.
179. Anonymous (ed.), *Bahthi dar Bareh-ye Marja'iyyat va Ruhaniyyat*, p. 74.
180. Anonymous (ed.), *Bahthi dar Bareh-ye Marja'iyyat va Ruhaniyyat*, p. 74.
181. Anonymous (ed.), *Bahthi dar Bareh-ye Marja'iyyat va Ruhaniyyat*, pp. 74–75.
182. Anonymous (ed.), *Bahthi dar Bareh-ye Marja'iyyat va Ruhaniyyat*, p. 78.
183. Anonymous (ed.), *Bahthi dar Bareh-ye Marja'iyyat va Ruhaniyyat*, pp. 78–79.

184. Anonymous (ed.), *Bahthi dar Bareh-ye Marja'iyyat va Ruhaniyyat*, p. 81. For further discussion of the nature of political and religious authority in Shi'ism, see Tabataba'i, *Shi'ite Islam*, pp. 39–71.

185. Anonymous (ed.), *Bahthi dar Bareh-ye Marja'iyyat va Ruhaniyyat*, p. 83.

186. Anonymous (ed.), *Bahthi dar Bareh-ye Marja'iyyat va Ruhaniyyat*, p. 85.

187. Anonymous (ed.), *Bahthi dar Bareh-ye Marja'iyyat va Ruhaniyyat*, p. 85.

188. Anonymous (ed.), *Bahthi dar Bareh-ye Marja'iyyat va Ruhaniyyat*, p. 86.

189. Anonymous (ed.), *Bahthi dar Bareh-ye Marja'iyyat va Ruhaniyyat*, p. 86.

190. Anonymous (ed.), *Bahthi dar Bareh-ye Marja'iyyat va Ruhaniyyat*, p. 86.

191. Anonymous (ed.), *Bahthi dar Bareh-ye Marja'iyyat va Ruhaniyyat*, p. 89.

192. Anonymous (ed.), *Bahthi dar Bareh-ye Marja'iyyat va Ruhaniyyat*, pp. 89–90. For further elaboration of Allamah Tabataba'i's political and social ideas, see Tabataba'i, *Ravabet-e Ejtema'i dar Islam*.

193. Anonymous (ed.), *Bahthi dar Bareh-ye Marja'iyyat va Ruhaniyyat*, pp. 90–91.

194. Anonymous (ed.), *Bahthi dar Bareh-ye Marja'iyyat va Ruhaniyyat*, p. 91.

195. Anonymous (ed.), *Bahthi dar Bareh-ye Marja'iyyat va Ruhaniyyat*, p. 91.

196. Anonymous (ed.), *Bahthi dar Bareh-ye Marja'iyyat va Ruhaniyyat*, p. 92.

197. Anonymous (ed.), *Bahthi dar Bareh-ye Marja'iyyat va Ruhaniyyat*, p. 92.

198. Anonymous (ed.), *Bahthi dar Bareh-ye Marja'iyyat va Ruhaniyyat*, p. 94.

199. Compare this with his treatment of the "Authority Verse" in previous sections of this chapter.

200. Anonymous (ed.), *Bahthi dar Bareh-ye Marja'iyyat va Ruhaniyyat*, p. 95.

201. Anonymous (ed.), *Bahthi dar Bareh-ye Marja'iyyat va Ruhaniyyat*, p. 97.

202. Compare this part with the relevant sections of Khomeini's chapter.

203. Anonymous (ed.), *Bahthi dar Bareh-ye Marja'iyyat va Ruhaniyyat*, p. 98.

204. Anonymous (ed.), *Bahthi dar Bareh-ye Marja'iyyat va Ruhaniyyat*, p. 98.

205. Anonymous (ed.), *Bahthi dar Bareh-ye Marja'iyyat va Ruhaniyyat*, p. 99.

206. Anonymous (ed.), *Bahthi dar Bareh-ye Marja'iyyat va Ruhaniyyat*, p. 99.

207. Marx, *The Poverty of Philosophy*, p. 29.

208. The great Poundian dictum. See Bradbury, *The Modern World*, p. 3.

6. *Mehdi Bazargan*

1. See Dawson, *Confucius*, p. 64.

2. Dawson, *Confucius*, p. 64.

3. See Bazargan, *Modafe'at*, p. 39. For a concise account of Bazargan's political career and ideas, see Chehabi, "State and Society in Islamic Liberalism," pp. 85–98.

4. See Ja'fari (trans. and ed.), *Nehzat-e Bidar-gari dar Jahan-e Islam*, p. 157.

5. Bazargan, *Modafe'at*, p. 41.

6. Ja'fari (trans. and ed.), *Nehzat-e Bidar-gari dar Jahan-e Islam*, p. 158.

7. Siasi, *Gozaresh-e Yek Zendeqi*, p. 94.

8. Siasi, *Gozaresh-e Yek Zendeqi*, p. 119.

9. Bazargan, *Az Khoda-parasti ta Khod-parasti*, p. 7.

10. Bazargan, *Az Khoda-parasti ta Khod-parasti*, p. 36.

11. Bazargan, *Az Khoda-parasti ta Khod-parasti*, p. 42.

12. Bazargan, *Az Khoda-parasti ta Khod-parasti*, p. 46.
13. Bazargan, *Az Khoda-parasti ta Khod-parasti*, p. 47.
14. Bazargan, *Az Khoda-parasti ta Khod-parasti*, pp. 50–51.
15. Bazargan, *Az Khoda-parasti ta Khod-parasti*, p. 57.
16. Bazargan, *Az Khoda-parasti ta Khod-parasti*, p. 60.
17. Bazargan, *Az Khoda-parasti ta Khod-parasti*, p. 61.
18. Bazargan, *Az Khoda-parasti ta Khod-parasti*, p. 66.
19. Bazargan, *Az Khoda-parasti ta Khod-parasti*, p. 68. For a further discussion of Bazargan's political ideas, see Chehabi, *Iranian Politics and Religious Modernism*, pp. 53–60.
20. Bazargan, *Az Khoda-parasti ta Khod-parasti*, p. 74.
21. Bazargan, *Az Khoda-parasti ta Khod-parasti*, p. 76.
22. Bazargan, *Az Khoda-parasti ta Khod-parasti*, p. 78.
23. Bazargan, *Az Khoda-parasti ta Khod-parasti*, p. 85.
24. Ja'fari (trans. and ed.), *Nehzat-e Bidar-gari dar Jahan-e Islam*, p. 159.
25. Bazargan, *Eshq va Parastesh*, p. 4.
26. Bazargan, *Eshq va Parastesh*, p. 6.
27. Bazargan, *Eshq va Parastesh*, p. 13.
28. Bazargan, *Eshq va Parastesh*, pp. 16–17.
29. Bazargan, *Eshq va Parastesh*, p. 19.
30. Bazargan, *Eshq va Parastesh*, p. 30.
31. Bazargan, *Eshq va Parastesh*, p. 50.
32. Bazargan, *Eshq va Parastesh*, p. 67. For a further discussion of Bazargan on economics, in contradistinction with Taleqani's ideas, see Chehabi, *Iranian Politics and Religious Modernism*, pp. 63–64.
33. Bazargan, *Eshq va Parastesh*, pp. 191–192.
34. Bazargan, *Eshq va Parastesh*, p. 205.
35. Bazargan, *Eshq va Parastesh*, p. 207.
36. Bazargan, *Eshq va Parastesh*, p. 220.
37. Bazargan, *Eshq va Parastesh*, pp. 221–222.
38. Bazargan, *Angizeh va Angizandeh*, pp. 26–27.
39. Bazargan, *Angizeh va Angizandeh*, p. 33.
40. Bazargan, *Mosalman: Ejtema'i va Jahani*, p. 4.
41. Bazargan, *Mosalman: Ejtema'i va Jahani*, p. 2.
42. Bazargan, *Mosalman: Ejtema'i va Jahani*, p. 10.
43. Bazargan, *Mosalman: Ejtema'i va Jahani*, p. 12.
44. Bazargan, *Mosalman: Ejtema'i va Jahani*, pp. 16–17. For post-revolutionary reflections of Bazargan on the nature and social functions of religion, see Bazargan, *Bazyabi-ye Arzesh-ha*.
45. Bazargan, *Mosalman: Ejtema'i va Jahani*, p. 37.
46. Bazargan, *Mosalman: Ejtema'i va Jahani*, p. 47.
47. Bazargan, *Mosalman: Ejtema'i va Jahani*, p. 48.
48. Bazargan, *Mosalman: Ejtema'i va Jahani*, p. 67.
49. Bazargan, *Khaneh-ye Mardom*, p. 5.
50. Bazargan, *Khaneh-ye Mardom*, p. 13.
51. Bazargan, *Khaneh-ye Mardom*, p. 49.
52. Bazargan, *Khaneh-ye Mardom*, p. 56.

53. Bazargan, *Khaneh-ye Mardom,* p. 57.

54. See Bazargan, *Bad va Baran dar Qur'an,* passim.

55. See Bazargan, *Seyr-e Tahavvol dar Qur'an.*

56. See Ja'fari (trans. and ed.), *Nehzat-e Bidar-gari dar Jahan-e Islam,* p. 160.

57. For the most comprehensive study of the Freedom Movement of Iran, see Chehabi, *Iranian Politics and Religious Modernism.* For a critical Persian account, see Soltani, *Khat-e Sazesh.*

58. Anonymous (ed.), *Nehzat-e Azadi-ye Iran,* p. 20.

59. Anonymous (ed.), *Nehzat-e Azadi-ye Iran,* p. 31.

60. Anonymous (ed.), *Nehzat-e Azadi-ye Iran,* p. 32.

61. Anonymous (ed.), *Nehzat-e Azadi-ye Iran,* p. 33.

62. Anonymous (ed.), *Nehzat-e Azadi-ye Iran,* p. 36.

63. Anonymous (ed.), *Nehzat-e Azadi-ye Iran,* p. 38.

64. Anonymous (ed.), *Nehzat-e Azadi-ye Iran,* p. 39.

65. Anonymous (ed.), *Nehzat-e Azadi-ye Iran,* p. 45.

66. For the story of this split, see Abrahamian, *Radical Islam,* chap. 3; Chehabi, *Iranian Politics and Religious Modernism,* chap. 5.

67. Anonymous (ed.), *Nehzat-e Azadi-ye Iran,* p. 48.

68. Anonymous (ed.), *Nehzat-e Azadi-ye Iran,* pp. 49–62.

69. Anonymous (ed.), *Nehzat-e Azadi-ye Iran,* p. 53.

70. Bazargan, *Modafe'at,* p. 2.

71. Bazargan, *Modafe'at,* pp. 2–3.

72. Bazargan, *Modafe'at,* p. 206.

73. Bazargan, *Modafe'at,* p. 208.

74. Bazargan, *Modafe'at,* p. 211.

75. Bazargan, *Modafe'at,* p. 213.

76. The first part of Bazargan's defense concludes with the assertion of "why and how I agree with constitutional monarchy for Iran" (Bazargan, *Modafe'at,* p. 213), while the second part begins with the explanatory "why we are opposed to absolutism and advocate the constitution, the national government, or democracy" (p. 214).

77. See the publisher's Introduction to Bazargan's *Modafe'at,* p. Two.

78. Bazargan, *Modafe'at,* p. 218.

79. Bazargan, *Modafe'at,* p. 250.

80. Bazargan, *Modafe'at,* p. 255.

81. Bazargan, *Modafe'at,* p. 263. For a useful discussion of Bazargan's uses of history, see Chehabi, *Iranian Politics and Religious Modernism,* p. 78.

82. Bazargan, *Modafe'at,* p. 272.

83. Bazargan, *Modafe'at,* p. 276.

84. Bazargan, *Modafe'at,* p. 306.

85. Bazargan, *Modafe'at,* p. 349.

86. See Bazargan, "Entezarat-e Mardom az Maraje'," in Anonymous (ed.), *Bahthi dar Bareh-ye Marja'iyyat va Ruhaniyyat,* pp. 103–104.

87. Bazargan, "Entezarat-e Mardom az Maraje'," in Anonymous (ed.), *Bahthi dar Bareh-ye Marja'iyyat va Ruhaniyyat,* pp. 104–105.

88. Bazargan, "Entezarat-e Mardom az Maraje'," in Anonymous (ed.), *Bahthi dar Bareh-ye Marja'iyyat va Ruhaniyyat,* p. 105.

89. Bazargan, "Entezarat-e Mardom az Maraje^c," in Anonymous (ed.), *Bahthi dar Bareh-ye Marja'iyyat va Ruhaniyyat*, p. 107.

90. Bazargan, "Entezarat-e Mardom az Maraje^c," in Anonymous (ed.), *Bahthi dar Bareh-ye Marja'iyyat va Ruhaniyyat*, p. 107.

91. Bazargan, "Entezarat-e Mardom az Maraje^c," in Anonymous (ed.), *Bahthi dar Bareh-ye Marja'iyyat va Ruhaniyyat*, p. 107.

92. Bazargan, "Entezarat-e Mardom az Maraje^c," in Anonymous (ed.), *Bahthi dar Bareh-ye Marja'iyyat va Ruhaniyyat*, pp. 108–109.

93. Bazargan, "Entezarat-e Mardom az Maraje^c," in Anonymous (ed.), *Bahthi dar Bareh-ye Marja'iyyat va Ruhaniyyat*, p. 111. Here Bazargan's political rationalization of fundamental changes in the clerical establishment draws considerably on the Usuli tradition in the dominant Shi'i jurisprudence. See Modarressi, *An Introduction to Shi'i Law*, pp. 23–58, for an historical background with full bibliographical references.

94. Bazargan, "Entezarat-e Mardom az Maraje^c," in Anonymous (ed.), *Bahthi dar Bareh-ye Marja'iyyat va Ruhaniyyat*, p. 111.

95. Bazargan, "Entezarat-e Mardom az Maraje^c," in Anonymous (ed.), *Bahthi dar Bareh-ye Marja'iyyat va Ruhaniyyat*, p. 113.

96. Bazargan, "Entezarat-e Mardom az Maraje^c," in Anonymous (ed.), *Bahthi dar Bareh-ye Marja'iyyat va Ruhaniyyat*, p. 113.

97. Bazargan, "Entezarat-e Mardom az Maraje^c," in Anonymous (ed.), *Bahthi dar Bareh-ye Marja'iyyat va Ruhaniyyat*, p. 114.

98. Bazargan, "Entezarat-e Mardom az Maraje^c," in Anonymous (ed.), *Bahthi dar Bareh-ye Marja'iyyat va Ruhaniyyat*, p. 114.

99. Bazargan, "Entezarat-e Mardom az Maraje^c," in Anonymous (ed.), *Bahthi dar Bareh-ye Marja'iyyat va Ruhaniyyat*, p. 115.

100. Bazargan, "Entezarat-e Mardom az Maraje^c," in Anonymous (ed.), *Bahthi dar Bareh-ye Marja'iyyat va Ruhaniyyat*, p. 115.

101. Bazargan, "Entezarat-e Mardom az Maraje^c," in Anonymous (ed.), *Bahthi dar Bareh-ye Marja'iyyat va Ruhaniyyat*, p. 115.

102. See, for example, Tonekaboni, *Qesas al-Ulama'*, p. 8. For an English translation of this passage, to which Tonekaboni refers in his discussion of Sayyid Muhammad Baqir al-Musavi, see my "Lives of Prominent Nineteenth-Century Ulama' from Tonekaboni's Qisas al-Ulama'," in Amir Arjomand (ed.), *Authority and Political Culture in Shi'ism*, p. 319.

103. Bazargan, "Entezarat-e Mardom az Maraje^c," in Anonymous (ed.), *Bahthi dar Bareh-ye Marja'iyyat va Ruhaniyyat*, pp. 119–121.

104. See the encounter between Allamah Tabataba'i and Ayatollah Borujerdi in the Tabataba'i chapter.

105. Bazargan, "Entezarat-e Mardom az Maraje^c," in Anonymous (ed.), *Bahthi dar Bareh-ye Marja'iyyat va Ruhaniyyat*, p. 122.

106. Bazargan, "Entezarat-e Mardom az Maraje^c," in Anonymous (ed.), *Bahthi dar Bareh-ye Marja'iyyat va Ruhaniyyat*, pp. 125–126.

107. Bazargan, "Entezarat-e Mardom az Maraje^c," in Anonymous (ed.), *Bahthi dar Bareh-ye Marja'iyyat va Ruhaniyyat*, p. 126.

108. Bazargan, *Bad va Baran dar Qur'an*, p. 8.

109. Bazargan, *Bad va Baran dar Qur'an*, p. 15.

110. Bazargan, *Bad va Baran dar Qur'an*, pp. 15–16.
111. Bazargan, *Bad va Baran dar Qur'an*, p. 16.
112. Bazargan, *Bad va Baran dar Qur'an*, p. 18.
113. Bazargan, *Bad va Baran dar Qur'an*, p. 90.
114. Bazargan, *Bad va Baran dar Qur'an*, p. 164. Bazargan's writings at this pseudo-scientific level represent a wider exegetical development whose primary function and purpose were to "prove" the Qur'an "scientifically" valid. See Khorramshahi, *Tafsir va Tafasir-e Jadid*, pp. 103–111 and 121–127, for further discussions of such pseudo-scientific readings of the Qur'an in modern times.
115. Bazargan, *Be'that va Ideology*, pp. 1–2.
116. Bazargan, *Be'that va Ideology*, p. 2.
117. Bazargan, *Be'that va Ideology*, p. 2.
118. Bazargan, *Be'that va Ideology*, p. 3.
119. Bazargan, *Be'that va Ideology*, p. 11.
120. Bazargan, *Be'that va Ideology*, pp. 12–54.
121. Bazargan, *Be'that va Ideology*, p. 56.
122. Bazargan, *Be'that va Ideology*, pp. 57–63.
123. Bazargan, *Be'that va Ideology*, p. 63–69.
124. Bazargan, *Be'that va Ideology*, p. 71. See also Chehabi, *Iranian Politics and Religious Modernism*, pp. 67–73.
125. Bazargan, *Be'that va Ideology*, pp. 72–73.
126. Bazargan, *Be'that va Ideology*, p. 75.
127. Bazargan, *Be'that va Ideology*, pp. 78–79.
128. Bazargan, *Be'that va Ideology*, p. 77.
129. Bazargan, *Be'that va Ideology*, p. 80.
130. Bazargan, *Be'that va Ideology*, p. 81.
131. Bazargan, *Be'that va Ideology*, p. 86.
132. Bazargan, *Be'that va Ideology*, p. 91.
133. I have heard this anecdote from some former students of the Engineering School at Tehran University.
134. Bazargan, *Be'that va Ideology*, pp. 92–93.
135. Bazargan, *Be'that va Ideology*, p. 94.
136. Bazargan, *Be'that va Ideology*, p. 96.
137. Bazargan, *Be'that va Ideology*, p. 98.
138. Bazargan, *Be'that va Ideology*, p. 103.
139. Bazargan, *Be'that va Ideology*, pp. 107–108.
140. Bazargan, *Be'that va Ideology*, p. 115. For a critical assessment of Bazargan's views on the relationship between religion and politics, see Soltani, *Khat-e Sazesh*, pp. 146–147.
141. Bazargan, *Be'that va Ideology*, p. 126.
142. Bazargan, *Be'that va Ideology*, p. 133.
143. Bazargan, *Be'that va Ideology*, p. 142.
144. Bazargan, *Be'that va Ideology*, pp. 107 and 143.
145. Bazargan, *Be'that va Ideology*, pp. 144–145.
146. Bazargan, *Be'that va Ideology*, p. 158.
147. Bazargan, *Be'that va Ideology*, p. 169.
148. Bazargan, *Be'that va Ideology*, p. 172.

149. Bazargan, Be'that va Ideology, p. 184.
150. Bazargan, Be'that va Ideology, p. 193. For a critical reading of Bazargan's understanding of Islam, principally accusing him of a "Westoxicated" grasp of his own faith, see Soltani, Khat-e Sazesh, pp. 150–152.
151. Bazargan, Be'that va Ideology, p. 198.
152. Bazargan, Be'that va Ideology, pp. 211–212.
153. Bazargan, Be'that va Ideology, pp. 216–217.
154. Bazargan, Be'that va Ideology, pp. 217–218.
155. Bazargan, Be'that va Ideology, p. 225. For similar views of Taleqani, see the related passages in Chapter 4.
156. Bazargan, Be'that va Ideology, p. 225.
157. Bazargan, Be'that va Ideology, p. 226.
158. Bazargan, Be'that va Ideology, p. 232.
159. Bazargan, Be'that va Ideology, p. 233.
160. Bazargan, Be'that va Ideology, p. 236.
161. See the publisher's Introduction to Bazargan, Azadi-ye Hend, p. 3.
162. Introduction to Bazargan, Azadi-ye Hend, p. 4.
163. Introduction to Bazargan, Azadi-ye Hend, p. 4.
164. Bazargan, Azadi-ye Hend, p. 13.
165. Bazargan, Azadi-ye Hend, p. 13–14.
166. Bazargan, Azadi-ye Hend, p. 15.
167. Bazargan, Azadi-ye Hend, p. 15.
168. Bazargan, Azadi-ye Hend, pp. 15–16. See also Chehabi, Iranian Politics and Religious Modernism, pp. 55 and 71.
169. Bazargan, Azadi-ye Hend, pp. 23–32.
170. Bazargan, Azadi-ye Hend, p. 32.
171. Bazargan, Azadi-ye Hend, p. 37.
172. Bazargan, Azadi-ye Hend, p. 95.
173. Bazargan, Azadi-ye Hend, pp. 95–96.
174. Bazargan, Azadi-ye Hend, p. 96.
175. Bazargan, Azadi-ye Hend, p. 95.
176. Bazargan, Azadi-ye Hend, p. 95.
177. Bazargan, Azadi-ye Hend, p. 96.
178. Bazargan, Azadi-ye Hend, p. 96. Compare this with Bazargan's later relationship with Khomeini; see Chehabi, Iranian Politics and Religious Modernism, especially pp. 238–239.
179. Bazargan, Azadi-ye Hend, p. 96.
180. Bazargan, Azadi-ye Hend, p. 122.
181. Bazargan, Azadi-ye Hend, p. 122.
182. Bazargan, Azadi-ye Hend, p. 122.
183. Bazargan, Azadi-ye Hend, p. 123.
184. Bazargan, Azadi-ye Hend, p. 205.
185. Bazargan, Azadi-ye Hend, p. 209.
186. Bazargan, Azadi-ye Hend, p. 210. Kawthar, the title of a Qur'anic chapter (108), is believed to be a spring in paradise. It literally means "abundance." The word appears in the Qur'an (108:1–3):

1. Lo! We have given thee Abundance *(al-Kawthar)*;
2. So pray unto thy Lord, and sacrifice.
3. Lo It is thy insulter (and not you) who is without posterity.

187. Bazargan, *Azadi-ye Hend,* p. 189.
188. Bazargan, *Azadi-ye Hend,* p. 189.
189. Bazargan, *Azadi-ye Hend,* p. 189.
190. Bazargan, *Azadi-ye Hend,* p. 190.
191. Bazargan, *Azadi-ye Hend,* p. 191.
192. Bazargan, *Azadi-ye Hend,* p. 191.
193. Bazargan, *Azadi-ye Hend,* p. 192.
194. Bazargan, *Azadi-ye Hend,* p. 311.
195. Bazargan, *Azadi-ye Hend,* p. 311.
196. Bazargan, *Azadi-ye Hend,* p. 312.
197. Bazargan, *Azadi-ye Hend,* p. 312.
198. The Qur'an, 2:134, and as quoted in Bazargan, *Azadi-ye Hend,* p. 314.
199. See Ahmad Aram's Introduction to Bazargan, *Dars-e Dindari,* p. Nine.
200. Bazargan, *Dars-e Dindari,* pp. 1–14.
201. Bazargan, *Dars-e Dindari,* p. 23.
202. Bazargan, *Dars-e Dindari,* pp. 26–27.
203. Bazargan, *Dars-e Dindari,* p. 40.
204. Bazargan, *Dars-e Dindari,* pp. 42–43.
205. Bazargan, *Dars-e Dindari,* p. 54.
206. Bazargan, *Dars-e Dindari,* p. 61.
207. Bazargan, *Dars-e Dindari,* p. 69.
208. Bazargan, *Dars-e Dindari,* p. 79. For a sympathetic reading of this passage, see Ja'fari (trans. and ed.), *Nehzat-e Bidar-gari dar Jahan-e Islam,* p. 161. For a critical review, see Soltani, *Khat-e Sazesh,* pp. 143–146.
209. Bazargan, *Dars-e Dindari,* p. 80.
210. Bazargan, *Dars-e Dindari,* p. 82.
211. Bazargan, *Dars-e Dindari,* p. 89.
212. Bazargan, *Dars-e Dindari,* pp. 89–90.
213. Bazargan, *Dars-e Dindari,* p. 94.
214. Bazargan, *Dars-e Dindari,* p. 114.
215. Bazargan, *Dars-e Dindari,* p. 118.
216. Bazargan, *Dars-e Dindari,* p. 118. For a critical reading, see Soltani, *Khat-e Sazesh,* p. 52. On the same page, notice the reference to the passage from Al-e Ahmad, *Dar Khedmat va Khianat-e Roshanfekran,* where Bazargan's writings are labelled "Westoxicated."
217. Bazargan, *Dars-e Dindari,* p. 125.
218. Bazargan, *Dars-e Dindari,* p. 131.
219. Bazargan, *Dars-e Dindari,* p. 132.
220. Bazargan, *Dars-e Dindari,* p. 136.
221. Bazargan, *Dars-e Dindari,* pp. 139 ff.
222. Bazargan, *Dars-e Dindari,* p. 147.
223. Bazargan, *Dars-e Dindari,* p. 149.

224. Bazargan, *Dars-e Dindari*, p. 156.
225. Bazargan, *Dars-e Dindari*, p. 160.
226. Bazargan, *Dars-e Dindari*, p. 161.
227. Bazargan, *Khaneh-ye Mardom*, p. 70.
228. Bazargan, *Khaneh-ye Mardom*, p. 77. These passages are almost identical with those of Shariʿati and Al-e Ahmad when they visited their fellow Muslims in Mecca.
229. Bazargan, *Khaneh-ye Mardom*, p. 79.
230. Bazargan, *Khaneh-ye Mardom*, p. 80.
231. Bazargan, *Khaneh-ye Mardom*, p. 81.
232. Bazargan, *Khaneh-ye Mardom*, p. 82.
233. Bazargan, *Khaneh-ye Mardom*, p. 19.
234. Bazargan, *Khaneh-ye Mardom*, p. 22.
235. Bazargan, *Khaneh-ye Mardom*, pp. 24–30. These passages of Bazargan are very much reminiscent of Shariʿati's repoliticization of the Shiʿi sacred memory. Compare these parts of Bazargan's understanding of the Muslim pilgrimage to Shariʿati, *Miʿad ba Ibrahim*.
236. Bazargan, *Khaneh-ye Mardom*, p. 33.
237. Bazargan, *Khaneh-ye Mardom*, p. 44.
238. Bazargan, *Khaneh-ye Mardom*, p. 59.
239. Bazargan, *Khaneh-ye Mardom*, pp. 61–62.
240. See Dawson, *Confucius*, p. 65.
241. Dawson, *Confucius*, p. 65.

7. Abolhasan Bani-Sadr

1. See Moggridge, *John Maynard Keynes*, p. 133.
2. Moggridge, *John Maynard Keynes*, p. 133.
3. Moggridge, *John Maynard Keynes*, p. 133.
4. See Bani-Sadr, *Kish-e Shakhsiyyat*, pp. 51–62. For a short biography of Bani-Sadr, see Deldam, *Enqelab beh Ravayat-e Enqelab-Sazan*, pp. 153–165. For a short statement on his ideological disposition, see Keddie, *Roots of Revolution*, pp. 202–230.
5. Bani-Sadr, *Kish-e Shakhsiyyat*, pp. 105–179.
6. Bani-Sadr, *Kish-e Shakhsiyyat*, pp. 179–230.
7. Bani-Sadr, *Kish-e Shakhsiyyat*, pp. 231–251.
8. Bani-Sadr, *Kish-e Shakhsiyyat*, pp. 269–303.
9. Bani-Sadr, *Kish-e Shakhsiyyat*, p. 299.
10. Bani-Sadr, *Kish-e Shakhsiyyat*, p. 314.
11. Bani-Sadr, *Movazeneh-ha*, p. 1. In his Introduction to this text, Bani-Sadr emphatically asserts that "apparently, the modern history of the world inevitably will have to be known as an extension of the European history" (p. A). His stated agenda is to find an alternative, what he calls unitarian (or monotheistic = Towhidi), Muslim self-understanding, only to plunge deeply into "The Western" construction of his collective imagination.
12. Bani-Sadr, *Movazeneh-ha*, p. 3.
13. Bani-Sadr, *Movazeneh-ha*, p. 4.

14. Bani-Sadr, *Movazeneh-ha*, p. 12.
15. Bani-Sadr, *Movazeneh-ha*, p. 14.
16. Bani-Sadr, *Movazeneh-ha*, p. 16.
17. Bani-Sadr, *Movazeneh-ha*, p. 15.
18. Bani-Sadr, *Movazeneh-ha*, p. 18.
19. Bani-Sadr, *Movazeneh-ha*, p. 19.
20. Bani-Sadr, *Movazeneh-ha*, p. 19.
21. Bani-Sadr, *Movazeneh-ha*, pp. 21–23.
22. Bani-Sadr, *Movazeneh-ha*, p. 23.
23. Bani-Sadr, *Movazeneh-ha*, p. 27. For post-revolutionary reflections on the same theme, see Bani-Sadr, "Dialectic-e har Qodrat-talabi bar Mabna'-ye Hadaf ast."
24. Bani-Sadr, *Movazeneh-ha*, pp. 27–37.
25. Bani-Sadr, *Movazeneh-ha*, p. 30.
26. Bani-Sadr, *Movazeneh-ha*, p. 32.
27. Bani-Sadr, *Movazeneh-ha*, p. 31.
28. Bani-Sadr, *Movazeneh-ha*, p. 33.
29. Bani-Sadr, *Movazeneh-ha*, p. 34.
30. Bani-Sadr, *Movazeneh-ha*, p. 35.
31. Bani-Sadr, *Movazeneh-ha*, pp. 35–36.
32. Bani-Sadr, *Movazeneh-ha*, p. 36.
33. Bani-Sadr, *Movazeneh-ha*, p. 40.
34. Bani-Sadr, *Movazeneh-ha*, p. 43.
35. Bani-Sadr, *Movazeneh-ha*, pp. 43 and 54.
36. Bani-Sadr, *Movazeneh-ha*, pp. 65–72.
37. See Weber, "Politics as a Vocation," in Weber, *From Max Weber*, p. 78.
38. Vieille and Bani-Sadr, *Petrole et Violence*, p. 11. For further expansions on the relationship between economics and politics, see Bani-Sadr, "Sarmayeh-daran-e ma Kar-farma-ye Siasi Budand." All these statements ought to be put in a context best provided in Katouzian, *The Political Economy of Modern Iran*, pp. 213–373.
39. Vieille and Bani-Sadr, *Petrole et Violence*, p. 70.
40. Vieille and Bani-Sadr, *Petrole et Violence*, p. 71.
41. Vieille and Bani-Sadr, *Petrole et Violence*, p. 89, Table II.
42. Vieille and Bani-Sadr, *Petrole et Violence*, p. 73.
43. Vieille and Bani-Sadr, *Petrole et Violence*, p. 93, Table VI.
44. Vieille and Bani-Sadr, *Petrole et Violence*, p. 77.
45. Vieille and Bani-Sadr, *Petrole et Violence*, pp. 80–82.
46. Vieille and Bani-Sadr, *Petrole et Violence*, p. 84. For a balancing perspective on the political economy of oil in Iran, see Melamid, "Petroleum Product, Distribution and the Evolution of Economic Regions in Iran," in Korterpeter (ed.), *Oil and the Economic Geography of the Middle East and North Africa*, pp. 49–64.
47. Bani-Sadr, *Naft va Solteh*, p. I.
48. Bani-Sadr, *Naft va Solteh*, p. II. For a cogent account of the relationship between the repressive measures of the Pahlavi regime and its economic policies, see Halliday, *Iran*.
49. Bani-Sadr, *Naft va Solteh*, p. II.
50. Bani-Sadr, *Naft va Solteh*, p. III.

51. Bani-Sadr, *Naft va Solteh*, p. 1.
52. Bani-Sadr, *Naft va Solteh*, p. 2.
53. Bani-Sadr, *Naft va Solteh*, p. 3.
54. Bani-Sadr, *Naft va Solteh*, p. 10.
55. Bani-Sadr, *Naft va Solteh*, p. 11. See also Melamid, "Satellization in Iranian Crude-Oil Production," in Korterpeter (ed.), *Oil and the Economic Geography of the Middle East and North Africa*, pp. 65–81.
56. Bani-Sadr, *Naft va Solteh*, pp. 13–14.
57. Bani-Sadr, *Naft va Solteh*, p. 14.
58. Bani-Sadr, *Naft va Solteh*, p. 20.
59. Bani-Sadr, *Naft va Solteh*, p. 21.
60. Bani-Sadr, *Naft va Solteh*, p. 22.
61. Bani-Sadr, *Naft va Solteh*, p. 23. For a critical assessment of Bani-Sadr's positions on this and other economic issues, see Katouzian, "Shi'ism and Islamic Economics: Sadr and Bani-Sadr," in Keddie (ed.), *Religion and Politics in Iran*, pp. 145–165.
62. Bani-Sadr, *Naft va Solteh*, p. 25.
63. Bani-Sadr, *Naft va Solteh*, p. 26.
64. Bani-Sadr, *Naft va Solteh*, pp. 26–27.
65. Bani-Sadr, *Naft va Solteh*, p. 28.
66. Bani-Sadr, *Naft va Solteh*, p. 29.
67. Bani-Sadr, *Naft va Solteh*, p. 29.
68. Bani-Sadr, *Naft va Solteh*, pp. 123–128.
69. Bani-Sadr, *Naft va Solteh*, p. 124.
70. Bani-Sadr, *Naft va Solteh*, p. 126.
71. Bani-Sadr, *Naft va Solteh*, p. 127.
72. Bani-Sadr, *Naft va Solteh*, p. 127.
73. Bani-Sadr, *Naft va Solteh*, p. 145. See also Halliday, *Iran*, pp. 249–284.
74. Bani-Sadr, *Naft va Solteh*, p. 178.
75. Bani-Sadr, *Naft va Solteh*, p. 203.
76. Bani-Sadr, *Naft va Solteh*, p. 208.
77. Bani-Sadr, *Naft va Solteh*, p. 225.
78. Bani-Sadr, *Naft va Solteh*, p. 236.
79. Bani-Sadr, *Naft va Solteh*, p. 244.
80. Bani-Sadr, *Naft va Solteh*, p. 245.
81. Bani-Sadr, *Naft va Solteh*, p. 331.
82. Bani-Sadr, *Naft va Solteh*, p. 364.
83. See Katouzian, "Shi'ism and Islamic Economics: Sadr and Bani Sadr," in Keddie (ed.), *Religion and Politics in Iran*, p. 147.
84. Katouzian, "Shi'ism and Islamic Economics: Sadr and Bani Sadr," in Keddie (ed.), *Religion and Politics in Iran*, p. 146.
85. For an analysis, see Katouzian, "Shi'ism and Islamic Economics: Sadr and Bani Sadr," in Keddie (ed.), *Religion and Politics in Iran*, pp. 147 ff.
86. See Katouzian, "Shi'ism and Islamic Economics: Sadr and Bani Sadr," in Keddie (ed.), *Religion and Politics in Iran*, pp. 149 ff.
87. See Katouzian, "Shi'ism and Islamic Economics: Sadr and Bani Sadr," in Keddie (ed.), *Religion and Politics in Iran*, p. 152.

88. See Katouzian, "Shi'ism and Islamic Economics: Sadr and Bani Sadr," in Keddie (ed.), *Religion and Politics in Iran*, p. 153.

89. See Katouzian, "Shi'ism and Islamic Economics: Sadr and Bani Sadr," in Keddie (ed.), *Religion and Politics in Iran*, p. 154.

90. See Katouzian, "Shi'ism and Islamic Economics: Sadr and Bani Sadr," in Keddie (ed.), *Religion and Politics in Iran*, pp. 154–155.

91. As argued in Katouzian, "Shi'ism and Islamic Economics: Sadr and Bani Sadr," in Keddie (ed.), *Religion and Politics in Iran*, pp. 157–158. For a contrasting perspective to Bani-Sadr's, see also Melamid, "The Geographical Pattern of Iranian Oil Development," in Korterpeter (ed.), *Oil and the Economic Geography of the Middle East and North Africa*, pp. 23–47.

92. Bani-Sadr, *Eqtesad-e Towhidi*, p. I. For a general critical assessment of modern Islamic economic thought, reflecting on their impracticalities, see Kuran, "Behavioral Norms in the Islamic Doctrine of Economics."

93. Bani-Sadr, *Eqtesad-e Towhidi*, p. IV.

94. Bani-Sadr, *Eqtesad-e Towhidi*, p. VI.

95. Bani-Sadr, *Eqtesad-e Towhidi*, p. IX.

96. Bani-Sadr, *Eqtesad-e Towhidi*, p. IX.

97. Bani-Sadr, *Eqtesad-e Towhidi*, pp. 26–33.

98. Bani-Sadr, *Eqtesad-e Towhidi*, p. 44.

99. Bani-Sadr, *Eqtesad-e Towhidi*, p. 108. For further expansions of these ideas, see Bani-Sadr, "Dar Islam Asas Kar ast nah Sarmayeh."

100. Bani-Sadr, *Eqtesad-e Towhidi*, p. 111.

101. Bani-Sadr, *Eqtesad-e Towhidi*, p. 126.

102. Bani-Sadr, *Eqtesad-e Towhidi*, p. 161.

103. Bani-Sadr, *Eqtesad-e Towhidi*, p. 176.

104. Bani-Sadr, *Eqtesad-e Towhidi*, pp. 204–207.

105. Bani-Sadr, *Eqtesad-e Towhidi*, pp. 221–222.

106. Bani-Sadr, *Eqtesad-e Towhidi*, p. 228.

107. Bani-Sadr, *Eqtesad-e Towhidi*, p. 228.

108. Bani-Sadr, *Eqtesad-e Towhidi*, p. 231.

109. Bani-Sadr, *Eqtesad-e Towhidi*, pp. 231 and 239.

110. Bani-Sadr, *Eqtesad-e Towhidi*, p. 239.

111. Bani-Sadr, *Eqtesad-e Towhidi*, p. 239.

112. Bani-Sadr, *Eqtesad-e Towhidi*, p. 239.

113. Bani-Sadr, *Eqtesad-e Towhidi*, pp. 239–240.

114. Bani-Sadr, *Eqtesad-e Towhidi*, p. 239.

115. Bani-Sadr, *Eqtesad-e Towhidi*, p. 235.

116. See Deldam, *Enqelab beh Ravayat-e Enqelab-sazan*, p. 155.

117. Bani-Sadr, *Eqtesad-e Towhidi*, pp. 243–244. For a post-revolutionary reflection on the nature of the political economy in Iran, see Clawson, "Islamic Iran's Economic Politics and Prospects," and Turner, "Iranian Oil Workers in the 1978–79 Revolution," in Nore and Turner (eds.), *Oil and Class Struggle*, pp. 272–292. See also Razavi and Vakili, *The Political Environment of Economic Planning in Iran, 1971–1983*, pp. 101–122.

118. Bani-Sadr, *Eqtesad-e Towhidi*, p. 247.

119. Bani-Sadr, *Eqtesad-e Towhidi*, p. 250.

120. Bani-Sadr, *Eqtesad-e Towhidi*, p. 257.

121. Bani-Sadr, *Eqtesad-e Towhidi*, p. 262.

122. Bani-Sadr, *Eqtesad-e Towhidi*, p. 262.

123. Bani-Sadr, *Eqtesad-e Towhidi*, p. 262.

124. Bani-Sadr, *Eqtesad-e Towhidi*, p. 262.

125. Bani-Sadr, *Eqtesad-e Towhidi*, p. 264.

126. Bani-Sadr, *Eqtesad-e Towhidi*, p. 317.

127. Bani-Sadr, *Moqe'iyyat-e Iran va Naqsh-e Modarres*, p. I. See also Chehabi, *Iranian Politics and Religious Modernism*, pp. 45–46.

128. Bani-Sadr, *Moqe'iyyat-e Iran va Naqsh-e Modarres*, pp. A-B.

129. Bani-Sadr, *Moqe'iyyat-e Iran va Naqsh-e Modarres*, p. 3.

130. Bani-Sadr, *Moqe'iyyat-e Iran va Naqsh-e Modarres*, pp. 5–6.

131. Bani-Sadr, *Moqe'iyyat-e Iran va Naqsh-e Modarres*, p. 7.

132. Bani-Sadr, *Moqe'iyyat-e Iran va Naqsh-e Modarres*, p. 8.

133. Bani-Sadr, *Moqe'iyyat-e Iran va Naqsh-e Modarres*, p. 12.

134. Bani-Sadr, *Moqe'iyyat-e Iran va Naqsh-e Modarres*, p. 27.

135. Bani-Sadr, *Moqe'iyyat-e Iran va Naqsh-e Modarres*, p. 28.

136. Bani-Sadr, *Moqe'iyyat-e Iran va Naqsh-e Modarres*, p. 28.

137. Bani-Sadr, *Moqe'iyyat-e Iran va Naqsh-e Modarres*, p. 28.

138. Bani-Sadr, *Moqe'iyyat-e Iran va Naqsh-e Modarres*, p. 30. Bani-Sadr's expansion of his conception of "The West" to include Alexander and the Crusades indicates how the geographical and ideological constructions of this term feed on each other to divide the entire human history into an "East-West" dichotomy.

139. Bani-Sadr, *Moqe'iyyat-e Iran va Naqsh-e Modarres*, p. 31.

140. Bani-Sadr, *Moqe'iyyat-e Iran va Naqsh-e Modarres*, p. 49.

141. Bani-Sadr, *Moqe'iyyat-e Iran va Naqsh-e Modarres*, p. 54.

142. Bani-Sadr, *Moqe'iyyat-e Iran va Naqsh-e Modarres*, p. 56.

143. Bani-Sadr, *Moqe'iyyat-e Iran va Naqsh-e Modarres*, p. 56, footnote 88.

144. Bani-Sadr, *Moqe'iyyat-e Iran va Naqsh-e Modarres*, p. 58.

145. Bani-Sadr, *Moqe'iyyat-e Iran va Naqsh-e Modarres*, p. 66. Here Bani-Sadr shares an obsessive national preoccupation with such conspiratorial concepts of history that release all Iranians from any measure of responsibility in their historical destiny. For an example of such preoccupations, see Parsons, *The Pride and the Fall*, pp. x-xi.

146. Bani-Sadr, *Moqe'iyyat-e Iran va Naqsh-e Modarres*, p. 72.

147. Bani-Sadr, *Moqe'iyyat-e Iran va Naqsh-e Modarres*, p. 73.

148. Bani-Sadr, *Moqe'iyyat-e Iran va Naqsh-e Modarres*, pp. 79–80.

149. Bani-Sadr, *Moqe'iyyat-e Iran va Naqsh-e Modarres*, p. 82.

150. Bani-Sadr, *Moqe'iyyat-e Iran va Naqsh-e Modarres*, p. 86.

151. Bani-Sadr, *Moqe'iyyat-e Iran va Naqsh-e Modarres*, p. 90.

152. Bani-Sadr, *Moqe'iyyat-e Iran va Naqsh-e Modarres*, p. 96.

153. Bani-Sadr, *Moqe'iyyat-e Iran va Naqsh-e Modarres*, p. 99.

154. Bani-Sadr, *Moqe'iyyat-e Iran va Naqsh-e Modarres*, p. 100.

155. Bani-Sadr, *Moqe'iyyat-e Iran va Naqsh-e Modarres*, p. 102. Bani-Sadr's argument in this and other sections of this text is founded squarely on a long list of primary and secondary sources in Iranian history. He has equal access to Persian,

Arabic, French, and English sources. This gives his discourse a certain aura of authenticity usually wished for but rarely attained by these ideologues.

156. Bani-Sadr, *Moqe'iyyat-e Iran va Naqsh-e Modarres*, p. 104.
157. Bani-Sadr, *Moqe'iyyat-e Iran va Naqsh-e Modarres*, p. 107.
158. Bani-Sadr, *Moqe'iyyat-e Iran va Naqsh-e Modarres*, p. 112.
159. Bani-Sadr, *Moqe'iyyat-e Iran va Naqsh-e Modarres*, p. 113.
160. Bani-Sadr, *Moqe'iyyat-e Iran va Naqsh-e Modarres*, p. 116.
161. Bani-Sadr, *Moqe'iyyat-e Iran va Naqsh-e Modarres*, p. 117.
162. Bani-Sadr, *Moqe'iyyat-e Iran va Naqsh-e Modarres*, p. 118.
163. Bani-Sadr, *Moqe'iyyat-e Iran va Naqsh-e Modarres*, pp. 119–120.
164. Bani-Sadr, *Moqe'iyyat-e Iran va Naqsh-e Modarres*, p. 121.
165. Bani-Sadr, *Moqe'iyyat-e Iran va Naqsh-e Modarres*, p. 123.
166. Bani-Sadr, *Moqe'iyyat-e Iran va Naqsh-e Modarres*, p. 123. See also Bani-Sadr, "Barqarari-ye Fascism dar Iran Mosavi ast ba Enhedam-e Jame'eh."
167. Bani-Sadr, *Moqe'iyyat-e Iran va Naqsh-e Modarres*, p. 124.
168. Bani-Sadr, *Moqe'iyyat-e Iran va Naqsh-e Modarres*, p. 124.
169. Bani-Sadr, *Moqe'iyyat-e Iran va Naqsh-e Modarres*, p. 124.
170. Bani-Sadr, *Moqe'iyyat-e Iran va Naqsh-e Modarres*, p. 125.
171. Bani-Sadr, *Moqe'iyyat-e Iran va Naqsh-e Modarres*, p. 125.
172. Bani-Sadr, *Moqe'iyyat-e Iran va Naqsh-e Modarres*, p. 126.
173. Bani-Sadr, *Moqe'iyyat-e Iran va Naqsh-e Modarres*, p. 127.
174. Bani-Sadr, *Moqe'iyyat-e Iran va Naqsh-e Modarres*, p. 128.
175. Bani-Sadr, *Moqe'iyyat-e Iran va Naqsh-e Modarres*, p. 131.
176. Bani-Sadr, *Moqe'iyyat-e Iran va Naqsh-e Modarres*, p. 134.
177. Bani-Sadr, *Moqe'iyyat-e Iran va Naqsh-e Modarres*, p. 135.
178. Bani-Sadr, *Moqe'iyyat-e Iran va Naqsh-e Modarres*, p. 137.
179. Bani-Sadr, *Moqe'iyyat-e Iran va Naqsh-e Modarres*, p. 137. Compare these ideological positions with Bani-Sadr's *Realpolitik* in early 1980. See Amir Arjomand, *The Turban for the Crown*, pp. 141–146.
180. Bani-Sadr, *Moqe'iyyat-e Iran va Naqsh-e Modarres*, p. 138.
181. Bani-Sadr, *Moqe'iyyat-e Iran va Naqsh-e Modarres*, p. 139.
182. Bani-Sadr, *Moqe'iyyat-e Iran va Naqsh-e Modarres*, p. 140.
183. Bani-Sadr, *Moqe'iyyat-e Iran va Naqsh-e Modarres*, p. 141.
184. Bani-Sadr, *Moqe'iyyat-e Iran va Naqsh-e Modarres*, p. 142.
185. Bani-Sadr, *Moqe'iyyat-e Iran va Naqsh-e Modarres*, p. 143.
186. Bani-Sadr, *Moqe'iyyat-e Iran va Naqsh-e Modarres*, p. 144.
187. Bani-Sadr, *Moqe'iyyat-e Iran va Naqsh-e Modarres*, p. 144.
188. Bani-Sadr, *Moqe'iyyat-e Iran va Naqsh-e Modarres*, p. 144.
189. Bani-Sadr, *Moqe'iyyat-e Iran va Naqsh-e Modarres*, p. 145.
190. Bani-Sadr, *Moqe'iyyat-e Iran va Naqsh-e Modarres*, p. 145. Compare with Bani-Sadr's own final political demise in June 1981. See Amir Arjomand, *The Turban for the Crown*, p. 146.
191. Bani-Sadr, *Moqe'iyyat-e Iran va Naqsh-e Modarres*, p. 145.
192. Bani-Sadr, *Moqe'iyyat-e Iran va Naqsh-e Modarres*, pp. 145–146.
193. Bani-Sadr, *Moqe'iyyat-e Iran va Naqsh-e Modarres*, p. 148.
194. Bani-Sadr, *Moqe'iyyat-e Iran va Naqsh-e Modarres*, p. 152.

195. Bani-Sadr, *Moqe'iyyat-e Iran va Naqsh-e Modarres*, p. 155.

196. Bani-Sadr, *Moqe'iyyat-e Iran va Naqsh-e Modarres*, p. 157.

197. Bani-Sadr, *Moqe'iyyat-e Iran va Naqsh-e Modarres*, p. 123.

198. Bani-Sadr, *Bayaniyyeh-ye Jomhuri-ye Islami*, p. A. For an English version of similar ideas expressed in this text, see Bani-Sadr, *The Fundamental Principles and Precepts of Islamic Government*.

199. Bani-Sadr, *Bayaniyyeh-ye Jomhuri-ye Islami*, p. B.

200. Bani-Sadr, *Bayaniyyeh-ye Jomhuri-ye Islami*, p. J.

201. Bani-Sadr, *Bayaniyyeh-ye Jomhuri-ye Islami*, p. H.

202. Bani-Sadr, *Bayaniyyeh-ye Jomhuri-ye Islami*, p. H.

203. Bani-Sadr, *Bayaniyyeh-ye Jomhuri-ye Islami*, p. KH.

204. Bani-Sadr, *Bayaniyyeh-ye Jomhuri-ye Islami*, p. KH.

205. Bani-Sadr, *Bayaniyyeh-ye Jomhuri-ye Islami*, p. KH.

206. Bani-Sadr, *Bayaniyyeh-ye Jomhuri-ye Islami*, p. R.

207. Bani-Sadr, *Bayaniyyeh-ye Jomhuri-ye Islami*, p. 1.

208. Bani-Sadr, *Bayaniyyeh-ye Jomhuri-ye Islami*, p. 3.

209. Bani-Sadr, *Bayaniyyeh-ye Jomhuri-ye Islami*, p. 8. Khomeini had a similarly dismissive attitude towards the "Religious Corps." See the relevant sections of the Khomeini chapter.

210. Bani-Sadr, *Bayaniyyeh-ye Jomhuri-ye Islami*, p. 15.

211. Bani-Sadr, *Bayaniyyeh-ye Jomhuri-ye Islami*, p. 16.

212. Bani-Sadr, *Bayaniyyeh-ye Jomhuri-ye Islami*, p. 28.

213. Bani-Sadr, *Bayaniyyeh-ye Jomhuri-ye Islami*, p. 34.

214. Bani-Sadr, *Bayaniyyeh-ye Jomhuri-ye Islami*, p. 39.

215. Bani-Sadr, *Bayaniyyeh-ye Jomhuri-ye Islami*, p. 42.

216. Bani-Sadr, *Bayaniyyeh-ye Jomhuri-ye Islami*, p. 45.

217. Bani-Sadr, *Bayaniyyeh-ye Jomhuri-ye Islami*, p. 51, footnote.

218. Bani-Sadr, *Bayaniyyeh-ye Jomhuri-ye Islami*, p. 61.

219. Bani-Sadr, *Bayaniyyeh-ye Jomhuri-ye Islami*, p. 62.

220. Bani-Sadr, *Bayaniyyeh-ye Jomhuri-ye Islami*, p. 63.

221. Bani-Sadr, *Bayaniyyeh-ye Jomhuri-ye Islami*, pp. 65–66, footnote. See also Katouzian, "Oil Boycott and the Political Economy: Musaddiq and the Strategy of Non-Oil Economics," in Bill and Louis (eds.), *Musaddiq, Iranian Nationalism, and Oil*, pp. 203–227.

222. Bani-Sadr, *Bayaniyyeh-ye Jomhuri-ye Islami*, p. 67.

223. Bani-Sadr, *Bayaniyyeh-ye Jomhuri-ye Islami*, p. 68.

224. Bani-Sadr, *Bayaniyyeh-ye Jomhuri-ye Islami*, p. 77.

225. Bani-Sadr, *Bayaniyyeh-ye Jomhuri-ye Islami*, p. 78.

226. Bani-Sadr, *Bayaniyyeh-ye Jomhuri-ye Islami*, p. 82.

227. Bani-Sadr, *Bayaniyyeh-ye Jomhuri-ye Islami*, pp. 79–83.

228. Bani-Sadr, *Bayaniyyeh-ye Jomhuri-ye Islami*, p. 83.

229. Bani-Sadr, *Bayaniyyeh-ye Jomhuri-ye Islami*, p. 88.

230. Bani-Sadr, *Bayaniyyeh-ye Jomhuri-ye Islami*, p. 90.

231. Bani-Sadr, *Bayaniyyeh-ye Jomhuri-ye Islami*, p. 94.

232. Bani-Sadr, *Bayaniyyeh-ye Jomhuri-ye Islami*, p. 94.

233. Bani-Sadr, *Bayaniyyeh-ye Jomhuri-ye Islami*, p. 96.

234. Bani-Sadr, *Bayaniyyeh-ye Jomhuri-ye Islami*, p. 98.

235. Bani-Sadr, *Bayaniyyeh-ye Jomhuri-ye Islami*, p. 101. Implicit in this statement is the future formation of some sort of radical alliance among the "Third World" or perhaps "Muslim" nations in which oil will be used as a political instrument for confrontation with "The West."

236. Bani-Sadr, *Bayaniyyeh-ye Jomhuri-ye Islami*, p. 107.

237. Bani-Sadr, *Bayaniyyeh-ye Jomhuri-ye Islami*, p. 112.

238. Bani-Sadr, *Bayaniyyeh-ye Jomhuri-ye Islami*, p. 115.

239. Bani-Sadr, *Bayaniyyeh-ye Jomhuri-ye Islami*, p. 115.

240. Bani-Sadr, *Bayaniyyeh-ye Jomhuri-ye Islami*, p. 122.

241. Bani-Sadr, *Bayaniyyeh-ye Jomhuri-ye Islami*, p. 124.

242. Bani-Sadr, *Bayaniyyeh-ye Jomhuri-ye Islami*, p. 125.

243. Bani-Sadr, *Bayaniyyeh-ye Jomhuri-ye Islami*, p. 126.

244. Bani-Sadr, *Bayaniyyeh-ye Jomhuri-ye Islami*, p. 130.

245. Bani-Sadr, *Bayaniyyeh-ye Jomhuri-ye Islami*, pp. 133–139. Bani-Sadr's predilection towards enumeration of the variety of ways to be pursued, or steps to be taken, for re-Islamization of the Iranian social, political, and economic culture is matched by Shari'ati's and Motahhari's equally determined ways to construct a sustained program of revolutionary action. Yet Bani-Sadr's approach appears to be much more mechanical and institutional than spontaneous or historically nuanced.

246. Bani-Sadr, *Bayaniyyeh-ye Jomhuri-ye Islami*, p. 138.

247. Bani-Sadr, *Bayaniyyeh-ye Jomhuri-ye Islami*, p. 143.

248. Bani-Sadr, *Bayaniyyeh-ye Jomhuri-ye Islami*, p. 144.

249. See Moggridge, *John Maynard Keynes*, p. 92.

250. Moggridge, *John Maynard Keynes*, p. 93.

251. Moggridge, *John Maynard Keynes*, p. 93.

252. In answer to a question about why the Bazaaries participated in the Revolution, Khomeini said, "It is because of their religious beliefs that they rebel against tyranny and dictatorship." See Khomeini, *Sahifeh-ye Nur*, vol. IV, p. 194.

8. Ayatollah Khomeini

1. See McNeill, *The History and Character of Calvinism*, p. 226.

2. McNeill, *The History and Character of Calvinism*, pp. 227–228.

3. For extensive biographical data on Ayatollah Khomeini, see Ruhani, *Nehzat-e Imam Khomeini*. Equally informative is Anonymous, *Biography-e Pishva'*. For a good bibliographical guide to Khomeini's writings, see Ostadi, "Ketab-ha va Athar-e Elmi-ye Imam Khomeini."

4. For a range of extremely important anecdotes about the life and character of Ayatollah Khomeini, see Vejdani and She'r-baf (eds.), *Sargozasht-ha-ye Vizheh az Zendegi-ye Hazrat-e Imam Khomeini*.

5. See Ruhani, *Nehzat-e Imam Khomeini*, vol. I, pp. 31–32.

6. For a short account of Khomeini's life, his teachers, students, and writings, see Ma'rufi (comp.), *Zendegi-nameh-ye Imam Khomeini*. This short biography is an abridged account from Ruhani's two-volume text.

7. Ma'rufi (comp.), *Zendegi-nameh-ye Imam Khomeini*, pp. 23–24. For a full discussion of Khomeini's juridical and political disposition, see Sobhani, "Jame'iyyat-e Elmi va Amali-e Imam Khomeini."

8. The Usuli nature of Khomeini's juridical disposition is to be seen in his *Tahrir al-Wasilah*, particularly in the second volume on "al-Muʿamilat." See especially his discussion of more contemporary issues under the general rubric of "al-bahth hawl al-masa'il al-mustahdathah" where he discusses, among other things, modern banking, artificial insemination, autopsy, trans-sexual operations, and radio and television on pp. 547–577.

9. See Sayyid Ali Khamenei's Introduction to Khomeini's collected speeches and proclamations, *Sahifeh-ye Nur*, vol. I, p. 1.

10. Khomeini, *Sahifeh-ye Nur*, vol. I, p. 1.

11. Khomeini, *Sahifeh-ye Nur*, vol. I, p. II.

12. Khomeini, *Sahifeh-ye Nur*, vol. I, p. II.

13. Khomeini, *Sahifeh-ye Nur*, vol. I, p. II.

14. Khomeini, *Sahifeh-ye Nur*, vol. I, p. II.

15. There is no critical study available of the June 1963 uprising. Hamid Algar's pioneering essay, "The Oppositional Role of the Ulama in Twentieth-Century Iran," in Keddie (ed.), *Scholars, Saints, and Sufis*, pp. 231–255, remains the only tangential account of the event. For two alternative accounts to Algar's view, see Tabari, "The Role of the Clergy in Modern Iranian Politics," in Keddie (ed.), *Religion and Politics in Iran*, pp. 47–72, and Floor, "The Revolutionary Character of the Ulama: Wishful Thinking or Reality?" in the same source, pp. 73–97. Considerable primary data on the June 1963 uprising have become available since Algar's essay. But that essay remains a good introduction to the dynamic organism of the Shiʿi clerical order. Abrahamian's chapter on "Clerical Opposition (1963–1977)," in his *Iran between Two Revolutions*, pp. 473–495, is an equally valuable account. Despite its occasional hagiographic intonations, Algar's recent article on "Imam Khomeini, 1902–1962: The Pre-Revolutionary Years," in Burke and Lapidus (eds.), *Islam, Politics and Social Movements*, pp. 263–288, provides a good premise upon which the June 1963 uprising may be assayed.

16. For an account of the left radical movements in this period, see Zabih, *The Left in Contemporary Iran*, especially Chapter Five, pp. 113–157.

17. For a general account of the Fada'ian-e Islam organization and its radical activities, see Alamuti, *Iran dar Asr-e Pahlavi*, vol. V, pp. 136–147. See also Kazemi, "State and Society in the Ideology of the Devotees of Islam." Ayatollah Kashani was affiliated with this organization. Their targets of assassination included Sayyid Ahmad Kasravi, the social reformist with radical anticlerical views, and Abdolhossein Hazhir, then the minister of court.

18. "Iran," President Carter toasted his first champagne of 1978, sometime after midnight, "because of the great leadership of the Shah, is an island of stability in one of the more troubled areas of the world." See Pahlavi, *Faces in a Mirror*, p. 198. Upon this speech, Princess Ashraf Pahlavi, the late Shah's twin sister, had the following immediate reaction: "As he spoke, I looked at his pale face. I thought his smile was artificial, his eyes icy—and I hoped I could trust him. But within that very year he sent emissaries to Khomeini, sent a military envoy to Tehran to undermine my brother's army, and hedged his own political bets by abandoning my brother as Iran moved toward revolution" (pp. 198–199). As for Khomeini, he had the following immediate assessment of Carter's meeting with the Iranian monarch. "And the Shah and his gang ought to know that whether or not he is successful in

his meeting with the American President to renew his servitude and consolidate his illegal power, the Iranian people do not want him and they will not abandon their struggle until they revenge their massacred youth, and until they save Islam and its principles from this dynasty." See Khomeini, *Sahifeh-ye Nur*, vol. I, p. 254.

19. On Molla Ahmad Naraqi, see my "Early Propagation of *Wilayat-i Faqih* and Mulla Ahamd Naraqi," in Nasr, Dabashi, and Nasr (eds.), *Expectation of the Millenium*, pp. 287–300.

20. For a full account of the notion of *velayat-e faqih* in Shiʿi Islam, see Montazeri, *Dirasat fi Vilayah al-Faqih*. For an English version of a similarly advocative account, see Sachedina, *The Just Ruler in Shiʿite Islam*. This latter book, despite a massive body of scholarship that has gone into its production, is not, alas, totally reliable. There are grave misrepresentations in it that have been admirably detected by Hossein Modarresi in "The Just Ruler or the Guardian Jurist: An Attempt to Link Two Different Shiʿite Concepts."

21. For a reliable discussion of these issues, see Amir Arjomand, *The Shadow of God and the Hidden Imam*, especially Chapter One, pp. 32–65. For a critical review of the central thesis of this seminal work in the sociology of Shiʿism, see my "Shiʿite Islam: The Theology of Discontent."

22. These letters and proclamations are all published in Khomeini, *Sahifeh-ye Nur*.

23. Khomeini, *Sahifeh-ye Nur*, vol. I, p. 117.

24. Khomeini, *Sahifeh-ye Nur*, vol. I, p. 118.

25. Khomeini, *Sahifeh-ye Nur*, vol. I, p. 120.

26. Khomeini, *Sahifeh-ye Nur*, vol. I, p. 120.

27. Khomeini, *Sahifeh-ye Nur*, vol. I, p. 120.

28. For further information on these putitative letters, see Payandeh (ed.), *Seh Nameh az Peyghambar*.

29. Khomeini, *Sahifeh-ye Nur*, vol. I, p. 119.

30. Khomeini, *Sahifeh-ye Nur*, vol. I, p. 119.

31. Khomeini, *Sahifeh-ye Nur*, vol. I, p. 120.

32. Khomeini, *Sahifeh-ye Nur*, vol. I, p. 120.

33. Khomeini, *Sahifeh-ye Nur*, vol. I, p. 122.

34. Khomeini, *Sahifeh-ye Nur*, vol. I, p. 122.

35. Khomeini, *Sahifeh-ye Nur*, vol. I, p. 124.

36. Khomeini, *Sahifeh-ye Nur*, vol. I, p. 126.

37. See Khomeini, *Resaleh-ye Towzih al-Masa'il*, p. 411.

38. See the collection of Khomeini's writings on "Insurance" in Motahhari, *Barrasi-ye Feqhi-e Mas'aleh-ye Bimeh*, p. 81.

39. See the collection of Khomeini's writings on "Insurance" in Motahhari, *Barrasi-ye Feqhi-e Mas'aleh-ye Bimeh*, p. 82.

40. Khomeini, *Sahifeh-ye Nur*, vol. I, p. 127.

41. Khomeini, *Sahifeh-ye Nur*, vol. I, p. 129. For wonderful accounts of Khomeini's student followers abroad, see Fischer and Abedi, *Debating Muslims*, pp. 88, 269, 279, 296–297, and 300.

42. Khomeini, *Sahifeh-ye Nur*, vol. I, p. 130.

43. Khomeini, *Sahifeh-ye Nur*, vol. I, p. 130.

44. Khomeini, *Sahifeh-ye Nur*, vol. I, p. 130.

45. Khomeini, *Sahifeh-ye Nur,* vol. I, p. 131.
46. Khomeini, *Sahifeh-ye Nur,* vol. I, p. 130.
47. Khomeini, *Sahifeh-ye Nur,* vol. I, p. 132.
48. Khomeini, *Sahifeh-ye Nur,* vol. I, p. 132. For an excellent account of Khomeini's mobilization of public sentiments for his revolutionary purposes, see Ashraf, "Theocracy and Charisma: New Men of Power in Iran," especially pp. 113–121. For a sample of genuine sentiments Khomeini did generate in his followers, see Fazel, "Shareh-e Shari'at-e Islam." For a more general discussion of the process of legitimation in the Middle East, see Razi, "Legitimacy, Religion, and Nationalism in the Middle East."
49. Khomeini, *Sahifeh-ye Nur,* vol. I, p. 132.
50. Khomeini, *Sahifeh-ye Nur,* vol. I, p. 132.
51. Khomeini, *Sahifeh-ye Nur,* vol. I, p. 133.
52. Khomeini, *Sahifeh-ye Nur,* vol. I, p. 132.
53. Khomeini, *Sahifeh-ye Nur,* vol. I, p. 132.
54. Khomeini, *Sahifeh-ye Nur,* vol. I, p. 133.
55. Khomeini, *Sahifeh-ye Nur,* vol. I, p. 141.
56. Khomeini, *Sahifeh-ye Nur,* vol. I, p. 141. For a full discussion of Khomeini's position on the function and significance of religious seminaries, see Jenati, "Feqh-e Ejtehadi va Eslah-e Howzeh-ha az Did-gah-e Imam Khomeini."
57. Khomeini, *Sahifeh-ye Nur,* vol. I, p. 141.
58. Khomeini, *Sahifeh-ye Nur,* vol. I, p. 140.
59. Khomeini, *Sahifeh-ye Nur,* vol. I, p. 140. There are also indications that Khomeini was in indirect contact with Jalal Al-e Ahmad. In a letter to Amir Pishdad and his friends, dated 12 October 1965, Al-e Ahmad reports that he is sending a message to Khomeini with his brother-in-law. See Dehbashi (ed.), *Nameh-ha-ye Jalal Al-e Ahmad,* p. 185.
60. Khomeini, *Sahifeh-ye Nur,* vol. I, p. 142.
61. Khomeini, *Sahifeh-ye Nur,* vol. I, p. 136.
62. Khomeini, *Sahifeh-ye Nur,* vol. I, p. 136.
63. Khomeini, *Sahifeh-ye Nur,* vol. I, p. 138.
64. Khomeini, *Sahifeh-ye Nur,* vol. I, p. 144.
65. Khomeini, *Sahifeh-ye Nur,* vol. I, p. 143.
66. Khomeini, *Sahifeh-ye Nur,* vol. I, p. 143.
67. Khomeini, *Sahifeh-ye Nur,* vol. I, p. 143.
68. Khomeini, *Sahifeh-ye Nur,* vol. I, p. 143. For a further discussion of Khomeini's *"Kulturkampf"* against the Westernized intellgentsia, see Amir Arjomand, *The Turban for the Crown,* pp. 101–102.
69. Khomeini, *Sahifeh-ye Nur,* vol. I, p. 147.
70. Khomeini, *Sahifeh-ye Nur,* vol. I, p. 147.
71. Khomeini, *Sahifeh-ye Nur,* vol. I, p. 148.
72. Khomeini, *Sahifeh-ye Nur,* vol. I, p. 148. For further information about Sa'idi, see Davani, *Nehzat-e Ruhaniun-e Iran,* vol. 5, pp. 309–23.
73. Khomeini, *Sahifeh-ye Nur,* vol. I, p. 148.
74. Khomeini, *Sahifeh-ye Nur,* vol. I, p. 148.
75. Khomeini, *Sahifeh-ye Nur,* vol. I, p. 148.
76. Khomeini, *Sahifeh-ye Nur,* vol. I, p. 148.

77. Khomeini, *Sahifeh-ye Nur*, vol. I, p. 148.

78. Khomeini, *Sahifeh-ye Nur*, vol. I, p. 149.

79. Khomeini, *Sahifeh-ye Nur*, vol. I, p. 149.

80. Khomeini, *Sahifeh-ye Nur*, vol. I, p. 150. Later on these and similar themes are explored to their fullest extent in Khomeini's will. See Khomeini, *Sahifeh-ye Enqelab*.

81. Khomeini, *Sahifeh-ye Nur*, vol. I, p. 152.

82. Khomeini, *Sahifeh-ye Nur*, vol. I, p. 152.

83. Khomeini, *Sahifeh-ye Nur*, vol. I, pp. 154–155.

84. Khomeini, *Sahifeh-ye Nur*, vol. I, p. 155.

85. Khomeini, *Sahifeh-ye Nur*, vol. I, p. 155.

86. My references are all to the Tehran (offset) edition of the text, Khomeini, *Velayat-e Faqih*. The only reliable English translation of this text is Hamid Algar's in Khomeini, *Islam and Revolution*. For minor consideration, see my review of this translation in *The Middle East Journal*.

87. Gregory Rose, the author of a useful exposition of Khomeini's *Velayat-e Faqih*, has the following observation about Algar's translation: "Algar seems to be under the impression that the lectures were delivered in Persian; however, persons present during the lectures, including Sayyid Ahmad Khomeini, indicate that they were delivered in Arabic, as one might expect in the *dars al-Kharij*." See Rose, "*Velayat-e Faqih* and the Recovery of Islamic Identity in the Thought of Ayatollah Khomeini," in Keddie (ed.), *Religion and Politics in Iran*, p. 167. Rose's report is highly dubious. Some Iraqi students at Najaf Seminary report that they did not attend Khomeini's lectures on Fiqh because they did not understand Persian.

88. See Khomeini, *al-Hukumah al-Islamiyyah*. The publisher's Introduction to the Arabic edition is dated March 1979, years after the original Persian edition. Here is a comparison of the first two sentences of the Persian text and their abbreviated Arabic:

1. (Original Persian, in Algar's translation) The subject of the governance of the Faqih *(velayat-e faqih)* provides us with the opportunity to discuss certain related matters and questions. The governance of the *Faqih* is a subject that in itself elicits immediate assent and has little need of demonstration, for anyone who has some general awareness of the beliefs and ordinances of Islam will unhesitatingly give his assent to the principle of the governance of the *Faqih* as soon as he encounters it; he will recognize it as necessary and self-evident.

2. (Arabic abridgment in my translation) *Velayat al-Faqih* is a self-evident and scientific notion which is in no need of proof. That is to say, whoever knows Islam, its principles and doctrines, recognizes its inevitability.

This comparison should leave little doubt that the original was delivered in (Khomeini's rather distinct) Persian, and that the Arabic translation is an abridgment of the original text.

89. See Khomeini, *Sharh Du*ᶜ*a Sahar*.

90. Khomeini, *Velayat-e Faqih*, pp. 172–173.

91. See the Arabic translation, Khomeini, *al-Hukumah al-Islamiyyah*, p. 116.

92. Khomeini, *Velayat-e Faqih*, p. 18. See also Maᶜrefat, "Vaqeᶜ-negari dar Binesh-e Feqhi-ye Imam Khomeini."

93. Khomeini, *Velayat-e Faqih*, p. 6.
94. Khomeini, *Velayat-e Faqih*, p. 8.
95. Khomeini, *Velayat-e Faqih*, p. 10.
96. Khomeini, *Velayat-e Faqih*, p. 10.
97. Khomeini, *Velayat-e Faqih*, p. 11.
98. Khomeini, *Velayat-e Faqih*, p. 14.
99. Khomeini, *Velayat-e Faqih*, p. 16. It is important to remember that Khomeini's repoliticization of Shi'i doctrines was not limited to *Velayat-e Faqih*. For his political rereading of the hajj pilgrimage, for example, see Khomeini, *Hajj*, and Khomeini, *Faryad-e Bera'at*.
100. Khomeini, *Velayat-e Faqih*, p. 19.
101. Khomeini, *Velayat-e Faqih*, p. 21.
102. Khomeini, *Velayat-e Faqih*, p. 22.
103. Khomeini, *Velayat-e Faqih*, p. 23.
104. Khomeini, *Velayat-e Faqih*, p. 24.
105. Khomeini, *Velayat-e Faqih*, p. 26.
106. Khomeini, *Velayat-e Faqih*, pp. 26–27.
107. Khomeini, *Velayat-e Faqih*, p. 28, footnote.
108. Khomeini, *Velayat-e Faqih*, p. 30. "The lesser occultation," or *Gheybat-e Soghra'*, is the period between 873 C.E. and 940 C.E., when the Hidden (Twelfth) Imam of the Shi'ites is believed to have been in contact with his community through four emissaries *(novvab-e arba'eh)*.
109. Khomeini, *Velayat-e Faqih*, p. 39. For an assessment of Khomeini's juridical encounter with the modern world, see Bi-azar-e Shirazi, "Binesh-e Feqhi-ye Imam dar Bar-khord-e ba Ruydad-ha-ye Novin-e Jahan."
110. Khomeini, *Velayat-e Faqih*, p. 41.
111. Khomeini, *Velayat-e Faqih*, p. 43.
112. Khomeini, *Velayat-e Faqih*, p. 47.
113. Khomeini, *Velayat-e Faqih*, p. 48.
114. Khomeini, *Velayat-e Faqih*, p. 49.
115. Khomeini, *Velayat-e Faqih*, p. 51.
116. Khomeini, *Velayat-e Faqih*, p. 52.
117. Khomeini, *Velayat-e Faqih*, pp. 52–53. For a discussion of the politial ramifications of Khomeini's ideas in the course of the revolutionary process, see Zonis, "The Rule of the Clerics in the Islamic Republic of Iran." This is an informed and insightful article, yet it has a puzzling footnote. Quoting a statement made in 1985 by Khamenei, then the President of the Islamic Republic, in which he had said, "The United States . . . enforces an extensive dictatorship on nations throughout the world. She has spread her dictatorial domination as far as her material and military powers permit. She appears wherever she thinks she has interests and does whatever she likes regardless of the aspirations, wishes, rights, and interest of the people of those regions. In our opinion, it is the ugliest and most difficult form of dictatorship," Zonis adds in his footnote that "The implications of his [that is, Khamenei's] referring to the United States as a female are yet to be analyzed" (p. 97). Khamenei could not have referred to the United States with "she" in his original Persian. This, as the translators of Khamenei's speech must have known at *Keyhan International*, is an old English affectation to refer to the names of coun-

tries, and ships, with the feminine pronoun. There is no need for further analysis here if we simply remember that Khamenei does not speak English (especially when addressing an Iranian audience), and that in the Persian language there is no gender-specific pronoun.

118. Khomeini, *Velayat-e Faqih*, p. 53.
119. Khomeini, *Velayat-e Faqih*, p. 54.
120. Khomeini, *Velayat-e Faqih*, p. 58.
121. Khomeini, *Velayat-e Faqih*, p. 58.
122. Khomeini, *Velayat-e Faqih*, p. 60.
123. Khomeini, *Velayat-e Faqih*, p. 60.
124. Khomeini, *Velayat-e Faqih*, p. 63.
125. Khomeini, *Velayat-e Faqih*, p. 63.
126. Khomeini, *Velayat-e Faqih*, p. 64.
127. Khomeini, *Velayat-e Faqih*, p. 65.
128. Both *vajeb-e aiyni* and *vajeb-e kefa'i* are juridical terms. *Vajeb* means a mandatory religious injunction incumbent upon the believer; failing to perform it is sinful. *Vajeb-e aiyni* is a *vajeb* act incumbent upon all Muslims. *Vajeb-e kefa'i* is a *vajeb* act that once one or more Muslims perform it, others are relieved of their duty.
129. Khomeini, *Velayat-e Faqih*, p. 69. For a discussion of Khomeini's contribution to modern Islamic political thought, see Sahebi, "Naqsh-e Imam Khomeini dar Tadvin va Tanqih-e Falsafeh-ye Siasi."
130. Khomeini, *Velayat-e Faqih*, p. 74.
131. Khomeini, *Velayat-e Faqih*, p. 80.
132. Khomeini, *Velayat-e Faqih*, p. 82.
133. On Molla Ahmad Naraqi's own disposition on *velayat-e faqih*, see my "Early Propagation of *Wilayat-i Faqih* and Mulla Ahmad Naraqi," in Nasr, Dabashi, and Nasr (eds.), *Expectation of the Millennium*, pp. 287–300.
134. Khomeini, *Velayat-e Faqih*, p. 88.
135. Khomeini, *Velayat-e Faqih*, p. 92.
136. Khomeini, *Velayat-e Faqih*, p. 97.
137. Khomeini, *Velayat-e Faqih*, p. 100.
138. Khomeini, *Velayat-e Faqih*, p. 98.
139. Khomeini, *Velayat-e Faqih*, p. 102. For a pioneering study of Khomeini's concept of *velayat-e faqih*, see Enayat, "Iran: Khumayni's Concept of the 'Guardianship of the Jurisconsult,' " in Piscatori (ed.), *Islam in the Political Process*, pp. 160–180. See also Hoogland and Royce, "The Shi'i Clergy of Iran and the Conception of an Islamic State," for a comparative assessment of Khomeini's and Shari'at-Madari's ideas. On the latter issue, see Menashri, "Shi'ite Leadership: In the Shadow of Conflicting Ideologies."
140. Khomeini, *Velayat-e Faqih*, p. 104.
141. Khomeini, *Velayat-e Faqih*, p. 106.
142. Khomeini, *Velayat-e Faqih*, pp. 116–117 and 123.
143. Khomeini, *Velayat-e Faqih*, p. 118.
144. Khomeini, *Velayat-e Faqih*, p. 122.
145. Khomeini, *Velayat-e Faqih*, p. 127.
146. Khomeini, *Velayat-e Faqih*, p. 129.

147. Khomeini, *Velayat-e Faqih*, p. 130.
148. Khomeini, *Velayat-e Faqih*, pp. 131–142.
149. Khomeini, *Velayat-e Faqih*, p. 142.
150. Khomeini, *Velayat-e Faqih*, p. 143.
151. Khomeini, *Velayat-e Faqih*, pp. 143–144.
152. Khomeini, *Velayat-e Faqih*, p. 144.
153. Khomeini, *Velayat-e Faqih*, p. 158. For a discussion of the relation of the Iranian military to Khomeini before and after the Revolution, see Milani, *The Making of Iran's Islamic Revolution*, pp. 230–231 and 257–258. See also Amir Arjomand, *The Turban for the Crown*, pp. 120–128.
154. Khomeini, *Velayat-e Faqih*, p. 163.
155. Khomeini, *Velayat-e Faqih*, p. 164.
156. Khomeini, *Velayat-e Faqih*, p. 165.
157. Khomeini, *Velayat-e Faqih*, p. 172.
158. Khomeini, *Velayat-e Faqih*, pp. 172–173.
159. Khomeini, *Velayat-e Faqih*, p. 174.
160. Khomeini, *Velayat-e Faqih*, p. 175.
161. Khomeini, *Velayat-e Faqih*, pp. 175–176.
162. Khomeini, *Velayat-e Faqih*, p. 179.
163. Khomeini, *Velayat-e Faqih*, p. 183.
164. Khomeini, *Velayat-e Faqih*, p. 199.
165. Khomeini, *Velayat-e Faqih*, p. 208. For a discussion of the nature of Khomeini's public appeal, see Savory, "Ex Oriente Nebula: An Inquiry into the Nature of Khomeini's Ideology," in Chelkowski and Pranger (eds.), *Ideology and Power in the Middle East*, pp. 339–362. For a more thorough examination of popular sentiments in the course of the revolutionary mobilization, see Vieille and Khosrokhavar, *Le Discours Populaire de la Revolution Iranienne*, vol. II.
166. Khomeini, *Sahifeh-ye Nur*, vol. I, p. 156.
167. Khomeini, *Sahifeh-ye Nur*, vol. I, p. 157. For a full discussion of Khomeini's appeal to the Muslim world at large, see al-Ghanushi, "Imam Khomeini va Rahbari-ye Nehzat-ha-ye Islami-ye Moʿaser-e Jahan." For a brief reference to the significance of Khomeini in the Islamic movement in Afghanistan, see Navvab-e Yusof-zadeh-ye Afghani, "Baztab-e Nehzat-e Imam dar Harekat-e Islami-ye Afghanistan." Both of these assessments gloss over the internal dyanmics that separate and animate the Muslim world. Despite its unusually deprecatory attitude towards Iran, Keddie's "Is There a Middle East?" provides an insightful deconstruction of that internal dynamics. Although certain aspects of this article have been rendered dubious by recent events in the Muslim world, it still brings out some enduring forces operative in the Muslim collective identity.
168. Khomeini, *Sahifeh-ye Nur*, vol. I, p. 157.
169. Khomeini, *Sahifeh-ye Nur*, vol. I, pp. 157–158.
170. Khomeini, *Sahifeh-ye Nur*, vol. I, p. 158.
171. Khomeini, *Sahifeh-ye Nur*, vol. I, pp. 158–159.
172. Khomeini, *Sahifeh-ye Nur*, vol. I, p. 160.
173. Khomeini, *Sahifeh-ye Nur*, vol. I, p. 161.
174. Khomeini, *Sahifeh-ye Nur*, vol. I, p. 162.
175. Khomeini, *Sahifeh-ye Nur*, vol. I, p. 162.

176. Khomeini, *Sahifeh-ye Nur,* vol. I, p. 165.

177. Khomeini, *Sahifeh-ye Nur,* vol. I, p. 166.

178. Khomeini, *Sahifeh-ye Nur,* vol. I, p. 166. For a pioneering study of Khomeini's revolutionary asceticism, see Mazlish, "The Hidden Khomeini." For a more thorough study of revolutionary asceticism, see Mazlish, *The Revolutionary Ascetic.*

179. Khomeini, *Sahifeh-ye Nur,* vol. I, p. 166.

180. Khomeini, *Sahifeh-ye Nur,* vol. I, p. 168.

181. Khomeini, *Sahifeh-ye Nur,* vol. I, p. 168.

182. Khomeini, *Sahifeh-ye Nur,* vol. I, p. 170.

183. Khomeini, *Sahifeh-ye Nur,* vol. I, p. 173.

184. Khomeini, *Sahifeh-ye Nur,* vol. I, p. 174.

185. Khomeini, *Sahifeh-ye Nur,* vol. I, p. 171.

186. Khomeini, *Sahifeh-ye Nur,* vol. I, p. 172.

187. Khomeini, *Sahifeh-ye Nur,* vol. I, p. 177.

188. Khomeini, *Sahifeh-ye Nur,* vol. I, p. 179.

189. Shahid-e Thani, *Sharh-e Lum'ah,* vol. I, p. 192, as quoted in Sajjadi, *Farhang-e Ma'aref-e Islami,* vol. I, pp. 297–298.

190. Khomeini, *Sahifeh-ye Nur,* vol. I., p. 181.

191. Khomeini, *Sahifeh-ye Nur,* vol. I, p. 181.

192. See Madani, *Tarikh-e Siasi-e Mo'aser-e Iran,* p. 204.

193. Khomeini, *Sahifeh-ye Nur,* vol. I, p. 182.

194. Khomeini, *Sahifeh-ye Nur,* vol. I, p. 183.

195. Khomeini, *Sahifeh-ye Nur,* vol. I, p. 183.

196. Khomeini, *Sahifeh-ye Nur,* vol. I, p. 184. For further details of the expulsion of Iranians from Iraq at this time and Khomeini's reaction to it, see Davani, *Nehzat-e Ruhaniun-e Iran,* vol. 6, pp. 73–74.

197. Khomeini, *Sahifeh-ye Nur,* vol. I, p. 184.

198. Khomeini, *Sahifeh-ye Nur,* vol. I, p. 185.

199. Khomeini, *Sahifeh-ye Nur,* vol. I, p. 186.

200. Khomeini, *Sahifeh-ye Nur,* vol. I, p. 186.

201. Khomeini, *Sahifeh-ye Nur,* vol. I, p. 189.

202. Khomeini, *Sahifeh-ye Nur,* vol. I, p. 190. See also Pahlavi, *Mission for My Country.*

203. Khomeini, *Sahifeh-ye Nur,* vol. I, p. 190.

204. Khomeini, *Sahifeh-ye Nur,* vol. I, pp. 190–191.

205. Khomeini, *Sahifeh-ye Nur,* vol. I, p. 192. The date on this letter of Khomeini as it appears in this official edition is wrong. The third of Ramadan 1392, on which occasion he wrote this letter, coincides with Wednesday, 19 Mehr, not 19 Aban, 1351, which is equal to 11 October 1972.

206. Khomeini, *Sahifeh-ye Nur,* vol. I, p. 193.

207. Khomeini, *Jehad-e Akbar,* p. 11. For a further discussion of Khomeini's mystical perspectives, see Hosseini-ye Qa'em-maqami, "Qur'an va Erfan az Manzareh-ye Imam."

208. Khomeini, *Jehad-e Akbar,* p. 12.

209. Khomeini, *Jehad-e Akbar,* p. 14.

210. Khomeini, *Jehad-e Akbar,* p. 15.

211. Khomeini, *Jehad-e Akbar,* p. 5. For a further discussion of Khomeini's

concern with ethical and mystical dimensions of a revolutionary character, see Mottahedeh, *The Mantle of the Prophet*, pp. 242–243. See also Anonymous, "Tajalli-ye Eshq dar Adab va Erfan-e Imam Khomeini," and Nezhad-Salim, "Jelveh-ye Eshq dar Ghazal-ha-ye Imam."

212. Khomeini, *Jehad-e Akbar*, p. 6.

213. Khomeini, *Jehad-e Akbar*, pp. 6–7.

214. Khomeini, *Jehad-e Akbar*, p. 8.

215. Khomeini, *Jehad-e Akbar*, p. 8.

216. Khomeini, *Jehad-e Akbar*, p. 10.

217. Khomeini, *Jehad-e Akbar*, p. 19.

218. Khomeini, *Jehad-e Akbar*, p. 19.

219. Khomeini, *Jehad-e Akbar*, p. 19.

220. Khomeini, *Jehad-e Akbar*, p. 22.

221. For further reflections on the moral and ascetic dimensions of Khomeini's revolutionary character, see Mazlish, "The Hidden Khomeini."

222. Khomeini, *Jehad-e Akbar*, p. 23.

223. Khomeini, *Jehad-e Akbar*, p. 26.

224. Khomeini, *Jehad-e Akbar*, p. 35.

225. Khomeini, *Jehad-e Akbar*, p. 38.

226. Khomeini, *Jehad-e Akbar*, p. 44.

227. Khomeini, *Jehad-e Akbar*, p. 44.

228. Khomeini, *Jehad-e Akbar*, p. 44.

229. Khomeini, *Jehad-e Akbar*, p. 44.

230. Khomeini, *Jehad-e Akbar*, p. 44.

231. Khomeini, *Jehad-e Akbar*, pp. 44–45.

232. For a brilliant exposition of Ibn Arabi's ideas, see Chittick, *The Sufi Path of Knowledge;* on Ibn Arabi's conception of *wahdat al-wujud*, see pp. 3, 79, 226, etc., of this book.

233. For a full exposition of a representative text of Molla Sadra, see his *The Wisdom of the Throne*, brilliantly translated and annotated by James Winston Morris.

234. Khomeini, *Jehad-e Akbar*, p. 44.

235. Khomeini, *Jehad-e Akbar*, p. 48.

236. Khomeini, *Jehad-e Akbar*, p. 49.

237. The Qur'an, 2:30: "And when thy Lord said unto the angels: Lo! I am about to place a viceroy in the earth, they said: Wilt thou place therein one who will do harm therein and will shed blood, while we, we hymn Thy praise and sanctify Thee? He said: Surely I know that which ye know not." The Qur'anic expression of man as God's "viceroy in the earth" is central to Khomeini's argument.

238. Khomeini, *Jehad-e Akbar*, p. 55.

239. Khomeini, *Jehad-e Akbar*, p. 56.

240. Khomeini, *Jehad-e Akbar*, p. 56.

241. For example, notice Sayyid Jalal al-Din Ashtiani's sweeping condemnation of the institutions of higher learning in Iran in his introduction to his edition of *Montakhabati az Athar-e Hokama'-ye Ilahi-ye Iran*, pp. Six-Twenty.

242. Khomeini, *Sahifeh-ye Nur*, vol. I, p. 196.

243. Khomeini, *Sahifeh-ye Nur*, vol. I, p. 196.
244. Khomeini, *Sahifeh-ye Nur*, vol. I, p. 197.
245. Khomeini, *Sahifeh-ye Nur*, vol. I, p. 201.
246. Khomeini, *Sahifeh-ye Nur*, vol. I, p. 202.
247. Khomeini, *Sahifeh-ye Nur*, vol. I, p. 203.
248. Khomeini, *Sahifeh-ye Nur*, vol. I, p. 204.
249. Khomeini, *Sahifeh-ye Nur*, vol. I, p. 207.
250. Khomeini, *Sahifeh-ye Nur*, vol. I, pp. 207–208.
251. Khomeini, *Sahifeh-ye Nur*, vol. I, p. 210. For a full discussion of Khomeini's interest in, and impact on, the rest of the Muslim world, see a collection of very good articles in Esposito (ed.), *The Iranian Revolution*.
252. Khomeini, *Sahifeh-ye Nur*, vol. I, p. 211.
253. Khomeini, *Sahifeh-ye Nur*, vol. I, p. 211.
254. Khomeini, *Sahifeh-ye Nur*, vol. I, p. 211.
255. Khomeini, *Sahifeh-ye Nur*, vol. I, pp. 211–212.
256. Khomeini, *Sahifeh-ye Nur*, vol. I, p. 212.
257. Khomeini, *Sahifeh-ye Nur*, vol. I, p. 213.
258. Khomeini, *Sahifeh-ye Nur*, vol. I, p. 214.
259. Khomeini, *Sahifeh-ye Nur*, vol. I, p. 214.
260. Khomeini, *Sahifeh-ye Nur*, vol. I, p. 214.
261. Khomeini, *Sahifeh-ye Nur*, vol. I, p. 214.
262. Khomeini, *Sahifeh-ye Nur*, vol. I, p. 214. These sentiments are central to the air of "expectation" awaiting Khomeini's return to Iran in the late 1970s. For an assessment of Khomeini's own revolutionary disposition in the wake of the Revolution, see Chapter Five of Amir Arjomand, *The Turban for the Crown*, pp. 91–102. See also Ashraf, "Theocracy and Charisma: New Men of Power in Iran," pp. 115–121.
263. Khomeini, *Sahifeh-ye Nur*, vol. I, p. 215.
264. Khomeini, *Sahifeh-ye Nur*, vol. I, p. 215.
265. Khomeini, *Sahifeh-ye Nur*, vol. I, p. 215.
266. Khomeini, *Sahifeh-ye Nur*, vol. I, p. 216.
267. Khomeini, *Sahifeh-ye Nur*, vol. I, p. 216.
268. Khomeini, *Sahifeh-ye Nur*, vol. I, p. 217.
269. Khomeini, *Sahifeh-ye Nur*, vol. I, pp. 219–220.
270. Khomeini, *Sahifeh-ye Nur*, vol. I, p. 219.
271. Khomeini, *Sahifeh-ye Nur*, vol. I, p. 221.
272. Khomeini, *Sahifeh-ye Nur*, vol. I, p. 223. For a full discussion of these and other problems fueling Khomeini's revolutionary mobilization of public sentiments, see Amir Arjomand, *The Turban for the Crown*, pp. 147–154. For a post-revolutionary reflection, see Rouleau, "Khomeini's Iran."
273. Khomeini, *Sahifeh-ye Nur*, vol. I, p. 226.
274. Khomeini, *Sahifeh-ye Nur*, vol. I, p. 227.
275. Khomeini, *Sahifeh-ye Nur*, vol. I, p. 227.
276. Khomeini, *Sahifeh-ye Nur*, vol. I, p. 227.
277. Khomeini, *Sahifeh-ye Nur*, vol. I, p. 228.
278. Khomeini, *Sahifeh-ye Nur*, vol. I, p. 228.
279. Khomeini, *Sahifeh-ye Nur*, vol. I, p. 228.

280. Khomeini, *Sahifeh-ye Nur*, vol. I, p. 229.

281. Khomeini, *Sahifeh-ye Nur*, vol. I, p. 229.

282. Khomeini, *Sahifeh-ye Nur*, vol. I, p. 229.

283. Khomeini, *Sahifeh-ye Nur*, vol. I, p. 229.

284. See the appropriate sections of the Taleqani chapter in this book.

285. Khomeini, *Sahifeh-ye Nur*, vol. I, p. 223.

286. Khomeini, *Sahifeh-ye Nur*, vol. I, p. 223.

287. Rumi, *The Mathnawi*, vol. III, lines 3901–3906.

288. Khomeini, *Sahifeh-ye Nur*, vol. I, p. 234.

289. See Nasafi, *Kitab al-Insan al-Kamil*, p. 4.

290. Khomeini, *Sahifeh-ye Nur*, vol. I, p. 234.

291. Khomeini, *Sahifeh-ye Nur*, vol. I, p. 234.

292. Khomeini, *Sahifeh-ye Nur*, vol. I, pp. 234–235.

293. Khomeini, *Sahifeh-ye Nur*, vol. I, p. 235.

294. Khomeini, *Sahifeh-ye Nur*, vol. I, p. 235.

295. Khomeini, *Sahifeh-ye Nur*, vol. I, p. 236.

296. Khomeini, *Sahifeh-ye Nur*, vol. I, p. 236.

297. Khomeini, *Sahifeh-ye Nur*, vol. I, p. 236.

298. Khomeini, *Sahifeh-ye Nur*, vol. I, p. 237. See the related passages on Qur'anic exegesis in Taleqani's chapter. For the significance of these Qur'anic interpretations for the "Liberation Movement of Iran," see Chehabi, *Iranian Politics and Religious Modernism*, pp. 50–51 and 107.

299. Khomeini, *Sahifeh-ye Nur*, vol. I, p. 237.

300. Khomeini, *Sahifeh-ye Nur*, vol. I, p. 238.

301. Khomeini, *Sahifeh-ye Nur*, vol. I, p. 240.

302. Khomeini, *Sahifeh-ye Nur*, vol. I, p. 241.

303. Khomeini, *Sahifeh-ye Nur*, vol. I, p. 241.

304. Khomeini, *Sahifeh-ye Nur*, vol. I, p. 243.

305. Khomeini, *Sahifeh-ye Nur*, vol. I, p. 244.

306. For a useful discussion of the general ideology transformation of Islam, regardless of the Sunni-Shi'i schism, see Tibi, "The Renewed Role of Islam in the Political and Social Development of the Middle East."

307. For a thorough overview of the general radicalization of the Islamic world in the vicinity of the Islamic Revolution in Iran, see Scholl-Latour, *Allah ist mit den Standhaften*, and Mongin and Roy (eds.), *Islam, le grand malentendu*.

308. For the ascendancy of the Islamic discourse over its secular alternatives, see the useful argument of Najmabadi, "Iran's Turn to Islam: From Modernism to Moral Order."

309. See Mazlish, "The Hidden Khomeini." My attention to the ascetic dimensions of Khomeini's discourse is greatly indebted to this essay and to a brilliant paper, "Khomeini as a Revolutionary Leader," that Professor Mazlish delivered at a conference on the comparative study of the Iranian Revolution, held at Harvard University, 19–20 January 1989.

310. Here I read Khomeini's asceticism differently from Bruce Mazlish. He maintains that Khomeini's "personal ascetic qualities . . . do allow him to symbolize properly the opposition to the corrupt, impure, and overly sensual image of the Shah and his regime." See Mazlish, "The Hidden Khomeini," p. 52. I think the

relation is reversed. Khomeini's asceticism is a negational response, an unconscious projection of the opposite, to the Shah's actual and presumed over-indulgence. Khomeini identifies his arch-enemy with supreme wickedness and then, in order to identify himself with supreme goodness, he personifies the opposite attributes of the image of the brutish King. Mazlish's account considers Khomeini's asceticism as a given—and thus a fortuitous—point of comparison against the monarch's extravagance. I think that although a certain degree of asceticism is integral to Khomeini's mystical training and disposition, irrespective of his revolutionary character, it still extends further to border on conscious or subconscious *reactions* to qualities he invests and then despises in his arch-enemy.

311. For a complete discussion of the delegitimating process of the Pahlavi state, see Shahrough Akhavi's account in *Religion and Politics in Contemporary Iran*, pp. 159–180.

312. See the related passages in Al-e Ahmad's chapter in this book.

313. See Ahani, *Koliyyat-e Falsafeh-ye Islami*, p. 3.

314. For a useful chronological narrative that puts Khomeini's decision to accept a cease-fire in the proper context, see Menashri, *Iran*, pp. 389–392.

Conclusion

1. Durkheim, *The Elementary Forms of the Religious Life*, p. 474.

2. Durkheim, *The Elementary Forms of the Religious Life*, pp. 474–475. Everett C. Hughes's brilliant article reflects on the social and historical mechanisms of how new conceptions of collectivity are formed from the old ones. See Hughes, "New Peoples," in Hughes, *The Sociological Eye*, pp. 174–190.

3. Durkheim, *The Elementary Forms of the Religious Life*, p. 475.

4. Durkheim, *The Elementary Forms of the Religious Life*, p. 475.

5. Durkheim, *The Elementary Forms of the Religious Life*, p. 475.

6. Durkheim, *The Elementary Forms of the Religious Life*, p. 475.

7. Durkheim, *The Elementary Forms of the Religious Life*, p. 475.

8. Weber, "Politics as a Vocation," in Weber, *From Max Weber*, p. 79.

9. Durkheim, *The Elementary Forms of the Religious Life*, p. 475.

10. Bell, *The End of Ideology*, p. 393.

11. Fukuyama, "The End of History." For a challenge, see Lewis, "The Return of History."

12. Durkheim, *The Elementary Forms of the Religious Life*, p. 475.

13. Durkheim, *The Elementary Forms of the Religious Life*, p. 476.

14. Durkheim, *The Elementary Forms of the Religious Life*, p. 476.

15. Durkheim, *The Elementary Forms of the Religious Life*, p. 476.

16. Durkheim, *The Elementary Forms of the Religious Life*, p. 476. For a remarkable testimony to the central significance of religious sentiments in revolutionary mobilizations, see the chronological reflections of an active participant in Khalili, *Gam beh Gam ba Enqelab*.

17. Durkheim, *The Elementary Forms of the Religious Life*, p. 476.

18. Durkheim, *The Elementary Forms of the Religious Life*, p. 476.

19. See Amir Arjomand, *The Shadow of God and the Hidden Imam*, pp. 85–100.

20. See Lambton, "Concepts of Authority in Persia: Eleventh to Nineteenth Centuries A.D."

21. See Lewis, *The Political Language of Islam*, p. 53–57.

22. For a full account of this first group of Iranian students abroad, see Minovi, "Avvalin Karevan-e Ma'refat," in Minovi, *Tarikh va Farhang*, pp. 380–437.

23. See Shirazi, *Safar-nameh*.

24. See Lahidji, "Constitutionalism and Clerical Authority," in Amir Arjomand (ed.), *Authority and Political Culture in Shi'ism*, pp. 133–158. For a fuller and more sympathetic account, see Ha'eri. *Tashayyo' va Mashrutiyyat dar Iran*.

25. See, for example, Martin, *Islam and Modernism*, p. 1.

26. See Foucault, "Iran: The Spirit of a World without Spirit," in Kritzman (ed.), *Michel Foucault*, pp. 211–224.

27. See Robinson, "When Will Revolutionary Movements Use Religion?" in Robbins and Robertson (eds.), *Church-State Relations*, pp. 53–63. For a pioneering study of the various modes of mobilization in the course of the Islamic Revolution and a balanced view of the significance of the clerical forces in it, see Ashraf and Banuazizi, "The State, Classes, and Modes of Mobilization in the Iranian Revolution."

28. Robinson, "When Will Revolutionary Movements Use Religion?" in Robbins and Robertson (eds.), *Church-State Relations*, p. 53.

29. Robinson, "When Will Revolutionary Movements Use Religion?" in Robbins and Robertson (eds.), *Church-State Relations*, p. 54.

30. See my review of Amir Arjomand, *The Shadow of God and the Hidden Imam*, "Shi'ite Islam: The Theology of Discontent," for one central debate.

31. See my review of Amir Arjomand, *The Shadow of God and the Hidden Imam*, "Shi'ite Islam: The Theology of Discontent," p. 180.

32. Robinson, "When Will Revolutionary Movements Use Religion?" in Robbins and Robertson (eds.), *Church-State Relations*, p. 56.

33. Robinson, "When Will Revolutionary Movements Use Religion?" in Robbins and Robertson (eds.), *Church-State Relations*, p. 58.

34. Robinson, "When Will Revolutionary Movements Use Religion?" in Robbins and Robertson (eds.), *Church-State Relations*, p. 58.

35. Robinson, "When Will Revolutionary Movements Use Religion?" in Robbins and Robertson (eds.), *Church-State Relations*, p. 59.

36. See Mead, *Mind, Self, and Society*, pp. 144–152.

37. Marx and Engels, *The German Ideology*, pp. 12–14 and 92–94.

38. See Mannheim, *Ideology and Utopia*, pp. 192–196. For further expansions on Mannheim's theme, see Ricoeur, *Lectures on Ideology and Utopia*. For a thorough study of "Ideology," see Thompson, *Studies in the Theory of Ideology*. Equally informative is the first chapter of the same author's *Ideology and Modern Culture*, pp. 28–73. For a critical outline of the history of "Ideology" as a volatile concept, see Eagleton, *Ideology*. For further explanations on the Mannheimian theory of ideology and utopia, see Neisser, *On the Sociology of Knowledge*, pp. 63–72.

39. See Ricoeur, *Lectures on Ideology and Utopia*, Chapters 11 and 12, pp. 181–215.

40. See Ricoeur, *Lectures on Ideology and Utopia*, Chapter 15, pp. 254–266.

41. See Rieff, *Fellow Teachers*, p. 99.

42. See Khomeini, *Sahifeh-ye Nur*, vol. IV, p. 57.

43. For a sound assessment of the Islamic reaction to "The West," see Voll, "Muslim Responses to Colonialism," in Kelly (ed.), *Islam*, pp. 157–172. "The West" is turning Muslims into marginal (wo)men in their own lands. There is the root of the revolt. On the social and inner dynamics of "the marginal man," see Hughes, "Social Change and Status Protest: An Essay on the Marginal Man," in Hughes, *The Sociological Eye*, pp. 220–228. The central consequence of this historical deconstruction of collective identity is *ressentiment* at a massive cultural level. For a classical study of *ressentiment,* expanding on the initial Nietzschean insight, see Scheler, *Ressentiment.*

44. Joyce, *A Portrait of the Artist as a Young Man*, pp. 37–39.

45. Joyce, *A Portrait of the Artist as a Young Man*, p. 35.

46. Daneshvar, *Savushun*, p. 31.

Bibliography

Abdulghani, Iasim. *Iraq and Iran: The Years of Crisis*. Baltimore: Johns Hopkins University Press, 1984.

Abedi, Mehdi, and Gary Legenhausen, eds. *Jihad and Shahadat: Struggle and Martyrdom in Islam*. Houston: The Institute for Research and Islamic Studies, 1986.

Abidi, A. H. H. "The Iranian Revolution: Its Origins and Dimensions." *International Studies* 18:2 (April-June 1979): 129–61.

Abrahamian, Ervand. *Iran between Two Revolutions*. Princeton: Princeton University Press, 1982.

———. *Radical Islam: The Iranian Mojahedin*. London: I. B. Tauris & Co., Ltd., 1989.

———. "Structural Causes of the Iranian Revolution." *MERIP Reports* 10 (May 1980): 21–29.

Adamiyyat, Fereydun. *Andisheh-ha-ye Mirza Aqa Khan-e Kermani*. Tehran: Payam, 1357/1978.

———. *Fekr-e Demokrasi-e Ejtema'i dar Nehzat-e Mashrutiyyat-e Iran*. Tehran: Payam, 2535/1976.

Afkhami, Gholam R. *The Iranian Revolution: Thanatos on a National Scale*. Washington, DC: The Middle East Institute, 1985.

Afrasiabi, B., ed. *Pedar Taleqani dar Zendan*. Tehran: N.p., 1359/1980.

Afshar, Haleh, ed. *Iran: A Revolution in Turmoil*. London: Macmillan, 1985.

Ahani, Gholam Hossein. *Koliyyat-e Falsafeh-ye Islami*. Tehran: Ilmi, 1362/1983.

Ahlstrom, Sydney E. *A Religious History of the American People*. New Haven: Yale University Press, 1972.

Ahmed, Ishtiaq. *The Concept of an Islamic State: An Analysis of the Ideological Controversy in Pakistan*. New York: St. Martin's Press, 1987.

Ajami, Fuad. *The Vanished Imam: Musa al-Sadr and the Shia of Lebanon*. Ithaca: Cornell University Press, 1986.

Akhavi, Shahrough. "Elite Factionalism in the Islamic Republic of Iran." *The Middle East Journal* 41:2 (Spring 1987): 181–201.

———. *Religion and Politics in Contemporary Iran: Clergy-State Relations in the Pahlavi Period*. Albany: State University of New York Press, 1980.

595

Al-e Ahmad, Jalal. *Arzyabi-ye Shetab-zadeh*. Tehran: Ibn-e Sina, 1344/1965.
————. *By the Pen*. Translated by M. R. Ghanoonparvar. Introduction by Michael Hillmann. Austin: Center for Middle Eastern Studies at the University of Texas at Austin, 1988.
————. "The Cursing of the Land: A Plot Summary." Prepared by M. R. Ghanoonparvar. *Literature East and West* 20:1–4 (January-December 1976): 240–44.
————. *Dar Khedmat va Khianat-e Roshanfekran*. 2 vols. Tehran: Kharazmi, 1357/1978.
————. *Did va Bazdid*. Tehran: Amir Kabir, 1349/1960.
————. *Gharbzadegi*. Tehran: Ravaq, 1344/1962.
————. *Gharbzadegi [Weststruckness]*. Translated from the Persian by John Green and Ahmad Alizadeh. Lexington: Mazda Publishers, 1982.
————. *Haft Maqaleh.*.Tehran: Ravaq, 1332/1953.
————. *Hezb-e Tudeh, Khalil Maleki, va Nezam-e Shahanshahi*. Breman, FRG: Nehzat-e Melli-ye Iran, 1981.
————. *Iranian Society: An Anthology of Writings*. Compiled and edited by Michael C. Hillmann. Lexington, KY: Mazda Publishers, 1982.
————. *Kar-nameh-ye Seh Saleh*. Tehran: Ravaq, 1357/1978.
————. *Kharg: Dorr-e Yatim Khalij*. Tehran: Amir Kabir, 1339/1960.
————. *Khasi dar Miqat*. Tehran: Amir Kabir, 1357/1978.
————. *Lost in the Crowd*. Translated by John Green et al. Introduced by Michael C. Hillmann. Washington, DC: Three Continent Press, 1985.
————. "The Mobilization of Iran." Translated by David C. Champagne, with an Introductory Note by Michael C. Hillmann. *Literature East and West* 20:1–4 (January-December 1976): 61–70.
————. *Modir-e Madreseh*. Tehran: Ravaq, 1362/1983.
————. *Nefrin-e Zamin*. Tehran: Ravaq, 1357/1978.
————. *Nun Va al-Qalam*. Tehran: Ravaq, 1357/1978.
————. *Occidentosis: A Plague from the West*. Translated by R. Campbell. Edited by Hamid Algar. Berkeley: Mizan Press, 1984.
————. *Safar beh Velayat-e Isra'il*. Introduction by Shams Al-e Ahmad. Tehran: Ravaq, 1363/1984.
————. *Sangi bar Guri*. Tehran: Ravaq, 1360/1981.
————. *Sargozasht-e Kandu-ha'*. Tehran: Ravaq, 1333/1954.
————. *Seh Maqaleh-ye Digar*. Tehran: Ravaq, 1337/1958.
————. *Seh Tar*. Tehran: Javdan, n.d.
————. *Tat-neshin-ha'-ye Boluk-e Zahra'*. Tehran: Amir Kabir, 1337/1958.
————. *Urazan*. Tehran: Danesh, 1333/1954.
————. "What Are the University and Education Doing?" *Literature East and West* 20:1–4 (January-December 1976): 174–77.
————. *Yek Chah va Do Chaleh va Masalan Sharh-e Ahvalat*. Tehran: Ravaq, 1357/1978.
————. *Zan-e Ziadi*. Tehran: Ravaq, 1331/1952.
Alamuti, Mostafa'. *Iran dar Asr-e Pahlavi*. 10 vols. to date. London: N.p., 1367–70/1988–91.
Alaolmolki, Nazar. "The New Iranian Left." *The Middle East Journal* 41:2 (Spring 1987): 218–33.

Alavi, Bozorg. *Panjah-o Seh Nafar*. Tehran: Amir Kabir, 1357/1978.

Alexander, Yonah, and Allan Nanes, eds. *The United States and Iran: A Documentary History*. Frederick, MD: University Publications of America, Inc., 1980.

Algar, Hamid. *Religion and State in Iran, 1785–1906: The Role of the Ulama in the Qajar Period*. Berkeley: University of California Press, 1969.

———. *The Roots of the Islamic Revolution*. London: The Open Press, 1983.

Althusser, Louis. *For Marx*. Translated by Ben Brewster. New York: Vintage Books, 1970.

Amanat, Abbas. *Resurrection and Renewal: The Making of the Babi Movement in Iran, 1844–1850*. Ithaca: Cornell University Press, 1989.

Amir Ahmadi, Hooshang, and M. Parvin, eds. *Post-Revolutionary Iran*. Boulder, CO: Westview Press, 1988.

Amir Arjomand, Said. "A la Rechèrche de la Conscience Collective: Durkheim's Ideological Impact in Turkey and Iran." *The American Sociologist* 17:2 (1982): 94–102.

———. "The Causes and Significance of the Iranian Revolution." *State, Culture, and Society*. 1:3 (Spring 1985): 41–66.

———. "Religion and Revolution in Iran." *Contemporary Sociology* 2 (July 1982): 391–409.

———. "Religion, Political Order and Societal Change: With Special Reference to Shiʿite Islam." *Current Perspectives in Social Theory* 6 (1985): 1–16.

———. *The Shadow of God and the Hidden Imam: Religion, Political Order and Societal Change in Shiʿite Iran from the Beginning to 1890*. Chicago: University of Chicago Press, 1984.

———. "Shiʿite Islam and the Revolution in Iran." *Government and Opposition* 16:3 (1981): 293–316.

———. "Social Change and Movements of Revitalization in Contemporary Islam." In *New Religious Movements and Rapid Social Change*, edited by J. A. Beckford. London and Beverly Hills: Sage Publications, 1986.

———. "Traditionalism in Twentieth Century Iran." In *From Nationalism to Revolutionary Iran*. London: Macmillan; Albany: State University of New York Press, 1984.

———. *The Turban for the Crown: The Islamic Revolution in Iran*. New York: Oxford University Press, 1988.

———. "The *Ulama's* Traditionalist Opposition to Parliamentarianism: 1907–1909." *Middle Eastern Studies* 17:2 (1981): 174–190.

———, ed. *Authority and Political Culture in Shiʿism*. Albany: State University of New York Press, 1988.

———, ed. *From Nationalism to Revolutionary Islam*. Forward by Ernest Gellner. Albany: State University of New York Press, 1984.

Amirsadeghi, Hossein, and R. W. Ferrier, eds. *Twentieth Century Iran*. London: Heinemann; New York: Holmes & Meier Publishers, Inc., 1977.

Amoli, Hasan Hasan-Zadeh-ye. "Allamah Tabataba'i dar Manzareh-ye Erfan-e Nazari va Amali." *Keyhan-e Andisheh* 26 (Mehr-Aban 1368/October-November 1989): 3–12.

Anonymous. *Bahthi Piramun-e Velayat-e Faqih*. New York: Mostazafan Foundation of New York, 1360/1981.

Anonymous. *Biography-e Pishva'*. N.p.: N.p., 1394/1974.
──────. "Dar Yadman-e Mo^callem-e Andishidan." *Keyhan-e Farhangi* 7:2, Serial
No. 74 (May 1990): 5–10.
──────. *Gozashteh Cheragh-e Rah-e Ayandeh Ast*. vol. 1. Tehran: Zebarjad, n.d.
──────. *Nehzat-e Azadi-ye Iran*. Tehran: Nehzat-e Azadi Iran, 1361/1982.
──────. *Seyri dar Athar-e Ostad-e Shahid Motahhari*. Tehran: Setad-e Bargozari-ye
Marasem-e Bozorg-dasht-e Salgard-e Ostad, 1359/1980.
──────. *Tafsir va Tahlil-e Velayat-e Motlaqeh-ye Faqih*. N.p.: Nehzat-e Azadi-ye
Iran, n.d.
──────. "Tajalli-ye Eshq dar Adab va Erfan-e Imam Khomeini." *Keyhan-e Andi-*
sheh 29 (Farvardin-Ordibehesht 1369/March-April 1990): 168–71.
──────. *Velayat-e Motlaqeh-ye Faqih*. Tehran: Nehzat-e Azadi Iran, c1366/
c1987.
──────. *Yadnameh-ye Abu Dharr-e Zaman*. Tehran: N.p., 1360/1981.
──────, ed. *Az Azadi ta Shahadat*. Tehran: Sherkat-e Sahami-ye Enteshar (Entesharat-e Abu Dharr), 1358/1979.
──────, ed. *Bahthi dar Bareh-ye Marja^ciyyat va Ruhaniyyat*. Tehran: Enteshar,
1341/1962.
──────, ed. *Dovvomiyn Yadnameh-ye Allamah Tabataba'i*. Tehran: Cultural Studies and Research Institute, 1363/1984.
──────, ed. *Majmu^ceh-ye Goftar-e Pedar Taleqani: (1) Khotbeh-ha-ye Namaz-e*
Jom^ceh va Id-e Fetr; (2) Ba Qur'an dar Sahneh. Long Beach, CA: Sazeman-e
Mojahedin-e Khalq-e Iran, 1359/1980.
──────, ed. *Sahih al-Bukhari: Arabic-English*. Lahore: N.p., 1971.
──────, ed. *Sargozasht-ha-ye vizheh az Zendeqi-ye Ostad-e Shahid Morteza Motah-*
hari. Vol. 1. Tehran: Mo'aseseh-ye Nashr va Tahqiqat-e Dhekr, 1366/1987.
──────, ed. *Yadnameh-ye Allamah Tabataba'i*. Tehran: Cultural Studies and Re-
search Institute, 1362/1983.
Ansari, Shaykh Morteza. *Fara'id al-Usul*. Tehran: N.p., n.d.
Ansari-ye Kermani, Hojat al-Islam. *Vizhegiha'-'i az Zendegi-ye Imam Khomeini*.
Tehran: Nashr-e Sobhan, 1362/1983.
Ansarian, Ali, ed. *Dastur al-Jumhuriyyah al-Islamiyyah al-Iraniyyah*. Damascus: al-
Mustashariyyah al-Thuqafiyyah li al-Jumhuriyyah al-Islamiyyah al-Iraniyyah bi
Dimashq, 1405/1985.
Aram, Abbas. *Bot-Shekani va Jedal-e Kheyr va Shar: Az Ibrahim ta Khomeini*.
Tehran: Ata^ci, 1358/1979.
Arasteh, Reza. *Education and Social Awakening in Iran, 1850–1968*. Leiden: E. J.
Brill, 1969.
Ardakani, Reja Davari, *Defa^caz Falsateh*. Tehran: Vezarat-e Farhang va Ershad-e
Islami, 1366/1987.
Ashraf, Ahmad. "Bazaar and Mosque in Iran's Revolution." Interview given to
Ervand Abrahamian. *MERIP Reports* 13 (March-April 1983): 16–23.
──────. "Dehqanan, Zamin va Enqelab." In *Ketab-e Agah*. Tehran: Agah, 1361/
1982.
──────. "Historical Obstacles to the Development of a Bourgeoisie in Iran." In
Studies in the Economic History of the Middle East from the Rise of Islam to
the Present Day, edited by M. A. Cook. Oxford: Oxford University Press, 1978.

————. "The Roots of Emerging Dual Class Structure in Nineteenth-Century Iran." *Iranian Studies* 14 (Winter-Spring 1981): 5–27.

————. "Theocracy and Charisma: New Men of Power in Iran." *International Journal of Politics, Culture, and Society* 4:1 (1990): 113–52.

Ashraf, Ahmad, and Ali Banuazizi. "The State, Classes, and Modes of Mobilization in the Iranian Revolution." *State, Culture and Society* 1:3 (Spring 1985): 3–40.

Ashraf, Ahmad, and H. Hekmat. "Merchants and Artisans in the Development Processes of Nineteenth-Century Iran." In *The Islamic Middle East, 700–1900: Studies in Economic and Social History,* edited by A. L. Udovitch. Princeton, NJ: Darwin Press, 1981.

Ashtiani, Sayyid Jalal al-Din, ed. *Montakhabati az Athar-e Hokama'-ye Elahi-ye Iran.* Tehran: N.p., 1351/1972.

————. *Sharh-e Hal va Ara'-e Falsafi-ye Molla Sadra.* N.p.: N.p., n.d.

Avery, Peter W. *Modern Iran.* London: Ernest Benn; New York: Praeger, 1965.

Ayatollahi, Sayyid Muhammad Taqi. *Velayat-e Faqih: Zir-bana'-ye Fekri-ye Mash-ruteh-ye Mashru'eh (Seyri dar Afkar va Mobarezat-e Sayyid Abdolhossein-e Lari).* Tehran: Amir Kabir, 1363/1984.

Badla, Sayyid Hossein. "*Kashf-e Asrar* va Zamineh-ye peydayesh-e An." *Keyhan-e Andisheh* 29 (Farvardin-Ordibehesht 1369/March-April 1990): 162–67.

Bahar, Malak al-Shu'ara. *Tarikh-e Ahzab-e Siasi-ye Iran.* 2 vols. Tehran: Jibi, 1357/ 1978 (vol. 1); Tehran: Amir Kabir, 1363/1984.

Bakhash, Shaul. *Iran, Monarchy, Bureaucracy and Reform under the Qajars, 1858–1896.* London: Ithaca Press, 1978.

————. *The Reign of the Ayatollahs: Iran and the Islamic Revolution.* New York: Basic Books, 1984.

Baldwin, George. *Planning and Development in Iran.* Baltimore, MD: Johns Hopkins University Press, 1967.

Ball, Nicole, and Milton Leitenberg. "The Iranian Domestic Crisis: Foreign Policy Making and Foreign Policy Goals of the United States." *Journal of South Asian and Middle Eastern Studies* 2:3 (Spring 1979): 36–56.

Banani, Amin. *The Modernization of Iran: 1921–1941.* Stanford: Stanford University Press, 1961.

Bani-Sadr, Abolhasan. "Barqarari-ye Fascism dar Iran Mosavi ast ba Enhedam-e Jame'eh." *Keyhan* (17 Ordibehesht 1358/1979): 8.

————. *Bayaniyyeh-ye Jomhuri-ye Islami.* Tehran: Imam, 1358/1979.

————. "Dar Islam Asas Kar ast nah Sarmayeh." *Keyhan* (12 Esfand 1357/1978): 6.

————. "Dialectic-e har Qodrat-talabi bar Mabna'-ye Hadaf ast." *Keyhan* (9 Farvardin 1358/1979): 6.

————. *The Fundamental Principles and Precepts of Islamic Government.* Translated from the Persian by Mohammad R. Ghanoonparvar. Lexington, KY: Mazda Publishers, 1981.

————. *Eqtesad-e Towhidi.* N.p.: N.p., 1357/1978.

————. *Khianat beh Omid.* N.p.: N.p., 1360/1981.

————. *Kish-e Shakhsiyyat.* N.p.: N.p., 1355/1976.

————. *Moqe'iyyat-e Iran va Naqsh-e Modarres.* Vol. 1. N.p.: Modarres, 1356/ 1977.

Bani-Sadr, Abolhasan. *Movazeneh-ha.* Tehran: Jahed, n.d.
———. *Naft va Solteh.* N.p.: Mosaddeq, 1356/1977.
———. "Sarmayeh-daran-e ma Kar-farma-ye Siasi Budand." *Keyhan* (12 Farvardin 1358/1979): 6.
———. *Zan va Zanashu'i.* Tehran: Entesharat-e Enqelab-e Islami, 1366/1985.
Banuazizi, Ali. "Iran's Revolution Reappraised." *Third World Quarterly* 10:2 (April 1988): 1041–47.
———. "Iranian 'National Character': A Critique of Some Western Perspectives." In *Psychological Dimensions of Near Eastern Studies,* edited by L. Karl Brown and Norman Itzkowitz, 210–39. Princeton Studies on the Near East. Princeton, NJ: The Darwin Press, 1977.
Banuazizi, Ali, and Myron Weiner, eds. *The State, Religion, and Ethnic Politics: Afghanistan, Iran, and Pakistan.* Syracuse: Syracuse University Press, 1986.
Bashiriyeh, Hossein. *The State and Revolution in Iran.* New York: St. Martin's Press, 1984.
Bataille, George. *The Accursed Share.* Translated by Robert Hurley. Vol. 1. New York: Zone Books, 1988.
Bayat, Mangol. "The Iranian Revolution of 1978–1979: Fundamentalist or Modern?" *The Middle East Journal* 37:1 (Winter 1983): 30–42.
———. *Mysticism and Dissent: Socioreligious Thought in Qajar Iran.* Syracuse: Syracuse University Press, 1982.
———. "A Phoenix Too Frequent: The Concept of Historical Continuity in Modern Iranian Thought." *Asian and African Studies* 12 (1978): 203–20.
Bazargan, Mehdi. *Angizeh va Angizandeh.* Houston: Book Distribution Center, 1356/1977.
———. *Az Khoda-parasti ta Khod-parasti.* Houston: Book Distribution Center, 1355/1976.
———. *Azadi-ye Hend.* Tehran: Omid, n.d.
———. *Bad va Baran dar Qur'an.* Tehran: Sherkat-e Sahami-ye Enteshar, 1353/1974.
———. *Bazyabi-ye Arzesh-ha.* 3 vols. Tehran: Nehzat-e Azadi Iran, 1362/1983.
———. *Be'that va Ideology.* Houston: Book Distribution Center, 1355/1976.
———. *Dars-e Dindari.* Introduction by Ahmad Aram. Tehran: Enteshar, 1344/1965.
———. *Enqelab-e Iran dar do Harakat.* Tehran: Naraqi, 1363/1984.
———. *Eshq va Parastesh.* Houston: Book Distribution Center, 1357/1978.
———. *Khaneh-ye Mardom.* Houston: Book Distribution Center, 1356/1977.
———. *Modafe'at.* Bellville, IL: Nehzat-e Azadi Iran, 1343/1964.
———. *Mosalman: Ejtema'i va Jahani.* Tehran: Ershad, 1344/1965.
———. *Seyr-e Tahavvol dar Qur'an.* Tehran: Sherkat-e Sahami-ye Enteshar, 1358/1979.
Beeman, William O. *Language, Status, and Power in Iran.* Bloomington, IN: Indiana University Press, 1986.
Behnam, M. Reza. *Cultural Foundations of Iranian Politics.* Salt Lake City, UT: University of Utah Press, 1986.
Bell, Daniel. *The End of Ideology: On the Exhaustion of Political Ideas in the Fifties.* Rev. ed. New York: The Free Press, 1960.

Bell, Richard, and W. M. Watt. *Introduction to the Qur'an*. Edinburgh: Edinburgh University Press, 1970.

Berger, Peter L. *The Sacred Canopy: Elements of a Sociological Theory of Religion*. New York: Anchor Books, 1969.

Bernard, Cheryl, and Zalman Khalilzad. *"The Government of God": Iran's Islamic Republic*. New York: Columbia University Press, 1984.

Bharier, J. *Economic Development of Iran, 1900–1970*. London: Oxford University Press, 1971.

Bi-azar-e Shirazi, Abdolkarim. "Binesh-e Fiqhi-e Imam dar Bar-khord-e ba Ruydad-ha-ye Novin-e Jahan." *Keyhan-e Andisheh* 29 (Farvardin-Ordibehesht 1369/ March-April 1990): 45–55.

Bierstedt, Robert. *Power and Progress: Essays on Sociological Theory*. New York: McGraw-Hill, 1974.

Bill, James A. *The Eagle and the Lion: The Tragedy of American-Iranian Relations*. New Haven: Yale University Press, 1988.

———. *The Politics of Iran: Groups, Classes, and Modernization*. Columbus, OH: Charles E. Merrill Publishing Co., 1972.

———. "Power and Religion in Revolutionary Iran." *Middle East Journal* 36:1 (Winter 1982): 22–47.

Bill, James A., and William Roger Louis, eds. *Musaddiq, Iranian Nationalism, and Oil*. Austin: University of Texas Press, 1988.

Binder, Leonard. *Iran: Political Development in a Changing Society*. Berkeley and Los Angeles: University of California Press, 1964.

———. *Islamic Liberalism: A Critique of Development Ideologies*. Chicago: University of Chicago Press, 1988.

Blachère, Régis. *Introduction au Coran*. Paris: Besson & Chantemerle, 1959.

Bloom, Allan. *The Closing of the American Mind: How Higher Education Has Failed Democracy and Impoverished the Souls of Today's Students*. New York: Simon and Schuster, 1987.

Bonine, Michael E., and Nikki R. Keddie, eds. *Modern Iran: The Dialectics of Activity and Change*. Albany: State University of New York Press, 1981.

Boyce, Mary. *Zoroastrianism: Their Religious Beliefs and Practices*. London: Routledge & Kegan Paul, 1979.

Bradbury, Malcolm. *The Modern World: Ten Current Writers*. New York: Viking Press, 1988.

Brière, Claire, and P. Blanchet. *Iran: la révolution au nom de Dieu*. Paris: Seuil, 1979.

Brzezinski, Zbigniew. *Power and Principle: Memoirs of the National Security Advisor, 1977–1981*. New York: Farrar, Straus and Giroux, 1983.

Burke, Edmund III, and Ira M. Lapidus, eds. *Islam, Politics, and Social Movements*. Berkeley: University of California Press, 1988.

Calder, Norman. "Accommodation and Revolution in Imami Shi'i Jurisprudence; Khumayni and the Classical Tradition." *Middle Eastern Studies* 18:1 (1982): 3–20.

Campbell, W. R., and Djamchid Darvich. "Global Implications of the Islamic Revolution for the Status Quo in the Persian Gulf." *Journal of South Asian and Middle Eastern Studies* 5 (Fall 1981): 31–51.

Carter, Jimmy. *Keeping Faith*. New York: Bantam Books, 1983.

Cassirer, Ernst. *The Myth of the State*. New Haven: Yale University Press, 1946.

Chehabi, H. E. *Iranian Politics and Religious Modernism: The Liberation Movement of Iran under the Shah and Khomeini*. Ithaca: Cornell University Press, 1990.

———. "State and Society in Islamic Liberalism." *State, Culture, and Society* 1:3 (Spring 1985): 85–101.

Chelkowski, Peter J., ed. *Iran: Continuity and Variety*. New York: New York University Press, 1971.

Chelkowski, Peter J., and Robert J. Pranger, eds. *Ideology and Power in the Middle East*. Studies in Honor of George Lenczowski. Durham, NC: Duke University Press, 1988.

Chittick, William C. *The Sufi Path of Knowledge: Ibn al-Arabi's Metaphysics of Imagination*. Albany: State University of New York Press, 1989.

Christopher, W. et al. *American Hostages in Iran: The Conduct of a Crisis*. New Haven: Yale University Press, 1985.

Clawson, Patrick. "Islamic Iran's Economic Politics and Prospects." *The Middle East Journal* 42:3 (Summer 1988): 371–88.

Cole, Juan R. I., and Nikki R. Keddie, eds. *Shi'ism and Social Protest*. New Haven: Yale University Press, 1986.

Constitution of the Islamic Republic of Iran. Translated by Hamid Algar. Berkeley, CA: Mizan Press, 1980.

Cook, J. M. *The Persian Empire*. New York: Schocken Books, 1983.

Corbin, Henri. *En Islam iranien, aspects spirituels et philosophiques*. 4 vols. Paris: Galimard, 1971–72.

Cottam, Richard. *Nationalism in Iran*. Pittsburgh, PA: University of Pittsburgh Press, 1979.

———. "The United States and Iran's Revolution: Goodbye to America's Shah." *Foreign Policy* 34 (Spring 1979): 3–14.

Crone, Patricia, and Martin Hind. *God's Caliph: Religious Authority in the First Centuries of Islam*. Cambridge: Cambridge University Press, 1986.

Dabashi, Hamid. "'Ali Shari'ati's Islam: Revolutionary Uses of Faith in a Post-Traditional Society," *The Islamic Quarterly* 27:4 (1983): 203–22.

———. *Authority in Islam: From the Rise of Muhammad to the Establishment of the Umayyads*. New Brunswick, NJ: Transaction Books, 1989.

———. "Imam Khomeini, *Islam and Revolution: Writing and Declarations of Imam Khomeini* (trans. Hamid Algar), and Ayatullah Murtaza Mutahhari, *Social and Historical Change: An Islamic Perspective* (trans. R. Campbell)." *The Middle East Journal* 42:3 (Summer 1988): 513–15.

———. Review of William O. Beeman, *Language, Status, and Power in Iran*. *Iranian Studies* 21:3–4 (1988): 122–27.

———. "The Revolutions of Our Time: Religious Politics in Modernity." *Contemporary Sociology* 13:6 (November 1984): 673–76.

———. "Shi'ite Islam: The Theology of Discontent." *Contemporary Sociology* 15:2 (March 1986): 178–81.

———. "The Sufi Doctrine of 'The Perfect Man' and a View of the Hierarchical Structure of Islamic Culture." *Islamic Quarterly* 30:2 (1986).

———. "A View of Mulla Sadra's Social Thought: Social Order in a Sacred Order." *Iran Nameh* 3:3 (Spring 1985): 407–28.

Daneshvar, Simin. *Savushun: A Novel about Modern Iran.* Translated by M. R. Ghanoonparvar. Washington, DC: Mage Publishers, 1990.

———. "Shohar-e Man Jalal." *Andisheh va Honar.* Special Commemorative Issue on Jalal Al-e Ahmad, New Series No. 4, 1343/1964.

Davani, Ali. *Nehzat-e Ruhaniun-e Iran.* 10 vols. [Tehran?]: Bonyad-e Farhangi-e Imam Reza, 1358/1979.

Dawson, Raymond S. *Confucius.* New York: Hill & Wang, 1982.

de Mause, Lloyd. "The Real Target Wasn't Terrorism." *The Journal of Psychohistory* 13:4 (Spring 1986): 413–26.

Dehbashi, Ali, ed. *Nameh-ha-ye Jalal Al-e Ahmad.* Vol. 1. Tehran: Bozorgmehr, 1367/1988.

———. *Yadnameh-ye Jalal Al-e Ahmad.* Tehran: Pasargad, 1364/1985.

Dekmejian, R. H. "The Anatomy of Islamic Revival: Legitimacy Crisis, Ethnic Conflict and the Search for Islamic Alternatives." *Middle East Journal* 34:1 (Winter 1980): 1–12.

Deldam, Eskandar. *Ayatollah Taleqani: Rehlat ya Shahadat.* Tehran: Behruz, 1359/1980.

———. *Enqelab beh Ravayat-e Enqelab-Sazan.* Tehran: Mo'aseseh-ye Matbuʿati-ye Ata'i, 1358/1980.

al-Dhahabi, Muhammad Husayn. *al-Ittijahat al-Munharifah fi Tafsir al-Quran al-Karim.* Cairo: N.p., 1971.

———. *al-Tafsir wa al-Mufassirun.* Cairo: N.p., 1961.

Droysen, J. C. *Outline of the Principles of History.* Translated by E. Benjamin Andrews. Boston: N.p., 1893.

Durkheim, Emile. *The Elementary Forms of the Religious Life.* New York: The Free Press, 1915.

Dynani, Gholamhossein Ebrahim. "Allamah Tabataba'i va Nazar-e Motekalleman dar bareh-ye Elm-e Khodavand beh Joz'iyyat." *Keyhan-e Farhangi* 6:8, Serial No. 68 (November 1989): 8–9.

Eagleton, Terry. *Ideology: An Introduction.* New York: Verso, 1991.

———. *The Ideology of the Aesthetic.* London: Basil Blackwell, 1990.

Eickelman, Dale R. *The Middle East: An Anthropological Approach.* Englewood Cliffs, NJ: Prentice-Hall, 1981.

Eliade, Mircea. *Myth and Reality.* New York: Harper & Row, 1963.

Eliash, Joseph. "The Ithna ʿAshari Shiʿi Juristic Theory of Political and Legal Authority." *Studia Islamica* 29 (1969): 17–30.

———. "Some Misconceptions Regarding the Juridical Status of the Iranian Ulama." *International Journal of Middle East Studies* 10 (February 1979): 9–25.

Elliott, Frank A. "Biological Roots of Violence." Paper presented at the annual meeting of the American Philosophical Society, Philadelphia, November 11, 1982.

Elliott, J. H. "Revolution and Continuity in Early Modern Europe." *Past and Present* 42 (1969): 35–57.

Ellmann, Richard, and Charles Feidelson, eds. *The Modern Tradition: Backgrounds of Modern Literature.* New York: Oxford University Press, 1965.

Elwell-Sutton, L. P. *Modern Iran*. London: George Routledge and Sons, 1941.

Enayat, Hamid. *Modern Islamic Political Thought*. London: Macmillan; Austin: University of Texas Press, 1982.

Esposito, John L., ed. *The Iranian Revolution: Its Global Impact*. Miami: Florida International University Press, 1990.

————. *Voices of Resurgent Islam*. New York: Oxford University Press, 1983.

Fallaci, Oriana. *Interview with History*. Boston: Houghton Mifflin Company, 1977.

Fateh, Mostafa'. *Panjah sal Naft*. Tehran: Kavosh, n.d.

Fathi, Asghar. "Role of the Traditional Leader in the Modernization of Iran, 1890–1910." *International Journal of Middle East Studies* 10:1 (February 1980): 87–98.

Fazel, Mojtaba'. "Shareh-e Shari'at-e Islam." *Keyhan-e Andisheh* 29 (Farvardin-Ordibehesht 1369/March-April 1990): 196–97.

Fernea, Elizabeth Warnock. *Guests of the Sheik: An Ethnography of an Iraqi Village*. New York: Anchor Books, 1965.

Ferrarotti, Franco. "The Paradox of the Sacred." *International Journal of Sociology* 14:2 (Summer 1984): 3–108.

Ferrier, R. W. *The History of the British Petroleum Company*. Vol. 1: *The Developing Years, 1901–1932*. Cambridge: Cambridge University Press, 1982.

Fischer, Michael M. J. *Iran: From Religious Dispute to Revolution*. Cambridge, MA: Harvard University Press, 1980.

Fischer, Michael M. J., and Mehdi Abedi. *Debating Muslims: Cultural Dialogues in Postmodernity and Tradition*. Madison: University of Wisconsin Press, 1990.

Forbis, William H. *Fall of the Peacock Throne: The Story of Iran*. New York: Harper & Row, 1980.

Frankfurt, Henri. *Kingship and the Gods*. Chicago: University of Chicago Press, 1948.

Fukuyama, Francis. "The End of History?" *The National Interest* 16 (Summer 1989): 3–19.

Gasiorowski, Mark. "The 1953 Coup d'État in Iran." *International Journal of Middle East Studies* 19:3 (August 1987): 261–86.

Gätje, Helmut. *The Qur'an and Its Exegesis: Selected Texts with Classical and Modern Muslim Interpretations*. Berkeley: University of California Press, 1976.

Geertz, Clifford. *The Interpretation of Cultures*. New York: Basic Books, 1973.

————. *Local Knowledge: Further Essays in Interpretive Anthropology*. New York: Basic Books, 1983.

Gellner, E. *Muslim Society*. New York: Cambridge University Press, 1981.

Gerth, Hans. "Speier's Critique of Karl Mannheim." *State, Culture and Society* 1:3 (Spring 1985): 198–208.

al-Ghanushi, Rashid. "Imam Khomeini va Rahbari-ye Nehzat-ha-ye Islami-ye Mo'aser-e Jahan." *Keyhan-e Andisheh* 29 (Farvardin-Ordibehesht 1369/March-April 1990): 110–29.

Gibb, H. A. R., and J. M. Kramers, eds. *Shorter Encyclopaedia of Islam*. Ithaca: Cornell University Press, 1953.

Gide, André. *Bazgasht-e Az Shoravi*. Translated by Jalal Al-e Ahmad. Tehran: Amir Kabir, 1356/1977.

Göbel, Karl-Heinrich. *Moderne schiitische politik und Staatsidee.* Schriften des Deutschen Orient-Instituts. Opladen: Leske Verlag, Budrich, 1984.

Graham, R. *Iran: The Illusion of Power.* London: Croom Helm, 1978; New York: St. Martin's Press, 1979.

Green, Jerrold D. *Revolution in Iran: The Politics of Countermobilization.* New York: Praeger, 1982.

Grisoni, D. A., comp. and ed. "Levi-Strauss en 33 Mots." *Magazine litteraire* 223 (October 1985): 26–27.

Grousset, René. *La Face de l'Asie.* Paris: Payot, 1955.

Habermas, Jürgen. *Legitimation Crisis.* Boston, MA: Beacon Press, 1973.

Haddad, Yvonne Yazbeck. *Contemporary Islam and the Challenge of History.* Albany: State University of New York Press, 1982.

———. "The Qur'anic Justification for an Islamic Revolution: The View of Sayyid Qutb." *The Middle East Journal* 37:1 (Winter 1983): 14–29.

Ha'eri, Abdolhadi. *Shi'ism and Constitutionalism in Iran: A Study of the Role Played by the Persian Residents of Iraq in Iranian Politics.* Leiden: E. J. Brill, 1977.

———. *Tashayyo' va Mashrutiyyat dar Iran.* Tehran: Amir Kabir, 1364/1985.

Hakimi, Muhammad Reza. *Tafsir-e Aftab: Negareshi beh Resalat-e Islam va Hamasah-ye Insan dar Rahbari-ye Imam Khomeini.* Tehran: Daftar-e Nashr-e Farhang-e Islami, 1357/1978.

Halliday, Fred. *Iran: Dictatorship and Development.* London and New York: Penguin, 1979.

Halliday, Fred, and Hamza Alavi, eds. *State and Ideology in the Middle East and Pakistan.* New York: Monthly Review Press, 1988.

al-Harrani, Ibn Shu'bah. *Tuhaf al-Uqul.* Beirut: N.p., 1974.

Hasan-zadeh Amoli, Hasan. "Allamah Tabataba'i dar Manzareh-ye Erfan-e Nazari va Amali." *Keyhan-e Andisheh* 26 (Mehr-Aban 1368/October-November 1989): 3–12.

Heidegger, Martin. *The Question of Being.* Translated by William Kluback and Jean T. Wilde. Boston: Twayne, 1958.

Heikal, Mohamed. *Iran: The Untold Story.* New York: Pantheon Books, 1981.

———. *The Return of the Ayatollah.* London: Andre Deutsch Limited, 1981.

Helms, Cynthia. *An Ambassador's Wife in Iran.* New York: Dodd, Mead & Co., 1981.

Hetherington, Norris. "Industrialization and Revolution in Iran: Forced Progress or Unmet Expectations." *Middle East Journal* 36:3 (Summer 1983): 362–73.

al-Hilli, Muhaqqiq. *Sharayi' al-Islam.* Tehran: Ilmiyyah Islamiyyah, 1958.

Hillmann, Michael C. *Iranian Culture: A Persianist View.* Lanham, MD: University Press of America, 1990.

Hiro, Dilip. *Holy Wars: The Rise of Islamic Fundamentalism.* New York: Routledge, 1989.

———. *Iran under the Ayatollahs.* Boston, MA: Routledge and Kegan Paul, 1985.

Hobsbawm, Eric, and Terence Ranger, eds. *The Invention of Tradition.* Cambridge: Cambridge University Press, 1983.

Homayun, Daryush. *Diruz va Farda: Seh Goftar dar Bareh-ye Iran-e Enqelabi.* N.p.: N.p., 1981.

Hoogland, Eric. *Land and Revolution in Iran, 1960–1980.* Austin: University of Texas Press, 1982.

Hoogland, Eric, and William Royce. "The Shiʻi Clergy of Iran and the Conception of an Islamic State." *State, Culture, and Society* 1:3 (Spring 1985): 102–17.

Hosseini-ye Qa'em-maqami, Sayyid Abbas. "Qur'an va Erfan az Manzareh-ye Imam." *Keyhan-e Andisheh* 29 (Farvardin-Ordibehesht 1369/March-April 1990): 66–109.

Hosseini-ye Tehrani, Sayyid Muhammad Hossein. *Mehr-e Taban* N.p.: Entesharat-e Baqer al-Olum, n.d.

Hoveyda, Fereydoun. *La Chute du Shah.* Paris: Editions Duchet/Chastel, 1979.

Hughes, Everett C. *The Sociological Eye: Selected Papers.* New York: Aldine-Atherton, 1971.

Hughes, H. Stuart. *Consciousness and Society: The Reorientation of European Social Thought, 1890–1930.* New York: Vintage Books, 1958.

Hunter, Shireen T. "Iran and the Spread of Revolutionary Islam." *Third World Quarterly* 10:2 (April 1988): 730–49.

———, ed. *The Politics of Islamic Revivalism: Diversity and Unity.* Bloomington, IN: Indiana University Press, 1988.

Huyser, Robert E. *Mission to Tehran.* New York: Harper & Row, 1986.

Inlow, E. Burke. *Shahanshah: The Monarchy of Iran.* Delhi: Motilal Banarsidass, 1979.

Issawi, C. *The Economic History of Iran 1800–1914.* Chicago: University of Chicago Press, 1971.

Izadi, Mostafa'. *Faqih-e Aliqadr.* 2 vols. Tehran: Sorush, 1361–66/1982–87.

Izadi, Mostafa', and Qasim Meskub, eds. *Did-gah-e Towhidi.* Vol. 1. Tehran: Daftar-e Nashr-e Farhang-e Islami, 1356/1977.

Jabbari, Ahmad, and Robert Olsen, eds. *Iran: Essays on a Revolution in the Making.* Lexington, KY: Mazda Publishers, 1981.

al-Jadili, Muhammad Abd al-Rahman. *Nazarat Hadithah fi al-Tafsir.* Beirut: N.p., 1963.

Jaʻfari, Sayyid Muhammad Mehdi, trans. and ed. *Nehzat-e Bidar-gari dar Jahan-e Islam.* Tehran: N.p., 1362/1983.

Jalali, Sadeq. *Bar Zedd-e Esteʻmar.* Tehran: Elmi, 1352/1973.

Javanshir, F. M., ed. with an Introduction. *Hamasah-ye 23 Tir: Gusheh-'i az Mobarezat-e Kargaran-e Naft-e Khuzestan.* N.p.: Hezb-e Tudeh, 1359/1980.

Jazani, Bizhan. *Capitalism and Revolution in Iran: Selected Writings of Bizhan Jazani.* London: Zed Press, 1980.

———. *Jonbesh-e Zedd-e Esteʻmari.* N.p.: N.p., 1346/1967.

———. *Nabard ba Dictatory. . . .* Tehran: Chaman, 1357/1978.

———. *Ta'rikh-e si Saleh-ye Iran.* Tehran: N.p., 1357/1978.

Jenati, Muhammad Ibrahim. "Feqh-e Ejtehadi va Eslah-e Howzeh-ha az Did-gah-e Imam Khomeini." *Keyhan-e Andisheh* 29 (Farvardin-Ordibehesht 1369/March-April 1990): 15–38.

Joyce, James. *A Portrait of the Artist as a Young Man.* New York: Penguin Books, 1964.

Jünger, Ernst. *Über die Linie.* Frankfurt: Klostermann, 1958.

———. *Ubur az Khat*. Translated by Mahmud Human and Jalal Al-e Ahmad. Tehran: N.p., 1346/1967.

Kapuscinski, Ryszard. *Shah of Shahs*. New York: Hellen and Kurt Wolff Books, 1982.

Karpat, Kemal, ed. *Political and Social Thought in the Contemporary Middle East*. New York: Praeger, 1968.

Kasravi, Ahmad. *Emruz Chareh Chist?* Tehran: Chapak, 1357/1978.

———. *Sarnevesht-e Iran Cheh Khahad Bud?* Tehran: Chapak, 1357/1978.

Katouzian, Homa. *Musaddiq and the Struggle for Power in Iran*. London: I. B. Tauris Co., Ltd., 1990.

———. "Nationalist Trends in Iran, 1921–1926." *International Journal of Middle East Studies* 10 (1979): 533–51.

———. *The Political Economy of Modern Iran: Despotism and Pseudo-Modernism, 1926–1979*. New York: New York University Press, 1981.

———, ed. with an Introduction. *Khaterat-e Siasi-ye Khalil Maleki*. N.p.: N.p., 1360/1981.

Kazemi, Farhad. *Politics and Culture in Iran*. Ann Arbor: Institute for Social Research, University of Michigan, 1988.

———. *Poverty and Revolution in Iran*. New York: New York University Press, 1980.

———. "State and Society in the Ideology of the Devotees of Islam." *State, Culture, and Society* 1:3 (Spring 1985): 118–35.

Keddie, Nikki R. "Iranian Revolutions in Comparative Perspective." *The American Historical Review* 88:3 (June 1983): 579–98.

———. *An Islamic Response to Imperialism: The Political and Religious Writings of Jamal-al-Din "al-Afghani."* Berkeley and Los Angeles: University of California Press, 1983.

———. "Is There a Middle East?" *International Journal of Middle East Studies* 4 (1973): 255–71.

———. "The Origins of the Religious-Radical Alliance in Iran." *Past and Present* 34 (1966): 70–80.

———. *Religion and Rebellion in Iran: The Tobacco Protests of 1891–92*. London: Frank Cass, 1966.

———. *Roots of Revolution: An Interpretative History of Modern Iran*. New Haven: Yale University Press, 1981.

———. "The Roots of the Ulama's Power in Modern Iran." In *Scholars, Saints, and Sufis: Muslim Religious Institutions since 1500*. Berkeley and Los Angeles: University of California Press, 1972.

———, ed. *Religion and Politics in Iran: Shi'ism from Quietism to Revolution*. New Haven: Yale University Press, 1982.

———, ed. *Scholars, Saints, and Sufis: Muslim Religious Institutions in the Middle East since 1500*. Berkeley: University of California Press, 1972.

Keddie, Nikki R., and Michael E. Bonine, eds. *Continuity and Change in Modern Iran*. Albany: State University of New York Press, 1981.

Keddie, Nikki R., and Mark J. Gasiorowski, eds. *Neither East Nor West: Iran, the Soviet Union, and the United States*. New Haven: Yale University Press, 1990.

Keddie, Nikki R., and Eric Hooglund, eds. *The Iranian Revolution and the Islamic Republic.* Washington, DC: Middle East Institute, 1982; Syracuse: Syracuse University Press, 1986.

Kedourie, Elie. "Khomeini's Political Heresy." *Policy Review* 12:5 (Spring 1980): 133–46.

Kedourie, Elie, and Sylvia G. Haim, eds. *Towards a Modern Iran: Studies in Thought, Politics and Society.* London: Frank Cass, 1980.

Kelidar, Abbas. "Ayatollah Khomeini's Concept of Islamic Government." In *Islam and Power,* edited by Alexander Cudsi and Ali Dessouki, 75–92. Baltimore, MD: Johns Hopkins University Press, 1981.

Kelly, Marjorie. *Islam: The Religious and Political Life of a World Community.* New York: Praeger, 1984.

Kenny, Anthony. *Aquinas.* Oxford: Oxford University Press, 1980.

———. *Thomas More.* Oxford: Oxford University Press, 1983.

Khadduri, Majid. *The Gulf War: The Origins and Implications of the Iraq-Iran Conflict.* New York: Oxford University Press, 1988.

Khalili, Akbar. *Gam beh Gam ba Enqelab.* Tehran: Sorush, 1360/1981.

Khamenei, Ali. *Manshur-e Tadavom-e Enqelab.* Tehran: Vezarat-e Farhanq va Ershad-e Islami, 1368/1989.

Khameh'i, Anvar. *Khaterat-e Anvar-e Khameh'i.* 3 vols. Tehran: Hafteh Publisher, 1362/1983.

Khanlari, Parviz Natel. *Haftad Sokhan: She'r va Honar.* 2 vols. Tehran: Tus, 1367/1988.

Khayyam, Omar. *Rubaiyat of Omar Khayyam.* Rendered in English verse by Edward Fitzgerald. New York: Heritage Club, 1940.

Kho'i, Isma'il. *Siahkal.* London: Shoma Publishers, 1364/1985.

Khomeini, Ahmad. *Ranj-nameh.* N.p.: N.p., n.d.

Khomeini, Ruhollah. *Asrar-e Namaz.* N.p.: N.p., 1358/1979.

———. *Faryad-e Bera'at.* Tehran: Vezarat-e Farhang va Ershad-e Islami, 1366/1987.

———. *Hajj.* Tehran: Vezarat-e Farhang va Ershad-e Islami, 1366/1987.

———. *al-Hukumah al-Islamiyyah.* Beirut: Dar al-Tali'ah li al-Tiba'ah wa al-Nashr, 1979.

———. *Imam va Enqelab-e Farhangi.* Tehran: Anjoman-ha-ye Islami va Sazeman-ha-ye Daneshjuyan-e Mosalman-e Daneshgah-ha va Madares-e Ali-ye Keshvar, n.d.

———. *Imam's Final Discourse.* Tehran: Ministry of Guidance and Islamic Culture, n.d.

———. *Islam and Revolution: Writings and Declarations of Imam Khomeini.* Translated and annotated by Hamid Algar. Berkeley, CA: Mizan Press, 1981.

———. *Jehad-e Akbar.* Tehran: Payam-i Azadi, n.d..

———. *Kashf al-Asrar.* N.p.: N.p., n.d.

———. *Majmu'eh-'i az Maktubat, Sokhan-rani-ha, Payam-ha va Fatavi-ye Imam Khomeini.* Tehran: Chapakhsh, 1360/1981.

———. *Majmu'eh-ye Goftar.* Paris: N.p., 1357/1978.

———. *Manasek-e Hajj.* Tehran: Entesharat-e Vahed-e Farhangi-ye Bonyad-e Shahid, 1361/1982.

———. *Mobarezeh ba Nafs ya Jehad-e Akbar.* Tehran: Amir Kabir, 1357/1978.
———. *Mobarezeh bah Nafs ya Jehad-e Akbar.* Tehran: Entesharat-e Payam-e Azadi, n.d.
———. *Naqsh-e Ruhaniyyat dar Islam.* Qom: Entesharat-e Dar al-Fekr, n.d.
———. *Parvaz dar Malakut (Moshtamel-e bar Adab al-Salat).* Edited by Sayyid Ahmad Fahri. Vol. 1. Tehran: Nehzat-e Zanan-e Mosalman, 1359/1980.
———. *Payam-e Hazrat-e Imam Khomeini beh Monasebat-e Eftetah-e Dovvomin Dowreh-ye Majles-e Shora-ye Islami.* Tehran: Ravabet-e Omumi-ye Majles-e Shora-ye Islami, 1363/1984.
———. *Rah-tusheh-ha-ye Pasdar.* Tehran: Daftar-e Siasi-ye Pasdaran-e Enqelabi-ye Islami, 1361/1982.
———. *Resaleh-ye Ahkam.* Tehran: Entesharat-e Isma'ilian, n.d.
———. *Resaleh-ye Novin.* Translated and edited by Abdolkarim Bi-azar-e Shirazi. 2 vols. Tehran: Mo'aseseh-ye Anjam-e Ketab, 1363–64/1984–85.
———. *Resaleh-ye Towzih al-Masa'il.* Tehran: Vezarat-e Farhang va Ershad-e Islami, 1367/1988.
———. *Sabu-ye Eshq: Ghazal-ha-ye Arefaneh-ye Hazrat-e Imam Khomeini.* Tehran: Sorush, 1368/1989.
———. *Sahifeh-ye Enqelab: Vasiyyat-nameh-ye Siasi-Elahi-ye Rahbar-e Kabir-e Enqelab-e Islami va Bonyan-gozar-e Jomhuri-ye Islami-ye Iran Hazrat-e Ayatollah al-Ozma' Imam Khomeini Qaddasa Sirrahu.* Tehran: Vezarat-e Farhang va Ershad-e Islami, 1368/1989.
———. *Sahifeh-ye Nur.* Introduction by Sayyid Ali Khamenei. 16 vols. Tehran: Markaz-e Madarek-e Farhangi-ye Enqelab-e Islami, 1361/1982.
———. *Sharh Du'a Sahar.* Translated by Sayyid Ahmad Fahri. Tehran: Markaz-e Entesharat-e Elmi va Farhangi, 1363/1984.
———. *Seda va Sima dar Kalam-e Imam Khomeini.* Tehran: Sorush, 1363/1984.
———. *Tahrir al-Wasilah.* 2 vols. Beirut: Dar al-Muntazir (Damascus: Sifarah al-Jumhuriyyah al-Islamiyyah al-Iraniyyah), 1405/1985.
———. *Velayat-e Faqih (Hokumat-e Islami).* Tehran: Amir Kabir, 1357/1978.
Khurasani, Muhammad Va'ez-Zadeh. "Seyri dar Zendegi-ye Elmi va Enqelabi-ye Ostad-e Shahid Morteza Motahhari." In Abdolkarim Sorush, ed., *Yadnameh-ye Ostad-e Shahid Morteza Motahhari,* pp. 319–80. Tehran: Sazeman-e Entesharat va Amuzesh-e Enqelab-e Islami, 1360/1981.
Khorramshahi, Baha' al-Din. *Tafsir va Tafasir-e Jadid.* Tehran: N.p., 1985.
Korterpeter, C. Max, ed. *Oil and the Economic Geography of the Middle East and North Africa: Studies by Alexander Melamid.* Princeton, NJ: The Darwin Press, Inc., 1991.
Kritzman, Lawrence D., ed. *Michel Foucault: Politics, Philosophy, Culture, Interviews and Other Writings, 1977–1984.* New York: Routledge, 1988.
Kuran, Timur. "Behavioral Norms in the Islamic Doctrine of Economics: A Critique." *Journal of Economic Behavior and Organization* 4 (1983): 353–79.
Ladjevardi, Habib. *Labor Unions and Autocracy in Iran.* Syracuse: Syracuse University Press, 1985.
Lambton, A. K. S. "Concepts of Authority in Persia: Eleventh to Nineteenth Centuries A.D." *Iran: Journal of the British Institute of Persian Studies* 26 (1988): 95–103.

Lambton, A. K. S. "A Reconsideration of the Position of the *Marja' al-Taqlid* and the Religious Institution." *Studia Islamica* 20 (1964): 115–35.

———. "Some New Trends in Islamic Political Thought in Late 18th and Early 19th Century Persia." *Studia Islamica* 39 (1973): 95–128.

Laqueur, Walter. "Why the Shah Fell." *Commentary* 67:3 (March 1979): 4–55.

Ledeen, Michael, and William Lewis. *Debacle: The American Failure in Iran.* New York: Knopf, 1982.

Lenczowski, George. "The Arc of Crisis: Its Central Sector." *Foreign Affairs* 57:4 (Spring 1979): 796–820.

———, ed. *Iran under the Pahlavis.* Stanford: Hoover Institution Press, 1978.

Lerman, Eran. "Mawdudi's Concept of Islam." *Middle Eastern Studies* 17:4 (1981): 492–509.

Lesani, Abolfazl. *Tala-ye Siah ya Bala-ye Iran.* Tehran: Amir Kabir, 1357/1978.

Levi-Strauss, Claude. *Myth and Meaning.* New York: Schocken Books, 1979.

Lewis, Bernard. *The Political Language of Islam.* Chicago: University of Chicago Press, 1988.

Lewis, Flora. "The Return of History." *SAIS Review: A Journal of International Affairs* 10:2 (Summer-Fall 1990): 1–11.

Lonney, Robert. *Economic Origins of the Iranian Revolution.* New York: Pergamon Press, 1982.

Madani, Jalal al-Din. *Ta'rikh-e Siasi-e Mo'aser-e Iran.* [Qom?]: Entesharat-e Islami, 1361/1983.

Madelung, Wilfred. "Authority in Twelver Shi'ism in the Absence of the Imam." In George Makdisi et al., eds., *La Notion d'Authorité au Moyen Age: Islam, Byzance, occident.* Paris: Presses Universitaires de France, 1982.

———. *Religious Trends in Early Islamic Iran.* Bibliotheca Persica. Albany: State University of New York Press, 1988.

Mannheim, Karl. *Ideology and Utopia.* Translated by Louis Worth and Edward Shils. New York: Harcourt, Brace Jovanovich, 1936.

Ma'rifat, Muhammad Hadi. "Vaqe'-negari dar Binesh-e Feqhi-ye Imam Khomeini." *Keyhan-e Andisheh* 29 (Farvardin-Ordibehesht 1369/March-April 1990): 39–44.

Martin, Vanessa. *Islam and Modernism: The Iranian Revolution of 1906.* London: I. B. Tauris & Co., Ltd., 1989.

Ma'rufi, Fatemah al-Sadat, ed. *Zendegi-nameh-ye Imam Khomeini.* Tehran: Entesharat-e Rah-e Imam, 1362/1983.

Marx, Karl. *The Poverty of Philosophy.* With an Introduction by Frederick Engels. New York: International Publishers, [1963].

Marx, Karl, and Fredrich Engels. *The German Ideology.* Edited with an Introduction by C. A. Arthur. New York: International Publishers, 1970.

Massignon, Louis. *The Passion of al-Hallaj: Mystic and Martyr of Islam.* Translated by Herbert Mason. Princeton: Princeton University Press, 1982.

———. *Salman-e Pak.* Edited and translated by Ali Shari'ati. Tehran: Entesharat-e Alburz, 2536/1977.

Mauss, Marcel. *Sociology and Psychology.* Translated by Ben Brewster. Boston, MA: Routledge & Kegan Paul, 1979.

Mazlish, Bruce. "The Hidden Khomeini." *New York* 24 (December 1979): 49–54.

————. "Khomeini as a Revolutionary Leader." Paper presented at the Conference on the Comparative Study of the Iranian Revolution, Harvard University, 19–20 January 1989.

————. *The Revolutionary Ascetic: Evolution of a Political Type.* New York: McGraw-Hill, 1976.

Mazlumi, Rajab Ali. *Tafsir-e Shi'eh.* Tehran: N.p., 1983.

McNeill, John T. *The History and Character of Calvinism.* New York: Oxford University Press, 1954.

Mead, George Herbert. *Mind, Self, and Society: From the Standpoint of a Social Behaviorist.* Edited and with an Introduction by Charles W. Morris. Vol. 1. Chicago: University of Chicago Press, 1934.

Menashri, David. *Iran: A Decade of War and Revolution.* New York: Holmes and Meier, 1990.

————. "Shi'ite Leadership: In the Shadow of Conflicting Ideologies." *Iranian Studies* 13:1–4 (1980): 119–45.

Merad, Ali. "The Ideologization of Islam in the Contemporary Muslim World." In *Islam and Power,* edited by Alexander S. Cudsi and Ali E. Hillal Dessouki. London: Croom Helm, 1981.

Merton, Robert K. *Social Theory and Social Structure.* New York: The Free Press, 1968.

Meskub, Shahrokh. *Meliyyat va Zaban.* [Paris:] Entesharat-e Ferdowsi, 1981.

Milani, Mohsen M. *The Making of Iran's Islamic Revolution: From Monarchy to Islamic Republic.* Boulder, CO: Westview Press, 1988.

Minovi, Mojtaba'. "Avvalin Karevan-e Ma'refat." In *Ta'rikh va Farhang.* Tehran: Kharazmi, 1352/1973.

Mishkat al-Dini, Abdolhossein. *Nazari beh Falsafeh-ye Sadr al-Din Shirazi.* Tehran: N.p., 1982.

Modarressi, Hossein. *An Introduction to Shi'i Law.* London: Ithaca Press, 1984.

————. "The Just Ruler or the Guardian Jurist: An Attempt to Link Two Different Shi'ite Concepts." *Journal of the American Oriental Society* 111:3 (July–September 1991): 549–562.

Moggridge, Donald E. *John Maynard Keynes.* New York: Praeger Books, 1976.

Mojtahed-e Shabastari, Muhammad. "Dianat va Siasat." *Keyhan-e Farhangi* 7:2, Serial No. 74 (May 1990): 5–10.

Momen, Moojan. *An Introduction to Shi'i Islam: The History and Doctrines of Twelver Shi'ism.* New Haven: Yale University Press, 1985.

Mommsen, Wolfgang J. *The Age of Bureaucracy: Perspectives on the Political Sociology of Max Weber.* New York: Harper Torchbooks, 1974.

————. *The Political and Social Theory of Max Weber: Collected Essays.* Chicago: University of Chicago Press, 1989.

Mongin, Olivier, and Olivier Roy, eds. *Islam, le grand malentendu.* Paris: Autrement, 1927.

Montazeri, Hossein-Ali. *Dirasat fi Vilayah al-Faqih: Fiqh al-Dawlah al-Islamiyyah.* 2 vols. Beirut: al-Dar al-Islamiyyah li al-Tiba'ah wa al-Nashr wa al-Tawzi' 1409/1988.

Mortimer, Edward. *Faith and Power: The Politics of Islam.* New York: Vintage, 1982.

Mosaddeq, Mohammad. *Khaterat va Ta'allomat-e Mosaddeq.* Edited by Iraj Afshar, with an Introduction by Gholam Hossein Mosaddeq. Tehran: Elmi, 1365/
1986.

————. *Musaddiq's Memoirs.* Edited with an Introduction by Homa Katouzian.
London: Jebhe, National Movement of Iran, 1988.

Motahhari, Morteza. *Akhlaq-e Jensi dar Islam va Jahan-e Gharb.* Qom: Sadra,
n.d.

————. *Ashna'i ba Olum-e Islami: Manteq va Falsafeh.* Qom: Sadra, 1358/1979.

————. *Bar-rasi-ye Feqhi Mas'aleh-ye Bimah.* Tehran: Miqat, 1361/1982.

————. *Bist Goftar.* Qom: Sadra, 1358/1979.

————. *Dastan-e Rastan.* 2 vols. Qom: Sadra, 1364/1985.

————. *Ehya'-ye Tafkkor-e Islami.* Qom: Daftar-e Entesharat-e Islami, 1361/1982.

————. *Elal-e Gerayesh beh Maddi-gari (beh Zamimeh-ye) Materialism dar Iran.*
Qom: Sadra, 1357/1978.

————. *Fundamentals of Islamic Thought.* Introduction by Hamid Algar. Berkeley,
CA: Mizan Press, 1985.

————. *Goftari dar bareh-ye Jomhuri-ye Islami.* Tehran: Hezb-e Jomhuri-ye Islami,
1361/1982.

————. *Hamaseh-ye Hosseini.* 2 vols. Qom: Sadra, 1361/1982.

————. *Haq va Batel (beh Zamimeh-ye) Ehya'-ye Tafakkor-e Islami.* Qom: Sadra,
1365/1986.

————. *Hejrat va Jehad.* Tehran: Daftar-e Markazi-ye Hezb-e Jomhuri-ye Islami,
1360/1981.

————. *Imamat va Rahbari.* Tehran: Sadra, 1364/1985.

————. *Imdad-ha-ye Gheybi dar Zendegi-ye Bashar (beh Zamimeh-ye) Chahar
Maqaleh-ye digar.* Qom: Sadra, 1354/1975.

————. *Insan va Iman, Insan dar Qur'an, Zendegi-ye Javid.* Qom: Sadra, n.d.

————. *Islam va Moqtaziat-e Zaman.* Vol. 1. Qom: Sadra, 1365/1986.

————. *Jahan-bini-ye Towhidi.* 2 vols. Qom: Sadra, n.d.

————. *Jazebeh va Dafe'eh-ye Ali.* Qom: Sadra, 1365/1986.

————. *Khadamat-e Motaqabel-e Islam va Iran.* Qom: Sadra, 1362/1983.

————. *Moqaddameh-'i bar Jahanbini-ye Islami.* Qom: Sadra, n.d.

————. *Naqdi bar Marxism.* Qom: Sadra, 1363/1984.

————. *Nehzat-ha-ye Islami dar Sad Saleh-ye Akhir.* Qom: Daftar-e Entesharat-e
Islami, 1365/1986.

————. *Nezam-e Hoquq-e zan dar Islam.* Tehran: Daftar-e Nashr-e Farhang-e
Islami, 1353/1974.

————. *Piramun-e Enqelab-e Islami.* Qom: Sadra, n.d.

————. *Qiam va Enqelab-e Mehdi, Shahid, Insan va Sar-nevesht.* Qom: Sadra,
1361/1982.

————. *Rahbari-ye Nasl-e Javan.* Tehran: Kanun-e Khadamat-e Farhangi-ye Alast,
1361/1982.

————. *Seyri dar Nahj al-Balaghah.* Qom: Sadra, 1354/1975.

————. *Sharh-e Manzumeh.* 2 vols. Tehran: Hekmat, 1360/1981.

————. *Shesh Maqaleh.* Qom: Sadra, 1363/1984.

————. *Sireh-ye Nabavi.* Tehran: Sadra, 1361/1982.

————. *Takamol-e Ejtema'i-ye Insan (beh Zamimeh-ye) Hadaf-e Zendegi, Elhami*

az Shaykh al-Ta'ifah, Mazaya va Khadamat-e Marhum Ayatollah Borujerdi.
Qom: Sadra, 1365/1986.
———. *Ta'lim va Tarbiat dar Islam.* Tehran: al-Zahra', 1362/1983.
———. *Tamasha-gah-e Raz: Mabahethi Piramun-e Shenakht-e Vaqe'i-ye Hafez.*
Qom: Sadra, 1359/1980.
———. *Vahy va Nobovvat.* Qom: Daftar-e Entesharat-e Islami, n.d.
———. *Vala'-ha va Velayat-ha.* Tehran: Entesharat-e Islami, 1362/1983.
Mottahedeh, Roy P. *The Mantle of the Prophet: Religion and Politics in Iran.* New
York: Pantheon Books, 1985.
Mozaffari, Mehdi. *Authority in Islam: From Muhammad to Khomeini.* Armonk,
NY: M. E. Sharpe, Inc., 1987.
Mughniyah, Muhammad Jawad. *al-Khumayni wa'l-dawlah al-Islmaiyah.* Beirut:
N.p., 1979.
Munson, Henry, Jr. *Islam and Revolution in the Middle East.* New Haven: Yale
University Press, 1988.
Na'ini, Shaykh Muhammad Hossein. *Tanbih al-Ummah va Tanzih al-Millah: ya
Hokumat az Nazar-e Islam.* Introduction and Explanatory Notes by Sayyid
Mahmud Taleqani. Tehran: Sherkat-e Sahami Enteshar, 1334/1955.
Naipaul, V. S. *Among the Believers.* New York: Vintage Books, 1981.
Najmabadi, Afsaneh. "Iran's Turn to Islam: From Modernism to a Moral Order."
The Middle East Journal 41:2 (Spring 1987): 202–17.
Naraqi, Molla Ahmad. *Awa'id al-Ayyam.* Tehran: Basirati Publisher, n.d.
al-Nasa'i, al-Hafiz Abi Abd al-Rahman ibn Shu'ayb. *Khasa'is al-Imam Amir al-
Mu'minim.* Beirut: N.p., n.d.
Nasafi, Aziz. *Kitab al-Insan al-Kamil.* Tehran: Institut Francais d'Iranologie de
Tehran, 1362/1983.
Nasr, Seyyed Hossein. *Sadr al-Din Shirazi & His Transcendent Theosophy.* Tehran:
Imperial Iranian Academy of Philosophy, 1978.
Nasr, Seyyed Hossein, Hamid Dabashi, and Seyyed Vali Reza Nasr, eds. *Expecta-
tion of the Millennium: Shi'ism in History.* Albany: State University of New
York Press, 1989.
———. *Shi'ism: Doctrines, Thought, and Spirituality.* Albany: State University of
New York Press, 1988.
Nava'i, A. H. *Fath-e Tehran: Gusheh-ha-'i az Tarikh-e Mashrutiyyat.* Tehran:
Babak, 1357/1978.
Navvab-e Yusof-zadah-ye Afghani, Muhammad. "Baztab-e Nehzat-e Imam dar
Harekat-e Islami-ye Afghanistan." *Keyhan-e Andisheh* 29 (Farvardin-Ordibe-
hesht 1369/March-April 1990): 198–99.
Neisser, Hans. *On the Sociology of Knowledge.* New York: James H. Heineman,
Inc., 1965.
Neske, Günther, and Emil Kettering, eds. *Martin Heidegger and National Social-
ism: Questions and Answers.* Introduction by Karsten Harries; translated by
Lisa Harries. New York: Paragon House, 1990.
Nezhad-Salim, Rahim. "Jelveh-ye Eshq dar Ghazal-ha-ye Imam." *Keyhan-e Andi-
sheh* 29 (Farvardin-Ordibehesht 1369/March-April 1990): 181–85.
Nobari, Ali-Reza. *Iran Erupts.* Stanford, CA: Iran-America Documentation Group,
1978.

Nore, Petter, and Terisa Turner, eds. *Oil and Class Struggle*. London: Zed, 1980.

Norton, Augustus Richard. *Amal and the Shi'a: Struggle for the Soul of Lebanon*. Austin: University of Texas Press, 1987.

Oestereicher, Emil. "Politics, Class and the Socially Unattached Intellectuals: A Re-Examination of Mannheim's Thesis." *State, Culture and Society* 1:3 (Spring 1985): 209–24.

Olmstead, Albert T. *History of the Persian Empire*. Chicago: University of Chicago Press, 1948.

Ostadi, Reza. "Ketab-ha va Athar-e Elmi-ye Imam Khomeini." *Keyhan-e Andisheh* 29 (Farvardin-Ordibehesht 1369/March-April 1990): 143–61.

Pahlavi, Ashraf. *Faces in a Mirror: Memoirs from Exile*. Englewood Cliffs, NJ: Prentice-Hall, 1980.

Pahlavi, Mohammad Reza. *Answer to History*. New York: Stein and Day, 1980.

——. *Mission for My Country*. London: Hutchinson, 1961.

——. *Pasokh beh Tarikh*. Paris: Imprimerie Aubin, 1980.

Parham, Mehdi. *Farhang-e Sokut*. Tehran: N.p., 1357/1978.

Parham, Sirus. *Enqelab-e Iran va Mabani-ye Rahbari-ye Imam Khomeini*. Tehran: Amir Kabir, 1357/1978.

Parsa, Misagh. *Social Origins of the Iranian Revolution*. New Brunswick, NJ: Rutgers University Press, 1989.

Parsons, Anthony. *The Pride and the Fall: Iran 1974–1979*. London: Jonathan Cape, 1984.

Parsons, Talcott. *Essays in Sociological Theory Pure and Applied*. Glencoe: The Free Press, 1949.

Pasaran, M. H. "The System of Development in Pre- and Post-Revolutionary Iran." *International Journal of Middle East Studies* 14:4 (November 1982): 501–22.

Payandeh, Abolqasem, ed. *Seh Nameh az Peyghambar*. Tehran: Javidan, n.d.

Pickthall, Marmaduke, trans. *The Glorious Koran*. London: George Allen & Unwin, 1976.

Piscatori, James P., ed. *Islam in the Political Process*. New York and Cambridge: Cambridge University Press, 1983.

Qanun-e Asasi-ye Jomhuri-ye Islami-ye Iran. Qom: Daftar-e Entesharat-e Islami, 1362/1983.

Qomi, Hajj Shaykh Abbas. *Safinah al-Bahar*. Tehran: N.p., n.d.

Rahimi, Mostafa'. *Osul-e Hokumat-e Jomhuri*. Tehran: Amir Kabir, 1358/1979.

Rahman, Fazlur. *Islam & Modernity: Transformation of an Intellectual Tradition*. Chicago: University of Chicago Press, 1982.

——. *The Philosophy of Mulla Sadra*. Albany: State University of New York Press, 1975.

Rajaee, Farhang. *Islamic Values and World Views: Khomayni on Man, the State and International Politics*. Lanham, MD: University Press of America, 1983.

Ramazani, Rouhollah K. "The Autonomous Republics of Azerbaijan and Kurdistan: Their Rise and Fall." In *The Anatomy of Communist Takeovers*, edited by Thomas T. Hammond. New Haven: Yale University Press, 1975.

——. *Iran's Foreign Policy: A Study of Foreign Policy in Modernizing Nations*. Charlottesville, VA: University Press of Virginia, 1975.

———. *Revolutionary Iran: Challenge and Response in the Middle East.* Baltimore, MD: Johns Hopkins University Press, 1986.

———. *The United States and Iran: The Patterns of Influence.* New York: Praeger, 1982.

———. "Who Lost America: The Case of Iran." *Middle East Journal* 36 (Winter 1982): 5–21.

Razavi, Hossein, and Firouz Vakili. *The Political Environment of Economic Planning in Iran, 1971–1983: From Monarchy to Islamic Republic.* Boulder, CO, and London: Westview Press, 1984.

Razi, G. Hossein. "Legitimacy, Religion, and Nationalism in the Middle East." *American Political Science Review* 84:1 (March 1990): 69–91.

Ricoeur, Paul. *History and Truth.* Evanston: Northwestern University Press, 1965.

———. *Lectures on Ideology and Utopia.* Edited by George H. Taylor. New York: Columbia University Press, 1986.

Rieff, Philip. *Fellow Teachers.* New York: Delta Books, 1972.

———. *Fellow Teachers: Of Culture and Its Second Death.* Chicago: University of Chicago Press, 1985.

———. *Freud: The Mind of the Moralist.* Chicago: University of Chicago Press, 1959.

———. "Toward a Theory of Culture: With Special Reference to the Psychoanalytic Case." In *Imagination and Precision in the Social Sciences, Essays in Memory of Peter Nettl,* edited by T. J. Nossiter, A. H. Hanson, and Stein Rokkan. London: Faber & Faber, 1972.

———. *The Triumph of the Therapeutic: Uses of Faith after Freud.* London: Chatto and Windus, 1966.

———, ed. *On Intellectuals: Theoretical Studies, Case Studies.* Garden City, NY: Doubleday, 1969.

Robbins, Thomas, and Roland Robertson, eds. *Church-State Relations: Tensions and Transitions.* New Brunswick, NJ: Transaction Books, 1987.

Rodinson, Maxime. *Islam and Capitalism.* Translated by Brian Pearce. Austin: University of Texas Press, 1966.

———. *Marxism and the Muslim World.* New York: Monthly Review Press, 1981.

Roosevelt, Kermit. *Counter Coup: The Struggle for the Control of Iran.* New York: McGraw-Hill, 1979.

Rose, Gregory F. "The Post-Revolutionary Purge of Iran's Armed Forces: A Revisonist Assessment." *Iranian Studies* 17:2–3 (1984): 153–194.

Rosen, Bary M., ed. *Iran since the Revolution.* New York: Brooklyn College Program on Society in Change, 1985.

Rouleau, Eric. "Khomeini's Iran." *Foreign Affairs* 59:1 (Fall 1980):1–20.

Rubin, Barry. *Paved with Good Intentions: The American Experience in Iran.* London and New York: Oxford University Press, 1980.

Ruhani, Fo'ad. *San'at-e Naft-e Iran: Bist sal pas az Melli Shodan.* Tehran: N.p., 2536/1356/1977.

———. *Ta'rikh-e Melli Shodan-e Naft-e Iran.* Tehran: Jibi, 1353/1974.

Ruhani (Ziarati), Sayyid Hamid. *Bar-rasi va Tahlili az Nehzat-e Imam Khomeini.* 2

vols. Vol 1—Tehran: Entesharat-e Rah-e Imam, 1360/1981; vol. 2—Tehran: Vahed-e Farhangi-ye Bunyad-e Shahid, 1364/1985.

Rumi, Maulana Jalal al-Din. *The Mathnawi*. Edited and translated by Reynold A. Nicholson. 6 vols. London: Luzac, 1982.

Ruzegar-e Now (monthly journal), Serial No. 89, Tir 1368/June-July 1989.

Sachedina, Abdulaziz Abdulhussein. *Islamic Messianism: The Idea of the Mahdi in Twelver Shiʿism*. Albany: State University of New York Press, 1981.

———. *The Just Ruler (al-sultan al-ʿadil) in Shiʿite Islam: The Comprehensive Authority of the Jurist in Imamite Jurisprudence*. Oxford: Oxford University Press, 1988.

Sadr, Hasan. *Defaʿ-e Doktor Mosaddeq az Naft dar Zendan-e Zerehi*. Tehran: Amir Kabir, 1357/1978.

Sadra, Molla. *Asrar al-Ayat*. Tehran: N.p., 1984.

———. *al-Shawahid al-Rububiyyah fi al-Manahij al-Sulukiyyah*. Edited, annotated, with an Introduction by Sayyid Jalaloddin Ashtiani. Tehran: Markaz-e Nashr-e Daneshgahi, 1360/1981 (1346/1967).

———. *The Wisdom of the Throne: An Introduction to the Philosophy of Mulla Sadra*. Translated and annotated by James Winston Morris. Princeton: Princeton University Press, 1981.

Sadri, Mahmoud, and Ahmad Sadri. "*The Mantle of the Prophet*: A Critical Postscript." *State, Culture, and Society* 1:3 (Spring 1985): 136–47.

al-Sahar, Abd al-Hamid Jawdah. *Abu Dharr Ghifari: Khoda-Parast-e Socialist*. Translated and revised by Ali Shariʿati. Tehran: Nashr-e Shahadat, 1337/1958.

———. *Abu Dharr Ghifari: Mardi az Rabdhah*. Translated by Ali Shariʿati. Tehran: N.p., 1356/1977.

Saheb-Ekhtiari, Behruz. "Aql va Eshq dar Adab va Erfan-e Farsi." *Keyhan-e Andisheh* 29 (Farvardin-Ordibehesht 1369/March-April 1990): 172–80.

Sahebi, Muhammad Javad. "Falsafeh-ye Siasi az Did-gah-e Allamah Tabataba'i." *Keyhan-e Andisheh* 26 (Mehr-Aban 1368/October-November 1989): 13–19.

———. "Naqsh-e Imam Khomeini dar Tadvin va Tanqih-e Falsafeh-ye Siyasi." *Keyhan-e Andisheh* 29 (Farvardin-Ordibehesht 1369/March-April 1990): 130–42.

Said, Edward. *Covering Islam: How the Media and the Experts Determine How We See the Rest of the World*. New York: Pantheon Books, 1981.

———. "Yeats and Decolonization." In Terry Eagleton et al., *Nationalism, Colonialism, and Literature*, pp. 67–95. Introduction by Seamus Deane. Minneapolis: University of Minnesota Press, 1940.

Saikal, Amin. *The Rise and Fall of the Shah*. Princeton: Princeton University Press, 1980.

Sajjadi, Sayyid Jaʿfar. *Farhang-e Maʿaref-e Islami*. 4 vols. Tehran: Sherkat-e Mo'allefan va Motarjeman-e Iran, 1362–63/1983–84.

Salehi, Najaf-abadi. *Velayat-e Faqih: Hokumat-e Salehan*. Tehran: Moʿaseseh-ye Khadamat-e Farhangi-ye Rasa, 1363/1984.

Salehi-Isfahani, Djavad. "The Political Economy of Credit Subsidy in Iran, 1973–1978." *International Journal of Middle East Studies* 21 (1989): 359–79.

Salinger, Pierre. *America Held Hostage: The Secret Negotiation.* London: Andre Deutsch, 1981.

Sanjabi, Karim. *Omid-ha va Na-Omidi-ha: Khaterat-e Siasi.* London: Nashre Ketab, 1368/1989.

Schama, Simon. *Citizens: A Chronicle of the French Revolution.* New York: Viking Press, 1989.

Scheler, Max. *Ressentiment.* Edited with an Introduction by Lewis A. Coser. Translated by William W. Holdheim. New York: The Free Press of Glencoe, 1961; reprinted New York: Schocken, 1972.

Schlossmann, Siegmund. *Persona und* ΠΡΟΣΩΠΟΝ *im Recht und im Christlichen Dogma.* Reprinted from *Festschrift der Universität Kiel Zum Gebürtstage S. M. des Kaisers am 27/1/1906.* Leipzig: Lipsius and Tischer, 1906.

Scholl-Latour, Peter. *Allah ist mit den Standhaften: Begegnungen mit der Islamischen Revolution.* Stuttgart: Deutsche Verlags-Anstalt, 1983.

Schutz, Alfred. "Max Scheller's Epistemology and Ethics." *Review of Metaphysics,* I-II 2 (December 1957, March 1958): 304–14, 486–501.

Segalen, Victor. *Essai sur l'Exotisme: Une Esthetique du Divers* (Notes). Paris: Explorations, Editions Fata Morgana, 1978.

Sha'bani, Ali. *Tarrah-e Coup d'état.* Tehran: Amir Kabir, 2535/1976.

Shahatah, Abd Allah Mahmud. *Ta'rikh al-Qur'an wa al-Tafsir.* Cairo: N.p., 1972.

Shahid al-Thani, Zayn al-Din Amili. *al-Rawdah al-Bahiyyah fi Sharh al-Lum'ah al-Mushfiqiyyah.* Tehran: Ilmiyyah Islamiyyah, 1929.

Shamlu, Ahmad. *Collected Works.* 2 vols. Giessen: Bamdad Verlag, 1368/1989.

———. *Shekoftan dar Meh.* Tehran: Zaman, 1349/1970.

Shari'ati, Ali. *Abu Dharr.* Collected Works No. 3. Tehran: Hoseyniyyeh Ershad, 1357/1978.

———. *Agar Pope va Marx Nabudand.* Tehran: N.p., n.d.

———. *Ali: Maktab, Vahdat, Edalat.* Houston: Book Distribution Center, 1355/1976.

———. *Az Hejrat ta Vafat.* N.p.: Ettehadiyyeh-ye Anjoman-ha-ye Islami-ye Daneshjuyan dar Orupa va Anjoman-e Islami-ye Daneshjuyan dar America va Canada, 1355/1976.

———. *Az Koja' Aghaz Konim.* N.p.: Ettehadiyyeh-ye Anjoman-ha-ye Islami-ye Daneshjuyan dar Orupa va Anjoman-e Islami-ye Daneshjuyan dar America va Canada, 1351/1972.

———. *Bazgasht.* Tehran: Hoseyniyyeh-ye Ershad, 1357/1978.

———. *Bazgasht-e beh Khish.* N.p.: n.p., n.d.

———. *Beh Sar-e Aql Amadan-e Sarmayeh-dari.* Houston: Anjoman-e Islami-ye Daneshjuyan dar America va Canada, n.d.

———. *Cheh bayad Kard?* N.p.: N.p., n.d.

———. *Fatemeh Fatemeh Ast.* Tehran: N.p., 1350/1976.

———. *Hajj.* Collected Works No. 6. Tehran: Hosseyniyyeh-ye Ershad, 1357/1978.

———. *Hajj.* Translated by Ali A. Behzadnia and N. Denny. Houston: Free Islamic Literatures, 1980.

———. *Hobut dar Kavir.* Collected Works No. 13. Tehran: Chapakhsh, 1365/1986.

Shari'ati, Ali. *Hossein: Vareth-e Adam.* Collected Works No. 19. Tehran: Entes-harat-e Qalam, 1367/1988.

————. *Insan, Marxism, Islam.* Rome: Centro Culturale Islamico Europeo, 1361/1982.

————. *Islamshenasi.* 3 vols. Collected Works Nos. 16, 17, and 18. Tehran: Entes-harat-e Shari'ati, 1360/1981.

————. *Jahan-bini va Ideology.* Collected Works No. 23. Tehran: Entesharat Muna, 1361/1982.

————. *Jahat-giri-ye Tabaqati-e Islam.* N.p.: Daftar-e Tadvin va Tanzim-e Majmu'eh-ye Athar-e Mo'alem-e Shahid Dr. Ali Shari'ati, 1359/1980.

————. *Jame'eh-shenasi-ye Adyan.* N.p.: N.p., n.d.

————. *Kavir.* Tehran: N.p., 1349/1970.

————. *Khodi-sazi-ye Enqelabi.* Collected Works No. 2. Tehran: Hosseyniyyeh-ye Ershad, 1356/1977.

————. *Ma va Iqbal.* Collected Works No. 5. Tehran: Hosseyniyyeh-ye Ershad, 1357/1978.

————. *Madhhab alayh-e Madhhab.* Tehran: N.p., 2536/1977.

————. *Man and Islam.* Translated by Fatollah Marjani. Houston: FILINC, 1981.

————. *Mi'ad ba Ibrahim.* Tehran: Mo'aseseh-ye Entesharat-e Athar-e Be'that, 1354/1975.

————. *Niayesh.* Tehran: N.p., 1352/1973.

————. *Niayesh.* Collected Works No. 8. Tehran: Hosseyniyyeh-ye Ershad, n.d.

————. *On Marxism and Other Western Fallacies.* Translated by R. Campbell. Berkeley: Mizan Press, 1980.

————. *On the Sociology of Islam.* Translated by Hamid Algar. Berkeley, CA: Mizan Press, 1979.

————. *Payam-e Omiyd beh Roshanfekr-e Mas'ul (Tafsiri bar Sureh-ye Rum).* Solon, OH: Ettehadiyyeh-ye Anjoman-ha-ye Islami-ye Daneshjuyan dar Orupa va Anjoman-e Islami Daneshjuyan dar America va Canada, 1358/1979.

————. *Pedar, Madar, Ma Mottahamim.* N.p.: N.p., n.d.

————. *Qesseh-ye Hasan va Mahbubeh.* N.p.: Ettehadiyyeh-ye Anjoman-ha-ye Islami-ye Daneshjuyan dar Orupa va Anjoman-e Islami-ye Daneshjuyan dar America va Canada, 1356/1977.

————. *Shahadat.* Solon, OH: Ettehadiyyeh-ye Anjoman-ha-ye Islami-ye Dane-shjuyan dar Orupa va Anjoman-e Islami-ye Duneshjuyan dar America va Can-ada, 1358/1979.

————. *Shi'ah.* Collected Works No. 7. Tehran: Hoseyniyyeh-ye Ershad, 1357/1978.

————. *Shi'ah: Yek Hezb-e Tamam.* Houston: Book Distribution Center, 1355/1976.

————. *Sima-ye Muhammad.* Solon, OH: Anjoman-e Islami-ye Daneshjuyan dar America va Canada, 1358/1979.

————. *Ta'rikh va Shenakht-e Adyan.* 2 vols. Collected Works Nos. 14 and 15. Tehran: Sherkat-e Sahami-ye Enteshar, 1362/1983.

————. *Ta'rikh-e Tamaddun.* 2 vols. Collected Works Nos. 11 and 12. Tehran: Entesharat-e Agah, 1361/1982.

————. *Tashayyoᶜ-e Alavi va Tashayyoᶜ-e Safavi*. Tehran: Hoseyniyyeh Ershad, 1350/1971.

————. *Vizheh-gi-ha-ye Qorun-e Jadid*. Collected Works No. 31. Tehran: Chapakhsh, 1361/1982.

————. *Zan*. Collected Works No. 21. Tehran: Entesharat-e Sabz, 1362/1983.

————. *Ziba-tarin Ruh-e Parastandeh*. Tehran: Mo'seseh-ye Entesharat-e Beᶜthat, n.d.

Shawcross, William. *The Shah's Last Ride: The Fall of an Ally*. New York: Simon and Schuster, 1988.

Shaygan, Daryush. *Le regard mutilé: Schizophrenie culturelle: pays traditionnels face à la modernité*. Paris: Editions Albin Michel S. A., 1989.

————. *Qu'est-ce qu'une revolution religieuse?* Paris: Les Presses d'aujourd'hui, 1982.

————. "Seyr va Soluk-e Corbin: Az Heidegger ta Sohrevardi," I and II. *Iran Nameh* 7:3 (Spring 1989): 461–92; 7:4 (Summer 1989): 584–617.

Shirazi, Mirza Saleh. *Safar-nameh*. Edited by Ismaᶜil Ra'in. Tehran: Rozan, 1347/1968.

Shuster, Morgan. *Ekhtenaq-e Iran*. Translated, edited, annotated, amended by new documents by Abolhasan Musavi Shushtari, with an Introduction by Faramarz Barzegar and Ismai'il Ra'in. Tehran: Safi Ali Shah, 1351/1972.

Siasi, Ali Akbar. *Gozaresh-e Yek Zendegi*. London: Paka, 1366/1987.

Sick, Gary. *All Fall Down: America's Tragic Encounters with Iran*. New York: Random House, 1985.

Skinner, Quentin. *The Foundations of Modern Political Thought*. 2 vols. Cambridge: Cambridge University Press, 1978.

Skocpol, Theda. "Rentier State and Shiᶜa Islam in the Iranian Revolution." *Theory and Society* 11:3 (May 1982): 265–83.

————. *States and Social Revolutions*. London and New York: Cambridge University Press, 1979.

Smith, Donald. *Religion and Political Development: An Analytic Study*. Boston: Little, Brown, 1970.

Sobhani, Jaᶜfar. "Jameᶜiyyat-ye Elmi va Amali-ye Imam Khomeini." *Keyhan-e Andisheh* 29 (Farvardin-Ordibehesht 1369/March-April 1990): 3–14.

————. "Maqam-e Elmi va Farhangi-ye Allamah Tabataba'i." *Keyhan-e Farhangi* 6:8, Serial No. 68 (November 1989): 5–7.

Soltani, Mojtaba'. *Khat-e Sazesh*. Vol. 1. Tehran: Sazeman-e Tablighat-e Islami, 1367/1988.

Soltani, Muhammad Ali. "Sima-ye Zan dar 'al-Mizan.' " *Keyhan-e Farhangi* 6:8, Serial No. 68 (November 1989): 14–16.

Sorel, G. *Reflections on Violence*. New York: Free Press, 1950.

Sorush, Abdolkarim. *Roshanfekri va Dindari*. Tehran: Nashr-e Puya', 1367/1988.

————, ed. *Yadnameh-ye Ostad-e Shahid Morteza Motahhari*. Tehran: Sazeman-e Entesharat va Amuzesh-e Enqelab-e Islami, 1360/1981.

Speir, Hans. "Karl Mannhein's Ideology and Utopia." *State, Culture and Society* 1:3 (Spring 1985): 183–97.

Stempel, John D. *Inside the Iranian Revolution*. Bloomington, IN: Indiana University Press, 1981.

Stone, Robert L., ed. *Essays on the Closing of the American Mind*. Chicago: Chicago Review Press, 1989.

Storr, Anthony. *Solitude: A Return to the Self*. New York: The Free Press, 1988.

Sullivan, William. "Dateline Iran: The Road Not Taken." *Foreign Policy* 40 (Fall 1980): 175–86.

———. *Mission to Iran*. New York: Norton, 1981.

al-Tabarsi, al-Fadl ibn al-Hasan. *Majmaʿ al-Bayan fi Tafsir al-Qurʿan*. Qom: Maktabah Ayatollah al-Uzma' al-Marʿashi al-Najafi, 1403/1983.

Tabataba'i, Allamah Sayyid Muhammad Hossein. *Falsafeh-ye Eqtesad-e Islam*. Tehran: Ata'i, 1361/1982.

———. *Islamic Teachings: An Overview*. Translated by R. Campbell. New York: Mostazafan Foundation, 1989.

———. "Kish-e Mehr." *Keyhan-e Farhangi* 6:8, Serial No. 68 (November 1989): 4.

———. *al-Mizan fi Tafsir al-Qur'an*. Beirut: al-Ilmi, n.d.

———. *Nahayah al-Hikmah*. Vol. 1. With commentaries by Muhammad Taqi al-Misbah al-Yazdi. N.p.: Entesharat-e al-Zahra', 1363/1984.

———. *Osul-e Falsafeh va Ravesh-e Realism*. Introduction and annotations by Morteza Motahhari. 5 vols. Qom: Entesharati-ye Sadra, 1332–64/1953–85.

———. *Osul-e Falsafeh-ye Realism*. Edited by Sayyid Hadi Khosrow-shahi. Qom: Center of Islamic Studies, 1397/1976.

———. *Qur'an dar Islam*. Mashhad: Entesharat-e Toluʿ n.d.

———. *Ravabet-e Ejtemaʿi dar Islam*. Tehran: Entesharat-e Azadi, n.d.

———. *Shiʿah dar Islam*. Qom: Daftar-e Tablighat-e Islam, 1348/1969.

———. *Shiʿah: Majmuʿeh-ye Modhakerat ba Professor Henri Corbin*. Edited with commentaries by Ali Ahmadi and Sayyid Hadi Khosrow-shahi. Qom: Entesharat-e Hejrat, 1397/1976.

———. *Shiʿite Islam*. Translated and edited with an introduction by Seyyed Hossein Nasr. London: Allen & Unwin, 1975.

———. *Tafsir al-Mizan*. 40 vols. Qom: Dar al-Ilm, 1344/1965.

———. *Ta'rikh-e Qur'an*. Translated by Soheyla' Din-parvar. Edited by Muhammad Ali Lesani-ye Fesharaki. Tehran: Sherkat-e Nashr-e Farhang-e Qurʿan, 1361/1982.

———. *Zohur-e Shiʿah (beh Zamimeh-ye Mosahebeh-ye Professor Henri Corbin)*. Tehran: Entesharat-e Faqih va Kanun-e Khadamat-e Farhangi-ye Alast, 1360/1981.

———. *Zohur-e Shiʿah: Majmuʿeh-ye Mosahebeh ba Professor Henri Corbin (beh Zamimeh-ye Pasokh beh Naqd-e Nashriyyeh-ye Shiʿah)*. Tehran: Nashr-e Shariʿat, n.d.

Tabari, Ihsan. *Barkhi Bar-rasi-ha dar Bareh-ye Jahan-bini-ha va Jonbesh-ha-ye Ejtemaʿi dar Iran*. N.p.: N.p., 1981.

———. *Foru-pashi-ye Nezam-e Sonnati va Zayesh-e Sarmayeh-dari dar Iran*. N.p.: Hezb-e Tudeh-ye Iran, 1354/1975.

Tabrizi, Hamid, ed. *Jalal Al-e Ahmad: Mardi dar Keshakesh-e Ta'rikh-e Moʿaser*. Tabriz: Kaveh, 1357/1978.

Ta'eb, Sayyid Hossein. *Tahlili az Terror-e Motafakker-e Shahid Ostad Motahhari (beh Zamimeh-ye) Maqaleh-'i Keh bah Khun Neveshteh Shod.* Berkeley, CA: Daftar-e Farhangi-ye Anjoman-e Islami-ye Daneshjuyan dar America va Canada, n.d.

Taleqani, Sayyid Mahmud. *Do Shahid-e Ershad.* N.p.: N.p., n.d.

———. *Hedayat-e Qur'an.* Tehran: N.p., 1359/1980.

———. *Islam and Ownership.* Translated by Ahmad Jabbari and Farhang Rajaee. Lexington, KY: Mazda, 1983.

———. *Islam va Malekiyyat dar Moqayeseh ba Nezam-ha-ye Eqtesadi-ye Gharb.* N.p.: N.p., n.d.

———. *Majmu^ceh Goftar-e Pedar Taleqani.* Long Beach, CA: N.p., 1980.

———. *Partovi az Qur'an.* 3 vols. Solon, OH: Ettehadiyyeh-ye Anjoman-ha-ye Islami-ye Daneshjuyan dar Orupa va Anjoman-e Islami-ye Daneshjuyan dar America va Canada, 1354–59/1975–80.

———. *Partovi az Qur'an.* 4 vols. Tehran: Sherkat-e Sahami-ye Enteshar, 1358–62/1979–83.

———. *Society and Economics in Islam.* Translated by R. Campbell; Introduction by Hamid Algar. Berkeley, CA: Mizan Press, 1983.

Thompson, John. *Ideology and Modern Culture.* Stanford: Stanford University Press, 1990.

———. *Studies in the Theory of Ideology.* Berkeley: University of California Press, 1984.

Tibi, Bassam. "The Renewed Role of Islam in the Political and Social Development of the Middle East." *Middle East Journal* 37:1 (Winter 1983): 3–13.

Tonekaboni, Mirza Muhammad. *Qesas al-Ulama.* Tehran: Intisharat Ilmiyyah Islamiyyah, 1364/1985.

Tully, James, ed. *Meaning and Context: Quentin Skinner and His Critics.* Princeton: Princeton University Press, 1988.

al-Tusi, Abu Ja^cfar Muhammad ibn Hasan. *al-Mabsut fi Figh al-Imami.* Tehran: Maktabah Murtazavi, 1969.

Ulmstead, Albert T. *History of the Persian Empire.* Chicago: University of Chicago Press, 1948.

Vance, Cyrus. *Hard Choices: Critical Years in America's Foreign Policy.* New York: Simon and Schuster, 1983.

Vejdani, Mostafa', and Reza She^cr-baf, eds. *Sargozasht-ha-ye Vizheh az Zendegi-ye Hazrat-e Imam Khomeini.* 6 vols. Tehran: Entesharat-e Payam-e Azadi, 1362–64/1983–85.

Vieille, Paul. "Notes sur la revolution iranienne avec une interview du President de la Republique." *Peuples Mediterranieens/Mediterranean Peoples* 12 Juillet-Septembre 1980): 109–40.

Vieille, Paul, and Abolhasan Bani-Sadr. *Petrole et Violence.* Paris: Editions Anthropos, 1974.

Vieille, Paul, and Farhad Khosrokhavar. *Le Discours Populaire de la Revolution Iranienne.* 2 vols. Paris: Contemporaneité, 1990.

Von Grunebaum, Gustave E. *Muhammadan Festivals.* London: Curson Press, 1976.

Weber, Max. *Economy and Society.* Edited by G. Roth and C. Wittich. Berkeley: University of California Press, 1978.

Weber, Max. *From Max Weber: Essays in Sociology.* Translated, edited, and with an Introduction by H. H. Gerth and C. Wright Mills. New York: Oxford University Press, 1946.

———. *Gesammelte Politische Schriften.* Tübingen: J. C. B. Mohr (Paul Siebeck), 1958 (1980).

———. *The Theory of Social and Economic Organization.* New York: The Free Press, 1947.

———. *Wirtschaft und Gesellschaft.* Tübingen: J. C. B. Mohr (Paul Siebeck), 1980.

Werblowsky, R. J. Zwi. *Beyond Tradition and Modernity: Changing Religions in a Changing World.* London: Athlone Press, 1976.

Wright, Robin. *In the Name of God: The Khomeini Decade.* New York: Simon and Schuster, 1989.

Wrong, Dennis H. *Power: Its Forms, Bases, and Uses.* Chicago: University of Chicago Press, 1979.

Yodfat, Aryeh Y. *The Soviet Union and Revolutionary Iran.* New York: St. Martin's Press, 1984.

Yusofi Oshkuri, Hasan. *Naqdi bar Ketab-e "Shahid Motahhari Efsha-gar-e Tote᷾eh. . . ."* Tehran: Enteshar, 1364/1985.

Yusofiyyeh, Valiollah. *Resalat-e Shariᶜati.* Tehran. Ataᶜi, 2537/1978.

Zabih, Sepehr. *The Communist Movement in Iran.* Berkeley and Los Angeles: University of California Press, 1966.

———. *Iran since the Revolution.* Baltimore: Johns Hopkins University Press, 1982.

———. *The Left in Contemporary Iran.* Stanford: Hoover Institute Press; Kent: Croom Helm, 1986.

Zamakhshari, Mahmud ibn Umar. *al-Kashshaf an Haqa'iq Ghavamiz al-Tanzil.* Beirut: Dar al-Kitab al-Arabi, n.d.

Zamani-nia, Mostafa', ed. *Farhang-e Jalal Al-e Ahmad.* 2 vols. Tehran: Pasargad, 1362/1983.

Zanjani, Izzoddin. "Allamah Tabataba'i: Jameᶜ-e Hekmat va Shariᶜat." *Keyhan-e Farhangi* 6:8, Serial No. 68 (November 1989): 1–4.

Zitrone, Leon. *Farah: Une cruelle destinée.* Paris: Le Signe, 1979.

Zonis, Marvin. "Iran: A Theory of Revolution from Accounts of the Revolution." *World Politics* 35:4 (1983): 586–606.

———. *Majestic Failure: The Fall of the Shah.* Chicago: The University of Chicago Press, 1991.

———. *The Political Elite of Iran.* Princeton: Princeton University Press, 1971.

———. "The Rule of the Clerics in the Islamic Republic of Iran." *The Annals of the American Academy of Political and Social Science* 482 (November 1985): 85–108.

Index

Obedience, 200, 229, 259, 333, 344, 361, 365, 372, 393, 419, 420, 440, 445, 482, 483, 488, 489, 505, 508; to God, 310, 370; and *Hossein-e Mazlum*, 302; and "Imam," 385, 397; to Muhammad, 310; in politics and economics, 383; and the Qur'an, 239. *See also* Command and obedience

Oil, 53, 56, 59, 62, 374, 378–80, 389, 400, 453; concessions, 48–49, 375, 393; embargo, 424, 468; in Islamic government, 403; nationalization of, 86, 90, 224, 330, 368, 375–76, 378, 401; political economy of and Pahlavi regime, 374–78; as a political weapon, 378–79, 579 n. 235; prices, 379; production rates, 377; Western companies, 374, 378

"Old Man Was Our Eyes, The" (Al-e Ahmad), 51

On the Services and Treasons of the Intellectuals (Dar Khedmat va Khiyanat-e Roshanfekran) (Al-e Ahmad), 56, 61–62, 79, 88–91, 98, 99

Ontology, Islamic, 185, 285

OPEC, 374, 376

Organization of People's Mojahedin, 238

"Orient, The," 500

"Oriental despotism," 391–92

Orientalists, 416, 436, 438, 446

Osul-e Falsafeh va Ravesh-e Realism (The Principles of Philosophy and the Realistic Method) (Tabataba'i), 278, 279, 283, 295, 306, 313–14; commentary and edited version of Motahhari, 149, 150–51, 153, 156, 159, 174–75, 184

"Other," 5, 14, 19, 20, 25–26, 28, 58, 85, 197, 322, 366, 395, 404, 500, 507–8, 510–12, 513–18

Ottomans, 390

Ownership, 225, 226, 352, 371, 383, 384–85, 387, 398

Pacifism, 185, 372–73; criticism of, 176–77; paradox, 398

Pahlavi regime, 82, 119, 121, 172, 195, 204, 267, 368, 402; and clerical order, 342, 454, 467, 469; economic policies of, 373; and death of Mohammad Reza Sa'idi, 436; (il)legitimacy of, 9–10, 132, 191, 194, 399, 431, 448, 453, 481, 502, 506; and legal system, 212; myth of, 83; and oil, 374–78; opposition to and criticism of, 231, 268, 276–77, 336–37, 337–39, 413–15, 416, 420, 421–23, 424, 431–33, 440, 451–53, 457, 466–68, 469–70, 478, 481, 501–2; image of religiosity of, 498; and suppression of dissent, 183, 191, 393, 394, 395, 411, 413, 415–16, 423–24, 457, 498

Palestine Liberation Organization, 481; and religious taxes, 433

Palestinians, 69, 129, 224, 447, 458, 468, 472–73, 479

Parsons, Talcott, 32

Partovi az Qur'an (A Ray from the Qur'an) (Taleqani), 236, 242, 243–44, 475, 477

Pasandideh, Ayatollah Sayyid Morteza (brother of Khomeini), 410

Pascal, Blaise, 29

Pasdars, 256

Passion d'Hallaj, La (Massignon), 107

Passive resistance, as political strategy, 453, 470. *See also* Pacifism

Passivity, and piety, 192

Patriarchal politics, 392

Paul, Saint, 507

Peace, universal, 287

Peasantry, 406; and call to resistance, 470

"People, The," 246, 263, 264, 340, 354, 364

"Perfect Man, The," 181, 413, 442, 476–77, 483. *See also Insan-e Kamel*

Perse au contact de l'occident, La (Siasi), 327

Persepolis, 451

Persianization, vs. Westernization, 395

Persian language, 13; importance of in discourse of Al-e Ahmad, 63, 80

Pétrole et Violence (Oil and Violence) (Bani-Sadr and Vielle), 373

Pharaoh, in the Qur'an, 369

Philosopher king, 413; Islamicized, 443

Philosophy: comparative, 299–301; financial support of, 279–81; Greek, on women, 312; and ideology, 156, 273–74; Islamic, 154, 482; and Islamic jurisprudence, 275, 286–87, 297–98, 309, 314–15; and mysticism, 289–90; and nationalism, 151–57; opposition to, 281–84; and Shi'i theological dogma, 284–85; teaching of in Qom seminary, 274–75, 278–79, 281–84; Western/European, 151–54, 278–79, 299–301, 313–14

Piety, 231, 286, 301, 366, 398, 409; and legitimate authority, 321–22; revolutionary redefinition of, 192–95

Pirandello, Luigi, 204

Pishevari Democratic Party, 47, 48

Pishevari, Sayyid Ja'far, 47; separatist movement of, 224

Plato, 207–208, 225, 413

Poetry, 292, 303, 416

Police, 394; expenditures on, 373–74. *See also* SAVAK

Politics: climate of in Iran, 399; re-Islamicized discourse of, 493–96; radical discourse of, 494–95; economy of and Islamic Ideology, 380–82; and legitimacy, 518; and mysticism, 287–90; parties and organizations, 469–70, 498; and religion, 398–99; and mandatory responsibility of jurist *(vajeb-e aiyni)*, 444

Polyandry, 208

Polygyny, 208–9, 242, 313

Polytheism, 131–32, 143, 339, 360, 393, 396